Lecture Notes in Computer Science   11241

Commenced Publication in 1973
Founding and Former Series Editors:
Gerhard Goos, Juris Hartmanis, and Jan van Leeuwen

More information about this series at http://www.springer.com/series/7412

George Bebis · Richard Boyle
Bahram Parvin · Darko Koracin
Matt Turek · Srikumar Ramalingam
Kai Xu · Stephen Lin
Bilal Alsallakh · Jing Yang
Eduardo Cuervo · Jonathan Ventura (Eds.)

Advances in Visual Computing

13th International Symposium, ISVC 2018
Las Vegas, NV, USA, November 19–21, 2018
Proceedings

 Springer

Editors

George Bebis
University of Nevada
Reno, USA

Richard Boyle
NASA Ames Research Center
Moffett Field, USA

Bahram Parvin
University of Nevada
Reno, USA

Darko Koracin
Desert Research Institute
Reno, USA

Matt Turek
DARPA
Arlington, USA

Srikumar Ramalingam
University of Utah
Salt Lake City, USA

Kai Xu
National University of Defense Technology
Changsha, China

Stephen Lin
Microsoft Research Asia
Beijing, China

Bilal Alsallakh
Bosch Research
Farmington Hills, MI, USA

Jing Yang
University of North Carolina at Charlotte
Charlotte, USA

Eduardo Cuervo
Microsoft Research
Redmond, USA

Jonathan Ventura
University of Colorado at Colorado Springs
Colorado Springs, USA

ISSN 0302-9743   ISSN 1611-3349 (electronic)
Lecture Notes in Computer Science
ISBN 978-3-030-03800-7   ISBN 978-3-030-03801-4 (eBook)
https://doi.org/10.1007/978-3-030-03801-4

Library of Congress Control Number: 2018960439

LNCS Sublibrary: SL6 – Image Processing, Computer Vision, Pattern Recognition, and Graphics

This Springer imprint is published by the registered company Springer Nature Switzerland AG
The registered company address is: Gewerbestrasse 11, 6330 Cham, Switzerland

Preface

It is with great pleasure that we welcome you to the proceedings of the 13th International Symposium on Visual Computing (ISVC 2018), which was held in Las Vegas, Nevada, USA. ISVC provides a common umbrella for the four main areas of visual computing including vision, graphics, visualization, and virtual reality. The goal is to provide a forum for researchers, scientists, engineers, and practitioners throughout the world to present their latest research findings, ideas, developments, and applications in the broader area of visual computing.

This year, the program consisted of 12 oral sessions, three special tracks, and six keynote presentations. We received 91 submissions for the main symposium from which we accepted 54 papers for oral presentation. Special track papers were solicited separately through the Organizing and Program Committees of each track. A total of 12 papers were accepted for oral presentation in the special tracks.

All papers were reviewed with an emphasis on the potential to contribute to the state of the art in the field. Selection criteria included accuracy and originality of ideas, clarity and significance of results, and presentation quality. The review process was quite rigorous, involving two to three independent blind reviews followed by several days of discussion. During the discussion period we tried to correct anomalies and errors that might have existed in the initial reviews. Despite our efforts, we recognize that some papers worthy of inclusion may have not been included in the program. We offer our sincere apologies to authors whose contributions might have been overlooked.

We wish to thank everybody who submitted their work to ISVC 2018 for review. It was because of their contributions that we succeeded in having a technical program of high scientific quality. In particular, we would like to thank the ISVC 2018 area chairs, the organizing institutions (UNR, DRI, LBNL, and NASA Ames), the industrial sponsors (BAE Systems, Intel, Ford, Hewlett Packard, Mitsubishi Electric Research Labs, Toyota, General Electric), the international Program Committee, the special track organizers and their Program Committees, the keynote speakers, the reviewers, and especially the authors who contributed their work to the symposium. In particular, we would like to express our appreciation to Springer for sponsoring the best paper award this year.

We sincerely hope that ISVC 2018 offered participants opportunities for professional growth.

September 2018

George Bebis
Richard Boyle
Darko Koracin
Bharam Parvin
Srikumar Ramalingam
Matt Turek
Kai Xu
Stephen Lin
Jonathan Ventura
Eduardo Cuervo
Jing Yang
Bilal Alsallakh

Organization

Program Committee

Mahmoud Abou-Nasr	Ford Motor Company
Nicoletta Adamo-Villani	Purdue University, USA
Emmanuel Agu	Worcester Polytechnic Institute, USA
Bilal Alsallakh	BOSCH Research
Gholamreza Amayeh	Arraiy
Amol Ambardekar	Microsoft
Mehdi Ammi	LIMSI-CNRS
Mark Apperley	University of Waikato, Japan
Antonis Argyros	Foundation for Research and Technology - Hellas, Greece
Alessandro Artusi	University of Cyprus, Cyprus
Vijayan K Asari	University of Dayton, USA
Vassilis Athitsos	University of Texas at Arlington, USA
Melinos Averkiou	University of Cyprus, Cyprus
George Baciu	The Hong Kong Polytechnic University, SAR China
Selim Balcisoy	Sabanci University, Turkey
Reneta Barneva	SUNY Fredonia
Ronen Barzel	Independent
George Bebis	University of Nevada, USA
Michael Behrisch	Harvard University, USA
Alexander Belyaev	Heriot-Watt University, UK
Jan Bender	RWTH Aachen University, Germany
Bedrich Benes	Purdue University, USA
Ayush Bhargava	Clemson University, USA
Harsh Bhatia	Lawrence Livermore National Laboratory, USA
Sanjiv Bhatia	University of Missouri – St. Louis, USA
Ayan Biswas	Los Alamos National Laboratory, USA
Dobrina Boltcheva	Université de Lorraine - LORIA, France
Rita Borgo	King's College London, UK
Jose Braz Pereira	EST Setúbal/IPS, Portugal
Valentin Brimkov	Buffalo State College, USA
Gerd Bruder	University of Central Florida, USA
Chris Bryan	University of California, Davis, USA
Tolga Capin	TED University
Sek Chai	SRI International, USA
Jian Chang	Bournemouth University, UK
Sotirios Chatzis	Cyprus University of Technology
Aashish Chaudhary	Kitware Inc.

Abon Chaudhuri	WalmartLabs
Rama Chellappa	University of Maryland, USA
Jian Chen	The Ohio State University, USA
Jie Chen	University of Oulu, Finland
Yang Chen	HRL Laboratories, LLC
Zhonggui Chen	Xiamen University, China
Yi-Jen Chiang	New York University, USA
Isaac Cho	UNC Charlotte, USA
Jia-Kai Chou	University of California, Davis, USA
Amit Chourasia	San Diego Supercomputer Center, UCSD, USA
Sabine Coquillart	Inria, France
Adam Czajka	Warsaw University of Technology, Poland
Aritra Dasgupta	New York University, USA
Jeremie Dequidt	University of Lille, France
Alok Desai	CubiScan
Sotirios Diamandaras	University of Nevada, Reno, USA
Alexandra Diehl	University of Konstanz, Germany
Cosimo Distante	CNR
Ralf Doerner	RheinMain University of Applied Sciences, Germany
Gianfranco Doretto	West Virginia University, USA
Anastasios Doulamis	Technical University of Crete, Greece
Ye Duan	University of Missouri at Columbia, USA
Achim Ebert	University of Kaiserslautern, Germany
Parris Egbert	Brigham Young University, USA
Mohamed El Ansari	University of Ibn Zohr, Morocco
Luis Miguel Encarnacao	Innovation by Design Intl. Consulting
Barrett Ens	University of South Australia, Australia
Alireza Entezari	University of Florida, USA
Ali Erol	Sigun Information Technologies
Mohammad Eslami	Technical University of Munich, Germany
Matteo Ferrara	University of Bologna, Italy
Nivan Ferreira	Universidade Federal de Pernambuco, Brazil
Francesco Ferrise	Politecnico di Milano, Italy
Rony Ferzli	Intel
Julian Fierrez	Universidad Autonoma de Madrid, Spain
Gian Luca Foresti	University of Udine, Italy
Steffen Frey	Visualisierunsginstitut der Universität Stuttgart, Germany
Ioannis Fudos	University of Ioannina, Greece
Issei Fujishiro	Keio University, Japan
Aphrodite Galata	The University of Manchester, UK
Christoph Garth	University of Kaiserslautern, Germany
M. Gavrilova	University of Calgary, Canada
Robert Geist	Clemson University, USA
Randy Goebel	University of Alberta, Canada
Wooi-Boon Goh	Nanyang Technological University, Singapore

Gustavo Olague	CICESE
Marc Olano	University of Maryland, Baltimore County, USA
Francisco Ortega	Florida International University, USA
Masaki Oshita	Kyushu Institute of Technology, Japan
Oyewole Oyekoya	Clemson University, USA
Volker Paelke	Hochschule Bremen, Germany
Daniele Panozzo	New York University, USA
Yorgos Papagian	University of Crete, Greece
Michael Papka	University of Chicago, USA
Giuseppe Patanè	CNR-IMATI
Maurizio Patrignani	Roma Tre University, Italy
Shahram Payandeh	Simon Fraser University, Canada
Euripides Petrakis	Technical University of Crete, Greece
Claudio Pinhanez	IBM Research, Brazil
Giuseppe Placidi	University of L'Aquila, Italy
Nick Porcino	Oculus Research
Fatih Porikli	Australian National University, Australia
Nicolas Pronost	Université Claude Bernard Lyon 1, France
Hong Qin	Stony Brook University, USA
John Quarles	University of Texas at San Antonio, USA
Srikumar Ramalingam	University of Utah, USA
Emma Regentova	UNLV
Guido Reina	University of Stuttgart, Germany
Erik Reinhard	Technicolor
Paolo Remagnino	Kingston University, UK
Benjamin Renoust	Osaka University, Japan
Theresa-Marie Rhyne	Consultant
Eraldo Ribeiro	Florida Institute of Technology, USA
Peter Rodgers	University of Kent, UK
Paul Rosen	University of South Florida, USA
Isaac Rudomin	BSC
Amela Sadagic	Naval Postgraduate School
Filip Sadlo	Heidelberg University, Germany
Punam Saha	University of Iowa, USA
Naohisa Sakamoto	Kobe University, Japan
Kristian Sandberg	Computational Solutions, Inc.
Allen Sanderson	SCI Institute
Nickolas S. Sapidis	University of Western Macedonia, Greece
Muhammad Sarfraz	Kuwait University, Kuwait
Andreas Savakis	Rochester Institute of Technology, USA
Jacob Scharcanski	UFRGS
Thomas Schultz	University of Bonn, Germany
Hans-Joerg Schulz	Aarhus University, Denmark
Timothy Shead	Sandia National Laboratories, USA
Mohamed Shehata	Memorial University, Canada
Yun Sheng	East China Normal University, China

Yueming Yang	Mount Holyoke College, USA
Mohammed Yeasin	University of Memphis, USA
Hsu-Chun Yen	National Taiwan University, Taiwan
Hong Yi	Renaissance Computing Institute
Lijun Yin	State University of New York at Binghamton, USA
Zeyun Yu	University of Wisconsin-Milwaukee, USA
Chunrong Yuan	TH Köln, Germany
Xiaoru Yuan	Peking University, China
Xenophon Zabulis	Foundation for Research and Technology - Hellas, Greece
Jiri Zara	Czech Technical University in Prague, Czech Republic
Wei Zeng	Florida International University, USA
Dong Zhang	NVIDIA
Jian Zhang	Bournemouth University, UK
Zhao Zhang	Soochow University, China
Ye Zhao	Kent State University, USA
Jianmin Zheng	Nanyang Technological University, Singapore
Yuanjie Zheng	Shandong Normal University, China
Changqing Zou	University of Maryland, USA
Vitomir Štruc	University of Ljubljana, Slovenia

Additional Reviewers

Dutta, Soumya	Müller, Jonas
Fu, Siwei	Park, Sanghun
Geist, Robert	Saglam, Ahmet
Gong, Xun	Vosinakis, Spyros
Huang, Jida	Wang, Li
Li, Xiangjia	Wang, Zhao
Liu, Dongyu	Zhang, Jinglu
Mei, Chao	Zhang, Zhuming
Murphy, Nick	

Contents

ST: Computational Bioimaging

Automatic Registration of Serial Cerebral Angiography:
A Comparative Review 3
  Alice Tang, Zhiyuan Zhang, and Fabien Scalzo

Skull Stripping Using Confidence Segmentation Convolution
Neural Network 15
  Kaiyuan Chen, Jingyue Shen, and Fabien Scalzo

Skin Cancer Segmentation Using a Unified Markov Random Field 25
  Omran Salih and Serestina Viriri

Heart Modeling by Convexity Preserving Segmentation and Convex
Shape Decomposition 34
  Xue Shi, Lijun Tang, Shaoxiang Zhang, and Chunming Li

Computer Graphics I

PSO-Based Newton-Like Method and Iteration Processes in the Generation
of Artistic Patterns 47
  Ireneusz Gościniak and Krzysztof Gdawiec

An Evaluation of Smoothing and Remeshing Techniques to Represent
the Evolution of Real-World Phenomena 57
  José Duarte, Paulo Dias, and José Moreira

Biomimetic Perception Learning for Human Sensorimotor Control 68
  Masaki Nakada, Honglin Chen, and Demetri Terzopoulos

Porous Structure Design in Tissue Engineering Using Anisotropic Radial
Basis Functions. 79
  Ye Guo, Ke Liu, and Zeyun Yu

Visual Surveillance

Accurate and Efficient Non-Parametric Background Detection
for Video Surveillance. 93
  *William Porr, James Easton, Alireza Tavakkoli, Donald Loffredo,
  and Sean Simmons*

A Low-Power Neuromorphic System for Real-Time Visual
Activity Recognition   106
  Deepak Khosla, Ryan Uhlenbrock, and Yang Chen

Video-Based Human Action Recognition Using Kernel
Relevance Analysis   116
  Jorge Fernández-Ramírez, Andrés Álvarez-Meza,
  and Álvaro Orozco-Gutiérrez

Robust Incremental Hidden Conditional Random Fields for Human
Action Recognition   126
  Michalis Vrigkas, Ermioni Mastora, Christophoros Nikou,
  and Ioannis A. Kakadiaris

Pattern Recognition

Rotation Symmetry Object Classification Using Structure Constrained
Convolutional Neural Network   139
  Seunghwa Yu and Seugnkyu Lee

A Hough Space Feature for Vehicle Detection   147
  Chunling Tu and Shengzhi Du

Gender Classification Based on Facial Shape and Texture Features   157
  Mayibongwe H. Bayana, Serestina Viriri, and Raphael Angulu

Authentication-Based on Biomechanics of Finger Movements Captured
Using Optical Motion-Capture   167
  Brittany Lewis, Christopher J. Nycz, Gregory S. Fischer,
  and Krishna K. Venkatasubramanian

Specific Document Sign Location Detection Based on Point Matching
and Clustering   180
  Huaixin Xiong

Virtual Reality I

Training in Virtual Environments for Hybrid Power Plant   193
  Max G. Chiluisa, Rubén D. Mullo, and Víctor H. Andaluz

Visualizing Viewpoint Movement on Driving by Space
Information Rendering   205
  Satoru Morita

Virtual Reality System for Children Lower Limb Strengthening
with the Use of Electromyographic Sensors 215
  Eddie E. Galarza, Marco Pilatasig, Eddie D. Galarza,
  Victoria M. López, Pablo A. Zambrano, Jorge Buele, and Jhon Espinoza

A Comparative Study of Virtual UI for Risk Assessment and Evaluation 226
  Naila Bushra, Daniel Carruth, and Shuchisnigdha Deb

Sensory Fusion and Intent Recognition for Accurate Gesture Recognition in
Virtual Environments. 237
  Sean Simmons, Kevin Clark, Alireza Tavakkoli, and Donald Loffredo

Deep Learning I

Accuracy of a Driver-Assistance System in a Collision Scenario 251
  Waqar Khan and Reinhard Klette

Classify Broiler Viscera Using an Iterative Approach on Noisy Labeled
Training Data 264
  Anders Jørgensen, Jens Fagertun, and Thomas B. Moeslund

Instance-level Object Recognition Using Deep Temporal Coherence 274
  Miguel Lagunes-Fortiz, Dima Damen, and Walterio Mayol-Cuevas

DUPL-VR: Deep Unsupervised Progressive Learning
for Vehicle Re-Identification. 286
  Raja Muhammad Saad Bashir, Muhammad Shahzad,
  and Muhammad Moazam Fraz

Motion and Tracking

Particle Filter Based Tracking and Mapping 299
  Nils Höhner, Anna Katharina Hebborn, and Stefan Müller

Multi-branch Siamese Networks with Online Selection
for Object Tracking. 309
  Zhenxi Li, Guillaume-Alexandre Bilodeau, and Wassim Bouachir

Deep Convolutional Correlation Filters for Forward-Backward
Visual Tracking 320
  Yong Wang, Robert Laganière, Daniel Laroche, Ali Osman Ors,
  Xiaoyin Xu, and Changyun Zhu

The Bird Gets Caught by the WORM: Tracking Multiple Deformable
Objects in Noisy Environments Using Weight ORdered Logic Maps 332
  Debajyoti Karmaker, Ingo Schiffner, Michael Wilson,
  and Mandyam V. Srinivasan

A Mumford Shah Style Unified Framework for Layering: Pitfalls
and Solutions 344
    Fareed ud din Mehmood Jafri, Martin Fritz Mueller,
    and Anthony Joseph Yezzi

Visualization

Visualization of Parameter Sensitivity of 2D Time-Dependent Flow 359
    Karsten Hanser, Ole Klein, Bastian Rieck, Bettina Wiebe, Tobias Selz,
    Marian Piatkowski, Antoni Sagristà, Boyan Zheng,
    Mária Lukácová-Medvidová, George Craig, Heike Leitte,
    and Filip Sadlo

Non-stationary Generalized Wishart Processes for Enhancing Resolution
over Diffusion Tensor Fields 371
    Jhon F. Cuellar-Fierro, Hernán Darío Vargas-Cardona,
    Andrés M. Álvarez, Álvaro A. Orozco, and Mauricio A. Álvarez

Reduced-Reference Image Quality Assessment Based on Improved Local
Binary Pattern. 382
    Xi-kui Miao, Dah-Jye Lee, Xiang-zheng Cheng, and Xiao-yu Yang

Web System for Visualization of Weather Data of the Hydrometeorological
Network of Tungurahua, Ecuador 395
    Jaime Santana, Fernando A. Chicaiza, Víctor H. Andaluz,
    and Patrick Reuter

Analysis and Visualization of Sports Performance Anxiety
in Tennis Matches. 407
    Shiraj Pokharel and Ying Zhu

Object Detection and Recognition

Detailed Sentence Generation Architecture for Image
Semantics Description 423
    Imran Khurram, Muhammad Moazam Fraz, and Muhammad Shahzad

Pupil Localization Using Geodesic Distance 433
    Radovan Fusek

Parallel Curves Detection Using Multi-agent System 445
    Shengzhi Du and Chunling Tu

Can Deep Learning Learn the Principle of Closed Contour Detection? 455
    Xinhua Zhang, Yijing Watkins, and Garrett T. Kenyon

Deep Learning II

DensSiam: End-to-End Densely-Siamese Network with Self-Attention
Model for Object Tracking.   463
  Mohamed H. Abdelpakey, Mohamed S. Shehata,
  and Mostafa M. Mohamed

Convolutional Adaptive Particle Filter with Multiple Models
for Visual Tracking.   474
  Reza Jalil Mozhdehi, Yevgeniy Reznichenko, Abubakar Siddique,
  and Henry Medeiros

Scale-Aware RPN for Vehicle Detection   487
  Lu Ding, Yong Wang, Robert Laganière, Xinbin Luo, and Shan Fu

Object Detection to Assist Visually Impaired People: A Deep Neural
Network Adventure.   500
  Fereshteh S. Bashiri, Eric LaRose, Jonathan C. Badger,
  Roshan M. D'Souza, Zeyun Yu, and Peggy Peissig

Large Scale Application Response Time Measurement Using Image
Recognition and Deep Learning   511
  Lan Vu, Uday Kurkure, Hari Sivaraman, and Aravind Bappanadu

Applications I

Vision-Depth Landmarks and Inertial Fusion for Navigation in Degraded
Visual Environments   529
  Shehryar Khattak, Christos Papachristos, and Kostas Alexis

Efficient Nearest Neighbors Search for Large-Scale
Landmark Recognition.   541
  Federico Magliani, Tomaso Fontanini, and Andrea Prati

Patient's Body Motion Study Using Multimodal RGBDT Videos   552
  Mohammad A. Haque, Simon S. Kjeldsen, Federico G. Arguissain,
  Iris Brunner, Kamal Nasrollahi, Ole Kæseler Andersen,
  Jørgen F. Nielsen, Thomas B. Moeslund, and Anders Jørgensen

Marker Based Thermal-Inertial Localization for Aerial Robots in Obscurant
Filled Environments   565
  Shehryar Khattak, Christos Papachristos, and Kostas Alexis

Shape-Based Smoothing of Binary Digital Objects Using Signed
Distance Transform.   576
  Xiaoliu Zhang, Cheng Chen, Gregory Chang, and Punam K. Saha

Segmentation

Patch-Based Potentials for Interactive Contour Extraction................ 587
Thoraya Ben Chattah, Sébastien Bougleux, Olivier Lézoray,
and Atef Hamouda

A New Algorithm for Local Blur-Scale Computation and Edge Detection ... 598
Indranil Guha and Punam K. Saha

Semantic Segmentation by Integrating Classifiers for Different
Difficulty Levels.. 607
Daisuke Matsuzuki and Kazuhiro Hotta

Applications II

Fast Image Dehazing Methods for Real-Time Video Processing 619
Yang Chen and Deepak Khosla

GPU Accelerated Non-Parametric Background Subtraction.............. 629
William Porr, James Easton, Alireza Tavakkoli, Donald Loffredo,
and Sean Simmons

Budget-Constrained Online Video Summarisation of Egocentric Video
Using Control Charts.. 640
Paria Yousefi, Clare E. Matthews, and Ludmila I. Kuncheva

p-Laplacian Regularization of Signals on Directed Graphs 650
Zeina Abu Aisheh, Sébastien Bougleux, and Olivier Lézoray

A Dense-Depth Representation for VLAD Descriptors in Content-Based
Image Retrieval 662
Federico Magliani, Tomaso Fontanini, and Andrea Prati

Virtual Reality II

Augmented Reality System for Training and Assistance in the Management
of Industrial Equipment and Instruments 675
Edison A. Chicaiza, Edgar I. De la Cruz, and Víctor H. Andaluz

Alternative Treatment of Psychological Disorders Such as Spider Phobia
Through Virtual Reality Environments................................ 687
Joseph Armas and Víctor H. Andaluz

The Skyline as a Marker for Augmented Reality in Urban Context 698
Mehdi Ayadi, Leo Valque, Mihaela Scuturici, Serge Miguet,
and Chokri Ben Amar

Oil Processes VR Training 712
  Víctor H. Andaluz, José L. Amaquiña, Washington X. Quevedo,
  Jorge Mora-Aguilar, Daniel Castillo-Carrión, Roberto J. Miranda,
  and María G. Pérez

ST: Intelligent Transportation Systems

Multiple Object Tracking in Urban Traffic Scenes with a Multiclass
Object Detector 727
  Hui-Lee Ooi, Guillaume-Alexandre Bilodeau, Nicolas Saunier,
  and David-Alexandre Beaupré

Autonomous Bus Boarding Robotic Wheelchair Using Bidirectional
Sensing Systems 737
  Shamim Al Mamun, Hisato Fukuda, Antony Lam, Yoshinori Kobayashi,
  and Yoshinori Kuno

Road User Abnormal Trajectory Detection Using a Deep Autoencoder 748
  Pankaj Raj Roy and Guillaume-Alexandre Bilodeau

Traffic Flow Classification Using Traffic Cameras 758
  Mohammad Shokrolah Shirazi and Brendan Morris

Author Index 769

ST: Computational Bioimaging

513 Computational Bioimaging

Automatic Registration of Serial Cerebral Angiography: A Comparative Review

Alice Tang, Zhiyuan Zhang, and Fabien Scalzo[✉]

Department of Neurology and Computer Science,
University of California Los Angeles (UCLA), Los Angeles, USA
fab@cs.ucla.edu

Abstract. Image registration can play a major role in medical imaging as it can be used to identify changes that have occurred over a period of time, thus mirroring treatment effectiveness, recovery, and detection of diseases onset. While medical image registration algorithms have been largely evaluated on MRI and CT, less attention has been given to Digital Subtraction Angiography (DSA). DSA of the brain is the method of choice for the diagnosis of numerous neurovascular conditions and is used during neurovascular surgeries. Numerous studies have relied on semi-automated registration that involve manual selection of matching features to compute the mapping between images. Nevertheless, there are currently a variety of automatic registration methods which have been developed, although the performance of these methods on DSA have not been fully explored. In this paper, we identify and review a variety of automatic registration methods, and evaluate algorithm performance in the context of serial image registration. We find that intensity-based methods are consistent in performance, while feature-based methods can perform better, but are also more variable in success. Ultimately a combined algorithm may be optimal for automatic registration, which can be applied to analyze vasculature information and improve unbiased treatment evaluation in clinical trials.

Keywords: Digital Subtraction Angiography · Image registration
Serial imaging · Co-registration · Angiogram

1 Introduction

Digital Subtraction Angiography (DSA) is the gold standard imaging method for vessel visualization in the diagnosis and treatment of neurovascular disorders [3,22]. DSA is a sequence of x-ray images showing contrast bolus passage through the vessels with background elements removed. One application of DSA is in the guidance of catheters for endovascular thrombectomy in the treatment of acute ischemic stroke [10]. In this context, image registration of DSA images is useful for providing information on stroke diagnosis, diseased vessel location, treatment planning, and treatment effect. Image registration is an important aspect of this

© Springer Nature Switzerland AG 2018
G. Bebis et al. (Eds.): ISVC 2018, LNCS 11241, pp. 3–14, 2018.
https://doi.org/10.1007/978-3-030-03801-4_1

process for comparing serial changes in DSA images or evaluating differences across neurovascular treatments and across patients.

Image co-registration is a process where two images are mapped onto the same coordinate frame. This process is widely used in the medical fields for integrating or comparing image data obtained from different time points, viewing angles, and modalities [16,24]. Currently, registration in the clinical setting is performed by manual selection of matching features between two DSA images to compute the affine transformation, which is then verified through visual inspection. However, manual image registration is inefficient, and can be arduous when the image datasets becomes large. Automatic methods for image co-registration are desired to provide a more efficient approach for analyzing large scale studies, and providing consistency to remove inter-reader variability [4]. Yet, there has not yet been an extensive study identifying and comparing registration algorithms in the application of DSA registration.

Algorithms for image registration can be classified generally into feature-based and intensity-based methods [11,25]. Feature-based methods include feature detection and matching steps, where corresponding distinctive regions are identified between images. Some feature detection algorithm include Speeded-Up Robust Features (SURF) [2], Scale-Invariant Feature Transform (SIFT) [13], and SIFT-like algorithms [7]. After matching, some algorithms find the optimal transform with RANSAC [9] or MSAC [28]. For intensity-based methods, images are represented with descriptors such as area based representations, landmark based representations [5], or gradient based representations [1,12,14]. Registration is performed by optimizing a criterion, such as mutual information [26], squared error, or correlation metrics [8]. Optimization is then performed either directly such as with gradient descent or heuristically such as with simplex methods [18]. Other types of registration methods exist such as iterative closest point (ICP) for point cloud registration [21], or alignment in the Fourier domain. While there are many algorithms and approaches to registration, there has not yet been an investigation on how the algorithms perform relative to each other for the application of DSA registration.

In this paper, we identify and evaluate the performance of existing registration algorithms that can potentially be used for DSA co-registration. This work will be beneficial for future image analysis on DSA images for physicians or researchers. This paper is organized as follows: We first describe how we identified existing image co-registration methods in Sect. 2.2. Then we describe in Sect. 2.3 the strategy we used to evaluate the performance of different image co-registration methods. In Sect. 3, we present the registration and evaluation results for each method, and discuss in Sect. 4 the methods with the best performance. Finally we conclude with a discussion on the influence our research may have in relevant medical area in Sect. 5.

2   Methods

2.1   Dataset

The image dataset used in this study to evaluate our framework was collected from patients admitted at the UCLA stroke center and diagnosed with symptoms of acute ischemic stroke. The use of this dataset was approved by the local Institutional Review Board (IRB). Inclusion criteria for this study included: (1) final diagnosis of acute ischemic stroke, (2) last known well time within six hours at admission, (3) Digital Subtraction Angiography (DSA) of the brain performed prior and at completion of a clot retrieval procedure. Therefore, an important feature of the dataset is that additional vessels may be present in the images acquired after the procedure; due to the recanalization of those vessels. A total of 32 patients satisfied the above criteria and were included in this study. The patients had various success in revascularization. DSA images had a resolution of 1024×1024 pixels.

2.2   Methods Identification

To start our evaluation, we identify available 2D-2D image co-registration methods that can potentially be applied to DSA registration. The search is performed on Google and Github with the following keyword combinations: 'image registration', '2d2d', and 'matlab source code'.

The 14 different methods we identified as potential algorithms for registering DSA images are as follows:

1. **iat-aba-LKWarp:** A gradient-based direct alignment method based upon the Lucas-Kanade algorithm [14], which is a local differential method using optical flow estimation. The optimum transformation T is found by minimizing the sum of squared errors between images as the criterion [1].
2. **iat-aba-ECCWarp:** A gradient-based direct alignment method which finds the optimum transformation T by maximizing the Enhanced Correlation Coefficient (ECC) between images as a similarity metric [8].
3. **iat-fba:** A feature-based registration method using Speeded Up Robust Features (SURF) algorithm to first detect interest points in the images and represent them by an area descriptor invariant to scale and rotation [2]. These features are matched based on arc-cosine angle between descriptor vectors to determine correspondences. Registration is achieved by estimating the optimum transform after minimizing the distance between corresponding features based upon a RANSAC scheme [9].
4. **matlab-inner:** An intensity-based registration method which represents the extent of image matching with mutual information similarity metric [17, 26]. Optimization is performed iteratively with one-plus-one evolutionary algorithm to find the optimum transform [23].
5. **MI-Opt:** This is an intensity-based registration algorithm with mutual information similarity metric and optimization with Nelder-Mead simplex method [18].

6. **lkwq007:** An FFT-based technique for registration by applying a high-pass filter and representing the spectra in log-polar coordinates. Rotation, scale, and translation parameters are extracted via phase correlation [20].

7. **ZeLianWen-sift:** A feature-based method using scale-invariant feature transform (SIFT) to identify and represent features [13]. The features are matched and clustered via Hough transform voting. The optimal transformation is then found via least squares optimization.

8. **ZelianWen-sar-sift:** A method using a SIFT-like algorithm robust to speckle noise for feature detection, originally used for synthetic-aperture radar (SAR) images [7,15]. The features are matched, clustered, and the optimal transform is found via least squares.

9. **hlpassion:** A feature-based algorithm utilizing Matlab's image processing tools [17]. Features are detected with a SURF algorithm and matched [2]. The optimal transformation is found using an M-estimator Sample Consensus (MSAC) algorithm.

10. **MinhazPalasara:** A method originally created for locating possible tumors in mammograms. The algorithm uses SIFT method to detect features in the images. The features are matched, outliers are computed via MSAC algorithm, and the optimal transformation found by aligning inlier features.

11. **tonycao:** This method was originally created for registration of multi-modal microscopy images using image analogies [5]. Example matches are used to create a dictionary of appearance relations, and a sparse representation model is used to obtain image analogies. Registration is then performed via least squares method.

12. **homography:** This method uses SURF to detect features which are matched via direct linear transformation (DLT). The 2D-2D projective homography is then estimated using RANSAC and Levenberg Marquardt optimization [6].

13. **ImageRegistrationApp:** An intensity-based method utilizing Matlab's image processing toolbox. The optimum transform is found by minimizing mean square error with gradient descent strategy.

14. **demon:** A non-rigid fluid-like registration method where a velocity (or movement) is defined on each pixel using gradient information [19,27]. The velocity field is used to transform one image onto the other, and the optimal transformation is found with gradient descent [12].

15. **ICP:** Iterative Closest Point (ICP) is a widely used surface matching algorithm for point clouds. DSA images are thresholded by Otsu's method and randomly sampled for points. Registration is performed by assuming closest points between point clouds are corresponding, and minimizing the distances between point correspondences [21].

2.3   Methods Evaluation

We evaluate the co-registration algorithms on 32 DSA image pairs. As a pre-processing step, we first extract vessels each image with a Frangi filter.

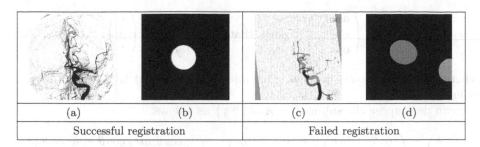

(a)	(b)	(c)	(d)
Successful registration		Failed registration	

Fig. 1. Example of Registration. An example of well registered image pairs (a) with low circle overlap error (b) on the left. The right shows an example of failed registration (c) with high circle overlap error (d).

We then compute groundtruth registration parameters for each image pair by manual selection of six corresponding points in each image pair, and then acquiring the affine transformation matrix as our groundtruth. Each reference point was placed at established anatomical locations by a Neurologist who was blinded to any information in the study. This groundtruth transformation will be compared to those obtained from the co-registration algorithms identified above in order to evaluate algorithm performance.

Circle Overlap Error. To evaluate algorithm accuracy, we define a circle overlap error metric. For each image pair, we have a groundtruth affine transformation $T_{groundtruth}$ and estimated affine transformations $T_{estimated}$ from each registration method. We apply the inverse transform for both the groundtruth and estimated transformation on a unit circle C. This will result in two elliptical shapes that may or may not overlap.

The calculation for circle overlap error is represented in the following equation:

$$Circle\,Overlap\,Error = 1 - \frac{|M \cap F|}{|M \cup F|} \qquad (1)$$

where $M = T_{estimated}^{-1}(C)$ is the elliptical region generated by applying the inverse estimated transform on the unit circle and $F = T_{groundtruth}^{-1}(C)$ is the elliptical region generated by applying the inverse groundtruth transform to the unit circle. Note that a greater overlap between elliptical regions such as in Fig. 1 corresponding to a more accurate estimated transformation will result in a smaller circle overlap error.

Parameter Error Calculation. Since circle overlap error can result in a value of 1 when there is no overlap in elliptical regions, we introduce a second error metric, parameter error. Parameter is computed from the difference between the transformation parameters from the groundtruth transformation and the estimated transformation. Total parameter error is obtained from the Euclidean error between all the groundtruth and estimated transform parameters. The affine transformation can be represented as a matrix

$$T = \begin{pmatrix} a & b & t_x \\ c & d & t_y \\ 0 & 0 & 1 \end{pmatrix} \quad \text{such that} \quad \begin{pmatrix} x' \\ y' \\ 1 \end{pmatrix} = T \begin{pmatrix} x \\ y \\ 1 \end{pmatrix} \quad (2)$$

where $(x, y, 1)$ are points in the original image and $(x', y', 1)$ are the transformed points.

We can decompose the sub-matrix $A = \begin{pmatrix} a & b \\ c & d \end{pmatrix}$ as follows:

$$\begin{pmatrix} a & b \\ c & d \end{pmatrix} = \begin{pmatrix} \cos\theta & -\sin\theta \\ \sin\theta & \cos\theta \end{pmatrix} \begin{pmatrix} s_x & 0 \\ 0 & s_y \end{pmatrix} \begin{pmatrix} 1 & m \\ 0 & 1 \end{pmatrix} = \begin{pmatrix} s_x\cos\theta & ms_x\cos\theta - s_y\sin\theta \\ s_x\sin\theta & ms_x\sin\theta + s_y\cos\theta \end{pmatrix}$$

Note that $\det(A) = ad - bc = s_x s_y$.

We can then compute 6 transformation parameters from T:

Translation along x-axis and y-axis : t_x and t_y

$$\text{Rotation} : \theta = \arctan 2\left(\frac{c}{a}\right)$$

$$\text{Scale along x-axis} : s_x = \frac{a}{\cos\theta} \text{ or } \frac{c}{\sin\theta} \quad (3)$$

$$\text{Scale along y-axis} : s_y = \frac{\det A}{s_x}$$

$$\text{Shear along y-axis} : m = \frac{b + s_y\sin\theta}{a} = \frac{d - s_y\sin\theta}{c}$$

Table 1. Algorithm Registration Absolute Errors. The mean absolute error and standard deviation values for parameter error and circle overlap error are listed. Underlined values emphasize the 3 lowest errors for each category.

Alg	err(s_x)	err(s_y)	err(t_x)	err(t_y)	err(θ)	err(m_y)	Circle overlap error
1*	**0.152 ± .1**	0.154 ± .1	**96.6 ± 100**	160 ± 160	**0.103 ± .1**	**0.097 ± .1**	0.757 ± .3
2	0.153 ± .1	0.154 ± .1	101 ± 100	166 ± 160	0.113 ± .1	0.105 ± .1	0.76 ± .3
3	0.175 ± .2	0.203 ± .4	**75.2 ± 100**	308 ± 380	0.138 ± .2	0.222 ± .3	0.800 ± .3
4	0.189 ± .2	0.155 ± .1	137 ± 120	222 ± 200	0.176 ± .2	0.180 ± .2	0.842 ± .3
5*	**0.144 ± .1**	0.159 ± .2	**94 ± 100**	158 ± 160	**0.098 ± .09**	**0.097 ± .1**	0.741 ± .3
6	**0.125 ± .1**	**0.135 ± .1**	377 ± 380	443 ± 420	0.425 ± .8	**0.089 ± .1**	0.851 ± .1
7	0.284 ± .5	**0.108 ± .2**	174 ± 280	300 ± 470	0.331 ± .6	0.366 ± .6	**0.633 ± .4**
8	0.270 ± .4	**0.125 ± .2**	243 ± 360	260 ± 410	0.686 ± .8	166 ± 720	**0.676 ± .4**
9	0.398 ± 1	0.341 ± 1	198 ± 330	373 ± 400	0.288 ± .6	0.559 ± 2	0.828 ± .3
10	0.678 ± 2	0.299 ± .9	573 ± 2.3k	458 ± 1k	0.450 ± .8	0.225 ± .4	**0.548 ± .4**
11	18 ± 76	208 ± 820	14k ± 58k	15k ± 66k	0.605 ± .8	14.1 ± 60	0.879 ± .3
12	3.2 ± 14	101 ± 550	2k ± 9k	1.7k ± 6k	0.580 ± .8	33 ± 190	0.737 ± .3
13	0.363 ± .3	0.342 ± .4	244 ± 230	195 ± 200	0.240 ± .3	0.476 ± .9	0.853 ± .3
14	0.229 ± .3	0.199 ± .2	103 ± 120	163 ± 160	0.161 ± .2	**0.093 ± .1**	0.836 ± .3
15	0.210 ± .2	0.176 ± .2	111 ± 120	160 ± 160	0.098 ± .09	0.148 ± .2	0.804 ± .3

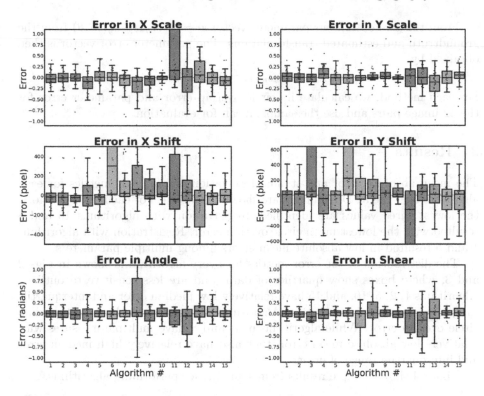

Fig. 2. Parameter Error. Parameter error plots for the 6 registration parameters. Box plot lines represent median and interquartile range over the errors of the 32 DSA pairs for each algorithm, with outliers outside the whiskers.

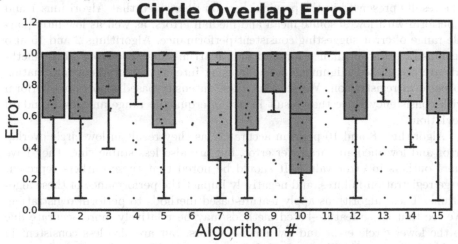

Fig. 3. Circle Overlap Error. Box plot lines represent median and interquartile range over the distribution of circle overlap errors of the 32 DSA registration pairs for each algorithm. Outliers lie outside of the whiskers. A lower circle overlap error value represents a better registration result.

From this, we obtain our parameter vector $p = (t_x, t_y, s_x, s_y, m, \theta)$ from the groundtruth and estimated transformations. The parameter error vector is then obtained by

$$p_{err} = p_{estimated} - p_{groundtruth} \tag{4}$$

For each method, we calculate its circle overlap error and parameter error for the 32 image pairs and use the sample mean for evaluation.

3 Results

The mean absolute error and standard deviation of the error metrics for each algorithm over the 32 DSA images are shown in Table 1. For each error category, the lowest three values are identified. Registration with algorithms 10 and 8 resulted with the lowest mean circle overlap error. Registration with algorithms 1 and 5 resulted in low absolute mean errors among multiple parameters.

The distribution of the error metrics for every algorithm is shown in Figs. 2 and 3, where boxes show quartiles of data, and are less sensitive to outliers. Algorithms 1, 2, 5, 10, and 15 have relatively low median error and interquartile ranges across all six parameters. Algorithms 10 and 8 has the lowest median circle overlap error. While algorithms 6, 7, and 8 have multiple measures with relatively low absolute mean error, they also have relatively high median error and interquartile range of error.

Figure 4 shows sample results from some higher performing algorithms.

4 Discussion

The results presented in the previous Section illustrated that Algorithms 1 and 5 perform with low absolute mean and median errors, as well as low interquartile range of error suggesting consistent performance. Algorithms 2 and 15 also demonstrate low median error and interquartile range of error. These methods are area-based alignment methods using intensity or gradient information to perform registration. We see that these intensity-based algorithms perform with consistency since they result in low interquartile range and low standard deviation.

Algorithms 8 and 10 perform accurately as they result in low circle overlap error and low median parameter error, but are also less stable since they have more outliers in error values. It should be noted that these outliers represent large registration failures, and negatively impact the performance of these algorithms. These algorithms apply feature-based methods to perform registration. We see that these feature-based methods may be relatively more accurate due to the lower circle error and low median errors, but are also less consistent in performance due to high standard deviation and higher number of outliers.

Algorithms 1 and 2 are area-based direct alignment algorithms relying on the brightness constancy assumption:

$$I_1(x, y) = I_2(T(x, y)) \tag{5}$$

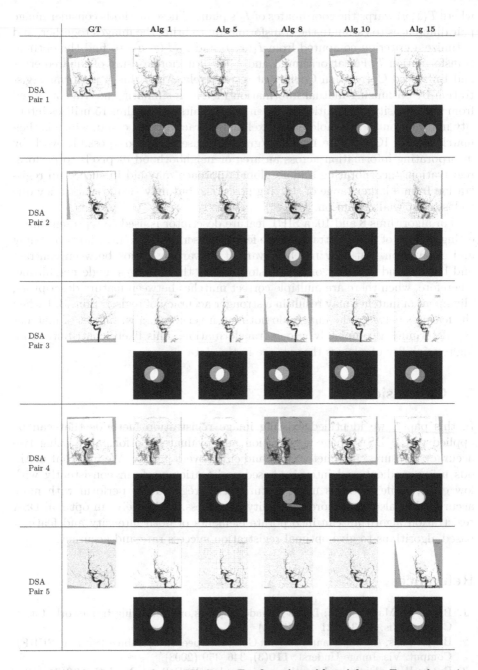

Fig. 4. Sample Results from Highest Performing Algorithms. Example registration results from 5 algorithms are shown. Pink vessels represent the pre-treatment DSA images, and green vessels represent the post-treatment DSA images. Circle overlap error visualization is shown under each registration result. (Color figure online)

where $T(x, y)$ warps the coordinates of I_2's plane. These methods consider image pair differences to estimate the transformation to bring the images together, and optimize a criterion computed from $I_1(x, y)$ and $I_2(T(x, y))$ to find the optimal transformation T. For algorithms 1 and 2, the criterion are sum of squared error and Enhanced Correlation Coefficient respectively. Algorithm 5 performs registration by optimizing mutual information metric, a similarity metric computed from the intensity distribution between image pairs. Algorithm 15 utilizes intensity information to threshold each pixel and extract a point cloud, which is then matched with ICP. These intensity/gradient based methods possibly work by incorporating information across an area or neighborhood of pixels to perform registration. Incorporating a more global approach may aid in successful registration from a larger range of starting positions, but may also lose accuracy due to loss of spacial resolution.

For algorithms 8 and 10, a SIFT feature descriptor is used to represent interesting regions of high contrast. These feature descriptors are invariant to scaling and orientation, but may not be invariant to varying ratios between contrast and background intensity or to transformations that changes angle magnitude. Therefore, when there are multiple correct matches between feature descriptors, alignment of matches may result in a stronger accuracy of registration. But when the features between the images do not match very well, a wrong set of matches can determine a completely wrong transformation. This likely contributes to a high variability of success that we see in the data.

5   Conclusion

In this paper, we identified existing image registration methods that can be applied to 2D DSA image registration and evaluated performance using two accuracy measures: parameter error and circle overlap error. We find that methods using gradient and intensity-based registration perform consistently with low error, while methods using feature-based registration perform with more accuracy but also with more variability in success. Ultimately, an optimal DSA registration algorithm can incorporate elements of both intensity and feature-based algorithms to give optimal registration success rate and accuracy.

References

1. Baker, S., Matthews, I.: Lucas-Kanade 20 years on: a unifying framework. Int. J. Comput. Vis. **56**(3), 221–255 (2004)
2. Bay, H., Ess, A., Tuytelaars, T., Van Gool, L.: Speeded-up robust features (SURF). Comput. Vis. Image Underst. **110**(3), 346–359 (2008)
3. Brody, W.R.: Digital subtraction angiography. IEEE Trans. Nucl. Sci. **29**(3), 1176–1180 (1982)
4. Brown, L.G.: A survey of image registration techniques. ACM Comput. Surv. **24**, 325–376 (1992)

5. Cao, T., Zach, C., Modla, S., Powell, D., Czymmek, K., Niethammer, M.: Multimodal registration for correlative microscopy using image analogies. Med. Image Anal. **18**(6), 914–926 (2014)
6. Chum, O., Pajdla, T., Sturm, P.: The geometric error for homographies. Comput. Vis. Image Underst. **97**(1), 86–102 (2005)
7. Dellinger, F., Delon, J., Gousseau, Y., Michel, J., Tupin, F., Tupin, F.: SAR-SIFT: a SIFT-like algorithm for SAR images. IEEE Trans. Geosci. Remote. Sens. **53**, 453–466 (2015)
8. Evangelidis, G.D., Psarakis, E.Z.: Parametric image alignment using enhanced correlation coefficient maximization. IEEE Trans. Pattern Anal. Mach. Intell. **30**(10), 1858–1865 (2008)
9. Fischler, M.A., Bolles, R.C.: Random sample consensus: a paradigm for model fitting with applications to image analysis and automated cartography. Commun. ACM **24**(6), 381–395 (1981)
10. Font, M.A., Arboix, A., Krupinski, J.: Angiogenesis, neurogenesis and neuroplasticity in ischemic stroke. Curr. Cardiol. Rev. **6**(3), 238–244 (2010)
11. Goshtasby, A.A.: 2D and 3-D Image Registration: For Medical, Remote Sensing, and Industrial Applications. Wiley-Interscience, New York (2005)
12. Kroon, D.J., Slump, C.H.: MRI modality transformation in demon registration. In: Proceedings of the IEEE International Symposium on Biomedical Imaging: From Nano to Macro, ISBI 2009, pp. 963–966. IEEE Signal Processing Society (2009)
13. Lowe, D.G.: Distinctive image features from scale-invariant keypoints. Int. J. Comput. Vis. **60**(2), 91–110 (2004)
14. Lucas, B.D., Kanade, T.: An iterative image registration technique with an application to stereo vision. In: Proceedings of the 7th International Joint Conference on Artificial Intelligence, IJCAI 1981, vol. 2, pp. 674–679 (1981)
15. Ma, W., et al.: Remote sensing image registration with modified sift and enhanced feature matching. IEEE Geosci. Remote. Sens. Lett. **14**(1), 3–7 (2017)
16. Maintz, J.B.A., Viergever, M.A.: A survey of medical image registration. Med. Image Anal. **2**, 1–36 (1998)
17. Mattes, D., Haynor, D.R., Vesselle, H., Lewellyn, T.K., Eubank, W.: Nonrigid multimodality image registration (2001)
18. Nelder, J.A., Mead, R.: A simplex method for function minimization. Comput. J. **7**(4), 308–313 (1965)
19. Pennec, X., Cachier, P., Ayache, N.: Understanding the "Demon's Algorithm": 3D non-rigid registration by gradient descent. In: Taylor, C., Colchester, A. (eds.) MICCAI 1999. LNCS, vol. 1679, pp. 597–605. Springer, Heidelberg (1999). https://doi.org/10.1007/10704282_64
20. Reddy, B.S., Chatterji, B.N.: An FFT-based technique for translation, rotation, and scale-invariant image registration. IEEE Trans. Image Process. **5**(8), 1266–1271 (1996)
21. Rusinkiewicz, S., Levoy, M.: Efficient variants of the ICP algorithm. In: Proceedings of Third International Conference on 3-D Digital Imaging and Modeling (2001)
22. Scalzo, F., Liebeskind, D.S.: Perfusion angiography in acute ischemic stroke. Comput. Math. Methods Med. **2016**, 2478324 (2016)
23. Styner, M., Brechbühler, C., Székely, G., Gerig, G.: Parametric estimate of intensity inhomogeneities applied to MRI. IEEE Trans. Med. Imaging **19**, 153–165 (2000)
24. Szeliski, R.: Image alignment and stitching: a tutorial. Technical report, MSR-TR-2004-92, Microsoft Research, 2004 (2005)
25. Szeliski, R.: Computer Vision: Algorithms and Applications, 1st edn. Springer, London (2011). https://doi.org/10.1007/978-1-84882-935-0

26. Thévenaz, P., Unser, M.: Optimization of mutual information for multiresolution image registration. IEEE Trans. Image Process. **9**(12), 2083–2099 (2000)
27. Thirion, J.P.: Image matching as a diffusion process: an analogy with Maxwell's demons. Med. Image Anal. **2**, 243–260 (1998)
28. Torr, P.H.S., Zisserman, A.: MLESAC: a new robust estimator with application to estimating image geometry. Comput. Vis. Image Underst. **78**, 138–156 (2000)

Skull Stripping Using Confidence Segmentation Convolution Neural Network

Kaiyuan Chen, Jingyue Shen, and Fabien Scalzo[✉]

Department of Computer Science and Neurology, University of California,
Los Angeles (UCLA), Los Angeles, USA
{chenkaiyuan,brianshen}@ucla.edu, fab@cs.ucla.edu

Abstract. Skull stripping is an important preprocessing step on cerebral Magnetic Resonance (MR) images because unnecessary brain structures, like eye balls and muscles, greatly hinder the accuracy of further automatic diagnosis. To extract important brain tissue quickly, we developed a model named Confidence Segmentation Convolutional Neural Network (CSCNet). CSCNet takes the form of a Fully Convolutional Network (FCN) that adopts an encoder-decoder architecture which gives a reconstructed bitmask with pixel-wise confidence level. During our experiments, a crossvalidation was performed on 750 MRI slices of the brain and demonstrated the high accuracy of the model (dice score: 0.97 ± 0.005) with a prediction time of less than 0.5 s.

Keywords: MRI · Machine learning · Skull stripping
Semantic segmentation

1 Introduction

Computer-aided diagnosis based on medical images from Magnetic Resonance Imaging (MRI) is used widely for its 'noninvasive, nondestructive, flexible' properties [3]. With the help of different MRI techniques like fluid-attenuated inversion recovery (FLAIR) and Diffusion-weighted (DW) MRI, it is possible to obtain the anatomical structure of human soft tissue with high resolution. For brain disease diagnosis, in order to check interior and exterior of brain structures, MRI can produce cross-sectional images from different angles. However, those slices produced from different angles pose great challenges in skull stripping. It is hard to strip those tissue of interest, from extracranial or non-brain tissue that has nothing to do with brain diseases such as Alzheimer's disease, aneurysm in the brain, arteriovenous malformation-cerebral and Cushings disease [3].

As a prerequisite, skull stripping needs to produce fast prediction speed and accurate representation of original brain tissue. In addition, since the MR

K. Chen and J. Shen—Equal Contribution.

© Springer Nature Switzerland AG 2018
G. Bebis et al. (Eds.): ISVC 2018, LNCS 11241, pp. 15–24, 2018.
https://doi.org/10.1007/978-3-030-03801-4_2

images can be taken from different angles, depth and light conditions, the algorithm needs to have great generalization power while maintaining high accuracy. Figure 1 illustrates the challenging nature of 2D skull stripping with some examples from our dataset. It can be seen that the non-brain structure appears very similar to the brain tissue. Sometimes brain tissue only occupies small part of the image and the boundaries between brain tissue and non-brain structures are not clear. The parameters of the MRI may lead to different intensity profiles. In addition, the image structure varies from one slice to another. Sometimes the slices do not hold any brain tissue.

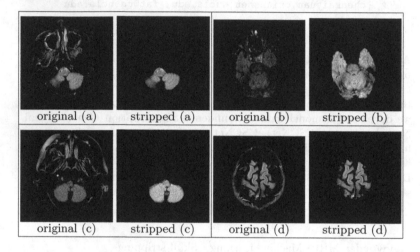

Fig. 1. Illustration of challenges posed during skull stripping.

Our contributions are as follows:

- We design CSCNet, a deep learning architecture that can be applied to skull stripping with confidence level.
- We use series of experiments to show our model is fast and accurate for reconstructing skull stripped images.

We organize this paper as following: we first introduce basic terms like CNN and related algorithms on skull stripping in Sect. 2; then we continue to strip skulls with confidence level in Sect. 3; we show our experimental results in Sect. 4; conclusion and future work are in Sect. 5.

2   Basic Concepts and Related Works

2.1   Traditional Skull Stripping Algorithms

As a preliminary step for further diagnosis, skull stripping needs both speed and accuracy in practice, so these two factors should be considered in any algorithms proposed. By Kalavathi et al. [3], skull stripping algorithms can be classified into five categories: mathematical morphology-based methods, intensity-based methods, deformable surface-based methods, atlas-based methods, and hybrid methods. In past few years, machine learning-based methods also show great results in skull stripping. For example, Yunjie et al. [6] developed a skull stripping method with an adaptive Gaussian Mixture Model (GMM) and a 3D mathematical morphology method. The GMM is used to classify brain tissue and to estimate the bias field in the brain tissue. Butman et al. [10] introduced a robust machine learning method that detects the brain boundary by random forest. Since random forest has high expressive power on voxels of brain boundary, this method can reach high accuracy. However, these methods of skull stripping usually take local patches and conduct prediction pixel by pixel. So if the training dataset is not complete or testing data contains too much noise, the resulting images will have high variance as we shown in our experiments.

2.2 Convolutional Neural Networks

Convolutional Neural Networks. Convolutional Neural Networks (CNNs) have shown great success in vision-related tasks like image classification, as shown in the performance of AlexNet [12], VGGNet [13], GoogLeNet [14]. Compared to traditional pixel-wise prediction by feeding local patches to linear or nonlinear predictors, CNNs can give better results due to their ability of joint feature and classifier learning [15].

Semantic Segmentation. In this paper, we model skull stripping as a special case of semantic segmentation. Semantic Segmentation is a process that associates each image pixel with a class label. Fully Convolutional Network (FCN), proposed by Long et al. [8] provides a hierarchical scheme for this problem. Many works on semantic segmentation like SegNet [1]and U-Net [2] are built on top of FCN [8]. FCN and most of its variations take an encoder-decoder architecture, where encoders try to learn features at different granularity while decoders try to upsample these feature maps from lower resolution to higher resolution for pixelwise classification. The encoder part is usually modified version of pre-trained deep classification network like VGG [13] or ResNet [16], and the decoder part is where most works differ. In FCN, each decoder layer takes the combination of the corresponding encoder max-pooling layer's prediction result (by applying a 1×1 convolution on the max-pooling layer) and previous decoder layer's result as input to do $2\times$ upsampling, in an effort to make local predictions that respect global structure [8]. In U-Net, a major modification from FCN is that it keeps the feature channels in upsampling. Instead of combining prediction results from corresponding encoder layer and the previous decoder layer, it combines feature maps of the two layers as input to next decoder layer, allowing the network to propagate context information to higher resolution [2]. For SegNet, it is more efficient in terms of memory and computation time during inference, and produces similar or better performance than FCN on different metrics. SegNet discards the fully connected layers of VGG16 in encoder part, which makes the network much smaller and easier to train. It features a more memory-efficient decoding technique compared to FCN and U-Net. It uses unpooling [19] rather than deconvolution to do upsampling [1]. Instead of remembering the whole feature maps in encoder part, SegNet only memorizes the indices selected during max-pooling, which only requires 2 bits to store per 2×2 pooling window, and uses them to perform upsampling [1]. This method eliminates the need for learning in upsampling step, and further reduces the number of parameters.

Architectures not based on FCN [8] are also proposed for semantic segmentation, like ENet [5] and PSPNet [9]. ENet also takes the general encoder-decoder approach, but designs its own encoder and decoder part from ground up. It has very fast inference time while having similar performance compared to SegNet, which shows great potential in applying to real-time low-power mobile devices [5]. PSPNet uses global scene context of an image as prior to help better predict pixels' labels. It utilizes a Pyramid Pooling Module to extract global contextual prior of input images and combines the feature map from its modified ResNet architecture with the prior to produce final prediction map [9].

Another work worth mentioning is Baysian SegNet by Kendall et al. [17]. The authors tried to model predictive system's uncertainty and produce probabilistic segmentation output by adding several dropout [18] layers in SegNet. They trained the model with dropout, and at test time they used dropout to do Monte Carlo dropout sampling over the network's weights to get the softmax class probabilities. This method shows better results than SegNet, but can lead to longer inference time due to sampling [17].

CNN-related Works on Skull Stripping. For 3D CT images, Kleesiek et al. [7] used non-parametric 3D Convolutional Neural Network (CNN) to learn important features from input images. However, 3D images usually contain more structural information than 2D images, so for models applying to 2D gray scale MRI should rely less on positional and spacial structures than 3D CNN. Some recent works also proposed FCN-based architecture and achieved better performance than traditional methods. For example, Zeynettin et al. [11] utilized fully convolutional network similar to U-Net to perform skull stripping. Raunak and Yi proposed an architecture called CompNet [4] that learns features from both brain tissue and its complementary part outside the brain to do skull stripping.

3 Proposed Method

In this section we introduce our proposed Confidence Segmentation convolutional Neural Network (CSCNet). We model this problem as semantic segmentation, and adopt an architecture similar to SegNet [1]. By making use of properties of gray scale MR images, we generate a confidence level matrix as a bitmask and apply the bitmask to the original MR Image.

3.1 Semantic Segmentation with Confidence Level

We model 2D Skull Stripping problem as a semantic segmentation problem, i.e. given an image as matrix $\mathbf{X}$, we can view it as a sum of skull matrix $\mathbf{S}$ and stripped matrix $\mathbf{X}'$ with dimension w and h, i.e.

$$X = S + X'$$

Given $\mathbf{X}$, our algorithm will produce a confidence matrix Θ that, with a hyper-parameter confidence level α, it will give a skull matrix

$$\mathbf{S}_{ij} = \begin{cases} \mathbf{X}_{ij} & \Theta_{ij} < \alpha \\ 0 & \Theta_{ij} \geq \alpha \end{cases}$$

and reconstructed image

$$\mathbf{X}'_{ij} = \begin{cases} \mathbf{X}_{ij} & \Theta_{ij} \geq \alpha \\ 0 & \Theta_{ij} < \alpha \end{cases}$$

3.2 Architecture

Encoder-Decoder Architecture. To handle pixel-wise labeling, most Fully Convolutional Network (FCN)s adopt an encoder-decoder scheme. FCN is translation invariant since it leverages operations like convolution, pooling and activation functions on relative distance space.

Under this encoder-decoder scheme, input images first go through convolutions and pooling layers to reduce to a more compact low dimensional embedding, and then the target images are reconstructed by deconvolutions and upsampling. Because of the characteristics of FCN, models are usually trained in an end-to-end fashion by back-propagation and weights are updated by Stochastic Gradient Descent (SGD) efficiently.

Encoder network for our model (Fig. 2) has 8 convolutional layers. For each encoder layer, it uses a filter bank to do convolutional with bias, followed by batch normalization and element-wise rectified linear non-linearity (ReLU), i.e. $\max(0, x)$. After going through encoder's convolution, batch normalization and ReLU, we perform a max-pooling operation. Our pooling window is 2×2 and to prevent overlapped pooling, our stride is also 2.

In decoder network starting from low dimensional encoded embedding, we adopted a deconvolutional scheme similar to Semantic Segmentation Fully Convolutional Networks [8]. We have 8 deconvolutional layers with upsampling and deconvolutions. These decoder layers upsample from input using transferred pool indices to generate feature maps. However, instead of strictly applying softmax in original SegNet, we apply a ReLU activation function and compare the results with gray scale images. The Relu is applied to construct a confidence level for each pixel in the image.

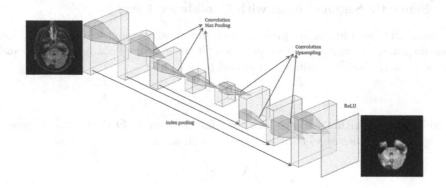

Fig. 2. Illustration of the CSCNet architecture for skull stripping.

From Confidence Level to Output Image. The segmented output image is produced by creating a binary mask. We use the output of the activation function based on the target image, which is expected to have higher confidence for brain tissue. The binary masking is performed as described in Sect. 3.1. Empirically, we set $\alpha=0.5$ in our experiments described in Sect. 4 and illustrated in Fig. 3. Tuning the parameter a could potentially improve the trade-off between true negative and false positive reflected by classification results.

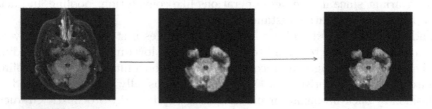

Fig. 3. Constructing brain-tissue images from confidence level matrix.

4   Experiment

In this section, we describe our experimental protocol and present the results.

4.1   Dataset Description

Our dataset consists of around 750 manually labeled skull stripped fluid-attenuated inversion recovery (FLAIR) brain slices from 35 patients provided by University of California, Los Angeles. The use of this dataset was approved by the Institutional Review Board (IRB). Each patient's brain MRI was composed of between 15 to 30 MR slices. The difficulty of skull stripping lies in the fact that brain structure varies due to different diseases patients have, and the challenges mentioned in Fig. 1 in Sect. 1.

4.2 Metrics

We use Dice Score as our major evaluation metric, which is defined as:

$$DiceScore = \frac{2|X \cap Y|}{|X| + |Y|},$$

where X represents the skull stripping results of our model and Y represents the ground truth stripped images. $|X \cap Y|$ means the intersection between ground truth and model's result. Here, for each image in our dataset, we consider $|X \cap Y|$ as the number of correctly classified pixels in an image. Beside this metric, which is commonly used in skull stripping, we also evaluate our model on other traditional classification metrics like Precision and Recall. In the context of classification problem, they are defined as follows:

$$Precision = \frac{TruePositive}{TruePositive + FalsePositive}$$

$$Recall = \frac{TruePositive}{TruePositive + FalseNegative}$$

4.3 Experiments Setup

We performed five-fold crossvalidation with 600 images as training set and remaining 150 images as validation set. The images are of size 256×256 pixels. We treated each patient as a learning unit and put all images of one patient either in training set or in test set. By this way all testing models are able to see different structures of brain and skull in both training and validation set. This approach increases the validity of our experiments' results. As a trade-off between accuracy and prediction time, we choose filter size 16 and 32.

4.4 Descriptions of Competing Models

We choose traditional pixel-by-pixel prediction random forest classifier as our baseline model. There are many existing classifiers like SVM, logistic regression, random forest that take in a local patch surrounding a single pixel and predict as a bitmask. Taking into account the training efficiency and prediction time, we choose random forest [10] as our baseline model and use 3×3 local patches along with brightness and position information as features.

Other competing state-of-the-art models include FCN [11] and CompNet [4]. For FCN [11], the architecture consists of two parts. The first part has three convolutional layers with three max pooling layers. The second part consists of three convolutional layers with three deconvolutional layers and one final reconstruction layer. For all models, we treat the outputs as bitmasks and then applied them to unstripped images to generate clearer and better results.

The accuracy of the competing models are shown in Table 1:

Table 1. Accuracy of models in different metrics

Model	Accuracy	Dice Score	Precision	Recall
Random Forest [10]	0.8538	0.6439	0.8816	0.50621
FCN [8]	0.9647	0.9066	0.9005	0.9213
CompNet [4]	0.9804	0.9468	0.9276	0.9711
CSCNet-16 (our model)	0.9787	0.9510	0.97664	0.9344
CSCNet-32 (our model)	0.9859	0.9701	0.96157	0.9830

4.5 Prediction Time Experiment

We ran all predictions on a personal laptop with single-core Skylake processor and 8G RAM without GPU to simulate actual scenario.

Table 2. Prediction time of the models

Model	Prediction time
Random Forest	35.32
FCN	0.88
CompNet	75.46
CSCNet-16 (our model)	0.31
CSCNet-32 (our model)	0.43

As shown in Table 1 and Table 2, our models (both CSCNet-16 and CSCNet-32) have high accuracy and dice score. They outperform the baseline Random Forest model and other state-of-art FCN-based models. Although CompNet has high prediction accuracy, its reliance on dense convolutional blocks makes its prediction time not applicable to be used in practice, since skull stripping is only a preprocessing step which requires both accuracy and fast speed.

4.6 Examples of Skull Stripped Results

Fig. 4 illustrates some of our skull stripping results. Our model is able to strip skulls from brain tissue given slices of a brain taken from different levels. During our experiments, we found that brain tissue in some images cannot be stripped cleanly from skulls. Such challenging case is illustrated in the upper right corner of Fig. 4. This could be caused by the blurry boundary condition in images, perhaps due to a motion artifact during the acquisition.

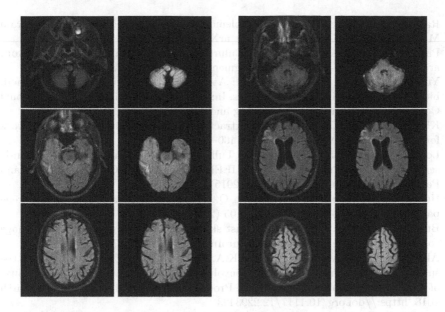

Fig. 4. Some test results of the skull stripping model on different brain slices.

5   Conclusion

The challenging part of skull stripping on MRI is that, given the limited structural information, the model needs to identify brain tissue and distinguish it from skull which usually has similar intensity and appearance. Thus, modeling MRI brain skull stripping in terms of semantic segmentation shows a way to think about labeling these images with pixel confidence level. We propose Confidence Segmentation CNN, a deep learning neural network that augments semantic segmentation models and makes use of the knowledge that higher pixel intensity implies higher confidence in skull classification. Based on a series of experiments, our model has high dice score, precision and recall and is faster that state-of-the-art models.

References

1. Badrinarayanan, V., Kendall, A., Cipolla, R.: SegNet: a deep convolutional encoder-decoder architecture for image segmentation (2015). arXiv:1511.00561
2. Ronneberger, O., Fischer, P., Brox, T.: U-Net: convolutional networks for biomedical image segmentation. In: Navab, N., Hornegger, J., Wells, W.M., Frangi, A.F. (eds.) MICCAI 2015. LNCS, vol. 9351, pp. 234–241. Springer, Cham (2015). https://doi.org/10.1007/978-3-319-24574-4_28
3. Kalavathi, P., Surya Prasath, V.B.: Methods on Skull Stripping of MRI Head Scan Images - a Review. Advances in Pediatries. U.S. National Library of Medicine (2016). www.ncbi.nlm.nih.gov/pmc/articles/PMC4879034

4. Raunak, D., Yi, H.: CompNet: complementary segmentation network for brain MRI extraction (2018). arXiv preprint arXiv:1804.00521v2
5. Paszke, A., Chaurasia, A., Kim, S., Culurciello, E.: ENet: a deep neural network architecture for real-time semantic segmentation (2016). arXiv:1606.02147v1
6. Yunjie, C., Jianwei, Z., Shunfeng, W.: A new fast brain skull stripping method, biomedical engineering and informatics. In: Tianjin: Proceedings 2nd International Conference on Biomedical Engineering and Informatics, BMEI 2009 (2009)
7. Kleesiek, J., et al.: Deep MRI brain extraction: a 3D convolutional neural network for skull stripping. NeuroImage, **129**, 460–469 (2016)
8. Long, J., Shelhamer, E., Darrell, T.: Fully convolutional networks for semantic segmentation. In: Proceedings of the IEEE Conference on Computer Vision and Pattern Recognition, pp. 3431–3440 (2015)
9. Hengshuang Z., Jianping S., Xiaojuan Q., Xiaogang W., Jiaya J. Pyramid scene parsing network. CoRR, abs/1612.01105 (2016)
10. Butman, J., Roy, S., Pham, D.: Robust skull stripping using multiple MR image contrasts insensitive to pathology. NeuroImage **146**, 132–147 (2017)
11. Akkus, Z., Kostandy, P.M., Philbrick, K.A., Erickson, B.J.: Extraction of brain tissue from CT head images using fully convolutional neural networks. In: Proceedings of SPIE, Medical Imaging 2018: Image Processing, vol. 10574, p. 1057420, 2 March 2018. https://doi.org/10.1117/12.2293423
12. Krizhevsky, A., Sutskever, I., Hinton, G.E.: ImageNet classification with deep convolutional neural networks. In: Pereira, F., Burges, C.J.C., Bottou, L., Weinberger, K.Q. (eds.) Advances in Neural Information Processing Systems, vol. 25, pp. 1097–1105. Curran Associates Inc. (2012)
13. Simonyan, K., Zisserman, A.: Very deep convolutional networks for large-scale image recognition. CoRR, abs/1409.1556 (2014)
14. Szegedy, C., et al.: Going deeper with convolutions. CoRR, abs/1409.4842 (2014)
15. Gu, J., et al.: Recent advances in convolutional neural networks. CoRR, abs/1512.07108 (2015)
16. He, K., Zhang, X., Ren, S., Sun, J.: Deep Residual Learning for Image Recognition. CoRR, abs/1512.03385 (2015)
17. Kendall, A., Badrinarayanan, V., Cipolla, R.: Bayesian SegNet: model uncertainty in deep convolutional encoder-decoder architectures for scene understanding. CoRR, abs/1511.02680 (2015)
18. Srivastava, N., Hinton, G., Krizhevsky, A., Sutskever, I., Salakhutdinov, R.: Dropout: a simple way to prevent neural net- works from overfitting. J. Mach. Learn. Res. **15**(1), 1929–1958 (2014)
19. Zeiler, M.D., Fergus, R.: Visualizing and Understanding Convolutional Networks. CoRR, abs/1311.2901 (2013)

Skin Cancer Segmentation Using a Unified Markov Random Field

Omran Salih and Serestina Viriri[✉]

School of Maths, Statistics and Computer Science,
University of KwaZulu-Natal, Durban, South Africa
omran@aims.ac.za, viriris@ukzn.ac.za

Abstract. Most of the medical institutions still use manual methods to detect the skin cancers tumors. However, melanoma detection using human vision alone can be subjective, inaccurate and poorly reproducible even among experienced dermatologists. This is attributed to the challenges in the automatic segmentation of skin cancer due to many factors, such as different skin colors and the presence of hair, diverse characteristics including lesions of varying sizes and shapes, lesions that may have fuzzy boundaries. To address these factors, a Unified Markov Random Field (UMRF) is used to segment both pixel information and regional information corresponding to skin lesions from the images, where UMRF model lies in two aspects. First, it combines the benefits of the pixel-based and the region-based Markov Random Field (MRF) models by decomposing the likelihood function into the product of the pixel likelihood function and the regional likelihood function. The experimental results show that the employed method has high precision 83.08% (Jaccard Index).

Keywords: Unified Markov Random Field · Markov Random Field
Skin lesion · Segmentation

1 Introduction

The skin cancer foundation in the United States has stated that the greatest frequent form of cancer is skin cancer. Skin cancer increase over time in many regions in the world such as Singapore [13], Slovakia [4], and The Netherland [14]. To date, the best way to stop spreading of skin cancer is through detecting the skin cancer in the early stage to be able to identify the abnormalities of skin cancer. In particular, detecting abnormalities of skin in the early stage is very important, since these abnormalities might lead to skin cancer. It is important to distinguish between non-melanoma skin cancer and melanoma skin cancer during the skin cancer examination, to be able to give the right treatment. Unfortunately, care health systems are facing a problem to provide potential patients of a large population with skin examination because of a small number of experts who deliver proper skin diagnosis and the difficulties of their location at the larger centre.

© Springer Nature Switzerland AG 2018
G. Bebis et al. (Eds.): ISVC 2018, LNCS 11241, pp. 25–33, 2018.
https://doi.org/10.1007/978-3-030-03801-4_3

Malignant melanoma has one of the most rapidly increasing incidences in the world and has a considerable mortality rate. Early diagnosis is particularly important since melanoma can be cured with prompt excision. Dermoscopy images play an important role in the noninvasive early detection of melanoma [1]. However, melanoma detection using human vision alone can be subjective, inaccurate and poorly reproducible even among experienced dermatologists. This is attributed to the challenges in interpreting images with diverse characteristics including lesions of varying sizes and shapes, lesions that may have fuzzy boundaries, different skin colors and the presence of hair [2]. Therefore, the automatic analysis of dermoscopy images is a valuable aid for clinical decision making and for image based diagnosis, to identify diseases such as melanoma.

The aim of this paper is to segment the skin lesion tumors. Automatic skin cancer detection system is an ill-posed problem and depends on certain parts such as lesion segmentation, detection and localization of visual dermoscopic features and disease classification. Each of the previous parts depend on certain criteria, for example lesion segmentation needs to be grouped in a pixels such as range of intensity value, texture or gradient information. Automatic skin cancer tumor detection is not an easy task. It needs a lot of image analytical knowledge and experience but in general most of medical institution still use manual methods to detect the skin cancers tumors where expert clinician segment out the tumor manually which is time-consuming. The domain of applications detect the skin cancer but they do not lead to the desired solutions. This lead to the fact that the chance of improving the existing techniques of skin cancer detection still available due to the availability of newer and more computationally efficient techniques yielding potentially more accurate results than those previously used.

2   Method

Unified Markov Random Field (UMRF) model is a probabilistic model [3] based on Markov Random Field (MRF). UMRF model seeking to put into account the advantages of two MRF models: The region-based MRF model and the pixel-based MRF model. This combination of the two MRF models gives the UMRF model more segmentation accuracy compared to state-of-the-art. The description of the UMRF model is basically as follows, first an input image is used to extract the pixel values, second an input image is used to over-segment using one of the over-segmented algorithm (mean shift, Ncut, watersheld, turbopixel), because the initial segmentation is very important since it could directly affect the final segmentation accuracy. Then regional feature formula provided by UMRF is used to obtain the regional features image. Finally both pixel values and regional feature is used to solve the maximum a posteriori (MAP) estimation to find the best estimation which leads to the desired image segmentation. Figure 1 shows the flowchart of UMRF model: First, extract the pixel features Y^P, and the regional features Y^P from the over-segmented image. Then, these features together are combined using likelihood function, and integrates them with spatial information of the posterior probability. Finally, the segmentation result can be given by finding the MAP estimation problem. UMRF model is described in more details below.

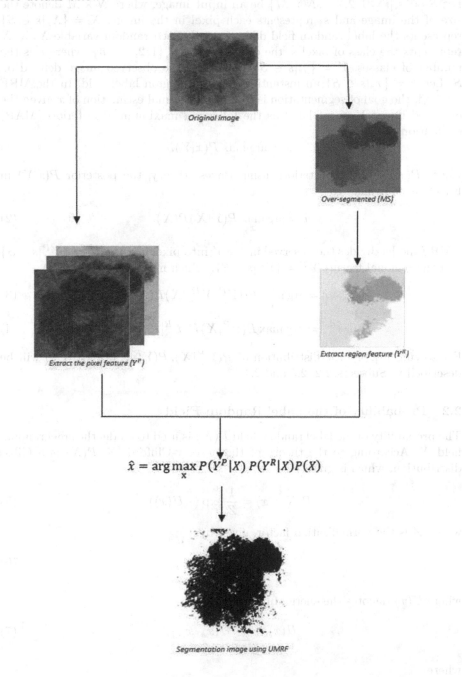

Original image

Over-segmented (MS)

Extract the pixel feature (Y^P)

Extract region feature (Y^R)

$$\hat{x} = \arg\max_{\mathbf{x}} P(Y^P|X)\, P(Y^R|X) P(X)$$

Segmentation image using UMRF

Fig. 1. Flowchart of the UMRF model using an example.

2.1 Problem Formulation

Let $S = \{s_i | i = 1, 2, \cdots, N \times M\}$ be an input image, where $N \times M$ denote the size of the image and s_i represents each pixel in the image. $X = \{X_s | s \in S\}$ represents the label random field defined on S. Each random variable X_s in X represents the class of pixel s, the class set is $\Lambda = \{1, 2, \cdots, n\}$, where n is the number of classes. $Y = \{y_s | s \in S\}$ represents the observed image defined on S. Let $x = \{x_s | s \in S\}$ an instantiation of the region label field. In the MRF method, the goal of segmentation is to find an optimal estimation of x given the observed image Y, formulated as the following maximum a posteriori (MAP) estimation problem:

$$\hat{x} = \arg\max_x P(x|Y), \tag{1}$$

where $P(x|Y)$ is the posteriori, using Bayes' theory, the posterior $P(x|Y)$ in Eq. (1) is equivalent to

$$\hat{x} = \arg\max_x P(Y|X)P(X). \tag{2}$$

UMRF model divides the observed image Y into pixel feature $Y^P = \{Y_s^P | s \in S\}$ and the regional feature $Y^R = \{Y_s^R | s \in S\}$, which means $Y = (Y^P, Y^R)$.

$$\hat{x} = \arg\max_x P((Y^P, Y^R)|X)P(X) \tag{3}$$

$$= \arg\max_x P(Y^P|X)P(Y^R|X)P(X). \tag{4}$$

For solving Eq. (4), the distribution of $P(Y^P|X), P(Y^R|X)$, and $P(X)$ will be described in Subsects. 2.2, 2.3 and 2.4.

2.2 Probability of the Label Random Field

The probability of the label random field $P(X)$ is used to model the label random field X. According to the theory of Harmercley-Clifford [9], $P(X)$ is a Gibss distribution, which is given by

$$P(X = x) = \frac{1}{Z}\exp\left(-U(x)\right) \tag{5}$$

where Z is the normalisation factor, given by:

$$Z = \sum_x U(x) \tag{6}$$

where $U(x)$ denotes the energy function, that is

$$U(x) = \sum_{s \in S} U(x_s, x_{N_s}) \tag{7}$$

where

$$U(x_s, x_{N_s}) = \sum_{t \in N_s} V(x_s, x_t) \tag{8}$$

where N_s is the set of pixels neighbouring pixel s and each $V(x_s, x_t)$ is the potential function between pixel s and pixel $t, t \in N_s$. The potential function $V(x_s, x_t)$ is defined by the multilevel logistic (MLL) model [9], which is

$$V(x_s, x_t) = \begin{cases} \beta & \text{if } x_s = x_t \\ -\beta & \text{if } x_s \neq x_t \end{cases} \tag{9}$$

where $\beta > 0$ is the potential parameter and $t \in N_s$.

2.3 Conditional Probability Function

In UMRF model, the likelihood function is divided in two parts: the pixels values and the regional feature, Both are described below in more details.

The Pixel Likelihood Function. Extract spectral value as the pixel feature to model the micro texture pattern and the detailed information using the likelihood function $P(Y_s^P | X)$. For solving $P(Y_s^P | X)$ UMRF model, we use Gaussian distribution to determine the distribution of the likelihood function of $P(Y_s^P | X)$, which is

$$P(Y_s^P | X_s = h) = \frac{1}{(2\pi)^{D/2} \sqrt{\det(\Sigma_h^P)}} \exp\left(-\frac{(Y_s^P - \mu_h^P)^T \cdot (Y_s^P - \mu_h^P)}{2\Sigma_h^P}\right) \tag{10}$$

where Y_s^P is the pixel feature for every pixel s, the Gaussian distribution parameters are μ_h^P, Σ_h^P, and D is the dimension of Y_s^P.

The Regional Likelihood Function. UMRF model provide a method of extracting the regional feature of an input image. It highlighted that one of over-segmented algorithm should be used to obtain the initial segmentation, since it is very important in the final segmentation accuracy. Several algorithms of over-segmented are proposed in the literature to provide a better over-segmentation result, such as watershed [5], mean shift (MS) [6], normalisation cut (Ncut) [7], and tuberpixel [8]. In this paper, MS is used to extract the over-segmented. The regional feature Y_s^R for UMRF model is presented to extract the spectral value information from over-segmented image for each pixel s, the regional feature Y_s^R is given as follow:

$$Y_s^R = p_{R_s} [1 - \log(p_{R_s})] + \frac{1}{|N_{R_s}|} \sum_{T \in N_{R_s}} p_T [1 - \log(p_T)] \tag{11}$$

where R_s represents the initial over-segmented region including s. p_{R_s} denotes the area ration of the region R_s to the whole image, and N_{R_s} is the set of neighbour regions of R_s. For solving the likelihood function of regional feature

$P(Y_s^R|X)$ UMRF model, we use Gaussian distribution to determine the distribution of the likelihood function of $P(Y_s^P|X)$, which is

$$P(Y_s^R|X_s = h) = \frac{\sqrt{\alpha}}{(2\pi)^{D'/2}\sqrt{\det(\Sigma_h^P)}} \exp\left(-\frac{(Y_s^P - \mu_h^P)^T \cdot (Y_s^P - \mu_h^P)}{2(\Sigma_h^P/\alpha)}\right) \quad (12)$$

where D' is the dimension of Y_s^R, μ_h^R, and Σ_h^R are the parameters of Gaussian distribution, $\det(\Sigma_h^R)$ is the determinant of Σ_h^R, $1 \leq h \leq n$, and α is proposed to show the interaction between the regional feature and the pixel feature, for more details [3].

2.4 Parameters Setting

UMRF model has six parameters, $\beta, \mu_h^P, \Sigma_h^P, \mu_h^R, \Sigma_h^R$ and α which are used in Eqs. (9), (10) and (12) respectively. Furthermore, they known as the mean value and the variance value for the Gaussian distribution, which can be calculated as follows.

$$\mu_h^P = \frac{1}{|X^h|}\sum_{s \in X^h} Y_s^P, \qquad \Sigma_h^P = \frac{1}{|X^h|}\sum_{s \in X^h}\left(Y_s^P - \mu_h^P\right)'\left(Y_s^P - \mu_h^P\right). \quad (13)$$

and

$$\mu_h^R = \frac{1}{|X^h|}\sum_{s \in X^h} Y_s^R, \qquad \Sigma_h^R = \frac{1}{|X^h|}\sum_{s \in X^h}\left(Y_s^R - \mu_h^R\right)'\left(Y_s^R - \mu_h^R\right). \quad (14)$$

β is the potential parameter in Eq. (9), which is used for finding $P(X)$, and α is used to reflect the interaction between $P(Y_s^P|X_s = h)$ and $P(Y_s^R|X_s = h)$.

2.5 Evaluations Metric

Evaluation of the segmentation has been done using three types of evaluation metric, to evaluate the effectiveness of the UMRF model segmentation. Firstly, sensitivity refers to the test's ability to correctly detect ill patients who do have the condition, given by

$$\textbf{Sensitivity} = \frac{TP}{P} = \frac{TP}{TP + TN} \quad (15)$$

where TP is the number of true positives, P is the number of actually positive samples, TN is the number of true negatives. The second type, specificity relates to the test's ability to correctly reject healthy patients without a condition, which is given by

$$\textbf{Specificity} = \frac{TN}{N} = \frac{TN}{TN + FP} \quad (16)$$

where N is the number of actually negatives samples, FP is the number of false negatives. The final type is Jaccard similarity coefficient which is used in the

2017 ISBI Challenge on Skin lesion analysis towards melanoma detection [16]. The Jaccard similarity coefficient measures similarity between finite sample sets, and is defined as the size of the intersection divided by the size of the union of the sample sets:

$$J(A, B) = \frac{|A \cap B|}{|A \cup B|} = \frac{|A \cap B|}{|A| + |B| - |A \cap B|}. \tag{17}$$

where $J(A, B)$ is Jaccard index $0 \leq J(A, B) \leq 1$. Another Jaccard similarity coefficient is used to measure the similarity between finite sample sets, which is called the Jaccard distance:

$$d_J(A, B) = 1 - J(A, B) = \frac{|A \cup B| - |A \cap B|}{|A \cup B|}. \tag{18}$$

where $d_J(A, B)$ is the Jaccard distance $0 \leq d_J(A, B) \leq 1$.

2.6 Algorithm for a UMRF Model

Algorithm 1 shows the steps of UMRF practical implementation, firstly gets an input image Y, and the number of the classes n. It gets over-segmented regions using MS algorithm, then extracts the pixel and regional feature, finally obtains the segmentation result.

Algorithm 1. UMRF model

1: **procedure** UMRF(Y)   ▷ Y is an input image
2:     Extract the spectral value of Y as the pixel feature Y^F;
3:     Use MS to obtain over-segmented regions;
4:     Extract the regional feature Y^R from over-segmented using equation (11);
5:     Get the initial label field X^0 by using k-mean algorithm cluster the feature into
       n classes;
6:     Start iteration. Set **itr** = 0;
7:     **while** True **do**
8:         Estimate $\mu_h^P, \Sigma_h^P, \mu_h^R$, and Σ_h^R respectively, for all the n classes given X^{itr};
9:         Compute: $P(Y_s^P|X_s = h), P(Y_s^R|X_s = h)$, and $P(X_s|X_{N_s})$;
10:        Obtain the best estimation $\hat{x} = \{\hat{x}_s | s \in S\}$ using equation (4);
11:        Set $X^{\text{itr}+1} = \hat{x}$;
12:        **if** $X^{\text{itr}+1} == X^{\text{itr}}$ **then**
13:            Stop and $X^{\text{itr}+1}$ is the best segmentation;
14:        **else if** $X^{\text{itr}+1} == X^{\text{itr}}$ **then**
15:            itr = itr + 1;
16:            repeat;
17:    **return** $X^{\text{itr}+1}$ ▷ $\hat{x} = \{\hat{x}_s | s \in S\}$

---

3 Experimental Results and Discussion

To achieve the goal of this research, Segmentation was preformed on 170 images containing 70 melanoma cases and 100 naevus cases from the MED-NODE database [15]. The image segmentation method is implemented using MATLAB.

Image segmentation of UMRF model is compared with others methods. These methods were used in the 2017 ISBI challenge on skin lesion analysis towards melanoma detection [16]. The top methods are chosen for the comparison. The segmentation performance of the metric on 170 real macroscopic images are shown in Table 1, and shed several important insights on the performance and particularities of the UMRF model. Firstly, the UMRF model methods achieved the lowest Jaccard Distance, which indicates that the UMRF model has the strongest over all performance when compared to the CDN, SLA, and DRN methods. Secondly, based on the Jaccard Index, it can be observed that the UMRF model has the highest performance when compared to the CDN, SLA, and DRN methods. Finally, the proposed method is performed equally on both melanoma and naevus cases. Figure 2 shows the segmentation of some image from our dataset.

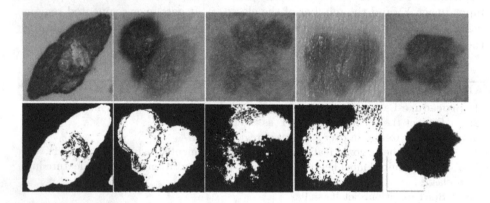

Fig. 2. Example images from MED-NODE database: the first row depict 8 melanoma cases, the second row contain the segmentation results obtained by the UMRF model.

Table 1. Segmentation performance metric.

Method	Jaccard index	Jaccard distance	Sensitivity	Specificity
UMRF model	0.8308	0.1692	0.78	0.22
CDN method [10]	0.7650	0.2350	–	–
SLA method [11]	0.7620	0.2380	–	–
DRN method [12]	0.7600	0.2400	–	–

4   Conclusion

In this paper, a UMRF model for image segmentation is employed. The results are found to be highly accurate compared with others methods. The UMRF model can be part of a system designed to assist automatic skin lesions in the health sector. Skin lesion experimental result using UMRF model indicate that UMRF model potentially can provide more accurate skin lesions segmentation from images than comparable methods existing in the literature. We plan to employ the model in a full automatic skin lesion detection.

References

1. Celebi, M.E., et al.: A methodological approach to the classification of dermoscopy images. Comput. Med. Imaging Graph. **31**(6), 362–373 (2007)
2. Celebi, M.E., et al.: Automatic detection of Blue-White veil and related structures in dermoscopy images. Comput. Med. Imaging Graph. **32**(8), 670–677 (2008)
3. Xiaouhui, C., Chen, Z., Hongtai, Y., Bingxue, W.: Image segmentation using a unified Markov random field. Inst. Eng. Technol. **10**(11), 860–869 (2017)
4. Rogers, H.W., Weinstock, M.A., Feldman, S.R., Coldiron, B.M.: Incidence estimate of nonmelanoma skin cancer (keratinocyte carcinomas) in the US population, 2012. JAMA Dermatology **151**(10), 1081–1086 (2015)
5. Chien, S.Y., Huang, Y.W., Chen, L.W.: Predictive watershed: a fast watershed algorithm for video segmentation. IEEE Trans. Circ. Syst. Video Technol. **13**(5), 453–461 (2003)
6. Comaniciu, D., Meer, P.: Mean Shift: a robust approach toward feature space analysis. IEEE Trans. Pattern Anal. Mach. Intell. **24**(5), 603–619 (2002)
7. Shi, J., Malik, J.: Normalized cuts and image segmentation. IEEE Trans Pattern Anal. Mach. Intell. **22**(8), 888–905 (2000)
8. Levinshtein, A., Stere, A., Kutulakos, K.N.: Turbopixels: fast superpixels using geometric flows. IEEE Trans Pattern Anal. Mach. Intell. **31**(12), 2290–2297 (2009)
9. Li, S.Z.: Markov Random Field Modeling in Image Analysis, 3rd edn. Springer, London (2009). https://doi.org/10.1007/978-1-84800-279-1
10. Yading, Y.: ISIC 2017: Automatic skin lesion segmentation with fully convolutional-deconvolutional networks. https://arxiv.org/pdf/1703.05165.pdf. Accessed 27 June 2018
11. Matt, B.: ISIC 2017- Skin Lesion Analysis Towards Melanoma Detection. https://arxiv.org/ftp/arxiv/papers/1703/1703.00523.pdf. Accessed 27 June 2018
12. Lei, B, Jinman, K, Euijoon A, and Dagan F.: ISIC 2017- Automatic Skin Lesion Analysis using Large-scale Dermoscopy Images and Deep Residual Networks. https://arxiv.org/ftp/arxiv/papers/1703/1703.04197.pdf. Accessed 27 June 2018
13. National Cancer Center Singapora. https://www.nccs.com.sg. Accessed 20 June 2018
14. Nijsten, T., Louwman, M.W., Coebergh, J.W.: Skin cancer epidemic in the Netherlands. Nederlands tijdschrift voor geneeskunde **153**, A768–A768 (2009)
15. Giotis, I., Molders, N., Land, S., Biehl, M., Jonkman, M.F., Petkov, N.: MED-NODE: a computer-assisted melanoma diagnosis system using non-dermoscopic images. Expert Syst. Appl. **42**(19), 6578–6585 (2015)
16. ISIC 2017: Skin Lesion Analysis Towards Melanoma Detection. https://challenge.kitware.com/#challenges. Accessed 26 June 2018

Heart Modeling by Convexity Preserving Segmentation and Convex Shape Decomposition

Xue Shi[1(✉)], Lijun Tang[2], Shaoxiang Zhang[3], and Chunming Li[1]

[1] University of Electronic Science and Technology of China (UESTC),
Chengdu, China
chunming.li@uestc.edu.cn
[2] The First Affiliated Hospital Nanjing Medical University, Nanjing, China
[3] Third Military Medical University, Chongqing, China

Abstract. This paper proposes a convexity-preserving level set (CPLS) and a novel modeling of the heart named Convex Shape Decomposition (CSD) for segmentation of Left Ventricle (LV) and Right Ventricle (RV) from cardiac magnetic resonance images. The main contributions are two-fold. First, we introduce a convexity preserving mechanism in the level set framework, which is helpful for overcoming the difficulties arised from the overlap between intensities of papillary muscles and trabeculae and intensities of myocardium. Furthermore, such a generally contrained convexity-preserving level set method can be useful in many other potential applications. Second, by decomposing the heart into two convex structures, and essentially converting RV segmentation into LV segmentation, we can solve both LV and RV segmentation in a unified framework without training any specific shape models for RV. The proposed method has been quantitatively validated on open datasets, and the experimental results and comparisons with other methods demonstrate the superior performance of our method.

Keywords: Level set · Ventricle segmentation · Geometric property

1 Introduction

Segmentation of cardiac magnetic resonance images (MRIs) provides important information for the diagnosis of left ventricle (LV) and right ventricle (RV) for the diagnosis and treatment of cardiovascular diseases. But the segmentation of LV and RV is a challenging task mainly because of the following reasons [17]: (1) myocardium, papillary muscle, and trabeculae have similar intensities; (2) different patients have considerable different shape of LV and RV, especially in the pathological cases; (3) RV has the thin structure and complex shape.

Due to the different challenges presented in LV and RV segmentation, most of the previous work deal with LV only. There are three main types of LV segmentation methods in the literature:statistical shape prior models [1,11,12], atlas-based methods [2,21], and anatomical knowledge based methods [8]. statistical

G. Bebis et al. (Eds.): ISVC 2018, LNCS 11241, pp. 34–43, 2018.
https://doi.org/10.1007/978-3-030-03801-4_4

shape prior based models often require a big training data set with manually segmentation obtained by experts, which may not be available in practice. Atlas-based approaches do not require a training set, but they depend on the accuracy of image registration, which may be erroneous in case of significant shape variability between the atlas image and target image. In the literature of cardiac LV segmentation, it is commonly assumed that endocardial and epicardial contours are convex. Anatomical knowledge based approaches incorporate the geometric property of LV to improve segmentation accuracy [19].

Due to its complicated crescent shape, segmentation of RV is much more challenging [14,18]. Segmentation methods dealing with RV can be found in the literature [6,10,18]. To take benefit from the relative positions of the two ventricles, some other methods segment LV and RV simultaneously [21,21]. Algorithms that incorporating the anatomical knowledge of the heart have also been proposed [16,20]. However, these methods still require a training shape model for RV, because it is very hard to use anatomical knowledge of the heart to release the training step completely due to the complicated shape of RV.

Liu and Li et al.proposed distance regularized two-layer level set (DR2LS) method for LV segmentation in [8] to take advantage of the property that the distance between the endocardium and epicardium is smoothly varying. In recent years, convexity shape prior has been used in LV segmentation. More general convex shape priors have been proposed in [5,15], the convexity term of the energy in the methods is 3rd order which make the energy minimization procedure computationally expensive.

In this paper, endocardium, epicardium, and myocardium of the two ventricles are collectively referred to as the heart. Our goal is to segment LV and RV from cardiac MRIs. We propose a novel convexity-preserving mechanism in the level set framework and a novel heart modeling technique, named Convex Shape Decomposition (CSD). The main contributions are two-fold. First, incorporating the convexity constraint into the level set framework is crucial for overcoming the difficulties arised from the intensity overlap between papillary muscles and myocardium in LV and RV segmentation. Moreover, such a generally contrained convexity-preserving level set method can be available in many other potential applications. Second, by decomposing the heart into two overlapping convex structures, and essentially converting RV segmentation into the same convex shape segmentation as LV segmentation, we can solve both LV and RV segmentation in a unified framework without training any specific shape models for RV.

2   Convexity-Preserving Segmentation of LV

In cardiac MR images, myocardium, papillary muscle, and trabeculae have similar intensities, as shown in Fig. 1. Therefore, it is hard to obtain desired boundaries of LV and RV using the segmentation algorithm including level set methods, in case of the heart shape prior or anatomical knowledge is not incorporated, as shown in Fig. 1(b). In clinical practice, the inclusion of papillary muscles and trabeculae in the LV cavity is more reproducible (i.e., agreed by most experts). A representative example of expert segmented endocardium is given in Fig. 1(a). Therefore, the desired endocardial and epicardial boundaries of LV should be convex and smooth for a better reproducibility. According to this, it is natural to propose a convexity-preserving mechanism in the segmentation algorithm, which ensures the resulting boundaries to be convex in addition to being similar to the true boundaries, as shown in Fig. 1(c).

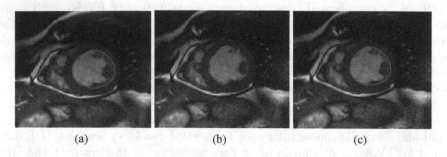

(a)   (b)   (c)

Fig. 1. LV convexity-preserving segmentation. (a) expert-delineated endocardium, (b) segmentation result without anatomical knowledge, and (c) resultant endocardium.

In [19] we proposed the two-layer convexity-preserving level set method. The endocardial contours and epicardial contours are expressed by the 0-level and k-level, which defined by

$$\{x : \phi(x) = 0\}, \quad \text{endocardial} \quad \text{contour} \tag{1}$$
$$\{x : \phi(x) = k\}, \quad \text{epicardial} \quad \text{contour} \tag{2}$$

Respectively. It is important to solve the intensities similarity difficulties between myocardium, myocardium, papillary muscle, trabeculae, and other tissues within the LV cavity.

The image domain is $\Omega \subset R^2$, $I : \Omega \to R$ an image, and $\phi : \Omega \to R$ a level set function. We define the curvature of ϕ as follows:

$$\kappa = div\left(\frac{\nabla\phi}{|\nabla\phi|}\right), \tag{3}$$

where $div(\cdot)$ is the divergence operator.

We define a Curvature Sign Indicator (CSI) function to keep the evolving contour convex, as follows:

$$\beta(\kappa) = \begin{cases} 1, & \kappa \geq 0, \\ 0, & \kappa < 0. \end{cases} \tag{4}$$

The contour is convex at positions where $\kappa \geq 0$ and concave where $\kappa < 0$. So we can obtain the convex contour, which the propagating countour be evolved adaptively through the CSI function.

We use the following evolution equation with the convexity-preserving mechanism to evolve the level set function regardless of the contour regularization terms

$$\frac{\partial \phi}{\partial t} = \beta(\kappa)D(\phi; I) + \nu(1 - \beta(\kappa))\kappa\delta(\phi),$$
(5)

The first term $D(\phi; I)$ is the data term, which drives the evolving contour towards the desired object boundary. The second term $\kappa\delta(\phi)$ is the convexity-preserving term, which expands the contour in case of $\kappa < 0$ and shrinks the contour in case of $\kappa \geq 0$, it only allows two directional motions of the contour. ν is a nonnegative coefficient of the convexity-preserving term.

The choice of the data term is varied with the scope of region-based and edge-based level set methods. In this paper, we propagate the contour using the Distance Regularized Level Set Evolution (DRLSE) model proposed in [7] . Thus, $D(\phi; I)$ can be obtained by

$$D(\phi; I) = \lambda\delta_\epsilon(\phi)div\left(g\frac{\nabla\phi}{|\nabla\phi|}\right) + \alpha g\delta_\epsilon(\phi),$$
(6)

where λ is a nonnegative coefficient of length term, α is the coefficient of the balloon force term. δ is the Dirac function which is approximated by

$$\delta_\epsilon(x) = \frac{1}{\pi}\frac{\epsilon}{\epsilon^2 + x^2},$$
(7)

and g is the edge indicator function defined by,

$$g \triangleq \frac{1}{1 + |\nabla G_\sigma * I|^2},$$
(8)

where $G_\sigma * I$ means filtering I by a Gaussian kernel function.

As mentioned above, literature [13] can produce the segmentation results with the best reproducibility without including papillary muscles and trabeculae (egrender luminal walls) in the myocardium. Based on this, the convexity-preserving mechanism is applied to maintain the two level countours convex. More precisely, endocardium and epicardium of LV and RV can be obtained by using the following evolution equation

$$\frac{\partial \phi}{\partial t} = \beta(\kappa)[\lambda_0\delta_\epsilon(\phi)div\left(g\frac{\nabla\phi}{|\nabla\phi|}\right) + \alpha_0 g\delta_\epsilon(\phi)$$
$$+ \lambda_k\delta_\epsilon(\phi - k)div\left(g\frac{\nabla\phi}{|\nabla\phi|}\right) + \alpha_k g\delta_\epsilon(\phi - k)]$$
$$+ (1 - \beta(\kappa))[\nu_0\kappa\delta(\phi) + \nu_k\kappa\delta(\phi - k)] + R(\phi),$$
(9)

where λ_0 and α_0 are the parameters for 0 level contour, λ_k and α_k for k level contour, and ν_0 and ν_k are nonnegative coefficients defined previously.

3   Segmentation of LV and RV by Convex Shape Decomposition (CSD)

The proposed convexity-preserving level set has been successfully applied to LV segmentation [19]. In this paper, we will extend the convexity preserving level set to segment both LV and RV. But it can not be directly used to segment RV due to its non-convex shape. In order to exploit the CPLS method, we propose to decompose the heart (i.e., endocardium, epicardium, and myocardium of LV and RV, to be precise) into two convex structures, the LV and the extended RV, which is defined as follows. The extented RV is introduced to represent a convexified version of the real RV. The extented RV is not a real anatomical structure, but it is convenient for us to apply the CPLS to obtain a convex shape which include the whole RV and a part of LV. Then we can easily remove the LV part from the extented RV.

The aim of our method is to segment endocardium, epicardium, and myocardium of LV and RV. The proposed of the CSD method consists of the following steps: (1) LV is segmented by CPLS method, (2) the extented RV is segmented by the same method, (3) the real RV can be obtained by subtracting the LV and myocardium of LV from the extented RV, as shown in Fig. 2.

Since the convex shape decomposition is performed by set operations, it is necessary to define their level set representation. Note that the level set functions in this paper take negative values inside Region Of Interests (ROI), and positive values outside. For a given region A, it can be defined as $A = \{x : \phi_A(x) \leq 0\}$, where $\phi_A(x)$ is a level set function which takes negative values for points $x \in A$ and nonnegative values for points $x \notin A$. We call the level set function ϕ_A the level set representation of the region A. Similarly, the region B can be represented by a level set function ϕ_B. It is easy to show that the level set representation of the union operation $A \cup B$ is represented by

$$\phi_{A \cup B}(x) = min(\phi_A(x), \phi_B(x)), \tag{10}$$

and the level set representation of the difference operation $A \setminus B$ is given by

$$\phi_{A \setminus B}(x) = max(\phi_A(x), -\phi_B(x)). \tag{11}$$

With such level set representations of the set operations, the corresponding boundaries of region $A \cup B$ and region $A \setminus B$ are denoted by $\phi_{A \cup B}(x) = 0$ and $\phi_{A \setminus B}(x) = 0$.

In this section, the level set representation of CSD is discribed in detail. To segment the entire heart, we employ two level set functions to represent these two structures, respectively. The two level set functions are then independently evolved by Eq. 9. Finally, the desired myocardial boundaries are obtained through set operations.

Figure 2 depicts the level set representation of CSD (better viewed in color). In (a), the entire endocardium and epicardium of the heart are denoted by the red and the green contours. Two level set functions ϕ_L and ϕ_R represent LH and RH respectively, as shown in (b). The black and blue curves, denoted by 0 level and k_L level of ϕ_L, correspond to endocardium and epicardium of LH, and 0 level (red curve) and k_R level (green curve) represent the inner and outer boundaries of RH. Note that k_L and k_R are set to two distinct values since the thickness of LV and RV myocardium may be significantly different.

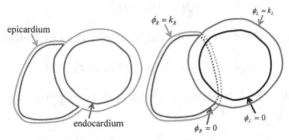

(a) Myocardial boundaries   (b) Level set representation

Fig. 2. Myocardial boundaries and its two-layer level set representation. (a) the true endocardium and epicardium. (b) two layer level set representation of LH and RH.

Before applying set operations to the two segmented structures, it is necessary to define the following four regions: the region inside 0 level of ϕ_L

$$V_L = \{x : \phi_L(x) < 0\}, \tag{12}$$

the region inside k_L level of ϕ_L

$$H_L = \{x : \phi_L(x) < k_L\}, \tag{13}$$

and the regions inside 0 level and k_R level of ϕ_R

$$\tilde{V}_R = \{x : \phi_R(x) < 0\}, \tag{14}$$

$$H_R = \{x : \phi_R(x) < k_R\}, \tag{15}$$

Then we employ set operations and their level set representation to define the regions to be extracted. The RV cavity V_R is the difference set of $\tilde{V}_R$ and H_L

$$V_R = \tilde{V}_R \setminus H_L. \tag{16}$$

From Eq. 11, we obtain the level set representation of V_R

$$\bar{\phi}_R(x) = max(\phi_R(x), -(\phi_L(x) - k_L)). \tag{17}$$

Then, the RV endocardium can be represented by zero level contour of $\bar{\phi}_R$.

The LV myocardium can be represented by

$$M_L = H_L \setminus V_L \tag{18}$$

According to Eq. 11, the level set representation of M_L is given by

$$\phi_{ML}(x) = max(\phi_L(x) - k_L, -\phi_L(x)). \qquad (19)$$

The LV myocardial boundaries is thus represented by $\phi_{ML}(x) = 0$.

The real whole heart is given by

$$H = H_L \cup H_R \qquad (20)$$

From Eq. 10, the level set representation of H can thus be obtained by

$$\phi_H(x) = min(\tilde{\phi}_L(x) - k, \tilde{\phi}_R(x) - k) \qquad (21)$$

where k stands for the k level, $\tilde{\phi}_R = \frac{k}{k_R}\phi_R$ and $\tilde{\phi}_L = \frac{k}{k_L}\phi_L$. The epicardium is then denoted by $\phi_H(x) = 0$.

4   Experimental Results

Unless otherwise stated, the parameters in this paper are set as follows: Gaussian filter σ is set to 1, $\epsilon = 1$, $\mu = 0.4$, coefficient of the data term for ϕ_L and ϕ_R are set the same, α_0, α_k, λ_0, and λ_k are set to -0.8, 0.1,5, 0.5, respectively. Since the thickness of LV myocardium and RV myocardium are may be significantly different, the outer level contours of ϕ_L and ϕ_R are respectively chosen as 8 and 3. ν_0 and ν_k are both set to 1.

Figure 3 shows the process of our method. (a) presents final result of the right structure, and the two colored curves correspond to inner and outer boundaries of RH. (b) depicts final result of LH, and the yellow curve and blue curve are endocardium and epicardium of LV, respectively. The results of the left structure and right structure are simultaneously superimposed to the original image before set operations in (c). The dashed boundaries of RH are not the true endocardium and epicardium of RV. The whole myocardial boundaries are shown in (d). The red curve represents endocardium of LV and RV, and the green curve is epicardium of LV and RV. It is worth noting that the segmented right structure and left structure are both convex, which is in accord with the convex shape decomposition modeling of the heart.

Our method has been taken effect on the Medical Image Computing and Computer-Asisted Intervention (MICCAI) 2012 grand challenge training and validation data set on Right ventricular segmentation. Contour accuracies in accordance with dice metric (DM) is employed to quantitatively evaluate the performance of our method. The dice metric is defined as

$$DM(R_1, R_2) = \frac{|R_1 \cap R_2|}{|R_1 \cup R_2|} \qquad (22)$$

where $|\cdot|$ stands for the area of a region of interest. R_1 is the region segmented using our method to be evaluated, and R_2 is the ground truth region. It can

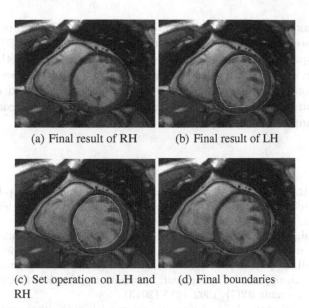

(a) Final result of RH   (b) Final result of LH

(c) Set operation on LH and   (d) Final boundaries
RH

Fig. 3. The whole process of our method. (a) final boundaries of RH. (b) resultant endocardium and epicardium of LH. (c) se operations on segmented LH and RH. (d) the entire final myocardial boundaries.

be easily seen that the closer DM is to 1, the better the performance of the algorithm.

Table 1 lists the comparison of our method with other RV segmentation approaches [3,4,9,21] on the contour accuracy of endocardium in terms of DM. It can be easily concluded that our method obtains a much larger average DM value while the deviation is significantly smaller, which also demonstrates the higher accuracy and robustness of our method.

Table 1. Contour accuracy of RV endocardium in terms of dice metric (average value ± standard deviation)

	CMIC [21]	BIT-UPM [9]	ICL [3]	LITIS [4]	Our method
DM (%)	0.78 ± 0.23	0.80 ± 0.19	0.78 ± 0.20	0.76 ± 0.20	0.87 ± 0.03

5   Conclusions

In this paper, we have used a convexity-preserving mechanism in the level set framework and proposed a novel heart modeling method, which is named convex shape decomposition. We extended the method in [19] to segment the both LV and RV by using the convex shape decomposition model. The proposed method has been validated on a number of cardiac MR images and compared with other methods. The quantitative evaluation showed advantage of our method in terms of segmentation accuracy. Given the generality of its formulation, we expect that the proposed convexity-preserving level set and the convex shape decomposition of heart will can be apply to more general objects that can be decomposed into a number of simple convex shape.

References

1. Avendi, M.R., Kheradvar, A., Jafarkhani, H.: A combined deep-learning and deformable-model approach to fully automatic segmentation of the left ventricle in cardiac MRI. Med. Image Anal. **30**, 108–119 (2016)
2. Bai, W., Shi, W., Ledig, C., Rueckert, D.: Multi-atlas segmentation with augmented features for cardiac MR images. Med. Image Anal. **19**(1), 98–109 (2015)
3. Bai, W., et al.: A probabilistic patch-based label fusion model for multi-atlas segmentation with registration refinement: application to cardiac MR images. IEEE Trans. Med. Imaging **32**(7), 1302–1315 (2013)
4. ElBaz, M.S., Fahmy, A.S.: Active shape model with inter-profile modeling paradigm for cardiac right ventricle segmentation. In: Ayache, N., Delingette, H., Golland, P., Mori, K. (eds.) MICCAI 2012. LNCS, vol. 7510, pp. 691–698. Springer, Heidelberg (2012). https://doi.org/10.1007/978-3-642-33415-3_85
5. Gorelick, L., Veksler, O., Boykov, Y., Nieuwenhuis, C.: Convexity shape prior for segmentation. In: Fleet, D., Pajdla, T., Schiele, B., Tuytelaars, T. (eds.) ECCV 2014. LNCS, vol. 8693, pp. 675–690. Springer, Cham (2014). https://doi.org/10.1007/978-3-319-10602-1_44
6. Grosgeorge, D., Petitjean, C., Dacher, J.N., Ruan, S.: Graph cut segmentation with a statistical shape model in cardiac MRI. Comput. Vis. Image Und. **117**(9), 1027–1035 (2013)
7. Li, C., Xu, C., Gui, C., Fox, M.D.: Distance regularized level set evolution and its application to image segmentation. IEEE Trans. Image Process. **19**(12), 3243–3254 (2010)
8. Liu, Y., et al.: Distance regularized two level sets for segmentation of left and right ventricles from CINE-MRI. Magn. Reson. Imaging **34**(5), 699–706 (2016)
9. Maier, O.M.O., Jimnez, D., Santos, A., Ledesma-Carbayo, M.J.: Segmentation of RV in 4D cardiac MR volumes using region-merging graph cuts. In: Proceedings of the IEEE CinC, pp. 697–700 (2012)
10. Moolan-Feroze, O., Mirmehdi, M., Hamilton, Markand Bucciarelli-Ducci, C.: Segmentation of the right ventricle using diffusion maps and markov random fields. In: Proceedings of the MICCAI, pp. 682–689 (2014)
11. Nambakhsh, C.M.S., et al.: Left ventricle segmentation in MRI via convex relaxed· distribution matching. Med. Image Anal. **17**(8), 1010–1024 (2013)
12. Ngo, T.A., Carneiro, G.: Fully automated non-rigid segmentation with distance regularized level set evolution initialized and constrained by deep-structured inference. In: Proceedings of the CVPR, pp. 3118–3125 (2014)
13. Park, E.A., Lee, W., Kim, H.K., Chung, J.W.: Effect of papillary muscles and trabeculae on left ventricular measurement using cardiovascular magnetic resonance imaging in patients with hypertrophic cardiomyopathy. Korean J. Radiol. **16**(1), 4–12 (2015)

14. Petitjean, C., et al.: Right ventricle segmentation from cardiac MRI: a collation study. Med. Image Anal. **19**(1), 187–202 (2015)
15. Qi, J., et al.: Drosophila eye nuclei segmentation based on graph cut and convex shape prior. In: Proceedings of the ICIP, pp. 670–674 (2013)
16. Qin, X., Cong, Z., Fei, B.: Automatic segmentation of right ventricular ultrasound images using sparse matrix transform and a level set. Phys. Med. Biol. **58**(21), 7609 (2013)
17. Queirs, S.: Fast automatic myocardial segmentation in 4D cine CMR datasets. Med. Image Anal. **18**(7), 1115–1131 (2014)
18. Ringenberg, J., Deo, M., Devabhaktuni, V., Berenfeld, O., Boyers, P., Gold, J.: Fast, accurate, and fully automatic segmentation of the right ventricle in short-axis cardiac MRI. Comput. Med. Imaging Graph. **38**(3), 190–201 (2014)
19. Yang, C., Shi, X., Yao, D., Li, C.: A level set method for convexity preserving segmentation of cardiac left ventricle. In: 2017 IEEE International Conference on Image Processing (ICIP), pp. 2159–2163. IEEE (2017)
20. Zhu, L., et al.: Automatic delineation of the myocardial wall from CT images via shape segmentation and variational region growing. IEEE Trans. Bio-med. Eng. **60**(10), 2887–2895 (2013)
21. Zuluaga, M.A., Cardoso, M. Jorgeand Modat, M.O.S.: Multi-atlas propagation whole heart segmentation from MRI and CTA using a local normalised correlation coefficient criterion. In: Proceedings of the FIMH, pp. 174–181 (2013)

Computer Graphics I

PSO-Based Newton-Like Method and Iteration Processes in the Generation of Artistic Patterns

Ireneusz Gościniak$^{(\boxtimes)}$ and Krzysztof Gdawiec

Institute of Computer Science, University of Silesia, Będzińska 39,
41-200 Sosnowiec, Poland
{ireneusz.gosciniak,krzysztof.gdawiec}@us.edu.pl

Abstract. In artistic pattern generation one can find many different approaches to the generation process. One of such approaches is the use of root finding methods. In this paper, we present a new method of generating artistic patterns with the use of root finding. We modify the classical Newton's method using a Particle Swarm Optimization approach. Moreover, we introduce various iteration processes instead of the standard Picard iteration used in the Newton's method. Presented examples show that using the proposed method we are able to obtain very interesting and diverse patterns that could have an artistic application, e.g., in texture generation, tapestry or textile design etc.

Keywords: Generative art · Root finding · Dynamics · Iterations
Visualization

1 Introduction

One of the most elusive goals in computer aided design is artistic design and pattern generation. This involves diverse aspects: analysis, creativity and development [1]. A designer has to deal with all of these aspects in order to obtain an interesting pattern, which later could be used in jewellery design, carpet design, as a texture etc. Usually the most work during the design stage is carried out by a designer manually, especially in the cases in which the designed pattern should contain some unique, unrepeatable artistic features. Therefore, it is highly useful to develop methods (e.g. automatic, semi-automatic) that will assist pattern generation, and will make the whole process easier.

In the literature we can find many artistic pattern generation methods. They involve different approaches to the generation process, e.g., fractals [2], neural networks [3], shape grammars [4] etc. One of the popular methods of generating artistic patterns is the use of root finding methods and visualization of their behaviour. This method is called polynomiography [5] and images created by it are called polynomiographs. In the generation process one can use a single root finding method [6] or a combination of them [7].

© Springer Nature Switzerland AG 2018
G. Bebis et al. (Eds.): ISVC 2018, LNCS 11241, pp. 47–56, 2018.
https://doi.org/10.1007/978-3-030-03801-4_5

Evolutionary algorithms are algorithms for optimization – particularly for solving the minimization problem, but they can also be adopted to root finding. One of very popular algorithms in this group is the Particle Swarm Optimization (PSO). The particle movement in PSO can be described by the following equation:

$$\mathbf{z}_i' = \mathbf{z}_i + \mathbf{v}_i', \tag{1}$$

where $\mathbf{z}_i'$ – the current position of the ith particle in a D dimensional environment, $\mathbf{z}_i$ – the previous position of the ith particle, $\mathbf{v}_i'$ – the current velocity of the ith particle in a D dimensional environment that is given by the following formula:

$$\mathbf{v}_i' = \omega \mathbf{v}_i + \eta_1 r_1(\mathbf{z}_{pbest\,i} - \mathbf{z}_i) + \eta_2 r_2(\mathbf{z}_{gbest} - \mathbf{z}_i), \tag{2}$$

where $\mathbf{v}_i$ – the previous velocity of the ith particle, ω – inertia weight ($\omega \in [0,1]$), η_1, η_2 – acceleration constants ($\eta_1, \eta_2 \in (0,1]$), r_1, r_2 – random numbers generated uniformly in the $[0,1]$ interval, $\mathbf{z}_{pbest\,i}$ – the best position of the ith particle, $\mathbf{z}_{gbest}$ – the global best position of the particles. The best position and the global best position of particles are updated in each iteration. The particle behaviour depends on inertia weight (ω) and acceleration constants (η_1, η_2). The inertia weight helps particle to escape from a not promising area and acceleration constants direct the particle to an extreme – the values of the parameters are selected during the tuning process.

The behaviour of particles can be very complicated in evolutionary algorithms [8,9]. So the use of this algorithms group – especially the PSO algorithm – can give rise to new artistic patterns. Thus, in this paper we propose modification of the Newton's method using the PSO approach and various iteration processes.

The rest of the paper is organized as follows. Section 2 introduces a root finding algorithm that is based on the Newton method and the PSO approach. Next, Sect. 3 introduces iteration processes known in literature. Then, in Sect. 4 an algorithm for creating artistic images is presented. Some examples of patterns obtained with the proposed algorithm are presented in Sect. 5. Finally, Sect. 6 gives short concluding remarks.

2   PSO-Based Newton Method

The Newton method is one of methods to solve a system of D non-linear equations with D variables [10]. Let $f_1, f_2, \ldots, f_D : \mathbb{R}^D \to \mathbb{R}$ and let

$$\mathbf{F}(z^1, z^2, \ldots, z^D) = \begin{bmatrix} f_1(z^1, z^2, \ldots, z^D) \\ f_2(z^1, z^2, \ldots, z^D) \\ \vdots \\ f_D(z^1, z^2, \ldots, z^D) \end{bmatrix} = \begin{bmatrix} 0 \\ 0 \\ \vdots \\ 0 \end{bmatrix} = \mathbf{0}. \tag{3}$$

Assume that $\mathbf{F} : \mathbb{R}^D \to \mathbb{R}^D$ is a continuous function which has continuous first partial derivatives. Thus, to solve the equation $\mathbf{F}(\mathbf{z}) = \mathbf{0}$, where

$\mathbf{z} = [z^1, z^2, \ldots, z^D]$, using the Newton method we select a starting point $\mathbf{z}_0 = [z_0^1, z_0^2, \ldots, z_0^D]$ and then use the following iterative formula:

$$\mathbf{z}_{n+1} = \mathbf{z}_n - \mathbf{J}^{-1}(\mathbf{z}_n)\mathbf{F}(\mathbf{z}_n) \quad n = 0, 1, 2, \ldots, \tag{4}$$

where

$$\mathbf{J}(\mathbf{z}) = \begin{bmatrix} \frac{\partial f_1}{\partial z_1}(\mathbf{z}) & \frac{\partial f_1}{\partial z_2}(\mathbf{z}) & \ldots & \frac{\partial f_1}{\partial z_D}(\mathbf{z}) \\ \frac{\partial f_2}{\partial z_1}(\mathbf{z}) & \frac{\partial f_2}{\partial z_2}(\mathbf{z}) & \ldots & \frac{\partial f_2}{\partial z_D}(\mathbf{z}) \\ \vdots & \vdots & \vdots & \vdots \\ \frac{\partial f_D}{\partial z_1}(\mathbf{z}) & \frac{\partial f_D}{\partial z_2}(\mathbf{z}) & \ldots & \frac{\partial f_D}{\partial z_D}(\mathbf{z}) \end{bmatrix} \tag{5}$$

is the Jacobian matrix of $\mathbf{F}$ and $\mathbf{J}^{-1}$ is its inverse.

Introducing $\mathbf{N}(\mathbf{z}) = -\mathbf{J}^{-1}(\mathbf{z})\mathbf{F}(\mathbf{z})$ the Newton method can be represented in the following form:

$$\mathbf{z}_{n+1} = \mathbf{z}_n + \mathbf{N}(\mathbf{z}_n), \quad n = 0, 1, 2, \ldots. \tag{6}$$

To solve (3) the following PSO approach can be used:

$$\mathbf{z}_{n+1} = \mathbf{z}_n + \mathbf{v}_{n+1}, \tag{7}$$

where $\mathbf{z}_0 \in \mathbb{R}^D$ is a starting position, $\mathbf{v}_0 = [0, 0, \ldots, 0]$ is a starting velocity, $\mathbf{v}_{n+1}$ is the current velocity of particle, $\mathbf{z}_n$ is the previous position of particle. The algorithm sums the position of the particle $\mathbf{z}_n$ with its current velocity $\mathbf{v}_{n+1}$. The current velocity of the particle is determined by the inertia weight and the acceleration constants:

$$\mathbf{v}_{n+1} = \omega \mathbf{v}_n + \eta \mathbf{N}(\mathbf{z}_n), \tag{8}$$

where $\mathbf{v}_n$ – the previous velocity of particle, $\omega \in [0, 1)$ – inertia weight, $\eta \in (0, 1]$ – acceleration constant.

The inertia weight (ω) and the acceleration constant (η) selection allows to change particle dynamics, which in consequence creates different patterns.

3   Iteration Processes

The Picard iteration is widely used in computational tasks which are based on iterative processes. This iteration has the following form

$$\mathbf{z}_{n+1} = \mathbf{T}(\mathbf{z}_n). \tag{9}$$

Let us notice that (7) uses the Picard iteration, where $\mathbf{T} : \mathbb{R}^D \to \mathbb{R}^D$ is given by the following formula

$$\mathbf{T}(\mathbf{z}_n) = \mathbf{z}_n + \mathbf{v}_{n+1}. \tag{10}$$

In the literature there exist many other types of iterations. The three most widely used iterations are the following:

1. The Mann iteration [11]:

$$\mathbf{z}_{n+1} = (1 - \alpha_n)\mathbf{z}_n + \alpha_n \mathbf{T}(\mathbf{z}_n), \ n = 0, 1, 2, \ldots, \tag{11}$$

where $\alpha_n \in (0, 1]$ for all $n \in \mathbb{N}$. The Mann iteration for $\alpha_n = 1$ reduces to the Picard iteration.

2. The Ishikawa iteration [12]:

$$\mathbf{z}_{n+1} = (1 - \alpha_n)\mathbf{z}_n + \alpha_n \mathbf{T}(\mathbf{u}_n),$$
$$\mathbf{u}_n = (1 - \beta_n)\mathbf{z}_n + \beta_n \mathbf{T}(\mathbf{z}_n), \ n = 0, 1, 2, \ldots, \tag{12}$$

where $\alpha_n \in (0, 1]$ and $\beta_n \in [0, 1]$ for all $n \in \mathbb{N}$. The Ishikawa iteration reduces to the Mann iteration when $\beta_n = 0$ and to the Picard iteration when $\alpha_n = 1$, $\beta_n = 0$ for all $n \in \mathbb{N}$.

3. The Agarwal iteration [13] (S-iteration):

$$\mathbf{z}_{n+1} = (1 - \alpha_n)\mathbf{T}(\mathbf{z}_n) + \alpha_n \mathbf{T}(\mathbf{u}_n),$$
$$\mathbf{u}_n = (1 - \beta_n)\mathbf{z}_n + \beta_n \mathbf{T}(\mathbf{z}_n), \ n = 0, 1, 2, \ldots, \tag{13}$$

where $\alpha_n, \beta_n \in [0, 1]$ for all $n \in \mathbb{N}$. The S-iteration reduces to the Picard iteration when $\alpha_n = 0$, or $\alpha_n = 1$ and $\beta_n = 0$.

A review of various iteration processes and their dependencies can be found in [14].

The introduced so far iterations used only one mapping $\mathbf{T}$, but in the literature we can find also the use of iterations that use more than one mapping [7]. The most basic iteration of this type are the following:

1. The Das-Debata iteration [15]:

$$\mathbf{z}_{n+1} = (1 - \alpha_n)\mathbf{z}_n + \alpha_n \mathbf{T}_2(\mathbf{u}_n),$$
$$\mathbf{u}_n = (1 - \beta_n)\mathbf{z}_n + \beta_n \mathbf{T}_1(\mathbf{z}_n), \ n = 0, 1, 2, \ldots, \tag{14}$$

where $\alpha_n \in (0, 1]$ and $\beta_n \in [0, 1]$ for all $n \in \mathbb{N}$. The Das-Debata iteration for $\mathbf{T}_1 = \mathbf{T}_2$ reduces to the Ishikawa iteration.

2. The Khan-Cho-Abbas iteration [16]:

$$\mathbf{z}_{n+1} = (1 - \alpha_n)\mathbf{T}_1(\mathbf{z}_n) + \alpha_n \mathbf{T}_2(\mathbf{u}_n),$$
$$\mathbf{u}_n = (1 - \beta_n)\mathbf{z}_n + \beta_n \mathbf{T}_1(\mathbf{z}_n), \ n = 0, 1, 2, \ldots, \tag{15}$$

where $\alpha_n \in (0, 1]$ and $\beta_n \in [0, 1]$ for all $n \in \mathbb{N}$. The Khan-Cho-Abbas iteration reduces to the Agarwal iteration when $\mathbf{T}_1 = \mathbf{T}_2$.

3. The generalized Agarwal's iteration [16]:

$$\mathbf{z}_{n+1} = (1 - \alpha_n)\mathbf{T}_3(\mathbf{z}_n) + \alpha_n \mathbf{T}_2(\mathbf{u}_n),$$
$$\mathbf{u}_n = (1 - \beta_n)\mathbf{z}_n + \beta_n \mathbf{T}_1(\mathbf{z}_n), \ n = 0, 1, 2, \ldots, \tag{16}$$

where $\alpha_n \in (0, 1]$ and $\beta_n \in [0, 1]$ for all $n \in \mathbb{N}$. The generalized Agarwal iteration reduces to the Khan-Cho-Abbas iteration when $\mathbf{T}_1 = \mathbf{T}_3$ and to the Agarwal iteration when $\mathbf{T}_1 = \mathbf{T}_2 = \mathbf{T}_3$.

4   Artistic Patterns Generation Method

To generate the artistic patterns we use Algorithm 1, which is very similar to the polynomiography. In the algorithm one of the iteration methods I_q presented in Sec. 3 is selected. Moreover, we select parameters ω, η for a single mapping $\mathbf{T}$ or $\omega_1, \omega_2, \omega_3$ and η_1, η_2, η_3 for $\mathbf{T}_1, \mathbf{T}_2, \mathbf{T}_3$ (depending on the chosen iteration). The maximum number of iterations m which algorithm should make, accuracy of the computations ε and a colouring function $C : \mathbb{N} \to \{0, 1, \ldots, 255\}^3$ are also chosen. Then, for each $\mathbf{z}_0$ in the considered area $\mathbf{A}$ we iterate it using the chosen iteration and mappings. The iterations of the algorithm proceed till the convergence criterion:

$$\|\mathbf{F}(\mathbf{z}_n)\| < \varepsilon \tag{17}$$

is satisfied or the maximum number of iterations is reached. A colour corresponding to the performed number of iterations is assigned to $\mathbf{z}_0$ using colouring function C.

Algorithm 1. Artistic Patterns Generation Method

Input: $\mathbf{F}$ – function, $\mathbf{A} \subset \mathbb{R}^D$ – solution space, m – the maximum number of
   iterations, I_q – iteration method, $q \in [0, 1]^N$ – parameters of the
   iteration I_q, ω, ω_1, ω_2, ω_3, η, η_1, η_1, η_2, η_3 – parameters defining
   functions $\mathbf{T}$, $\mathbf{T}_1$, $\mathbf{T}_2$, $\mathbf{T}_3$, C – colouring function, ε – accuracy
Output: visualization of the dynamics

1 **foreach** $\mathbf{z}_0 \in \mathbf{A}$ **do**
2 | $n = 0$
3 | $\mathbf{v}_0 = [0, 0, \ldots, 0]$
4 | **while** $n \leq m$ **do**
5 | | **if** $\|\mathbf{F}(\mathbf{z}_n)\| < \varepsilon$ **then**
6 | | | **break**
7 | | $\mathbf{z}_{n+1} = I_q(\mathbf{z}_n)$
8 | | $n = n + 1$
9 | colour $\mathbf{z}_0$ with $C(n)$

The solution space $\mathbf{A}$ is defined in a D-dimensional space, thus the algorithm returns patterns in this space. For $D = 2$, a single image is obtained. When $D > 2$ cross section of $\mathbf{A}$ with a two-dimensional plane for visualization can be made.

5   Examples

In this section we present some examples obtained with the proposed method.

Let $\mathbb{C}$ be the field of complex numbers with a complex number $c = x + iy$ where $i = \sqrt{-1}$ and $x, y \in \mathbb{R}$. In the examples we will use the following complex polynomials:

1. $p_1(c) = c^3 - 1 = x^3 - 3xy^2 - 1 + (3x^2y - y^3)i$
   the roots: $1,\ -0.5 - 0.866025i,\ -0.5 + 0.866025i$,
2. $p_2(c) = c^4 - 10c^2 + 9 = x^4 - 6x^2y^2 + y^4 - 10x^2 + 10y^2 + 9 + (4x^3y - 4xy^3 - 20xy)i$
   the roots: $-3,\ -1,\ 1,\ 3$,
3. $p_3(c) = c^5 - c = x^5 - 10x^3y^2 + 5xy^4 - x + (5x^4y - 10x^2y^3 + y^5 - y)i$
   the roots: $-1,\ -i,\ 0,\ i,\ 1$,
4. $p_4(c) = c^6 + 10c^3 - 8 = x^6 - 15x^4y^2 + 15x^2y^4 - y^6 + 10x^3 - 30xy^2 - 8 + (6x^5y - 20x^3y^3 + 6xy^5 + 30x^2y - 10y^3)i$
   the roots: $-2.207,\ -0.453 - 0.785i,\ -0.453 + 0.785i,\ 0.906,\ 1.103 - 1.911i,$
   $1.103 + 1.911i$.

Having a complex polynomial equation $p(c) = 0$ we can transform it into a system of two equations with two real variables, i.e.,

$$\mathbf{F}(x, y) = \begin{bmatrix} \Re(p(x + iy)) \\ \Im(p(x + iy)) \end{bmatrix} = \begin{bmatrix} 0 \\ 0 \end{bmatrix} = \mathbf{0}, \tag{18}$$

where $\Re(c), \Im(c)$ denote the real and imaginary part of a complex number c, respectively.

In the examples the same colourmap will be used, which is presented in Fig. 1. The other common parameters used in the examples are the following: $m = 128$, $\varepsilon = 0.1$, image resolution 800×800 pixels. The areas depend on the polynomial and are the following: $\mathbf{A}_1 = [-2.0, 2.0]^2$, $\mathbf{A}_2 = [-4.0, 4.0] \times [-2.0, 2.0]$, $\mathbf{A}_3 = [-2.0, 2.0]^2$, $\mathbf{A}_4 = [-2.3, 1.7] \times [-2.0, 2.0]$.

Fig. 1. Colour map used in the examples

The particles behaviour (dynamics) depends on the acceleration constant (η) and inertia weight (ω). The increase in values of acceleration constant and inertia weight increases the number of image details (increases the image dynamics). Moreover, also the parameters used in the various iteration processes influence particle's dynamics.

Examples of patterns generated with the use of the Picard iteration for the four considered polynomials and different values of ω and η are presented in Fig. 2. The patterns for the Mann iteration for the considered test functions are presented in Fig. 3. The same values of the parameters were used to create these patterns. We can observe that the obtained patterns have similar features. Comparing the images obtained with the Mann iteration with the ones obtained with the Picard iteration we see that the shapes of the patterns have change in a significant way. The most noticeable change is observed in case of the second polynomial (Fig. 2(b) and Fig. 3(b)).

The patterns for the Ishikawa iteration for the considered test functions are presented in Fig. 4. Images (a) and (b) were generated using $\omega = 0.7$ and $\eta = 0.3$,

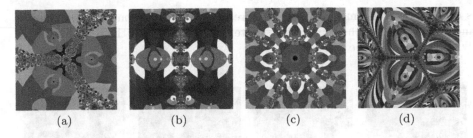

Fig. 2. Patterns generated with the Picard iteration: (a) $\omega = 0.9$, $\eta = 0.1$; (b) $\omega = 0.6$, $\eta = 0.9$; (c) $\omega = 0.4$, $\eta = 0.5$; (d) $\omega = 0.9$, $\eta = 0.03$

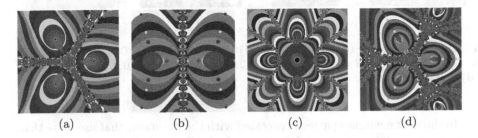

Fig. 3. Patterns generated with the Mann iteration for $\alpha = 0.3$, $\omega = 0.5$, $\eta = 0.6$

whereas the images (c) and (d) were generated using $\omega = 0.8$ and $\eta = 0.2$. The obtained patterns have similar dynamics – the increase in the inertia weight can be compensated by the decrease of the acceleration constant. The introduction in the iteration process of the second step and in consequence adding a second parameter (β) increases the possibilities of dynamics control. From the obtained images we see that the shapes of the patterns have changed in a significant way comparing to the patterns obtained with the Picard and Mann iterations.

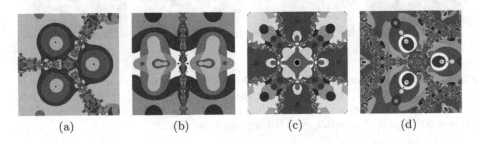

Fig. 4. Patterns generated with the Ishikawa iteration for $\alpha = 0.9$, $\beta = 0.9$ and: (a), (b) $\omega = 0.7$, $\eta = 0.3$; (c), (d) $\omega = 0.8$, $\eta = 0.2$

The patterns generated with the last iteration that uses only one function – the Agarwal iteration – are presented in Fig. 5. In this iteration the function is evaluated three times. This gives more possibilities to control the dynamics and in consequence the shape of the pattern. The impact of the α parameter on dynamics seems to be smaller.

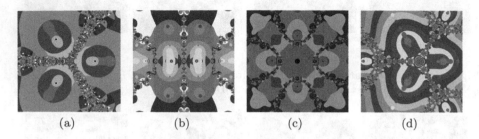

(a)   (b)   (c)   (d)

Fig. 5. Patterns generated with the Agarwal iteration for: (a) $\alpha = 0.7$, $\beta = 0.5$, $\omega = 0.7$, $\eta = 0.3$; (b) $\alpha = 0.5$, $\beta = 0.9$, $\omega = 0.6$, $\eta = 0.6$; (c) $\alpha = 0.9$, $\beta = 0.9$, $\omega = 0.3$, $\eta = 0.9$; (d) $\alpha = 0.9$, $\beta = 0.5$, $\omega = 0.3$, $\eta = 0.3$

In the next examples pattens generated with the iterations that use more than one function will be presented. We start with the Das-Debata iteration. Patterns generated with this iteration are presented in Fig. 6. Patterns were generated for different values of the parameters. Changes in the value of the α parameter more strongly affect the dynamics change than the changes in the value of parameter β. Moreover, we can observe more complex change of patterns' shape comparing to the iterations with one function.

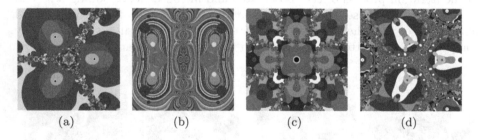

(a)   (b)   (c)   (d)

Fig. 6. Patterns generated with the Das-Debata iteration for: (a) $\alpha = 0.7$, $\beta = 0.9$, $\omega_1 = 0.5$, $\eta_1 = 0.6$, $\omega_2 = 0.5$, $\eta_2 = 0.2$; (b) $\alpha = 0.5$, $\beta = 0.9$, $\omega_1 = 0.6$, $\eta_1 = 0.5$, $\omega_2 = 0.9$, $\eta_2 = 0.3$; (c) $\alpha = 0.9$, $\beta = 0.6$, $\omega_1 = 0.7$, $\eta_1 = 0.3$, $\omega_2 = 0.9$, $\eta_2 = 0.2$; (d) $\alpha = 0.6$, $\beta = 0.8$, $\omega_1 = 0.9$, $\eta_1 = 0.3$, $\omega_2 = 0.5$, $\eta_2 = 0.2$

The patterns generated with the Khan-Cho-Abas iteration for the considered test functions are presented in Fig. 7. Similarly to the Das-Debata iteration the change of patterns' shape is very complex. Moreover, its use gives more possibilities to obtain diverse patterns.

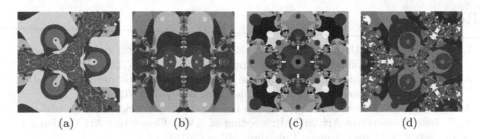

Fig. 7. Patterns generated with the Khan-Cho-Abas iteration for: (a) $\alpha = 0.5$, $\beta = 0.9$, $\omega_1 = 0.6$, $\eta_1 = 0.6$, $\omega_2 = 0.8$, $\eta_2 = 0.8$, $\omega_3 = 0.6$, $\eta_3 = 0.6$; (b) $\alpha = 0.7$, $\beta = 0.5$, $\omega_1 = 0.7$, $\eta_1 = 0.3$, $\omega_2 = 0.3$, $\eta_2 = 0.7$, $\omega_3 = 0.7$, $\eta_3 = 0.3$; (c) $\alpha = 0.9$, $\beta = 0.5$, $\omega_1 = 0.3$, $\eta_1 = 0.3$, $\omega_2 = 0.6$, $\eta_2 = 0.6$, $\omega_3 = 0.3$, $\eta_3 = 0.3$; (d) $\alpha = 0.9$, $\beta = 0.5$, $\omega_1 = 0.3$, $\eta_1 = 0.3$, $\omega_2 = 0.6$, $\eta_2 = 0.6$, $\omega_3 = 0.3$, $\eta_3 = 0.3$

In the last example – Fig. 8 – patterns generated using the generalized Agarwal iteration are presented. The possibility of independent setting of all parameters of the algorithm gives the greatest possibilities to control the dynamics of the created pattern. It gives the possibility to obtain differentiated image features.

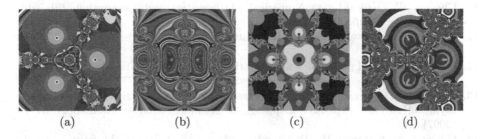

Fig. 8. Patterns generated with the generalized Agarwal iteration for: (a) $\alpha = 0.5$, $\beta = 0.7$, $\omega_1 = 0.9$, $\eta_1 = 0.3$, $\omega_2 = 0.3$, $\eta_2 = 0.9$, $\omega_3 = 0.5$, $\eta_3 = 0.3$; (b) $\alpha = 0.9$, $\beta = 0.9$, $\omega_1 = 0.3$, $\eta_1 = 0.9$, $\omega_2 = 0.9$, $\eta_2 = 0.3$, $\omega_3 = 0.1$, $\eta_3 = 0.9$; (c) $\alpha = 0.7$, $\beta = 0.7$, $\omega_1 = 0.7$, $\eta_1 = 0.7$, $\omega_2 = 0.3$, $\eta_2 = 0.3$, $\omega_3 = 0.5$, $\eta_3 = 0.5$; (d) $\alpha = 0.7$, $\beta = 0.5$, $\omega_1 = 0.7$, $\eta_1 = 0.3$, $\omega_2 = 0.3$, $\eta_2 = 0.7$, $\omega_3 = 0.9$, $\eta_3 = 0.3$

6 Conclusions

In this paper, we presented a modification of the Newton's method using the PSO approach and various iteration processes. Moreover, we proposed artistic patterns generation method that is based on the introduced PSO-based Newton's method. The presented examples showed that using the proposed method we are able to obtain very interesting and diverse artistic patterns.

References

1. Wannarumon, S., Unnanon, K., Bohez, E.: Intelligent computer system for jewelry design support. Comput. Aided Des. Appl. **1**(1–4), 551–558 (2004)
2. Soo, S., Yu, K., Chiu, W.: Modeling and fabrication of artistic products based on IFS fractal representation. Comput. Aided Des. **38**(7), 755–769 (2006)
3. Setti, R.: Generative dreams from deep belief networks. In: Soddu, C., Colabella, E. (eds.) Generative Art 2015: Proceeding of XVIII Generative Art Conference, pp. 260–273. Domus Argenia Publisher, Milan (2015)
4. Jia, C., Ming-Xi, T.: Integrating shape grammars into a generative system for Zhuang ethnic embroidery design exploration. Comput. Aided Des. **45**(3), 591–604 (2013)
5. Kalantari, B.: Polynomiography and applications in art, education and science. Comput. Graph. **28**(3), 417–430 (2004)
6. Kalantari, B.: Polynomial Root-Finding and Polynomiography. World Scientific, Singapore (2009)
7. Gdawiec, K.: Fractal patterns from the dynamics of combined polynomial root finding methods. Nonlinear Dyn. **90**(4), 2457–2479 (2017)
8. Gosciniak, I.: Immune algorithm in non-stationary optimization task. In: 2008 International Conference on Computational Intelligence for Modelling Control Automation, pp. 750–755, December 2008
9. Gosciniak, I.: Discussion on semi-immune algorithm behaviour based on fractal analysis. Soft Comput. **21**(14), 3945–3956 (2017)
10. Cheney, W., Kincaid, D.: Numerical Mathematics and Computing, 6th edn. Brooks/Cole, Pacific Grove (2007)
11. Mann, W.: Mean value methods in iteration. Proc. Am. Math. Soc. **4**(3), 506–510 (1953)
12. Ishikawa, S.: Fixed points by a new iteration method. Proc. Am. Math. Soc. **44**(1), 147–150 (1974)
13. Agarwal, R., O'Regan, D., Sahu, D.: Iterative construction of fixed points of nearly asymptotically nonexpansive mappings. J. Nonlinear Convex Anal. **8**(1), 61–79 (2007)
14. Gdawiec, K., Kotarski, W.: Polynomiography for the polynomial infinity norm via Kalantari's formula and nonstandard iterations. Appl. Math. Comput. **307**, 17–30 (2017)
15. Das, G., Debata, J.: Fixed points of quasi-nonexpansive mappings. Indian J. Pure Appl. Math. **17**(11), 1263–1269 (1986)
16. Khan, S., Cho, Y., Abbas, M.: Convergence to common fixed points by a modified iteration process. J. Appl. Math. Comput. **35**(1), 607–616 (2011)

An Evaluation of Smoothing and Remeshing Techniques to Represent the Evolution of Real-World Phenomena

José Duarte$^{(\boxtimes)}$, Paulo Dias, and José Moreira

DETI/IEETA, University of Aveiro, Aveiro, Portugal
{hfduarte, paulo.dias, jose.moreira}@ua.pt

Abstract. In this paper we investigate the use of morphing techniques to represent the continuous evolution of deformable moving objects, representing the evolution of real-world phenomena. Our goal is to devise processes capable of generating an approximation of the actual evolution of these objects with a known error. We study the use of different smoothing and remeshing methods and analyze various statistics to establish mesh quality metrics with respect to the quality of the approximation (interpolation). The results of the tests and the statistics that were collected suggest that the quality of the correspondence between the observations has a major influence on the quality and validity of the interpolation, and it is not trivial to compare the quality of the interpolation with respect to the actual evolution of the phenomenon being represented. The Angle-Improving Delaunay Edge-Flips method, overall, obtained the best results, but the Remeshing method seems to be more robust to abrupt changes in the geometry.

Keywords: Deformable moving objects · Spatiotemporal data management Morphing techniques

1 Introduction

Morphing techniques can be used to represent the continuous transformation of a geometry, e.g. a polygon or a polyline, between two observations, i.e. a source and a target known geometries, and their main goal is to obtain a smooth and realistic transformation. However, the geometric characteristics of the observations can influence the quality of the interpolation. For example, a low-quality mesh is more likely to cause numerical problems and generate self-intersecting (invalid) geometries during interpolation. A high-quality mesh is more likely to generate natural transformations. This is a well-known problem, and several smoothing and remeshing methods and metrics have been proposed in the literature to measure and improve mesh quality [6, 11, 13]. However, to the best of our knowledge, there are no established methodologies to assess the quality of the interpolation with respect to the actual evolution of the object being represented.

In this paper we use the compatible triangulation method proposed in [6], and the rigid interpolation method proposed in [1, 3], with smoothing and remeshing methods,

© Springer Nature Switzerland AG 2018
G. Bebis et al. (Eds.): ISVC 2018, LNCS 11241, pp. 57–67, 2018.
https://doi.org/10.1007/978-3-030-03801-4_6

to represent the continuous evolution of deformable moving objects from a set of observations. Our main goal is to devise automatic processes to generate an approximation of the actual evolution of real-world phenomena with a known error, in the context of spatiotemporal data management and spatiotemporal databases. We implemented several smoothing and remeshing methods to improve the quality of the observations and studied its influence on the quality and validity of the intermediate geometries.

This paper is organized as follows. Section 2 introduces some background and related work. Section 3 presents the methods that were implemented and studied. The experimental results are presented and discussed in Sects. 4 and 5 presents the conclusions and future work.

2 Background

We use the *sliced representation* proposed in [5] to represent deformable moving objects, also known as moving regions. In the *sliced representation*, a moving object is an ordered collection of units, a unit represents the continuous evolution, i.e. the changes in position, shape and extent, of the moving object between two consecutive observations, and the evolution of the moving object within a unit is given by a function (Fig. 1) that should provide a good (realistic) approximation of the actual evolution of the object being represented, generate only valid intermediate geometries, and allow the processing of large datasets.

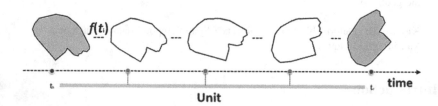

Fig. 1. Sliced representation.

The first algorithm proposed in the spatiotemporal databases literature to create the so-called moving regions from observations was proposed in [12]. This method was extended in more recent works [7–9]. These methods use the concept of moving segments to represent the evolution of a moving region during a unit. The authors main focus is on the robustness and complexity of the algorithms, and they make tradeoffs that have a significant impact on the quality of the intermediate geometries. Indeed, these more recent algorithms are robust and have low complexity, but may cause deformation of the intermediate geometries, and the approximation error can be too big to be neglected in scientific work, e.g. if a rotation exists the intermediate geometries tend to inflate at the middle of the interpolation, and the methods used to handle concavities either do not perform well with noisy data [7, 10, 12] or make the intermediate geometries approximately convex during interpolation, causing deformation [8, 9].

On the other hand, several morphing techniques exist to represent the continuous evolution of a geometry between a source and a target geometry. These methods are successfully used in animation packages and computer graphics, and their main goal is to obtain a smooth and realistic interpolation. For example, when using compatible triangulation and rigid interpolation methods there are two main steps to compute the evolution of a deformable moving object between two observations. In step 1, we find a compatible triangulation between the two observations. The compatible triangulation method receives two polygons, P and Q, and generates two triangular meshes, P* and Q*. P and Q must have a one-to-one correspondence between their vertices, and P* and Q* must have a one-to-one correspondence between their triangles. In step 2, the rigid interpolation method is used to generate the evolution of the deformable moving object between P* and Q*.

3   Methods

The following methods were implemented: an angle-improving (Delaunay) edge-flips method, the weighted angle-based smoothing, the area equalization smoothing, the remeshing, and the edge-splits refinement methods proposed in [6], the classical Laplacian smoothing method, and the smoothing methods proposed in [2]. A new position is used if it improves the current geometry given some criteria, the new positions are updated sequentially, i.e. immediately, (Another option is to update them simultaneously, but we did not consider it.) and if not mentioned explicitly, the method is applied individually to each mesh.

3.1   Compatible Angle-Improving (Delaunay) Edge-Flips

To check if an edge is locally Delaunay we can perform two tests [4]. The edge p_1p_3 (Fig. 2, left) is locally Delaunay if the sum of the angles at the points p_2 and p_4 is less than or equal to 180°, or if the circumcircle (the dashed circle) of one of its adjacent triangles does not contain the opposite point in the other triangle. In this case, edge p_1p_3 is non-locally Delaunay and needs to be flipped to become edge p_2p_4, which is locally Delaunay. This method is applied to two compatible meshes simultaneously and preserves their compatibility. An edge is only flipped if it is non-locally Delaunay in both meshes.

3.2   Weighted Angle-Based Smoothing

In [6] the authors propose using two rules to improve the angles of the triangles incident on a point c (Fig. 2, right). In the first one, the new position c_{new} is the average of all the c_i computed for all the neighbors, p_i, of c, namely:

$$c_{new} = \frac{1}{k}\sum_{i=1}^{k} c_i \tag{1}$$

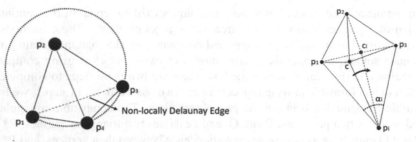

Fig. 2. Delaunay edge-flips (*left*) and weighted angle-based smoothing (*right*).

where k is the number of neighbors of c, and c_i is obtained by rotating c around p_i to coincide with the bisector of α_i (the angle formed at p_i). The second rule introduces weights to take small angles into account, and Eq. (1) becomes:

$$c_{new} = \frac{1}{\sum_{i=1}^{k} \frac{1}{\alpha_i^2}} \sum_{i=1}^{k} \frac{1}{\alpha_i^2} c_i \qquad (2)$$

where α_i is the angle formed at p_i. We implemented both rules. They are called W. Avg and W. Angle, respectively.

3.3   Area Equalization Smoothing

This method finds the new position of an interior point c which makes the areas of its k adjacent triangles as close as possible, by minimizing the following function:

$$(x', y') = \arg\min \sum_{i=1}^{k} \left(A_i - \frac{A}{k} \right)^2 \qquad (3)$$

where (x', y') is the new position of c, A_i is the area of the i-th adjacent triangle to c, and A is the area of the polygon containing the k triangles adjacent to c.

3.4   Compatible Edge-Splits Refinement

The edge-splits refinement method was implemented using the criterion proposed in [6], given by the following rule

$$e = \arg\max_{e \in P \cup Q} \frac{|e|}{(\theta_{min}(e))^2} \qquad (4)$$

where e is an edge, $|e|$ is the length of the edge, and $\theta_{min}(e)$ is the minimum angle adjacent to e. This refinement is performed simultaneously on two compatible meshes and preserves their compatibility.

3.5   Laplacian Smoothing and Simple Smoothing

Laplacian smoothing defines the new position of an interior point c as the average of the positions of its k adjacent points

$$c' = \frac{1}{k} \sum_{i=1}^{k} p_i \qquad (5)$$

where c' is the new position of c, k is the number of points adjacent to c, and p_i is the position of the i-th adjacent point.

The 'Simple' smoothing method was proposed in [2], and it works by performing a circular search with a decreasing radius around an interior point, to find new valid positions for that point that maximize the minimum area or angle, depending on the parameterization, of the triangles connected to it. If a new valid position is not found, the search radius decreases by a fixed factor. This method is called S. Max Area and S. Max Angle, depending on the criterion used.

3.6   The Remeshing Algorithm

The remeshing algorithm is presented in Algorithm 1. We have not yet established metrics to define the quality of a mesh, and its optimum number of Steiner (interior) points. Therefore, we define a maximum number of iterations to control the execution of the algorithm.

Algorithm 1. Remeshing algorithm outline.

While the maximum number of iterations is not reached.
  1. Alternate between angle-based smoothing and angle-improving edge-flips.
  2. Refine both meshes using k splits.
  3. Alternate between angle-based smoothing and angle-improving edge-flips.
  4. Perform a single iteration of area equalization.
  5. Alternate between angle-based smoothing and angle-improving edge-flips.

---

4   Experimental Results

We performed tests to study the quality of the interpolation with respect of the actual evolution of real-world phenomena.

4.1   Dataset

We used a dataset obtained from a sequence of satellite images tracking the movement of two icebergs in the Antarctic. The data and the procedures used to obtain this dataset are described in [10]. The one-to-one point correspondences defined in the original dataset were refined manually.

4.2   Tests

We studied the evolution of the area and the perimeter, the validity, and the geometric similarity (with respect to a known geometry) of the intermediate geometries during interpolation, when using the various smoothing and remeshing methods presented, the compatible triangulation method proposed in [6], and the rigid interpolation method proposed in [1, 3]. We collected statistics on the meshes representing observations: the number of triangles and Steiner points, the minimum and maximum angles, the number of angles lower and bigger than a given angle, the maximum and minimum triangle areas and the ratio between them, and information about the area, the perimeter, and the position of the centroid.

To compute the geometric similarity between two geometries we used the Haus-dorff distance. The geometries being compared may have a different number of vertices and are aligned using partial Procrustes superimposition before measuring their similarity. The alignment is performed using a set of 'landmarks', i.e. points that exist in the source, target, and intermediate geometries, and whose position does not change significantly between them.

We are interested in a smooth and realistic evolution of the intermediate geometries. It makes sense that under these circumstances the evolution of the properties studied follows approximately monotonically increasing or decreasing functions. As such, we assume that during a unit the properties being studied evolve smoothly, and their expected minimum and maximum values are given by the source and target known geometries. Therefore, we consider a lower and upper bound, a deviation with respect to these bounds, and the inflection points of the functions that approximate the evolution of the properties studied during interpolation (Fig. 3, right). This allows us to compare the results obtained when using the different methods. For example, in (Fig. 3, left) we can observe that in some cases the area of the intermediate geometries is bigger or lower than the source and target areas. This may be an indication of an unnatural behavior. Inflection points can also be an indication of local or global deformation during interpolation. It makes sense to 'penalize' these situations.

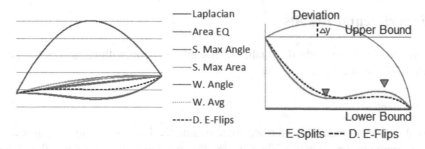

Fig. 3. Evolution of the area of 1000 intermediate geometries (*left*), and upper and lower bounds, deviation and inflection points (*right*).

Area Evolution During Interpolation. For each method 1000 samples (intermediate geometries) were generated and their areas were recorded. Tests were performed to study the effect of using a different number (1, 5, 10, 20, and 40) of splits and iterations when using the Edge-Splits and the Remeshing methods, respectively.

The results suggest that the evolution of the area during interpolation follows approximately linear, quadratic and cubic functions. A method does not always follow the same function (although quadratic functions seem to be more common), and the evolution of the area can be represented differently by different methods (Fig. 3, left).

The results show that the Edge-Flips and the Edge-Splits (using 10 splits) are the least penalized methods (Fig. 4). The Remeshing method (using 5 iterations) is the most penalized. Increasing the number of iterations did not improve the results significantly, and, in general, as the number of iterations increases the enlargement of the geometry tends to become more and more evident. The biggest area deviations were 5% and 21% of the maximum expected area when using the Remeshing and the S. Max Area methods, respectively. In the case of the Edge-Splits method, the smallest area deviation was obtained when using 10 or less splits, and in some cases when using 40 splits. The results obtained using 10, 20, and 40 splits are similar, suggesting that there

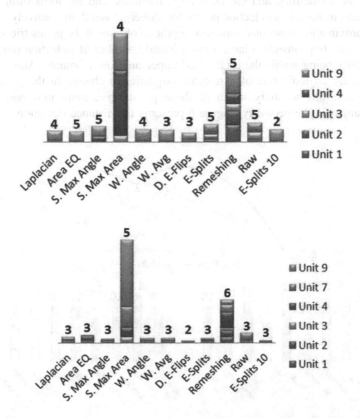

Fig. 4. Maximum area deviation by method and unit (using Steiner points) for Iceberg 1 (*top*) and Iceberg 2 (*bottom*).

exists a 'saturation'. The numbers on top of the bars in Fig. 4 indicate the number of times the area exceeded the expected upper and lower bounds during interpolation, e.g. the S. Max Area method was penalized in 4 of the 5 units representing the evolution of Iceberg 1 (Fig. 4, top), and the blocks stacked in the bars correspond to the percentage of the maximum area deviation for each method and unit. The results show that the S. Max Area method is the most unstable: it is the second most penalized method and reaches deviations larger than 20%. The other smoothing methods obtained similar results, and there is not a method that obtains the smallest area deviation in all cases.

Geometric Similarity During Interpolation. We studied the geometric similarity of the intermediate geometries with respect to a known geometry (the source geometry of each unit). This can give information on how smoothly the geometry evolves during interpolation. For each unit, representing the continuous evolution of the iceberg between two observations, we generated 1000 intermediate geometries and collected data on the Hausdorff distance between each intermediate geometry and the source geometry. This metric is very sensitive to changes in the geometry. We consider inflexion points the most relevant indicator, e.g. the inflection point marked with a triangle (Fig. 5, top) may indicate an abrupt change in the geometry. (Figure 5, bottom-left and bottom-right) shows that the Remeshing and the D. E-Flips methods, and the Remeshing and the E-Splits methods, have less inflection points for iceberg 1 and 2, respectively.

The approximation functions (representing the evolution of the geometric similarity of the intermediate geometries) have a considerable number of inflection points, with more than 50% being within the established upper and lower bounds. And, not all of these points are an indication of a relevant (significant) change in the geometry. It would be interesting to study which of these points give more information about relevant changes in the geometry. Figure 6 presents the distance deviation.

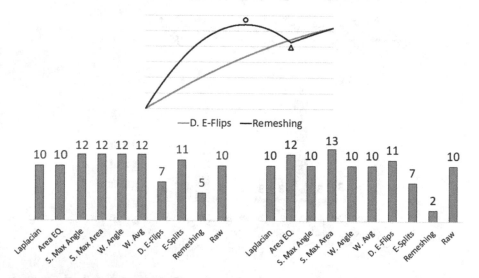

Fig. 5. Example of inflection points (*top*), and number of inflection points by method for Iceberg 1 (*bottom-left*) and Iceberg 2 (*bottom-right*).

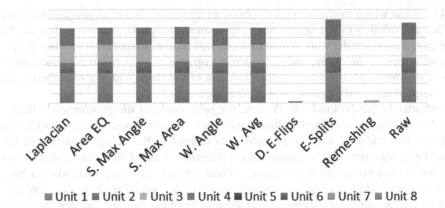

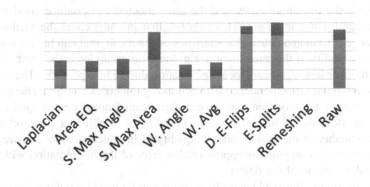

Fig. 6. Distance deviations, Iceberg 1 (*top*), and Iceberg 2 (*bottom*).

We also studied the evolution of the perimeter, but it is not presented here. The area and the perimeter can evolve in different ways, and a method can represent the evolution of one property better than the other, e.g. the Remeshing method tends to increase the area of the meshes during interpolation but gives the best results for the perimeter. We also observed that the one-to-one point correspondence between the source and target geometries has a significant influence on the results obtained and can produce invalid intermediate geometries. We obtained valid intermediate geometries for all the units used in the tests when using appropriate correspondences.

5 Conclusions and Future Work

We implemented and studied various smoothing and remeshing methods to improve the quality of triangular meshes, used with morphing techniques to represent the continuous evolution of deformable moving objects. While previous research on morphing techniques has focused on smooth and visually natural interpolations, our goal is to find which methods to use to obtain an interpolation, i.e. an approximation of the actual evolution of the object being represented, with a known error, that can be used in applied scientific work. These methods will be used to represent moving objects in spatiotemporal databases, and to implement operations to perform numerical analysis of real-world phenomena, e.g. the evolution of the shape and size of icebergs and cell morphology, or the propagation of forest fires.

We studied the evolution of the area, the perimeter and the geometric similarity, and the validity, of the intermediate geometries to study mesh quality metrics to evaluate the quality of the interpolation with respect to the actual evolution of the object being represented. The analysis of the statistics collected from the meshes shows that two meshes processed with different smoothing and remeshing methods can have exact or similar statistics but produce different results. This suggest that the statistics collected are not sufficient to characterize the quality of the meshes, and that there may be other factors that influence the evolution of the intermediate geometries. There is no method that is the best in all cases, and the same method can produce good results in some cases, and worse in others. This suggests that in some cases the method is not able to change certain geometric characteristics of the mesh, that can have a significant impact on the quality of the interpolation, e.g. long thin triangles at the mesh boundary can cause more or less significant local deformation during interpolation. The quality of the one-to-one point correspondence between two geometries can give rise to invalid geometries during interpolation and have a significant impact on the quality of the interpolation. Because of this, it was not possible to establish a clear relationship between the quality of the meshes and the quality of the interpolation, and we did not establish a metric to compute the approximation error of the interpolation with respect to the actual evolution of the object.

The Angle-Improving (Delaunay) Edge-Flips can be used by default since it is the method that, overall, obtains the best results, and its algorithmic complexity is reasonable (because of space constraints the algorithmic complexity of the methods is not presented here). This also applies when the evolution of the area or the algorithmic complexity are critical. In situations where the perimeter or the geometric similarity are a critical factor the Remeshing method can be used instead. The tests results suggest that the Remeshing method is more robust to abrupt local changes in the intermediate geometries.

In the future, we will collect and analyze other mesh statistics, study the relevance of the different inflection points, use more and diverse datasets, study which are the geometric features that are more relevant to the quality of the interpolation, and the use of well-known, well-established mesh quality improvement toolkits, e.g. the Mesh Quality Improvement Toolkit (MESQUITE) and the VERDICT library, to improve the quality of the meshes and collect mesh quality metrics.

Acknowledgments. This work is partially funded by National Funds through the FCT (Foundation for Science and Technology) in the context of the projects UID/CEC/00127/2013 and POCI-01-0145-FEDER-032636, and by the Luso-American Development Foundation 2018 "Bolsas Papers@USA" programme. José Duarte has a research grant also awarded by FCT with reference PD/BD/142879/2018.

References

1. Alexa, M., et al.: As-rigid-as-possible shape interpolation. In: Proceedings of the 27th annual Conference on Computer Graphics and Interactive Techniques—SIGGRAPH 2000, pp. 157–164 (2000)
2. Amaral, A.: Representation of Spatio-Temporal Data Using Compatible Triangulation and Morphing Techniques. Aveiro University, Aveiro (2015)
3. Baxter, W., et al.: Rigid shape interpolation using normal equations. In: NPAR 2008 Proceedings of the 6th International Symposium on Non-photorealistic Animation and Rendering, pp. 59–64 (2008)
4. De Berg, M. et al.: Computational Geometry: Algorithms and Applications, 3rd ed. Springer-Verlag Berlin Heidelberg (2008). https://doi.org/10.1007/978-3-540-77974-2
5. Forlizzi, L., et al.: A Data model and data structures for moving objects databases. In: Proceedings of the 2000 ACM SIGMOD International Conference on Management of Data, pp. 319–330 (2000)
6. Gotsman, C., Surazhsky, V.: High quality compatible triangulations. Eng. Comput. **20**(2), 147–156 (2004)
7. Heinz, F., Güting, R.H.: Robust high-quality interpolation of regions to moving regions. GeoInformatica **20**(3), 385–413 (2016)
8. McKenney, M., Webb, J.: Extracting moving regions from spatial data. In: Proceedings of the 18th SIGSPATIAL International Conference on Advances in Geographic Information Systems, San Jose, California, pp. 438–441 (2010)
9. McKennney, M., Frye, R.: Generating moving regions from snapshots of complex regions. ACM Trans. Spat. Algorithms Syst. **1**(1), 1–30 (2015)
10. Moreira, J., et al.: Representation of continuously changing data over time and space: modeling the shape of spatiotemporal phenomena. In: 2016 IEEE 12th International Conference on e-Science (e-Science), October 2016, pp. 111–119 (2016)
11. Mortara, M., Spagnuolo, M.: Similarity measures for blending polygonal shapes. Comput. Graph. (Pergamon) **25**(1), 13–27 (2001)
12. Tøssebro, E., Güting, R.H.: Creating representations for continuously moving regions from observations. In: Jensen, C.S., Schneider, M., Seeger, B., Tsotras, V.J. (eds.) SSTD 2001. LNCS, vol. 2121, pp. 321–344. Springer, Heidelberg (2001). https://doi.org/10.1007/3-540-47724-1_17
13. Veltkamp, R.C.: Shape matching: similarity measures and algorithms. In: Proceedings - International Conference on Shape Modeling and Applications, SMI 2001, pp. 188–197 (2001)

Biomimetic Perception Learning
for Human Sensorimotor Control

Masaki Nakada$^{(\boxtimes)}$, Honglin Chen, and Demetri Terzopoulos

University of California, Los Angeles, USA
nakada@cs.ucla.edu

Abstract. We present a simulation framework for biomimetic human perception and sensorimotor control. It features a biomechanically simulated, musculoskeletal human model actuated by numerous skeletal muscles, with two human-like eyes whose retinas have spatially nonuniform distributions of photoreceptors. Our prototype sensorimotor system for this model incorporates a set of 20 automatically-trained, deep neural networks (DNNs), half of which are neuromuscular DNN controllers comprising its motor subsystem, while the other half are devoted to visual perception. Within the sensory subsystem, which continuously operates on the retinal photoreceptor outputs, 2 DNNs drive eye and head movements, while 8 DNNs extract the sensory information needed to control the arms and legs. Exclusively by means of its egocentric, active visual perception, our biomechanical virtual human learns efficient, online visuomotor control of its eyes, head, and four limbs to perform tasks involving the foveation and visual pursuit of target objects coupled with visually-guided reaching actions to intercept the moving targets.

Keywords: Sensorimotor control · Active vision
Foveated perception · Biomimetic vision · Deep learning

1 Introduction

Biological vision has inspired computational approaches that mimic the functionality of neural mechanisms. Recent breakthroughs in machine learning with artificial (convolutional) neural networks have proven to be effective in computer vision; however, the application of Deep Neural Networks (DNNs) to sensorimotor systems has received virtually no attention in the computer vision field.

Sensorimotor functionality in biological organisms refers to the process of continually acquiring and interpreting sensory information necessary to produce appropriate motor responses in order to perform actions that achieve desired goals. We have recently introduced a simulation framework for investigating biomimetic human perception and sensorimotor control [4,5]. Our framework is unique in that it features a biomechanically simulated, human musculoskeletal model, which currently includes 823 skeletal muscle actuators. Our virtual

© Springer Nature Switzerland AG 2018
G. Bebis et al. (Eds.): ISVC 2018, LNCS 11241, pp. 68–78, 2018.
https://doi.org/10.1007/978-3-030-03801-4_7

• SENSORY SUBSYSTEM (top): (a) Each retinal photoreceptor casts a ray into the virtual world to compute the irradiance captured by the photoreceptor. (b) The arrangement of the photoreceptors (black dots) on the left (b)L and right (b)R foveated retinas. Each retina outputs an Optic Nerve Vector (ONV). There are 10 vision DNNs. The two (yellow) foveation DNNs (c) (1,6) input the ONV and produce eye movements to foveate visual targets. (d) The other eight (green) vision DNNs—(d)L (7,8,9,10) for the left eye (e)L and (d)R (2,3,4,5) for the right eye (e)R—also input the ONV and output limb-to-target visual discrepancy estimates.

• MOTOR SUBSYSTEM (bottom): There are 10 motor DNNs. The (orange) cervicocephalic neuromuscular motor controller (f) (DNNs 11,12) inputs the average of the foveation DNN responses and outputs activations to the neck muscle group. The four (blue) limb neuromuscular motor controllers (g),(h) (DNNs 13–20) of the limb musculoskeletal complexes input the average of the left (d)L and right (d)R limb vision DNN responses and output activations to the respective arm and leg muscle groups.

• NEUROMUSCULAR MOTOR CONTROLLER (above): The voluntary motor controller inputs a target discrepancy δ and, recurrently, the muscle activations a, and outputs adjustments Δa_v to the muscle activations that induce the desired actuation of the associated musculoskeletal complex. The reflex controller inputs the changes in muscle strains e and strain rates $\dot{e}$ and produces muscle-stabilizing activation adjustments Δa_r. The output of the neuromuscular motor controller is $a(t \mid \Delta t) = a(t) + (\Delta a_v(t) + \Delta a_r(t))$.

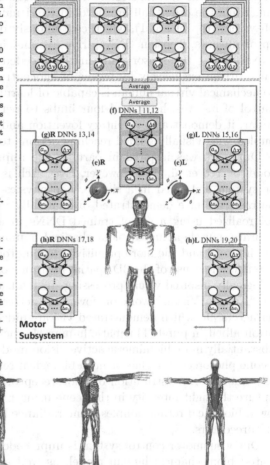

Fig. 1. The sensorimotor system architecture, whose controllers include a total of 20 DNNs, numbered 1–20, and the neuromuscular motor controller architecture. The complete biomechanical model (bottom), showing the skeletal system with its 103 bones and the 823 Hill-type muscle actuators.

human perceives its environment using two eyes whose foveated retinas contain photoreceptors arranged in spatially nonuniform distributions.

As illustrated in Fig. 1, we have developed a prototype visuomotor control system for our biomechanical human musculoskeletal model that incorporates a set of 20 automatically-trained, fully-connected DNNs, half of which are employed in neuromuscular motor controllers comprising its motor subsystem, while the other half are devoted to visual perception. Within its sensory subsystem (top of Fig. 1), which continuously operates on the retinal photoreceptor outputs, 2 vision DNNs drive eye and head movements, while 8 vision DNNs extract the sensory information needed to control the arms and legs. Thus, driven exclusively by means of egocentric, active visual perception, our biomechanical virtual human is capable of learning efficient and effective, online control of its eyes, head, and four limbs to perform visuomotor tasks. In particular, it demonstrates voluntary foveation and visual pursuit of target objects coupled with visually-guided reaching actions to intercept the moving targets.

Our work was inspired in part by the impressive visuomotor "EyeCatch" model of Yeo et al. [10]. However, EyeCatch is a non-learning-based visuomotor system embodied in a simple, non-physics-based humanoid character. By contrast, we have demonstrated dramatically more complex sensorimotor control realized using a set of trained DNNs in a comprehensive, anatomically-accurate, muscle-actuated biomechanical human model. Furthermore, the EyeCatch model and the more primitive visuomotor model of Lee and Terzopoulos [3] made direct use of the 3D spatial positions of virtual visual targets, without biologically-inspired visual processing. Instead, we have built upon the pioneering "Animat Vision" work on foveated, active computer vision for animated characters [9], which demonstrated vision-guided bipedal locomotion and navigation albeit in purely kinematic human characters [6]. In particular, we offer a substantially more biomimetic active vision model based on the foveated pattern of cone photoreceptor placement in biological retinas [7]. Given their fundamentally nonuniform distribution of photoreceptors, the retinas in our eye models capture the light intensity in the scene using raytracing, which better emulates how a biological retina samples scene radiance from the incidence of light on its photoreceptors.

Our visuomotor control system is unprecedented both in its use of a sophisticated biomechanical human model, as well as in its use of modern machine learning methodologies to control a realistic musculoskeletal system and perform online visual processing for active, foveated perception, all through a modular set of DNNs that are automatically trained from data synthesized by the human model itself.

The remainder of this paper is organized as follows: In Sect. 2, we overview our biomechanical human musculoskeletal model and its neuromuscular motor control subsystem (additional details are found in [5]). In Sect. 3 we describe its ocular and retinal models and in Sect. 4 we describe its sensory subsystem (additional details are found in [4]). Section 5 presents one of our experimental results. Section 6 summarizes our contributions and plans for future work.

2   Biomechanical Model and Motor Subsystem

The musculoskeletal system of our anatomically accurate biomechanical human model is shown at the bottom of Fig. 1. It includes all of the relevant articular bones and muscles—103 bones connected by joints comprising 163 articular degrees of freedom, plus a total of 823 muscle actuators. Each skeletal muscle is modeled as a Hill-type uniaxial contractile actuator that applies forces to the bones at its points of insertion and attachment. The human model is numerically simulated as a force-driven articulated multi-body system (see [2] for the details).

Each muscle actuator is activated by an independent, time-varying, efferent activation signal $a(t)$. The overall challenge in the neuromuscular motor control of our human model is to determine the activation signals for each of its 823 muscles necessary to carry out various motor tasks. For the purposes of the present paper, we mitigate complexity by placing our virtual human in a seated position, immobilizing the pelvis as well as the lumbar and thoracic spinal column vertebra and other bones of the torso, leaving free to articulate only the cervico-cephalic, two arm, and two leg musculoskeletal complexes (displayed within the lower box in Fig. 1).

The cervicocephalic musculoskeletal complex is rooted at the thoracic vertebra (T1), with its seven vertebrae, C7 through C1 (atlas), progressing up the cervical spine to the skull, which is an end-effector of substantial mass. A total of 216 short, intermediate, and long Hill-type uniaxial muscle actuators arranged in deep, intermediate, and superficial layers, respectively, actuate the seven 3-degree-of-freedom joints of the cervicocephalic musculoskeletal complex.

Each arm musculoskeletal complex is rooted at the clavicle and scapula, and includes the humerus, ulnar, and radius bones. A total of 29 Hill-type uniaxial muscles actuate the shoulder, elbow, and wrist joints in each arm. The hands, which currently are actuated kinematically, serve as end effectors.

Each leg musculoskeletal complex, which includes the femur, patella, tibia, and fibula bones, is rooted by the pelvis. A total of 39 Hill-type uniaxial muscles actuate the hip, knee, and ankle joints in each leg. The feet, which currently are actuated kinematically, serve as end effectors.

The motor subsystem (lower box of Fig. 1) includes 10 motor DNNs (numbered 11–20 in the figure) comprising five recurrent neuromuscular motor controllers. Two DNNs control the 216 neck muscles that balance the head atop the cervical column against the downward pull of gravity and actuate the neck-head biomechanical complex, thereby producing controlled head movements. Two DNNs control each limb; in particular, the 29 muscles in each of the two arms and the 39 muscles in each of the two legs. Additional details about our biomechanical human musculoskeletal model and the five recurrent neuromuscular controllers comprising its motor subsystem, are presented elsewhere [5]. The next two sections describe the sensory subsystem, which is illustrated in the upper box of Fig. 1.

3   Ocular and Retinal Models

We modeled the eyes by taking into consideration the physiological data from an average human. As shown in Fig. 1e, we model the virtual eye as a sphere of 12 mm radius, that can be rotated with respect to its center around its vertical y axis by a horizontal angle of θ and around its horizontal x axis by a vertical angle of ϕ. The eyes are in their neutral positions looking straight ahead when $\theta = \phi = 0°$. For now, we have modeled the eye as an idealized pinhole camera with aperture at the center of the pupil and with horizontal and vertical fields of view of 167.5°.

We can compute the irradiance at any point on the hemispherical retinal surface at the back of the eye using the conventional raytracing technique of computer graphics rendering [8]. Sample rays from the positions of photoreceptors on the hemispherical retinal surface are cast through the pinhole and out into the 3D virtual world where they recursively intersect with the visible surfaces of virtual objects and query the virtual light sources according to the Phong local illumination model. The irradiance values returned by these rays determine the light impinging upon the retina at the photoreceptor positions. Figure 2a,b illustrates this retinal imaging process.

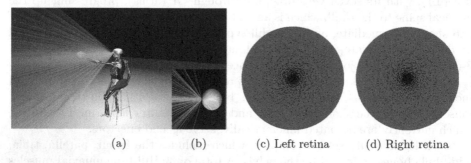

(a)   (b)   (c) Left retina   (d) Right retina

Fig. 2. Via raytracing (blue rays), the biomechanical virtual human's eyes (b) visually sample the environment (a) to compute the irradiance at RGB photoreceptors (black dots) on their foveated retinas (c) (d), which are nonuniformly positioned according to a noisy log-polar distribution. (Color figure online)

To simulate foveated perception, we use a noisy log-polar distribution to determine the nonuniform 2D positions of the photoreceptors on the retina. Figure 2c,d illustrates the arrangement of the photoreceptors. By drawing different random numbers, the 3,600 photoreceptors are placed in slightly different positions on each of the two hemispherical retinas. Of course, other placement patterns are possible, including more elaborate biomimetic procedural models or photoreceptor distributions empirically measured from biological eyes, all of which deviate dramatically from the uniformly-sampled Cartesian pixel images commonly used in vision and graphics.

The foveated retinal RGB "image" captured by each eye is output for further processing down the visual pathway, not as a conventional 2D array of pixels, but as a 1D vector of length $3,600 \times 3 = 10,800$, which we call the Optic Nerve Vector (ONV). The raw sensory information encoded in this vector feeds the vision DNNs that directly control eye movements and whose outputs also feed the motor networks that control head movements and the reaching actions of the limbs.

4   Sensory Subsystem

We next present the 10 vision DNNs (numbered 1–10 in Fig. 1) that implement the sensory subsystem. The sensory subsystem includes two types of fully-connected feedforward DNNs (Fig. 3), which will be described in the next two sections. These DNNs input the sensory information provided by the 10,800-dimensional ONV. The first type (Fig. 3a) controls the eye movements, as well as the head movements via the neck motor DNN. The second type (Fig. 3b) produces arm-to-target 3D error vectors $[\Delta x, \Delta y, \Delta z]^T$ that drive the limbs via the limb motor DNNs.

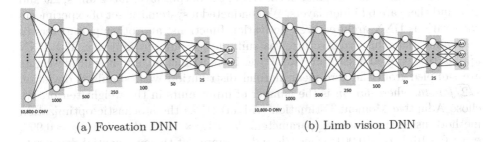

(a) Foveation DNN   (b) Limb vision DNN

Fig. 3. The vision DNN architecture.

4.1   Foveation DNNs (1,6)

The first role of the left and right foveation DNNs is to induce saccadic eye movements to foveate visible objects of interest by rotating the eyes to look directly at those visual targets, thereby observing them with maximum visual acuity. Both eyes verge naturally to focus together on a foveated target. This is illustrated in Fig. 4 for a white ball in motion that enters the eye's field of view from the lower right, stimulating several peripheral photoreceptors at the upper left of the retina. The maximum speed of saccadic eye movements is 900 degrees/sec, and the eye almost instantly foveates the visual target. Fine adjustments comparable to microsaccades can be observed during fixation.

The eye movements are tightly coupled with head movements that facilitate foveation, fixation, and visual tracking. By quickly saccading to and then pursuing the visual target, the eyes look directly at it, whereas the head follows, albeit

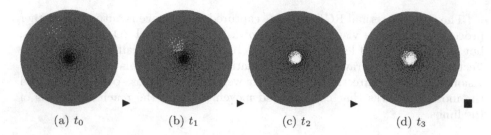

(a) t_0 (b) t_1 (c) t_2 (d) t_3

Fig. 4. Time sequence (a)–(d) of photoreceptor responses in the left retina during a saccadic eye movement that foveates and tracks a moving white ball. At time t_0 the ball becomes visible in the periphery, at t_1 the eye movement is bringing the ball towards the fovea, and the moving ball is being fixated in the fovea at times t_2 and t_3.

much more sluggishly due to its substantial mass. Hence, the second role of these two DNNs is to control head movement, which is accomplished by driving the neck neuromuscular motor controller (11,12) (Fig. 1f) with the average of their outputs.

As shown in Fig. 3a, the input layer to the foveation DNN comprises 10,800 units, due to the dimensionality of the ONV, the output layer has 2 units, $\Delta\theta$ and $\Delta\phi$, and there are 6 hidden layers. We conducted a systematic set of experiments with various DNN architectures, activation functions, and other parameters to determine that this architecture was suitable for our purposes [4]. The DNN applies the rectified linear unit (ReLU) activation function, and its initial weights are sampled from the zero-mean normal distribution with standard deviation $\sqrt{2/fan\_in}$, where fan_in is the number of input units in the weight tensor. We chose Adaptive Moment Estimation (Adam) [1] as the stochastic optimization method, using the following parameters: $lr = 1.0 \times 10^{-6}$, $\beta_1 = 0.9$, $\beta_2 = 0.999$, $\epsilon = 1.0 \times 10^{-8}$, $\alpha = 0.001$, where β_1 and β_2 represent the exponential decay rate for momentum estimates taking an average and an average of squared gradients, respectively, ϵ prevents a divide-by-zero error, lr is the learning rate, and α is the step size. An early stopping condition is set to avoid overfitting and mean squared error serves as the loss function.

We use our virtual human model to train the network, as follows: We presented a white sphere within the visual field. By raytracing the 3D scene, the photoreceptors in the retinas of each eye are stimulated, and the visual stimuli are presented as the RGB components of the respective ONV. Given this ONV as input, the desired output of the network is the angular differences $\Delta\theta$ and $\Delta\phi$ between the actual gaze directions of the eyes and the known gaze directions that would foveate the sphere. Repeatedly positioning the sphere at random locations in the visual field, we generated a large training dataset of 1M input-output pairs. The backpropagation DNN training process converged to a small error after 80 epochs, which triggered the early stopping condition (no improvement for 10 successive epochs) to avoid overfitting.

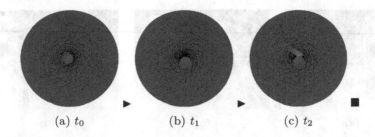

(a) t_0 (b) t_1 (c) t_2

Fig. 5. Retinal images during an arm reaching motion that deflects a moving red ball. The photoreceptors are simultaneously stimulated by the fixated ball and by the (green) arm entering the eye's field of view from the lower right (upper left on the retina). (Color figure online)

4.2 Limb Vision DNNs (2,3,4,5 and 7,8,9,10)

The role of the left and right limb (arm and leg) vision DNNs is to estimate the separation in 3D space between the position of the end effector (hand or foot) and the position of a visual target, thus driving the associated limb motor DNN to extend the limb to touch the target. This is illustrated in Fig. 5 for a fixated red ball and a (green) arm that enters the eye's field of view from the lower right, stimulating several peripheral photoreceptors at the upper left of the retina.

The architecture of the limb vision DNN (Fig. 3b) is identical to the foveation DNN except for the size of the output layer, which has 3 units, Δx, Δy, and Δz, to encode the estimated discrepancy between the 3D positions of the end effector and the visual target.

Again, we use our virtual human model to train the four limb networks, as follows: We present a red ball in the visual field and allow the trained foveation DNNs to foveate the ball. Then, we extend a limb (arm or leg) towards the ball. Again, by continually raytracing the 3D scene, the photoreceptors in the retinas of each eye are stimulated and the visual stimuli are presented as the RGB components of the respective ONV. With the ONV as input, the desired output of the network is the 3D discrepancy, Δx, Δy, and Δz, between the known 3D positions of the end effector and the visual target. Repeatedly placing the sphere at random positions in the visual field and randomly articulating the limb to reach for it in space, we again generated a large training dataset of 1M input-output pairs. The backpropagation DNN training process converged to a small error after 388 epochs, which triggered the early stopping condition to avoid overfitting. As expected, due to the greater complexity of this task, the training speed is significantly slower than that of the foveation DNN.

5   Experimental Results

Figure 6 shows a sequence of frames from a simulation demonstrating the active sensorimotor system. A cannon shoots a ball towards the virtual human, which actively perceives the ball on its foveated retinas. The ONVs from the eyes are

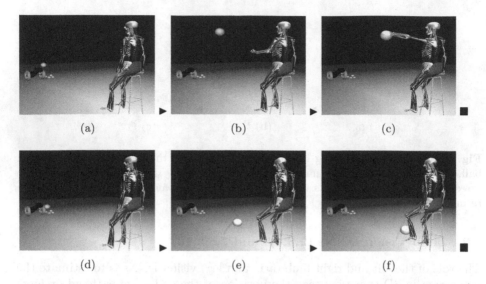

Fig. 6. Frames from a simulation of the biomechanical virtual human sitting on a stool, demonstrating active visual perception and simultaneous motor response; in particular, a left-arm reaching action (a)–(c) and a left-leg kicking action (d)–(f) to intercept balls shot by a cannon. Each incoming ball is perceived by the eyes, processed by the perception DNNs, foveated and tracked through eye movements in conjunction with muscle-actuated head movements controlled by the cervicocephalic neuromuscular motor controller, while visually guided, muscle-actuated limb movements are controlled by the left arm and left leg neuromuscular motor controllers.

processed by the vision DNNs to enable foveation and visual tracking of the incoming ball. Simultaneously fed by the vision DNNs, the motor DNNs control the extension of the arms and legs to intercept the incoming ball and deflect it out of the way. Thus, given just the high level objective of deflecting the incoming ball, the virtual human successfully controls itself to carry out this nontrivial dynamic sensorimotor control task. A number of additional demonstrations are presented in [5].

6   Conclusion

We have introduced a simulation framework for biomimetic human perception and sensorimotor control. It is unique in that it features an anatomically accurate, biomechanical human musculoskeletal model that is actuated by numerous contractile skeletal muscles. The novel contributions of our framework include the following primary ones:

- A biomimetic, foveated retinal model, which is deployed in a pair of human-like foveated eyes capable of realistic eye movements, that employs raytracing to compute the irradiance captured by a nonuniform distribution of photoreceptors.

- A fully functional prototype sensorimotor system, which in addition to deep-learning-based neuromuscular control of the neck-head, arms, and legs (under the influence of gravity), includes a sensory subsystem that incorporates a set of 10 automatically-trained deep neural networks driven by the optic nerve outputs from the eyes.
- Demonstration of the performance of our innovative sensorimotor system in nontrivial tasks. These simultaneously involve eye movement control for saccadic foveation and pursuit of a visual target in conjunction with appropriate dynamic head motion control, plus visually-guided dynamic limb control to generate natural limb reaching actions in order to deflect moving visual targets.

Our approach has been to train the deep neural networks with very large quantities of training data that are synthesized by the biomechanical human musculoskeletal model itself. Our work to date confirms that our innovative deep learning approach to strongly biomimetic sensorimotor control works remarkably well. Nevertheless, our prototype visuomotor system inevitably has some limitations that we plan to address in future work. These include appropriately detailed biomechanical modeling of the eye and development of neuromuscular controllers for the 6 extraocular muscles, the incorporation of visual attention and stereoscopic vision mechanisms, which will require a substantial increase in the number of retinal photoreceptors in conjunction with sparsely-connected vision DNN architectures, and ultimately fully unconstraining our virtual human and successfully training thoracic/lumbar neuromuscular controllers, which would enable us to address a variety of more complex sensorimotor tasks.

References

1. Kingma, D., Ba, J.: Adam: a method for stochastic optimization. arXiv preprint arXiv:1412.6980 (2014)
2. Lee, S.H., Sifakis, E., Terzopoulos, D.: Comprehensive biomechanical modeling and simulation of the upper body. ACM Trans. Graph. **28**(4), 99:1–17 (2009)
3. Lee, S.H., Terzopoulos, D.: Heads up! biomechanical modeling and neuromuscular control of the neck. ACM Trans. Graph. **23**(212), 1188–1198 (2006)
4. Nakada, M., Chen, H., Terzopoulos, D.: Deep learning of biomimetic visual perception for virtual humans. In: ACM Symposium on Applied Perception (SAP 18), pp. 20:1–8. Vancouver, BC, August 2018
5. Nakada, M., Zhou, T., Chen, H., Weiss, T., Terzopoulos, D.: Deep learning of biomimetic sensorimotor control for biomechanical human animation. ACM Trans. Graph. **37**(4), 56:1–15 (2018). (in Proc. ACM SIGGRAPH 2018)
6. Rabie, T.F., Terzopoulos, D.: Active perception in virtual humans. In: Proceedings of Vision Interface 2000, pp. 16–22. Montreal, Canada (2000)
7. Schwartz, E.L.: Spatial mapping in the primate sensory projection: analytic structure and relevance to perception. Biol. Cybern. **25**(4), 181–194 (1977)
8. Shirley, P., Morley, R.K.: Realistic Ray Tracing, 2nd edn. A. K. Peters Ltd, Natick (2003)

9. Terzopoulos, D., Rabie, T.F.: Animat vision: active vision with artificial animals. In: Proceedings of International Conference on Computer Vision (ICCV), pp. 840–845. Cambridge, MA (1995)
10. Yeo, S.H., Lesmana, M., Neog, D.R., Pai, D.K.: Eyecatch: simulating visuomotor coordination for object interception. ACM Trans. Graph. (TOG) **31**(4), 42 (2012)

Porous Structure Design in Tissue Engineering Using Anisotropic Radial Basis Functions

Ye Guo[1](✉), Ke Liu[2], and Zeyun Yu[3]

[1] University of Wisconsin - Milwaukee, Milwaukee, WI 53211, USA
yeguo@uwm.edu
[2] Lattice Engines Inc., San Mateo, CA 94404, USA
lkhoho@gmail.com
[3] University of Wisconsin - Milwaukee, Milwaukee, WI 53211, USA
yuz@uwm.edu

Abstract. The rapid development of additive manufacturing in last decades has greatly improved the quality of medical implants and widened its applications in tissue engineering. For the purpose of creating realistic porous scaffolds, a series of diverse methodologies are attempted to help simplify the manufacturing process and to improve the scaffold quality. Among these approaches, implicit surface methods based on geometric models have gained much attention for its flexibility to generate porous structures. In this paper, an innovative heterogeneous modeling method using anisotropic radial basis functions (ARBFs) is introduced for designing porous structures with controlled porosity and various internal architectures. By re-defining the distance method for the radial basis functions, the interpolated porous shape can be customized according to different requirements. Numerous experiments have been conducted to show the effectiveness of the proposed method.

Keywords: Porous structure design · Bio-scaffolds
Anisotropic radial basis functions · Implicit surface modeling

1 Introduction

With recent development and prosperity of additive manufacturing (AM) techniques [12,15], various 3D printed porous scaffolds have been widely applied in the field of tissue engineering (TE) in order to repair damaged tissues or organs. The design of artificial scaffolds usually requires some specific properties on the pore architectures, such as pore shape, mechanical stiffness, porosity, and rate of degradation. In fact, native human tissues and organs, including skin, femur, tibia, are not solid but inherently heterogeneous structures with fracture and complex pore texture. The naturally formed inner interconnected porous network not only facilitates the inflow of nutrients and disposal of metabolic wastes, but also provides 3D scaffolds for cell growth and attachment.

© Springer Nature Switzerland AG 2018
G. Bebis et al. (Eds.): ISVC 2018, LNCS 11241, pp. 79–90, 2018.
https://doi.org/10.1007/978-3-030-03801-4_8

While exactly reproducing internal micro-architectures of authentic human tissue is extremely hard, the prior work in literature has been mainly focused on designing simplified prototypes that have similar bio-functionalities. Numerous methodologies have been proposed to fabricate two types of porous scaffolds [7, 24], namely regular porous scaffolds and irregular porous scaffolds as listed in Table 1. Computer-aided design (CAD) based methods make full use of existing modeling software tools to manipulate standard solid primitives (cylinders, spheres, cubes, etc.) and bio-featured solid cells through Boolean operations to produce complicated patterns [1, 20]. Imaged-based methods combine image processing and freeform fabrication techniques to visualize and simplify scaffold design [8]. Space-filling curve is an improvement of extrusion-based techniques, which consist of the extrusion of a micro-diameter polymeric filament terminating with a nozzle having an orifice diameter in hundreds of microns [27]. Among these approaches, implicit surface modeling (ISM), especially triply periodic minimal surface (TPMS), has captured most attention in tissue engineering scaffold design due to its high interconnectivity and smooth surface. A majority of TPMSs, such as Schwartz's Primitive Surface (P-surface), Schwartz's Diamond Surface (D-surface), and Schoen's Gyroid Surface (G-surface), have demonstrated their efficacy in high-precision fabrication of functional scaffolds [4]. Although traditional TPMS could perfectly form a uniform porous network, it is only applicable to regular hexahedron and the external surface is possibly disconnected or containing some sharp edges for irregular shapes. As it is demonstrated in Fig. 1, some structures from the superficial layer are broken and deformed. To address these problems, Yoo et al. proposed a comprehensive system using TPMSs to create heterogeneous porous scaffolds for complex models [25, 26]. Other alternative solutions include combing TPMSs with T-spline [5] and parameterized hexahedral mesh [3].

The radial basis function (RBF) interpolation is one of the primary methods to reconstruct functions from multi-dimensional scattered data. The present paper uses anisotropic radial basis function (ARBF), a variant of RBF, as the basis to construct customized porous structures by interpolating values into tetrahedrons or hexahedrons.

The rest of paper is organized as follows. Section 2.1 introduces conventional RBF interpolation, followed by description of anisotropic RBF in Sect. 2.2. Section 2.3 gives more details of the algorithm implementation. Section 3 provides some experimental results and discussions. Section 4 concludes this paper.

2   Methods

2.1   Radial Basis Function (RBF) Interpolation

The conventional radial basis function interpolation is given by

$$f(\mathbf{x}) = \sum_{i=1}^{N} w_i \phi(\|\mathbf{x} - \mathbf{x}_i\|), \qquad (1)$$

where the interpolated function $f(\mathbf{x})$ is represented as a weighted sum of N radial basis functions $\phi(\cdot)$ and each function is centered differently at $\mathbf{x}_i$ and weighted by w_i. Once the values of f_i where $i = 1 \cdots N$ are given at $\mathbf{x}_i$, the weights w_i can be solved through

$$
\begin{bmatrix}
\phi_{11} & \cdots & \phi_{1N} \\
\vdots & \ddots & \vdots \\
\phi_{N1} & \cdots & \phi_{NN}
\end{bmatrix}
\begin{bmatrix}
w_1 \\
\vdots \\
w_N
\end{bmatrix}
=
\begin{bmatrix}
f_1 \\
\vdots \\
f_N
\end{bmatrix}
\tag{2}
$$

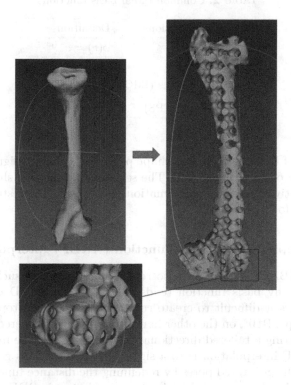

Fig. 1. Porous femur bone scaffold designed by TPMS. From the close-up view, one can see broken and deformed structures of the surface layer.

Table 1. Category of methods to design porous scaffolds in tissue engineering.

Type of scaffolds	Method
Regular porous scaffolds	CAD-based methods [1,20]
	Image-based methods [8]
	Implicit surface modeling (ISM) [3–5,18,25,26]
	Space-filling curves [27]
Irregular porous scaffolds	An optimization method proposed by [9]
	Stochastic methods using Voronoi models [17,19]
	A hybrid Voronoi-spline method [16]
	Methods using volumetric meshes [13]

where $\phi_{ji} = \phi(\|\mathbf{x}_j - \mathbf{x}_i\|)$. Accordingly, the value at an arbitrary point can be evaluated through Eq. 1.

In conventional RBF method, the distance between point $\mathbf{x} \in \mathbb{R}^d$ and center of basis function $\mathbf{x}_i \in \mathbb{R}^d$ is measured by Euclidean distance denoted as $r = \|\mathbf{x} - \mathbf{x}_i\|$. Some commonly used radial basis functions are listed in Table 2.

Table 2. Common radial basis functions

Types of basis functions	Definition
Gaussian	$\phi(r) = e^{-(cr)^2}$
Multiquadrics (MQ)	$\phi(r) = \sqrt{r^2 + c^2}$
Inverse multiquadrics (IMQ)	$\phi(r) = \dfrac{1}{\sqrt{r^2+c^2}}$
Thin plate spline (TPS)	$\phi(r) = r^2 ln(r)$

The choice of basis function and shape parameter c have a significant impact on the accuracy of an RBF method. The selection of adaptive shape parameter has been an active topic in approximation theory [22]. Interested readers can refer to [10,21] for more details.

2.2 Anisotropic Radial Basis Function (ARBF) Interpolation

Conventional RBF interpolation is isotropic to all directions such that the target domain of any basis function tends to be circular in 2D or spherical in 3D, which makes it difficult to create comprehensive porous topological structures. Anisotropic RBF, on the other hand, could perfectly overcome the limitation of constructing a tailored directional porous network. The major feature of anisotropic RBF interpolation is to assign the basis functions consistent directionality with the generated pores by redefining the distance functions. Figure 2 (a) and (b) depict the support domains by using isotropic RBF and anisotropic RBF in a 2D triangular mesh, respectively.

In anisotropic RBF interpolation, a new basis function centered at a line segment rather than a point is introduced such that the resulting surface is connected along the line's direction. Given a combination of line segments and single points $L = \{l_j\}_{j=1,...,N}$ as the centers of basis functions, the anisotropic RBF interpolation is described as

$$\Phi(u) = \sum_{j=1}^{N} w_j \phi(\|u - l_j\|_L), \tag{3}$$

where $\|u - l_j\|_L$ defines the distance between two points or two line segments or a point and a line segment.

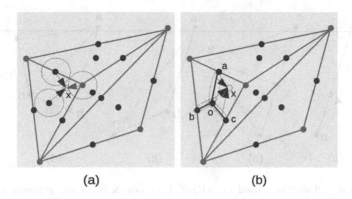

(a)   (b)

Fig. 2. 2D interpolation schemes. x is the pixel to be interpolated. Dashed circle (for RBF) or ellipses (for anisotropic RBF) describe the support domains of underlying basis functions. (a) RBF interpolation. (b) Anisotropic RBF interpolation.

The distance between two points are still measured using Euclidean distance in ARBF. However, the distance between two line segments or between a point and a line segment is redefined as follows. Assume we are calculating the distance between point $\mathbf{x}$ and line segment $(\mathbf{a}, \mathbf{b})$, there are three possible cases.

(1) For case 1, if point $\mathbf{x}$ is on the line segment $(\mathbf{a}, \mathbf{b})$, then the distance between $\mathbf{x}$ and $(\mathbf{a}, \mathbf{b})$ directly equals to 0.
(2) For case 2, if point $\mathbf{x}$ and the endpoints of line segment $(\mathbf{a}, \mathbf{b})$ form an acute triangle, the distance is evaluated as the perpendicular distance from $\mathbf{x}$ to line segment $(\mathbf{a}, \mathbf{b})$.
(3) For case 3, if $\mathbf{x}$ and the endpoints of line segment $(\mathbf{a}, \mathbf{b})$ form an obtuse triangle, the distance is defined as $min\{\|\mathbf{x} - \mathbf{a}\|, \|\mathbf{x} - \mathbf{b}\|\}$.

Figure 3(a–c) illustrates the three distances between point $\mathbf{x}$ and line segment $(\mathbf{a}, \mathbf{b})$ under the above circumstances. Besides, the distance between two line segments $(\mathbf{a}, \mathbf{b})$ and $(\mathbf{c}, \mathbf{d})$ is defined as $min\{\|\mathbf{a} - \mathbf{c}\|, \|\mathbf{a} - \mathbf{d}\|, \|\mathbf{b} - \mathbf{c}\|, \|\mathbf{b} - \mathbf{d}\|\}$. An example is provided in Fig. 3(d).

The new distance functions of ARBF take both magnitude and direction into account to change the support domain of the basis function from a regular circle or sphere to an ellipse or ellipsoid, which enables the conventional RBF method with some new properties to control the shapes of internal pore structures.

2.3   Algorithm Description

Anisotropic RBF interpolation mainly involves three stages. The first is function-fitting by solving a linear system corresponding to the interpolation conditions. To figure out the weight coefficients of the basis functions in Eq. 2, some specified values are assigned to the given mesh. In the current method, the values of all mesh vertices are assigned 1. For 2D meshes, the middle point of each edge, the

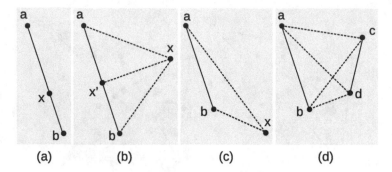

Fig. 3. Distance definitions used by ARBF. (a) Point **x** is on line segment (**a, b**). (b) Point **x** and line segment (**a, b**) form an acute triangle. (c) Point **x** and line segment (**a, b**) form an obtuse triangle. (d) Distance between line segments (**a, b**) and (**c, d**).

face (triangle or quadrangle) center and also the line segments from the center to the middle point are all set to -1. For 3D meshes, the centers of surfaces and the centers of sub-volume (tetrahedron or hexahedron) are assigned -1. Moreover, the line segments from the volume center to the face centers are assigned -1 as well. Figure 4(a–c) demonstrates the distribution of values at the centers of all radial basis functions in a 2D triangular mesh, a 3D tetrahedral mesh, and a 3D hexahedral mesh, respectively. Secondly, once the weight coefficients of the basis functions are solved using the revised distance definitions, the function values of the interpolated points could be easily calculated through Eq. 3. In our algorithm, the bounding box of the target object is partitioned into a matrix of small cubes of the same size, and the vertices of the small cubes are chosen as the interpolation points. Lastly, an iso-surface is extracted using the well-known Marching Cube algorithm [11].

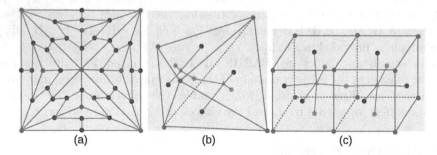

Fig. 4. Values assigned to mesh nodes. Red dots indicate value 1 is assigned while blue dots indicate value -1 is assigned. Brown lines indicate value -1 is assigned as well. In 3D meshes, green dots represent interior nodes. (a) Sample distribution of node values in the 2D triangular mesh. (b) Sample distribution of node values in the 3D tetrahedral mesh. (c) Sample distribution of node values in the 3D hexahedral mesh.

In general, a finite number of mesh nodes can be used to initialize the matrix in Eq. 2 with a reasonable size for simple scaffolds. Nonetheless, the matrix will become singular or extremely time-consuming to solve when a complex model is given as the input. To this end, the global interpolation method can be substituted with a local ARBF interpolation method. Instead of solving the coefficients for all nodes at once, a set of adaptive coefficients are figured out for each unit domain. At the same time, the nodes from neighboring domains will be taken into consideration to ensure the connectivity and smoothness between the target domain with surrounding domains. To identify the neighboring domain of each point instantly and accurately, we integrate the well-known k-d tree algorithm [2] into our local interpolation scheme.

3   Results and Discussion

Given an iso-value and a specified shape parameter, a variety of porous architectures can be obtained by determining the locations of various centers of the radial basis functions within a given boundary constraint. In this section, we choose the inverse multiquadric (IMQ) function as basis functions and use a constant $C = 0.1$ as its shape parameter. A proper iso-value is applied to each independent porous structure. Figure 5 (a) shows a pore structure obtained from single regular tetrahedron whose opening grows from the center of the tetrahedron toward the centers of its four triangle surfaces. Figure 5 (b) presents a surface inserted into two adjacent regular tetrahedrons. Figure 5 (c) describes a pore network comprised of the ARBF surface pieces from twenty tetrahedrons. Figure 6 (a) shows the surface interpolated from a single hexahedron. Figure 6 (b) presents the structure obtained from eight hexahedrons in a cube shape. Figure 6 (c) describes the surface obtained from a rod comprised of four hexahedrons in a row. Furthermore, diverse basis functions lead to distinctive patterns of morphology. Interpolated results using different basis functions, including multiquadric (MQ) function, inverse multiquadric (IMQ) function, Gaussian function and thin plate spline (TPS) function, are illustrated in Fig. 7. To further study the practicality of ARBF surfaces in biomedical engineering, we manufactured a realistic porous femur scaffold in 3D vision. At first, a scanned femur model was tiled into 989 pieces of arbitrary tetrahedrons. Here we use a body-centered cubic (BCC) lattice [14] based tetrahedral mesh generation algorithm followed by a quality tetrahedral mesh smoothing via boundary-optimized Delaunay triangulation (B-ODT) [6,23]. For each tetrahedron, we use the four vertices, the centers of four triangle faces, the tetrahedron center, and the line segments from the triangle centers to the tetrahedron center as the centers of basis functions. Moreover, the basis functions from the first layer of surrounding tetrahedrons are included in current tetrahedron's linear system to ensure the pore surface smoothly connected with the surfaces from adjacent tetrahedrons. Consequently, a large number of connected porous structures are formed tetrahedron by tetrahedron as illustrated in Fig. 8.

The randomness of porous distribution can be enhanced by moving the centers of basis functions toward arbitrary directions, which is a viable method to manufacture more realistic tissue scaffold with complex physiological architectures. Figure 9 shows some randomized mesh surfaces generated from a single hexahedron domain. Moreover, the surface appearance and the porosity would change hugely when the iso-value or the shape parameter varies. Figure 10(a–d) reveal that the porosity increases as the iso-value augments. In addition, Fig. 11 reflects the relationships between the porosity and the two factors respectively.

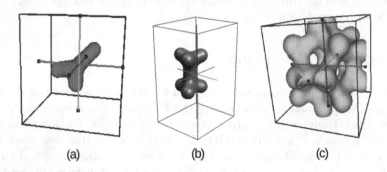

(a)   (b)   (c)

Fig. 5. Generated porous surfaces in regular tetrahedrons. (a) Surface in single regular tetrahedron. (b) Surface in two connecting tetrahedrons. (c) Surface in an icosahedron.

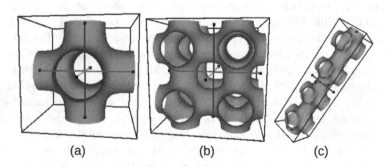

(a)   (b)   (c)

Fig. 6. Generated porous surfaces in regular hexahedrons. (a) Surface in single hexahedron. (b) Surface in 2×2 stack of hexahedrons. (c) Surface in 4 hexahedrons arranged to form a rod.

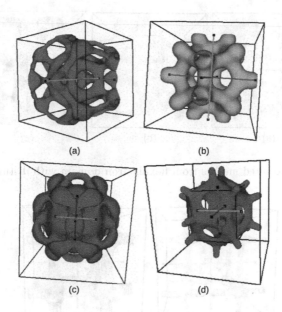

(a)   (b)

(c)   (d)

Fig. 7. Results obtained from icosahedron domain using different basis functions. (a) multiquadrics (MQ). (b) inverse multiquadrics (IMQ). (c) Gaussian. (d) thin plate spline (TPS).

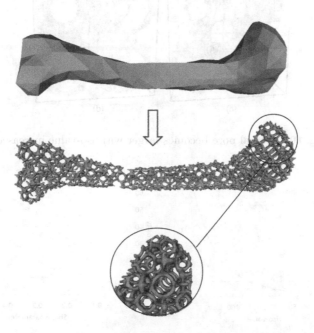

Fig. 8. Interpolated porous inner structure of femur scaffold.

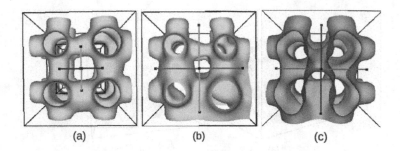

Fig. 9. Resulted meshes from hexahedron domain with disturbance.

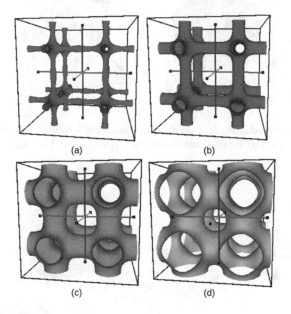

Fig. 10. Internal pore becomes larger with iso-value increased.

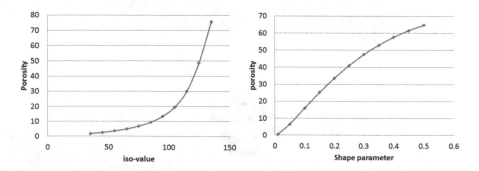

Fig. 11. Relationship between porosity and iso-value(left)/shape parameter(right).

4   Conclusions

In tissue engineering, the design of internal structures plays a critical role in determining the functionality of a scaffold in terms of equivalent internal connectivity and mass transportation. In this article, we presented a new ARBF implicit surface approach to generating inhomogeneous porous tissue scaffolds. Comparing to other implicit surface methods such as TPMS, our proposed method has three significant advantages. Firstly, in most methods based on periodic porous structures a small modification to the cell structure would change the appearance of the entire porous architecture. Nevertheless, local modifications of pore shape, size or distribution can be achieved by accordingly adjusting the local configuration of sub-volumes. Secondly, our approach is flexible to choose different meshes as inputs (tetrahedral mesh or hexahedral mesh). Thirdly, unlike many implicit methods requiring post-actions like Boolean operations (e.g. intersection) to get the final pieces built, the only post-action in our approach is to retrieve iso-surface using Marching Cube algorithm. In general, our method is superior in flexibility and easy to implement.

Although our ARBF interpolation method has been tested with some heterogeneous 3D models such as the human femur in Sect. 3, the performance of the experimental result is very dependent on the construction of tetrahedral meshes. In the future, we will use adaptive scattered point clouds as the inputs of our program to increase the pores' autonomous randomness.

References

1. Bucklen, B.S., Wettergreen, W.A., Yuksel, E., Liebschner, M.A.K.: Bone-derived CAD library for assembly of scaffolds in computer-aided tissue engineering. Virtual Phys. Prototyp. **3**, 13–23 (2008)
2. Chandran, S.: Introduction to kd-trees. Department of Computer Science, University of Maryland, Technical report (2004)
3. Chen, H., Guo, Y., Rostami, R., Fan, S., Tang, K., Yu, Z.: Porous structure design using parameterized hexahedral meshes and triply periodic minimal surfaces. In: Proceedings of Computer Graphics International 2018, CGI 2018, pp. 117–128. ACM, New York (2018)
4. Elomaa, L., Teixeira, S., Hakala, R., Korhonen, H., Grijpma, D.W., Seppala, J.V.: Preparation of poly(e-caprolactone)-based tissue engineering scaffolds by stereolithography. Acta Biomaterialia **7**, 3850–3856 (2011)
5. Feng, J., Fu, J., Shang, C., Lin, Z., Li, B.: Porous scaffold design by solid t-splines and triply periodic minimal surfaces. Comput. Methods Appl. Mech. Eng. **336**, 333–352 (2018)
6. Gao, Z., Yu, Z., Holst, M.: Quality tetrahedral mesh smoothing via boundary-optimized Delaunay triangulation. Comput. Aided Geom. Des. **29**(9), 707–721 (2012)
7. Giannitelli, S.M., Accoto, D., Trombetta, M., Rainer, A.: Current trends in the design of scaffolds for computer-aided tissue engineering. Acta Biomaterialia **10**, 580–594 (2014)
8. Hollister, S.J.: Porous scaffold design for tissue engineering. Nat. Mater. **4**, 518–524 (2005)

9. Khoda, A.K., Ozbolat, I.T., Koc, B.: Engineered tissue scaffolds with variational porous architecture. J. Biomech. Eng. **133**, 011001 (2011)
10. Kosec, G., Sarler, B.: Local RBF collocation method for Darcy flow. Comput. Model. Eng. Sci. **25**, 197–208 (2008)
11. Lorensen, W.E., Cline, H.E.: Marching cubes: a high resolution 3d surface construction algorithm. SIGGRAPH Comput. Graph. **21**(4), 163–169 (1987)
12. Melchels, F.P.W., Domingos, M.A.N., Klein, T.J., Malda, J., Bartolo, P.J.S., Hutmacher, D.W.: Additive manufacturing of tissues and organs. Prog. Polym. Sci. **37**, 1079–1104 (2012)
13. Melchels, F.P.W., Wiggenhauser, P.S., Warne, D., Barry, M., Ong, F.R., Chong, W.S., Hutmacher, D.W., Schantz, J.T.: CAD/CAM-assisted breast reconstruction. Biofabrication **3**, 034114 (2011)
14. Molino, N., Bridson, R., Teran, J., Fedkiw, R.: A crystalline, red green strategy for meshing highly deformable objects with tetrahedra. In: In 12th International Meshing Roundtable, pp. 103–114 (2003)
15. Peltola, S.M., Melchels, F.P.W., Grijpma, D.W., Kellomaki, M.: A review of rapid prototyping techniques for tissue engineering purposes. Ann. Med. **40**, 268–280 (2008)
16. Schaefer, D.W., Keefer, K.D.: Structure of random porous materials: silica aerogel. Phys. Rev. Lett. **56**, 2199–2202 (1986)
17. Schroeder, C., Regli, W.C., Shokoufandeh, A., Sun, W.: Computer-aided design of porous artifacts. Comput.-Aided Des. **37**, 339–353 (2005)
18. Shi, J., Yang, J., Zhu, L., Li, L., Li, Z., Wang, X.: A porous scaffold design method for bone tissue engineering using triply periodic minimal surfaces. IEEE Access **6**, 1015–1022 (2018)
19. Sogutlu, S., Koc, B.: Stochatic modeling of tissue engineering scaffolds with varying porosity levels. Comput.-Aided Des. Appl. **4**, 661–670 (2007)
20. Sun, W., Starly, B., Nam, J., Darling, A.: Bio-CAD modeling and its applications in computer-aided tissue engineering. Comput.-Aided Des. **37**, 1097–1114 (2005)
21. Vertnik, R., Sarler, B.: Solution of incompressible turbulent flow by a mesh-free method. Comput. Model. Eng. Sci. **44**, 65–95 (2009)
22. Wang, J., Liu, G.: On the optimal shape parameters of radial basis functions used for 2-d meshless methods. Comput. Methods Appl. Mech. Eng. **191**, 2611–2630 (2002)
23. Wang, J., Yu, Z.: Feature-sensitive tetrahedral mesh generation with guaranteed quality. Comput.-Aided Des. **44**(5), 400–412 (2012)
24. Wang, X., Xu, S., Zhou, S., Xu, W., Leary, M., Choong, P., Qian, M., Brandt, M., Xie, Y.: Topological design and additive manufacturing of porous metals for bone scaffolds and orthopaedic implants: A review. Biomaterials **83**, 127–141 (2016)
25. Yoo, D.J.: Computer-aided porous scaffold design for tissue engineering using triply periodic minimal surfaces. Int. J. Precis. Eng. Manuf. **12**, 61–67 (2011)
26. Yoo, D.J.: Porous scaffold design using the distance field and triply periodic minimal surface models. Biomaterials **32**, 7741–7754 (2011)
27. Zein, I., Hutmacher, D.W., Tan, K.C., Teoh, S.H.: Fused deposition modeling of novel scaffold architectures for tissue engineering applications. Biomaterials **23**, 1169–1185 (2002)

Visual Surveillance

Accurate and Efficient Non-Parametric Background Detection for Video Surveillance

William Porr[1], James Easton[2], Alireza Tavakkoli[3]([✉]), Donald Loffredo[4], and Sean Simmons[4]

[1] University of California-Berkeley, Berkeley, CA 94720, USA
porrliam@gmail.com
[2] University of Texas, Austin, TX 78712, USA
jweaston99@gmail.com
[3] University of Nevada, Reno, NV 89557, USA
tavakkol@unr.edu
[4] University of Houston-Victoria, Victoria, TX 77901, USA
{LoffredoD,SimmonsS}@uhv.edu

Abstract. In this paper, we propose an adaptive, non-parametric method of separating background from foreground in static camera video feed. Our algorithm processes each frame pixel-wise, and calculates a probability density function at each location using previously observed values at that location. This method makes several improvements over the traditional kernel density estimation model, accomplished through applying a dynamic learning weight to observed intensity values in the function, consequentially eradicating the large computational and memory load often associated with non-parametric techniques. In addition, we propose a novel approach to the classic background segmentation issue of "ghosting" by exploiting the spatial relationships among pixels.

Keywords: Background detection · Background subtraction
Change detection · Nonparametric modeling · Incremental learning

1 Introduction

Accurate separation of foreground from background is essential for many video surveillance applications. The separation serves as a basis from which other, higher level surveillance applications can be conducted more efficiently. Such higher-level applications include tasks such as object tracking or, as what was done in [2], the segmentation of body parts. The general approach is to create a statistical model of the background at either each pixel or a larger surrounding region using the known values from the video feed. Then for each incoming frame, the pixel or region models are referenced using the incoming values. This "referencing" will then return a value which reflects how closely the incoming

© Springer Nature Switzerland AG 2018
G. Bebis et al. (Eds.): ISVC 2018, LNCS 11241, pp. 93–105, 2018.
https://doi.org/10.1007/978-3-030-03801-4_9

value corresponds to the background model. Those values with low probabilities of belonging to the background model are to be designated as foreground.

Unfortunately, this approach is not without its faults. Because the background models are generally based on the pixel intensity values alone, we run into issues when those values change for reasons other than the inclusion of foreground objects. For example, Global illumination change is a common problem because it changes the values of each pixel for most, if not all pixels in the frame, often leading to many false foreground detections. Shadows are also often falsely detected as foreground, as they decrease the pixel values that they cover. However, techniques such as the use of chromasticity variables as done in [1] have been able to solve this issue. Intermittent object motion is another notorious problem with these algorithms because it produces "ghosts". These "ghosts" are falsely detected foreground regions left behind by the exit of objects that were previously considered background. Slow moving objects can be difficult to detect in certain algorithms that incorporate blind updating as well because the background model updates faster than the object itself moves. Blind updating refers to updating the probability density function, or pdf, with the incoming value regardless of whether it was detected as a foreground or background value.

In any case, much of the challenge is in creating an algorithm that is both precise and computationally efficient. Many algorithms are able to produce fantastic benchmarking results, but are too costly to be used in real time applications or embedded systems because the processing speed is slower than the rate at which new frames are coming in. Other algorithms are simple and rapid in their execution, but lack enough accuracy to be depended on in higher level applications. Here, we attempt to strike an effective balance between speed and precision.

2   Related Work

If one were to invest even the smallest fraction of time investigating the field of computer vision, they would quickly become aware of the vast and diverse stores of literature addressing the problem of background subtraction. However diverse and unique these approaches may be, the majority tend to fall into a combination of a few structural categories. The most prominent of these categories being pixel based vs. region based model jurisdiction, parametric vs. non-parametric modeling, and conservative vs. blind updating.

Pixel-based vs. Region-based For most methods, background models are formed by a matrix of statistical models. Each individual model forms the background at either one particular pixel or a larger region of N × N pixels. Some other region based approaches also use superpixels to define regions rather than using a grid approach. The benefit of modeling at the pixel level, such as in [3,7,11], is the potential for sharper foreground segmentation and better capture of small foreground objects. The drawback of this approach is an increased potential for random noise affecting the background segmentation, since the spatial relationships between pixels are not taken advantage of, and a higher computational and memory cost. Region-based modeling, such as in [1,4], has the benefit of lower computational and memory cost, lower levels of noise, and a more cohesive capture of foreground objects (less holes, gaps, etc). The main drawbacks, as implied, are less precise foreground segmentation, poor detection of small objects, and inaccurate modeling along edges separating different background objects.

Parametric vs. Non-Parametric Parametric models, such as [3], are often structured with underlying assumptions about the arrangement of the true background, while non-parametric models, such as [1,2,5], are designed to conform to the true background almost solely using observed input from the video sequence. The benefit of parametric models is that they often are less computationally demanding than their non-parametric counterparts, but the structural assumptions made can result in inaccuracies when they are not consistent with the true background. Non-parametric models have the benefit of being more flexible, however, as stated in [9], they are highly dependent on data.

Conservative vs. Blind Updating Blind updating schemes, such as [2,5,7], use both observed foreground and background pixel values in order to model the background, while conservative updating schemes only make use of pixel values detected as background in order to create a background model. Blind updating schemes are better able to adapt to changes in scenery, but are typically poor in detecting slow moving foreground objects. Conservative updating schemes, as stated in [9], prevent "pollution" of the background model from foreground pixels. This comes at the cost of having to devise a method of including static foreground objects into the background after a period of time and having to create a means of initializing the background model using frames that include foreground objects as done in [1].

As stated before, the many modern algorithms contain a combination of these features along with other novel structural attributes. Maddalena et al. developed the SOBS system, which makes use of artificial neural networks inspired by biological systems in order to create an adaptive background model. This network of neurons is able to model the background in a self-organizing manner and has many resemblances of a non-parametric system [5]. Hati et al. are able to compute a background model using their LIBS scheme by establishing an intensity range for each pixel location in the scene. This intensity range defines the upper and lower extremities for which a value can be considered background [3]. Elgammal et al. used a non-parametric approach which makes use of kernel density estimation to create a probability density function at each pixel. Sampled values at a pixel location are each assigned a weighted kernel function. These kernel functions collectively create a weighted density function from which newly observed values can be predicted as foreground or background [2].

The ViBe algorithm models the background at the pixel level, while simultaneously incorporating spatial relationships among pixels into the individual background models. An incoming value is predicted to be background if they are within a certain proximity in 3-D space of enough previously observed values at that location or its neighbor. Also, in order to update the background models and allow adaptation, ViBe randomly selects which values in the model to substitute with incoming values that are designated to be incorporated into the background model [1]. Lu in [4] developed a region based approach which creates a background model using various levels of a Gaussian pyramid. Foreground information is detected not only by observing the difference between different regions in the input frame and background model at the finest Gaussian scale, but also by the motion probability contributed by the coarser Gaussian scales. Zivkovic in [11] improves upon the widely used parametric Gaussian Mixture Model system by incorporating an on-line clustering algorithm. Manzanera in [7] uses a simple and effective non-linear background subtraction method which simply uses increment and decrement to update current estimates. It is popular in embedded systems because of its low computational cost.

3   Non-Parametric Background Detection

A primary motivation in the design of our model is to improve upon the traditional Kernel Density Estimation model as used in [2]. There are certain drawbacks in the KDE model which can be improved upon significantly within the context of background subtraction for better efficiency and accuracy. One major issue with kernel density estimation is that since N kernels must be summed and averaged for computation of $P(\mathbf{x}^t|BG)$, the computational complexity of the basic method becomes $O(N)$, causing a large degree of inefficiency as N becomes larger over time. In addition, when using kernel density estimation one must store each individually observed intensity in order to keep track of the kernel locations. This is obviously undesireable as it would dramatically increase the memory demand in an implementation. Also, the user only has access to individual values of $P(\mathbf{x}^t|BG)$, rather than the function as a whole since only the kernel locations are stored. Our model is inherently able to solve these problems through its incremental design.

Our scheme builds a pixel-wise non-parametric density function using observed values from the various frames of a video feed. Each function represents the probability density function for one channel of one pixel in the video frame, and this model is updated as new intensities are observed at the pixel location. A model for one channel of location $\mathbf{x}$ can be represented at time t by:

$$\overset{\sim t}{\theta}(\mathbf{x}) = \alpha \overset{\sim t-1}{\theta}(\mathbf{x}^t) - \beta \overset{\sim t-1}{\theta}(\sim \mathbf{x}^t) \tag{1}$$

such that the model $\overset{\sim}{\theta}$ is normalized.

$\mathbf{x}^t$ is the most recently observed channel intensity at location $\mathbf{x}$, $\sim \mathbf{x}^t$ reflects all values in the function that are not $\mathbf{x}^t$, and D is the size of the domain of the function. α is the value by which $\overset{\sim t-1}{\theta}(\mathbf{x}^t)$ is updated at time t, and β is the value by which all unobserved values of the function are forgotten. In this sense,

α reflects the learning rate of the function, and β the forgetting rate. For our purposes, α and β can be substituted by linear functions, such that:

$$\alpha = \frac{N^{t-1} - (\overset{\sim t-1}{\theta}(\mathbf{x}^t) \cdot N^{t-1})}{(N^{t-1})^2 + N^{t-1}} \quad \text{and} \quad \beta = \frac{\overset{\sim t-1}{\theta}(\mathbf{x}^t) \cdot N^{t-1}}{(N^{t-1})^2 + N^{t-1}} \quad (2)$$

where N^t is the number of samples in the function with relation to time t. These functions reflect decreasing values of α and β which approach 0 as N approaches infinity. We chose these dynamic values of α and β for the computational efficiency and accuracy it provides. A decreasing learning and forgetting rate allows for the formation of a general model quickly in the beginning of the video sequence since earlier frames will have the largest influence. This rough model is then finely tuned during latter frames of the sequence using the lowered rates.

One may desire for a learning rate which approaches a constant value rather than zero as N approaches infinity. In that case, the Eq. 1 could be reworked as:

$$\overset{\sim t}{\theta}(\mathbf{x}) = \frac{\alpha \overset{\sim t-1}{\theta}(\mathbf{x^t})}{1 + \alpha} + \frac{\overset{\sim t-1}{\theta}(\sim \mathbf{x^t})}{1 + \alpha} \quad \text{where} \quad \alpha = \frac{1 + Z \cdot N^{t-1}}{N^{t-1}} \quad (3)$$

Here, Z is the constant α will approach as N approaches infinity. This approach would have the benefit of increased adaptability at later frames.

In order to determine if location $\mathbf{x}$ is a background pixel, the process used in Eq. 1 to model the function at time t is then repeated for the other two channels of pixel $\mathbf{x}$. In order to calculate the probability of $\mathbf{x}$ being a part of the background using the three probabilistic values gathered from Eq. 1, we use the following:

$$P(BG|\mathbf{x}) = \overset{\sim t}{\theta}(\mathbf{x}_B^t) \cdot \overset{\sim t}{\theta}(\mathbf{x}_G^t) \cdot \overset{\sim t}{\theta}(\mathbf{x}_R^t) \quad (4)$$

By multiplying these probabilities, we are able to acquire a probabilistic value which assumes a statistical independence at each channel. To decide which values are associated with the background and which are to be considered foreground, we establish a global threshold value th. Now, we determine that pixel $\mathbf{x}$ is a background pixel only if its probability as gathered from Eq. 4 is greater than th. Also, for the purposes of computational efficiency and improving end results, we adopted a parameter σ to serve as a bandwidth for the probability density function. This bandwidth should be chosen in such a way that the effect of random noise in the video sequence is diminished, while avoiding the effects of oversmoothing.

After each frame is processed and a binary output frame is produced, a Gaussian blur filter is applied to the binary image to soften the effect of these missclassified pixels. This image is then fed into a median filter. This filter operates by filtering out misclassified foreground pixels based on the presence of foreground pixels in the surrounding neighborhood. For example, if we have a binary output frame B, and pixel B_i is detected as a foreground pixel, then pixel

B_i shall remain a foreground pixel only if more than half of the pixels surrounding it within a 5×5 space are *also* detected as pixels associated with a foreground object. These simple solutions have shown to improve results significantly.

3.1   Global Illumination Change

As we stated before, Global Illumination Change is a characteristic problem associated with algorithms such as the one we propose here. Our method of background subtraction is unable to natively consider global changes in illumination, so we must make an exception. Also, since our algorithm fundamentally assumes that the video feed comes from a stationary source, we run into issues when a camera is shifted for whatever intentional or unintentional reason. If either condition arises, the native algorithm will adapt only slowly, which is undesirable for the vast majority of applications as it would inhibit accurate background segmentation during that period. For this reason, we have the program attempt to predict a global illumination change or some other significant change in the background. This is simply done by setting a threshold of foreground pixels. This threshold is arranged such that if the proportion of detected foreground pixels to background pixels exceeds that threshold, we clear the probability density function for every channel of every pixel in the frame. It is a simple addition which saves the program from a large number of false detections, ensuring that it can run smoothly through abnormal conditions.

3.2   Ghost Detection

Ghosts refer to the presence of a falsely detected foreground region when an object is removed from the scene. This represent a notoriously difficult issue to resolve. A continuously updating algorithm can adapt over time to include foreground objects into the background model. However, as was the case with global illumination changes, this adaptation is too slow to be desirable in real time applications when dealing with a falsely detected foreground region. Differentiating between true foreground objects and ghosts historically has been a difficult task to solve, yet we have devised a method to do just that. To alleviate this problem we proposed the following procedure to detect and eliminate the ghosting effect.

The Procedure. The proposed ghost detection procedure makes use of the fact that, as stated in [1], the values of the background surrounding the ghost object tend to be similar to those values of the ghost itself. Using this information, we devised a method of comparing nearly all the values near the edge of a ghost with those background values in the same vicinity. By using this information, we are able to effectively differentiate between ghosts and true foreground objects, where we can proceed to make appropriate adjustments.

In order to make these comparisons, the proposed method first gathers the silhouette of the detected foreground region in question using the binary output frame. For each pixel along the silhouette (or just a portion for improved performance, the logic still holds), two nearby values from the *original* frame are gathered, one outside the boundary of the silhouette and one inside. These two values are then subtracted. The subtraction result in absolute value form is then added to an accumulating sum. This sum is then divided by half of the total number of samples gathered for that particular foreground object. If in fact the object is a ghost and the surrounding background region shares similar values, the average difference should be about zero.

However, we do not always end up with such a result simply because backgrounds themselves can, for instance, have elaborate patterns and edges. This, with the addition of the inaccuracies caused by random noise, leads us to establish a threshold *near* zero in order to distinguish ghosts from static foreground objects, while still compensating for backgrounds that contain elaborate textures and edges. For example, say we have a silhouette and two arrays (O and I) of sampled values, one corresponding to values gathered outside the silhouette boundary and one corresponding to those values gathered inside the boundary. Each value was gathered according to its proximity to a silhouette pixel, meaning that pixel O_i should be within the same neighborhood as I_i. We then take the average difference of the corresponding values between the two arrays and compare it to a designated threshold value by

$$(\sum_{k=0}^{N} O_k - I_k)/N < t \tag{5}$$

N being the size of each array and t representing the set threshold value. If this Boolean operation returns true, then we designate that foreground region as a ghost. If the operation does not return true, then we designate the region as a static foreground region, since detectable foreground objects are presumed to have no predictable correlation with the background. A visual example of this situation is given in Fig. 1.

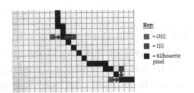

Fig. 1. Ghost detection

If the foreground region is detected as a ghost, we will clear all the observed values of each probability density function contained within the ghost object. Therefore, what has become irrelevant data about foreground object will be discarded to allow the model to reform to the background.

4 Experimental Results

To accomplish an accurate comparison of performance between various methods, we chose to use the 2014 dataset from changedetection.net workshop held in conjunction with the Computer Vision and Pattern Recognition (CVPR) conference

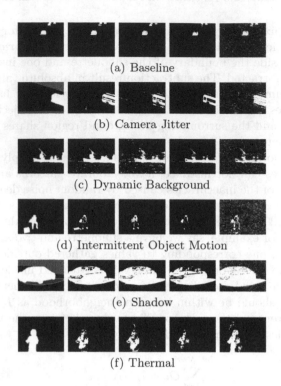

(a) Baseline

(b) Camera Jitter

(c) Dynamic Background

(d) Intermittent Object Motion

(e) Shadow

(f) Thermal

Fig. 2. Qualitative results comparison between methods. From left, GroundTruth, SOBS, Our Method, ViBe, and ZipFian.

[10]. This dataset provides a variety of environmental conditions which may be experienced in real-world usage of background-subtraction programs, resulting in a useful benchmarking tool that highlights the strengths and weaknesses of the methods used. An overview of the 2014 dataset can be found here [10].

4.1   Parallelized Implementation

To further increase performance, the proposed algorithm is parallelized by employing CPU multithreading. We believed that this was an appropriate addition considering how multi-core CPUs have been widely adopted and will likely be adopted even further as time progresses [8]. Therefore, we have provided an implementation of our method which will accurately reflect how the algorithm would perform in modern applications.

4.2   Choice of Other Methods

We used three state-of-the-art algorithms with superior results to test against our program, namely, SOBS [5], ViBe [1], and the Zipfian method [7]. The purpose of this comparison is to show how our algorithm performs relative to established

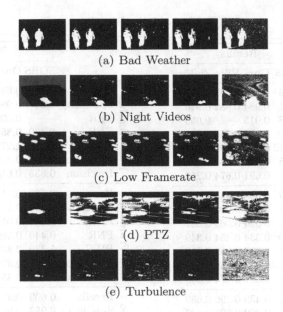

(a) Bad Weather

(b) Night Videos

(c) Low Framerate

(d) PTZ

(e) Turbulence

Fig. 3. Qualitative results comparison between methods. From left, GroundTruth, SOBS, Our Method, ViBe, and ZipFian.

methods. SOBS was chosen to serve as an example of the best segmentation precision possible today. This top-quality performance comes at the cost of its often slow computational times. On the other end of the spectrum, the Zipfian method was chosen as an example of the relative upper boundary in computational time. ViBe was chosen as one of the better-established methods which seeks to strike the same balance between computational speed and precision as we do in this paper.

4.3 Parameters of Other Methods and Specifications

The parameters of SOBS are $e1 = 1.0$, $e2 = 0.008$, $c1 = 1.0$, $c2 = 0.05$; any parameters not listed were left at default as given in [6]. The raw TP, FP, FN, and TN numbers were computed using the C++ comparator program provided by changedetection.net. The ViBe and Zipfian methods, as well as our method, were built from source and tested on Linux Mint 18 Cinnamon 64-Bit with Linux Kernel version 4.4.0-21-generic, while the SOBS method was tested on Windows 10 using the executable found on the author's website [6]. All methods were tested using an Intel core i5-4690k clocked at 4.3 GHz with four cores/threads and 16 GB of RAM.

4.4 Comparisons

Figures 2 and 3 show qualitative comparisons between the proposed method and the selected approaches from the literature applied on sample videos from

Table 1. Method results

		Results						Results			
		SOBS	Our	ViBe	ZipFian			SOBS	Our	ViBe	ZipFian
Obj. Motion	Recall	0.549	0.365	0.263	0.357	**Bad Weather**	Recall	0.569	0.643	0.434	0.787
	Specificity	0.901	0.984	0.982	0.946		Specificity	0.997	0.993	0.996	0.855
	FPR	0.098	0.015	—	0.053		FPR	—	0.006	—	0.144
	FNR	0.450	0.634	0.736	0.642		FNR	0.430	0.356	0.565	0.212
	PWC	11.012	6.136	6.905	9.638		PWC	0.872	1.277	1.287	14.630
	F-Measure	0.495	0.379	0.330	0.272		F-Measure	0.666	0.609	0.555	0.236
	Precision	0.554	0.691	0.674	0.269		Precision	0.835	0.618	0.857	0.166
Shadow	Recall	0.729	0.665	0.545	0.650	**Low Framerate**	Recall	0.550	0.419	0.263	0.486
	Specificity	0.988	0.975	0.994	0.932		Specificity	0.955	0.988	0.982	0.928
	FPR	0.011	0.024	0.005	0.067		FPR	0.044	0.011	—	0.071
	FNR	0.270	0.334	0.454	0.349		FNR	0.449	0.580	0.736	0.513
	PWC	2.234	3.737	2.399	7.912		PWC	5.779	2.873	6.905	8.238
	F-Measure	0.731	0.588	0.659	0.407		F-Measure	0.472	0.379	0.330	0.248
	Precision	0.740	0.581	0.874	0.305		Precision	0.548	0.451	0.674	0.184
Thermal	Recall	0.482	0.439	0.296	0.639	**Night Video**	Recall	0.603	0.491	0.283	0.638
	Specificity	0.996	0.990	0.999	0.882		Specificity	0.958	0.967	0.993	0.862
	FPR	0.003	0.009	—	0.117		FPR	0.041	0.032	0.006	0.137
	FNR	0.517	0.560	0.703	0.360		FNR	0.396	0.508	0.716	0.361
	PWC	2.641	5.071	4.591	13.570		PWC	4.944	4.326	2.147	14.225
	F-Measure	0.594	0.519	0.434	0.391		F-Measure	0.363	0.308	0.331	0.179
	Precision	0.862	0.699	0.984	0.317		Precision	0.301	0.267	0.483	0.115

all categories from the changedetection.net benchmark dataset. As it can be observed, the proposed technique produces superior results compared to the state-of-the-art, while enjoying the least computational complexity among the compared techniques.

Tables 1 and 2 show a quantitative comparison of the proposed method with the three methods from the tree methods selected from the literature. From the results gathered in this experiment, it is evident that there are certain categories which some methods execute better than others, and that no one solution completely dominates the other three. In particular, it can be seen through the results that the ViBe implementation excels at datasets which incorporate noise, small camera displacement, or dynamic background movements. This is a result of ViBe's use of spatial relationships in updating pixel models, effectively suppressing noise and dynamic background movements such as trees or waves. The SOBS algorithm took the lead in accuracy in most categories, which can be attributed to its use of a sophisticated artificial neural network. However, its level of sophistication caused it to be the slowest of all the methods that were used. For our method, we see strong results in a number of categories, especially with the F-measure and recall measurements. This means that our method does well at covering most of the foreground objects without sacrificing too much precision. The categories we performed well in include the baseline, low frame-rate,

Table 2. Method Results

		Results						Results			
		SOBS	Our	ViBe	ZipFian			SOBS	Our	ViBe	ZipFian
Baseline	Recall	0.771	0.609	0.534	0.648	PTZ	Recall	0.699	0.582	0.313	0.483
	Specificity	0.998	0.996	0.998	0.856		Specificity	0.682	0.866	0.904	0.722
	FPR	0.001	0.003	0.001	0.143		FPR	0.317	0.133	0.095	0.277
	FNR	0.228	0.390	0.465	0.351		FNR	0.300	0.417	0.686	0.516
	PWC	0.902	1.989	1.954	15.278		PWC	31.780	13.681	10.152	28.103
	F-Measure	0.839	0.709	0.680	0.296		F-Measure	0.040	0.195	0.089	0.033
	Precision	0.920	0.868	0.994	0.23		Precision	0.021	0.170	0.059	0.018
Jitter	Recall	0.717	0.594	0.452	0.604	Turbulence	Recall	0.631	0.672	0.578	0.696
	Specificity	0.972	0.960	0.998	0.869		Specificity	0.994	0.971	0.999	0.898
	FPR	0.027	0.039	0.011	0.130		FPR	0.005	0.028	—	0.101
	FNR	0.282	0.405	0.547	0.359		FNR	0.368	0.327	0.421	0.303
	PWC	3.737	5.323	3.311	13.951		PWC	0.750	3.013	0.269	10.248
	F-Measure	0.616	0.492	0.521	0.267		F-Measure	0.463	0.234	0.674	0.062
	Precision	0.545	0.429	0.638	0.174		Precision	0.438	0.163	0.822	0.034
Dynamic	Recall	0.726	0.636	0.443	0.524						
	Specificity	0.985	0.979	0.997	0.966						
	FPR	0.014	0.020	—	0.033						
	FNR	0.273	0.363	0.556	0.475						
	PWC	1.643	2.448	0.822	3.840						
	F-Measure	0.528	0.443	0.504	0.215						
	Precision	0.467	0.402	0.671	0.153						

object motion, thermal, and bad weather categories. Our success in the baseline category shows the method's ability to increasingly approach the true density when left relatively undisturbed.

The results in the latter mentioned category can be attributed to our non-parametric model and lack of an initialization phase, such as that used in [1,5]. This allows our model to adapt over time and prevent initial misclassifications from persisting throughout execution. These missclassifications would be accentuated by a low framerate sequence where foreground objects are likely to appear in more areas of the scene due to the increased frame-interval time. It is evident that many categories, aside from the few mentioned above, show similar outcomes between our algorithm and ViBe. Also, due to our increment-decrement approach, the computational complexity of the proposed method is $O(1)$, leading to an extremely efficient implementation. Consequentially, though when multi-threaded the proposed method is far more efficient than ViBe or SOBS, in single threaded applications it is still able to outperform ViBe by 42 frames per second and SOBS by 154 frames per second, while still providing sufficient accuracy most surveillance scenarios. Based on these results, it seems that the proposed method would be useful in typical surveillance applications, especially where high resolution and high frame-rate surveillance videos are needed. Additionally, the efficiency and accuracy of this solution would also prove useful in situations where low power and low memory embedded systems are used.

Additionally, though it was not included during benchmarking, the ghost detection method has proven its potential. The best use of the method would likely be in applying it only to stationary objects. This, as opposed to simply applying it to all foreground objects, would significantly reduce the computational cost of its addition.

5   Conclusions

In this paper, we presented a non-parametric solution to background subtraction in video surveillance applications. Our method operates on the pixel level using probability density functions built from observed values in the video feed to create a background model. These models then naturally develop to represent the true background of the video. We also developed a novel approach to solving the classic issue of ghosting. This was achieved by taking the difference between the pixel values at the edge of a detected foreground object and the pixel values of the background surrounding the object to distinguish true foreground objects from ghosts. Our algorithm has proven to be computationally efficient while still maintaining a level of precision comparable to established methods. This, when coupled with the method's extreme multithreading potential, makes it a viable option for modern surveillance systems.

Acknowledgments. This material is based upon work supported in part by the U. S. Army Research Laboratory and the U. S. Department of Defense under grant number W911NF-15-1-0024, W911NF-15-1-0455, and W911NF-16-1-0473. This support does not necessarily imply endorsement by the DoD or ARL.

References

1. Barnich, O., Droogenbroeck, M.V.: ViBe: a universal background subtraction algorithm for video sequences. IEEE Trans. Image Process. **20**(6), 1709–1724 (2011). https://doi.org/10.1109/TIP.2010.2101613
2. Elgammal, A., Duraiswami, R., Harwood, D., Davis, L.S.: Background and foreground modeling using nonparametric kernel density estimation for visual surveillance. Proc. IEEE **90**(7), 1151–1163 (2002). https://doi.org/10.1109/JPROC.2002.801448
3. Hati, K.K., Sa, P.K., Majhi, B.: Intensity range based background subtraction for effective object detection. IEEE Signal Process. Lett. **20**(8), 759–762 (2013)
4. Lu, X.: A multiscale spatio-temporal bakcground model for motion detection. In: IEEE International Conference on Image Processing (ICIP) (2014)
5. Maddalena, L., Petrosino, A.: A self-organizing approach to background subtraction for visual surveillance applications. IEEE Trans. Image Process. **17**(7), 1168–1177 (2008). https://doi.org/10.1109/TIP.2008.924285
6. Maddalena, L., Petrosino, A.: A self-organizing approach to background subtraction for visual surveillance applications. IEEE Trans. Image Process. **17**(7), 1168–1177 (2008)

7. Manzanera, A.: $\sigma - \delta$ background subtraction and the zipf law. In: Rueda, L., Mery, D., Kittler, J. (eds.) CIARP 2007. LNCS, vol. 4756, pp. 42–51. Springer, Heidelberg (2007). https://doi.org/10.1007/978-3-540-76725-1_5

8. Min, J.: Multicore goes mainstream (2014). http://embedded-computing.com/articles/multicore-goes-mainstream/

9. Piccardi, M.: Background subtraction techniques: a review. In: IEEE International Conference on Systems, Man and Cybernetics (2005)

10. Wang, Y., Jodoin, P.M., Porikli, F., Konrad, J., Benezeth, Y., Ishwar, P.: CDnet 2014: an expanded change detection benchmark dataset. In: Proceedings IEEE Workshop on Change Detection (CDW-2014) at CVPR-2014 (2014)

11. Zivkovic, Z.: Improved adaptive Gaussian mixture model for background subtraction. In: Proceedings of the 17th International Conference on Pattern Recognition (ICPR) (2004)

A Low-Power Neuromorphic System for Real-Time Visual Activity Recognition

Deepak Khosla[(⊠)], Ryan Uhlenbrock, and Yang Chen

HRL Laboratories, Malibu, CA 90265, USA
dkhosla@hrl.com

Abstract. We describe a high-accuracy, real-time, neuromorphic method and system for activity recognition in streaming or recorded videos from static and moving platforms that can detect even small objects and activities with high-accuracy. Our system modifies and integrates multiple independent algorithms into an end-to-end system consisting of five primary modules: object detection, object tracking, convolutional neural network image feature extractor, recurrent neural network sequence feature extractor, and an activity classifier. We also integrate neuromorphic principles of foveated detection similar to how the retina works in the human visual system and the use of contextual knowledge about activities to filter the activity recognition results. We mapped the complete activity recognition pipeline to the COTS NVIDIA Tegra TX2 development kit and demonstrate real-time activity recognition from streaming drone videos at less than 10 W power consumption.

Keywords: Activity recognition · Behavior recognition · Foveated detection
Neuromorphic · Aerial surveillance · Onboard video processing
Deep learning

1 Introduction

Visual activity recognition has many applications for surveillance and autonomous vehicles. For these applications it is necessary to recognize activities in unconstrained videos. Much activity recognition research focuses on more constrained videos, where the activity is spatially the center, dominant focus of the video, and temporally the video is trimmed to contain mostly only the activity of interest. Such constrained videos are easier to collect and label, so large datasets for training and evaluation more often consist of videos of this type. Leveraging activity recognition models trained on such datasets can be a benefit for models in the unconstrained domain, but applying them is non-trivial. We propose a visual activity recognition system that can apply pre-trained models and overcome the spatial and temporal challenges of unconstrained videos. We make use of recent advances in convolutional neural network-based object detection and classification systems combined with tracking as an initialization for activity detection candidates. Further, we use a foveated object detection technique to improve object localization and small object detection. We use the objects detected in the foveation phase as context to inform constraints on the activity classification.

© Springer Nature Switzerland AG 2018
G. Bebis et al. (Eds.): ISVC 2018, LNCS 11241, pp. 106–115, 2018.
https://doi.org/10.1007/978-3-030-03801-4_10

We temporally integrate the activity classification model and context information to identify short duration activities in long, untrimmed videos.

2 Related Work

There are many methods for activity recognition in videos [1–9]. The state of the art is in using deep learning methods. One main limitation of many of these methods is that they only address the activity classification problem: they assume the input is an activity video clip that is centered on and contains just the activity of interest. They are not applicable to detect and classify applications where the scene may contain multiple objects, clutter, and the actual activity of interest occupies a small spatio-temporal segment of the video. In this class of problems, the objects of interest first need to be detected, classified and tracked before activity classification can be carried out. In addition, the platform may be aerial or ground and static or moving.

3 Method

Figure 1 shows our system block diagram for real-time activity recognition in streaming or recorded videos from static or moving platforms. We describe the individual components in the following subsections.

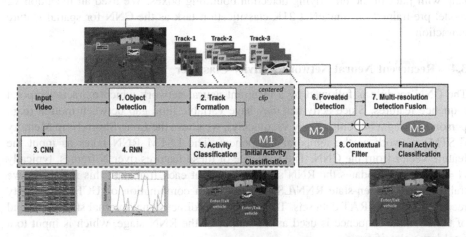

Fig. 1. Block diagram of our activity recognition approach. Blue box (left, dashed) shows the baseline architecture. Yellow box (right, solid) shows improvements via foveation and context. M1, M2 and M3 are the three main methods we compared in Sect. 4.3. (Color figure online)

3.1 Object Detection

The object detection module finds and recognizes objects of interest in the input video and outputs their bounding box location and class label. For example, if the objective is human activity recognition, then this module detects and classifies all human objects in the incoming video. If the objective is vehicle activity recognition, then this detects and classifies all vehicle objects in the incoming video. This module uses our prior work for real-time object recognition from aerial platforms [10].

3.2 Track Formation

Activity tracks are now formed by tracking detected objects across frames. The matching of bounding boxes from the current frame to the previous frame is done with the Munkres version of the Hungarian algorithm. The cost is computed using bounding box overlap ratio between the predicted bounding box and the previous bounding box. The algorithm is used to compute an assignment which minimizes the total cost. Sporadic detections of moving trees, shadows, etc. are removed by only considering tracks with a minimum duration of T seconds (e.g., T is nominally 2 s). The output of this module is persistent object tracks that have a minimum duration of T seconds. For example, if a person is carrying a gun in the video and visible for 5 s, this module will output a track of that object with a unique track number during those 5 s.

3.3 Convolutional Neural Network Feature Extraction

Persistent tracks are input to a convolutional neural network feature extractor. Track bounding boxes may be enlarged by X% (typically 20%) before feature extraction to help with jitter in the underlying detection bounding boxes. We used an Inception v2 model pre-trained on ImageNet 21K classification task as the CNN for spatial feature extraction.

3.4 Recurrent Neural Network Activity Classifier

The CNN module is followed by a recurrent neural network which extracts temporal sequence features. Since activities may have variable time gap between motion (e.g., person entering a building slowly vs. quickly), we chose the Long Short-Term Memory (LSTM) network as the temporal component. The LSTM RNN takes as input the feature vector from the CNN. The sequence of these features over N frames, typically N = 16 frames, updates the RNN's internal state at each frame. In this invention, we train the 256-hidden-state RNN/LSTM stage on a combination of UCF-101 activity recognition and VIRAT data sets. The RNN's 256-dimensional internal state at the end of the N frame sequence is used as the output of the RNN stage, which is input to a final layer classifier.

3.5 Activity Classifier

Assuming we have K activities to classify, a final fully-connected layer with K outputs gives the final class probability. Alternatively the RNN features can be sent to a Support Vector Machine (SVM) classifier with K outputs. The final output is a probability or confidence score (range 0–1) for each of the K classes. In the case where we only intend to recognize certain types of activity, no softmax is used, and instead a threshold is placed on the output response of the K output nodes to determine when an activity of interest is detected. Other activities, e.g. a person walking, should have no output above the threshold and receive effectively a label of "no relevant activity". In case of a winner take all embodiment, the activity with the high confidence is the activity label of that track. Modules 3–5 are run in parallel for each track from Module 2.

3.6   Foveated Detection

We leverage the relationship between entity detection and activity detection to design a foveated detection system in which the detection network is first run on the full frame resolution, then for each detected and robust track, the detection network is run again on a foveated region around the track center and expanded larger than the track size (1.5x the size corresponding to the track box). Detections from this second pass replace those in the foveated region from the first pass.

3.7   Multi-resolution Detection Fusion

We run our object detector twice on the incoming video. During the first pass, it analyzes the full video at the native resolution and detects potential objects. A tracker is initiated on every detected object. During the second pass, it analyzes the bounding boxes corresponding to all robust tracks at its resolution to further detect any objects within them that may have been missed in the first pass. This second pass is foveated detection. If the first pass detection is accurate, then no new information is gained in the second pass; it only serves as a confirmation. In some cases (e.g., person in front of car), the first pass misses detection of the smaller object (e.g., person), whereas the second pass run on the car track bounding box detects a new object. Although it is possible, we did not see any instance where the first pass detects more objects than the second pass in our data. We append the detected objects from the first and second pass into a single detected-objects list and use that for context in the next contextual filtering step.

3.8   Contextual Filter

We experimented with combining foveated detection and an entity-based contextual filter on our activity classification probabilities to improve activity recognition. Our activities of interest involve people interacting with vehicles or people alone. So the presence or absence of a person or vehicle is closely tied to what activities are possibly occurring in a given region of interest. Our convolutional and recurrent neural networks don't explicitly have this entity information as input. Our entity detection and localization is generally robust for these two classes. We implemented a filter logic that modifies the activity class probabilities from the neural network based on the detected entities (i.e., context). The logic is based on common sense intuition about the activities. The possible activities are Open/Close Trunk, In/Out Vehicle, In/Out Facility, Person Walking, Person Carrying Weapon, and Person Aiming Weapon. When there are no vehicles or people in a region of interest, no activity is possible. When a vehicle is present, In/Out Facility is not possible; its class probability is set to 0. When a person is present without a vehicle, Open/Close Trunk and In/Out Vehicle are not possible; their probabilities are set to 0. Softmax is applied after the filter to renormalize the activity class probability distribution.

4 Results

4.1 VIRAT Dataset

We first evaluated our approach on the Video and Image Retrieval and Analysis Tool (VIRAT) dataset. This dataset is designed to be realistic, natural and challenging for video surveillance domains in terms of its resolution, background clutter, diversity in scenes, and human activity and event categories than existing action recognition datasets. We used a subset of the dataset contains several HD videos of people performing various everyday activities. The ground truth annotation specifies the type of activity as well as bounding box and temporal range for activities in each video. There are 12 classes of activities annotated. We combined three pairs of similar activities to pose this as a K = 3-class activity classification problem: Open/Close Trunk, In/Out Vehicle, and In/Out Facility (see Fig. 2).

Fig. 2. Example of In/out facility activity classification.

For this evaluation, we focused on activity classification only (i.e., Integrated modules 3, 4 and 5 of Fig. 1). We evaluated four different methods using ground-truth based video clips (16 evenly spaced frames from each activity and rescaling the images to 360 × 360 pixels). We used the CNN-RNN as a 256-dimensional feature extractor and trained a new SVM last layer classifiers for K = 3 activities. The SVMs were trained on either the CNN features-averaged across the 16 frames, RNN features-averaged, RNN features-concatenated, or RNN features selected from the last frame. We evaluated the performance with cross-validation using a split of 80% training and 20% testing. Table 1 shows the activity classification scores with these four methods.

Table 1. Classification accuracy of 3-class VIRAT dataset.

Method	Classification accuracy
1. CNN only	90.8%
2. CNN + RNN averaged	88.6%
3. CNN + RNN concatenated	90.9%
4. CNN + RNN last frame	92.8%

4.2 HRL Parking Lot Dataset

We collected additional activity videos on the HRL campus in order to test the generalization performance of our classifiers. Two pan-tilt-zoom cameras looking down to a parking lot were mounted on a campus building. We recorded 45 min of video while people went through the parking lot, specifically performing the activities of opening/closing a trunk and getting in/out of a vehicle (see Fig. 3). The videos are in color with resolution 704 × 480. We annotated the videos with bounding boxes and start/stop times as the ground truth. This resulted in 47 trunk open/close and 40 vehicle in/out sequences. We used a classifier trained on features extracted by a CNN from the VIRAT dataset on three classes (open/close trunk, in/out vehicle, in/out building). Table 2 shows the activity recognition accuracy.

Fig. 3. Example video footage collected from HRL campus using EO cameras.

Table 2. Global activity recognition accuracy of 80.5% from HRL parking lot dataset.

	Open/Close Trunk	In/Out Vehicle	In/Out Facility	Accuracy %
Open/Close Trunk	32	15	0	68%
In/Out Vehicle	2	38	0	95%
In/Out Facility	0	0	0	NA

4.3   HRL Drone Dataset

We also evaluated our approach on multiple video datasets collected from a DJI quadcopter drone at a helipad and parking lot. The dataset involves multiple people and cars performing various activities with the drone hovering over and collecting data from two different viewpoints. The videos are in color with 4K resolution. We completed ground-truth annotation of the videos with bounding boxes and start/stop times. We annotated seven classes of activities: {In/Out Vehicle, Open/Close Trunk, In/out Facility, Person walking, Person Carrying Weapon, Person Aiming Weapon, None} (Fig. 4).

Fig. 4. Example annotations created for HRL August drone data set for In Vehicle (top) and Out Vehicle (bottom) from two different angles.

As described in Modules 3.3 and 3.4, we trained our deep learning architecture based on CNN and RNN for these 7 classes of activities. We used an Inception v2 model pre-trained on ImageNet 21K classification task as the CNN for spatial feature extraction, and a 256-hidden-state RNN/LSTM stage for activity recognition trained on a combination of UCF-101 activity recognition and VIRAT data sets.

The test protocol for the online streaming processing scheme uses an object detector to seed an object tracker. When the tracker has accumulated 16 frames of a tracked object, the activity classifier will be invoked. Since In/out Facility and Person walking are under-represented in the data, we only present results of the other activities in Tables 3 and 4 below. Figure 5 shows a typical result.

Table 3. Summary results across all activities on HRL drone dataset. Method M3 generally performs better than M1 or M2 (high PC, low FPPI).

Method	PD	PC	FPPI
M1	0.87	0.38	2.03
M2	0.91	0.40	1.82
M3	0.88	0.71	1.72

Table 4. Individual class activity results on HRL drone dataset.

M1	PD	PC	FPPI
In/Out Vehicle	0.90	0.90	2.42
Open/Close Trunk	0.97	0.05	2.60
Aim/Carry Weapon	0.73	0.18	0.26
M2	**PD**	**PC**	**FPPI**
In/Out Vehicle	0.89	0.89	2.09
Open/Close Trunk	0.93	0.25	2.55
Aim/Carry Weapon	0.87	0.27	0.27
M3	**PD**	**PC**	**FPPI**
In/Out Vehicle	0.80	0.73	2.06
Open/Close Trunk	0.91	0.64	2.41
Aim/Carry Weapon	0.92	0.80	0.35

Fig. 5. Typical recognized activity (see text above box) and detected entities (see text below box) using M3.

We evaluated the performance of three methods (M1, M2, and M3) as shown in Fig. 1. Method 1 (M1) is the system without foveated detection. Method 2 (M2) uses foveated detection and contextual filter path. Method 3 (M3) uses multi-resolution detection fusion and contextual filter.

4.4   Hardware Setup

Figure 6 shows a typical setup to collect and process video data from the DJI Inspire quadcopter. In the current invention, we can process results on either a computer with a GPU card or the NIVIDIA Tegra TX1 board. The desktop software and demonstration system runs under Ubuntu Linux 14.04 and requires a NVIDIA GPU to function.

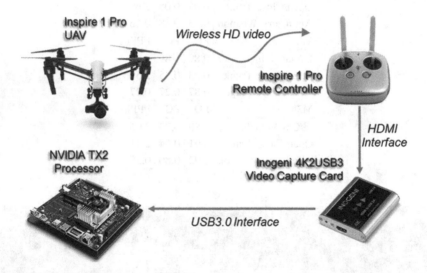

Fig. 6. Drone aerial video processing architecture.

We have mapped the complete activity recognition pipeline to the NVIDIA Tegra TX2 development board and systematically evaluated algorithmic performance in terms of frames per second and the power consumptions. As can be seen in Table 5, we can achieve a throughput of 9.9 frames per second for the full HD video at a processing power of 10 W.

Table 5. Processing throughput and power consumption for full video activity recognition.

	Display live video	Object recognition	Activity recognition (localized)	Activity recognition (full video)
Frames per second	158	16.4	47.8	9.9
Processing power (W)	5.5	8	7.5	10

Acknowledgments. This material is based upon work supported by the Office of Naval Research (ONR) under Contract No. N00014-15-C-0091. Any opinions, findings and conclusions or recommendations expressed in this material are those of the author(s) and do not necessarily reflect the views of the Office of Naval Research (ONR).

References

1. Kalogeiton, V., et al.: Action tubelet detector for spatio-temporal action localization. In: ICCV-IEEE International Conference on Computer Vision (2017)
2. Kuhn, H.W.: The Hungarian method for the assignment problem. Naval Res. Logist. (NRL) **2**(1–2), 83–97 (1955)
3. Karpathy, A., et al.: Large-scale video classification with convolutional neural networks. In: Proceedings of the IEEE Conference on Computer Vision and Pattern Recognition (2014)
4. Simonyan, K., Zisserman, A.: Two-stream convolutional networks for action recognition in videos. In: Advances in Neural Information Processing Systems (2014)
5. Vrigkas, M., Nikou, C., Kakadiaris, I.A.: A review of human activity recognition methods. Front. Robot. AI **2**, 28 (2015)
6. Donahue, J., et al.: Long-term recurrent convolutional networks for visual recognition and description. In: Proceedings of the IEEE Conference on Computer Vision and Pattern Recognition (2015)
7. Oh, S., et al.: A large-scale benchmark dataset for event recognition in surveillance video. In: 2011 IEEE Conference on Computer Vision and Pattern Recognition (CVPR). IEEE (2011)
8. Soomro, K., Zamir, A.R., Shah, M.: UCF101: a dataset of 101 human actions classes from videos in the wild (2012)
9. Redmon, J., Farhadi, A.: YOLO9000: better, faster, stronger. arXiv preprint (2017)
10. Khosla, D., Chen, Y., Kim, K.: A neuromorphic system for video object recognition. Front. Comput. Neurosci. **8**, 147 (2014)

Video-Based Human Action Recognition Using Kernel Relevance Analysis

Jorge Fernández-Ramírez[1,2]([✉]), Andrés Álvarez-Meza[1,2],
and Álvaro Orozco-Gutiérrez[1,2]

[1] Automatics Research Group, Pereira, Colombia
[2] Universidad Tecnolgica de Pereira, Pereira, Colombia
jorgeferram17@utp.edu.co

Abstract. This paper presents a video-based Human Action Recognition using kernel relevance analysis. Our approach, termed HARK, comprises the conventional pipeline employed in action recognition, with a two-fold post-processing stage: (i) A descriptor relevance ranking based on the centered kernel alignment (CKA) algorithm to match trajectory-aligned descriptors with the output labels (action categories), and (ii) a feature embedding based on the same algorithm to project the video samples into the CKA space, where the class separability is preserved, and the number of dimensions is reduced. For concrete testing, the UCF50 human action dataset is employed to assess the HARK under a leave-one-group-out cross-validation scheme. Attained results show that the proposed approach correctly classifies the 90.97% of human actions samples using an average input data dimension of 105 in the classification stage, which outperforms state-of-the-art results concerning the trade-off between accuracy and dimensionality of the final video representation. Also, the relevance analysis allows to increase the video data interpretability, by ranking trajectory-aligned descriptors according to their importance to support action recognition.

Keywords: Human action recognition · Relevance analysis
Feature embedding · Kernel methods

1 Introduction

Human action recognition has become an important research area in the computer vision field due to its wide range of applications, including automatic video analysis, video indexing and retrieval, video surveillance, and virtual reality [5]. As a result of the increasing amount of video data available both on internet repositories and personal collections, there is a strong demand for understanding the content of complex real-world data. However, different challenges arise for action recognition in realistic video data [13]. First, there is large intra-class variation caused by factors such as the style and duration of the performed action, scale changes, dynamic viewpoint, and sudden motion. Second, background clutter, occlusions, and low-quality video data are known to affect robust recognition

© Springer Nature Switzerland AG 2018
G. Bebis et al. (Eds.): ISVC 2018, LNCS 11241, pp. 116–125, 2018.
https://doi.org/10.1007/978-3-030-03801-4_11

as well. Finally, for large-scale datasets, the data processing represents a crucial computational challenge to be addressed [3].

The most popular framework for action recognition is the Bag of visual Words (BOW) with its variations [11,12]. The BOW pipeline contains three main stages: feature estimation, feature encoding, and classification. Besides, there are several pre-processing and post-processing stages, such as relevance analysis and feature embedding to enhance data decorrelation, separability and interpretability [2]. Furthermore, different normalization techniques have been introduced for improving the performance of the recognition system. For the feature estimation step, the recent success of local space-time features like Dense Trajectories (DT) and Improved Dense Trajectories (iDT) has lead researchers to use them on a variety of datasets, obtaining excellent recognition performance [12,13]. Regarding the feature encoding step, super-vector based encoding methods such as Fisher Vector (FV) and Vector of Locally Aggregated Descriptors (VLAD) are presented as the state-of-the-art approaches for feature encoding in action recognition tasks [5,11]. Lastly, the classification stage has usually been performed by Support Vector Machines (SVM) in most recognition frameworks [8,10].

The feature encoding method that provides the final video representation is crucial for the performance of an action recognition system, as it influences directly the classifier ability to predict the class labels. However, video representations generated by methods such as FV or VLAD are known to provide high dimensional encoding vectors which increases the computational requirements in the classification stage [5,13]. On the other hand, the high dimensionality of the input data could affect the classifier accuracy adversely, by using redundant information and even noise, which do not enhance data separability. Therefore, the Dimensionality Reduction (DR), which consists of feature selection and feature embedding methods, is imperative to lighten the burden associated with the encoding stage, eliminate redundant information, and project samples into new spaces to increase separability [1]. Conventional methods, such as Principal Component Analysis (PCA) and Linear Discriminant Analysis (LDA) have been proposed to decorrelate the individual features of descriptors and reduce their length, in a pre-processing stage to the encoding [6]. Nevertheless, these methods are specially designated to work with real-valued vectors coming from flat Euclidean spaces. Thus, in modern computer vision due to real-world data and models, there has been growing interest to go beyond the extensively studied Euclidean spaces and analyse more realistic non-linear scenarios for better representation of the data [7].

In this work, we introduce a new human action recognition system using kernel relevance analysis. The system, based on a non-linear representation of the super-vector obtained by the FV encoding technique, seeks to reduce the input space dimensionality, as well as, enhance separability and interpretability of video data. Specifically, our approach includes a centered kernel alignment (CKA) technique to recognize relevant descriptors related to action recognition. Hence, we match trajectory-aligned descriptors with the output labels (action categories) through non-linear representations [2]. Also, the CKA-algorithm allows to compute a linear projection matrix, where the columns quantify the required number of dimensions to preserve the 90% of the input data variability. Therefore, by projecting the video samples into the CKA generated space, the class separability is preserved, and the number of dimensions is reduced. Attained results on the UCF50 database demonstrate that our proposal favors the interpretability of the commonly employed descriptors in action recognition, and presents a system able to obtain competitive recognition accuracy using a drastically reduced input space dimensionality to the classification stage.

The rest of the paper is organized as follows: Sect. 2 presents the main theoretical background, Sect. 3 describes the experimental set-up, Sect. 4 introduces the results and discussions. Finally, Sect. 5 shows the conclusions.

2   Kernel-Based Descriptor Relevance Analysis and Feature Embedding

Let $\{\boldsymbol{Z}_n \in \mathbb{R}^{T \times D}, y_n \in \mathbb{N}\}_n^N$ be an input-output pair set holding N video samples, each of them represented by T trajectories generated while tracking a dense grid of pixels, whose local space is characterized by a descriptor of dimensionality D, as presented in [13]. Here, the samples are related to a set of human action videos meanwhile the descriptor in turn is one of the following trajectory-aligned measure: trajectory positions (Trajectory), Histogram of Oriented Gradients (HOG), Histogram of Optical Flow (HOF), Motion Boundary Histograms (MBHx and MBHy), yielding a total of $F = 5$ descriptors. Likewise, the output label y_n denotes the human action being performed in the corresponding video representation. From $\boldsymbol{Z}_n$, we aim to encode T described trajectories concerning a Gaussian Mixture Model (GMM), trained to be a generative model of the descriptor in turn. Therefore, the Fisher Vector (FV) feature encoding technique is employed, as follows [9]:

Let $\boldsymbol{Z}_n$ be a matrix holding T described trajectories $\boldsymbol{z}_t \in \mathbb{R}^D$, and υ^λ be a GMM with parameters $\lambda = \{w_i \in \mathbb{R}, \boldsymbol{\mu}_i \in \mathbb{R}^D, \sigma_i^2 \boldsymbol{I} \in \mathbb{R}^{D \times D}\}_{i=1}^K$, which are respectively the mixture weight, mean vector, and diagonal covariance matrix of K Gaussians. We assume that $\boldsymbol{z}_t$ is generated independently by υ^λ. Therefore, the gradient of the log-likelihood describes the contribution of the parameters to the generation process:

$$\boldsymbol{x}_n^\lambda = \frac{1}{T} \sum_{t=1}^T \nabla_\lambda \log \upsilon_\lambda(\boldsymbol{z}_t) \tag{1}$$

where ∇_λ is the gradient operator w.r.t. λ. Mathematical derivations lead $\boldsymbol{x}_n^{\mu,i}$ and $\boldsymbol{x}_n^{\sigma,i}$ to be the D-dimensional gradient vectors w.r.t the mean and standard deviation of the Gaussian i, that is:

$$\boldsymbol{x}_n^{\mu,i} = \frac{1}{T\sqrt{w_i}} \sum_{t=1}^T \gamma_t(i) \left(\frac{\boldsymbol{z}_t - \boldsymbol{\mu}_i}{\sigma_i} \right), \tag{2}$$

$$\boldsymbol{x}_n^{\sigma,i} = \frac{1}{T\sqrt{2w_i}} \sum_{t=1}^T \gamma_t(i) \left[\frac{(\boldsymbol{z}_t - \boldsymbol{\mu}_i)^2}{\sigma_i^2} - 1 \right] \tag{3}$$

where $\gamma_t(i)$ is the soft assignment of trajectory z_t to the Gaussian i, that is:

$$\gamma_t(i) = \frac{w_i v_i(z_t)}{\sum_{j=1}^K w_j v_j(z_t)} \tag{4}$$

The final gradient vector x_n^λ is a concatenation of the $x_n^{\mu,i}$ and $x_n^{\sigma,i}$ vectors for $i = 1, \dots, K$ and is $2KD$-dimensional.

Assuming that the same procedure is performed for each descriptor, the concatenation of the resulting vectors generates the set $\{x_n \in \mathbb{R}^{2K(D_1 + \cdots + D_F)}, y_n \in \mathbb{N}\}_n^N$. Afterwards, a *Centered Kernel Alignment* (CKA) approach is performed to compute a linear projection matrix, and to determine the relevance weight from each trajectory-aligned descriptor individual feature, as follows [2]:

Let $\kappa_X : \mathbb{R}^S \times \mathbb{R}^S \to \mathbb{R}$, where $S = 2K(D_1 + \cdots + D_F)$, be a positive definite kernel function, which reflects an implicit mapping $\phi : \mathbb{R}^S \to \mathcal{H}_X$, associating an element $x_n \in \mathbb{R}^S$ with the element $\phi(x_n) \in \mathcal{H}_X$, that belongs to the Reproducing Kernel Hilbert Space (RKHS), $\mathcal{H}_X$. In particular, the Gaussian kernel is preferred since it seeks an RKHS with universal approximation capability, as follows [4,14]:

$$\kappa_X(x_n, x_{n'}; \sigma) = \exp\left(-v^2(x_n, x_{n'})/2\sigma^2\right); \; n, n' \in \{1, 2, \dots, N\}, \tag{5}$$

where $v(\cdot, \cdot) : \mathbb{R}^S \times \mathbb{R}^S \to \mathbb{R}$ is a distance function in the input space, and $\sigma \in \mathbb{R}^+$ is the kernel bandwidth that rules the observation window within the assessed similarity metric. Likewise, for the output labels space $\mathcal{L} \in \mathbb{N}$, we also set a positive definite kernel $\kappa_L : \mathcal{L} \times \mathcal{L} \to \mathcal{H}_L$. In this case, the pairwise similarity distance between samples is defined as $\kappa_L(y_n, y_{n'}) = \delta(y_n - y_{n'})$, being $\delta(\cdot)$ the Dirac delta function. Each of the above defined kernels reflects a different notion of similarity and represents the elements of the matrices $\mathbf{K}_X, \mathbf{K}_L \in \mathbb{R}^{N \times N}$, respectively. In turn, to evaluate how well the kernel matrix $\mathbf{K}_X$ matches the target $\mathbf{K}_L$, we use the statistical alignment between those two kernel matrices as [2]:

$$\hat{\rho}(\mathbf{K}_X, \mathbf{K}_L) = \frac{\langle \bar{\mathbf{K}}_X, \bar{\mathbf{K}}_L \rangle_F}{\sqrt{\langle \mathbf{K}_X \mathbf{K}_X \rangle_F \langle \mathbf{K}_L \mathbf{K}_L \rangle_F}}, \tag{6}$$

where the notation $\bar{\mathbf{K}}$ stands for the centered kernel matrix calculated as $\bar{\mathbf{K}} = \tilde{I} \mathbf{K} \tilde{I}$, being $\tilde{I} = I - \mathbf{1}^\top \mathbf{1}/N$ the empirical centering matrix, $I \in \mathbb{R}^{N \times N}$ is the identity matrix, and $\mathbf{1} \in \mathbb{R}^N$ is the ones vector. The notation $\langle \cdot, \cdot \rangle_F$ represents the matrix-based Frobenius norm. Hence, Eq. (6) is a data driven estimator that allows to quantify the similarity between the input feature space and the output label space [2]. In particular, for the Gaussian kernel κ_X, the Mahalanobis distance is selected to perform the pairwise comparison between samples:

$$v_A^2(x_n, x_{n'}) = (x_n - x_{n'}) A A^\top (x_n - x_{n'})^\top, \; n, n' \in \{1, 2, \dots, N\}, \tag{7}$$

where the matrix $A \in \mathbb{R}^{S \times P}$ holds the linear projection in the form $w_n = x_n A$, with $w_n \in \mathbb{R}^P$, being P the required number of dimensions to preserve the 90% of the input data variability, and $\boldsymbol{AA}^\top$ the corresponding inverse covariance matrix in Eq. (7), assuming $P \leq S$. Therefore, intending to compute the projection matrix $\boldsymbol{A}$, the formulation of a CKA-based optimizing function can be integrated into the following kernel-based learning algorithm:

$$\hat{\boldsymbol{A}} = \arg\max_{\boldsymbol{A}} \log\left(\hat{\rho}(\mathbf{K}_X(\boldsymbol{A};\sigma),\mathbf{K}_L)\right), \tag{8}$$

where the logarithm function is employed for mathematical convenience. The optimization problem from Eq. (8) is solved using a recursive solution based on the well-known gradient descent approach. After the estimation of the projection matrix $\hat{\boldsymbol{A}}$, we assess the relevance of the S input features. To this end, the most contributing features are assumed to have the higher values of similarity relationship with the provided output labels. Specifically, the CKA-based relevance analysis calculates the relevance vector index $\varrho\in\mathbb{R}^S$, holding elements $\varrho_s\in\mathbb{R}^+$ that allows to measure the contribution from each of the s-th input features in building the projection matrix $\hat{\boldsymbol{A}}$. Hence, to calculate those elements, a stochastic measure of variability is utilized as follows: $\varrho_s=\mathbb{E}_P\{|a_{s,p}|\}$; where $p\in\{1,2,\dots P\}$, $s\in\{1,\dots,S\}$, and $a_{s,p}\in\hat{\boldsymbol{A}}$.

3   Experimental Set-Up

Database. To test our *video-based human action recognition using kernel relevance analysis* (HARK), we employ the UCF50 database [10]. This database contains realistic videos taken from Youtube, with large variations in camera motion, object appearance and pose, illumination conditions, scale, etc. For concrete testing, we use $N = 5967$ videos concerning the 46 human action categories in which the human bounding box file was available [13]. The video frames size is 320×240 pixels, and the length varies from around 70–200 frames. The dataset is divided into 25 predefined groups. Following the standard procedure, we perform a leave-one-group-out cross-validation scheme and report the average classification accuracy overall 25 folds.

HARK Training. Initially, for each video sample in the dataset we employ the Improved Dense Trajectory feature estimation technique (iDT), with the code provided by the authors in [13], keeping the default parameter settings to extract $F = 5$ different descriptors: Trajectory (x, y normalized positions along 15 frames), HOG, HOF, MBHx, MBHy. The iDT technique is an improved version of the previously realized Dense Trajectory technique from the same author, which removes the trajectories generated by the camera motion and the inconsistent matches due to humans. Thus, the human detection is a challenging requirement in this technique, as people in action datasets appear in many different poses, and could only be partially visible due to occlusion or by being partially out-of-scene. These five descriptors are extracted along all valid trajectories and the resulting dimensionality D_f is 30 for the trajectory, 96 for HOG, MBHx and MBHy, and 108 for HOF.

We then randomly select a subsample of 5000×K trajectories from the training set to estimate a GMM codebook with $K = 256$ Gaussians, and the FV encoding is performed as explained in Sect. 2. Afterwards, we apply to the resulting vector a Power Normalization (PN) followed by the L2-Normalization ($\||\mathrm{sign}(x)|x|^{\alpha}\||$, where $0 \leq a \leq 1$ is the normalization parameter). The above procedure is performed per descriptor, fixing $\alpha = 0.1$. Next, all five normalized FV representations are concatenated together, yielding $S = 218112$ encoding dimension. The linear projection matrix $\hat{A} \in \mathbb{R}^{S \times P}$ and the relevance vector index $\varrho \in \mathbb{R}^{S}$ are computed as explained in section Sect. 2; where $P=104.8$, is the average required number of dimensions, through 25 leave-one-out iterations, to preserve the 90% of the input data variability.

For the classification step, we use a one-vs-all Linear SVM with regularization parameter equal to 1 and a Gaussian kernel SVM, varying the kernel bandwidth between the range $[0.1\sigma_o, \sigma_o]$, being $\sigma_o \in \mathbb{R}^{+}$ the median of the input space Euclidean distances; and searching the regularization parameter within the set $\{0.1, 1, 100, 500, 1000\}$, by nested cross-validation with the same leave-one-group-out scheme. Figure 1 summarizes the HARK training pipeline. It is worth noting that all experiments were performed using the Matlab software on a Debian server with 230 GB of RAM and 40 cores. The FV code is part of the open-source library VLFeat, the implementation is publicly available[1]. On the other hand, the CKA code was developed by Alvarez-Meza *et al.* in [2] and is also publicly available[2].

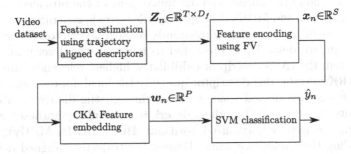

Fig. 1. Sketch of the proposed HARK-based action recognition system.

4   Results and Discussions

Figure 2, shows a visual example of feature estimation and encoding using trajectory-aligned descriptors and BOW. From the color points, where different colors represent the assignment of a given trajectory to one of the prototype vectors generated by the k-means algorithm, we can appreciate the hard assignment of trajectory descriptors in the BOW encoding. Also, different sizes of the points represent the scale in which the trajectory is generated. In contrast, this paper uses the soft assignment of the GMM-based FV encoding, which is not

---

[1] http://www.vlfeat.org/overview/encodings.html.
[2] https://github.com/andresmarino07utp/EKRA-ES.

as straightforward to express in a figure. It is worth noting that due to the human segmentation performed before the trajectory-based feature estimation, the encoding points are mainly grouped in the player whereabouts, which constrains the zone of interest to only characterize the player information. This strategy helps to reduce the uncertainty from the video representation, as the influence of the background is decreased.

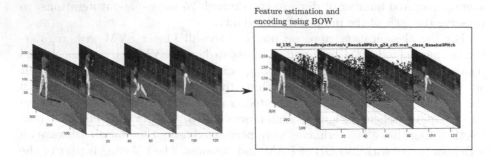

Fig. 2. Feature estimation and encoding using trajectory-aligned descriptors and BOW.

Figure 3(a) shows the normalized relevance value of the provided Trajectory, HOG, HOF, MBHx, and MBHy descriptors, this figure is generated by averaging the components of $\varrho \in \mathbb{R}^S$ which corresponds to each descriptor. Therefore, the mean and standard deviation is presented to represent the descriptor relevance vector. As seen, the HOG descriptor exhibit the highest relevance value regarding our HARK criteria, this descriptor quantify the local appearance and shape within the trajectory-aligned space window through the distribution of intensity gradients. Notably, all the others descriptors mainly quantifies the human local motion (Trajectory normalized positions, HOF, MBHx, MBHy), are very close regarding their relevance value. Hence, the trajectory-aligned descriptors match similarly the human actions labels concerning the CKA-based analysis presented in Sect. 2, as they are all local measures of appearance, shape, and motion equally important to support action recognition. Remarkable, the relevance value in Fig. 3(a) mainly depends upon the discrimination capability of the Gaussian kernel in Eq. 5, and the local measure being performed by the descriptor. Now, as seen in Fig. 3(b), the CKA embedding in its first two projections provides an insight into the data overlapping. The studied classes overlapping (human actions) can be attributed to similar intra-class variations in several categories, as videos with realistic scenarios have inherent attributes such as background clutter, scale changes, dynamic viewpoint and sudden motion, that may be affecting adversely the class separability.

Furthermore, as it is evidenced by the confusion matrix of the test set in Fig. 3(c), an RBF SVM over the CKA feature embedding can obtain $90.97 \pm 2.64\%$ of accuracy in classifying human actions on the employed dataset. From this matrix, the classes 22 and 23 are generating classification problems because the human movements performed in both are similar, these classes correspond to Nunchucks and Pizza tossing respectively. As expected, the RBF SVM can achieve more reliable recognition than a Linear SVM, as the data problem in Fig. 3(b) is non-linear, see the results presented for this paper in Table 1. Notable, our approach requires only 104.8 dimensions on average through 25 leave-one-out iterations to classify 46 actions of the UCF50 dataset, with competitive accuracy, which is very useful, because more elaborated classifiers (once discarded due to the data dimension) can be employed to increase the recognition rate further.

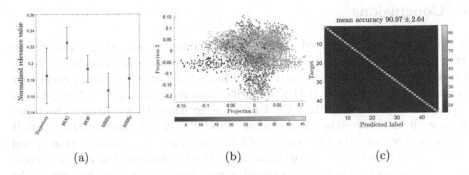

(a)   (b)   (c)

Fig. 3. Human action recognition on the UCF50 database. (a) Feature relevance values. (b) 2D input data projection from 46 action categories using CKA.(c) Confusion matrix for the test set under a nested leave-one-group-out validation scheme using an RBF SVM classifier.

In turn, Table 1 presents a comparative study of the results achieved by our HARK and other similar approaches from the state-of-the-art for human action recognition on the UCF50 database. To build this comparative analysis, approaches with similar experimental set-up are employed. Specifically, those approaches using iDT representation and similar descriptors. Primarily, the compared results exhibit a trade-off between data dimension and accuracy, more elaborate procedures such as the one presented in [5], uses Time Convolutional Networks (TCN) and Spatial Convolutional Networks (SCN) descriptors along with iDT descriptors, and Spatio-temporal VLAD (ST-VLAD) encoding to enhance the class separability. Thus, the mentioned approach obtain very high mean accuracy 97.7%. However, the data dimensionality is considerably high, which limits the usage of many classifiers. On the other hand, the approach presented in [13], enhances the spatial resolution of the iDT descriptors by using a strategy called spatiotemporal pyramids (STP) along with Spatial Fisher Vector encoding (SFV). Obtained results regarding the accuracy of [13] are comparable to ours. Nonetheless, the data dimension is drastically higher.

Table 1. Comparison with similar approaches in the state-of-the-art on the UCF50 dataset.

Reference	Representation	Descriptors	Feature encoding	Data dimension	Classification method	Accuracy [%]
Uijlings *et al* [11]	-	HOG+HOF+MBHx+MBHy	FV	36864	Linear SVM	81.8
Wang *et al* [13]	iDT	HOG+HOF+MBHx+MBHy	SFV + STP	611328	Linear SVM	91.7
Duta *et al* [5]	iDT+2St	HOG+HOF+MBHx+MBHy+SCN+TCN	ST-VLAD	258816	Linear SVM	97.7
HARK	iDT	Traj+ HOG+HOF+MBHx+MBHy	FV + CKA	**104.8**	Linear SVM	**87.9**
HARK	iDT	Traj+ HOG+HOF+MBHx+MBHy	FV + CKA	**104.8**	RBF SVM	**90.9**

5 Conclusions

In this paper, we introduced a video-based human action recognition system using kernel relevance analysis (HARK). Our approach highlights the primary descriptors to predict the output labels of human action videos using trajectory representation. Therefore, HARK quantifies the relevance of $F = 5$ trajectory-aligned descriptors towards a CKA-based algorithm, that matches the input space with the output labels, to enhance the descriptor interpretability, as it allows to determine the importance of local measures (appearance, shape, and motion) to support action recognition. Also, the CKA-algorithm allows to compute a linear projection matrix, through a non-linear representation, where the columns quantify the required number of dimensions to preserve the 90% of the input data variability. Hence, by projecting the video samples into the generated CKA space, the class separability is preserved, and the number of dimensions is reduced. Attained results on the UCF50 database show that our proposal correctly classified the 90.97% of human actions samples using an average input data dimension of 104.8 in the classification stage, through 25 folds under a leave-one-group-out cross-validation scheme. In particular, according to the performed relevance analysis, the most relevant descriptor is the HOG which quantifies the local appearance and shape through the distribution of intensity gradients. Remarkable, HARK outperforms state-of-art results concerning the trade-off between the accuracy achieved and the required data dimension (Table 1). As future work, authors plan to employ other descriptors such as the deep features presented in [5]. Also, a HARK improvement based on the enhancement of spatial and temporal resolution, as the one presented in [13], could be an exciting research line.

Acknowledgments. Under grants provided by the project 1110-744-55958 funded by COLCIENCIAS. Also, J. Fernández is partially founded by the COLCIENCIAS project "ATTENDO" - code: FP44842-424-2017, and by the Maestría en Ingeniería Eléctrica from the Universidad Tecnológica de Pereira.

References

1. Ai, S., Lu, T., Xiong, Y.: Improved dense trajectories for action recognition based on random projection and fisher vectors. In: MIPPR 2017: Pattern Recognition and Computer Vision, International Society for Optics and Photonics, vol. 10609, p. 1060915 (2018)
2. Alvarez-Meza, A.M., Orozco-Gutierrez, A., Castellanos-Dominguez, G.: Kernel-based relevance analysis with enhanced interpretability for detection of brain activity patterns. Front. Neurosci. **11**, 550 (2017)
3. Álvarez-Meza, A.M., Molina-Giraldo, S., Castellanos-Dominguez, G.: Background modeling using object-based selective updating and correntropy adaptation. Image Vis. Comput. **45**, 22–36 (2016)
4. Brockmeier, A.J., et al.: Information-theoretic metric learning: 2-D linear projections of neural data for visualization. In: EMBC, pp. 5586–5589. IEEE (2013)
5. Duta, I.C., Ionescu, B., Aizawa, K., Sebe, N.: Spatio-temporal VLAD encoding for human action recognition in videos. In: Amsaleg, L., Guðmundsson, G.Þ., Gurrin, C., Jónsson, B.Þ., Satoh, S. (eds.) MMM 2017. LNCS, vol. 10132, pp. 365–378. Springer, Cham (2017). https://doi.org/10.1007/978-3-319-51811-4_30
6. Guo, K., Ishwar, P., Konrad, J.: Action recognition from video using feature covariance matrices. IEEE Trans. Image Process. **22**(6), 2479–2494 (2013)
7. Harandi, M., Salzmann, M., Hartley, R.: Dimensionality reduction on spd manifolds: the emergence of geometry-aware methods. IEEE Trans. Pattern Anal. Mach. Intell. (2017)
8. Li, Q., Cheng, H., Zhou, Y., Huo, G.: Human action recognition using improved salient dense trajectories. Comput. Intell. Neurosci. (2016)
9. Perronnin, F., Snchez, J., Mensink, T.: Improving the fisher kernel for large-scale image classification. Lecture Notes in Computer Science (including subseries Lecture Notes in Artificial Intelligence and Lecture Notes in Bioinformatics), vol. 6314, LNCS (PART 4), pp. 143–156 (2010)
10. Reddy, K.K., Shah, M.: Recognizing 50 human action categories of web videos. Mach. Vis. Appl. **24**(5), 971–981 (2013)
11. Uijlings, J., Duta, I.C., Sangineto, E., Sebe, N.: Video classification with densely extracted hog/hof/mbh features: an evaluation of the accuracy/computational efficiency trade-off. Int. J. Multimedia Inf. Retrieval **4**(1), 33–44 (2015)
12. Wang, H., Kläser, A., Schmid, C., Liu, C.L.: Dense trajectories and motion boundary descriptors for action recognition. Int. J. Comput. Vis. **103**(1), 60–79 (2013)
13. Wang, H., Oneata, D., Verbeek, J., Schmid, C.: A robust and efficient video representation for action recognition. Int. J. Comput. Vis. **119**(3), 219–238 (2016)
14. Wang, Y., et al.: Tracking neural modulation depth by dual sequential monte carlo estimation on point processes for brain-machine interfaces. IEEE Trans. Biomed. Eng. **63**(8), 1728–1741 (2016)

Robust Incremental Hidden Conditional Random Fields for Human Action Recognition

Michalis Vrigkas[1]([⊠]), Ermioni Mastora[2], Christophoros Nikou[2],
and Ioannis A. Kakadiaris[1]

[1] Computational Biomedicine Laboratory, Department of Computer Science,
University of Houston, Houston, TX, USA
{mvrigkas,ikakadia}@central.uh.edu

[2] Department of Computer Science and Engineering, University of Ioannina,
Ioannina, Greece
{emastora,cnikou}@cse.uoi.gr

Abstract. Hidden conditional random fields (HCRFs) are a powerful supervised classification system, which is able to capture the intrinsic motion patterns of a human action. However, finding the optimal number of hidden states remains a severe limitation for this model. This paper addresses this limitation by proposing a new model, called robust incremental hidden conditional random field (RI-HCRF). A hidden Markov model (HMM) is created for each observation paired with an action label and its parameters are defined by the potentials of the original HCRF graph. Starting from an initial number of hidden states and increasing their number incrementally, the Viterbi path is computed for each HMM. The method seeks for a sequence of hidden states, where each variable participates in a maximum number of optimal paths. Thereby, variables with low participation in optimal paths are rejected. In addition, a robust mixture of Student's t-distributions is imposed as a regularizer to the parameters of the model. The experimental results on human action recognition show that RI-HCRF successfully estimates the number of hidden states and outperforms all state-of-the-art models.

Keywords: Student's t-distribution
Hidden conditional random fields · Hidden Markov model
Action recognition

1 Introduction

In recent years, a tremendous amount of human action video recordings has been made available. As a consequence, human action recognition has become a very popular task in computer vision with a wide range of applications such as visual surveillance systems, human-robot interaction, video retrieval, and sports video analysis [21]. The recognition of human actions in videos is a challenging

© Springer Nature Switzerland AG 2018
G. Bebis et al. (Eds.): ISVC 2018, LNCS 11241, pp. 126–136, 2018.
https://doi.org/10.1007/978-3-030-03801-4_12

task due to anthropometric differences (size, gender, shape) among subjects and variations in the way, spread, and speed of the action.

Hidden conditional random fields (HCRF) [13] are a generalization of conditional random fields (CRF) [9] and appear to be a very promising approach in many application domains, due to their ability of relaxing strong independence assumptions and exploiting spatio-temporal variations, via a graphical structure. A hybrid model that consists of a combination of generative and discriminative models to improve the performance of the classical models has been proposed in the literature [1]. Motivated by this approach, Soullard et al. [17] introduced an HMM-based weighting in the conditional probability of the HCRF, which constrains the discriminative learning, yielding improved accuracy. On the other hand, Zhang et al. [25] used HMMs to make hidden variables "observable" to HCRF so the objective function can be convex. Multi-modal action recognition (i.e., combination of audio and visual information) using HCRFs has also been given great focus [16,19,22].

However, previous works define the number of hidden variables in a intuitive manner or with exhaustive search, which is a computationally expensive and time-consuming task. Bousmalis et al. [2] introduced infinite hidden conditional random fields (iHCRF), a nonparametric model that estimates the number of hidden variables to recognize human behaviors. The model assumes that the HCRF potentials are sampled directly from a set of hierarchical Dirichlet processes and its hyper-parameters are learned using the sampling that removes hidden variables that are not presented in the samples. Moreover, Bousmalis et al. [3] proposed an extension of the previous model, called variational HCRF, which is a generalized framework for infinite HCRF modeling and variational inference in order to converge faster and reduce the computational cost.

Recently, deep leaning methods have shown outstanding results [5]. Although important progress has been made in the fields such as object detection and image classification, the understanding of human actions is still a difficult task due to pose variability, short duration of actions, and ambiguity in human annotations. Sigurdsson et al. [15] tried to answer a set of fundamental questions regarding the problem of action recognition to address the aforementioned limitations. Convolutional neural networks (CNNs or ConvNets) [7] are the most widely used approach to simultaneously learn spatio-temporal dynamics of human actions. A novel architecture that uses spatio-temporal fusion by combining the ConvNet towers was introduced by Feichtenhofer et al. [8]. Finally, an on-line frame-pooling method, which extracts only the most important frames that best describe human actions, was proposed by Wang et al. [23].

In this work, a robust incremental hidden conditional random field (RI-HCRF) is proposed, which addresses two major issues in standard HCRFs. At first, the proposed model incrementally estimates the optimal number of hidden variables using a Viterbi-based procedure. Additionally, it uses a mixture of Student's t-distributions as prior to the parameters of the model that leads to a model robust to outliers.

2   Model Formulation

The proposed RI-HCRF model is defined by a linear chained structured undi-rected graph $\mathcal{G} = (\mathcal{V}, \mathcal{E})$. Each variable, observed (video frame) and unobserved (hidden variable), is a node $\mathcal{V}$ in the graphical model $\mathcal{G}$ and any dependencies between them are presented by an edge $\mathcal{E}$. We consider a dataset $\mathcal{D} = \{\mathbf{x}^k, y^k\}_{k=1}^N$ of N labeled observations, where an observation $\mathbf{x}^k = \{\mathbf{x}_1, \mathbf{x}_2, \ldots, \mathbf{x}_T\}$ corre-sponds to the kth video sequence that consists of T frames, and y^k is the kth class label defined in a finite label set $\mathcal{Y}$. Each observation $\mathbf{x}_i^k$ can be represented by a feature vector $\phi(\mathbf{x}_i^k) \in \mathbb{R}^d$, which is a collection of several features extracted from the ith frame in the video sequence.

The goal of the proposed model is, for a given observation $\mathbf{x}$ and the model's parameter vector $\boldsymbol{\theta}$, to find the most probable label y by maximizing the condi-tional probability $P(y|\mathbf{x}; \boldsymbol{\theta})$. The RI-HCRF model is a member of the exponen-tial family and the conditional probability of the class label given an observation sequence is defined as:

$$P(y|\mathbf{x}; \boldsymbol{\theta}) = \sum_h P(y, \mathbf{h}|\mathbf{x}; \boldsymbol{\theta}) = \frac{\sum_h \exp \Psi(y, \mathbf{h}, \mathbf{x}; \boldsymbol{\theta})}{\sum_{y', \mathbf{h}} \exp \Psi(y', \mathbf{h}, \mathbf{x}; \boldsymbol{\theta})}, \tag{1}$$

where $\mathbf{h}$ is a set of hidden variables $\mathbf{h}^k = \{h_1, h_2, \ldots, h_T\}$, with $\mathbf{h}^k \in \mathcal{H}$, and $\Psi(\cdot)$ is the potential function that specifies dependencies between different nodes in the model given by:

$$\Psi(y, \mathbf{h}, \mathbf{x}; \boldsymbol{\theta}) = \sum_{j \in \mathcal{V}} \boldsymbol{\theta}_1 \cdot \psi_1(x_j, h_j) + \sum_{j \in \mathcal{V}} \boldsymbol{\theta}_2 \cdot \psi_2(y, h_j) + \sum_{(i,j) \in \mathcal{E}} \boldsymbol{\theta}_3 \cdot \psi_3(y, h_i, h_j). \tag{2}$$

The functions $\boldsymbol{\theta}_1 \cdot \psi_1(\cdot)$ and $\boldsymbol{\theta}_2 \cdot \psi_2(\cdot)$ are the node potentials N_p, which model the relationship between the hidden variable h_j and the feature vector x_j, and the relationship between the class label y and the hidden variable h_j, respectively, and $\boldsymbol{\theta}_3 \cdot \psi_3(\cdot)$ is the edge potential E_p, which models the relationship between the class label y and the hidden variables h_i and h_j.

3   Estimation of the Number of Hidden States

To estimate the optimal number of hidden variables, we propose an iterative method, which seeks for a sequence of hidden variables, where each variable participates in a maximum number of optimal paths. The variables with low participation in the optimal paths are rejected.

For a given label $y = \alpha$, the node potentials for all observations and all possible hidden variables can be represented in a matrix form:

$$N_p = [n_{p_{ij}}]_{S \times T} = \begin{bmatrix} \theta_{1_{11}} \cdot x_1 + \theta_{2_{1}\alpha} & \cdots & \theta_{1_{1T}} \cdot x_T + \theta_{2_{1}\alpha} \\ \theta_{1_{21}} \cdot x_1 + \theta_{2_{2}a} & \cdots & \theta_{1_{2T}} \cdot x_T + \theta_{2_{2}\alpha} \\ \vdots & \ddots & \vdots \\ \theta_{1_{S1}} \cdot x_1 + \theta_{2_{S}\alpha} & \cdots & \theta_{1_{ST}} \cdot x_T + \theta_{2_{T}\alpha} \end{bmatrix}, \tag{3}$$

where S is the number of hidden variables and T is the number of frames in the video sequence. The edge potentials, for a given label $y = \alpha$, express the compatibility between a pair of hidden variables and they can be represented by the following square matrix:

$$E_p = [e_{p_{ij}}]_{S \times S} = \begin{bmatrix} \theta_{3_{11}} & \theta_{3_{12}} & \cdots & \theta_{3_{1S}} \\ \theta_{3_{21}} & \theta_{3_{22}} & \cdots & \theta_{3_{2S}} \\ \vdots & \vdots & \ddots & \vdots \\ \theta_{3_{S1}} & \theta_{3_{S2}} & \cdots & \theta_{3_{SS}} \end{bmatrix}. \tag{4}$$

All values of the node potentials N_p matrix are transformed into the range $[0, 1]$ using min-max normalization, so that all input variables equally contribute in the model and the parameters of the node potential N_p are not scaled with respect to the units of the inputs. As a result, we end up with smaller standard deviations, which can suppress the effect of outliers. Also, we construct a stochastic matrix based on the edge potential E_p, with each row summing to one.

To determine the number of hidden variables, we employ multiple HMMs. Specifically, an HMM is defined by the set of hidden variables $\mathbf{h}$ and a set of parameters $\Lambda = \{\boldsymbol{\pi}, \mathbf{A}, \mathbf{B}\}$, where $\boldsymbol{\pi}$ is a vector that collects the prior probabilities of h_i being the first hidden variable of a state sequence, $\mathbf{A}$ is a matrix that collects the transition probabilities of moving from one hidden variable to another, and $\mathbf{B}$ is the matrix that collects the emission probabilities, which characterize the likelihood of a certain observation $\mathbf{x}$, if the model is in hidden variable h_i.

Let us consider that the normalized node potentials are the entries of the emission probability matrix, the edge potentials are the entries of the transition probability matrix, and there is a vector of initial probabilities $\boldsymbol{\pi}$, where each hidden variable is equally probable to be first in the sequence $\pi_{1 \times S} = \frac{1}{S} \cdot \mathbf{1}_S$.

Given the above definitions, for a given label $y = \alpha$, we can determine an HMM and the optimal hidden variable sequence using the Viterbi algorithm to estimate the probability of the most probable path ending $\delta_t(i)$ and keep track of the best path ending $\phi_t(i)$ in the ith hidden state at time t:

$$\delta_t(i) = \max_{h_1, \ldots, h_{T-1}} P(h_1, \ldots, h_{T-1}, h_T = i, x_1, \ldots, x_T | \pi, E_p, N_p), \tag{5}$$

$$\phi_t(i) = \operatorname*{argmax}_{h_1, \ldots, h_{T-1}} P(h_1, \ldots, h_{T-1}, h_T = i, x_1, \ldots, x_T | \pi, E_p, N_p). \tag{6}$$

Figure 1 depicts the flow of the proposed method for the estimation of the optimal number of hidden variables. The proposed method learns the optimal number of hidden variables following an incremental learning approach. It starts by setting an initial number $S = |\mathcal{H}| \geq 1$ for the hidden variables and the maximum number of iterations. In each iteration, all optimal paths, for every video sequence and for every label, are estimated using the Viterbi algorithm and the frequency of appearance of each hidden state in all paths is calculated. The termination criterion is reached when the frequency of each hidden variable is lower than a predefined threshold τ. If this criterion is not satisfied, the number

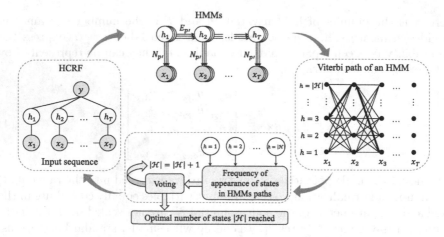

Fig. 1. Illustration of the iterative and incremental method for the estimation of the optimal number of the hidden variables. The grey nodes are the observed features (x_i), and the unknown labels (y). The white nodes are the hidden variables (h). At each iteration, an HCRF is built with an initial number of hidden states and then the Viterbi algorithm is used to estimate the optimal paths in the HMM setting. Then, the frequency of each hidden variable is computed and if the termination criterion is satisfied the number of hidden states is decided by majority voting, otherwise the number of hidden states is increased by one and the process is repeated.

of hidden variables is increased by one and the process is repeated. If the termination criterion is satisfied, we move to the next iteration and a voting for the most probable number of hidden variables in the current iteration is performed. Finally, when the maximum number of iterations is reached, the optimal number of hidden variables is the one with the majority of votes.

4   A Student's T-Mixture Prior on the Model Parameters

Let us assume that the parameters θ of the proposed RI-HCRF follow a mixture model with three Student's-t components. Taking into consideration that the parameter vector θ describes three different relationships among observations, hidden variables and labels, we expect that each component corresponds to one of these relationships. To this end, the proposed method relies on partitioning the parameter vector using a Student's t-mixture model to identify, preserve, and enhance the different characteristic of each partition and improve the classification model. The use of Student's t-mixture model is justified by the fact that it has a heavier tails pdf and provides smaller weights to the observations that lie in the tail area. Thus, it provides robustness to outliers and less extreme estimates of the posterior probabilities of the mixture model [11]. Additionally, each Student's t-component originates from a wider class of an elliptically symmetric distribution with an additional robustness tuning parameter that corresponds to the degrees of freedom ν.

However, by making the above assumption the problem of setting the mixture weights arises. To estimate the best weights for the mixture model, one might perform an exhaustive search to check multiple combinations of probable values of mixture weights. To avoid the prohibitive quadratic computational cost of this approach, we dynamically estimate the best fitted mixture model for parameters θ at the end of each iteration of the training process.

Let each parameter θ follows a univariate t-distribution with mean μ, variance σ^2, and $\nu \in [0, \infty)$ degrees of freedom then, given the weight u that follows a Gamma distribution (Γ) parameterized by ν, the parameter θ has the univariate normal with mean μ and variance σ^2/u, with u being a random variable distributed as $u \sim \Gamma(\nu/2, \nu/2)$.

By integrating out the weights from the joint density leads to the density function of the marginal distribution:

$$p(\theta; \nu, \mu, \lambda) = \frac{\Gamma(\frac{\nu+1}{2})}{\Gamma(\frac{\nu}{2})} \left(\frac{\lambda}{\pi\nu}\right)^{\frac{1}{2}} \left(1 + \frac{\lambda(\theta - \mu)^2}{\nu}\right)^{-\frac{\nu+1}{2}}, \tag{7}$$

where the inverse scaling parameter λ (similar to precision) is the reciprocal of variance ($\lambda = (\sigma^2)^{-1}$). Also, it can be shown that for $\nu \to \infty$ the Student's t-distribution tends to be a Gaussian distribution. Moreover, for $\nu > 1$, μ is the mean of θ and for $\nu > 2$, the variance of θ is $\nu(\lambda(\nu - 2))^{-1}$. The t-distribution is used to estimate probabilities based on incomplete data or small samples. A K-component mixture of t-distributions is given by:

$$\phi(\theta, \Omega) = \sum_{i=1}^{K} \pi_i p(\theta; \nu_i, \mu_i, \lambda_i), \tag{8}$$

where θ denotes the observed data vector, $\Omega = \{\Omega_i\}_{i=1}^{K}$ is the mixture parameter set with $\Omega_i = \{\pi_i, \nu_i, \mu_i, \lambda_i\}$, and π_i are the ith mixing proportions that satisfy the following constraints: $\sum_{i=1}^{K} \pi_i = 1$ and $0 \leq \pi_i \leq 1$. The best fitted mixture with Student's t-components can be obtained by maximizing the likelihood function using the EM algorithm [11].

During training a maximum likelihood approach is followed to estimate the parameters θ of the model by maximizing the following loss function:

$$\mathcal{L}(\theta) = \sum_{i=1}^{N} \log P(y_i|x_i; \theta) + \log \left(\sum_{k=1}^{K} \pi_k p(\theta; \nu_k, \mu_k, \lambda_k)\right), \tag{9}$$

where the first term is the conditional log-likelihood of the input data and the second term represents the best fitted Student'st-mixture model on parameter vector θ, obtained by the EM algorithm. The optimal weights $\theta^\star$ are learned by maximizing the objective function. The optimization of Eq. (9) is performed using the limited-memory BFGS (LBFGS) method [4], since the value and the derivative of the objective function may be calculated. Then, the corresponding label is estimated by maximizing the posterior probability:

$$y^\star = \underset{y \in \mathcal{Y}}{\operatorname{argmax}} P(y|\mathbf{x}; \theta^\star). \tag{10}$$

5   Experimental Results

To demonstrate the ability of the proposed method to recognize human actions, we compared it with several state-of-the-art methods in three publicly available benchmark datasets. First, we used the Parliament dataset [20], which consists of 228 video sequences of political speeches categorized in three behavioral classes: friendly, aggressive, and neutral. The TV human interaction (TVHI) dataset [12], is a collection of 300 video sequences depicting four kinds of interactions such as handshakes, high fives, hugs, and kisses. Finally, the SBU Kinect Interaction (SBU) dataset [24] is used, which contains approximately 300 video sequences of two-person interactions captured by a Microsoft Kinect sensor. Each video is labeled with one of the following actions: approaching, departing, pushing, kicking, punching, exchanging objects, hugging, and shaking hands.

For all datasets, we used spatio-temporal interest points (STIP) [10] as our basic representation. Also, for the Parliament and TVHI datasets, we extracted the mel-frequency cepstral coefficients (MFCC) [14] features along with their first and second order derivatives, while for the TPI dataset, we used the provided by the dataset poses. Additional to the hand-crafted features, we used CNNs both for end-to-end classification and for feature extraction by employing the pre-trained model of Tran *et al.* [18], which is a 3D ConvNet. Finally, we assessed the performance of the RI-HCRF by comparing with the following baseline methods: SVM [6], CRF [9], HCRF [13], and CNN (end-to-end) [18].

The threshold for the automatic learning of the optimal number of hidden variables was set to take values from a discrete set $\tau \in \{0.001, 0.005, 0.01, 0.02, 0.05\}$ and the maximum number of iterations were set to 30. The number of components for the mixture of Student's t-distribution was set to $K = 3$. The model parameters were randomly initialized and the experiments were repeated five times, while 5-fold cross validation was used to split into training and test sets. To examine the performance of the RI-HCRF model against the standard HCRF, we varied the number of hidden variables from 3 to 18.

The average recognition accuracies and the corresponding standard deviations for all datasets, for both hand-crafted and CNN features, are presented in Table 1. It can be observed that the proposed RI-HCRF method outperforms all the state-of-the-art methods for all datasets. It is worth noting that RI-HCRF show very small deviation compared with the rest of the methods, which indicates that the use of Student's t-distribution provides robustness and reduces the miss classification errors. It is also interesting to observe that for the Parliament and TVHI datasets, the absolute improvement of RI-HCRF over the CNN model is very high (11% and 33%, respectively). This improvement can be explained by the fact that the CNN model uses a linear classifier in the softmax layer, while RI-HCRF is more suitable to encode sequential data by modeling dependencies between consecutive frames in a more principled way.

Since the best results, for the RI-HCRF method, were achieved when CNN features were employed, the corresponding confusion matrices are depicted in Fig. 2. It can be observed that the misclassification errors are quite small for

Table 1. Comparison of the classification accuracies (%) for the Parliament [20], TVHI [12], and SBU [24] datasets. The results were averaged for all different configurations (mean ± standard deviation).

Method	Parliament [20]	TVHI [12]	SBU [24]
Hand-crafted features			
SVM [6]	75.5 ± 3.1	85.5 ± 4.8	81.5 ± 6.8
CRF [9]	82.1 ± 1.7	**100.0 ± 0.0**	87.3 ± 4.4
HCRF [13]	82.9 ± 2.5	99.5 ± 1.5	87.0 ± 2.6
RI-HCRF	**85.5 ± 3.1**	**100.0 ± 0.0**	**89.4 ± 2.7**
CNN-based features			
SVM [6]	73.3 ± 0.9	91.0 ± 0.6	94.3 ± 0.4
CRF [9]	85.5 ± 0.7	92.8 ± 0.3	93.7 ± 0.4
HCRF [13]	89.0 ± 0.8	93.0 ± 0.2	91.5 ± 0.4
CNN [18]	78.1 ± 0.4	60.5 ± 1.1	94.2 ± 0.8
RI-HCRF	**89.5 ± 0.7**	**93.5 ± 0.2**	**94.8 ± 0.3**

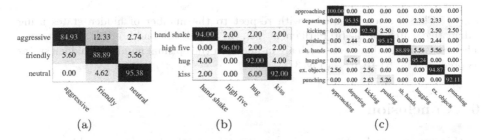

(a)   (b)   (c)

Fig. 2. Confusion matrices for the classification results using CNN features for the (a) Parliament [20], (b) TVHI [12], and (c) SBU [24] datasets.

the three datasets indicating that the proposed method can efficiently recognize human actions with high accuracy and small intra-class classification errors.

Figure 3 depicts the results for the prediction of the optimal number of hidden states for all three datasets, when CNN features are used for the classification. For the Parliament dataset, number 4 is the most suitable candidate, for TVHI number 7 seems to be the most probable case, and for the SBU dataset, number 9 turns out to be the candidate with the most votes estimated by the RI-HCRF model. The estimated number of hidden states obtained from the proposed model is in fully agreement with the results from the exhaustive search of the number of hidden states (Fig. 4). Also, we may observe that the number of candidates is much lower compared to the exhaustive search.

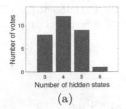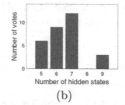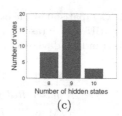

(a)   (b)   (c)

Fig. 3. Estimation of the optimal number of hidden variables by the proposed RI-HCRF algorithm using the CNN features for the (a) Parliament [20], (b) TVHI [12], and (c) SBU [24] datasets. The number of hidden states that do not appear in the horizontal axis received zero votes.

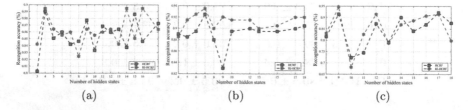

(a)   (b)   (c)

Fig. 4. Classification accuracies with respect to the number of hidden states using exhaustive search for the (a) Parliament [20], (b) TVHI [12], and (c) SBU [24] datasets. The results from exhaustive search are in-line with the optimal number of hidden states as predicted by RI-HCRF in Fig. 3.

6   Conclusion

In this paper, a video-based action recognition method using a graphical representation of human actions is introduced. The proposed approach is an extension of standard HRCFs, which can automatically infer the number of hidden states from the input data. The proposed model is a mixture of three Student's t-components coupled to the RI-HCRF model as a prior to the parameters providing robustness to outliers. An extented experimental evaluation demonstrated that the proposed method achieved promising results, while reduced the search space for the estimation of the number of hidden states.

Acknowledgments. This work has been co-funded by the European Union and Greek national funds through the Operational Program Competitiveness, Entrepreneurship and Innovation, under the call RESEARCH-CREATE-INNOVATE (project code: T1EDK04517) and by the UH Hugh Roy and Lillie Cranz Cullen Endowment Fund. The authors gratefully acknowledge the support of NVIDIA Corporation with the donation of the Titan Xp GPU used for this research. All statements of fact, opinion or conclusions contained herein are those of the authors and should not be construed as representing the official views or policies of the sponsors.

References

1. Bouchard, G.: Bias-variance tradeoff in hybrid generative-discriminative models. In: ICMLA, pp. 124–129 (2007)
2. Bousmalis, K., Zafeiriou, S., Morency, L.P., Pantic, M.: Infinite hidden conditional random fields for human behavior analysis. Trans. Neural Netw. Learn. Syst. **24**(1), 170–177 (2013)
3. Bousmalis, K., Zafeiriou, S., Morency, L.P., Pantic, M., Ghahramani, Z.: Variational hidden conditional random fields with coupled dirichlet process mixtures. In: Proceedings of Joint European Conference on Machine Learning and Knowledge Discovery in Databases, pp. 531–547 (2013)
4. Byrd, R.H., Nocedal, J., Schnabel, R.B.: Representations of quasi-Newton matrices and their use in limited memory methods. Math. Program. **63**(1), 129–156 (1994)
5. Carreira, J., Zisserman, A.: Quo vadis, action recognition? A new model and the kinetics dataset. In: CVPR, pp. 6299–6308, July 2017
6. Chang, C.C., Lin, C.J.: LIBSVM: a library for support vector machines. ACM Trans. Intell. Syst. Technol. **2**, 1–27 (2011)
7. Donahue, J., Hendricks, L.A., Guadarrama, S., Rohrbach, M., Venugopalan, S., Saenko, K., Darrell, T.: Long-term recurrent convolutional networks for visual recognition and description. In: CVPR, pp. 2625–2634, June 2015
8. Feichtenhofer, C., Pinz, A., Zisserman, A.: Convolutional two-stream network fusion for video action recognition. In: CVPR, June 2016
9. Lafferty, J.D., Pereira, F.C.N., McCallum, A.: Conditional random fields: probabilistic models for segmenting and labeling sequence data. In: ICML, pp. 282–289 (2001)
10. Laptev, I.: On space-time interest points. Int. J. Comput. Vis. **64**(2–3), 107–123 (2005)
11. McLachlan, G.J., Peel, D.: Robust mixture modelling using the t distribution. Stat. Comput. **10**(4), 335–344 (2000)
12. Patron-Perez, A., Marszalek, M., Reid, I., Zisserman, A.: Structured learning of human interactions in TV shows. IEEE Trans. Pattern Anal. Mach. Intell. **34**(12), 2441–2453 (2012)
13. Quattoni, A., Wang, S., Morency, L.P., Collins, M., Darrell, T.: Hidden conditional random fields. IEEE Trans. Pattern Anal. Mach. Intell. **29**(10), 1848–1852 (2007)
14. Rabiner, L., Juang, B.H.: Fundamentals of Speech Recognition. Prentice-Hall, Englewood Cliffs (1993)
15. Sigurdsson, G.A., Russakovsky, O., Gupta, A.: What actions are needed for understanding human actions in videos? In: Proceedings of IEEE International Conference on Computer Vision, pp. 2156–2165 (2017)
16. Song, Y., Morency, L.P., Davis, R.: Multi-view latent variable discriminative models for action recognition. In: CVPR, Providence, RI, June 2012
17. Soullard, Y., Artières, T.: Hybrid HMM and HCRF model for sequence classification. In: ESANN, pp. 453–458 (2011)
18. Tran, D., Bourdev, L., Fergus, R., Torresani, L., Paluri, M.: Learning spatiotemporal features with 3D convolutional networks. In: ICCV, pp. 4489–4497 (2015)
19. Vrigkas, M., Kazakos, E., Nikou, C., Kakadiaris, I.A.: Inferring human activities using robust privileged probabilistic learning. In: ICCVW, pp. 2658–2665 (2017)
20. Vrigkas, M., Nikou, C., Kakadiadis, I.A.: Classifying behavioral attributes using conditional random fields. In: Likas, A., Blekas, K., Kalles, D. (eds.) SETN 2014. LNCS (LNAI), vol. 8445, pp. 95–104. Springer, Cham (2014). https://doi.org/10.1007/978-3-319-07064-3_8

21. Vrigkas, M., Nikou, C., Kakadiaris, I.A.: A review of human activity recognition methods. Front. Robot. AI **2**(28), 1–26 (2015)
22. Vrigkas, M., Nikou, C., Kakadiaris, I.A.: Identifying human behaviors using synchronized audio-visual cues. IEEE Trans. Affect. Comput. **8**(1), 54–66 (2017)
23. Wang, L., Xiong, Y., Lin, D., Van Gool, L.: Untrimmednets for weakly supervised action recognition and detection. In: CVPR, pp. 4325–4334, July 2017
24. Yun, K., Honorio, J., Chattopadhyay, D., Berg, T.L., Samaras, D.: Two-person interaction detection using body-pose features and multiple instance learning. In: CVPRW, pp. 28–35 (2012)
25. Zhang, J., Gong, S.: Action categorization with modified hidden conditional random field. Pattern Recognit. **43**(1), 197–203 (2010)

Pattern Recognition

Rotation Symmetry Object Classification Using Structure Constrained Convolutional Neural Network

Seunghwa Yu and Seugnkyu Lee[✉]

Kyunghee University, Yong-in Gyeonggi 17104, Korea
sud0303@naver.com, seungkyu@khu.ac.kr
http://www.cvlab.khu.ac.kr

Abstract. Rotation symmetry is a salient visual clue in describing and recognizing an object or a structure in an image. Recently, various rotation symmetry detection methods have been proposed based on key point feature matching scheme. However, hand crafted representation of rotation symmetry structure has shown limited performance. On the other hand, deep learning based approach has been rarely applied to symmetry detection due to the huge diversity in the visual appearance of rotation symmetry patterns. In this work, we propose a new framework of convolutional neural network based on two core layers: rotation invariant convolution (RI-CONV) layer and symmetry structure constrained convolution (SSC-CONV) layer. Proposed network learns structural characteristic from image samples regardless of their appearance diversity. Evaluation is conducted on 32,000 images (after augmentation) of our rotation symmetry classification data set.

Keywords: Rotation symmetry classification · CNN

1 Introduction

Symmetry is an essential structural clue in recognizing single object, grouped objects or scene structure. Reflection and rotation symmetry detection in 2D and 3D visual data have been studied in the past half-century [10–12]. Recent improvements in rotation symmetry detection mostly depends on carefully developed representation of rotation symmetry structure based on salient and robust key point or region feature matching. Even skewed rotation symmetry is described in the representation based on the study of camera projection [11] or approximation by affine projection [3]. However, not all aspect of distortion and variation of rotation symmetry structure can be predetermined and described in the hand crafted representation revealing limitation in performance [12]. Deep learning approach has been shown significant improvement in many detection and recognition problems over existing methods employing hand crafted features and frameworks using shallow learning approaches. Yet, deep learning has

© Springer Nature Switzerland AG 2018
G. Bebis et al. (Eds.): ISVC 2018, LNCS 11241, pp. 139–146, 2018.
https://doi.org/10.1007/978-3-030-03801-4_13

**Rotation
symmetry image**   **None-rotation
symmetry image**

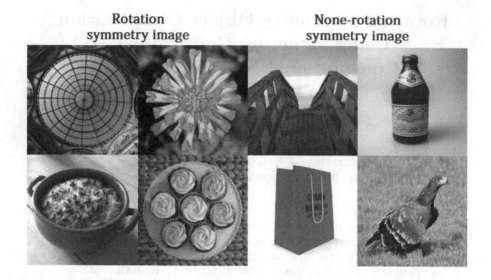

Fig. 1. Sample rotation and non-rotation symmetry images from our dataset

been rarely applied to symmetry detection due to the huge diversity of visual appearance that forms rotation symmetry patterns.

There have been deep learning approaches manipulating feature maps inside the network. While they are not able to learn a particular structure like rotation symmetry, they learn visual appearance regardless of any particular spatial structure variation. Jaderberg et al. [8] propose Spatial Transformer that allows the spatial manipulation of data within the network. This network is able to learn invariance to translation, scale, rotation. In Dieleman et al. [4], four operations (slice, pool, roll and stack) are inserted into convolutional neural network as a new layer to make it equivariant to rotations. Cheng et al. [2] make rotation invariance of a particular layer for object detection in VHR optical remote sensing images. The layer is trained for rotation invariance by additional loss function. Marcos et al. [13] encode rotation invariance directly in the convolutional neural network. They rotate convolution filters for each angles and pool in rotation dimension to extract rotation invariant features.

Brachmann and Redies [1] detect mirror symmetry from the filter responses of convolutional neural network that were trained on regular image data set. They compare the original and flipped max-pooling maps to find mirror pattern along the vertical axis. However, they use a conventional convolution layer working on visual appearance and there is no effort to develop a new network for structural characteristic. Ke et al. [9] propose side-output residual network to detect reflectional symmetries of objects. Funk and Liu [5] modifies existing CNN models [6,14] and detect both reflection and rotation symmetries. Even though this is the first work using CNN for rotation symmetry detection reporting

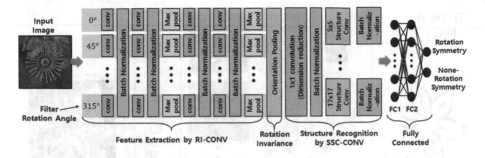

Fig. 2. Proposed network by combining RI-CONV and SSC-CONV learning structural characteristic from image samples regardless of their appearance diversity

competitive evaluation results, they employ existing convolution scheme capturing visual information not structure information.

In this paper, we propose a novel neural network to learn structural characteristic of rotation symmetry regardless of their appearance diversity. To this end, we propose to employ two core layers. We include rotation invariant convolution (RI-CONV) layer implemented similar to [13]. We propose a symmetry structure constrained convolution (SSC-CONV) layer that finds rotational repetition in the depth map of RI-CONV layer. The contribution of our work includes (1) rotation symmetry detection data set consists of total 2000 images (32,000 after augmentation) and (2) new framework of convolutional neural network by combining RI-CONV and SSC-CONV learning structural characteristic from image samples regardless of their appearance diversity.

2   Proposed Method

In order to recognize rotation symmetry pattern in an image, structure of visual information has to be learned instead of visual appearance itself mostly has been required in prior work such as object recognition. In other words, rotation symmetry has to be learned from common structural characteristic of rotation samples: (1) repeated patterns (2) spread along the angular direction with (3) circularly aligned orientations. Convolution filter in CNN is trained to extract a common shape that is required for discrimination between classes building hierarchically features from cascaded layers. Therefore, existing convolutional neural networks in rotation symmetry classification may learn unexpected common visual features of training samples that are nothing to do with rotation symmetry structure. We propose new convolutional neural network for rotation symmetry image classification consists of rotation invariant feature extraction step and symmetry structure recognition step.

2.1   Rotation Invariant Feature Extraction

First we incorporate rotation invariance in our new network to capture repeated similar patterns regardless of their orientation amount. This allows following

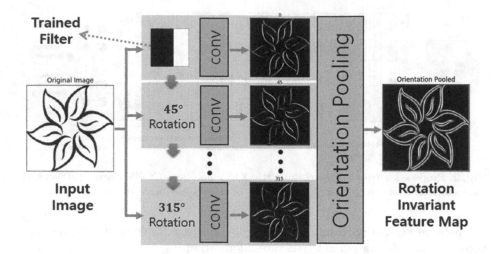

Fig. 3. Rotation invariant feature extraction by rotation invariant convolution (RI-CONV) with orientation pooling similarly built to [13]

rotation symmetry structure recognition step becomes easier task. Convolution layer responds differently with original and rotated shapes. One of ways that convolution layer become rotation invariant is that filter has same value at each rotation way (in case of 3×3 convolution filter, all values have to be same except value at center). Standalone rotation invariant filter has limited representation ability. To resolve the problem, we rotate convolution filters N times and convolve input image with each rotated filter [13]. Instead of filter rotation, input image can be rotated N times by corresponding angles and convoluted followed by back-rotation to original coordinate [4]. However, rotating input image is computationally expensive and requires additional back-rotation step. Given neural network and data set, batch normalization [7] and drop out [15] lead stable and optimal training. We use both batch normalization and drop out. Batch normalization normalize features in batch dimension to remove the covariate shift. Batch normalization in our network is conducted after convolutions considering all different rotation angles. Applying batch normalization to individual feature map is inappropriate, because what we want to obtain from the set of convolutions in different rotation angles is how single convolution filter grabs repeated patterns well regardless of their orientations. If we conduct the batch normalization at each feature map individually, different mean, variance, scaling and shifting factors will be applied to each feature maps which distort responses of following symmetry structure recognition step. We conduct batch normalization after concatenating all feature maps of rotation angles. After two sets of convolution and batch normalization, max-pooling on the feature map of each rotation is conducted. Finally after four sets of convolution and batch normalization including two times of max-pooling, orientation pooling is performed over the resultant N feature maps of rotation angles obtaining rotation invariant feature. Figure 2 shows all the layers of rotation invariant feature extraction step. Figure 3 gives example feature maps of each rotation angle and orientation pooling.

2.2 Symmetry Structure Recognition

In this step, we propose symmetry structure constrained convolution (SSC-CONV) layer to recognize the structure of rotation symmetry. Prior to this step, we insert 1×1 convolution to the output of orientation pooling. 1×1 convolution reduces the channels of feature map concentrating more on spatial structure rather than the variation in visual appearance. In general, plenty of appearance features can be extracted by convolutions in multiple channels. However in our network, diverse appearance features contained in such multiple channels are relatively less critical in recognizing symmetry structure. After 1×1 convolution, we apply a set of circularly constrained convolution filters concentrating on rotational patterns in different scale (Fig. 4). Circular nature of constrained convolution filters capture rotation symmetry characteristic better than original square filters. In other words, representation scope of the convolution is reduced to circular shapes by removing unnecessary part of filters. Corners of square in convolution filter are not needed to find circle shape. Number of constrained filters and their scales can be adjusted depending on the size of target rotation object and expected classification precision. Large filter can find large circle shape and vice-versa. We give a hole in the circle shape convolution filter to fit the each scale filter at corresponding scales. In real images, rotation symmetry patterns can be skewed due to perspective projection. We give appropriate thickness of the circular bands in the constrained convolution filters to be robust to skewed rotation symmetry detection. Finally, we obtain the outputs of structure constrained convolution. Fully-connected layers classify rotation symmetry images.

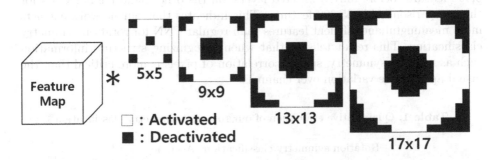

Fig. 4. Scheme of structure convolution symmetry structure constrained convolution (SSC-CONV)

3 Experimental Results

For the evaluation of our network, we built rotation symmetry classification dataset which have two classes (Rotation symmetry class and none-rotation symmetry class). Each class has 1000 images, images were collected by hand from free image website such as www.flickr.com and www.pixabay.com. In the network, input image size is 80×80. We employ 8 times rotation at filters considering computational work. The number of rotations can be higher such as 16, 32 and 64. We use 64 filters (filter size is 5×5) for the first two convolution layers and 128 filters for the next two convolution layers before the orientation pooling. After orientation pooling, we use 32 filters for 1×1 convolution layer. Size of the feature map before structure constrained convolution is $20 \times 20 \times 32$. Structure constrained convolution is applied with four different scale filters (5×5, 9×9, 13×13, 17×17). Size of the feature map before fully-connected layer is $20 \times 20 \times 16$. All convolution operations are followed by batch normalization. Fully-connected part has 3 layers (size of first two fully-connected layer is 4096). Drop out is applied to the fully-connected layer using the rate of 0.65. For quantitative evaluation, we construct another convolutional neural network, which has regular convolutional neural network shape with similar capacity. It has six convolution layers followed by respective batch normalization and three max pooling layers in a similar structure of our network. The number of filters of regular CNN are 64, 128, and 256 for each pair of convolution layers. Filter size and fully-connected layer are all identical with our proposed network. Drop out is also applied with same rate. In the training, we set batch size as 32, learning rate as 0.0001. We randomly divide dataset into 90% of train images and 10% of test images for each class. Training data is augmented by image rotation, flipping and gray-scale. As a result, total number of training image is 28,800. We selected test set in total image randomly. Training and testing are repeated 10 times.

In Table 1, our proposed network shows improved accuracy (78%) and standard deviation over regular CNN (76%). Furthermore, proposed network holds 6,400 features before fully-connected layers, on the other hand regular CNN for the comparison holds 25,600 features. This indicates that our network extracts more meaningful and efficient features than regular CNN for rotation symmetry classification. This result tells us that when recognizing structure information such as rotation symmetry, spatial correlation of pixels is more critical than the visual appearance variation over channels.

Table 1. Quantitative evaluation of our rotation symmetry classification

Rotation symmetry classification	Accuracy	
	Mean	Std.
Regular CNN	0.77	0.005
Our proposed network	**0.79**	**0.004**

Figure 5 shows examples of misclassified results. First misclassified rotation symmetry image in Fig. 5(a) has partially occluded symmetry object by image region. This example tells us that the current network is not trained or structured to capture such impaired structure. Indeed, our constrained convolution filters cares only perfectly circular patterns (Fig. 4). If we add additional constrained convolution filters reflecting occluded structure, our network can be improved to deal with such occlusion. Rotation symmetry in the second misclassified rotation image is not from an object, but from overall placement of lots of stars. Convolution layer may have difficulty in capturing this weak clue for rotation symmetry. In the last misclassified rotation symmetry image, only boundary edges support the rotation symmetry object. Again, convolution layer fails to capture such weak symmetry pattern. First misclassified non-rotation symmetry image in Fig. 5(b) does not have any symmetry pattern. However it has background smoothly changing its color with almost no textures where almost uniform but rotationally symmetric region can be found by similar uniform patterns. Second misclassified non-rotation symmetry image has roughly circular region in the background. Last example of misclassified non-rotation symmetry image has two identical objects and non-textured background. Rotation symmetry pattern with two times of repetition easily can be found from anywhere of images that is hardly considered as rotation symmetry pattern. However, our network does not exclude such singular case from rotation symmetry.

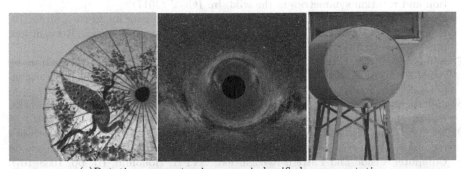

(a)Rotation symmetry images misclassified as non-rotation

(b)Non-rotation symmetry images misclassified as rotation

Fig. 5. Example misclassified result images

4   Conclusion

In this work, we propose a new convolutional neural network adopting rotation invariant convolution layer and proposing symmetry structure constrained convolution layer. We built dataset for rotation symmetry classification with 2000 real images. Our evaluation results show that our proposed network compared with regular CNN improved performance even if regular CNN has more features. Our study and following experimental evaluation highlight potential future research on structure constrained CNN for general symmetry detection tasks.

References

1. Brachmann, A., Redies, C.: Using convolutional neural network filters to measure left-right mirror symmetry in images. Symmetry **8**(12), 144 (2016)
2. Cheng, G., Zhou, P., Han, J.: Learning rotation-invariant convolutional neural networks for object detection in VHR optical remote sensing images. IEEE Trans. Geosci. Remote Sens. **54**(12), 7405–7415 (2016)
3. Cornelius, H., Loy, G.: Detecting rotational symmetry under affine projection. In: 18th International Conference on Pattern Recognition, ICPR 2006, vol. 2, pp. 292–295. IEEE (2006)
4. Dieleman, S., De Fauw, J., Kavukcuoglu, K.: Exploiting cyclic symmetry in convolutional neural networks. ICML (2016)
5. Funk, C., Liu, Y.: Beyond planar symmetry: Modeling human perception of reflection and rotation symmetries in the wild. In: ICCV (2017)
6. He, K., Zhang, X., Ren, S., Sun, J.: Deep residual learning for image recognition. In: Proceedings of the IEEE Conference on Computer Vision and Pattern Recognition, pp. 770–778 (2016)
7. Ioffe, S., Szegedy, C.: Batch normalization: accelerating deep network training by reducing internal covariate shift. In: International Conference on Machine Learning, pp. 448–456 (2015)
8. Jaderberg, M., Simonyan, K., Zisserman, A., et al.: Spatial transformer networks. In: Advances in Neural Information Processing Systems, pp. 2017–2025 (2015)
9. Ke, W., Chen, J., Jiao, J., Zhao, G., Ye, Q.: SRN: side-output residual network for object symmetry detection in the wild. In: Proceedings IEEE Conference on Computer Vision and Pattern Recognition, CVPR, Honolulu, HI, pp. 1068–1076 (2017)
10. Lee, S.: Symmetry-driven shape description for image retrieval. Image Vis. Comput. **31**(4), 357–363 (2013)
11. Lee, S., Liu, Y.: Skewed rotation symmetry group detection. IEEE Trans. Pattern Anal. Mach. Intell. **32**(9), 1659–1672 (2010)
12. Liu, Y., Dickinson, S.: Detecting symmetry in the wild. In: International Conference on Computer Vision (ICCV) Workshops (2017)
13. Marcos, D., Volpi, M., Tuia, D.: Learning rotation invariant convolutional filters for texture classification. In: 2016 23rd International Conference on Pattern Recognition (ICPR), pp. 2012–2017. IEEE (2016)
14. Simonyan, K., Zisserman, A.: Very deep convolutional networks for large-scale image recognition. In: ICLR (2014)
15. Srivastava, N., Hinton, G., Krizhevsky, A., Sutskever, I., Salakhutdinov, R.: Dropout: a simple way to prevent neural networks from overfitting. J. Mach. Learn. Res. **15**(1), 1929–1958 (2014)

A Hough Space Feature for Vehicle Detection

Chunling Tu$^{1(\boxtimes)}$ and Shengzhi Du^2

^{1} Department of Computer Systems Engineering, Tshwane University of Technology,
Pretoria 0001, South Africa
tclchunling@gmail.com
^{2} Department of Electrical Engineering, Tshwane University of Technology,
Pretoria 0001, South Africa

Abstract. This paper addresses the pattern of vehicle images in the Hough space, and presents a feature to detect and classify vehicle images from samples with no vehicle contains. Instead of detecting straight line by seeking peaks in the Hough space, the Hough transform is employed in a novel way to extract features of images. The standard deviation of the columns in the Hough data is proposed as a new kind of feature to represent objects in images. The proposed feature is robust with respect to challenges, such as object dimension, translation, rotation, occlusion, distance to camera, and camera view angle. To evaluate the performance of the proposed feature, a Neural Network pattern recognition classifier is employed to classify vehicle images and non-vehicle samples. The success rate is validated via various imaging environment (lighting, distance to camera, view angle, and incompleteness) for different vehicle models.

Keywords: Vehicle detection · Hough transform
Pattern recognition · Image classification

1 Introduction

The number of vehicles has been increasing very fast during these years. This also leads to many issues for contemporary cities, such as vehicle accidents, traffic congestion, vehicle crimes and so on. Automatic traffic control systems, anticrime systems, and driving assistance systems have been proposed with the purpose of decreasing accidents and crimes and of improving traffic security. As part of all these systems, vision-based vehicle detection is a fundamental component. Almost in all vision-based vehicle systems, the first task is to detect and track vehicles from images or video frames. Therefore robust and reliable techniques for extracting vehicles from the complex background are attracting popular attention [1–6]. Vision based methods are very sensitive to viewpoint

Funding: This study was funded by THUTHUKA FUNDING INSTRUMENT (National Research Foundation Rating Track) of South Africa under Grant No. 99383.

© Springer Nature Switzerland AG 2018
G. Bebis et al. (Eds.): ISVC 2018, LNCS 11241, pp. 147–156, 2018.
https://doi.org/10.1007/978-3-030-03801-4_14

of camera, illumination of environment, speed of vehicle, etc. Various researches were reported to overcome these affections [1–5], but it is still an open research topic. Vehicle detection systems commonly have two stages: firstly, the features of vehicle are extracted that include size, edge, color, texture and so on; and then classification algorithms based on desired features are employed to classify the vehicles and background. In such systems, features take critical role for the success of vehicle detection and classification. Various features of vehicles were considered, such as symmetry, color, edges, corners, text, motion etc. For example, a fast learning method was proposed to classify vehicles based on Haar-like feature extraction algorithm [1], and oriented gradients was studied to classify vehicle based on hypothesis generation and hypothesis verification from histogram.

In this paper, the vehicle images were mapped to Hough space, where some interesting patterns are discovered. Then statistics in the Hough space are extracted as a new type of features that can be used to detect vehicles from background samples. The patterns of vehicle images in the Hough space are demonstrated, and some interesting properties are studied. It is revealed that these patterns are robust with respect to imaging conditions and view angle of cameras, which in fact is valuable for vehicle detection in complex traffic context. To validate the effectiveness of the proposed feature, a Neural Network classifier is employed to classify the vehicle images from background samples. Experimental results show that the features are robust with respect to most of imaging conditions.

The remainder of the paper is organized as follows: Sect. 2 presents an overview of related works in features detection and classification. Section 3 introduces the proposed vehicle feature in the Hough space. Section 4 shows the experimental results. The last section concludes the paper.

2   Related Works

Features extraction and classification are the main tasks for vehicle detection systems. In fact, they are also common components of most applications in the field of computer vision. Object features are firstly extracted and then provided as input to classifiers, so that the properties of object features usually have significant effects on the classification performance.

2.1   Features Extraction

Features are important information about objects, especially for vision based systems where images and objects contained are the main contents to be considered. Common features of objects in images include color properties (intensity, histogram, contrastness, optical flow, etc.), spatial domain properties (size, shape, edges, texture, corner, local structure, etc.), and properties obtained from frequency domain methods (Discrete Cosine Transform, Wavelet Transform, Fast Fourier Transform, Laplace operator, etc.). These features are commonly used to represent objects in the feature spaces. Each feature space only reflects some aspects of objects. Therefore, in image processing techniques, combining features from multiple feature spaces becomes a common and important task for object detection and recognition. Then the combined features can be used to identify and isolate various desired objects in images. Many algorithms were developed to extract image features, for instance, Soble Operator, Laplacian of Gaussian, Candy operator were developed for edge detection.

When vehicle detection is concerned, a large number of algorithms were developed for feature extraction. Wen et al. [1] developed a feature selection method to extract harr-like feature from images and then using incremental learning method to classify the vehicles. A method is proposed to detect sides and linearity features of vehicles [2]. Monocular pre-crash vehicle detection system was presented [3], with the system using Gabor filter to extract rectangular features of vehicle.

Hough Transform (HT) [7] is one of traditional and robust techniques which can be used to detect straight lines and circles features embedded in images. HT converts pixels (commonly the edging pixels) in the image space into Hough space according parametric equation, for instance, Eq. (1) is used for straight line detection.

$$\rho = x \cos \theta + y \sin \theta \tag{1}$$

where the features point (x, y) in image space is mapped into a sine curve (ρ, θ) in the Hough space. A straight line in the image will generate a peak in Hough space. In this paper standard deviation of Hough space columns, instead of peaks, are extracted to represent the texture features in images.

2.2 Classifiers

Machine learning is a category of popular methods in the field of artificial intelligence that can be trained using sample data to detect and classify objects based on specific features. Several algorithms have been proposed in the machine learning field, such as neural network (NN) [3], support vector machine (SVM) [3], Naive Bayes Classifier, K-Nearest Neighbors (KNN), etc. All of these algorithms have been used to recognize or classify the vehicles. For example, an incremental learning method based on AdaBoost method for vehicle detection [1] was proposed. Hsieh et al. [3] used NN and SVM to classify the vehicle on the road. Among these machine learning algorithms, significant differences can be found when robustness to feature quality, classification performance, and computation requirements are concerned. Therefore, it is very important to select a suitable method according to requirements of applications. For example, SVM has high accuracy that can deal with high-dimensional feature space, however it requires large computation and memory resources. Naive Bayes is simple and suitable for small training data set, but it lacks the capability to learn interaction features. NN has high accuracy and strong learning ability, even for associated learning and memory. Providing plenty training set, NN is robust to noise. In this paper, NN is employed to classify the vehicle images from samples with no vehicle contained.

3   The Proposed Vehicle Feature in Hough Space

3.1   Mapping Between Image Space and Hough Space

The HT maps feature points (usually edging pixels) in binary images to the parameter space (Hough space) using Eq. (1). Local structures in images are mapped to some specific patterns in the Hough space, for instance, a straight-line segment is mapped to a butterfly-shape region with a peak in the center [9], as shown in Fig. 1. The butterfly-shape regions in Hough space can be used to detect straight-line segments [10].

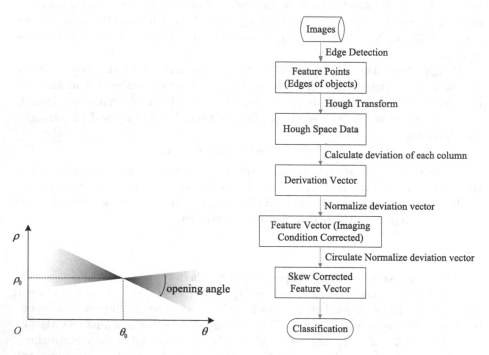

Fig. 1. The butterfly-shape pattern for straight segment detection [10]

Fig. 2. The diagram for the proposed method detection

3.2   Vehicle Image Features in Hough Space

In fact, various local spatial structures (such as shapes, corners) have their own features after mapped to Hough space. Because the edge intensity distribution of these local structures are different in images, one can expect to differentiate them in the Hough space as well. Due to the fact that Hough Transform is based on a voting scheme, the Hough features are more robust than the image space features. This motivates the consideration of using Hough space features for image space object recognition proposed in this paper.

Considering the common image space features of vehicles (such as existence of parallel lines, corners), the pattern mapped to Hough space can be helpful for object detection. Meanwhile, differences also exist among various models of vehicles, which can be considered for vehicle model classification.

For vision based applications, the image space usually contains lots of disturbances resulting from imaging condition, camera position, the pose of objects, incompleteness, perspective distortion, etc. Statistical variables are usually helpful to build robust features under these situations.

In this paper, firstly, the Hough Transform in Eq. (1) is used to map the feature points (edging pixels) in binary images to the Hough space. Secondly, the standard deviation of each column in the Hough space is calculated to build the feature vector. Thirdly, the deviation vector is normalized to accommodate the objects with different dimensions and imaging conditions. Finally, the normalized deviation vector is circulated by locating the column with highest deviation to the first column in the vector. This is to solve the problem of skew. Figure 2 demonstrates the procedure of the prosed method.

4   Experiment and Results

To validate the proposed Hough space vehicle feature, the dataset [11] is used. Experiments are designed to evaluate the reliability of the proposed feature under the challenges of imaging condition, camera position, and skew. The classification rates demonstrate the effectiveness. The resolution of the HT used in all experiments is $1°$ for θ and 1 pixel for ρ.

4.1   The Difference of Hough Space Features for Vehicle and None-Vehicle samples

In the dataset [11], 3425 images of vehicle rears were provided with different camera positions, and 3900 samples from road sequences without vehicles contained.

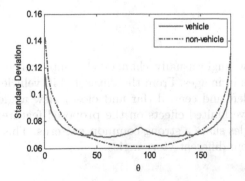

Fig. 3. Average features of vehicle and non-vehicle samples

Figure 3 depicts the average Hough space features for these two categories. Significant differences can be noted from the normalized standard deviation of columns in Hough data. For instance, the steeper edge of vehicle images and peak around the center of the vector. These differences will enable classifiers generate clear boundaries to separate the two classes.

4.2   Reliability to Imaging Condition

Imaging conditions, such as lighting and camera position, are a known challenge for vision-based applications. Experiments are designed to show the performance of the proposed feature under these challenges.

Lighting: In the dataset, vehicle images were intentionally captured under various lighting conditions, such as sunny weather, cloudy days, medium conditions (neither very sunny nor cloudy), poor illumination (down/dusk), light rain, and in tunnels (with artificial light). Figure 4 shows the average features under the lighting conditions, where one finds that the features did not have significant changes across various conditions.

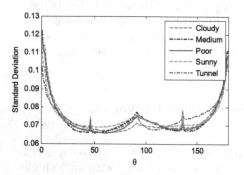

Fig. 4. Average vehicle image features on various lighting conditions

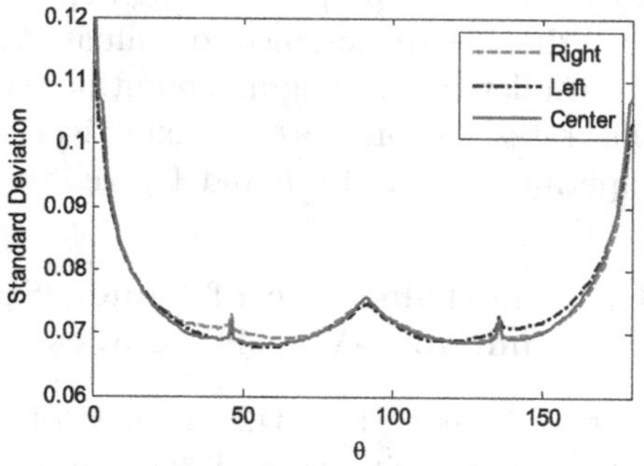

Fig. 5. Average vehicle image features with different view angles

View Angle: View angle usually changes the appearance and some spatial properties of objects in images. From the dataset [14], vehicle images were captured in the right, left and central (far and close) view angles. Figure 5 shows that view angles have limited effects on the proposed feature, and the features for various view angles share a strong common patterns. This enables classifiers recognize objects from different view angles.

Distance to Camera: The distance to camera results in the change of resolution for the same object. Objects closer to camera usually yield larger, higher resolution, and clearer images. When the object moves far from the camera, fewer effective pixels of the object remain. This affects the spatial features. In the dataset, there are vehicle images captured far from camera and close to camera. Figure 6 shows the average feature of vehicle images not sensitive to the distances to camera.

4.3   Reliability to Conformal Mapping

Conformal mapping, such as image rotation, translation, and change of dimension, is another factor should be considered in vision based applications. To study on these effects, the vehicle image shown in Fig. 7 is considered.

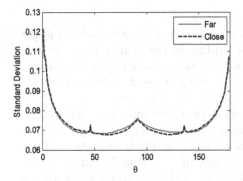

Fig. 6. Average vehicle image features with different distances to camera

Fig. 7. A vehicle image to be used to extract Hough space feature

Rotation: To study the effects of image rotation to the proposed feature, a vehicle image was rotated before extracting Hough space feature. Figure 8 depicts the features extracted from rotated images and the original image, where the general properties of the feature vector are almost not affected.

Translation: In image based object detection and recognition systems, objects are usually localized and the window containing the object is considered for feature extraction. However, the window cannot always exactly cut the boundaries of the object. In this situation, the object position in the window might change, which can be considered as translation.

This experiment takes the edging data of the image in Fig. 7, but insert columns of 0-pixels to the left, which mimics the translation of the object in a bigger image.

From Fig. 9 one finds that after moving all the pixels of the object by the same distance, the Hough space feature shows only minor changes, indicating the robustness of the proposed feature to image translation.

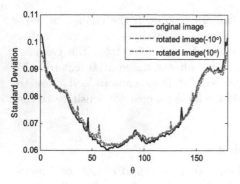

Fig. 8. Hough space features of rotated images

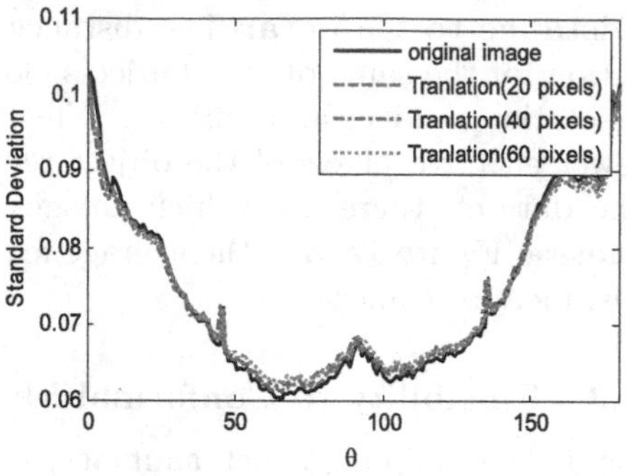

Fig. 9. The effects of translation on Hough space features

Dimension: Due to the different resolution for cameras, the same object might get various size in images. Another factor leading to the change of object size is the distance to the camera. The more close an object locating to the camera, the bigger object size is obtained in image. So the features for object detection and recognition have to be robust with respect to the object size.

For limited resolution, some properties of the local structure of an object might get lost in small images, which is a challenge for object detection/recognition.

In this experiment, the vehicle image is resized to study the effects of object size to the proposed feature. As shown in Fig. 10, the Hough feature is not strongly impacted by the change of object size, although some properties of local structure might get affected by the resizing operation.

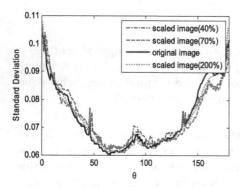

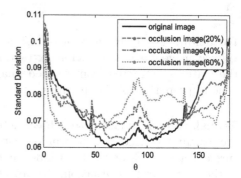

Fig. 10. The effects of object size on Hough space features

Fig. 11. The effects of image occlusion on Hough space features

4.4   Reliability to Occlusion

Occlusion usually happens when part of the object is blocked or moved out of the view of camera, which is a serious challenge since the image of the object loses spatial characteristics, even might lose the features that classifiers rely on.

The image in Fig. 7 is used to demonstrate the effects of occlusion on the proposed feature but a portion of the image was replaced by 0-pixels before extracting the Hough space feature. From Fig. 11 one finds the feature was significantly affected only after 60% of the image was occluded when most of the local structure properties are lost.

4.5   Classification

A Neural Network classifier for pattern recognition is employed to classify vehicle and non-vehicle samples under various situations. The classifier has 10 neurons in hidden layer and 2 in output layer. 70% samples are used for training, 15% for validation, and the rest 15% for testing. Table 1 listed the sample sizes and success rate of classification under different situations where the following points are noted:

- For the samples captured with right or left view angles, the classification success rate are similar.
- For different distances to the camera, higher classification rate can be expected for closer samples. The closer to the camera, the stronger local structure properties, which makes the classification easier.
- The better lighting condition the higher classification rate, because images become more sharp (higher contrast). It should be noted that for the tunnel case (artificial lighting), 100% classification rate was obtained, which might because the sample size is so small that over fitting happened.
- The total dataset was also given as input to the classifier, where all samples of vehicle are considered as the same class, and all the non-vehicle samples as the other class. In this way, it becomes more challenging because the differences among subset classes might disturb the classifier. However, from the experiment, the total classification rate is just slightly lower than other experiments.

Table 1. Success rate of classification

Image sets		Positive sample size	Negative sample size	Success rate
View angle	Left	975	975	91.8%
	Right	975	975	91.5%
Camera distance	Far	975	975	91.1%
	Close	500	975	94.2%
Lighting	Cloudy	210	210	88.9%
	Medium	392	392	92.4%
	Sunny	408	408	95.1%
	Tunnel	40	40	100%
Total		3425	3900	0.46	90.8%

5   Discussion and Future Work

A Hough space feature was proposed in the paper, by applying Hough Transform to images. The standard deviation of columns in Hough space was considered as the feature to describe the vehicle samples. Various challenges on lighting condition, distance to camera, conformal mapping, and object dimensions are considered in experiments to verify the reliability of the proposed feature. Experiments show the proposed feature is reliable under these challenges, and can be used in classification with high success rate.

The mean drawback of the proposed feature is the dimension. Currently it is a 1D vector with 180 elements. The future work includes the refining of the dimension of the feature.

References

1. Wen, X., Shao, L., Xue, Y., Fang, W.: A rapid learning algorithm for vehicle classification. Inf. Sci. **295**, 395–406 (2015)
2. Guo, E., Bai, L., Zhang, Y., Han, J.: Vehicle detection based on superpixel and improved HOG in aerial images. In: Zhao, Y., Kong, X., Taubman, D. (eds.) ICIG 2017. LNCS, vol. 10666, pp. 362–373. Springer, Cham (2017). https://doi.org/10.1007/978-3-319-71607-7_32
3. Hsieh, J.-W., Shih-Hao, Y., Chen, Y.-S., Wen-Fong, H.: Automatic traffic surveillance system for vehicle tracking and classification. IEEE Trans. Intell. Transp. Syst. **7**(2), 175–187 (2006)
4. Sun, Z., Bebis, G., Miller, R.: Monocular precrash vehicle detection: features and classifiers. IEEE Trans. Image Process. **15**(7), 2019–2034 (2006)
5. Tu, C., Du, S.: A following behavior detecting method for drive assistance. In: Proceedings of the 2016 International Conference on Intelligent Information Processing, p. 9 (2016)
6. Wen, X., Shao, L., Fang, W., Xue, Y.: Efficient feature selection and classification for vehicle detection. IEEE Trans. Circuits Syst. Video Technol. **25**(3), 508–517 (2015)
7. Paul V C Hough: Method and means for recognizing complex patterns. U.S. Patent 3,069,654, issued 18 December 1962
8. Sun, Z., Bebis, G., Miller, R.: On-road vehicle detection using Gabor filters and support vector machines. In: 2002 14th International Conference on Digital Signal Processing, DSP 2002, vol. 2, pp. 1019–1022 (2002)
9. Du, S., van Wyk, B.J., Tu, C., Zhang, X.: An improved hough transform neighborhood map for straight line segments. IEEE Trans. Image Process. **19**(3), 573–585 (2010)
10. Du, S., Tu, C., van Wyk, B.J., Chen, Z.: Collinear segment detection using HT neighborhoods. IEEE Trans. Image Process. **20**(12), 3612–3620 (2011)
11. Arrspide, J., Salgado, L., Nieto, M.: Video analysis based vehicle detection and tracking using an MCMC sampling framework. EURASIP J. Adv. Signal Process. **2012** (2012). Article ID 2012:2, https://doi.org/10.1186/1687618020122

Gender Classification Based on Facial Shape and Texture Features

Mayibongwe H. Bayana, Serestina Viriri$^{(\boxtimes)}$, and Raphael Angulu

School of Maths, Statistics and Computer Science,
University of Kwazulu Natal, Durban, South Africa
viriris@ukzn.ac.za

Abstract. This paper seeks to improve gender classification accuracy by fusing shape features, the Active Shape Model with the two appearance based methods, the Local Binary Pattern (LBP) and Local Directional Pattern (LDP). A gender classification model based on the fusion of appearance and shape features is proposed. The experimental results show that the fusion of the LBP and LDP with the Active Shape Model improved the gender classification accuracy rate to 94.5% from 92.8% before fusion.

Keywords: Active shape model · Local binary pattern
Local directional pattern · Fusion

1 Introduction

The influence of Artificial Intelligence is spreading to every aspect of human life from health, advertising to determining who goes to prison and who to lend money, which are tasks traditionally performed by humans but now have been entrusted to be performed by algorithms [1]. The human face is very important when it comes to communication as it conveys a lot of information, such as gender [2] or age [3] which helps one to know how to then approach an individual to initiate a conversation. With Artificial Intelligence making inroads into every corner of society the human face has been used as the source of information from age [3], ethnicity [4,5], emotion [6]. However this information may not be enough to uniquely identify an individual and in such cases it is referred to as a soft biometric [7]. Gender classification has been applied to the field of Human Computer Interaction which may improve interactions and services tailoring them to each gender [8], another important application of gender classification is with marketing electronic billboards which may be programmed to show male products when there are more males than females standing in front of it [9].

A number of methods have been put forward to obtain the gender of an individual given an image. Researchers have used the face as a whole, which may not always be possible as a result of environmental constraints and as a result fusion may be used put forward to enhance gender classification accuracies is

© Springer Nature Switzerland AG 2018
G. Bebis et al. (Eds.): ISVC 2018, LNCS 11241, pp. 157–166, 2018.
https://doi.org/10.1007/978-3-030-03801-4_15

fusion, which can occur at feature or classifier level. According to Yang et al. [10] there has been few papers which have discussed classification of gender by fusing global and local features.

This paper seeks to improve gender classification accuracies using the whole facial area as input by fusing the appearance (Local Binary Pattern, Local Directional Pattern) and the shape features (Active Shape Models). The Support Vector Machine is used as the classifier of choice inspired by findings of [11] who obtained improved results from fusing the DCT, LBP and a novel feature extractor they termed the Geometric Distance Feature using a Support Vector Machine as the preferred classifier. The authors of this research paper use the FG-Net dataset and the Pilots Parliament Benchmark project [1] which is made up of images of parliamentarians drawn from Africa and Europe.

1.1   Literature Review

Approaches to gender classification have been categorized into two which are the appearance and the geometric based approach [8]. The appearance based approach uses image pixels and performs statistical computations on them, on the other hand the geometric approach uses the distances between the facial features to determine an individuals gender. The appearance based approach hence makes use of an image as a high dimensional vector and extracts features from its statistical features making a decision based solely on it. Feature extraction attempts to develop a transformation of the input space onto the low-dimensional subspace whilst maintaining the most relevant information [12].

In the area of pattern recognition there are two categories when it comes to one is feature combination and the other being classifier combination [13]. A hybrid approach was put forward by Mozaffari et al. [11], in which they utilized two appearance based features the Discrete Cosine Transform (DCT), Local Binary Pattern (LBP) and the novel Geometric Distance Feature (GDF) to enhance gender classification and compared the results on two datasets, Ethnic and AR using ellipse fitting during the localization process. On the Ethnic dataset a combination of the LBP and DCT yielded a 84.6% compared to 97.1% for LBP, DCT and GDF showing an enhancement of 12.5%. On the AR dataset combination of the LBP and DCT yields a 80.3% a combination of LBP, DCT and GDF yield a 96% accuracy having and enhancement of 15.7% using frontal images.

A hybrid approach is proposed by Xu et al. [14] combining the Appearance based and geometric features. 83 landmarks are detected from the local features using the Active Appearance Model, leading to $3403(C_{83}^2)$ features from which 10 are selected to form a feature vector and as a result can be further optimized to detect fewer features for classification to improve efficiency. Global features are extracted using the Adaboost algorithm and a Support Vector Machine is used as the classifier of choice. The results from the hybrid method proposed by Xu et al. [14] led to a recognition rate of 92.38% compared to 82.97% and 88.55% for appearance and geometry features when used individually.

Other researchers have attempted to carry out fusion at classifier level [13] by combining four different Support Vector Machines for the eyes, nose, mouth and hair using the fuzzy integral. Of particular interest is the use of hair, as proposed by Lapedriza et al. [15] as previous researchers had shunned its use because of its large variations [13]. From their results [13] found that individually they eyes had the highest classification of 84.24% followed by the mouth and the hair had a better accuracy than the nose at 75.42% compared 70.94%. The fuzzy integral was used for classification after combining classifiers for the eyes, nose, mouth and hair recorded the highest accuracy, 90.61% compared to the weighted sum with 99.73%, the Maximum Margin Criterion using only facial features recorded 87.32%.

1.2 Local Binary Pattern

The Local Binary pattern is one the simplest texture based feature extraction techniques [2]. This technique makes use of pixel values to perform calculations on them. The LBP is a non parametric approach which summarizes local structures by comparing each pixel with its neighbouring pixels (denoted by P) [16]. In the equation below radius is denoted by(R), the central pixel which is being thresholded is denoted by g_c) converting them into a decimal number as shown in Eq. 1.

$$LBP_{P,r(X_c,Y_c)} = \sum_{P=0}^{P-1} s_{(g_p-g_c)}2^p$$

$$wheres(x) = \begin{cases} 1 & \text{if } x \geq 0 \\ 0 & \text{if } x < 0 \end{cases}$$

(1)

Although the LBP provides an invariant description in the presence of monotomic illumination it does not perform well under non-monotomic illumination. As a result various forms of the LBP have been introduced to make it more robust such as the uniform patterns, which contain at most two bitwise transitions from 0 to 1 or 1 to 0.

In previous research experiments Jabied et al. [17], showed that the LDP using an SVM classifier outperformed the LBP using an Adaboost classifier and the LBP using the weighted Chi-square classifier, as facial components have been shown to have different gender discriminatory levels. Classification accuracies of 95,05% against 92.25% and 81.90% are obtained respectively. The findings of the paper also further revealed that increasing block size affects accuracy as increasing the size from 5(5 by 5) to 10(10 by 10) only increased accuracy by 2% and further increasing it to 20 by 20 blocks the accuracy went back down by 1%.

Shape features can be extracted using the Active Shape Model [18] and Active Appearance Model [19]. The latter seeks to match the position of the model points against a representation of the texture of an object to the image whilst the ASM matches the model points to the image whilst being limited by a model of the shape. Lakshmiprabha et al. [20] compared the performance of four major classifiers the AAM, Gabor wavelet, LBP and Wavelet Decomposition for gender classification of the FG-NET dataset with a Neural Network with three layers being used. The AAM obtained 92.523%, Gabor 90.03%, LBP 90.34% and the Wavelet Decomposition (WD) had the least with 89.72% accuracy.

2   Method

The gender classification model proposed is composed of a few steps, first being converting the image to grayscale then detecting the face and extracting the facial components. After facial components have been detected they are extracted using the LBP and the Active Shape Model after which dimensionality reduction is carried out using PCA and LDA. The final stage is classification by the Support Vector Machine as illustrated in Fig. 1.

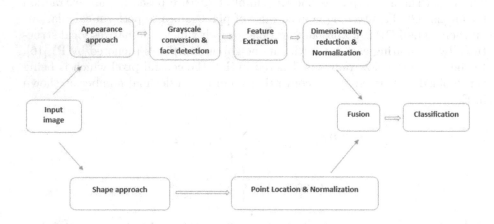

Fig. 1. Proposed model

2.1   Face Detection

Face detection is one of the most fundamental steps in gender classification and other face recognition tasks. The findings of previous researchers have shown us that the Viola-Jones algorithm [21] has outperformed all other facial detectors and hence it is used in this research. The goal of face detection is to find any face present in a given image returning the given face as an output [22]. There are three components which make the algorithm efficient which are the integral image which enables rapid computation of haar-like features, adaboost learning which combines weak classifier to find a accurate stronger classifier. The haar-like features, which are digital image features used in object detection in the form of rectangles of black and white. The integral image is calculated by summing the pixels in the white area which are then subtracted from those in the black area as shown in Eq. 2.

$$ii(x,y) = \sum_{x' \leq x, y' \leq y} i(x',y') \tag{2}$$

In Eq. 1, $ii(x,y)$ is the integral image at pixel location (x, y) which is used to find the sum of the rectangle where we subtract the white area from the black area as shown in the equation that follows. Given a rectangle WXYZ we then calculate the sum of pixels as shown by Eq. 3.

$$\sum_{(x,y)} \in WXYZ = ii(Z) + ii(W) - ii(X) - ii(Y) \tag{3}$$

The cascade structure increases efficiency by rejecting negative sub-windows before further processing.

2.2 Local Directional Pattern

The Local Directional Pattern [23] has been shown to have great resistance to noise and hence was chosen a the descriptor of choice. The LDP therefore computes the binary code for each pixel in the image by comparing edge responses of each pixel in the 8 different directions. The Kirsch edge detector is used in this paper. Hence when given a centre pixel in an image $P(i,j)$, 8-directional responses are computed by convolving the neighbouring pixels. The LDP determines the K significant directional responses setting them to a bit value of 1 and the rest to 0. The binary response bit for each bit is shown in Eq. 4.

$$LDP_K = \sum_{i=0}^{i=7} b_i((m_i - m_k) \times 2^i)$$

$$b_i(a) = \begin{cases} 1, \text{if } a \geq 0 \\ 0, \text{if } a < 0 \end{cases} \tag{4}$$

In Eq. 4, m_k is the Kth significant directional response. For $K = 3$ as used we generate $C_3^8(56)$ distinct patterns and a histogram $H(i)$ with C_k^8 bins can be used to represent an image $I_L(x,y)$, shown in Eq. 5. Where $where\,C_i$ is the ith LDP Pattern$(0 \leq i < 56)$.

$$H(i) = \sum_{x,y} P(I_L(x,y) = C_i),$$

$$where P(A) = \begin{cases} 1 \; if \; A \; is \; true \\ 0 \; if \; A \; is \; false \end{cases} \tag{5}$$

2.3   Active Shape Model

The Active Shape Model put proposed by Cootes [24] is used in medical segmentation and facial feature localization among others, it fits a set of local feature detectors to an object taking into account global shape considerations. A manually labelled training set is used to come up with a linear shape model shown by the Eq. 6.

$$x = \bar{x} + P_s b_s \tag{6}$$

In Eq. 6 above, $\bar{x}$ is the mean shape, with P_s being the set of orthogonal modes of variation and b_s is the set of shape parameters, hence fitting an ASM is a non-linear optimization problem to minimize a squared error measure of the output that is desired and that of the model. This is shown in the equation below in which Y represents feature points in an image plane, the shape model parameters b_s are determined by minimizing the expression as shown in Eq. 7.

$$|Y - T_t(\bar{x} + P_s b_s)| \tag{7}$$

Constraints are placed on the allowable shape parameters b_s the shape model estimate of the current feature points $T_t(\bar{x}) + P_s b_s)$ are constrained to form a plausible shape, an example of an image with the detected facial points is shown below.

2.4   Normalization and Feature Fusion

After feature extraction has been carried out normalization is carried out on both feature vectors of the Active Shape Models and the Local Binary Pattern, since we will add the features. From the various methods studied for normalization the Min-Max method is used as it is simpler [25]. The Min-max equation is shown in Eq. 8.

$$n = \frac{x - min}{max - min} \tag{8}$$

The end-points of the range are specified by max and min and x represents the new matrice value to be determined. Min-max maps the values to within the range $[-1, 1]$. After which feature fusion is carried out by addition and dimensionality reduction is carried out.

2.5   Dimensionality Reduction

The fact that the facial image data is always high dimensional has meant that it requires considerable computing time for classification [26]. Hence gender classification like other image recognition practices has the stumbling block of high dimensionality and hence dimensionality reduction improves the learning process and resulting in comprehensibility as irrelevant and redundant data are removed as we move the data from a high dimensional space to one with a low dimension as shown below:

$$
\begin{bmatrix} a_1 \\ a_2 \\ \vdots \\ a_n \end{bmatrix} dimensionality\ reduction->\ \begin{bmatrix} b_1 \\ b_2 \\ \vdots \\ b_n \end{bmatrix} \tag{9}
$$

Dimensionality reduction, Eq. 9, shows dimensionality reduction where the number of variables is reduced from N to K as $K \leq n$ from a high dimensional data space [N], representing our normalized matrice to a lower dimensional dataspace [k]. In this research we have used the Principle Component Analysis and the Local Discriminant Analysis. The Principal Component analysis is a supervised learning method which is also referred as the Singular Value Decomposition.

The PCA reduces dimensionality by finding the direction of greatest variance in the given data. The first principal components show most of the variance, hence the rest can be thrown away as they contain little information [27]. The LDA is also performed in this experiment as to maximize between the classes scatter and minimizing within class scatter without losing data and hence for all sample classes the LDA defines two measures, the first being the within class scatter.

$$
S_W = \sum_{j=1}^{c} \sum_{N_i=1}^{N_j} (x_i^j - \mu_j)(x_i^j - \mu_j)^T \tag{10}
$$

In Eq. 10, c is the number of classes and $x(i)^j$ is the i-th sample of the class j, μ_j and N_j the number of samples in class j. Below is the equation for the between class scatter.

$$
S_b = \sum_{j=1}^{c} (\mu_j - \mu)(\mu_j - \mu)^T \tag{11}
$$

In Eq. 11, μ represents the mean of all classes. After dimensionality reduction has been carried out the vector is then fed into a support Vector Machine [28], which finds the optimal linear hyperplane which will minimize the classification error for unseen test samples. The RBF kernel was chosen as previous researchers had found that it performed better than others [28], with the SVM type C-Support Vector classification being chosen as it applied on classes greater than or equal to two.

2.6 Datasets

The FG-NET dataset was used to determine gender estimation using either LDP or LBP for feature extraction and SVM classification. The dataset is built up of 1002 images, coming from 82 different individuals drawn up from ages 1–69 years. Images have a wide variation in illumination, color amongst others.

The Pilots Parliament Benchmark was used to provide a better intersectional representation on gender and skin type and consists of 1270 individuals drawn from three African and three European countries giving a good reflection on algorithm performance. Images from the FG-Net dataset are also used made up of 1002 images belonging to 82 different individuals with ages ranging from 0–69.

3   Results

The experiments carried out in this paper included feature using the LBP, LDP, ASM with the SVM as the classifier and the results are shown in Table 1.

Table 1. Gender classification using the SVM with various feature extractors

Feature extractor	FG-NET	PPB
LBP	85.33%	83.13%
LDP	92.85%	89.26%
LDP + ASM	94.53%	81.56%
LBP + ASM	89.53%	85.43%

4   Conclusion and Future Work

In this paper, a method for fusing shape and appearance based features is put forward, using the Local Binary Pattern (LBP) and Local Directional Pattern (LDP)to extract the appearance based features and the Active Shape Model to extract the shape features. Of particular interest is the fact that for all tests, the fusion based approach outperforms the singular feature extractor.

References

1. Buolamwini, J., Gebru, T.: Gender shades: intersectional accuracy disparities in commercial gender classification. Proc. Mach. Learn. Res. **81**, 1–15 (2018)
2. Cheung, Y.-m., Deng, J.: Ultra local binary pattern for image texture analysis. In: Secutrity, Pattern Analysis and Cybernetics (2014)
3. Angulu, R., Tapamo, J., Adewum, A.: Human age estimation using multifrequency biologically inspired features (mf-bif). In: IEEE AFRICON 2017 (2017)
4. Wang, Wei, He, Feixiang, Zhao, Qijun: Facial ethnicity classification with deep convolutional neural networks. In: You, Zhisheng, Zhou, Jie, Wang, Yunhong, Sun, Zhenan, Shan, Shiguang, Zheng, Weishi, Feng, Jianjiang, Zhao, Qijun (eds.) CCBR 2016. LNCS, vol. 9967, pp. 176–185. Springer, Cham (2016). https://doi.org/10.1007/978-3-319-46654-5_20

5. Boyseens, A., Viriri, S.: Component-based ethnicity identification from facial images. In: Chmielewski, L.J., Datta, A., Kozera, R., Wojciechowski, K. (eds.) ICCVG 2016. LNCS, vol. 9972, pp. 293–303. Springer, Cham (2016). https://doi.org/10.1007/978-3-319-46418-3_26
6. Luoh, L., Huang, C.: International coriference on system science and engineering image processing based emotion recognition. In: 2010 International Coriference on System Science and Engineering (2010)
7. Jain, A.K., Dass, S.C., Nandakumar, K.: Soft biometric traits for personal recognition systems. In: Zhang, D., Jain, A.K. (eds.) ICBA 2004. LNCS, vol. 3072, pp. 731–738. Springer, Heidelberg (2004). https://doi.org/10.1007/978-3-540-25948-0_99
8. Hoffmeyer-Zlotnik, J.H.P., Wolf, C. (eds.): Advances in Cross-National Comparison A European Working Book for Demographic and Socio-Economic Variables. Springer, New York (2003). https://doi.org/10.1007/978-1-4419-9186-7
9. Yu, S., Tan, T., Huang, K., Jia, K., Wu, X.: A study on gait-based gender classification. IEEE Trans. Image Process. 18(8) (2008)
10. Yang, W., Chen, C., Ricanek, K., Sun, C.: Gender classification via global-local features fusion. In: Sun, Z., Lai, J., Chen, X., Tan, T. (eds.) CCBR 2011. LNCS, vol. 7098, pp. 214–220. Springer, Heidelberg (2011). https://doi.org/10.1007/978-3-642-25449-9_27
11. Mozaffari, S., Behravan, H., Akbari, R.: Gender classification using single frontal image per person: combination of appearance and geometric based features. In: 20th International Conference on Pattern Recognition, ICPR 2010 (2010)
12. Chumerin, N., Hulle, M.M.V.: Comparison of two feature extraction methods based on maximization of mutual information. In: 2006 16th IEEE Signal Processing Society Workshop on Machine Learning for Signal Processing (2006)
13. Lian, X.-C., Lu, B.-L.: Gender classification by combining facial and hair information. In: Köppen, M., Kasabov, N., Coghill, G. (eds.) ICONIP 2008. LNCS, vol. 5507, pp. 647–654. Springer, Heidelberg (2009). https://doi.org/10.1007/978-3-642-03040-6_79
14. Ziyi Xu, L.L., Shi, P.: A hybrid approach to gender classification from face images. In: 2008 IEEE (2008)
15. Lapedriza, A., Masip, D., Vitria, J.: Are external face features useful for automatic face classification? In: CVPR 2005, vol. 3, pp. 151–157 (2005)
16. Cao, L., Dikmen, M., Fu, Y.: Gender recognition from body. In: MM 08 Proceedings of the 16th ACM International Conference on Multimedi (2008)
17. Jabid, K.M., Chae, O.: Local directional pattern for face recognition. In: International Conference on Consumer Electronics (2010)
18. Cootes, T.F., Taylor, C.J., Cooper, D.H., Graham, J.: Active shape modelstheir training and application. Comput. Vis. Image Underst. 61, 38–59 (1995)
19. Cootes, T.F., Edwards, G.J., Taylor, C.J.: Active appearance models. In: Burkhardt, H., Neumann, B. (eds.) ECCV 1998. LNCS, vol. 1407, pp. 484–498. Springer, Heidelberg (1998). https://doi.org/10.1007/BFb0054760
20. Lakshmiprabha, N.: Face image analysis using AAM, Gabor, LBP and WD features for gender age, expression and ethnicity classification. Comput. Vis. Pattern Recognit. (cs.CV) (2016)
21. Viola, P., Jones, M.: Robust real-time object detection. In: Second International Workshop on Statistical and Computational Theories of Vision-Modelling, Learning, Computing and Sampling (2001)
22. Yang, M.-H., Kriegman, D.J., Ahuja, N.: Detecting faces in images: a survey. IEEE Trans. Pattern Anal. Mach. Intell. 24(1) (2002)

23. Jabid, T., Kabir, H., Chae, O.: Robust facial expression recognition based on local directional pattern. ETRI J. (2010)
24. Cootes, T., Edwards, G., Taylor, C.: Comparing active shape models with active appearance models. In: British Machine Vision (1999)
25. Xu, Z., Lu, L., Shi, P.: A hybrid approach to gender classification from face images. In: 2008 19th International Conference on Pattern Recognition (2008)
26. Jadhao, V., Holambe, R.S.: Feature extraction and dimensionality reduction using radon and fourier transforms with application to face recognition. In: Conference on Computational Intelligence and Multimedia Applications (2007)
27. Pang, Y., Yuan, Y., Li, X.: Effective feature extraction in a high dimensinal space. IEEE Trans. Syst. (2008)
28. Yang, M.H., Moghaddam, B.: Support vector machines for visual gender classification. In: Proceedings 15th International Conference on Pattern Recognition, ICPR-2000 (2000)

Authentication-Based on Biomechanics of Finger Movements Captured Using Optical Motion-Capture

Brittany Lewis, Christopher J. Nycz, Gregory S. Fischer,
and Krishna K. Venkatasubramanian[✉]

Worcester Polytechnic Institute, Worcester, MA 01609, USA
{bfgradel,cjnycz,gfischer,kven}@wpi.edu

Abstract. In this paper, we propose an authentication approach based on the uniqueness of the biomechanics of finger movements. We use an optical-marker-based motion-capture as a preliminary setup to capture goniometric (joint-related) and dermatologic (skin-related) features from the flexion and extension of the index and middle fingers of a subject. We use this information to build a personalized authentication model for a given subject. Analysis of our approach using finger motion-capture from 8 subjects, using reflective tracking markers placed around the joints of index and middle fingers of the subjects shows its viability. In this preliminary study, we achieve an average equal error rate (EER)—when false accept rate and false reject rate are equal—of 6.3% in authenticating a subject immediately after training the authentication model and 16.4% ERR after a week.

Keywords: Authentication · Biometrics · Finger biomechanics
Motion-capture

1 Introduction

The idea behind biometrics is to use, in an automated manner, the *traits* of human physiology and/or behavior as a way to uniquely recognize (authenticate) a person and clearly distinguish this person from others. Biometric data are increasingly being used in a large number of governmental and private programs, such as airport security, school attendance, and public assistance programs [7]. The increase in the use of biometric data to control access to programs, services, and facilities raises the need for newer biometric modalities. Once we have linked an identity to a set of biometric traits collected from a person, we can then identify and/or authenticate them as well.

In this paper, we make the case for a novel biometric-based authentication approach that uses biometric traits from human fingers. Human fingers are extremely complex limbs. The way the fingers of a person move to bend (flexion), straighten (extension) and rotate (circumduction) is determined by their anatomy. That is, the combination of the ligaments, blood vessels, joints,

G. Bebis et al. (Eds.): ISVC 2018, LNCS 11241, pp. 167–179, 2018.
https://doi.org/10.1007/978-3-030-03801-4_16

bone structure, tissues, muscle, and skin that constitute fingers determine the type and extent of movements they make. We argue that by using notions from biomechanics we can capture these anatomical characteristics from a person's fingers and develop a rich new class of traits, which can be used as biometrics. Of course, finger-based biometrics is nothing new. Biometrics based on fingerprints [8], palm print [6], finger vein patterns [9], and even knuckle-print [4] have existed for a while. As important as these biometrics are, we argue that there is a whole slew of finger-centric biometrics that have not yet been explored, those based on the uniqueness of the *biomechanics of a person's* fingers. Finger biomechanics has many uses as a complementary biometric for people for whom existing biometrics fail. For example, the visually impaired. Fewer than 10% of people who are legally blind in the US are able to read Braille, they cannot easily use ubiquitous PIN/password-based authentication systems [2]. Hence, a solution based on biomechanics can be very useful for such a population.

In order to capture the biomechanics of a person's fingers, we explore an approach that uses marker-based optical motion-capture of the flexion and extension of a person's index and middle fingers to understand the unique patterns underlying such motion. We then build a machine learning-based *authentication model* that uses ensemble learning and subject-specific features, to capture the individual uniqueness of the finger flexions and extensions. This model can then be used to identify a person when they perform a single finger flexion and extension at a later time. Although we use motion capture to identify the key characteristics in this preliminary study due to the high precision and frame rate, ultimately these features are expected to be able to be identified using compact and economical sensors.

In this preliminary work, we use marker-based motion-capture to demonstrate the viability of finger biomechanics as a biometric for authentication. Analysis of our approach using finger motion-capture from 8 subjects, using reflective tracking markers placed around the joints of index and middle fingers, shows an average equal error rate (EER)[1] of ~6.3% in authenticating an individual immediately after training and around 16.4% EER after a week. The **contributions** of this work are: (1) a preliminary authentication approach based on biometrics derived from finger movement captured using a motion-capture system, (2) demonstration of the viability of the proposed approach using finger movement data collected longitudinally. Note that, in this work, we only aim to show the viability of the finger biomechanics as a biometric. There are several problems that still need to be addressed to make an authentication system that uses finger biomechanics, for instance, eliminating the need for markers in the motion capture, which we plan to consider in the future.

1.1 Problem Statement

We next detail our problem statement and the assumed threat model for this work. The principal problem that we address in this paper is *to determine if*

---

[1] Equal error rate is the value where the false accept and false reject rates for a model are equal.

the flexion and extension of index and middle fingers of a subject are capable of uniquely identifying them. We assume that the threat to our authentication approach comes from adversaries trying to declare themselves to be a particular subject (i.e., victim) and try to use their own finger movements to authenticate as the victim. For the purposes of this work, we assume that adversaries: (1) do not have access to the authentication model, and (2) cannot pollute the authentication model during the training stage.

2   Approach

Our approach to authentication based on flexion and extension of a person's fingers has four phases. *Data collection phase* describes our process for capturing a subject's index and middle finger flexion and extension using a marker-based motion-capture setup. The *feature extraction phase* then processes this motion-capture data to extract several biomechanical traits of the fingers. We then use these features to train an authentication model in the *training phase*. Finally, in the *authentication phase*, we used the authentication model to identify the subject at a later time. We now describe each of these phases in detail.

2.1   Motion-Capture-Based Data Collection

We collected data from 8 different subjects. Each subject had 21 reflective hemispherical markers (3 mm facial markers, NaturalPoint, Inc., Corvallis Oregon) [1] attached to the dorsum of their right hand using a cosmetic adhesive. We placed three markers over each presumed rigid segment of the index and middle fingers, establishing a 3DoF reference frame for each. No articulation (movement) is assumed to occur between the 2nd and 3rd metacarpal bones, hence a single set of three markers is placed over them, establishing the hand tracking frame H. The marker placement and their naming convention is shown in Fig. 1. Figure 1 shows the various joints in the hand for reference. We asked the participants to sit at a table with 8 optical tracking cameras (Optitrack Flex 13, NaturalPoint, Inc.,) placed to the left, right, front, and above the hand. We placed the cameras approximately 1 m from the center of the capture volume. Prior to data collection, for each subject, we calibrated the cameras with a 100 mm long calibration wand until an average residual error of less than 0.3 mm was achieved. Position data for the markers, relative to a global reference frame, was logged at 120 Hz. Markers were manually labeled in post-processing (we expect to automate this in the future).

Each subject was instructed to repeatedly perform flexion and extension within the motion-capture volume for both index and middle fingers. This results in 4 types of joint movements for flexion: (1) coupled flexion of the proximal interphalangeal (PIP) and distal interphalangeal (DIP) joints of the *index finger*, (2) flexion of the *index finger* metacarpophalangeal (MCP) joint, (3) coupled flexion of the proximal interphalangeal (PIP) and distal interphalangeal (DIP) joints of the *middle finger*, and (4) flexion of the *middle finger* metacarpophalangeal (MCP) joint.

A depiction of these movements for the index finger is shown in Figs. 2(a) and (b). Since every flexion is accompanied by an extension of the finger, we have the same 4 types of joint movements for extension as well. We demonstrated the finger movement to the participants before data collection. Even though, we ask the users to perform simple finger flexions and extensions, the exact angle of flexion/extension is not prescribed or controlled. We aim to build aggregate models characterizing the overall flexion/extension capability of the user based on a variety of characteristics (see next section), which turn out to be unique. For example, Fig. 3 shows the joint positions for the index fingers of 2 different subjects while they repeatedly flex their MCP. The viewpoint is set be orthogonal to the MCP axes of both subjects and their MCPs are fixed at 0,0. Their fingers are fully extended when the joints are near the

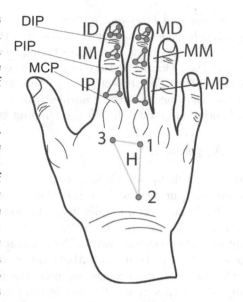

Fig. 1. An illustration of: (a) motion-capture marker placement and naming convention used for data collection. Here, D, M, P, and H stand for distal, medial, proximal, and hand, respectively. While I and M stand for index and middle, respectively.

line $x = 0$. It is easy to see that the joints for the two subjects follow distinct paths. Once the data was collected, we post-processed it to calculate the position and orientation of each joint throughout the performed finger movement. The positions and orientations of the joints were found from the motion-capture data using methods of Gamage et al. [5].

(a)   (b)

Fig. 2. An illustration of a set of performed movements for the index finger and its markers: (a) Coupled flexion and extension of the proximal interphalangeal (PIP) and distal interphalangeal (DIP) joints. (b) Flexion and extension of the metacarpophalangeal (MCP) joint.

2.2   Feature Extraction

For feature extraction, we considered not just the joints specifically being flexed, but rather all the joints of the index and middle fingers. Biomechanic and neurological features, such as muscle synergies and friction between adjacent tendons, typically prohibit decoupled movement of the fingers. These coupled movements may contain difficult-to-replicate signatures specific to an individual. For each of the two tracked fingers, there were 58 features captured which can be divided into two categories: (1) *goniometric features*, which describe joint rotations, and (2) *dermatologic features*, which describe skin movement. There were 48 goniometric and 10 dermatological features.

To define the start and end time of a flexion motion, we consider the point where the joint reaches 10% of its range of motion as the start and the point at which the joint reaches 90% of its range of motion as the end. Similarly for extension, we consider the point where the joint reaches 90% of its range of motion as the start and 10% as the end. These thresholds help to make repeated measurements of an individual consistent where measurement noise or small movements of the joints are not incorrectly identified as the start of an observed flexion or extension.

The goniometric features extracted can be classified into six categories of joint measurements for both flexion and extension. These include: (1) PIP joint-related measurements, (2) DIP joint-related measurements, (3) MCP joint-related measurements, (4) DIP-PIP interrelationship, (5) PIP-MCP interrelationship, and (6) DIP-MCP interrelationship. The latter 3 feature categories capture how the DIP, PIP, and MCP joints change in relation to each other during finger flexion and extension.

The PIP, DIP, and MCP joint-related measurements each are a set of 12 features (total $3 \times 12 = 36$ features) that capture: (1) the basic statistics of the angle of the joint at various times during flexion and extension (these fea-

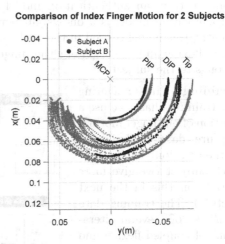

Fig. 3. Joint positions for the index fingers of 2 different subjects while they repeatedly flex their MCP.

tures pertain to the particular angle that the finer joints make during flexion and extension); (2) the trajectory of the joint during flexion and extension modeled as a quintic function, whose coefficients form the features (which captures both the angles and the broader trajectory of the finger movement); (3) the slope of a linear fit for the trajectory measuring the rate of change of the joint angle during flexion and extension (which represents the speed of the finger motion). Similarly, the DIP-PIP, PIP-MCP and DIP-MCP interrelationship feature categories are a list of 4 features (total $3 \times 4 = 12$ features) each that capture the maximum, median, and average of the ratio of the two joint angles, along with the slope of the linear fit of the scatter plot between the two joint positions during flexion and extension. Together we have a total of 48 $(36 + 12)$ goniometric features.

For the dermatologic features, we primarily measure how much the skin stretches at the proximal and medial phalanges when the finger flexes and extends. At both the phalanges, we extract 5 features, which capture the skin stretch at the beginning and end of the finger movement, the average and median skin stretch, and the skin stretch rate. Together we have a total of 10 (5×2) dermatologic features.

Since all of these features are measured for both the index and middle fingers, we extract a total of $(48+10) \times 2 = 116$ features during both flexion and extension of the index and middle fingers. A full list of our features can be seen at: https://tinyurl.com/ybrzx6g5.

2.3   Training and Authentication

Once we have the features from the motion-capture of finger flexion and extension, we train an authentication model for each subject in our dataset. The authentication model is a one-vs.-all personalized model for a subject. Subsequently, this model is used in the authentication phase, when a newly captured finger flexion and extension of either finger is evaluated by the model to see if it belongs to the subject.

Training Phase: During the training phase, we use a portion of our finger motion-capture data to build an authentication model for each subject (we give more details on this in the next section). The training data consists of several iterations of coupled flexion and extension of the PIP and DIP joints and the flexion and extension of the MCP joint as shown in Fig. 2 for both the index and middle fingers. For each flexion and it's corresponding

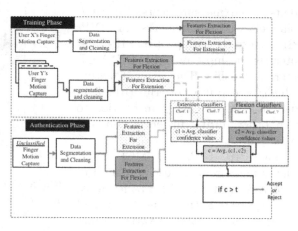

Fig. 4. Overview of our authentication approach.

extension, we extract a total of 116 features from the motion-capture of the fingers. Once the features are extracted, in order to build an authentication model, we train a *personalized model* for each subject in our dataset. We take the features extracted from the finger movements performed by a particular subject during the training phase as positive class feature points for the subject's personalized model. We then use the features from finger movements performed by all other subjects in our dataset during the training phase as negative class points for the personalized model. These negative class feature points simulate the condition when someone other than the subject, i.e., an adversary, tries to authenticate as the subject. We use both the negative and positive class points for training a machine-learning classifier that acts as the authentication model.

During training we have many more negative feature points than positive feature points. Therefore, we create an ensemble of several classifiers for our authentication model. This is needed to make sure the model does not get biased by the majority class during training. Therefore, instead of one classifier we use a group of 7 classifiers (as we have seven times as many negative feature points than positive feature points), each classifier uses all the positive feature points but using only 1/7th of the negative feature points, which are randomly selected without replacement. Since flexion and extension are two separate types of movements, whose features have different underlying characteristics, we build a total of 14 classifiers (7 that use flexion features and 7 that use extension features). Each of our 14 classifiers outputs a confidence value that describes how confident the classifier is that a new feature point belongs to the subject (whose model is being used). These confidence values from the classifiers are averaged independently for flexion and extension and then averaged again to produce a final confidence value. If this final confidence value is greater than the threshold, t, the model outputs that the new feature point belongs to the subject whose model is being used. All 14 classifiers use the same machine-learning algorithm in our setup.

Authentication Phase: Once the classifiers in the ensemble model are trained using the training data, they can be used to determine whether a new (yet unclassified) flexion and extension movement pair belongs to that subject or not. During the authentication phase, the subject is asked to flex and extend their index or middle finger once (either a coupled flexion and extension of the DIP and PIP joints or a flexion and extension of the MCP joint). The motion-capture system captures the movement and extracts two 116-dimensional features, one for flexion and one for extension. The feature from finger flexion is fed into the 7 classifier ensemble for the flexion features and the feature from finger extension is fed into the 7 classifier ensemble for the extension features. The average of the confidence values of each of these groups of classifiers are then compared against a threshold, t, as described above, to produce the final result that states whether these two new features belong to the subject or not. A diagram of our approach is illustrated in Fig. 4.

3   Experimental Setup

In this section we briefly discuss our experimental methodology to evaluate the efficacy of our authentication approach, the choice of machine-learning classifier chosen, and the customization of the feature set for each subject.

Dataset Curation: We obtained an institutional review board (IRB) approval from our university for the data collection. We then recruited eight subjects from the student population for this work. These includes 3 males and 5 females aged 22.1 ± 4.1 years (mean $\pm$ std deviation). During data collection we asked each subject to flex and extend their index and middle fingers 10 times in a *session*. We conducted our data collection over two sessions, which we refer to as **session 1** and **session 2**. Session 2 was conducted roughly 1 week after session 1, and data from all subjects were collected in both sessions. For training the models, we used the first 8 iterations of flexion and extension collected from the index and middle fingers for each subject from session 1. We refer to this subset of our dataset as the *training data*. The rest of the flexions and extensions from session 1 and all of session 2 are used to evaluate the models trained and are referred to as *test data*[2]. The use of data from two sessions allows us to evaluate the performance of our authentication model longitudinally. As the training data consists of eight iterations for IP extension, IP flexion, MCP extension, and MCP flexion collected from index and middle fingers for each subject, there are $(8 \times 4 \times 2) = 64$ movements in each subject's training set. Given the organization of our ensemble model, we split our training data into two different training groups of 32 flexion movements and 32 extension movements, each producing a positive feature point (116-dimensional feature) for our model. In addition, since each subject has their own model, all of the training data from the other subjects in the dataset is used to generate the negative feature points for that subject's authentication model. Therefore, for each subject there are a total of $32 \times 7 = 224$ flexion and 224 extension (116-dimensional) negative feature points.

Metrics: In order to evaluate the efficacy of our approach, we using two metric: receiver operating characteristic (ROC) curve and equal error rate (EER). An ROC curve plots true accept rate (TAR) vs. false accept rate (FAR) at various operating points of a classifier. The true accept rate (TAR) is the rate at which true positive feature points (i.e., points from the subject) are accepted by the model, while the false accept rate (FAR) is the rate at which true negative feature points

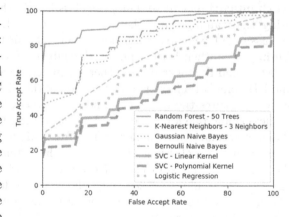

Fig. 5. ROC curves for 5-fold cross validation for various machine-learning classifiers

are accepted by the model. The EER is the rate at which the FAR and it's

---

complement false reject rate (FRR) are equal. This is a customary metric in the biometrics/authentication domain and is the point at which our model balances the accuracy of its detection with usability.

Classifier Selection: We examine several classifiers for our authentication model, by performing 5-fold cross validation on our ensemble classifier model using the training data. The classifiers that we considered are: Random Forest with 50 trees, K-nearest neighbors with k = 3, Gaussian Naive Bayes, Bernoulli Naive Bayes, Support Vector Machine (SVC) with a Linear Kernel, SVC with a polynomial kernel, and Logistic Regression. The reason we chose these classifiers is because of their simplicity and excellent tool support. Ultimately, Random Forest with 50 trees was chosen as it performed the best during cross validation. The Receiver Operating Characteristic (ROC curve) for cross validation of the classifiers can be seen in Fig. 5. An ROC curve plots TAR vs. FAR at various operating points of a classifier. The larger the area under the curve, the better the classifier's performance.

Feature Customization: Finally, as subjects are unique, systems are more effective if they are tuned to fit a particular subject [12]. As a result, we use greedy backward feature subset selection (i.e., slowly reduce the number of features used by a model until we reach about half the total number of features) in order to customize the feature set for each individual subject during the training phase. Given that we have 14 classifiers in our authentication model for a subject, we run the feature subset selection for each of the 14 random forest classifiers to produce a customized feature subset for each subject. Figure 6 shows a heat-map of how many of the classifiers, out of the 14 classifier set, for each subject contained a particular feature. The number of classifiers that choose a feature for a subject is written in the corresponding square in the heat map. Further, the larger this number, the darker its coloring. Features are ranked from left to right in descending order of the number of times they were chosen for all subjects. Only features which were chosen by at least three classifiers by every subject are shown in order to highlight the best performing features.

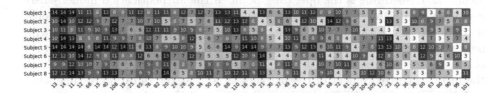

Fig. 6. Feature importance heat-map. Feature IDs align with the feature list provided at: https://tinyurl.com/ybrzx6g5.

4   Results

Once the classifiers in our model are chosen and trained, the next step is to see
how well the overall authentication model performs. In order to evaluate our
models longitudinally, we use as test data the features from finger movements
immediately after the training phase (4 flexion/extension combinations from
session 1), and from finger movements collected approximately a week later (at
least 8 flexion/extension combinations from session 2). For session 2, we had
to place the markers on the subject's fingers a second time. However, we did
not precisely place the markers in the exact same location as during the training
phase. This allows us to evaluate the performance of our model in a more realistic
setting, longitudinally.

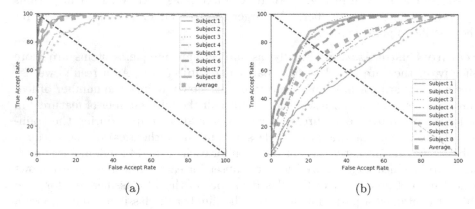

(a)   (b)

Fig. 7. ROC curves for (a) session 1 (immediately after training) of test features for
all subjects, (b) session 2 (∼1 week later) of test features for all subjects.

Figure 7(a) shows the performance in session 1 of our models, using the ROC
curve, broken down by subject performance. The point where the ROC curve
meets the dashed line is the operating point of the authentication model where
it reaches EER (lowest error). It can be seen that the accuracy is above the 80%
mark, approaching the dashed line for even the worst performing subjects, with
near-perfect performance on some subject models. The authentication accuracy
is lower in session 2 compared to session 1 as seen in Fig. 7(b). This is due to both
the inconsistent placement of the markers as well as the duration of time since
training. The average EER rates for session 1 was 6.3% and session 2 was 16.7%.
Even though we present the results in terms of EER, the advantage of showing
the ROC curves is that we can see what happens if we optimize the thresholds
to shift the balance to favor false acceptance or false rejection, depending on
the needs of the system being deployed. In many cases it could be argued that
we minimize false accepts at all costs while tolerating higher false rejects (i.e.,
entrance to a secure facility), while for others we do the opposite (i.e., entrance
to a commercial building).

Given these results, we then evaluated which of the two movement types we used in this work (i.e., coupled PIP-DIP flexion/extension or MCP flexion/extension) worked better during the authentication phase. Figure 8(a) shows the result in the form of the ROC curve. It can be seen that the overall difference between the two types of movement was largely nonexistent, with MCP flexion/extension performed better than coupled PIP-DIP flexion/extension immediately after training, while the latter performed better longitudinally. We also evaluated which of our two fingers was better in the authentication phase, given the trained models. As can be seen from the average ROC curves over all subjects in Fig. 8(b), the movement of the middle finger seems better at identifying a subject than the index finger.

However, overall it is clear that the motion-capture of finger movement and using fingers to capture the biomechanics of finger movements have the potential to uniquely identify an individual over time. Furthermore, the ability of the approach to authenticate based off of unseen test data shows that the system is effective even over natural variation in joint angles and motions during repetition. In the future, we plan to use larger datasets to explore these results in more detail, develop methods to reduce the longitudinal error rate of the authentication models, and explore methods for identifying joint centers and angles *without the use* of adhesive markers.

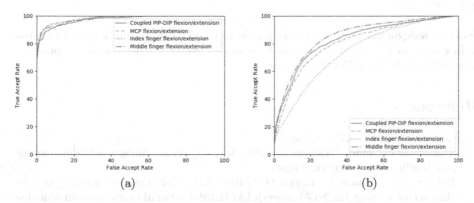

Fig. 8. Average ROC curve over all subjects for PIP-DIP and MCP flexion/extension, and index finger movement and middle finger movement for: (a) session 1 and (b) session 2.

5   Related Work

There has been a wide variety of interest in finger related biometrics in recent years. This includes biometrics based on: keyboard dynamics [10], in-air signatures [3], gestures [13], knuckle pattern [4], and fingerprint [8]. However, all of these approaches look at either the hand itself or focus on actions performed by the hand when accomplishing a particular task. They do not focus on the movement characteristics of the individual fingers, which, as we have shown, are themselves unique. In [11] the authors utilize a joint angle monitoring glove to measure joint angle changes while a person manipulates an object as a way to identify a subject. Compared to all of these approaches our work operates based on the biomechanics of the fingers by applying just the movement of the fingers without the use of any props.

6 Conclusion

In this paper we presented a novel authentication system based on biometrics derived from the biomechanics of fingers using a marker-based motion-capture system. Specifically, we focused on the flexion and extension movements of the index and middle fingers. We built personalized authentication models for subjects using goniometric and dermatologic features extracted via motion-capture and evaluated their performance longitudinally. This is a preliminary work intended to show the viability of this approach. In the future, we plan to extend this work in several ways: (1) deploying this system for visually impaired subjects with different finger sizes, genders, and age groups; (2) perform more stringent security analysis where adversaries try to copy a victim's finger movement; and (3) explore marker-less methods for capturing finger movement for authentication.

Acknowledgments. The authors would like to thank Tess Meier who helped with the data collection for this work. This work is supported by the defense health program grant DHP W81XWH-15-C-0030.

References

1. Opitrack. http://optitrack.com/
2. The Braille Literacy Crisis in America. https://nfb.org/images/nfb/documents/pdf/braille_literacy_report_web.pdf
3. Behera, S.K., Kumar, P., Dogra, D.P., Roy, P.P.: Fast signature spotting in continuous air writing. In: 2017 Fifteenth IAPR International Conference on Machine Vision Applications (MVA), pp. 314–317. IEEE (2017)
4. Choraś, M., Kozik, R.: Contactless palmprint and knuckle biometrics for mobile devices. Pattern Anal. Appl. **15**(1), 73–85 (2012)
5. Gamage, N., Kuang, Y.C., Akmeliawati, R., Demidenko, S.: Gaussian process dynamical models for hand gesture interpretation in sign language. Pattern Recogn. Lett. **32**(15), 2009–2014 (2011)
6. Gupta, P., Gupta, P.: Multi-biometric authentication system using slap fingerprints, palm dorsal vein and hand geometry. IEEE Trans. Ind. Electron., 1 (2018)
7. Lee, T.: Biometrics and disability rights: legal compliance in biometric identification programs. J. Law Technol. Policy **2016**(2), 209–244 (2016)
8. Marasco, E., Ross, A.: A survey on antispoofing schemes for fingerprint recognition systems. ACM Comput. Surv. (CSUR) **47**(2), 28 (2015)

9. Tagkalakis, F., Vlachakis, D., Megalooikonomou, V., Skodras, A.: A novel approach to finger vein authentication. In: 2017 IEEE 14th International Symposium on Biomedical Imaging (ISBI 2017), pp. 659–662 (2017)
10. Teh, P.S., Teoh, A.B.J., Yue, S.: A survey of keystroke dynamics biometrics. Sci. World J. **2013** (2013)
11. Vogiannou, A., Moustakas, K., Tzovaras, D., Strintzis, M.G.: A first approach to contact-based biometrics for user authentication. In: Tistarelli, M., Nixon, M.S. (eds.) ICB 2009. LNCS, vol. 5558, pp. 838–846. Springer, Heidelberg (2009). https://doi.org/10.1007/978-3-642-01793-3_85
12. Wobbrock, J.O., Kane, S.K., Gajos, K.Z., Harada, S., Froehlich, J.: Ability-based design: concept, principles and examples. ACM Trans. Accessible Comput. (TAC-CESS) **3**(3), 9 (2011)
13. Wu, J., Christianson, J., Konrad, J., Ishwar, P.: Leveraging shape and depth in user authentication from in-air hand gestures. In: 2015 IEEE International Conference on Image Processing (ICIP), pp. 3195–3199. IEEE (2015)

Specific Document Sign Location Detection Based on Point Matching and Clustering

Huaixin Xiong$^{(\boxtimes)}$

RICOH Software Research Center Beijing Co., Ltd., Beijing, China
huaixin.xiong@srcb.ricoh.com

Abstract. In this paper we describe a method for specific document sign location detection based on key point grouping correspondence. The proposed method extracts stable points determined only by each contour shape as key points, match point pairs based on contour Fourier shape descriptor; clusters point pairs into different scale level set and finally detects sign location by finding projective matrix in each point pairs set. The contribution of this paper includes 1. a novel concept of key point and its extraction method, 2. a clustering operation for grouping point pairs. 3. a fuzzy DBSCAN processing which response to the constraints of maximum clustering radius. The experimental results show that our method is effective way to process printing/scanning document sign detection, both in recall rate and in speed.

Keywords: Document sign location detection · Fourier descriptors
Key point · Clustering

1 Introduction

The document sign is refer to those specific graphs described by shape, color or symbols in a printed/scanned document (Fig. 1), such as a logo, or document stamp e.g. "copy prohibited". It plays important roles in document intelligent filing, removal of signs and security warning. More and more intelligent terminals pay attention to the sign detection before next smart processing for various propose.

Given two images, the reference image (document sign without any deformation) and the test image (scanned image), the task of sign detection is to determine whether the test image contains the reference sign and find a transformation to map the reference image to the best possible spatial correspondence in test image.

After document printing/scanning, the sign graph usually experiences scaling, rotation, translation transformation and a litter of deformation or pollution. The standard approach for matching local regions is to cut out patches and compare them with reference image. The SIFT [1]/SURF [2] descriptor and LBP [3] descriptor are widely used to describe local texture for establishing the correspondence of key points [4–6]. However local textures are easily affected by printing/scanning, the point texture matching sometimes falls into local similarity, and the time consumption is heavy for real time detection. Beside texture, contour shape, as an important distinguishing feature, is also widely adopted in object recognition [7]. The method [8] calculates the translation and rotation parameters by Iterative Closest Point (ICP) based on the most

© Springer Nature Switzerland AG 2018
G. Bebis et al. (Eds.): ISVC 2018, LNCS 11241, pp. 180–190, 2018.
https://doi.org/10.1007/978-3-030-03801-4_17

Fig. 1. Examples of document sign

similar edge shape. And other methods [9] give target region proposals and compare each region with reference image to determine its position and size, however it can't directly process rotation case.

In this paper, we propose a robust document sign detection algorithm for printing/scanning process which can be divided into 3 stages, (1) sign representation (2) sign discovery and (3) sign location. Firstly, closed curves and its key points are extracted, each contour is described by Fourier shape descriptor and the reference sign is represented as the set of those points and contour shapes. Then, the correspondence of similar shapes between two images is established based on shape matching, and after scale clustering, the correlation of those shape pairs in one cluster represent the possible existence of a potential sign object. Since all shape pairs can be converted to the key point correspondence directly, thus, a proper transformation matrix can be derived from each potential sign object. By verifying the target region under the projective mapping, the document sign location in target image is finally determined.

The rest of the paper is organized as follows: In the next section, all details related with sign representation are presented. Section 3 introduces the sign finding process, including shape matching and fuzzy clustering. Section 4 gives the calculation of sign location transformation matrix and its verification. Section 5 presents the experimental result and finally conclusion is given in Sect. 6.

2 Document Sign Representation

2.1 Overview

As an artificial graph, the most significant feature for document sign is shape line and the internal boundary formed by different color regions, which will not disappear or be altered due to printing/scanning or color distortion. Each contour shape can be considered as a component that makes up the entire sign graph, and its correlation of components is constrained by each key point. Thus the document sign can be represented as one set of key points and contour shapes.

2.2 Key Point Definition

In prior art, key point (Harris or SIFT/SURF) usually is "physical" pixel associated with its local neighborhood. Most of them are based on local gradient or based on a comparison of the pixels in the surrounding neighbors in current image and in the scales above and below. To ensure its uniqueness and robustness, multi-scale processing (Image Pyramids or Mean Pyramids) is needed in the extraction of key points.

Different with prior art, the key point in this method is defined as a special "virtual" position which is unique for a given contour shape, and also it is invariant for rotation and scaling. Each key point is only determined by a given contour shape and each contour shape can have several key points for different key point definitions, such as the center position of the smallest circle that surrounds a shape edge, or the centroid point of a shape, the centroid of an outer convex contour, etc. Both of them are stable even when the shape experiences rotating, scaling and shifting, the relative position of them will not change. This makes the key point in proposed method have the uniqueness of the usual key point. It should be noted that some special key points are associated only with special shapes, and not all shapes have the same number of key points.

2.3   Key Point Extraction

The key point is determined only by shape, so its extraction is converted to component shape extraction according its definition.

Shapes in this method include not only the various closed contours, but also the internal boundary formed by different color regions. One simple method for shape extraction is to find all internal and external contours in monochrome which is obtained using color segmenting followed by image binarization. Another method is utilized CANNY edge detection algorithm followed by edge link step [10] to obtain closed lines. Usually the small size shape is abandoned for acceleration due to its weak shape retention at the pixel level after scaling, rotating and blurring.

2.4   Key Point Descriptor Generation

As a "virtual" point the key point in proposed method has any pixel and texture characteristics like LBP or SIFT/SURF, but it is associated with the only shape, thus the shape feature can be treated as its description.

The normalized Fourier descriptor [11] is used for shape descriptor. A closed edge composed of N points (x, y) can be defined as a discrete complex function $z(n)$

$$z(n) = x(n) + iy(n), \quad \text{where the } n = 0, 1, 2, \ldots, N - 1.$$

Its discrete Fourier Transformation (DFT) for $z(n)$ is given by

$$a(v) = F(z(n)) = \frac{1}{N} \sum_{n=0}^{N-1} z(n) exp^{-2\pi nv/N},$$

$$\text{where the } v = 0, 1, 2, \ldots, N - 1$$

And the normalized Fourier descriptor of $a(v)$ is defined as

$$b(v) = \frac{\|a(v)\|}{\|a(1)\|}$$

Here $a(v)$ is Fourier coefficients and operator $\|.\|$ is the magnitude of $a(v)$. According to the properties of $a(v)$, the normalized FD $b(v)$ is invariant to translation, rotation and scaling.

The low frequency components of $a(v)$ describe the general shape and the high frequency components contain finer details. An approximate reconstruction of $z(n)$ can be expressed as below.

$$z'(n) = \sum_{v=0}^{M-1} a(v) exp^{2\pi n v/N}$$

Where the $M \leq N$, if the M equal to N, there is no any loss for reconstruction. Figure 2 shows an original sign and its reconstruction image with 30 low frequency coefficients from 256 point for each contour.

Fig. 2. An example of logo shape reconstruction from FD coefficients

The normalized FD is scaling-invariant, while each component shape of document sign are of different sizes, thus a 3-tuple feature $Sz(sz_1, sz_2, sz_3)$ is supplied to describe each shape size, Here the component sz_1 is the length of contours shape, sz_2 is the radius of outer circle of contours and sz_3 is the area of contours shape.

3 Document Sign Discovery

3.1 Overview

In proposed method, the target sign graph is decomposed into components, so a sign discovery can be carried out by following three steps: 1. the single component finding step which is archived by shape matching, 2. the potential target sign finding step base on the aggregation of components which is archived by clustering technique. 3. The target sign verification step to confirm each candidate. The step 3 is related with sign location so it will be given in next section.

3.2   Shape Similarity Matching

Given 2 detected contour C_i, and C_j from reference and test image respectively, their shape similarity $D(i,j)$ can be calculated through a weighted Euclidean distance between their normalized FDs defined as below:

$$D(i,j) = \sqrt{\begin{array}{l} \displaystyle\sum_{k=0}^{(M-1)/2} W(k) * \big(b_i(k+2) - b_j(k+2)\big)^2 \\ + \displaystyle\sum_{k=(M-1)/2}^{M-1} W(k) * \big(b_i(N-k-1) - b_j(N-k-1)\big)^2 \end{array}}$$

Where b_i b_j is FDs for contours C_i and C_j, 'M' is numbers of FD, and 'N' is total numbers of sampled point, the weighted coefficient $W(k)$ is defined as

$$W(k) = \begin{cases} \frac{M}{2} - k, & \text{if } k < M/2 \\ k - \frac{M}{2}, & \text{if } k \geq M/2 \end{cases}$$

Since the low frequency FD means more important roles in general shape description, so a big weight value is given to it for shape similarity calculation.

Compared with a given threshold value, all similar shape pairs can be found, each shape pairs represent a correspondence of two similar components independent of its location and size from reference and target image respectively.

3.3   Shape Pairs Clustering in Scale Space

The individual components shape matching does not take into account the differences in location and size, Not all matched shape are true part of an document sign instance in target image. To discover a potential target sign better, it is need to aggregate those truly related components from matched shape pairs, which is archived by an unsupervised clustering technique in scale space.

Firstly a $S(s_1, s_2, s_3)$ is derived to describe scale of each matched shape pair, which is defined as a ratio of the corresponding components of two 3-tuple Sz:

$$s_k = sz_k(CS_i)/sz_k(CT_j),$$

Where CS_i is i-th reference shape, CT_j is the j-th shape from target image. The vector S is corresponding to a point in 3-D scale space.

Although a sign graph in target image has different size from referent image, the S should keep similar for each matched components, in a word, all 3-D point S belong to a certain sign graph should come from the same distribution. The clustering is try to aggregate those matched shapes with the same distribution of S, make the members in a cluster more approximate to the requirements of a potential sign, so that the sign object can be found better.

In this proposed method DBSCAN (Density-Based Spatial Clustering of Applications with Noise) [12] is adopted to implement scale unsupervised clustering. Given a set of points S_k, DBSCAN groups together points that are closely packed together (points with many nearby neighbors), marking as outliers points that lie alone in low-density regions (whose nearest neighbors are too far away). It can be abstracted into the following 3 steps: 1. Find the ε neighbors of every point, and identify the core points with more than *minPts* neighbors. 2. Find the connected components of core points on the neighbor graph, ignoring all non-core points. 3. Assign each non-core point to a nearby cluster if the cluster is an ε neighbor, otherwise assign it to noise.

After DBSCAN clustering, all points S_k are assigned to different cluster. If a cluster point number is less than 4, the cluster and its member will be removed as noise. Figure 3 shows an example of logo shape pairs grouping process and result.

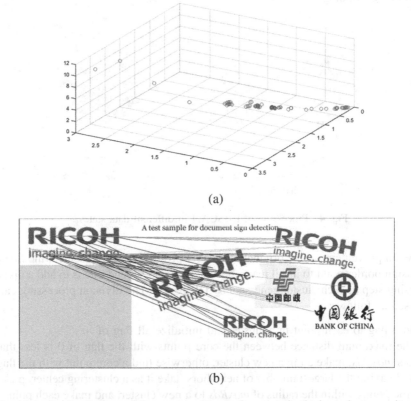

(a)

(b)

Fig. 3. (a) is the distribution of S corresponding to the example (b) in scale space, it can be clustered into 4 clusters, and those large discrete points are removed as noise. (b) shows the grouping correspondence of matched shape pair after scale clustering, the point pairs connected by the same color line are from the same cluster respectively (totally 4 color)

3.4 A Fuzzy Unsupervised Clustering Processing

Affected by shape edge pixel extraction error at different resolution, the S_k for all components which make up a sign is not a constant but is from an approximate joint

Gauss distribution. When there is a small overlap between two close Gauss as shown in Fig. 4(a), the overlap part corresponds to the non-core point (border point) in DBSCAN, it will be assigned to either Gauss, depending on the order the data are processed; When two Gauss are close together shown in Fig. 4(b), it is hard to make a distinction between each in DBSCAN which treat all reachable core points as one cluster. The lack of constraints on the clustering radius allows it to find arbitrarily shaped clusters, however it expands the clustering range, and contradicts the original intention of scale clustering in this proposed method that is to aggregate components around a certain scale level. To overcome above shortcomings, we improve the original DBSCAN algorithm by adding a parameter $maxRds$ to limit the maximum radius of clustering, make it have the ability of fuzzy processing, which can be better used in document sign finding.

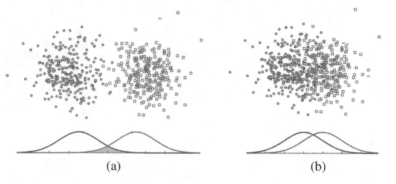

(a)   (b)

Fig. 4. Processing of DBSCAN in different data states.

Two improvements to the original DBSCAN processing are presented, the first one is to assign border point to its all reachable clusters, and second one is to add a division processing step to each cluster generated by DBSCAN. The division processing can be expressed as follows:

1. Add a flag to each point in a cluster and initialize all flag of '0'.
2. If the maximum distance between the core points with the flag of 0 is less than 2 times $maxRds$, make all in a new cluster, otherwise find a core point with the flag of 0 and having the largest number of neighbors, take it as a clustering center, pick out all the points within the radius of $maxRds$ to a new cluster, and make each point flag increased by 1 in new cluster.
3. Repeat the step 2 till any core point with the flag of 0 is processed.
4. Find the max flag and pick out all core points with the max flag (flag > 1) to make up a new point set, and find a core point with max neighbors from the new set, take it as a clustering center, pick out all the points within the radius of $maxRds$ to a new cluster, and make each point flag with 1 in new cluster.
5. Repeat the step 4 until all point flag is 1. Output all new clusters as new clustering result.

Due to the fuzzy processing in improved DBSCAN, one point can be assigned to more than one cluster. Although the final cluster number is increased, but the complexity of the member in each cluster is decreased, which is more convenient for the discovery of a single sign object.

4 Document Sign Location

4.1 Overview

In proposed method, component shapes matching and scale clustering is eventually converted to grouping corresponding between the key points from reference image and target image. Based on point pairs in a cluster, a transformation hypothesis can be given conveniently, so the location assumptions for potential targets are obtained accordingly. By verifying the consistency between candidate target graph and reference graph, the final location of document sign can be determined.

4.2 Perspective Projection and Location Hypothesis

The reference image of document sign is a rectangle, usually it appears in in the target image accompanied by rotation, scaling, translation and a small deformation, which forms a perspective projection transformation between the reference image and the target location. The transformation can be described by a 3x3 perspective projection matrix H.

$$(x, y, w) = (X, Y, 1) * H \tag{1}$$

$$x' = \frac{x}{w}, \quad y' = \frac{y}{w}$$

Here (X, Y) is the coordinates of the point in reference image, and (x', y') is its corresponding projection point in target image. The transformation matrix H can be computed by solving a series of linear equations derived from the four point-pairs using LU decomposition.

In this proposed method, 4 point-pairs are randomly picked out from one cluster to estimate its transformation and RANSAC (Random sample consensus) scheme [13] is applied to find a best matrix H for each cluster. Through removing all inliers (key point-pairs matched with H), we can continue estimate next H in rest of point-pairs.

Each matrix H represents a possible projective mapping, according to the Eq. (1), the location hypothesis for one potential document sign in target image can be getting by inputting 4 corner points of reference image.

4.3 Target Location Verifying

Based on the correspondence of key points, the location hypothesis for document sign in target image are put forward. Through verifying hypothesis, the final position for document sign in target image can be confirmed.

Some heuristic rules about target region can be used for primary judgment, for example, whether the shape of the target region is convex, whether the center point and the centroid point is close enough, and whether the area of target region is consistent with the scale information during components clustering.

Besides, the image HASH technique [14] can be applied for verifying, thus, the target region is cut out from target image, zoomed to a fixed small size, and the Hash value is extracted from it. Two hash values are compared to decide whether they are similar or not. In addition, the Siamese network [15] based on machine learning also can be used for similarity judgment of two images.

If a hypothesis has passed the verification, the region associated with the hypothesis is identified as a location of the document sign in target image. After removing the same location result or refining the similar results (due to the reason of the adoption of fuzzy clustering in object finding phase), the finial detection result can be output.

5   Experiments

To evaluate the performance of proposed method, we set up an image data set that consisted of 28 reference images and 120 test images. The 28 reference images are selected from internet, which are logo or stamp of document. The test images are divided into two groups, one containing 124 sign objects in 60 images which are generated by geometric transformation from the corresponding reference image, and the other containing 85 sign objects in 60 images which are get from a variety of printed documents through scanning, e.g. the business forms and the business cards. All test images are cut to 1000×1000 sizes

We also implemented other 2 methods based on SIFT/SURF descriptor extraction and matching techniques provided in OpenCV respectively, and then compared their accuracy against our method (PMSC). The IOU (Intersection over Union) metric is set to evaluate the detection accuracy which is defined as the ratio of overlapping region to joint region. If an IOU value for the ground-truth region and detected region both defined by 4 points is great than 0.8, the detection result is considered as a correct. Table 1 shows the experiment results, and Fig. 5 gives some example of detection result.

Table 1. Document sign location detection results.

	Group 1 (30 images, 124 signs)			Group 2 (60 scanned images, 85 signs)		
	Recall	Precision	Time (ms)	Recall	Precision	Time (ms)
SIFT	91.1%	86.9%	915	84.7%	85.7%	1231
SURF	68.5%	84.2%	725	58.8%	83.3%	816
PMSC	96.0%	90.1%	101	92.9%	84.7%	234

Fig. 5. Examples of detection result.

Since the 3 methods have shared the same process for perspective calculation and result verification except key point extraction and matching, so the precision is similar, and their performance differences are mainly reflected in the recall rate and time consumption, especially when the test objects are in different groups.

Test images in group 2 are scanned from real materials, its text, form and noise are more than group 1, which is the main reason for the decrease in the recall rate compared with the group 1 results. Due to the number of contours detected is more than group 1, the processing time of our method has increased largely. However, the results of the comprehensive experiment shows the presented algorithm provides stable detection results at low computational cost (five times shorter than that by SIFT), and it is more robust to printing/scanning.

6   Conclusion and Future Work

In this paper, we have proposed a document sign detection method based on key point grouping correspondence. Different with prior art, the key point in this method is not a physical pixel, but a special position associated with a specific component shape, accordingly, the correspondence of points is converted to component shape matching, and the point grouping is converted to component clustering in scale space. Shape is a stable feature to describe document sign and Fourier descriptors is powerful tool for shape describing. So their combination makes the correspondence of key point more robust and correct, therefore, it can achieve better results in document sign detection, especially for printing/scanning. Besides, most operations are not on time-consuming pixel level except contour extraction, so it is faster than SIFT/SURF method.

The component shape is a kind of middle level feature, the number of component usually is much smaller than the number of key points in other methods. When the number of matching components is less than the minimum number of projection transformations required,or all the matching key points are on the same line, for example, by removing the below text "imagine change" from the Ricoh logo (Fig. 2), the location will fail, that is a shortage compared to the SIFT/SURF methods. Thus, how to utilize the features of the shape itself in image alignment, or how to combine with local texture feature to strengthen its matching ability, is next research direction. Besides, in an intelligent terminal system in which multiple reference images are stored in advance, how to optimize the algorithm to further improve the detection response speed is also the main task for future work.

References

1. Lowe, D.: Distinctive image features from scale-invariant keypoints. Int. J. Comput. Vision **60**, 91–110 (2004)
2. Bay, H., et al.: Speeded-up robust features (SURF). Comput. Vis. Image Underst. **110**(3), 346–359 (2008)
3. Ojala, T., et al.: Multi resolution gray scale and rotation invariant texture classification with local binary patterns. IEEE Trans. PAMI **24**, 971–987 (2002)
4. Kabbai, L.: Image matching based on LBP and SIFT descriptor. In: IEEE 12th International Multi-Conference on Systems, Signals & Devices (SSD15) (2015)
5. Jiang, P.: Rotational invariant LBP-SURF for fast and robust image matching. In: 9th International Conference on Signal Processing and Communication Systems (ICSPCS) (2015)
6. Piccinini, P.: Real-time object detection and localization with SIFT-based clustering. Image Vis. Comput. **30**(8), 573–587 (2012)
7. Belongie, S., et al.: Shape matching and object recognition using shape contexts. IEEE Trans. Pattern Anal. Mach. Intell. **24**(4), 509–522 (2002)
8. Duan, W., et al.: Automatic object and image alignment using Fourier descriptors. Image Vis. Comput. Arch. **26**(9), 1196–1206 (2008)
9. Girshick, R., et al.: Rich feature hierarchies for accurate object detection and semantic segmentation. In: Computer Vision and Pattern Recognition (CVPR) (2014)
10. Ghita, O., et al.: Computational approach for edge linking. J. Electron. Imaging **11**(4), 479–485 (2002)
11. Zhang, D., Lu, G.: A comparison of shape retrieval using Fourier descriptors and short-time Fourier descriptors. In: Shum, H.-Y., Liao, M., Chang, S.-F. (eds.) PCM 2001. LNCS, vol. 2195, pp. 855–860. Springer, Heidelberg (2001). https://doi.org/10.1007/3-540-45453-5_111
12. Wikipedia Homepage. https://en.wikipedia.org/wiki/DBSCAN. Accessed 03 July 2018
13. Wikipedia Homepage. https://en.wikipedia.org/wiki/Random_sample_consensus. Accessed 03 July 2018
14. Weng, L., et al.: Shape-based features for image hashing. In: Proceedings of IEEE International Conference on Multimedia and Exposition (2009)
15. Melekhov, I.: Siamese network features for image matching. In: 23rd International Conference on Pattern Recognition (ICPR) (2016)

Virtual Reality I

Training in Virtual Environments for Hybrid Power Plant

Max G. Chiluisa$^{(\boxtimes)}$, Rubén D. Mullo, and Víctor H. Andaluz

Universidad de las Fuerzas Armadas ESPE, Sangolquí, Ecuador
{mgchiluisa, rdmullo, vhandaluz1}@espe.edu.ec

Abstract. This article describes a Virtual Environments application of a Hybrid Power Plant, for professionals in Electrical Power Systems training. The application is developed in the Game Engine Unity 3D and features three different modes as: immersion, interaction and failure modes, which enhance professional's skills through visualization of the plant components and different processes operation. Additionally, failure mode is proposed, it simulates wrong maneuvers consequences and effects. The Generation Environment is integrated by wind turbines and photovoltaic panels that interact through a mathematical model and enables manipulation of dependent variables bringing out a more realistic background.

Keywords: Virtual reality training · Hybrid power plant · Mathematical model
Game engine unity 3D · Immersive and interactive environments

1 Introduction

In recent years, technology has shown great interest in improving methods and skills in training processes in different areas such as education, medicine and especially in industrial processes, thus allowing an increasement in operators and instrumentalist's experience at work [1, 2]. The industrial technology has incorporated simulators and programming languages to represent and emulate the operation of different processes in real time, due to the fact that operation maintenance and maneuvers require meaningful resources, it is important to mention that by associating these technological tools with the different engineering branches, great advantages are obtained, *e.g.,* in Electromechanical Engineering, it allows to have a constant calibrations maintenance and electrical and mechanical components adjustments, where the main responsible is the operator at performing these procedures [3, 4]. On the other hand, Electric Power Systems are permanently delivering energy and require constant monitoring of the Generation and Transmission System, *i.e.,* their maintenance is essential and the maneuvers performed are dangerous [5, 6]. Although computational technologies are found in all engineering branches, lately it has grown significantly in renewable energies field, the main objective of it, is helping the designer in planning and impact assessment processes of wind and solar power plants [7, 8].

One of the computer technologies developed in recent years is virtual environments training, this tool leads the future of learning processes in education and professional fields, making a turn into traditional classroom-based method with exclusively

© Springer Nature Switzerland AG 2018
G. Bebis et al. (Eds.): ISVC 2018, LNCS 11241, pp. 193–204, 2018.
https://doi.org/10.1007/978-3-030-03801-4_18

theoretical learning and the limited availability of laboratories for practices and training due to different factors such as time, infrastructure, costs and other resources. Simulation software used in information technology and computing allow students and professionals to infer the problem in any experiment performed on a computer [9]. These immersive technologies are being used to undergo into new methods of training in engineering subjects, allowing the identification, analysis and diagnosis of failures that take place among man-machine interaction [10]. It is important to mention that Virtual Reality as a learning tool has two key concepts, immersion and interaction. There are several immersion software's, which help motivating learning and encourage interest in this type of teaching tool where visualization equipment and graphic software converge; while in the field of virtual interaction there is a certain difficulty, due to the complexity of developing them, in having complete dynamic control of all the components that intervene in their environment [11, 12].

The contribution generated by Virtual Reality in teaching and learning in all of engineering fields and especially in Electrical Power Systems, has allowed a strengthening in practice, due to the complexity and danger of real electrical equipment, Therefore, the performance of all these virtual maneuver tests represents a great advantage, allowing professionals to improve the operation protocols and constant maintenance of the electrical and mechanical installations [13]. Studies related above have proposed several applications of Virtual Immersion in EPS, such is the case, Barreto *et al.* Implements a methodology to create virtual scenes of electrical substations, which allows the acquisition of 3D models to improve communication between the operating room and the field [6]. Galván *et al.* Poses an application for the training of operators in underground electrical distribution lines, this system incorporates different maintenance and operation maneuvers for medium and low voltage underground distribution networks [14]. Barata *et al.* Incorporates a transformer testing system using a virtual reality application for maintenance and operations procedure for optimum performance [15]. The virtual applications mentioned above provide great advantages, however, there are some cons, because the user only has the feeling of being inside this environment, but not of being able to interact with it. Virtual reality has the advantage of being safe, controllable, less expensive and improves learning and training outcomes [16, 17].

This paper features the development of a VR application where students and professionals can be trained in Hybrid Generation Systems, ensuring a correct analysis and diagnosis of it, *i.e.,* can be trained not only in an immersive environment but can also interact with the different components of the application. In order to have a better dynamic interaction with the energy variables involved in the Hybrid Power Plant, a mathematical model of a wind turbine and a photovoltaic panel is determined. In addition, a substation is interlinked to the Generation Plant, which raises the voltage level for subsequent transmission systems, where it is possible to observe and interact with all the major components of the application, *e.g.;* instrument transformer, bus bars, circuit breakers, break switches, relays and the power transformer as a fundamental element of a substation. Additionally, it is possible to carry out all the operation protocols, observe the failures and destruction effects that the whole system can present due to bad maneuvers.

2 Problem Formulation

Nowadays, the teaching methods implemented in professional training in the area of Electrical Power Systems have certain limitations, because they do not provide adequate techniques to improve the skills of the operator. Many of these methods have been innovated by means of graphic simulators, notably replacing traditional and classical teaching such as 2D diagrams and plans. Therefore, in order to reduce risks, prevent damage to equipment and specially to involved personnel, the aim is to improve training through an application of a 3D virtual immersion and interaction environment, providing the professional the ability to analyze and make correct decisions in operation and maintenance procedures.

As described above, this work poses the development of a virtual reality application for the training of a Hybrid Generation Plant interlinked to an Elevation Substation. The application presents three training modalities: (*i*) *Presentation*, in this scene you will be able to visualize and monitor all the components of this application, such as, electrical substation, wind turbines, solar panels and control rooms; (*ii*) *Interaction*, in this mode, the operator will be trained by performing guided maneuvers through operating instructions within an electrical substation; (*iii*) *Failure Modes*, in this space there are failures shown in different stages of the generation process, where the damages that can be caused can be observed. To achieve immersion and interaction, a virtual reality helmet and haptic input controls are used to interact with the environment; In addition, a control system for the generation stage is developed using a mathematical model of a wind turbine and a photovoltaic panel. The link between these input devices and the control system will respond to the actions performed by the user through the virtual environment developed in the Game Engine Unity 3D.

The Fig. 1 presents the component interrelation diagram, the first phase contains the *Game Objects* required for the virtual appliance, where the interaction methods are linked to the *Grab Object Controller* to manipulate and verify the behavior of all 3D models in the virtual environment. In this phase, energy variables are used to simulate a generation process identical to a real one.

In the *Input* and *Output* phase many devices that allow immersion and interaction are considered with the virtual environment, e.g. virtual reality helmet types (*HTC VIVE* and *Gear VR*) and haptic input controls. This application has a universal code with different inputs and outputs, which allow to automatically detect the devices and their compatibility with various platforms, avoiding errors and project reconstructions.

The *Scripts Module* is responsible for managing communication between input, output and control block devices through the *APP Manager*, providing an efficient functionality of the virtual environment. The user will be able to select the virtual training mode through the user interface providing a dive (technical observation of the system) or interaction (operation and failure modes), where the *Grab Object Controller* will allow manipulation of the virtual environment components and the location within the Power Generation System. In addition, this application has a Multiuser Support allowing the interaction of several users in the application at the same time.

The *Mathematical Software Module* poses a modeling system for a wind turbine and a photovoltaic panel, in this process the input variables of wind and solar

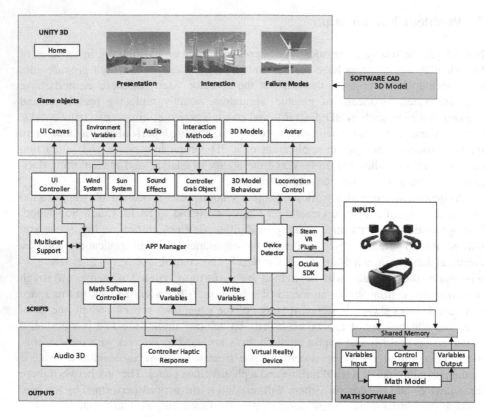

Fig. 1. Component interrelation diagram

irradiation originated in the Game Engine Unity 3D are directly linked to the modeling process through mathematical formulations and relationships between operating variables. Output energy variables such as power, voltage, current, rotor speed return to the virtual application through a shared memory, with the aim of visualizing and monitoring the generation system for better immersion and interaction.

Finally, the *Output Module* provides the user a real feeling through total immersive audio, a haptic response system to the inputs to increase the level of interaction and tracking of user movements within the virtual environment.

3   Virtual Interaction and Immersion

A Virtual Reality application must integrate aspects that, mixed together, allow users a complete immersion and interaction in a virtual environment. The virtual application is developed in Fig. 2.

Fig. 2. VR. Application developed in the Game Engine Unity 3D

To develop and perform this work, a multi-layer scheme that considers different types of blocks is proposed in Fig. 3.

Layer 1 is the first phase of the virtualization model, here a CAD software; SOLIDWORKS is being used, these design tool allows an integrated work flow that evolves creation steps, importing of parts, assembly and validation of all 3D parts that conform this virtual application, e.g., mechanical parts of the wind turbines, photovoltaic panels, electromechanical components of the substation, control room, and the entire hybrid generation plant, within others, as shown in Fig. 4. At the end of this phase every part needs to be saved or exported with a *.IGS extension which is compatible with 3DS MAX, software required for next phase of virtualization.

Layer 2. In this phase 3D models are imported and developed in the CAD software 3DS MAX, model parts hierarchy is defined, these are arranged according to the assembly, the number of elements, and positioning and movement restrictions of every single part. It also allows orientating and location of the parts of the model through reference parts (Pivot Points). Finally, a *.FBX file is obtained which is totally compatible with the Game Engine Unity 3D where de application will be developed.

Layer 3. In the third phase a platform will be developed where the simulation of virtual 3D will be performed being this Game Engine Unity 3D. In this application the scenes of different virtualization and training are built. The configuration of entries for interaction of mobile items which build the 3D model and input devices such as HTC VIVE and Gear VR that allow an interface between the user and the virtual application, it is developed using the OnTriggerEnter, OnTriggerStay, OnTriggerExit functions. For manipulation of mobile device and the Trigger or Grop, emphasizing the collider for object movements. The user in the virtual environment can transfer to a desired point in the surface, by pointing towards the reference point where it wants to locate, this by the implementation of teleportation.

Sublayer 3.1. This scene proposes a virtual interaction with photovoltaic panels and wind turbine environments with GamesObjects (Wind and Solar Zone).

Wind Zone, allows having a wind zone to interact directly with the blades of the wind turbine movements in a realistic mode, simulating primary wind generation conditions.

Solar Zone, the created environment for photovoltaic panels, has the solar light intensity, generating variables with irradiance characteristics and direction, causing a better sense of realism in the environment, as well as having the possibility to simulate

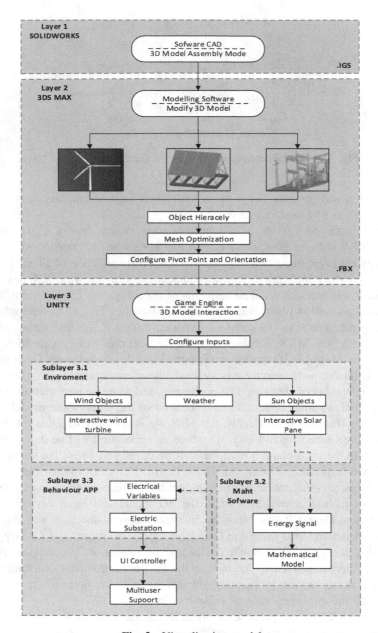

Fig. 3. Virtualization model

world places with weather conditions and interpret generation data according to geographic location.

Sublayer 3.2. The mathematic modeling is essential in the application, this allows having a better interaction with the electric generating objects which are wind turbines

Fig. 4. Electrical Substation developed in SolidWorks

and photovoltaic panels, improving its operation performance, based on an interactive variable from Game Engine Unity 3D, MATLAB and Simulink.

The wind turbine modeling as shown in Fig. 5 is provided directly from *Math-Works Simulink*. This is a high-level visual programing method tool, that works under MATLAB software, due to it, simulates physics, mathematic, hydraulic, and other systems in real time.

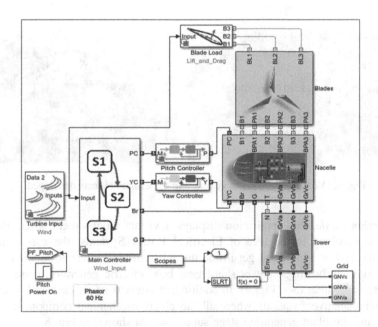

Fig. 5. Mathematical model of the wind turbine

Sublayer 3.3. This layer represents the electrical dependent variables obtained from the mathematical models and the independent variables involved in each of them. The data is obtained in the control room for its operation, monitoring and verifying its variation according to weather conditions for electric generation. Once this process is accomplished, transmission of electric energy is required through an elevation single bus bar substation. The training process in these electrical transformation centers is important because there is a lack of accessibility and several safety protocols, so the user can interact and activate the elements that are part of the substation, assuming safety and operation parameters, as well as maneuvering the control room.

Finally, the virtual environment has a multi-user interface, which allows several people to be connected at the same time for training, with an application with three modes: presentation, interaction and failure modes.

4   Results and Discussion

In this section, the virtual simulation environment of a Power Plant System is displayed (wind turbine, photovoltaic panels and electrical substation). The user can interact in a dynamic mode with the different elements and devices of the system as shown in Fig. 6.

Fig. 6. Virtual environment system and experimental tests developed

Immersion Mode, this application displays a virtual environment where the professional is involved in the area of Electrical Power Systems, the user is able to visualize the power wind plant get inside the wind turbine tower to identify interior elements, such as bearings, power shaft, gear box, electric generator, control panel, anemometer and other (See Fig. 7). In addition, it consists of an electrical substation, control and maneuvers stations where all the electromechanical components can be inspected and the plant generation stage supervised as shown in Fig. 8.

Interactive Mode, this method is important in the development of the application, the user will be able to interact directly with the parts and components of the virtual environment. It will be able to carry out maneuvering protocols in the entire substation under the respective safety standards. A comparison is made between the classical method and our virtual application in the Fig. 9. It can be appreciated that the training

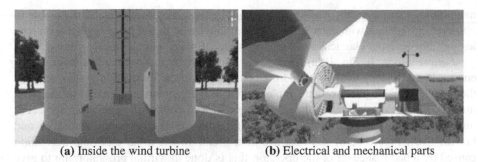

(a) Inside the wind turbine   **(b)** Electrical and mechanical parts

Fig. 7. Immersion in the wind turbine

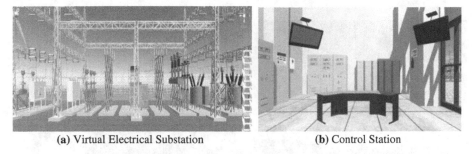

(a) Virtual Electrical Substation   **(b)** Control Station

Fig. 8. Supervision and maneuvering of the Power Plant

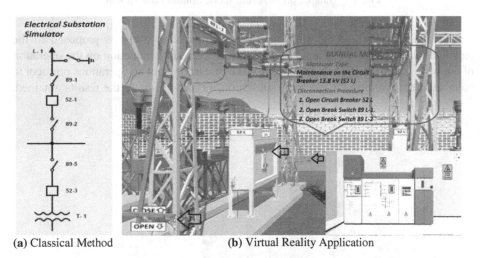

(a) Classical Method   **(b)** Virtual Reality Application

Fig. 9. Training methods

methodology surpasses the traditional method, because the professional will be able to observe and interact with each of the elements involved in the process of maneuvers, leaving obsolete the classical method consisting of plans and electrical symbols.

Failure Mode, In Fig. 10(a). It shows a wind turbine that suffered an overload of energy in the system, this originated the combustion of the lubrication system and fire the nacelle. This disturbance was implemented in the mathematical model of the wind turbine, specifically in the regulator, forcing it not to control the energy in the accumulators, which later led to an inevitable fire, thus losing economic resources and human lives. Figure 10(b) shows a fire of a break switch in an electrical substation caused by a bad maneuver of the operator, this is done by virtual programming to give the corresponding graphic and sound realism at the time of causing a fire and explosion.

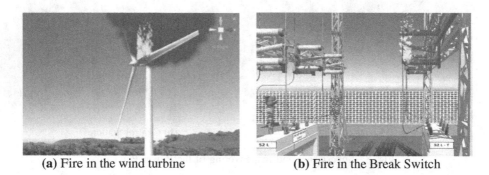

(a) Fire in the wind turbine   **(b)** Fire in the Break Switch

Fig. 10. Simulation of failure modes in the Power Plant

Finally, to determine the efficiency of the application a test is proposed to the technical participants in this area; each of them received an induction on the operation of the two training methods, with the objective of carrying out an operations protocol to connect and disconnect the electrical substation. Figure 11 shows the results obtained.

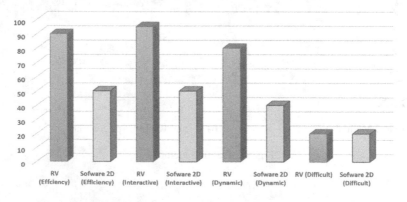

Fig. 11. Training system evaluation results

The results obtained indicate that our Virtual Application contributes with the learning and development of skills of the professional in this area, because it allows to identify and interact with all the electromechanical components of a Power Plant.

5 Conclusions

In this article, an application of virtual training in a Hybrid Power Plant is being proposed for Electrical Power Systems professionals. This virtual simulation environment is being developed in the Game Engine Unity 3D, where the user is able to have a better immersion and interaction with all the devices implemented during the learning process, optimizing economic resources, as well as infrastructure and time. The experimental results obtained show a greater efficiency of the application, developing a friendly human-machine interaction with the development of skills and strengths in the Electrical Power Systems.

Acknowledgements. The authors would like to thanks to the Corporación Ecuatoriana para el Desarrollo de la Investigación y Academia –CEDIA for the financing given to research, development, and innovation, through the CEPRA projects, especially the project CEPRA-XI-2017-06; Control Coordinado Multi-operador aplicado a un robot Manipula-dor Aéreo; also to ESPE, Universidad Técnica de Ambato, Escuela Superior Politécnica de Chimborazo, and Universidad Nacional de Chimborazo, and Grupo de Investigación en Automatización, Robótica y Siste-mas Inteligentes, GI-ARSI, for the support to develop this work.

References

1. Gyusung, L., Mija, L.: Investigation of the practical influence of the performance metrics from the virtual reality robotic surgery simulator on the skill learning and associated cognitive workloads. Accepted June (2017)
2. Andaluz, V.H., et al.: Immersive industrial process environment from a P&ID diagram. In: Bebis, G., et al. (eds.) ISVC 2016. LNCS, vol. 10072, pp. 701–712. Springer, Cham (2016). https://doi.org/10.1007/978-3-319-50835-1_633
3. Andaluz, V.H., et al.: Unity3D virtual animation of robots with coupled and uncoupled mechanism. In: De Paolis, L.T., Mongelli, A. (eds.) AVR 2016. LNCS, vol. 9768, pp. 89–101. Springer, Cham (2016). https://doi.org/10.1007/978-3-319-40621-3_6
4. Liang, H., Wen, Y., Chengzhong, H.: The platform design of practice teaching in the electromechanical major that based on the virtual reality technique. In: Du, Z. (ed.) Intelligence Computation and Evolutionary Computation. AISC, vol. 180, pp. 161–165. Springer, Heidelberg (2013). https://doi.org/10.1007/978-3-642-31656-2_23
5. Romero, G., Maroto, J., Felez, J., Cabanellas, J., Martínez, M., Carretero, A.: Virtual reality applied to a full simulator of electrical sub-stations. Electr. Power Syst. Res. **78**(3), 409–417 (2008)
6. Barreto, C., Cardoso, A., Lamounier, E., Carvalho, A., Mattioli, L.: Strategy to optimize the creation of arrangements in virtual electric power substations. In: IEEE 2017 XLIII Latin American Computer Conference (CLEI), p. 21 (2017)

7. de Sousa, M.P.A., Filho, M.R., Nunes, M.V.A., da Costa Lopes, A.: Maintenance and operation of a hydroelectric unit of energy in a power system using virtual reality. Int. J. Electr. Power Energy Syst. **32**(6), 599–606 (2010)
8. Lizcano, P.E., Manchado, C., Gomez-Jauregui, V., Otero, C.: Virtual reality to assess visual impact in wind energy projects. In: Eynard, B., Nigrelli, V., Oliveri, S., Peris-Fajarnes, G., Rizzuti, S. (eds.) Advances on Mechanics, Design Engineering and Manufacturing. LNME, pp. 717–725. Springer, Cham (2017). https://doi.org/10.1007/978-3-319-45781-9_72
9. Valdez, M.T., Ferreira, C.M., Martins, M.J.M., Barbosa, F.P.M.: Virtual labs in electrical engineering education the VEMA environment. In: IEEE 2014 Information Technology Based Higher Education and Training (ITHET), pp. 1–5 (2014)
10. Yasmín, H., Pérez, R.M.: Virtual reality systems for training improvement in electrical distribution substations. In: IEEE Third International Conference on Innovative Computing Technology (INTECH 2013), pp. 199–204, 04 November 2013
11. Kao, Y.-C., Tsai, J.-P., Cheng, H.-Y., Chao, C.-C.: Design and construction of a virtual reality wire cut electrical discharge machining system. In: International Symposium on Computer, Communication, Control and Automation (2010)
12. Enríquez, D.C., Pimentel, J.J.A., López, M.Á.H., García, O.S.N.: Uso didáctico de la Realidad Virtual Inmersiva enfocada en la inspección de Aerogeneradores, Apertura, pp. 8–23 (2017)
13. Araújo, R.T.S., Araújo, M.E.S., Medeiros, F.N.S., Oliveira, B.F.C., Araújo, N.M.S.: Interactive simulator for electric engineering training. In: IEEE, May 2016
14. Galvan-Bobadilla, I., Ayala-García, A., Rodríguez-Gallegos, E., Arroyo-Figueroa, G.: Virtual reality training system for the maintenance of underground lines in power distribution system. In: IEEE Third International Conference on Innovative Computing Technology, pp. 199–204 (2013)
15. Barata, P.N.A., Filho, M.R., Nunes, M.V.A.: Consolidating learning in power systems: virtual reality applied to the study of the operation of electric power transformers. IEEE Trans. Edu. **58**(4), 255–261 (2015)
16. Ortiz, J.S., et al.: Virtual training for industrial automation processes through pneumatic controls. In: De Paolis, L.T., Bourdot, P. (eds.) AVR 2018. LNCS, vol. 10851, pp. 516–532. Springer, Cham (2018). https://doi.org/10.1007/978-3-319-95282-6_37
17. Abulrub, A.H.G., Attridge, A.N., Williams, M.A., Virtual reality in engineering education: the future of creative learning. In: IEEE Global Engineering Education Conference, pp. 751–757 (2011)

Visualizing Viewpoint Movement on Driving by Space Information Rendering

Satoru Morita[✉]

The Graduate School of Sciences and Techonology Innovation, Yamaguchi University,
Tokiwadai 2-16-1, Ube, Japan
satoru.morita@gmail.com

Abstract. Automobiles are necessary for movement. However many people die as a result of automobile accident. Automobile accident does not decrease to at all. On the other hand, we measure a gaze point and a trial to detect person's interest is performed. The method measuring where person looks on an image is general in traditional eye movement measuring system. But we do not understand person's interest without image analysis in the traditional system. We propose the method directly calculating three dimensional position of interest object from person's eye images using virtual reality system without defining two dimensional position of interest object. We register all the candidate object with interest. We propose space information rendering technique to write in direct viewpoint information at virtual space by voting for the object when person watchs an object closely. We develop a driving simulator using virtual reality of a university neighborhood driving course. A beginner driver can know the eye movement of an expert driver by applying this proposed system for an expert driver and a beginner driver.

Keywords: Eye movement · Virtual reality · Driving

1 Introduction

Traffic accidents are more than 1,000 cases per a day while automatic driving technology progresses. There is lack of safe confirmation of a driver in a high rank of the traffic accident cause. Therefore we measure the gaze point of a driver. We try to improve driving technology and driving manner by adding it to education of driving schools. Eye trackers such as NAC and tobii measuring viewpoint movement are marketed [1–4]. When we measure viewpoint movement, the method which puts eyes on a viewpoint image is general. In this case it is difficult to identify which object you really watch without image analysis. With the rapid spread of cheap virtual reality applications, virtual reality systems are becoming more popular [5]. In using a virtual reality system comprising a viewpoint movement tracker in this paper, we propose a support system for

© Springer Nature Switzerland AG 2018
G. Bebis et al. (Eds.): ISVC 2018, LNCS 11241, pp. 205–214, 2018.
https://doi.org/10.1007/978-3-030-03801-4_19

driving. We propose a system which can observe eye movement in constant time by registering the objects which we should recognize. Though the method to put viewpoint information on an 2D image is popular, it is difficult to estimate where it is in real world from 2D image position. We do not put viewpoint information on an image in this paper, but we propose a method of how to write viewpoint information in the 3D world directly. Furthermore, we calculate the frequency that viewpoint is close to an object. We visualize viewpoint information intuitively by showing it with a color. We can display total space using the colored three plane drawing. In driving the world that was visualized, we can confirm gaze information. We show the space information visualization of viewpoint movement both before and after in Fig. 1. Whereas we see a mark as usual before the presentation, viewpoint information are shown by colored markers after the presentation. We make a virtual world course that is driveable in around 30 min of the university neighborhood, We show the effectiveness by driving this simulator.

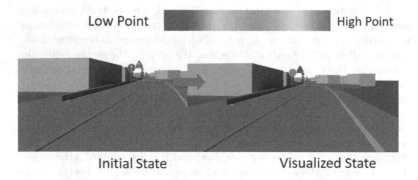

Fig. 1. Space information visualization of eye movement

2   Virtual Reality System and Eyes Movement

We show a calibration method of VR system and the basic computation method. The virtual reality system used in this paper is FOVE0 corresponding to eyes

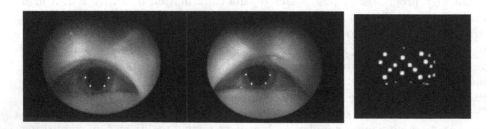

Fig. 2. (a) Eyes image (b) Position camera image

tracking. Vision field angle is $110°$, and the maximum refresh rate is $70\,Hz$. Resolution of a video panel is 2564×1440 pxel. A video panel uses organic electroluminescence.

2.1 The Necessary Condition of a VR System

- Driving with a steering wheel, brakes and accelerator.
- Reproducing the real 3D world of a specific small range
- Arranging traffic signs
- Installing traffic lights
- Existing an oncoming car and a walker
- Observing gaze points on driving after driving

We propose a system satisfying these conditions in this paper. A search coil method, a corneal reflex method, Linbus tracking method, image analyze method and EOG method [1–4] are proposed as a tracking method of viewpoint movement. Six infrared LEDs are implemented around a right and left lens by an expert skill method. The sensor which receives this red LED is implemented inside HMD. Infrared LED light which set inside HMD is irradiated to an eyeball, The red photo reflected on the retina side is received with a CMOS photo sensor installed in HMD. System calculate the position and angle of pupils from quantity information of the infrared LED light. We can presume what the drive observes from the position of two pupils. Quantity of LED light changes corresponding to position of two pupils. We calculate what the driver observes based on this information. Actually 10 points on a circle in a screen are shown for the calibration, The system calculates a position and an angle of eyes from quantity of the LED light which a CMOS photo sensor receives. Tracking of HMD correspond to six axis degree of freedom by a combination with a built-in sensor and an outside establishment sensor. Eyes tracking rate is $120\,HZ$, and Fig. 2(a) shows an image of eyes, and Fig. 2(b) shows image of a position camera.

2.2 Calculating the Rotations of Car, Head and Eye

The quaternion $P = (0; xp, yp, zp) = (0 : Vp)$ is used for composing rotation of car, head and eye. We assume a vector expressing a direction of an rotation axis as $v = (xv, yv, zv)$ and assume the rotation angle as θ. But the size of v is assumed as $|v| = 1$. We make the two quaternions Q and R from V. $Q = (cos(\frac{\theta}{2}), xv * sin(\frac{\theta}{2}), yv * sin(\frac{\theta}{2}), zv * sin(\frac{\theta}{2}))$ $R = (cos(\frac{\theta}{2}), -xv * sin(\frac{\theta}{2}), -yv * sin(\frac{\theta}{2}), -zv*sin(\frac{\theta}{2}))$ R is the conjugate quaternion of Q. A movement coordinate is $R * P * Q = (0; x, y, z)$ after a rotation. When we perform N time rotation $r_1, r_2, \cdots, r_n$ of a position vector, 1 time rotation is assumed as $r_2 = q_1 * r_1 * (q_1^*)$, 2 time rotation is assumed as $r_3 = q_2 * r_2 * (q_2^*)$, and N time rotation is assumes as $r_n = q_{N-1} * r_{N-1} * (q_{N-1}^*)$. The quaternion is $q = q_{N-1} \cdots q_2 q_1$.

If we use transform matrix without using quaternion, the 1 time rotation is assumed as $r_2 = A_1 r_1$, and the 2 time rotation is assumed as $r_3 = A_2 r_2$, and the N time rotation is assumed as $r_N = q_{N-1} * r_{N-1}$. The N time rotation is assumed as $r_N = Ar_1$ for $A = A_{N-1} \cdots A_2 A_1$. The order of products of a transform matrix is the same as the quaternion. When we perform rotation $r_1, r_2, \cdots, r_N$ of a coordinate system of a N time, the calculation become $q = q_1 q_2 \cdots q_{N-1}$ about the quaternion named $r_N = q r_1 q^*$. The calculation become $B = B_{N-1} \cdots B_2 B_1$ about a transform matrix named $r_N = Br_1$. The order of products of a transform matrix is reverse to the quaternion. We can calculate efficiently a movement vector of eyes by composing rotation of viewpoint, head and car. We register a polygon of the traffic sign which we want to recognize beforehand. We calculate the effective radius from three-dimensional central location (cx, cy, cz) and the size of an target object. We define target objects which driver must recognize for the safe driving. We register polygon of target objects with a database beforehand. And we define most proximity distance with target object center (cx, cy, cz) from eyes central location $EC = (ecx, ecy, ecz)$ and eyes vector $EV = (evx, evy, evz)$. EV vector is unit vector $EV = 1$. Furthermore, we calculate whether distance from the center is included in a traffic sign from the effective radius that we registered myself with. We divide it by the distance from the center using the effective radius. If it is less than 1, it is inside. If it is more than 1, it is outside.

Fig. 3. Virtual space on the road including traffic signs

3   Space Information Rendering of Viewpoint Movement

Methods to calculate the viewpoint using a view image are often popular by conventional technique. We propose a technique to write viewpoint information in real 3D space by saving all viewpoint information and space information in the computer. It becomes easy to confirm viewpoint information. The number that viewpoint is close to the object is recorded and the distance between viewpoint and object is recorded for every object registered with a database as the object which it should have been able to be recognized beforehand.

3.1 Collision Calculation Between Viewpoint and an Object

We reproduce the university neighborhood as the stage of a simulator. Figure 8 shows the whole of driving course overlooked from the top. The route of a course in a simulator is the order of ABC. We calculate the topography height by putting the measured topography data on map. As there are many slopes In the neighborhood of a university, a lot of incline differences are realized in this simulator. The real length 1 meter is normalized to 1. A z axial direction shows north and south. A x axial direction shows east and west. Figure 3 shows virtual space on a road with a traffic sign. We arrange 11 kinds of traffic signs as shown in Table 1 in virtual space. The alphabet show these objects in a following figure.

Table 1. Traffic signs used on the road of the virtual space

Alphabet	A	B	C
Name	Traffic light	Pedestrian traffic	No parking
Alphabet	D	E	F
Name	One way	No passing	Speed limit
Alphabet	G	H	I
Name	Train	School area	Stop
Alphabet	J	K	
Name	Parking	Car(red)	

4   Evaluation of Viewpoint Movement on Driving

4.1   Measuring the Eye Movement with a Virtual Reality System

Figure 4 shows a state at the time of driving of a proposing driving simulator. The proposing virtual reality system is composed of head mount display, handle, break, accelerator and note computer. A driver turns his face to a progress direction, and drive a car. A driver move eyes to various directions and watch a traffic sign. A driver turned eyes to all objects consciously to check whether objects reacted. The score increases if the sight line crosses to an object. Figure 8 shows a measurement result. A horizontal axis shows a traffic sign, and a vertical axis shows reactivity. The traffic sign installed 229 machine. As quantity of data is too big, the whole is divided into a 4 pieces. Figure 8 shows the 14 positions from A to N. The route composed of the route from A to E through C, the route from E to A through G, from A to J through L and from L to A trough N. A driver can drive whole experimental 3D space while memory buffer is changed for each region space because of the limitation of the memory size.

Fig. 4. Driving simulator

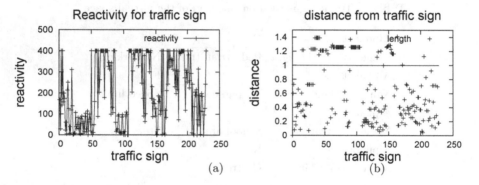

Fig. 5. (a) Points of all traffic signs (b) The difference between traffic sign and attention points

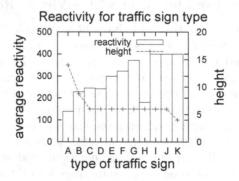

Fig. 6. Average points of traffic sign types

4.2   Analysis of a Measurement Result

Figure 5(a) shows scores of all traffic signs. Horizontal axis of graph shows traffic signs. Vertical axis of graph shows score. Figure 6 shows a average score according to a kind of a traffic sign and height from a road. Horizontal axis of graph shows type of traffic signs. Vertical axis of graph shows score. If the hight of object is high, a score tends to be low. We observe a minimum gap between a viewpoint and traffic sign. So we measure distance between a viewpoint and traffic sign in whole driving. We select minimum distance in all measured distances. An error is described as the ratio for 1 at a globe radius in Fig. 5(b) for the judgments whether he looked at the object. Traffic sign that error rate is less 1 is about 61% in all traffic signs. The average is 0.735550 and the standard deviation is 0.482295. It is found that we can detect viewpoint in 3D space. Figure 7 show the influence of road width and traffic sign arrangement. The possibility can be able to see a traffic sign is high if a driver can see only one traffic sign. The possibility can be able to see a traffic sign is low if a driver can see many traffic signs because a driver must see many traffic signs in a short time. If road width is narrow, a driver is close in distance with a traffic sign. If road width is wide, as for the driver is far in distance with a traffic sign. Therefore the possibility that a drive miss a traffic sign tends to be high. When it is a large main street of road width, as for the driver, distance with a traffic sign remotes Influence by crowd is not observed. A horizontal axis shows width, and a vertical axis shows a score in Fig. 7(b). The possibility that driver does not see a traffic sign tend to be high if road width is wide.

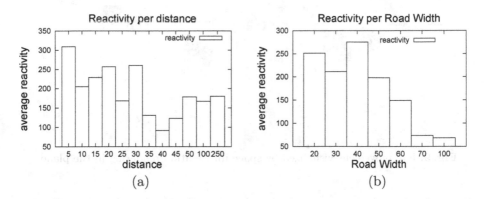

Fig. 7. Position state of traffic sign (a) The distance between neighbour traffic signs (b) road width

4.3   Visualization of Viewpoint Movement

A driver drives a course once, and the system records viewpoint information about traffic signs. The system paints over the traffic sign with a single color.

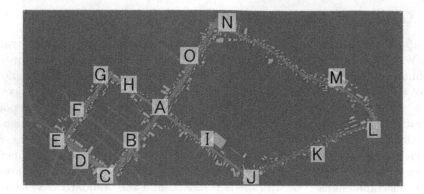

Fig. 8. Virtual space on the road in the neighbour of university

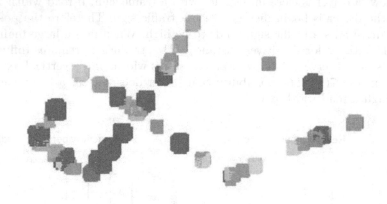

Fig. 9. Eye movement visualized by space information rendering in the plane

The traffic sign which we confirmed well is described with red. The traffic sign which a driver did not confirm very much is described with blue. We describe viewpoint information with color. Figure 9 shows visualizing of space information rendering. It is found that a driver can understands the viewpoint position clearly because it is described as colored 2D map. The color of traffic sign changed according to viewpoint information by the system, When a driver drive in a cource with changed color once again, a driver can be aware of a gaze point. Figure 10(a) shows the view that a driver at the time of a viewpoint movement measurement of EFLJKHA of Fig. 8 observes. Figure 10 shows the view that a

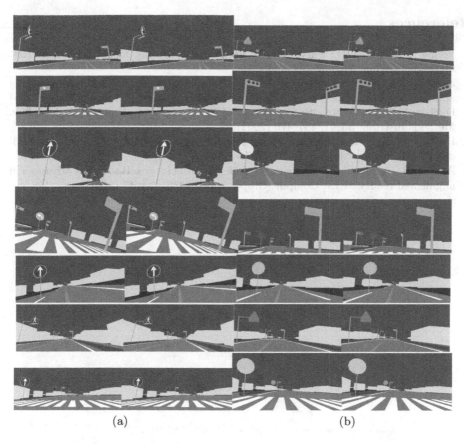

(a)   (b)

Fig. 10. (a) Observation before visualizing eye movements on EFLJKHA of Fig. 8 (b) Observation after visualizing eye movements on EFLJKHA of Fig. 8

driver observes after visualization by space information rendering of viewpoint movement of EFLJKHA of Fig. 8. A traffic sign shown in red is confirmed well, A traffic sign shown in blue is not confirmed well. A unit area of a mark of a traffic light is small. A position of a mark of a traffic light is high. It is regarded as the factor that evaluation value is lower. Figure 10(b) shows visualization of 3D of viewpoint movement by space information rendering.

5   Conclusion

We can visualize a reaction state by space information rendering technique. A driver can watch a viewpoint characteristic of himself at the time of driving. We introduce a visualization system which change the color of object according to the gaze degree of a subject. We succeeded in visualizing eye movement. A beginner driver can know the eye movement of an expert driver by applying this method for an expert driver.

References

1. Young, L., Sheena, D.: Survey of eye movement recording methods. Behav. Res. Methods Instrum. **7**(5), 397–429 (1975)
2. Jacob, R.J.K.: Eye tracking in advanced interface design. In: Virtual Environments and Advanced interface Design, vol. 7, pp. 258–291. Oxford University Press (1995)
3. Duchowski, A.T.: A breadth-first survey of eye-tracking applications. Behav. Res. Methods Instrum. **34**(4), 454–470 (2002)
4. Duchowski, A.T.: Eye Tracking Methodology: Theory and Practice. Springer, London (2003). https://doi.org/10.1007/978-1-84628-609-4
5. Azuma, R., Aaillot, Y., Begringer, R., Juiler, S., MacIntyre, B.: Recent advances in augmented reality. IEEE Comput. Graph. Appl. **21**(6), 34–47 (2001)

Virtual Reality System for Children Lower Limb Strengthening with the Use of Electromyographic Sensors

Eddie E. Galarza$^{(\boxtimes)}$, Marco Pilatasig, Eddie D. Galarza,
Victoria M. López, Pablo A. Zambrano, Jorge Buele,
and Jhon Espinoza

Universidad de las Fuerzas Armadas – ESPE, Sangolquí, Ecuador
comunicacion@espe.edu.ec

Abstract. This article presents a virtual system for children lower limb strengthening by using electromyographic sensors and the graphics motor Unity 3D. The system allows the acquisition and processing of electromyographic EMG signals through Bluetooth wireless communication which also allows to control virtual environments. Two videogames have been designed with different difficulty levels and easy execution, the interaction with the virtual environments generate muscle strengthening exercises. Moreover, five users have performed experimental tests (3 boys and 2 girls), the children are between 8 and 13 years old, the following inclusion criteria has been taken into account: users must have ages > 7 and < 14 years old and also must have any muscle affectation, additionally, the exclusion criteria is: the users who have any visual deficiency and/or several hearing impairment. Finally, users did perform the usability test SEQ with the following results (59.6 ± 0.33), which allows to know the acceptation level of the virtual system for children lower limb strengthening.

Keywords: Muscle strengthening · Virtual reality · Software unity 3D
Electromyographic sensor · SEQ

1 Introduction

Experimental outcomes determine that the adequate muscle training by using Virtual Reality can improve the walking capacity of people, especially the ones with any weakness [1, 2], additionally, training using this techniques is more effective than any other independent training [3]. One critical variable to induce plasticity of muscles for movement is that the sensory motor stimulation must be intensive, repetitive and compensated [4]. Training people with virtual reality systems produces improvements to their way of walking [5], the training also includes displacement tests which uses the knee as a fundamental element for the training results verification.

In the present, the postural alteration rates beneath the child student population has been increasing, there is not a proper Health system that allows the early detection of this anomaly [6]. In this phase of child's growth their posture suffer a lot of adaptation

© Springer Nature Switzerland AG 2018
G. Bebis et al. (Eds.): ISVC 2018, LNCS 11241, pp. 215–225, 2018.
https://doi.org/10.1007/978-3-030-03801-4_20

settings since there are a lot of body changes and also many demanding psychosocial factors.

The support and the upright walking may vary according to the load and effort, this could produce changes in the body, especially in the lower limbs and the spine [7]. It is important to determine that some alterations could show a natural improvement or an auto correction, possibly due to the psychosocial pressure of the environment surrounding the individual. This behavior is also observed in this study, where the scapula descended alterations, the front shoulder projection and the head inclination show a significant recovery without applying any muscular exercising program [8].

The muscle strengthening in children is presented specially for cases of minors with the difficulty of developing movement of their lower limbs. González-Agüero et al. [9], performs the study of the muscle mass, isometric force and the dynamics of children and teenagers lower limbs who have the Down Hosking et al. [10] syndrome, also the force measurement of the muscles and their performance in normal children and children who have muscles with diseases is performed. In [11–13] studies about muscular strengthening in children with cerebral palsy are performed. In [14, 15] it is shown virtual systems for the development of therapeutic exercises related to rehabilitation.

This work's objective is to develop a virtual system to strengthen the lower limbs of children through the usage of electromyographic sensor and the graphics motor Unity 3D. This system allows us to acquire and process the electromyographic (EMG) signals by using Bluetooth wireless communication elements to control the virtual environments. This article is divided in 5 sections, including the introduction. Section 2 presents the system's structure, Sect. 3 explains the way the virtual system is used. Section 4 show the tests and results, and finally, the conclusions and future work are presented in Sect. 5.

1.1 Strengthening Techniques for Lower Limbs

The main joints of a lower limb includes the ankle, the knee and the hip. The ankle's joint has the following movement range: dorsiflexion, plantar flexion, varus and valgus. Additionally, the knee's joint has the movement range of flexion and extension [16]. Remembering the detail of this movements is difficult for a user without medical assistance, hence, after suffering an accident or having an injury of the lower limbs it is important to perform an accurate rehabilitation with specific muscular strengthening exercises, to do this it is necessary to have a physiotherapist which has expertise with the diagnosis, prevention and treatment of the multiple pathological ailments with therapeutic techniques.

The proposed exercises to accomplish the established tasks in every videogame have been recommended by rehabilitation specialists from the IESS Hospital. Considering that children learn by playing, it was recommended to execute the following sequence of strengthening exercises which consist in performing the feet dorsiflexion and plantar flexion in an alternated and repetitive way.

1.2 Electromygraphic Sensors

Virtual interactions like picking up and dodging objects, are defined by the level of the required muscular activity [17]. Our emphasis uses electromyographic (EMG) signals that filter and measure every electric impulse generated by the muscle and also produces a rectified and amplified analogic signal that can be easily read by a microcontroller to be interpreted within an order.

The EMG are acquired over the muscle skin through surface electrodes, thus, it is a non-invasive method which shows important characteristics like the muscular effort [18]. This sensor provide an operation voltage of 2.9 to 5.7 volts and an adjustable gain, also, the have an inverse polarity protection and indicative LEDs which are activated when they detect any change in the muscular activity.

2 Structure of the System

The proposed system is comfortable, secure and easy to use, besides it also entertains the user when performing the strengthening exercises. Figure 1 shows each essential stage of the interactive process between the user and the virtual environments.

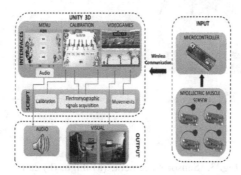

Fig. 1. Structure of the system

2.1 Signal Acquisition and Communication

The electromyographic sensors are in charge of detecting the EMG signals generated by the thigh and calf muscles from the lower limbs. The signals work through the measurement of the muscle activity which is produced by the muscular fiber cells when the individual is in repose or during the exercise; these are controlled by a Micro Arduino device.

To place the sensors over the skin of each muscle, it is used adhesive electrodes that are connected to the sensor through brooches, this electrodes are easy to place and provide good contact with the skin, additionally, two electrodes are used for signal acquisition and the third is used as neutral or for reference. According to the recommendations given by the European Concerted Action Surface EMG for non-invasive assessment of muscles, the measurements for the diameter of an electrode should be less or equal to 10 mm and the separation between both electrodes should be less or equal to 30 mm [19] as shown in Fig. 2.

Fig. 2. Electrodes measurements

In Fig. 3, it can be observed how the sensors must be correctly placed, if the sensors are placed wrong, then the EMG signals could be altered and there should be a low signal quality.

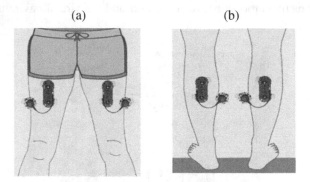

Fig. 3. Sensor placement: (a) thigh; (b) calf.

The electromyographic signals which are produced by the muscles are conditioned and sent via wireless to the computer. In the graphics motor Unity 3D, the signals are received and interpreted through control scripts and comparison algorithms, that is to say, the user controls the object movement in a virtual environment through the contraction of determined muscles.

The Bluetooth technology let the two devices to connect and interchange information in real time and via wireless, they eliminate the disorder and confusion that cables could bring.

3 Script Development

In this section, it is explained the development of every different control script, that is to say, how this plane text files manage the information obtained with the sensors, after the interpretation is done, the users finally make the interaction with the virtual environment. Figure 4 details how are the communication scripts linked with the reading and control so the user could control the object displacement within the virtual reality environment.

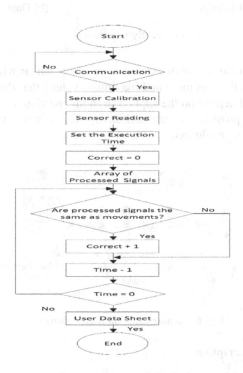

Fig. 4. System flowchart

3.1 Virtual Environment Design

Using the graphics motor Unity 3D there were created virtual reality environments by combining software and hardware in order to provide interaction between the real world and the virtual world. The designed videogames are focused in the repetition concept, ergo, the proposed activities are routed to the enrichment, recovery and compensation of the lower limb abilities and functions which are limited or deficient (Fig. 5).

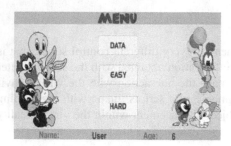

(a)   Menu Interface   (b) Data interface

Fig. 5. System menus

The virtual system has an environment where every sensor will be calibrated (see Fig. 6), that is to say, the minimum and maximum values that the user generates are measured and this will depend on the applied strength and also the physical conditions that the lower limbs provide. Getting and saving the starting data of each user is important to evaluate its evolution.

Fig. 6. Sensor calibration environment

3.2   Videogame Description

There are two levels of difficulty for the videogames, the easy level presents a soccer videogame where the user must catch the soccer balls, the screen show the execution time as well as the caught balls, this is shown in Fig. 7a.

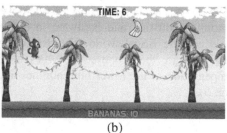

(a)   (b)

Fig. 7. (a) Easy level, (b) Hard level

The hard level has a virtual jungle environment where a running monkey eats bananas, also, like the easy level it has the execution time and the number of bananas that the monkey has caught or eaten, this could be seen in Fig. 7b.

To bring more realism, the two games have sounds that will be launched with every success, also when finishing the games, the system gives important data about the user that will be analyzed by the treating doctor to evaluate their progress.

3.3 Usage Mode of the Virtual System

To correctly use the system, the user must wear a holding belt and also he must clean the chosen area of the thigh and the calf of every lower limb where the sensors are going to be placed. Figure 8 presents a flow diagram of the execution beneath the virtual system.

To correctly use the system, the user must wear a holding belt and also he must clean the chosen area of the thigh and the calf of every lower limb where the sensors are going to be placed. Figure 8 presents a flow diagram of the execution beneath the virtual system.

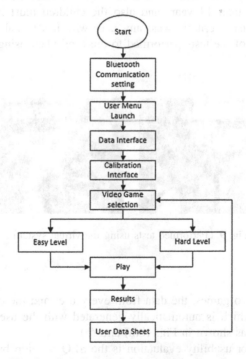

Fig. 8. Flow diagram of the system execution.

In the developed environments, first, the required data is entered, then every sensor is calibrated in order to obtain the starting movements value in every lower limb of the user.

In the first videogame the extended legs should be flexed alternately to the maximum that the user can and repetitively. In the second videogame the user must dorsiflexion and plantar flex the feet alternately and repetitively.

For this system, the therapist is the one in charge of adjusting the exercising time as well as supervising them for every videogame. When every videogame is finished, the system will give a data sheet with the number of success for every user, this is done in order to have a controlled follow-up; additionally, the system has visual and audible feedback thought to improve the concentration and learning process.

4 Tests and Results

4.1 Tests

In order to determine the implemented system's usability, the system was tested with 5 users (3 boys and 2 girls) with ages between 8 and 13 years, the users have been explained about the developed virtual system's operation, next, they finish the designed videogames with the described movements in Sect. 3 and finally they fill the SEQ questionnaire. The following inclusion criteria was used: Children who were older than 7 years and younger than 14 years and also the children must have any muscular affectation. The exclusion criteria was: any user who has visual or audible illness. Figure 9 show many of the tests performed to the user when using the virtual reality system.

Fig. 9. Performed tests using the virtual system

4.2 Results

When finishing the two games, the data from every user and the obtained values are saved in a text file which is automatically generated with the user's name that performed the exercises as shown in Fig. 10(a) and (b).

The chosen test for usability evaluation is the SEQ develop by Gil-Gómez et al. [20], it has 14 questions, which 13 of them has the values of 1 to 5 points according to the following schema: The first seven questions (Q1–Q7) are related to the acceptation level and the immersion after the user experienced the virtual system. The following four questions (Q8–Q11) are linked to the effects and discomfort that the system could cause like: nauseas, disorientation or eye discomfort; the next two questions are related

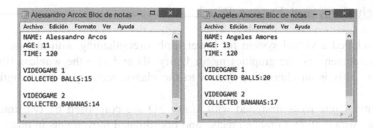

Fig. 10. User data files.

to the difficulty of performing the tests, finally the last question is open so the user could indicate if there is any discomfort when using the virtual system and its reasons.

If the obtained result is in the range of 40–65, the implemented system is considered as acceptable. The questions asked to the users about the virtual system and the results of the usability questionnaire SEQ are shown in Table 1.

Table 1. SEQ results

Question	Result (N = 5)	
	Mean	SD
1. How much did you enjoy your experience With the system?	3.8	0.75
2. How much did you sense to be in the environment of the system?	3.6	0.8
3. How successful were you in the system?	4.8	0.4
4. To what extent were you able to control the system?	3.8	0.75
5. How real is the virtual environment of the system?	4.8	0.4
6. Is the information provided by the system clear?	5.0	0
7. Did you feel discomfort during your experience with the system?	1.0	0
8. Did you experience dizziness or nausea during your practice with the system?	1.0	0
9. Did you experience eye discomfort during your practice with system?	1.2	0.4
10. Did you feel confused or disoriented during your experience with the system?	1.2	0.4
11. Do you think that this system will be helpful for your rehabilitation?	5.0	0
12. Did you find the task difficult?	1.8	0.4
13. Did you find the devices of the system difficult to use?	1.0	0
Global score (total)	59.6	0.33

The results for the SEQ test performed by 5 users after using the virtual system is: (59.6. ± 0.33). The obtained results are greater than 40, hence, it shows that the virtual system has good acceptance for the muscular strengthening of lower limbs.

5 Conclusions and Future Work

It was developed a virtual system for lower limb strengthening with the use of electromyographic sensors, the graphics motor Unity 3D and also the wireless Bluetooth technology. This is an alternative system to the classic techniques to strengthen the muscles.

The virtual interfaces designed with Unity 3D are composed by two interactive videogames which allow to make precise and coordinated movements in order to help the muscular strengthening. Also, the system has visual and audible feedback which allows a cognitive development in the users.

The obtained outcomes when using the SEQ test show that system has good acceptance to be used in the lower limb strengthening, this is because users enjoy the videogames, they don't have discomfort and they have little difficulty to use the system.

As future work it is thought to design a control system which will acquire and process the electromyographic signals to be used in the valuation of researches affecting the nervous system, as well as the muscle studies.

References

1. Bryanton, A., Bosse, J., Brien, M., Mclean, J., McCormick, A., Sveistrup, H.: Feasibility, motivation, and selective motor control: virtual reality compared to conventional home exercise in children with cerebral palsy. Cyberpsychol. Behav. **9**(2), 123–128 (2006)
2. Jang, S.H., et al.: Cortical reorganization and associated functional motor recovery after virtual reality in patients with chronic stroke. Arch. Phys. Med. Rehabil. **86**, 2218–2223 (2005)
3. Mirelman, A., Bonato, P., Deutsch, J.: Effects of training with a robot-virtual reality system compared with a robot alone on the gait of individuals after stroke. Stroke **40**(1), 169–174 (2009)
4. Cecatto, R.B., Chadi, G.: The importance of neuronal stimulation in central nervous system plasticity and neurorehabilitation strategies. Funct. Neurol. **22**(3), 137 (2007)
5. Deutsch, J.E., Merians, A.S., Adamovich, S., Poizner, H., Burdea, G.C.: Development and application of virtual reality technology to improve hand use and gait of individuals post-stroke. Restor. Neurol Neurosci. **22**, 371–386 (2004)
6. Penha, P., Amado Joao, S., Casarotto, R., Amino, C., Penteado, D.: Postural assessment of girls between 7 and 10 years of age. Clinics **60**(1), 9–16 (2005)
7. Baumgarter, R., Stinus, H.: Tratamiento ortésico del pie. Mason, Barcelona (1997)
8. Espinoza-Navarro, O., Valle, S., Berrios, G., Horta, J., Rodríguez, H., Rodríguez, M.: Prevalencia de alteraciones posturales en niños de Arica-Chile. Efectos de un programa de mejoramiento de la postura. Int. J. Morphol. **27**(1), 25–30 (2009)
9. González-Agüero, A., Villarroya, M.A., Rodríguez, G., Casajús, J.A.: Masa muscular, fuerza isométrica y dinámica en las extremidades inferiores de niños y adolescentes con síndrome de Down. Biomecánica **17**(2), 46–51 (2009)
10. Hosking, J.P., Bhat, U.S., Dubowitz, V., Edwards, R.H.: Measurements of muscle strength and performance in children with normal and diseased muscle. Arch. Dis. Child. **51**(12), 957–963 (1976)

11. Eek, M.N., Beckung, E.: Walking ability is related to muscle strength in children with cerebral palsy. Gait Posture **28**(3), 366–371 (2008)
12. Crompton, J., Galea, M.P., Phillips, B.: Hand-held dynamometry for muscle strength measurement in children with cerebral palsy. Dev. Med. Child Neurol. **49**(2), 106–111 (2007)
13. Vrijens, J.: Muscle strength development in the pre-and post-pubescent age. In: Pediatric Work Physiology, vol. 11, pp. 152–158. Karger Publishers, Berlin (1978)
14. Pruna, E., et al.: VRAndroid system based on cognitive therapeutic exercises for stroke patients. In: Rocha, Á., Correia, A.M., Adeli, H., Reis, L.P., Costanzo, S. (eds.) WorldCIST 2017. AISC, vol. 570, pp. 657–663. Springer, Cham (2017). https://doi.org/10.1007/978-3-319-56538-5_67
15. Pruna, E., et al.: 3D virtual system trough 3 space Mocap sensors for lower limb rehabilitation. In: De Paolis, L.T., Bourdot, P., Mongelli, A. (eds.) AVR 2017. LNCS, vol. 10325, pp. 119–128. Springer, Cham (2017). https://doi.org/10.1007/978-3-319-60928-7_10
16. Yeh, S.-C., Chang, S.-M., Chen, S.-Y., Hwang, W.-Y., Huang, T.-C., Tsai, T.-L.: A lower limb fracture postoperative-guided interactive rehabilitation training system and its effectiveness analysis. In: 2012 IEEE 14th International Conference on e-Health Networking, Applications and Services (Healthcom), Beijing, China, pp. 149–154. IEEE, Washington (2012). ISBN: 978-1-4577-2039-0
17. Ponto, K., Kimmel, R., Kohlmann, J., Bartholomew, A., Radwir, R.G.: Virtual exertions: a user interface combining visual information, kinesthetics and biofeedback for virtual object manipulation. In: 2012 IEEE Symposium on 3D User Interfaces (3DUI), March 4–5 2012, Costa Mesa, CA, USA, pp. 85–88. IEEE, Washington (2012). ISBN: 978-1-4673-1204-2
18. Jayarathne, M., Wickramanayake, D., Afsheenjinan, A., Ranaweera, R., Weerasingha, V.: EMG based biofeedback system using a virtual reality method. In: IEEE 10th ICIIS, Peradeniya, Sri Lanka, pp. 111–116. IEEE, Washington (2015). ISBN: 978-1-5090-1741-6
19. Merlo, A., Campanini, I.: Technical aspect of surface electromyography for clinicians. Open Rehabil. J. **3**, 100–106 (2010)
20. Gil-Gómez J.A., Lozano-Quilis, J.A., Manzano-Hernández, P., Albiol-Pérez, S., Aula-Valero, C.: SEQ: suitability evaluation questionnaire for virtual rehabilitation systems. application in a virtual rehabilitation system for balance rehabilitation. In: 2013 7th International Conference on Pervasive Computing Technologies for Healthcare and Workshops, Venice, Italy, pp. 335–338. IEEE, Washington (2013). ISBN: 978-1-4799-0296-5

A Comparative Study of Virtual UI
for Risk Assessment and Evaluation

Naila Bushra[1(✉)], Daniel Carruth[2], and Shuchisnigdha Deb[2]

[1] Department of CSE, Mississippi State University, Starkville, MS 39759, USA
nb921@msstate.edu
[2] Center for Advanced Vehicular Systems, Starkville, MS 39762, USA
{dwc2,deb}@cavs.msstate.edu

Abstract. The simulation of a real-life environment in VR greatly
reduces the time and cost to perform experiments. A useful application
of Virtual Reality (VR) can be training employees and measuring their
performances before their assignment in the real work environment. For
this study, an experimental environment was created using VR to represent a machine shop in an industrial manufacturing facility. The VR
provided with a safe environment for trainees to correctly identify hazards associated with each machine. A comparative study was conducted
to evaluate two different ways a trainee can interact with the training system within the VR environment. Participants in the study were
asked to perform training tasks with both user interfaces and complete
user experience and usability questionnaires. The evaluation of interfaces
played an important role in the design and selection of a useful mode of
interaction within the VR environment.

Keywords: Virtual-reality · Graphical-user-interface
Human-performance · VRTK

1 Introduction

Advances in technology have greatly enhanced the quality of life by helping people perform tasks in large volumes and do calculations within seconds. Virtual
Reality (VR) is one of the most important emerging technologies that has lead
scientific research method to a new dimension. VR allows users to inhabit a simulated real-world environment using a head-mounted display (HMD). There are
extended activities that can be performed within the VR environment through
the use of controllers or haptic systems. This VR technology can be used to
execute a broad range of real-life activities such as entertainment, education,
training, medical procedures, physical activities, and so on.

There are many costs associated with performing practical experiments:
experimental setup, replication of trials, change in scenarios, time and labor
cost, surveillance control factors, etc. VR environment can eliminate most of
these costs by providing a flexible mean for modification in scenarios and trials

© Springer Nature Switzerland AG 2018
G. Bebis et al. (Eds.): ISVC 2018, LNCS 11241, pp. 226–236, 2018.
https://doi.org/10.1007/978-3-030-03801-4_21

[5,14,15]. VR not only provides a three-dimensional (3D) environment but also the opportunity to interact with the objects to improve decision-making from both qualitative and quantitative perspectives [4]. Therefore, a useful application of Virtual Reality (VR) environment can be training employees to measure their performances before they are engaged in the real work environment [12,17]. This implementation can be more crucial when the actual work environment involves several risks and hazards. However, designing a proper training interface in a virtual training environment is challenging considering trainees' first-time exposure, experience level with the training module, and comfort with VR.

2   Related Work

Interface design in VR depends on users' mental representation of the environment and realistic interaction with it. The challenge is to ensure that all VR components function similarly to the way the user would interact with the real world. Interaction modes should be selected based on the spatial movement requirements and task-types a user needs to perform in the VE. For risk assessment training using a VR environment, trainees require to select objects and enter data for hazard related surveys. Therefore, to make their interaction easy and realistic with virtual objects, the interface should be familiar, user-friendly, and easy to use. Trainees should feel comfortable enough to select an object, respond to the surveys based on their selection, make changes in their responses, and have the ability to skip, retry, go back, and exit the survey anytime they want.

Previous studies have considered different interfaces types to input and output information. In order to support symbolic interaction in a three-dimensional (3D) VR environment, input devices use voice commands, gestural commands, gaze, or menus floating in space while output devices use mostly visual, auditory, and haptic cues [18,19]. Floating menu resembles a desktop screen or projector from the real world. In the virtual world, users require to use their fingers or some laser pointers, attached to the physical controllers of the VR system to interact with these floating menus. Schultheis et al. [16] reported that two-handed 3D interfaces to manipulate objects within the VR environment were considered natural and intuitive. In the real world, the user directly interacts with a physical object. Nevertheless, direct interaction is not possible in the virtual environment. In addition, the indirect interaction in VR takes much higher cognition levels and concentration to complete a task, which can eventually cause severe simulation sickness [7]. Having a VR interface similar to the real-world setting can reduce the cognition demands [7].

Literature shows different virtual windows types for 3D manipulation. Feiner et al. proposed 3 different windows types: surround-fixed windows (a fixed position interface in the VE that does not move with users' movement), view-fixed window (windows move along with the user as they look around within the VE), object-fixed window (window is fixed, relative to a specific object in the VE. If the object moves, the window moves along with it) [8]. Without a physical support for manipulation, these windows provide limited user precision. Also, if the floating menu moves with the user, it blocks their view for the part of the environment. On the other hand, a menu, fixed at one position, would increase user head movements. To counter these problems, the researchers have introduced the 'pen-and-tablet' interfaces [2,9]. With this approach, users can hold an object-fixed window in their non-dominant hand and interact with it using a finger from their dominant hand. These interfaces combine the use of a two-dimensional window interface with the necessary freedom provided by 3D manipulations. These hand-held windows are always within reach, move along with the user, and do not obstruct the user's view.

In our experiment, we have built a VR environment representing a machine shop in an industrial manufacturing facility. The employees, especially the new hires, at the facility need to be trained and evaluated on their ability to identify different types of work hazards associated with the tools and machines. The purpose of the VR environment we have created is to provide a safe environment for the workers where they will be trained to identify the hazards associated with the tools and machines. In this particular study, we have built two different graphical user interfaces (GUI) as input and output modes for the purpose of interaction in the training system. These are: (1) a floating menu interface controlled by pointers triggered using controllers and (2) a tablet interface controlled by touch with the virtual index finger. The project's scope was to compare the usability of these two user interfaces (UI) in a virtual reality (VR) environment. The participants of the study interacted separately with the two different user interfaces in the VR environment and filled out surveys afterward, reflecting on their experience with these user interfaces. Comparison and analysis have been performed on the collected feedback of the participants. The goal of this study was to analyze the survey results to understand how these interfaces can most effectively be designed to enhance user performance in training and evaluation.

3   Developed Virtual Reality Environment

3.1   VR Environment

We have developed a VR environment that represents a machine shop in an industrial manufacturing facility. Several machines and hand tools (drilling machine, toolbox, hammer, wrench, screwdriver etc.) were placed on the machine shop shelves, tables, and floor, within the environment.

3.2   Tools

Hardware. For this study, we used the Oculus Rift which comes with an Oculus Headset (HMD), left and right touch controllers, and two motion sensors. Using this VR hardware connected to a device which supports the VR application, i.e. a computer with enough memory and enhanced graphics cards, users can visualize and interact with the VR environment.

Software. We used Unity3D (version 2017.1.1f1), a very popular tool to build VR environments, to develop the virtual machine shop environment. The built-in models help to create a quick prototype of the intended environment. Unity 3D makes an asset store available that has thousands of free or purchasable assets that can be easily integrated with the environment that is being developed. Unity3D supports several virtual reality SDK packages that can be downloaded and used for various VR hardware types. Additionally, there are a lot of other tool-kits to build applications that can be run using any hardware. VRTK [1] is the toolkit we used for building our environment. It supports all major VR hardware and provides easy-to-use scripts. The VRTK toolkit also provides cross-platform open-source support for user interaction in VR.

4   Experimental Procedures

The Institutional Review Board of Mississippi State University reviewed and approved the protocol used in the study. The purpose of this proposed study was to investigate participants' perceptions of two different user interfaces (UI) for interacting with a virtual environment. These user interfaces were displayed to the participants as menus with which they interacted. Participant's interaction with the virtual environment was recorded using Camtasia. After completion of the interaction, participants filled out surveys. The survey results, as well as objective measures of the average interaction time required to complete the defined tasks, were used to evaluate the two interfaces in terms of usability and navigation measures.

4.1   Participants

Thirteen participants were recruited from the Starkville Mississippi area. Participants provided consent before participation. The participants, aged 18–60 years, were fluent English speakers, had normal vision, either naturally or with glasses or contact lenses, and had the physical ability to work in a machine shop environment. Participants who had limitations (such as tremors) that restrict their ability to hold and touch controllers to correctly point to objects, buttons, checkbox etc. were excluded from the study. For these people, it would be difficult and sometimes impossible to interact with the interface. Language efficiency and normal vision are necessary in order to interpret the interface contents and instructions correctly and perform tasks accordingly. The experiment took around 30 min to complete and participants were compensated with $10 for their time and participation. Table 1 presents an overview of the demographic information of the participants.

4.2   Experimental Setup

The experiment was performed in the Human Performance Lab at the Center for Advanced Vehicular Systems, Starkville, Mississippi (CAVS). This experiment

Table 1. Participant information for the VR interface comparison study.

Participants (n = 13)	Statistics (Proportions)
Previous experience with VR	Experienced: 76.9% | Not experienced: 23.1%
Gender	Male: 46.2% | Female: 53.8%
Age	18-24: 7.7% | 24-34: 15.4% | 34-44: 76.9%
Level of education	Bachelor's degree: 38.5% | Master's degree: 61.5%
Experience with digital UI	2 or less: 15.4% | 2-5: 7.7% | 5-10: 30.8% | 10 or more: 46.1%
Daily usage of digital user interfaces (Cell phone/tablet/computer)	Less than 2: 7.7% | 2-5: 7.7% | More than 5: 84.6%

did not require much movement from the participant around the VR environment; however, the lab had ample spaces to move freely around the environment after we set up the Oculus VR hardware. Two Oculus motion sensors were placed facing the participants' standing position. The Oculus headset and the touch controller were placed on a table, along with the computer that ran the experimental VR environment.

4.3   Study Design

The study was divided into 3 parts. The first part was a 'practice' session where the participants were asked to wear the headsets and use the touch controller to familiarize themselves with the VR environment and the general method for interacting with the components within the environment. The practice session took around 5 min to complete. In the second and third parts, they experienced two different interfaces: the floating menu and the tablet. The interfaces were randomly assigned; 7 participants used the floating menu as their first interface while the remaining 6 participants used the tablet as their first interface; afterwards, they switched. Each of these interactions lasted approximately 10 min (Fig. 1).

4.4   Task Description

Each participant was assigned a list of tasks for the risk assessment training within a VR machine shop environment using each interfaces. They needed to select an object from the machine shop, identify different hazard types associated with the object, determine each hazard's severity, and select personal protective equipment/s to protect themselves from that specific hazard. Participants then repeated these steps for another object in the environment and continued for the 10-minute interaction time. The participants had to pick their responses from the survey containing multiple choice-based questions. Two proposed interfaces provided different ways to interact with the objects and respond to hazard-related surveys.

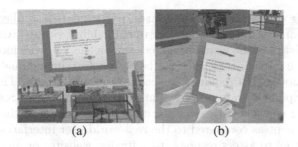

Fig. 1. Two interfaces tested in this study. (a) Floating menu and (b) Tablet

Floating Menu Interface. During their interaction with the floating menu, the participants pointed at and highlighted a particular object, then clicked on the touch controller's trigger button to bring up a floating interface. This interface appeared in the participants' perspective view displaying hazard-related information for the highlighted object. Then the participants used the controller's pointer to interact with other components on the floating menu interface (i.e. Check-box, radio button, button, etc.). The participants browsed through several pages on the interface to provide responses related to the selected object, such as hazard type, severity, required personal protective equipment, etc. After completing the data entry, the participants exited VR and completed the survey for the floating interface.

Tablet Interface. For the tablet interface, a virtual tablet (hand-held electronic device) was attached to the participant's touch controller. The participant performed the same steps to point, highlight and click on a particular object with the touch controller that had the tablet attached to it. The participants were able to view avatars of both of their hands attached to the controller. This helped them to visualize the different hand gestures performed on the virtual objects with the touch controllers such as touching, grabbing, trigger-clicking etc. Participants used their hands (index fingertip) to interact with the tablet interface through virtual touch and were able to take picture of an object using the camera button. These gestures are similar to the real-life tablet interactions. This session ended with the participants completing the data entry for this interface. After leaving VR, the participants completed a survey on the tablet interface.

4.5   Survey Instruments and Administration

The participants responded to a Simulation Sickness Questionnaire (SSQ, [11]) before their participation and after each time their exposure to one of the interfaces. The SSQ included 16 items, each having the ratings of "None = 1", "Slight = 2", "Moderate = 3" and "Severe = 4". Any rating that showed an SSQ score> 5 or any item scored as "Severe" would trigger the discontinuation of the study. In our study, no participants were withdrawn due to the SSQ score.

After interacting with each of the interfaces, participants also filled out surveys on the realism of the interfaces and System Usability Scale (SUS) rating [3]. Many characteristics of the visual interfaces within the VR were intended to successfully immerse participants, such as the screen size, image quality, text size, and the body movements required to accomplish tasks [6, 20]. The researchers asked the participants to rate proposed interfaces from "1" (Not realistic) to "5" (Realistic) for 11 characteristics in order to test the realism of the interfaces in the VR environment as compared to the real-world user interfaces. The SUS is a very popular tool to assess response to software, websites or any other digital interfaces. The SUS, modified for the interfaces used in the current study, contained 10 questions with a 5-point rating for each of them (from "1" denoting Strongly Disagree to "5" denoting Strongly Agree). At the end, the participants responded to the demographic questions (gender, age, education level, experience and frequency of daily usage of digital UIs) along with other surveys for the observed interface.

5   Results and Discussion

The survey results indicate the strengths and weaknesses of the two interface types. The evaluation of the interfaces will help in the design and selection of a useful mode of interaction within the VR. The following tables list the results collected from the survey responses of the 13 participants. Table 2 contains the means (M) and standard deviations (SD) of the ratings for different characteristics of the interfaces along with the pairwise comparison outcomes (t statistics and p values) for each of the items. Table 3 contains the same statistics for each of the interfaces' SUS ratings.

5.1   Realism

Face validity was conducted by testing realism for the interfaces based on several constructs related to their designs and factors affecting interaction with each interface. Pairwise comparisons using t-tests showed significant differences between the two interfaces with respect to interface placement, screen size, graphics and text quality. For each of the constructs, the tablet interface was rated to be more realistic than the floating menu. On a 5-point scale for realism rating, the tablet received scores greater than 3.5 for all of the constructs and scores greater than 4 for interface setting, placement, and size and for head movements required for interaction. These higher scores confirm the realistic appearance of a tablet interface in the VR environment which provided participants with better placement, reasonable size, and quality graphics and text within the VR.

Table 2. Analysis of realism test results.

Survey items	Floating menu		Tablet		T-test	
	M	SD	M	SD	t Stat. $df=12$	p-value
Interface setting	3.70	1.18	4.00	1.08	−0.887	0.39
Interface placement	**3.85**	**0.90**	**4.39**	**0.65**	**−2.214**	**0.04**
Screen size	**3.54**	**1.39**	**4.31**	**0.95**	**−2.245**	**0.04**
Graphics quality	**2.92**	**1.32**	**3.77**	**1.42**	**−1.389**	**0.01**
Text Size	3.23	1.54	3.69	1.18	−1.674	0.19
Text quality	**2.85**	**1.68**	**3.56**	**1.45**	**−2.188**	**0.02**
Ease of use pointing at object	4.15	1.14	3.85	1.21	0.433	0.57
Ease of use selecting object	4.00	1.16	3.77	1.36	0.762	0.67
Head movement required to read text	3.92	1.04	3.92	1.04	0.000	1.00
Head movement required to interact	3.85	1.21	4.08	0.64	−1.164	0.46
Hand movement required to interact	3.77	1.48	3.69	1.49	0.179	0.86

Consistent with previous studies using a tablet as an interaction interface within the VR environment [10,13], this study recommends using a tablet interface for object selection and data entry with novice and inexperienced employees. Tablets have a similar interface to cell phones which is familiar to almost everyone. Therefore, it is clear that people will know the basic functionality required to accomplish a task using the tablet interface. In addition, the participants' avatar hands may have made the interaction more realistic with a tablet. Watching themselves working on a tablet and getting the expected outcome could explain the results for this interface regarding realism.

5.2 System Usability Scale (SUS) Ratings

Pairwise comparisons and descriptive statistics for SUS scores revealed that participants only perceived significant differences between the two interfaces for two survey items. The results showed that participants found the floating interface to be a bit more cumbersome to use than the tablet. They responses indicated that significant technical support would be needed to use the floating menu as compared to the tablet interface. According to the standard definition of the SUS scaling factors, any interface with a SUS score higher than 68 can be considered to be good, and in both of the cases, the SUS scores are much higher than 68. In addition, no significant difference was found between the interfaces with respect to the overall SUS score. Therefore, it can be said that both interfaces were recognized to be useful for interacting within VR, but the tablet gives a more realistic interaction effect in terms of its placement, size, graphics and text quality.

Table 3. Analysis of system usability scale (SUS) ratings.

Survey items	Floating menu		Tablet		T-test	
	M	SD	M	SD	t Stat. $df = 12$	p-value
1. I'll use this interface frequently	3.69	1.44	3.77	0.83	−0.201	0.84
2. Interface is unnecessarily complex	4.46	0.66	4.08	1.19	1.443	0.18
3. Interface is easy to use	4.54	0.88	4.31	1.03	0.610	0.53
4. Need tech support to be able to use	**4.23**	**1.17**	**3.54**	**1.45**	**2.112**	**0.04**
5. Various functions are well integrated	4.23	0.83	4.54	0.78	−1.298	0.22
6. Too much inconsistency	3.92	1.12	3.92	1.26	0.000	1.00
7. Most people will learn to use very quickly	4.62	0.87	4.54	0.88	0.210	0.84
8. Very cumbersome to use	**4.08**	**1.19**	**3.15**	**1.28**	**3.207**	**0.01**
9. Very confident using this interface	4.54	0.78	4.38	0.77	0.562	0.58
10.Need to learn a lot before using	4.23	0.93	3.77	1.17	1.720	0.11
Total SUS score	85	13.78	80	13.64	1.293	0.22

5.3   Average Interaction Time

The average time to complete the tasks on one object (time between selecting an object and finishing the entering of hazard information) was found to be significantly different [t = −6.021, df = 12, p = > 0.0001]. For the tablet interface, the average time was about 68 s with a standard deviation of 9 s, while for the floating menu, this was around 93 s with a standard deviation of 4 s. With the floating menu, the participants required a longer start-up time as well as more time to locate the floating screen and point the trigger to the correct place. The longer time may be the reason for unfamiliar settings with the VR controllers for multiple functions, such as pointing at the object, selecting the object, and filling out surveys on the floating menu. With the tablet interface, the familiar camera button and hand avatar helped the participants to use the interfaces properly.

6   Conclusion

The current study investigated employees' preference for the virtual interface in risk assessment training and evaluation. The study allowed participants to experience a VR machine shop environment and interact with different objects using two proposed interfaces. Each interface had different methods of interaction, designed based on the task requirement and recommendations from previous studies in this area. The inclusion of 2D interfaces for 3D manipulation in risk assessment training and evaluation identified effective design criteria and suggestions for improvement.

The results of this study showed that the use of the standard metrics such as SUS, realism test with basic interface characteristics, and average task-completion time gave an overall idea of the usability of the interfaces. The quick and easy approach of the VR experiment brought out the important features of tablet interface (interface placement, screen size, and quality of graphics and text) that made it more appealing to the users. The study also revealed important aspects of the usability for a virtual UI. Users found the floating menu cumbersome to use and they needed more technical support to use the menu interface. However, further improvement of the interfaces will allow the user to respond more specifically which will make the comparison more robust.

Acknowledgement. The authors wish to thank Toyota Motor Manufacturing, Mississippi for their assistance with risk assessment training module development.

References

1. Vrtk - virtual reality toolkit (2018). http://vrtoolkit.readme.io. Accessed 5 June 2018
2. Bowman, D.A., Wineman, J.D., Hodges, L.F.: Exploratory design of animal habitats within an immersive virtual environment. Technical report, Georgia Institute of Technology (1998)
3. Brooke, J., et al.: SUS-A quick and dirty usability scale. In: Usability Evaluation in Industry, vol. 189(194), pp. 4–7 (1996)
4. Chen, P.Q.: Virtual reality in design and manufacturing. Ph.D. thesis, Nanyang Technological University, School of Mechanical and Production Engineering (2002)
5. Deb, S., Carruth, D.W., Sween, R., Strawderman, L., Garrison, T.M.: Efficacy of virtual reality in pedestrian safety research. Appl. Ergon. **65**, 449–460 (2017)
6. Ditton, T.B.: The unintentional blending of direct experience and mediated experience: the role of enhanced versus limited television presentations in inducing source-monitoring errors (1998)
7. Federoff, M.A.: Heuristics and usability guidelines for the creation and evaluation of fun in video games. Ph.D. thesis, Citeseer (2002)
8. Feiner, S., MacIntyre, B., Haupt, M., Solomon, E.: Windows on the world: 2D windows for 3D augmented reality. In: Proceedings of the 6th Annual ACM Symposium on User Interface Software and Technology, pp. 145–155. ACM (1993)
9. Fuhrmann, A., Loffelmann, H., Schmalstieg, D., Gervautz, M.: Collaborative visualization in augmented reality. IEEE Comput. Graph. Appl. **18**(4), 54–59 (1998)
10. Grudin, J.: The case against user interface consistency. Commun. ACM **32**(10), 1164–1173 (1989)
11. Kennedy, R.S., Lane, N.E., Berbaum, K.S., Lilienthal, M.G.: Simulator sickness questionnaire: an enhanced method for quantifying simulator sickness. Int. J. Aviat. Psychol. **3**(3), 203–220 (1993)

12. Mujber, T.S., Szecsi, T., Hashmi, M.S.: Virtual reality applications in manufacturing process simulation. J. Mater. Process. Technol. **155**, 1834–1838 (2004)
13. Rekimoto, J.: Tilting operations for small screen interfaces. In: Proceedings of the 9th Annual ACM Symposium on User Interface Software and Technology, pp. 167–168. ACM (1996)
14. Rizzo, A.A., Buckwalter, J.G., Neumann, U., Kesselman, C., Thiébaux, M.: Basic issues in the application of virtual reality for the assessment and rehabilitation of cognitive impairments and functional disabilities. CyberPsychology Behav. **1**(1), 59–78 (1998)
15. Rose, F., Attree, E.A., Brooks, B., Parslow, D., Penn, P.: Training in virtual environments: transfer to real world tasks and equivalence to real task training. Ergonomics **43**(4), 494–511 (2000)
16. Schultheis, U., Jerald, J., Toledo, F., Yoganandan, A., Mlyniec, P.: Comparison of a two-handed interface to a wand interface and a mouse interface for fundamental 3D tasks. In: 2012 IEEE Symposium on 3D User Interfaces (3DUI), pp. 117–124. IEEE (2012)
17. Squelch, A.: Virtual reality for mine safety training in south africa. J. South. Afr. Inst. Min. Metall. **101**(4), 209–216 (2001)
18. Stork, D.G., Hennecke, M.E.: Speechreading by Humans and Machines: Models, Systems, and Applications, vol. 150. Springer Science & Business Media, Heidelberg (2013)
19. Vo, M.T., Wood, C.: Building an application framework for speech and pen input integration in multimodal learning interfaces. In: 1996 IEEE International Conference on Acoustics, Speech, and Signal Processing, ICASSP-1996, Conference Proceedings, vol. 6, pp. 3545–3548. IEEE (1996)
20. Wang, J., Lindeman, R.: Coordinated 3D interaction in tablet-and HMD-based hybrid virtual environments. In: Proceedings of the 2nd ACM Symposium on Spatial User Interaction, pp. 70–79. ACM (2014)

Sensory Fusion and Intent Recognition for Accurate Gesture Recognition in Virtual Environments

Sean Simmons[1], Kevin Clark[2], Alireza Tavakkoli[3(✉)], and Donald Loffredo[1]

[1] University of Houston-Victoria, Victoria, TX 77901, USA
{SimmonsS,LoffredoD}@uhv.edu
[2] Rice University, Houston, TX 77005-1892, USA
kmc10@rice.edu
[3] University of Nevada, Reno, NV 89557, USA
Tavakkol@unr.edu

Abstract. With the rapid growth of Virtual Reality applications, there is a significant need to bridge the gap between the real world and the virtual environment in which humans are immersed. Activity recognition will be an important factor in delivering models of human actions and operations into the virtual environments. In this paper, we define an activity being composed of atomic gestures and intents. With this approach, the proposed algorithm detects predefined activities utilizing the fusion of multiple sensors. First, data is collected from both vision and wearable sensors to train Recurrent Neural Networks (RNN) for the detection of atomic gestures. Then, sequences of the gestures, as observable states, are labeled with their associated intents. These intents denote hidden states, and the sequences are used to train and test Hidden Markov Models (HMM). Each HMM is representative of a single activity. Upon testing, the proposed gesture recognition system achieves around 90% average accuracy with 95% mean confidence. The overall activity recognition performs at an average of 89% accuracy for simple and complex activities.

Keywords: Gesture recognition · Intent recognition
Activity recognition · Sensor fusion · Activity segmentation
Wearable sensors

1 Introduction

In certain applications in which human presence is prohibitively expensive or dangerous, as described in [15], remote robotic agents take the human operator's place as active operational agents. With rapid proliferation and commercialization of Virtual Reality (VR) technologies, it is natural to enhance traditional Teleoperation of remote robotic agents with the immersion afforded by VR, as illustrated in [9]. To enhance the presence and immersion felt by human operators in such applications, there needs to be mechanisms in place within the VR

© Springer Nature Switzerland AG 2018
G. Bebis et al. (Eds.): ISVC 2018, LNCS 11241, pp. 237–248, 2018.
https://doi.org/10.1007/978-3-030-03801-4_22

system to deliver potentially a large number of sensory information to the human operator as well as to the remotely operated agent in an efficient and intuitive manner. In this paper, we approach such a task through the implementation of learning techniques in which the robotic entity can efficiently identify the human actions meant for its operational tasks. Teleoperators experience greater immersion when more organic movements are used in place of traditional control methods as this bridges the gap between virtual and real world interaction. To further this task, we have investigated the recognition of atomic gestures, human intent, and human activity to improve both the accuracy and the speed at which activities are recognized. Along with this novel approach for activity recognition, we also utilized the fusion of heterogeneous sensors to provide a more complete and accurate representation of provided user input. We believe the way forward for teleoperation of a remote robotic agent is through the synthesis of data from varied sensor inputs in combination with recognition of activities that are defined by their structured sub-components.

2   Literature Review

Much research conducted in the areas of gesture, intent, and activity recognition primarily utilize single sensor computer vision techniques. Ajili et al. employ a Microsoft Kinect sensor to teleoperate a remote robotic agent by collecting visual motion data from a person performing a gesture, process the information, and send the commanded gesture to a remote robot in [1]. In [14], Sharma et al. conducted research centered on recognizing gestures made in the air and used image processing techniques on images obtained from an optic device. The advantage of using computer vision over other methods is the broadness of the provided data. Images provide a large amount of information, and a series of images provide more in-depth data of a dynamic scene. Although images are fairly easy to process and obtain, this ease-of-use comes at the cost of accuracy and reliability. Vision data is primarily two-dimensional, meaning it cannot accurately portray every possible action in the real world. This reduces the reliability of using computer vision and limits the capability of an area of research like gesture recognition to a much smaller scope than what would be practically ideal.

Other related research areas, rather than using computer vision methods, make use of wearable sensory devices. Lu et al. in [10] implement a data glove combined with Extreme Learning Machines to train and test human gestures. Luzhnica et al. in [11] developed a sliding window approach combined with a custom data glove to recognize gestures. The primary advantage in using wearable sensory technology is the accuracy of the data obtained. The frame data from a computer vision approach cannot use three-dimensional data as accurately as the accurate sensor information conveyed through a data glove. The disadvantages of using just data glove technology is the potential loss of position information provided by imaging. Environmental context can play a critical role in recognition circumstances, thus limiting the potential for variability and growth in the applied domain.

Activities, as defined in our work, are composed of atomic gestures and their intents. Literature review has shown that combining both gestures and intents into activities is a novel approach. The two closest to our work are the research taken by Wang et al. in [16] and the research taken by Bates et al. in [2]. Wang et al. in [16] detected gestures and used these to detect over-arching activities. Bates et al. in [2] designed a real-time learning and detection system capable of segmenting motion and identifying simple activities. Where Wang et al. in [16] lacked is the complexity of information provided by their wireless body sensors which were attached to the wrists, held in hand, and worn on the body. Activities may involve minute manipulations of smaller body parts not measured by wireless body sensors. This lack of compensation for the intricacies of human activities limits the research by Wang et al. in [16] to a small domain of study. Although the work by Bates et al. in [2] was unsupervised and required no prior training for real-time recognition, the activities detected were too simple in nature to be applied in a practical scenario. To provide a more accurate recognition of activities, training models before testing will prove to be a better approach than unsupervised real-time recognition.

The intent recognition performed in this research experiment is based on the work conducted by Kelley et al. in [7]. In [7], Kelley et al. developed a novel Hidden Markov Model approach to recognize and predict human intent, which is based on the theory of mind. The theory of mind states that an entity with such theory assigns a mental state to itself and another entity. This allows said individual to anticipate or "read" another's mind to determine their intended purpose for a series of actions. Although the accuracy of the intent recognition was high in the experimental results, the predefined intents were lacking in complexity and utilized only computer vision.

Other related works in recognition for teleoperation of a remote robotic agent can be found in [6,18]. In [18], Wolf et al. demonstrate the use of a wearable sensory device to detect atomic gestures for remote robotic control. In [6], Hauser develops a teleoperation system taking cursor input for task recognition. The research conducted in both [6,18] lack in activity complexity and do not utilize heterogeneous sensory fusion to provide rich data and promote accuracy of the human performed tasks.

3   The Proposed Approach

This paper proposes a novel approach to activity recognition for the teleoperation of remote robotic agents using virtual reality technologies. This technique is designed to extend and enhance the framework designed by Bounds et al. in [5], Regenbrecht et al. in [13], and Wilson et al. in [17], all of which are utilized as a comprehensive VR system for robotic teleoperation.

In this work activities are defined to be composed of observed gestures and their hidden intents. Through the utilization of sensor fusion from both wearable and vision devices, atomic gestures are obtained in sequences. These gesture sequences are labeled with a single intent per gesture which overall corresponds to a specifically defined activity as illustrated in Fig. 1.

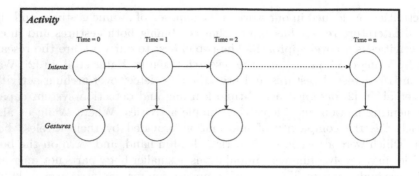

Fig. 1. Relationship between gesture, intent, and activity

Specifically, the devices used to capture gesture data consist of a Leap Motion controller and Virtual Motion Labs VMG 30 data gloves. The fusion of the collected sensor data is used to train Recurrent Neural Networks (RNN) for both the left and right hands. Once trained, these RNNs are used to collect sequences of gestures which are labeled with their appropriate intents. Once enough sequence data is obtained, we train Hidden Markov Models (HMM) for each unique sequence type that constitutes an activity. The activity sequences can then be used to test the accuracy of the trained models. Figure 2 displays the specified design of the research that we have taken.

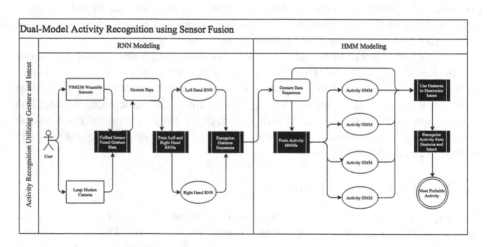

Fig. 2. Overall activity recognition workflow

3.1 Gesture Recognition

The novelty of our approach lies in the overall application of an RNN to read gestures by fusing data collected from both wearable and motion capture sensors.

The data gloves and the position and velocity information from the motion capture camera supply data that cannot be gathered from one tool alone. One of the fundamental goals of efficient HRI is effective gesture recognition [8]. The rich fused sensory data in the proposed mechanism facilitates a more effective gesture recognition technique. The temporal nature of the sequences lends itself to utilizing Recurrent Neural Networks as one of the most suitable choices for the implementation of the learning algorithm.

In the current system, the VMG30 data gloves from Virtual Motion Labs and a Leap Motion Capture Camera are employed. The data gloves contain 27 sensors including finger flexion sensors, attitude sensors, fingertip pressure sensors, and abduction sensors, while the Leap camera contains 3-dimensional position and velocity vectors. The data from these sensory systems is combined into one 33-valued input vector for both the left and right hands.

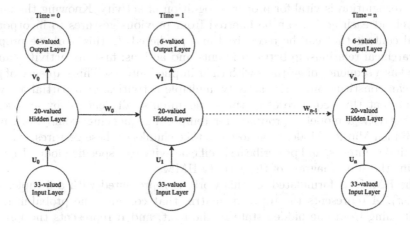

Fig. 3. The proposed RNN model for gesture recognition

The proposed RNN structure is represented in Fig. 3 and is loosely based on the RNN design described in [3]. The network takes the 33-valued vector as the input layer, signified as **i**. The RNN also has one 20 element hidden layer **h** and one output layer **o** comprising of 6 nodes. Each node in the output layer represents a recognizable gesture.

The hidden layer at time t is calculated as:

$$\mathbf{h}^t = \tanh(\mathbf{U} \cdot \mathbf{i}^t \oplus \mathbf{W} \cdot \mathbf{h}^{t-1}) \tag{1}$$

where $\oplus$ is element-wise addition, $\cdot$ is matrix multiplication, and $\mathbf{U}$ and $\mathbf{W}$ are $|\mathbf{i}| \times |\mathbf{h}|$ and $|\mathbf{h}| \times |\mathbf{h}|$ matrices of weights respectively.

The output layer at time t is calculated as:

$$\mathbf{o} = softmax(\mathbf{V} \cdot \mathbf{h}) \tag{2}$$

where $softmax(\cdot)$ is the element-wise softmax function, and $\mathbf{V}$ is a $|\mathbf{h}| \times |\mathbf{o}|$ matrix of weights.

Error L at time t is calculated for stochastic gradient descent training with the following formula:

$$L^t = \mathbf{y}^t \cdot \log \mathbf{o}^t - \left(1 - \mathbf{y}^t\right) \cdot \log\left(1 - \mathbf{o}^t\right) \tag{3}$$

where $\mathbf{y}^t$ is the vector that encodes the correct gesture at time t and $\mathbf{o}^t$ is the output of the RNN at time t.

Once trained, these RNNs were used to gather gesture sequence data. Four specific types of sequences were created, one for each of the predefined activities to be recognized. Half of the sequence data was labeled with intents per gesture while the other half remained unsupervised.

3.2   Intent and Activity Recognition

Intent recognition is vital for proper recognition of activity. Knowing the intention behind each action can be inferred from previous gestures to incorporate a local context that can be recognized and predicted. In this work we propose a hierarchical relationship between intents and actions: first, an activity can be defined as a sequence of gestures with their implied intents. This sequence of gestures can constitute an entire activity, multiple activities, or a partial activity. To represent this sequence of gestures and intents, all denoted by an overarching activity, a model appropriate for temporal sequencing would work best. The Hidden Markov Model was chosen to take chunks of these gestures, evaluate their hidden intents, and prescribe a specific activity to a specific model. Figure 4 contains the state diagram of the activity HMMs.

The HMM, as formulated for this work, is represented with a 3-tuple, $\lambda = (A, B, \pi)$. A represents the $|\mathbf{n}| \times |\mathbf{n}|$ matrix that contains the probabilities of transitioning from one hidden state to the next, and $\mathbf{n}$ represents the number of hidden states, or intents in our context. B represents the $|\mathbf{m}| \times |\mathbf{n}|$ matrix that contains the probabilities of hidden state q_t emitting the observation k_t, or gesture, at time t, and $\mathbf{m}$ is the number of possible observations, or possible gestures. The last element, π, is the $1 \times |\mathbf{n}|$ vector matrix that contains the probabilities of an intent sequence starting in state q.

Maximum Likelihood Estimation in conjunction with the Baum-Welch Algorithm were used to train the matrices representing each HMM using supervised and unsupervised training samples, respectively. In [4], Blunsom illustrates how to calculate the matrices with Maximum Likelihood Estimation.

The Forward and Backward algorithms calculate the α and β probabilities for every unsupervised sequence of gestures. These are the probabilities of viewing these gestures and their intent sequence probabilities for every possible intent state sequence, both forward and backward. With these probabilities, the Baum-Welch algorithm first calculates the probability of being in a certain state at time t and transitioning to another state at time $t + 1$. As defined in [12] by Rabiner, the Viterbi algorithm is used to test the models against unsupervised data to determine the most likely state sequence and model for a given set of observations. Under our context, the Viterbi algorithm took a sequence of

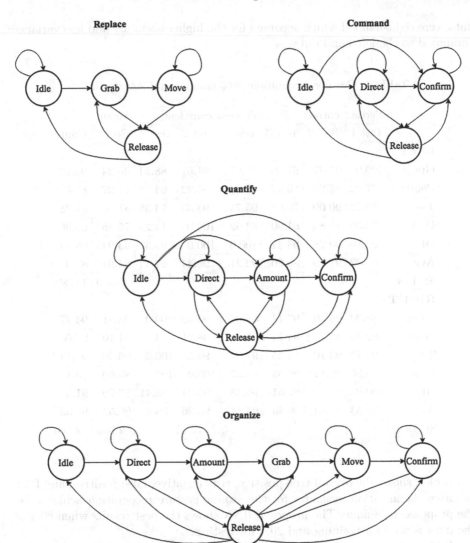

Fig. 4. The four predefined activity HMMs

gestures and determined the most likely sequence of intents as well as the most probable activity model.

4 Results

The gesture recognition system was trained with 80% and 100% total collected data set, and tested with 80%, 20%, and 100% of the data under specific circumstances as stated in Table 1. The majority of subjects used to collect gesture data were right-handed which accounts for the higher accuracy and less variance compared to the left hand data.

Table 1. Gesture recognition: 80% training and 20% testing

	Percent correct			Percent confident			Mean	
	Test 1	Test 2	Test 3	Test 1	Test 2	Test 3	Corr	Conf
LEFT								
Grasp	100.0	91.67	97.06	97.67	91.67	88.24	96.24	92.53
Point	67.92	97.22	66.67	83.02	97.22	64.58	77.27	81.61
Two	78.72	90.00	76.92	95.74	93.33	74.36	81.88	87.78
Four	74.36	89.80	61.90	84.62	100.0	14.29	75.35	66.30
OK	93.10	90.28	98.44	100.0	100.0	95.31	93.94	98.44
Avg	82.82	91.79	80.20	92.21	96.44	67.34	84.94	85.33
St. Dev.							8.589	11.005
RIGHT								
Grasp	88.00	96.30	97.14	88.00	96.30	100.0	93.81	94.77
Point	92.86	85.71	94.74	95.24	98.21	94.74	91.10	96.06
Two	95.74	93.10	82.35	97.87	96.55	100.0	90.40	98.14
Four	86.05	92.11	90.63	88.37	100.0	100.0	89.60	96.12
OK	100.0	80.49	82.61	96.08	90.24	88.41	87.70	91.58
Avg	92.53	89.54	89.49	93.11	96.26	96.63	90.52	95.33
St. Dev.							2.000	2.166

Table 2 shows the overall true positive, true negative, false positive, and false negative classification measures for the atomic gesture recognition achieved by the proposed technique. The proposed RNN shows the best results when 80% of the data is used for training and 20% for testing.

Table 3 shows the results of the proposed hierarchical activity recognition approach. Upon analysis of the results, the simpler activities of *Replace* and *Command* had more success in identifying the correct model or activity as well as the intent of each gesture. The more complex activities like that of *Quantify* and *Organize* had less successful results in being recognized. *Quantify* displayed accurate intent recognition while *Organize* had less accurate results for both categories of intent and activity recognition.

Because of the simple nature of both the *Replace* and *Command* activities, there is less variation in the possible sequence of gestures. Since there is less variation, the activities and intents were recognized with relative ease. *Quantify* is a more complex activity in that it is similar *Command* but with the added gestures of *Two* and *Four*. Because of slight similarities, the results of testing the *Quantify* data led to the activity recognizer to mistake some of the sequences for

Table 2. Gesture recognition measures

	80% Testing				20% Testing				100% Testing			
	TP	FP	FN	TN	TP	FP	FN	TN	TP	FP	FN	TN
Grasp	94.26	07.54	78.92	05.74	95.03	14.69	61.94	04.97	83.33	03.13	78.63	16.67
Point	83.98	01.91	81.29	16.02	84.19	02.53	62.91	15.81	80.09	01.18	79.27	19.91
Two	84.68	02.45	81.19	15.32	86.14	01.70	62.89	13.86	87.52	01.81	77.67	12.48
Four	83.04	03.94	81.52	16.96	82.47	07.27	63.38	17.53	59.48	00.63	83.74	40.52
OK	87.76	06.60	80.33	12.24	90.82	13.96	59.25	09.18	81.58	02.81	78.88	18.42

Table 3. Activity and intent recognition results

	Activity recognition %			Intent recognition %			Mean	
	Test 1	Test 2	Test 3	Test 1	Test 2	Test 3	Activity	Intent
Replace	100.0	99.00	100.0	96.07	92.47	93.13	99.67	93.89
Command	100.0	100.0	99.00	98.87	96.63	95.73	99.67	97.38
Quantify	87.60	90.00	79.00	94.00	95.07	93.07	85.53	94.05
Organize	71.00	67.00	81.00	76.73	75.00	79.59	73.00	77.11
Avg	89.65	89.00	89.75	91.38	90.50	90.60	89.47	90.83

Command. Organize is a combination of all three activities in that it incorporates all possible gestures. This accounts for a great variation in the possible gesture sequences that can be classified under the *Organize* activity category. Because of this high variance, a much lower percentage of both intents and activities were recognized in comparison to the other model results.

Table 4 shows the overall true positive, true negative, false positive, and false negative classification measures for the hierarchical activity recognition achieved by the proposed technique, as well as the intent recognition HMM approach.

In comparison with one other similar experiment, our proposed sensor-fused recognition approach yielded superior results. In [2], Bates et al. maintained a 92% accuracy for quite simple activity recognition only based on motion detection from a virtual reality environment. Our sensor-fused approach obtained nearly 100% accuracy for two of the four predefined activities. Our activities were also defined to cover a broad array of scenarios compared to being confined to washing dishes as was the case in [2].

Table 4. Activity and intent measures

	Percentage			
	TP	FP	FN	TN
ACTIVITY				
Replace	99.67	02.13	00.33	97.87
Command	99.67	11.69	00.33	88.31
Quantify	85.63	00.00	14.38	100.0
Organize	73.00	00.09	27.00	99.91
INTENT				
Idle	100.0	07.16	00.00	92.84
Grab	100.0	00.58	00.00	99.42
Direct	96.79	00.60	03.21	99.40
Move	75.59	04.12	24.41	95.88
Amount	89.36	01.80	10.64	98.20
Confirm	98.93	00.30	01.07	99.70
Release	93.56	01.08	06.44	98.92

5   Conclusion and Future Work

Our proposed sensor-fused activity recognition system produced accurate results under testing. Two of the predefined activity models were recognized nearly 100% of the time while the other two more complex activities were recognized at 85% and 73%. Intent recognition remained fairly high with three of the activities while the most complex activity had a lower intent recognition rate. Defining an activity to be composed of various sub-components and using multiple sensor in + puts proves to be a viable option for activity recognition under tele-operation of a remote robotic agent using virtual reality technologies.

To improve on our proposed activity recognition system, future work will consist of incorporating more sensors to obtain an even more accurate and complete picture of user input activities. More motion tracking cameras and possibly eye tracking tools may be utilized to enhance the effectiveness of the system. Other model combinations or processing techniques will be explored to improve gesture, intent, and activity recognition overall.

Acknowledgments. This material is based upon work supported in part by the U. S. Army Research Laboratory and the U. S. Department of Defense under grant number W911NF-15-1-0024, W911NF-15-1-0455, and W911NF-16-1-0473. This support does not necessarily imply endorsement by the DoD or ARL.

References

1. Ajili, I., Mallem, M., Didier, J.Y.: Gesture recognition for humanoid robot teleoperation. In: 26th IEEE International Symposium on Robot and Human Interactive Communication (RO-MAN) (2017)
2. Bates, T., Ramirez-Amaro, K., Inamura, T., Cheng, G.: On-line simultaneous learning and recognition of everyday activities from virtual reality performances. In: 2017 IEEE/RSJ International Conference on Intelligent Robots and Systems (IROS) (2017)
3. Bianchi, F.M.: Recurrent neural networks: A quick overview. University of Tromsø (2017)
4. Blunsom, P.: Hidden markov models. Utah State University (2004)
5. Bounds, M., Wilson, B., Tavakkoli, A., Loffredo, D.: An integrated cyber-physical immersive virtual reality framework with applications to telerobotics. In: Bebis, G., et al. (eds.) ISVC 2016. LNCS, vol. 10073, pp. 235–245. Springer, Cham (2016). https://doi.org/10.1007/978-3-319-50832-0_23
6. Hauser, K.: Recognition, prediction, and planning for assisted teleoperation of freeform tasks. Auton. Robot. **35**(4), 241–254 (2013)
7. Kelley, R., King, C., Tavakkoli, A., Nicolescu, M., Nicolescu, M., Bebis, G.: An architecture for understanding intent using a novel hidden markov formulation. Int. J. Hum. Robot. (2008)
8. Liu, H., Wang, L.: Gesture recognition for human-robot collaboration: A review (2017)
9. Liu, O., Rakita, D., Mutlu, B., Gleicher, M.: Understanding human-robot interaction in virtual reality. In: 2017 26th IEEE International Symposium on Robot and Human Interactive Communication (RO-MAN), pp. 751–757, August 2017. https://doi.org/10.1109/ROMAN.2017.8172387
10. Lu, D., Yu, Y., Liu, H.: Gesture recognition using data glove: An extreme learning machine method. In: Proceedings of the 2016 IEEE International Conference on Robotics and Biomimetics (2016)
11. Luzhnica, G., Simon, J., Lex, E., Pammer, V.: A sliding window approach to natural hand gesture recognition using a custom data glove. In: IEEE Symposium on 3D User Interfaces (2016)
12. Rabiner, L.: A tutorial on hidden Markov models and selected applications in speech recognition. Proc. IEEE **77**(2) (1989)
13. Regenbrecht, J., Tavakkoli, A., Loffredo, D.: A robust and intuitive 3D interface for teleoperation of autonomous robotic agents through immersive virtual reality environments. In: 2017 IEEE Symposium on 3D User Interfaces (3DUI), pp. 199–200, March 2017. https://doi.org/10.1109/3DUI.2017.7893340
14. Sharma, T., Kumar, S., Yadav, N., Sharma, K., Bhardwaj, P.: Air-swipe gesture recognition using opencv in android devices. In: 2017 International Conference on Algorithms, Methodology, Models and Applications in Emerging Technologies (ICAMMAET) (2017)
15. Sheridan, T.B.: Human-robot interaction: Status and challenges. Hum. Fac. **58**(4), 525–532 (2016). https://doi.org/10.1177/0018720816644364. pMID: 27098262
16. Wang, L., Gu, T., Chen, H., Tao, X., Lu, J.: Real-time activity recognition in wireless body sensor networks: from simple gestures to complex activities. In: 2010 IEEE 16th International Conference on Embedded and Real-Time Computing Systems and Applications (RTCSA) (2010)

17. Wilson, B., et al.: VETO: An immersive virtual environment for tele-operation. Robotics **7**(2) (2018). https://doi.org/10.3390/robotics7020026, http://www.mdpi.com/2218-6581/7/2/26
18. Wolf, M.T., Vernacchia, C.A.M.T., Fromm, J., Jethani, H.L.: Gesture-based robot control with variable autonomy from the JPL biosleeve. In: 2013 IEEE International Conference on Robotics and Automation (ICRA) (2013)

Deep Learning I

Accuracy of a Driver-Assistance System in a Collision Scenario

Waqar Khan[1,2](✉) and Reinhard Klette[1]

[1] Centre for Robotics and Vision, Auckland University of Technology, Auckland,
New Zealand
wkha011@aucklanduni.ac.nz
[2] Wellington Institute of Technology, Wellington, New Zealand

Abstract. Object tracking for collision avoidance systems benefits from current progress in object detection by deep learning. For the purpose of collision avoidance, a hazard has to be tracked in several frames before the safety system can determine its future trajectory and issue a necessary warning for braking.

Because the detected object is defined by a rectangular boundary, it can represent (a non-rectangular) object as well as its background, thus leading to misleading tracking information. Therefore, we rely on feature points identified in the detected regions over time for performing feature point tracking. Feature points in the background are removed by performing clustering in real-world co-ordinates using iterative semi-global matching stereo as well as an approximate size of the detected object type.

While matching the feature points between consecutive frames, a best match might not be found. In such circumstances, initially an optimally tracked feature point is used for updating the tracking information of the mismatched feature point. However, with too many mismatches (possibly due to occlusion) its information is overwritten by a more recently matched feature point. We evaluated our system on created test video data involving a controlled collision course.

1 Introduction

The *ego-vehicle* is the considered vehicle where a driver-assistance system is operating in. Given a pair of cameras mounted on an ego-vehicle observing a scene in a canonical stereo configuration, as part of a stereo vision-based safety system. The ultimate goal of this system is to assist the driver in identifying colliding hazards such that, in response to a braking warning, either a driver can apply brakes to avoid a collision, or the ego-vehicle applies brakes automatically.

In order to determine a true collision scenario, first, the system has to detect a hazard, then it has to track it over several frames (also called *observations*). With each observation, the confidence about the measured trajectory for the hazard should improve.

At each observation, the safety system needs to first locate the object in the (say) left camera image, called the *reference image L*. This process is also called

© Springer Nature Switzerland AG 2018
G. Bebis et al. (Eds.): ISVC 2018, LNCS 11241, pp. 251–263, 2018.
https://doi.org/10.1007/978-3-030-03801-4_23

object detection. Then, to predict the object trajectory, it has to measure its real-world location. For this purpose, the object has to be binocularly visible such that, based on its corresponding position in the right camera image (i.e. in the *match image R*), object disparities can be computed. This allows the safety system to measure the object's real-world position. For the sketched stereo vision functionalities, see textbooks such as [10].

Assuming that a tracked object as well as the ego-vehicle travel at constant velocity within a given local context (i.e. a limited time interval), we refer to modelled *safety systems* as previously proposed in [6]. Such a system also determines the accuracy of stereo configuration parameters to identify maximum-tolerable collision velocities (for the considered driver-assistance system).

In real-world scenarios, it is very rare for the ego-vehicle as well as the opposing hazard to be traveling at constant velocity, therefore, an alternate model was proposed in [7] where the hazard approached the ego-vehicle with a variable velocity. In both of these models it has been identified that a change in measured disparity is very important in determining a *timely warning* (i.e. a brake warning which provides a driver or the car sufficient time to apply brakes and avoid collision). A timely warning is possible because, due to observed changes in measured positions, the range of possible trajectories reduces significantly. In studies in both referenced papers it was also reflected that, due to discrete pixels, the depth is measured at integral steps; even when a stereo matching algorithm can produce sub-pixel disparities [9], this hypothesis is still applicable.

The farther the object is from the ego-vehicle, the trajectory estimation time can potentially be longer before timely warning becomes due. However, due to stereo measurement uncertainties, the depth resolution is also poor. This means, to observe a change in disparity, the system can also take longer. To mitigate this limitation to an extent, in [7], it was proposed to use several *feature points* (FPs). This would allow a FP being closer to the disparity change boundary, to be observed at a different disparity quickly.

With an assumption, that the object is rigid, velocity estimated by a FP over the object can represent all FPs. This assumption becomes very useful in the real-world where not all FPs are matched over time. This assumption will be dealt with differently for non-rigid objects (for example, pedestrians), and requires object detection algorithms which not only detect the location of hazards but do also classify those hazards.

This paper aims at refining the work reported in [7,9] for supporting even better accuracies in collision scenarios. The paper is structured as follows. In Sect. 2 we point to current options provided by *deep neural networks* (DNNs), and a subsequent use of FPs in object tracking. Section 3 specifies our performed processes, the used test data set, and the proposed feature tracker. Section 4 reports about the proposed collision warning system and experimental results. Section 5 concludes.

2   Reconsideration of Feature Points in Object Tracking

In recent years, due to the availability of classified datasets like PASCAL VOC 2007, 2012, and MS COCO, training of DNNs for the purpose of object detection and their classification has become relatively easy. The outcome of such algorithms is a detected location of the object in the form of a bounding box as well as the confidence of it belonging to a particular class. The accuracy of these outcomes depends upon the processing resources used. For example, [13] was able to achieve high accuracy on PASCAL VOC 2007, 2012 and MS COCO datasets on a GPU which was able to process 5 frames per second. If speed is more critical than performance, then [12] is an option for achieving a frame rate of at least 40 but at a cost of poor detection accuracy.

For supporting mobile platforms with limited memory resources, efficient *convolutional neural networks* (CNNs) can be used [4]. For building our safety system, we opted to use the Mobile-nets proposed by [4], trained by [3] firstly on the MS COCO dataset, followed by further training on the PASCAL VOC dataset; it can be used to detect twenty different type of objects [14].

Consider that an object, detected by DNN, is represented by a bounding box, also called the *region of interest* (ROI) around the object. The accuracy of this detection depends on the resolution of the input image. The larger the resolution the better should be the accuracy. But, at the same time, the processing time also increases accordingly. The DNN can also output a confidence value c for each detection. Using c, matches can be sorted, and the best one, encompassing other sub-matches, can be used to represent those other sub-matches as well.

Since a tracked object is not always a perfect rectangle, so a rectangular ROI is not only representing the object but also part of the background. So, for avoiding to track the background for too long, FPs are detected within the ROI. This concept re-connects the use of FPs, previously used for object detection and recently replaced by DNNs, again to the detection and tracking process, but *after* a DNN provided base-line detection and tracking.

Here, an FP is defined as a pixel location consisting of uniquely identifiable features. Like in the case of matching an object ROI from one frame to the following, it is also a challenge to identify the location where an FP has moved to in Frame k with respect to Frame $k - 1$.

With the ego-vehicle approaching closer to the object after a frame delay of δs s, the relative pose of the observed scene keeps on changing in every frame. This change in visual appearance effects FP matching as well as stereo-correspondence matching. Unique details, which were previously visible, are now self-occluded or occluded by other objects (e.g. closer to the ego-vehicle). In the context of FP matching, the same FP might not be detected in the current frame, hence mismatches become a possibility. Similarly, in the context of stereo correspondence, a disparity measured for the matched FP can be inaccurate.

Both of these issues influence the estimation of an FP trajectory in real-world co-ordinates. To an extent, mismatching FPs can be identified through outlier removal techniques, and can be excluded this way. However, the same is not possible for disparity mismatches. Instead, we rely on Kalman filter [5] trackers (i.e. one for each FP within the DNN's ROI). The goal of the tracker is to first train itself based on observations, and then start predicting the object trajectory as well. The prediction can be used for an estimation by when it is safe to issue a warning. The prediction can also be used to estimate an FP position when a mismatch occurs.

Research reported in this paper improves the findings in [8] where FP tracking was used for a pre-detected object to test a safety system on a choreographed collision scenario. Because object detection was missing in this previous study, features were only anchored to the first frame and then used for matching in all of the subsequent frames. In this study, however, we detect hazards by using a DNN for every frame, and we update matched features after the matching step. With the introduction of a DNN-based ROI, we evaluate the performance of various FP detectors and their descriptors.

3   Set-up and FP Tracker

The following **FP detectors** were used in our testing: the *difference of Gaussians* (DoG), and STAR (derived from the center-surrounded-extrema detector); see text books such as [10]. To describe the detected FPs, we used descriptors like: *scale-invariant feature transform* (SIFT), *speeded-up robust features* (SURF), *binary robust invariant scalable keypoints* (BRISK) descriptor [11], *binary robust independent elementary feature* (BRIEF) [2] descriptor, and *fast retina keypoint* (FREAK) descriptor [1].

For **stereo matching**, we use *iterative semi-global matching* (iSGM) which was winning the *Robust Vision Challenge* at ECCV 2012.[1] For matching in general, we used a brute-force matching strategy, but we also included a ratio test, a RANSAC approach, as well as a disparity check. In the disparity check, we computed the mean disparity of a ROI in the training frame, and then used this mean value to evaluate which matching FPs in the training frame are within an acceptable disparity tolerance; the acceptance criterion is based on a threshold $dT > 0$. This allowed us to gradually remove FPs detected in the ROI, but actually representing part of the background.

As **dataset**, we use pre-choreographed collision sequences. Figure 1 illustrates a frame of a sequence where issuing a warning before Frame $k = 110$ is considered to be a timely warning. For this sequence, the ego-vehicle was travelling at $\approx 11.1\,\text{m/s}$ (equivalent to $\approx 40\,\text{km/h}$). The stereo system captured 25 frames per second; the illustrated sequence consists of 111 frames. However, to be consistent with the study reported in [8], we start the processing at Frame $k = 50$. For the purpose of a driver assistance system, a warning issued before $k = 110$ (or within 60 observations) is a timely one.

We report now about the used **feature point tracker**. Assume that an object is detected in the left camera image only. For an object, a DNN can output several detections, however, by choosing the one with highest confidence

---

[1] See hci.iwr.uni-heidelberg.de/Robust_Vision_Challenge_2012.

Fig. 1. Frame of a choreographed sequence. A *marker on the road* is placed at the *safe braking distance* from the *colliding object*. The *observer* raises a flag when the ego-vehicle crosses this marker. In the illustrated sequence, the ego-vehicle was on *collision course* with constant speed until the observer raised the flag. The ego-vehicle's collision trajectory was bended towards the left. *Bottom*: SGM disparity map for the stereo pair illustrated by one frame at the top.

value c we select the best detection candidate, represented by a rectangular ROI defined by four coordinates $[roi_u, roi_v, roi_w, roi_h]$.

By using the DNN's best detection in the reference view, a ROI is identified in the first frame (i.e. the *query frame*). In this ROI, along with q detected FPs, one disparity d is used for initializing the Kalman filter (KF) tracker for each FP using real-world measurements in the frame of reference. Along with the KF, two parameters $nm[j]$ and $w[j]$ are also initialized, for each FP j:

- nm is an array of size q; it is initialized to be 0 at each position.
- w is also an array of size q; it is initialized to be 1 at each position.

Here, nm keeps track of all non-matched query FPs in the given frame, while w keeps track of how often a query FP gets matched.

nm is used for deleting query FPs i when $nm[i] > nmT$, where nmT is the threshold for keeping a query FP which did consistently not match. When such a point is not deleted, then its measurements are computed based on the KF_i prediction of a candidate FP m. A candidate FP is the one which has a maximum weight w_m, and it was most recently matched as well.

After δs seconds, a training frame is observed within which objects are detected; a ROI is defined; the mean disparity d_{avg} is computed; training FPs

---

Algorithm 1 FP tracker

---

collisionDecisionSystem$(c, nmT, dT, \delta, \mu, r_{exc})$ **returns** state S;
for each Observation k in $\{0, 1, \ldots\}$ **do**
  if $k == 0$ **then**
    Initialization: see Algorithm 2
  else
    Detect objects in training frame; choose those with confidence c at least;
    In each isolated neighbourhood select object $O(i)$ with highest confidence;
    Read ROI_i of $O(i)$ as $[roi_u, roi_v, roi_w, roi_h]$;
    Detect t train FPs in train frame within the ROI_i;
    Describe each FP with the feature descriptor;
    for each query FP j in $\{1, 2, \ldots, q\}$ **do**
      Match FP with trained FPs in t; remove outliers using dT;
      If matched: Increment $w[j]$, $nm[j] = 0$; Otherwise, $nm[j] = nm[j] + 1$;
    end for
    $m = $ FIND optimal tracker j with maximum $w[j]$ and minimum $nm[j]$;
    for each query FP j in $\{1, 2, \ldots, q\}$ **do**
      If $nm[j] \leq nmT$: KF_j prediction of position $\overrightarrow{O_j^r}$ and velocity $\overrightarrow{V_j^r}$;
      If $nm[j] > nmT$: Find measurements with old position measurement $\overrightarrow{O_j^r}$ and
      $\overrightarrow{V_m^r}$; Replace FP j with train FP;
      Update KF_j with new measurements;
    end for
    $l = $ FIND j with smallest predicted distance: $||\overrightarrow{O_j^r}||$;
    Using $\overrightarrow{O_l^r}$, $\overrightarrow{V_m^r}$, co-efficient of friction μ, and ego-vehicle exclusion zone r_{exc},
    compute braking distance D_b and braking time t_b;
    Estimate $\overrightarrow{O_l^r}$ position in real-world co-ordinates after $t_b + \delta s$ using $\overrightarrow{V_m^r}$;
    if "Definitely colliding" or "possibly colliding" **then**
      Issue definite braking warning $S \leftarrow$ **S4** or precautionary braking warning
      $S \leftarrow$ **S3**;
      return S
    end if
  end if
end for

---

get detected as well. Matching between query and training FPs is performed and followed by outlier removal tests. The outlier removal also consists of disparity checks, where potential background-matched FPs with $|d - d_{avg}| > dT$ are registered as being *non-matched*. Because a stereo matcher also has a correspondence error, so, instead of straight away deleting this point, its value w remains unchanged, and nm is incremented by 1.

All FPs j, which pass the outlier test, have their $w[j]$ value incremented by 1, with setting $nm[j] = 0$. Their real-world relative positions are computed and are used to update the Kalman filter KF_j. Their details in the query FP are updated with the matched training FP. The process of updating a FP, or deleting it, is illustrated in Fig. 2. The working principles of a FP tracker are summarised in Algorithm 1; the initialisation step is detailed in Algorithm 2.

Algorithm 2 Initialization

Detect objects in query frame; choose detections with a minimum confidence c;
In each isolated neighbourhood, select object $O(i)$ with highest confidence;
Read ROI_i of $O(i)$ as $[roi_u, roi_v, roi_w, roi_h]$;
Detect q query FPs in query frame within the ROI_i;
Describe each FP with the feature descriptor;
for each query FP j in $\{1, 2, \ldots, q\}$ **do**
    Compute real world position $\overrightarrow{O_j^r}$ of FP j in relative frame of reference; initialize
    KF_j using $\overrightarrow{O_j^r}$;
    Initialize not matched element $nm[j] = 0$, weight element $w[j] = 1$;
end for
System state $S \leftarrow \mathbf{S0}$;

---

4   Collision Warning System

In our experiments we use a confidence value $c = 0.40$ for identifying objects in the scene. For outlier removal with disparity check, we used $dT = 1$. To delete FPs, we used a threshold $nmT = 2$. The detector was able to detect vehicles in the scene, occasionally a vehicle as an aeroplane, and when the ego-vehicle was very close to the observer than a person as well.

Often a tree was wrongly detected as a person as well. However, by including a test for excluding detections outside the boundary of the image, those mis-detections were removed.

Specific confidence values for each detection allowed us to focus on a particular detection in a local neighbourhood. For example, in the given scene in Fig. 1, there are two objects of interest (i.e. a person and a vehicle); in this case our focus is mainly on the vehicle in this choreographed sequence.

We observed that the performance of the detector changed when image resolution changed. For images of reduced resolution, the confidence of detections was low and many overlaying objects were identified. However, the closer the resolution was to the resolution of the original image, the better the detections were. Figure 3 illustrates these findings for $k = 89$ in the reference image in the collision sequence. Note that in Fig. 3 for clarity purpose, the bounding boxes are drawn on the original resolution images only.

In our experiments we also observed that a change in the viewing angle, from left to right, impacted the confidence of the detector as well; see Fig. 4. In our experiments we relied only on the left camera view.

The location of an object in the real-world with respect to the ego-vehicle can be determined based on the measured location of FPs (as known from *visual odometry*). This location allows the KF tracker to train itself and to have accurate predictions. In fact, the more consistently a query FP is matched, the better is the estimation. The matching accuracy of an FP depends on its descriptor type as well as the detector type.

With a ROI detected by DNN, no matter which detector and descriptor is chosen, the test area remains consistent. Instead of identifying a good FP

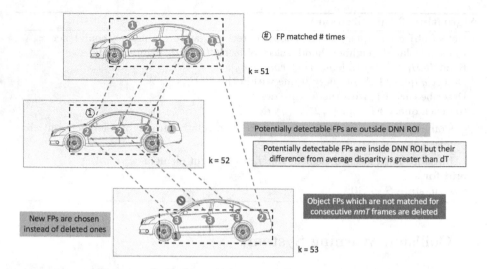

Fig. 2. Working principles of an FP tracker on training frames. Value $k = 51$ suggests the second processed frame. Matching FPs are those with label 1. At Frame $k = 52$, some FPs get matched, hence label 2 in this frame. They define the new descriptor in Frame $k = 52$, which are used for matching with the following frame. Those who do not get matched have unchanged descriptors. At Frame $k = 53$, a FP gets deleted if $nmT = 1$.

detector based on its detections, we instead rely on how it is matched with the query frame. So, in other words, we evaluate the performance of all descriptors on a given detector.

Figure 5 illustrates the matching performance of all considered descriptors for the DoG and STAR detectors. One clear observation is that when the object is farther away, the FPs are more likely detected in the background due to a larger ROI around the object. The FPs which are deleted are overwritten by FPs which are also in the background initially. However, when the object is closer, the ROI is also more accurate, hence fewer points are identified as outliers due to the disparity check.

The DoG detector with BRIEF descriptor illustrates an example case where the matching fails at $k = 85$ and onwards, but not all FPs are written off immediately. Instead, based on the nmT threshold, a few FPs still remain valid. Therefore, there are no steep peaks; they gradually increase as new FPs are chosen. There is a similar performance of the BRIEF descriptor with the STAR detector. The SIFT descriptor with both detectors seems to be a reliable choice.

The DoG detector with the FREAK descriptor is initially performing well; however, after $k = 95$, its FPs are removed as outliers due to the disparity check. This means that the likelihood that other FPs being assigned wrong disparities is also high. This can serve as a good test for evaluating the performance of the Kalman filter's role in handling the noise.

Fig. 3. Left camera image at $k = 89$ of resolution $[w \times h] = [960 \times 320]$ pixels. Top image resolution reduced to half resolution $[w \times h] = [480 \times 160]$ pixels. Middle image resolution reduced to $[w \times h] = [768 \times 256]$ pixels. Bottom image is of unchanged resolution.

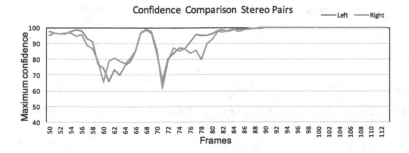

Fig. 4. Change in detection confidence for a changing viewing angle of the stereo camera pair for the collision sequence.

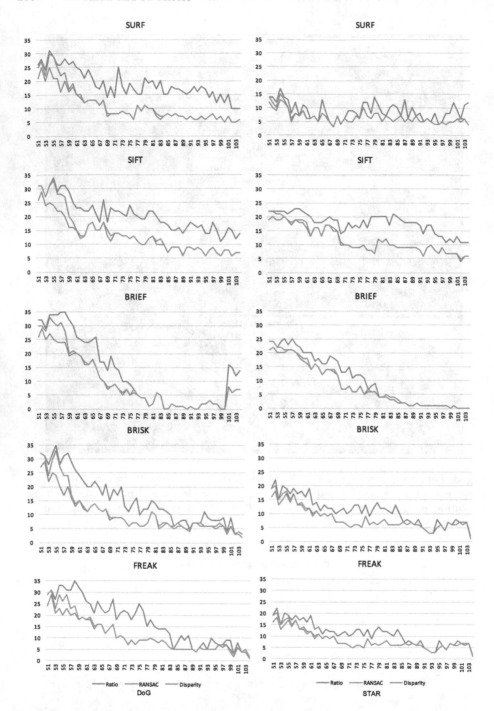

Fig. 5. Illustration of the performance of tested descriptors for the DoG and STAR detectors. Left column: DoG detector. Right column: STAR detector. The horizontal axis shows the frame number, and the vertical axis the number of FP matches.

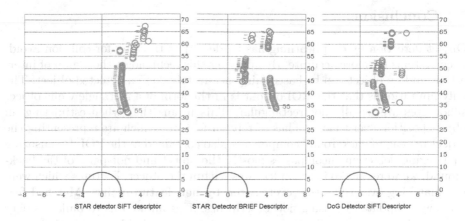

Fig. 6. Safety system results for STAR and DoG detector on SIFT and BRIEF descriptors. It illustrates only X and Z axes measurements in relative frame of reference from the ego-vehicle. The red circle is the exclusion zone.

The SIFT descriptor acts as a reliable source, no matter which FP detector is used. Note that the DoG detector matches 43 features initially with the brute force matcher. However, the STAR detector only matches 26 FPs. Because the STAR detector is more conservative in matching features initially, so over time it has fewer candidate FPs to describe the object's position. This can potentially become important when another object occludes the candidate FPs.

So, if a detector and descriptor combination is to be chosen based on the number of FPs available over time, then the SIFT descriptor can be combined with any of the detectors. Figure 6 further illustrates their comparison as a tracking output, along with a test case for the STAR detector with the BRIEF descriptor, which resulted in only a few matching FPs at later stages. Units of measurements are in metres; parameter r_{exc} has been set to 2 m.

The SIFT descriptor with the STAR detector is able to produce a candidate point that is consistently matched, from $Z = 52$ m until a warning is issued. The warning is issued after 55 observations. The same amount of time is taken by the STAR detector with the BRIEF descriptor, even though it demonstrated difficulties in producing FP matches. This figure, however, also illustrates that even with mismatches, an FP is acting as a candidate FP hence it is consistently matched over time. This candidate FP is able to support other FPs whose predictions are being re-initialized due to mismatches. Eventually, a warning is issued not due to the collision path of the candidate FP but due to an adjacent FP whose trajectory is predicted by candidate FP velocity.

The DoG detector with the SIFT descriptor has been able to switch between several candidate points, before a warning is issued after 54 observations. So, the method-of-choice is DoG detector with SIFT descriptor.

5 Conclusions

Object detection by deep learning has made object tracking for collision avoidance systems far more accurate. By applying this technology, the region of interest around an object can be based fairly accurately "on" a detected object. The only limitation is that this ROI output is in the form of a rectangle while object silhouettes are usually not rectangular. This means that when estimating an object position over time, one has to rely on features which are representing the object instead of background components also contained in the ROI. By ensuring that region detection encompasses mostly the object and not parts of the background, we were able to focus on features within the object. Features which were not matching over time were overwritten by new feature points. Matched features were updated by using new descriptors. This allowed us to build a safety system where more candidate feature points were available in case that some become partially occluded for some time.

We successfully tested our safety system on a head-on collision scenario. The system was able to generate timely braking warnings to the driver.

References

1. Alahi, A., Ortiz, R., Vandergheynst, P.: Freak: fast retina keypoint. In: Proceedings of the IEEE International Conference on Computer Vision Pattern Recognition (2012)
2. Calonder, M., Lepetit, V., Strecha, C., Fua, P.: BRIEF: binary robust independent elementary features. In: Daniilidis, K., Maragos, P., Paragios, N. (eds.) ECCV 2010. LNCS, vol. 6314, pp. 778–792. Springer, Heidelberg (2010). https://doi.org/10.1007/978-3-642-15561-1_56
3. Caffe implementation of Google MobileNet SSD detection network. github.com/chuanqi305/MobileNet-SSD
4. Howard, A., et al.: MobileNets: efficient convolutional neural networks for mobile vision applications. J. CoRR, vol. 1704.04861 (2017)
5. Kalman, R.E.: A new approach to linear filtering and prediction problems. J. Basic Eng. 82(1), 35–45 (1960)
6. Khan, W., Morris, J.: Safety of stereo driver assistance systems. In: Proceedings of the IEEE Symposium Intelligent Vehicles, pp. 469–475 (2012)
7. Khan, W., Klette, R.: Stereo accuracy for collision avoidance for varying collision trajectories. In: Proceedings of the IEEE Symposium Intelligent Vehicles (2013)
8. Khan, W., Klette, R.: Accuracy of trajectories estimation in a driver-assistance context. In: Huang, F., Sugimoto, A. (eds.) PSIVT 2013. LNCS, vol. 8334, pp. 47–58. Springer, Heidelberg (2014). https://doi.org/10.1007/978-3-642-53926-8_5
9. Khan, W., Klette, R.: Stereo-matching in the context of vision-augmented vehicles. In: Proceedings of the International Symposium Visual Computing (2015)
10. Klette, R.: Concise Computer Vision. UTCS. Springer, London (2014). https://doi.org/10.1007/978-1-4471-6320-6
11. Leutenegger, S., Chli, M., Siegwart, R.Y.: BRISK: binary robust invariant scalable keypoints. In: Proceedings of the IEEE International Conference on Computer Vision (2011)

12. Redmon, J., Divvala, S.K., Girshick, R.B., Farhadi, A.: You only look once: unified, real-time object detection. J. CoRR, vol. 1506.02640 (2015)
13. Ren, S., He, K., Girshick, R.B., Sun, J.: Faster R-CNN: towards real-time object detection with region proposal networks. J. CoRR, vol. 1506.01497 (2015)
14. Rosebank, A.: Object detection with deep learning and OpenCV. www.pyimagesearch.com/2017/09/11/ (2017)

Classify Broiler Viscera Using an Iterative Approach on Noisy Labeled Training Data

Anders Jørgensen[1,2(✉)] ⓘ, Jens Fagertun[2], and Thomas B. Moeslund[1] ⓘ

[1] University of Aalborg, Aalborg, Denmark
[2] IHFood A/S, Copenhagen, Denmark
andjor@create.aau.dk

Abstract. Poultry meat is produced and slaughtered at higher and higher rates and the manual food safety inspection is now becoming the bottleneck. An automatic computer vision system could not only increase the slaughter rates but also lead to a more consistent inspection. This paper presents a method for classifying broiler viscera into healthy and unhealthy, in a data set recorded in-line at a poultry processing plant. The results of the on-site manual inspection are used to automatically label the images during the recording. The data set consists of 36,228 images of viscera.

The produced labels are noisy, so the labels in the training set are corrected through an iterative approach and ultimately used to train a convolutional neural network. The trained model is tested on a ground truth data set labelled by experts in the field. A classification accuracy of 86% was achieved on a data set with a large in-class variation.

Keywords: Broiler · Viscera · Food safety · CNN · Classification

1 Introduction

The consumption of poultry meat has seen a large increase from 2.88 kg on average per person in 1961 to 14.99 kg in 2013 [10]. To keep up with the high demand, broilers are slaughtered at rates up to 13,500 birds per hour on a single conveyor [9]. The processing line is highly automated to achieve these rates, yet the food safety inspection is still done manually by veterinarians. Both the carcass and the viscera are inspected and with nearly four birds per second this is a task that requires constant attention. The inspectors are therefore relieved every 30 min for a break to avoid straining themselves, but these shifts cause inconsistency as the inspection can be very subjective. An automatic computer vision system could assist the veterinarians and result in a better and more consistent food safety inspection.

This paper focuses on the inspection of the viscera. The goal of a developed system is to detect and remove unhealthy sets of viscera from the conveyor. But

© Springer Nature Switzerland AG 2018
G. Bebis et al. (Eds.): ISVC 2018, LNCS 11241, pp. 264–273, 2018.
https://doi.org/10.1007/978-3-030-03801-4_24

getting labelled images is expensive and time consuming as the viscera must be graded by veterinarians. We developed a recording system utilizing the existing work procedures in the slaughter house to attain automatically labeled data albeit with a certain amount of noise in the labels. In an iterative approach the mislabeled samples were detected and relabeled and used to train a convolutional neural network (CNN). A small subset of data was graded by experts and used for validation and test.

2   Related Work

While others have worked on inline inspection of poultry carcasses [2,14], not much work have been done on the topic of inspection of poultry viscera. Early work showed that multi-spectral images of the heart could be used to classify four different diseases and healthy, with true positive rates between 84% and 100% [1]. The used data set contained 125 hearts, 25 in each category. [3] achieved a classification rate of 96% in detecting septicemia in chicken livers by utilizing the NIR spectrum. Their data set contained 200 livers used for training and 100 for testing. [13] used UV light to detect splenomegaly in poultry carcasses. 57 images were in the data set on which they achieved a 95% classification rate. All data sets were fairly small, and the heart and liver were separated from the rest of the viscera before the classification, which is impractical in real life scenarios where you should be able to track the viscera back to the broiler it came from. [7] developed a method for diagnosing broiler livers still attached to the viscera set. A data set of 1,476 images was used to separate the livers into four categories and achieved true positive rates between 71.0% and 80.3%.

Getting labelled data to use in supervised learning can be a challenge, especially when experts are needed to obtain ground truth. In some situations, labels can be gathered effortlessly, for example via Google image search or Instagram hash tags, but these labels will often we inaccurate. In a survey from 2014 [4] the author describes three ways to handle noisy labels; Noise-cleansing, Noise-tolerant and Noise-robust. Noise-cleansing models tries to remove or filter the noisy samples before training. Noise-tolerant models attempt to model the noise as part of the training, which requires some prior knowledge about the label noise. Noise-robust methods does neither of the previous, but trains with the noisy labels.

[11] proved that deep learning methods are fairly good at handling uniform noise, by showing a classification performance over 90% on the MNIST data set, with 100 noisy labels for each correct label. CIFAR-10 and ImageNet showed similar trends, but performance was hit harder by the number of noisy labels. All experiments, however, showed that the best performance was achieved with no noisy labels.

Many methods have been developed to utilize noisy training set. With the rise of deep learning, data sets need to be larger which often introduce more noise, as it gets more time consuming and costly to grade the samples manually. [5] proposed a technique using a complementary neural network and removed samples misclassified by both networks. The method gave a minor performance boost for all four tested data sets. [6] augmented a neural network with a noise model that is learned simultaneous with the base model. The noise model effectually denoises the noisy samples through back-propagation, which results in a more accurate model. The augmented network performed considerately better than the base model, especially at noise level above 30%.

The method presented in this paper utilizes the noise-robustness of neural networks to identify and relabel the mislabeled samples in the training set.

3   Data Set Acquisition

The data acquisition consists of two parts, first image recording and later automatic image labelling. To utilize the labels already given to the viscera by the on-site inspectors, one must understand the normal working procedure at the evisceration and inspection part of the processing line. This has been sketched in Fig. 1.

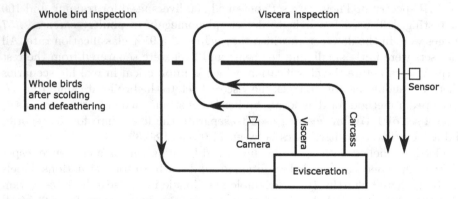

Fig. 1. Overview of the conveyor around the inspection and evisceration.

The birds are first inspected for diseases that are detectable on the carcass. This can be bruises, eczema and fractures among others. If the broiler is unfit for consumption it is removed from the line. The broilers are then transported into another room for evisceration. From here viscera and carcass, now separated, move back into the inspection room where the viscera are inspected for diseases. The evisceration happens in a different room due to high noise levels and as the use of water on the scolded carcasses causes a high humidity. As the camera and flash must not disturb the inspectors the recording system is installed in this room just after the evisceration.

As the viscera sets pass the inspection the unhealthy sets are removed, and the healthy sets stay on the conveyor. In order to utilize this knowledge a beam break sensor is placed on the viscera conveyor after the inspection. If the sensor detects that a hanger is empty it means that the viscera has been removed and the corresponding image can be labelled "unhealthy".

3.1   Data Handling

The images are recorded with a LW-AL-IMX253C-USB3 camera from ISG which is a global shutter color camera capable of capturing images at a resolution of 4096×3000. The broilers are slaughtered at a rate of around 3.75 birds per second, which means the camera generates 45 MiB every second. As the grade is not known by the time the viscera pass the camera all viscera sets are captured and saved. However, only around 0.7% of the broilers will be unhealthy [8] and many of these will be removed during the inspection of the carcass. To capture a more balanced data set the system automatically deletes most of healthy captured viscera sets. All images of unhealthy viscera are saved.

It must be assumed that each category contains a certain amount of noise. If the inspectors fail to remove an unhealthy viscera it will be labelled as "healthy". The risk of it being saved is small, however. It can also happen that the inspectors removed some healthy viscera sets by mistake or because it looks suspicious on the conveyor. Bear in mind that they only have around 1/4th of a second to make the decision and they will likely rather remove one too many than one too few. These will be labelled "unhealthy". If a viscera set falls out of the hanger between the camera and the sensor, it will also be categorized as "unhealthy".

Lastly, for some unhealthy viscera, the disease might be present in an area that is not visible in the image. These will end up in the unhealthy category but should for this purpose be regarded as healthy.

3.2   Resulting Data Set

The data set consist of 13,542 "healthy/not removed" images and 22,686 "unhealthy/removed" images captured in the period October 21th, 2016 to December 10th, 2017. Six examples of each class can be seen in Fig. 2. It is clear that there is a large variation in shape and appearance within both the healthy and unhealthy class.

A small set of the images were graded by veterinarians, which contains 1208 unhealthy and 1086 healthy images. 500 images from each class will be used in the test set and the rest will be used for validation. The final split can be seen in Table 1. The training images uses the noisy labels given during the acquisition.

Table 1. Number of samples in each set. Only the validation and the test set have been graded by veterinarians.

	Training	Validation	Test
Healthy (**H**) = Not removed	12456	586	500
Unhealthy (**U**) = Removed	21478	708	500

Fig. 2. Image examples from the data set. Top row is healthy, bottom row is unhealthy.

3.3 Preprocessing

The images have been captured over a period of a year and it was noticed that the images got brighter over time. This is primarily due to limescale accumulating on the glass in front of the lens which reflect light back into the lens. The images contain a large portion of the black background and all images are therefore corrected by simple subtraction to have a background color of 30, 30, 30 in R, G, and B, respectively.

4 Method

To obtain a CNN that can classify the viscera as healthy or unhealthy, we employ an iterative approach where we train using the noisy labelled data and after each iteration we grade the samples with the largest error. The next iteration is then trained on the same data, but with the new labels applied. A sample can also be removed from the training set if it contains no useful information for the classifier. This can be images where large parts of the viscera are missing or hanging half way out of the frame. These images were also removed from the validation and test set by the veterinarians during grading.

4.1 Training the CNN

All training is done in python with the CNTK framework from Microsoft [12]. The network is a simple neural network with three convolutional layers. The entire network are depicted in Table 2.

Table 2. Neural network. Each convolution layer is followed by an relu activation. MaxPooling uses a stride of 2 in each direction. Each convolution layer has 64 filters.

Convolution(5,5)(64)
MaxPooling(3,3)
Dropout(0.2)
Convolution(5,5)(64)
MaxPooling(3,3)
Dropout(0.35)
Convolution(5,5)(64)
MaxPooling(3,3)
Dropout(0.5)
AvgPool(8,8)
Dense(2,1)

For each iteration we train 300 epochs with a batch size of 64 and a constant learning rate of 0.005. Each epoch uses 100,000 samples each augmented with random crops and horizontal flips. The images are scaled to a resolution of 150×300 and the model is saved after each epoch. After each iteration we select a model with which to predict the training samples. This model must perform well on the validation set, but we also want to avoid overfitting, as the model should fail on the training samples that are mislabeled. The selected model is therefore the earliest model that is less than 5 correct validation samples from the minimum validation error. As the validation set contains 1294 images this corresponds to a maximum difference of 0.39%.

The incorrectly predicted training samples are ranked in descending order by the difference in their class predictions as in Eq. 1.

$$P_D = P_W - P_C \qquad (1)$$

P_W is the probability of the wrong class and P_C is the probability of the correct class. P_D will always be positive for wrongly classified samples and will be 0 when both classes are equally likely at 0.5 and 0.5. The first 1000 samples are then graded by the author as either healthy, unhealthy or invalid. Invalid samples are excluded from the training set for the following iterations. This grading is done after each iteration. When a sample has been graded once it is omitted in the following grading iterations, so that no sample is graded twice.

The last iteration will be validated and tested in two ways. First in the same way as for the previous iterations to compare the results of the final manual grading round. The model will then be trained again as the purpose is no longer to identify mislabeled training samples, but to get the optimal performance from the network. To make sure that the model has converged it will train for 1000 epochs, 500 with a learning rate of 0.005, then 300 epochs with 0.003 and 200 epochs with a learning rate of 0.001. The performance on the validation set will be used for early stopping.

5   Results

A total of seven iterations have been run, where the first, iteration 0, was without any manually graded training samples. For the next six iterations a total of 6000 training samples were manually inspected. The amount of samples that were either relabelled or discarded can be seen in Fig. 3, plotted for each iteration. The total number of relabeled samples is 2870 and 425 was discarded. The majority of relabels are from unhealthy to healthy which is in line with the assumption about the noise in the data set.

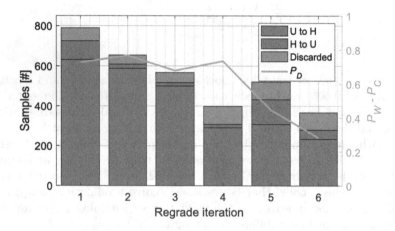

Fig. 3. Regrades for each iteration. 1000 samples were graded for each iteration. P_D describes the certainty of the wrong prediction.

Figure 3 also shows the average prediction difference, P_D, for the 1000 samples graded in each iteration. It drops rapidly for iteration 5 and 6, indicating that the model is no longer certain about the predictions. This also means that the samples get harder to grade as the viscera no longer are clearly unhealthy or clearly healthy. It was therefore chosen to stop grading after iteration 6.

Figure 4 shows the minimum train and validation error for each iteration. The training error drops rapidly for the first 3 iterations and seems to converge around 7%. The validation error shows a more linear decline from 13.60% at iteration 0 to 11.44% at iteration 6.

The results of the final training can be seen in Fig. 5. This model uses the training labels from iteration 6, but trains for 1000 epochs instead of 300. The training error seems to converge around 6% and the validation converges around 12.5%.

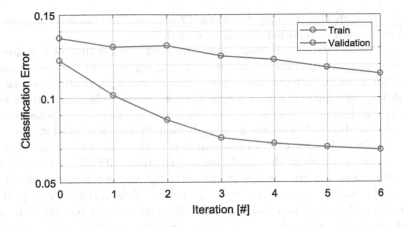

Fig. 4. Minimum training and validation error for the seven iterations. All iterations have been trained for 300 epochs.

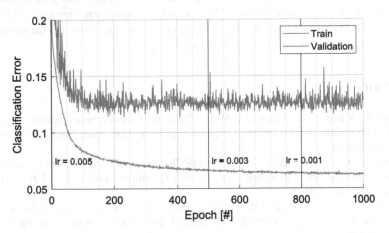

Fig. 5. The last iteration trained for 1000 epochs.

The smallest validation error is 11.36% at epoch 408, which is a small improvement compared to the model only trained for 300 epochs. The model at epoch 408 was then selected for testing and the classification error on the test set was 14.00%.

6 Conclusion

Automatic classification of viscera is a difficult task as there is a large variation is both the healthy and the unhealthy samples. In this work we presented a method that achieved a classification accuracy of 86%. Data graded by experts was used for validation and test only, while the training was performed on noisy labelled data. Of the 36,228 images in the data set only 6.33% were graded by experts. Through the training iterations 17.68% of the training samples were graded by the author and 8.46% was relabeled.

A fully graded data set is always desirable, but grading images is a slow and expensive process, especially when a correct grading requires the use of experts. The author is no expert but had a short introduction to grading viscera by a veterinarian. This proved good enough to spot and regrade crude errors in the automatically labelled training set, but when the incorrectly predicted samples became less and less obvious the grading became harder and harder.

The results indicate a clear improvement over the 6 grading iterations where the classification error on the validation set fell from 13.60% to 11.44%. Even though the input images are binary labelled, the content is very varying and there can be multiple reason to reject a viscera. This variation can probably explain some of the gap seen between the validation and the test error. It might be that the validation and test sets are simply too small to fully express the population variance.

The achieved accuracy of 86% is still below the bar of what you would want of a food-safety inspection system. But we need to examine the accuracy of the current manual inspection, before we can measure the true performance gap between automatic and human inspection.

References

1. Chao, K., Chen, Y.R., Hruschka, W.R., Park, B.: Chicken heart disease characterization by multi-spectral imaging. Appl. Eng. Agric. Am. Soc. Agric. Eng. **99**(171), 99–106 (2001)
2. Chao, K., Yang, C.C., Kim, M.S.: Spectral line-scan imaging system for high-speed non-destructive wholesomeness inspection of broilers. Trends Food Sci. Technol. **21**(3), 129–137 (2010)
3. Dey, B.P., Chen, Y.R., Hsieh, C., Chan, D.E.: Detection of septicemia in chicken livers by spectroscopy. Poult. Sci. **82**(2), 199–206 (2003). https://doi.org/10.1093/ps/82.2.199
4. Frenay, B., Verleysen, M.: Classification in the presence of label noise: a survey. IEEE Trans. Neural Netw. Learn. Syst. **25**(5), 845–869 (2014). https://doi.org/10.1109/TNNLS.2013.2292894
5. Jeatrakul, P., Wong, K.W., Fung, C.C.: Data cleaning for classification using misclassification analysis. J. Adv. Comput. Intell. Intell. Inform. **14**(3), 297–302 (2010). https://doi.org/10.20965/jaciii.2010.p0297
6. Jindal, I., Nokleby, M., Chen, X.: Learning Deep Networks from Noisy Labels with Dropout Regularization. In: 2016 IEEE 16th International Conference on Data Mining (ICDM), pp. 967–972. IEEE, December 2016. https://doi.org/10.1109/ICDM.2016.0121
7. Jørgensen, A., Fagertun, J., Moeslund, T.B.: Diagnosis of broiler livers by classifying image patches. In: Sharma, P., Bianchi, F.M. (eds.) SCIA 2017. LNCS, vol. 10269, pp. 374–385. Springer, Cham (2017). https://doi.org/10.1007/978-3-319-59126-1_31
8. Löhren, U.: Overview on current practices of poultry slaughtering and poultry meat inspection. EFSA Supporting Publications **9**(6), 1–58 (2012)

9. Marel Poultry: The world of Poultry Processing. Marel.com (2018). https://marel.com/files/pdf/world-of-stork-poultry-en.pdf

10. Ritchie, H., Roser, M.: Meat and Seafood Production & Consumption (2018). https://ourworldindata.org/meat-and-seafood-production-consumption

11. Rolnick, D., Veit, A., Belongie, S.J., Shavit, N.: Deep learning is robust to massive label noise. CoRR abs/1705.10694 (2017)

12. Seide, F., Agarwal, A.: Cntk: Microsoft's open-source deep-learning toolkit. In: Proceedings of the 22nd ACM SIGKDD International Conference on Knowledge Discovery and Data Mining, KDD 2016, pp. 2135–2135. ACM, New York (2016). http://doi.acm.org/10.1145/2939672.2945397

13. Tao, Y., Shao, J., Skeeles, K., Chen, Y.R.: Detection of splenomegaly in poultry carcasses by UV and color imaging. Trans. Asae $43(2)$, 469–474 (2000)

14. Yoon, S.C., Park, B., Lawrence, K.C., Windham, W.R., Heitschmidt, G.W.: Line-scan hyperspectral imaging system for real-time inspection of poultry carcasses with fecal material and ingesta. Comput. Electron. Agric. $79(2)$, 159–168 (2011). https://doi.org/10.1016/j.compag.2011.09.008

Instance-level Object Recognition Using Deep Temporal Coherence

Miguel Lagunes-Fortiz[1]([📧]) [iD], Dima Damen[2][iD], and Walterio Mayol-Cuevas[1,2]

[1] Bristol Robotics Laboratory, University of Bristol, Bristol, UK
[2] Computer Science Department, University of Bristol, Bristol, UK
{mike.lagunesfortiz,Dima.Damen,Walterio.Mayol-Cuevas}@bristol.ac.uk

Abstract. In this paper we design and evaluate methods for exploiting *temporal coherence* present in video data for the task of instance object recognition. First, we evaluate the performance and generalisation capabilities of a Convolutional Neural Network for learning individual objects from multiple viewpoints coming from a video sequence. Then, we exploit the assumption that on video data the same object remains present over a number of consecutive frames. A-priori knowing such number of consecutive frames is a difficult task however, specially for mobile agents interacting with objects in front of them. Thus, we evaluate the use of temporal filters such as Cumulative Moving Average and a machine learning approach using Recurrent Neural Networks for this task. We also show that by exploiting *temporal coherence*, models trained with a few data points perform comparably to when the whole dataset is available.

Keywords: Object recognition · Temporal modeling · Deep learning

1 Introduction

State-of-the-art object recognition using Convolutional Neural Networks (CNNs) is commonly achieved trough class-level learning [12].

However, the approach of using large databases is somewhat unsuitable to the widely encountered situation for intelligent agents performing tasks with *specific* and individual objects in front of them. This calls for methods capable of using only a few viewpoints of the objects of interest and being able to detect and re-detect these objects on subsequent unseen and possibly noisy scenarios.

This motivates our work for a model trained with few data (*i.e.* low hundreds of training examples per instance ,as available in a few seconds of video) that can achieve the same level of performance as one trained with an order of magnitude more of training data. To achieve this, we leverage the end-to-end nature of very deep CNNs for learning and extracting features and using temporal filters for exploiting the *temporal coherence* present on video data to make the predictions

This work was funded in part by the Mexican scientific agency Consejo Nacional de Ciencia y Tecnologia (CONACyT).

© Springer Nature Switzerland AG 2018
G. Bebis et al. (Eds.): ISVC 2018, LNCS 11241, pp. 274–285, 2018.
https://doi.org/10.1007/978-3-030-03801-4_25

more robust against the commonly encountered changes on perspective, scale, illumination, object's pose and adversarial noise.

First, we explore how the way of collecting data (*i.e.* different distributions of the training data) influences the performance of the CNN. This is, if acquiring images by following a vertical-slices trajectory leads to the same level of performance of a more methodical way, such as using a sphere with all Point-of-Views (POV). We evaluate too if frame-to-frame training leads to better results compared to skipping-frames in seeks to use data more efficiently and speed up the training.

Then, we exploit the *temporal coherence* trough filters applied across frame-to-frame CNN predictions. The first filter is a simple algorithm used for predicting the next element on a sequence and consists on averaging the predictions over a number of frames. This method already offers improvement and does not require a training stage but does requires a careful selection of the number of frames to be fused in order to avoid fusing a large number of predictions containing different objects. The second method is a recurrent neural network trained to produce a sequence of predictions with temporal coherence, the architecture is depicted in Fig. 1.

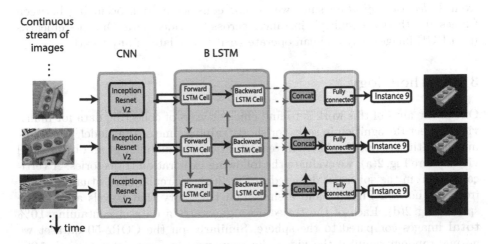

Fig. 1. A continuous stream of images goes trough a CNN and BLSTM for producing predictions with temporal coherence.

2 Related Work

Instance-level Object Recognition (*i.e.* learning specific objects) was broadly studied during the past decades trough the process of extracting and matching visual feature descriptors as in [1,5,16]. This is not necessarily a flawed approach *per se*, but one that can lead to flaws when integrating visual components together. The effectiveness of end-to-end methods via Convolutional Neural Networks, specifically showcased on class-level object recognition, aims to address such an integration problem.

CNNs tend on proposing deeper architectures for learning features at various levels of abstraction and achieve higher generalization capabilities. Such is case for the Inception-Resnet-V2 architecture [18]. While deeper architectures achieve lower error rates on large-scale image classification datasets, are still prone to recognition errors on real-world applications given a limited invariance to rotation [3], occlusions [17] and adversarial noise [7].

On the other hand, the use of recurrent architectures on top of CNNs has shown to be a useful approach for exploiting temporal information on video data for tasks such as Object Recognition as in *CortexNet* [2], 6-D camera re-localisation [4] and Object Tracking [19]. Within Recurrent Neural Networks, BLSTMs [9] posits as the state-of-the-art for visual sequence learning [8].

Our recognition framework operates in a less restrictive domain compared to existing work on data association like *Object Tracking*, where localization and identity of objects is known in the first frame and the tracker finds their localization on the subsequent ones. In contrast, no such *prior* information is required and we do not assume strong saliency of objects. Finally, it's different from *Video Classification* since we do not consider motion occurring between frames and there are multiple instances across the video data. Our model learns from RGB images only and can operate with video data of any length.

3   Methodology

One of the aims of this work is to find efficient ways of collecting data for multi-view Object Recognition in seeks for short training time of the model. Considering the ultimate, yet less likely in real situations, availability of an object's full view sphere Fig. 2(a), we evaluate the following exploration trajectories: A vertical slice from the sphere as depicted in Fig. 2(b), a circular slice situated at 45° from the horizon Fig. 2(c) and a sinusoidal trajectory that travels around the sphere Fig. 2(d). Each of the trajectories generates a dataset containing **10% total** images compared to the sphere. Similarly, on the CORe-50 dataset we normal-random sampled the video clip sequences to form datasets with **10%** and **50% total** images to evaluate how different distributions of the training data (e.g. frame-to-frame vs. normal-sampled images) affects on the recognition performance. We then perform the next steps for each training set generated.

Our approach starts with a pre-trained Network and replacing the last layer corresponding to the Fully Connected (FC) layer that produces the output predictions (*logits*); the replacement involves adjusting the dimensionality corresponding to the number of desired objects to learn. Then we keep all Convolutional layers fixed and only the last fully connected layer is first trained, with its weights and biases initialized with a normal-random distribution. This process is commonly referred as using the *CNN as a Feature Extractor* [14] and it will be useful for choosing hyper-parameters from the temporal filters later on. Once

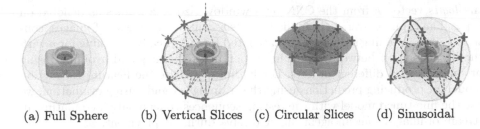

(a) Full Sphere   (b) Vertical Slices   (c) Circular Slices   (d) Sinusoidal

Fig. 2. Proposed Trajectories for extracting images, each forming a training set with a total of 90% less images compared to a full sphere (left) of Points of View.

the Feature Extraction model has converged, then a fine-tuning process takes place, retraining all the variables on the network until reaching convergence.

For both training phases we used the cross entropy as loss function H on its discrete form that reduces the error between the constructed probability distribution q by the CNN, and the distribution p from the ground truth, as denoted on Eq. 1:

$$H(p, q) = -\sum_x p(x) \log q(x) \tag{1}$$

Then, our approach for achieving temporal coherence is by considering both **current** visual information and predictions from **previous** frames. This relies on the assumption: *On the stream of images, a given object is likely to persist between adjacent frames* and thus, predicted *logits* from the CNN must be consistent over these frames. We only take into account the final predictions from the CNN, in contrast with methodologies used on video and action classification where information from middle and early layers is used by 3D convolutions [13] or recurrent connections [10] for modeling *motion* information which is not required for object recognition applications.

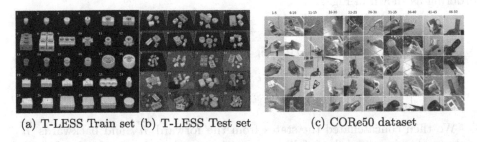

(a) T-LESS Train set (b) T-LESS Test set   (c) CORe50 dataset

Fig. 3. T-LESS and CORe50 datasets images borrowed from [11] and [15] respectively, we recommend using the digital version of this document for a closer inspection of the instances and their ID number.

As Temporal Filters we use two techniques: *Cumulative Moving Average*, a baseline and simple sum-rule in which an average calculation is performed over the *logits* vector x from the CNN by a window size of n frames as denoted on Eq. 2. The running average is applied across a continuous stream of images, consisting of the training sequences concatenated for empirically searching for n with the best trade-off between producing coherent predictions and avoiding fusing predictions with different objects. For finding n we use the Feature Extraction model for producing predictions using the training set and during evaluation, we use the fine-tuned model with the testing sequences concatenated, emulating an stream of images that an agent might receive during deployment.

$$x_{t+1} = \sum_{i=t}^{t-n} \frac{x_i}{n} \tag{2}$$

The second technique is to use a **Bidirectional Long-Short Term Memory (BLSTM)** Network that takes a sequence of n predictions from the CNN and filters them to have temporal coherence. To train the BLSTM we used the Feature Extraction model, previously obtained, for producing sequences using the training set and with the ground truth labels as targets to the BLSTM. We used the same training data used for training the backbone CNN and similarly to [2] all training video clips are concatenated and presented to the network until convergence. We used the Feature Extraction model since has a lower performance compared to the fine-tuned one (mainly because the majority of its weights comes from a different dataset) thus, it will produce erroneous predictions on the training set which allows the BLSTM to learn how to correct such incoherent predictions. During evaluation we used the same testing set concatenated as for the Moving Average.

The variables from the CNN are frozen and only the gates i (input), f (forget) and o (output) gates are trained using the activation function $tanh$ for the h (states) as shown in Eq. 3. The weights W and biased terms b are shared across all the cells. What makes the BLSTM unique to other recurrent approaches, is that the model processes the data sequence in both forward and backward ordering as shown in Fig. 1.

$$\begin{aligned}
i_t &= \sigma(W_{xi}^T x_t + W_{hi}^T h_{t-1} + b_i) \\
f_t &= \sigma(W_{xf}^T x_t + W_{hf}^T h_{t-1} + b_f) \\
o_t &= \sigma(W_{xo}^T x_t + W_{ho}^T h_{t-1} + b_o) \\
h_t &= o_t \otimes tanh(c_t)
\end{aligned} \tag{3}$$

We then concatenated the states from the forward $\overrightarrow{h}_t$ and backwards $\overleftarrow{h}_t$ states and train a single layer fully connected network with no activation function as shown on Eq. 4, this is for predicting the same number of instances as in the *logits* vector $\boldsymbol{x}$:

$$\overrightarrow{\boldsymbol{h}}_t = \sigma\big(W^T_{\overrightarrow{x}\overrightarrow{o}}\boldsymbol{x}_t + W^T_{\overrightarrow{h}\overrightarrow{o}}\overrightarrow{\boldsymbol{h}}_{t-1} + b_{\overrightarrow{o}}\big) \otimes tanh(\overrightarrow{\boldsymbol{c}}_t)$$

$$\overleftarrow{\boldsymbol{h}}_t = \sigma\big(W^T_{\overleftarrow{x}\overleftarrow{o}}\boldsymbol{x}_t + W^T_{\overleftarrow{h}\overleftarrow{o}}\overleftarrow{\boldsymbol{h}}_{t-1} + b_{\overleftarrow{o}}\big) \otimes tanh(\overleftarrow{\boldsymbol{c}}_t)$$

$$\boldsymbol{h}_t = \left[\overrightarrow{\boldsymbol{h}}_t, \overleftarrow{\boldsymbol{h}}_t\right]$$

$$\boldsymbol{y}_t = W^T_y \boldsymbol{h}_t + b_y$$

(4)

Since the BLSTM produces predictions for every image, we used the same Loss function H from Eq. 1 for training. The architecture is depicted in Fig. 1.

4   Results

The first dataset used is T-LESS [11] (Fig. 3(a) and (b)), which contains thirty industry-relevant objects with no significant texture and no discriminative colour, presenting symmetries and mutual similarities in shape and/or size and some of them are sub parts of others. T-LESS allowed us to evaluate the performance of a CNN for multi-POV instance-level recognition when training data comes with a nicely isolated object on a black background and testing data with increasing complexity.

The second dataset is CORe50 [15] and contains a collection of 50 domestic objects belonging to 10 categories: plug adapters, mobile phones, scissors, light bulbs, cans, glasses, balls, markers, cups and remote controls as shown in Fig. 3(c). CORe50 allowed us to evaluate the performance of the CNN on the presence of occlusions produced by a hand, alternating backgrounds and lighting conditions, which are well-suited for simulating a number of robotic applications.

For evaluating, **we use a single video containing all the testing scene concatenated**, which means there are different objects across the video data, where the models has to adapt for exploiting the temporal coherence correctly. As evaluation metric we used mean Average Precision (mAP) for T-LESS, consisting of first averaging precisions per class and then globally, due to the data unbalanced on the testing set (e.g. there are 8000 images of object 1 while only 1000 images of object 30) and Precision (P) for CORe50, which calculates the precision across all test set.

We used Inception-Resnet-V2 [18] as the backbone CNN architecture for extracting and learning features, since our temporal model uses the predictions only, smaller models can be used for fitting hardware requirements. The CNN was originally trained on the ILSVRC-2012-CLS dataset, for both re-training phases we used the Cross entropy as Loss. For the first phase of training the FC layer we used a batch size of 128 images and RMSProp (Root Mean Square Propagation algorithm) for solving the optimization problem, with the hyper-parameters: weight decay $w_d = 0.0004$, learning rate from $l_r = 0.001$ to $lr = 0.00001$, decay $\rho = 0.9$, momentum $m = 0.9$ and $\epsilon = 1^{-10}$, with decay occurring every 10 epochs as performed on [18]. For the *fine-tuning* phase we selected the same optimizer but with smaller learning rates, starting at $l_r = 0.0001$ to $l_r = 0.000001$.

4.1   Data Augmentation

In T-LESS, we deal with texture-minimal objects and varying lighting conditions. We initially performed the recommended data augmentation procedure in [6] regarding random cropping and modifications to colour and illumination. Initial results showed however, that the recommended augmentation for textured objects seems to produce inferior results when tested on texture-minimal objects. We thus do not use these data augmentation approaches for the remainder of the experiments. Applying random rotations *on-the-fly* resulted more useful on T-LESS to slightly boosting the performance. On CORe-50 we did not apply any data augmentation technique since video data shows objects with different pose, illumination and background conditions.

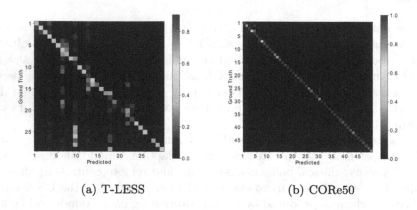

(a) T-LESS   (b) CORe50

Fig. 4. Normalized confusion matrices with frame-by-frame evaluation using 100% of training data, the instances ID numbers are consistent with Fig. 3.

In Fig. 4(a) and (b) we present the Normalized Confusion Matrices after training the CNN models using 100% of the data from each dataset. The numbering used on the matrices is consistent with the instances ID number presented in Fig. 3.

T-LESS (Fig. 4(a)) resulted a more challenging task for the CNN than CORe50 (Fig. 4(b)), we believe this is explained in part by the texture-minimal characteristic on the objects which makes them easier to be confused on cluttered, partial and fully occluded conditions, *e.g.* objects like the texture-less box #27 are easily misclassified when stronger features from other objects such as the holes from object #9 appear on the image. Additionally, the available training data doesn't contain occlusions or different background conditions which makes generalization more difficult to achieve.

On CORe50 (Fig. 4(b)) we notice that misclassification occurs mostly between objects from the same classes. For example, for the case of glasses (objects labelled from 26–30) present the same geometry and visual information when they are showed from the top view, then only the temples and top-bar are visible and thus, the model can get easily confused. This is indeed a challenging situation that was partially solved with the temporal filters.

4.2 Sampling Methods

T-LESS allowed us to test how training with views from different sampling methods affect recognition performance. The images were obtained following the sampling methods described above. The size of the training data from all trajectories is 10% relative to the initial full-sphere set. For CORe50 we tested frame-to-frame images versus normal-sampling from each training video clip, with a total of images of 10% and 50% relative to the total amount of training data available. We run each training session three times for 150 epochs.

Table 1. Sampling methods and amount of training data

T-LESS		CORe50	
Trajectory	mAP	Sampling Method	Precision
Vertical	0.430	10% continuous frames	0.871
Circular	0.311	10% normal-random sampled	0.906
Sinusoidal	**0.432**	50% continuous frames	0.921
		50% normal-random sampled	**0.941**
Baseline 100% training data	0.468	Baseline 100% training data	0.943

Table 1 contains the results about using trajectories for collecting data vs a full-POV sphere. We run every training session three times, showing only the best run. Results show that using more data leads to the best performance, however models trained with data containing enough variability, such images coming from the vertical or sinusoidal, offered close performance to a model trained with much more data (e.g. 10 times more data) and allows faster convergence times for the CNNs.

Additionally, Table 1 contains the results on CORe50 when different amounts of data are used, comparing frame-to-frame vs normal-random sampling from the video clips. Similarly, model trained with more data leads to the best performance, and normal-sampled slightly outperforms frame-to-frame sampling. However, interestingly the difference between 100 and 10% of training is only 3.7%. These results shows that diversity on the training data are key for training CNN models efficiently.

4.3 Temporal Component

Table 2 present the mean Average Precision, when the temporal filters are used on the models trained with 100% and 10% of data available.

For T-LESS, the 10% of data available comes from the sinusoidal sampling method since offered the best performance, related to the use of CMA, we varied the averaging window from 1 to 60 frames with steps of 5, we only showed the best performance achieved by a window with size of 25. For the Bidirectional LSTM we varied the number of hidden states (corresponding to the number of frames that the BLSTMs can process at the time) from 100 to 600 cells and we varied the number of neurons on the gates, going from 200 to 1000, we report only the best performance achieved by a length of 400 cells with 600 neurons.

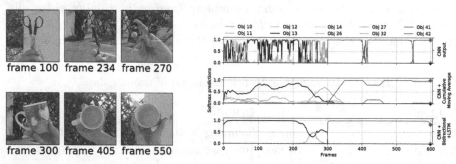

(a) First 600 testing frames   (b) Predictions from each model. The black line represents the black scissors and the red one the red and green mug.

Fig. 5. Fragment of Core50 testing sequence, showing object 13 -black scissors- and 41 - red and green mug-. The temporal filters resulted useful for correcting misclassifications caused by object's pose ambiguity. Please use the electronic version for a closer view and refer to Fig. 3(c) for the numbering of the instances. (Color figure online)

For CORe50 the 10% dataset comes from the normal-sampled method since outperformed the frame-by-frame one. We performed a similar search for the best window size for the CMA, which resulted in 40 and is consistent with the one reported on [15]. For Bidirectional LSTM the architecture with highest performance was the one with length 500 cells and 400 neurons. We used Adam Optimizer with learning rate $l_r = 1e - 4$ during 50 epochs, selecting such a small learning rate was crucial for training the BLSTM for avoiding the well-know *gradient vanishing problem* on Recurrent Neural Networks.

Both temporal filters boosted the performance on the Precision (mAP on T-LESS and P on CORe50); related to the BLSTM, the results are consistent on works like in [20], in which the performance gets better using more cells and with the number of neurons being not as relevant as the number of cells.

In Figs. 5 and 6 we show an example of the predictions produced by the three models (CNN, CNN + Cumulative Moving Average and CNN + BLSTM) using a fragment of the test set with two objects. On every Figure we present six images on the top, which corresponds to example frames from the testing sequence. Below, we present probabilities *per*-frame about what object is being

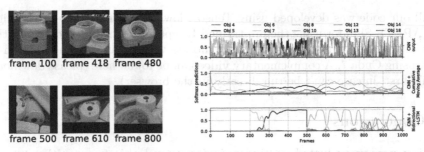

(a) First 500 testing frames (b) Predictions from each model. The black line represents the Object 5 and the red one the Object 4

Fig. 6. Fragment of T-LESS testing sequence showing objects 4 and 5. Highly occluded conditions resulted quite challenging for the CNN and this could not be alleviated by the use of Temporal Filters. Please use the electronic version for a closer view and refer to Fig. 3(a) for numbering of the instances.

Table 2. Temporal filters

Model	T-LESS		CORe50	
	100% training data (mAP)	10% training data (mAP)	100% training data (P)	10% training data (P)
CNN	0.468	0.432	0.943	0.906
CNN + CMA	0.524	0.479	0.971	0.944
CNN + BLSTM	**0.563**	**0.550**	**0.991**	**0.979**

predicted by each model. In order to maintain the plots readable, we only show the Top-10 objects detected across the presented sequence.

In Fig. 5 we show how both filters resulted useful for correcting the erroneous predictions from the CNN, caused by ambiguity at the given object's pose. This is, some views are quite similar among the five mugs (objects label 41–45) such as the top view. Which was alleviated by the using information from previous frames. The first 300 frames corresponds to the black scissors (object 13) and represented by the black line on the predictions plot. The rest 300 frames corresponds to the red and green mug (object 41), represented by a red line.

In Fig. 6 we show how the BLSTM performs better than the CMA, in this case by recovering faster after a set of erroneous predictions from the CNN, due to clutter conditions. Additionally, we present how neither of the filters can compensate from a majority of erroneous predictions caused in this case by highly cluttered and occluded objects. This limitation from the CNN on dealing with clutter and occlusions is more acute for minimal-texture objects, especially when objects are parts of other objects. We attribute the big gap on performance between the dataset to this CNNs limitations and how to overcome them remains as an open research question.

All our code was developed using TensorFlow 1.5, we made use of the high level API TF-Slim for using the pre-trained Inception-Resnet-V2 model and the Bidirectional LSTM implementation. All models where trained using a Titan-X GPU, using Cuda 7. A complementary video can be found here (please download the file first, in case can't be run directly in the browser).

5   Conclusions

In this paper we evaluated multi-view instance-level object recognition trough exploiting the temporal-coherence present on a continuous stream of images. We show how this way of learning can be specially useful when few data points are desired for training the models, accelerating the training process. This is useful for agents exploring the world in front of them and when they need to react and use these objects without delay. The BLSTM resulted more useful for exploiting the temporal coherence, but it does require to be trained while the simpler CMA filter shows itself useful, with the main disadvantage being the dimensionality of the window fusion. Overall our methods show useful improvements on the performance of commonly employed CNNs that do not exploit the temporal element.

References

1. Bay, H., Ess, A., Tuytelaars, T., Van Gool, L.: Speeded-up robust features (surf). Comput. Vis. Image Underst. **110**(3), 346–359 (2008). https://doi.org/10.1016/j.cviu.2007.09.014
2. Canziani, A., Culurciello, E.: Cortexnet: a generic network family for robust visual temporal representations. CoRR abs/1706.02735 (2017). http://arxiv.org/abs/1706.02735
3. Cheng, G., Zhou, P., Han, J.: Learning rotation-invariant convolutional neural networks for object detection in vhr optical remote sensing images. IEEE Trans. Geosci. Remote. Sens. **54**(12), 7405–7415 (2016). https://doi.org/10.1109/TGRS.2016.2601622
4. Clark, R., Wang, S., Markham, A., Trigoni, N., Wen, H.: Vidloc: 6-dof video-clip relocalization. CoRR abs/1702.06521 (2017). http://arxiv.org/abs/1702.06521
5. Damen, D., Bunnun, P., Calway, A., Mayol-Cuevas, W.: Real-time learning and detection of 3D texture-less objects: a scalable approach. In: British Machine Vision Conference. BMVA, September 2012. http://www.cs.bris.ac.uk/Publications/Papers/2001575.pdf
6. Donahue, J., et al.: Decaf: A deep convolutional activation feature for generic visual recognition. CoRR abs/1310.1531 (2013). http://arxiv.org/abs/1310.1531
7. Fawzi, A., Moosavi-Dezfooli, S., Frossard, P.: Robustness of classifiers: from adversarial to random noise. CoRR abs/1608.08967 (2016). http://arxiv.org/abs/1608.08967
8. Graves, A., Fernández, S., Schmidhuber, J.: Bidirectional LSTM networks for improved phoneme classification and recognition. In: Duch, W., Kacprzyk, J., Oja, E., Zadrożny, S. (eds.) ICANN 2005. LNCS, vol. 3697, pp. 799–804. Springer, Heidelberg (2005). https://doi.org/10.1007/11550907_126

9. Graves, A., Jaitly, N., Mohamed, A.: Hybrid speech recognition with deep bidirectional LSTM. In: 2013 IEEE Workshop on Automatic Speech Recognition and Understanding, Olomouc, Czech Republic, December 8–12, 2013, pp. 273–278 (2013). https://doi.org/10.1109/ASRU.2013.6707742

10. Hara, K., Kataoka, H., Satoh, Y.: Learning spatio-temporal features with 3D residual networks for action recognition. CoRR abs/1708.07632 (2017). http://arxiv.org/abs/1708.07632

11. Hodaň, T., Haluza, P., Obdržálek, Š., Matas, J., Lourakis, M., Zabulis, X.: T-LESS: An RGB-D dataset for 6D pose estimation of texture-less objects. In: IEEE Winter Conference on Applications of Computer Vision (WACV) (2017)

12. Huang, J., et al.: Speed/accuracy trade-offs for modern convolutional object detectors. In: The IEEE Conference on Computer Vision and Pattern Recognition (CVPR), July 2017

13. Ji, S., Xu, W., Yang, M., Yu, K.: 3D convolutional neural networks for human action recognition. IEEE Trans. Pattern Anal. Mach. Intell. 35(1), 221–231 (2013). https://doi.org/10.1109/TPAMI.2012.59

14. Li, Z., Hoiem, D.: Learning without forgetting. CoRR abs/1606.09282 (2016). http://arxiv.org/abs/1606.09282

15. Lomonaco, V., Maltoni, D.: Core50: a new dataset and benchmark for continuous object recognition. arXiv preprint arXiv:1705.03550 (2017)

16. Lowe, D.G.: Distinctive image features from scale-invariant keypoints. Int. J. Comput. Vision 60(2), 91–110 (2004). https://doi.org/10.1023/B:VISI.0000029664.99615.94

17. Osherov, E., Lindenbaum, M.: Increasing cnn robustness to occlusions by reducing filter support. In: 2017 IEEE International Conference on Computer Vision (ICCV), pp. 550–561, October 2017. https://doi.org/10.1109/ICCV.2017.67

18. Szegedy, C., Ioffe, S., Vanhoucke, V.: Inception-v4, inception-resnet and the impact of residual connections on learning. CoRR abs/1602.07261 (2016). http://arxiv.org/abs/1602.07261

19. Tripathi, S., Lipton, Z.C., Belongie, S.J., Nguyen, T.Q.: Context matters: refining object detection in video with recurrent neural networks. CoRR abs/1607.04648 (2016). http://arxiv.org/abs/1607.04648

20. Zamir, A.R., Wu, T., Sun, L., Shen, W., Malik, J., Savarese, S.: Feedback networks. CoRR abs/1612.09508 (2016). http://arxiv.org/abs/1612.09508

DUPL-VR: Deep Unsupervised Progressive Learning for Vehicle Re-Identification

Raja Muhammad Saad Bashir[1], Muhammad Shahzad[1(✉)], and Muhammad Moazam Fraz[1,2,3(✉)]

[1] School of Electrical Engineering and Computer Sciences (SEECS), National University Sciences and Technology (NUST), Islamabad, Pakistan
{rbashir.mscs16seecs,muhammad.shehzad,moazam.fraz}@seecs.edu.pk
[2] The Alan Turing Institute, London, UK
[3] Department of Computer Science, University of Warwick, Coventry CV47AL, UK

Abstract. Vehicle re-identification (Re-ID) is a search for the similar vehicles in a multi-camera network usually having non-overlapping field-of-views. Supervised approaches have been used mostly for re-ID problem but they have certain limitations when it comes to real life scenarios. To cope with these limitations unsupervised learning techniques can be used. Unsupervised techniques have been successfully applied in the field of person re-identification. Having this in mind, this paper presents an unsupervised approach to solve the vehicle re-ID problem by training a base network architecture with a self-paced progressive unsupervised learning architecture which has not been applied to solve the vehicle re-ID problem. The algorithm has been extensively analyzed over two large available benchmark datasets VeRi and VehicleID for vehicle re-ID with image-to-image and cross-camera search strategies and the approach achieved better performance in most of the standard evaluation metrics when compared with the existing state-of-the-art supervised approaches.

1 Introduction

Vehicle re-identification (re-ID) plays an important role in an automated visual surveillance system [14]. Moreover, it also plays an important part in the monitoring or tracking the vehicles from multiple cameras in real time video surveillance or doing forensic analysis on the backup data for various kind of tasks e.g. patterns recognition of different vehicles, traffic conditions [19] etc. Vehicle re-ID is an automated process to find the similar vehicles in a multi-camera network normally having non-overlapping camera views. It is done using the unique ID's assigned to the vehicles upon discovery in the multi-camera network and keeping track of the discovered vehicles through the multi-camera network as depicted in Fig. 1.

A trivial and easy to implement solution for vehicle re-ID is to match the license plates [20] as license plate number is a unique ID of the vehicle. But

© Springer Nature Switzerland AG 2018
G. Bebis et al. (Eds.): ISVC 2018, LNCS 11241, pp. 286–295, 2018.
https://doi.org/10.1007/978-3-030-03801-4_26

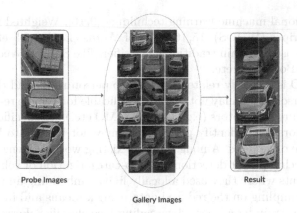

Probe Images   Result

Gallery Images

Fig. 1. Given the probe/query images finding the match in the gallery using similarity matching to find the most similar vehicles in gallery captured from different cameras having different viewpoints and illuminations.

there are few issues to this approach e.g., low resolution, environmental factors (e.g. fog, dust, rain, storm etc.), side viewpoints (i.e., neither frontal nor backward) and poor/improper illumination. A solution to these issues is to use additional appearance based approaches, which typically rely on visual and structural cues of the vehicles e.g., shape, color, texture [5,14] etc. However, these approaches work well in normal cases but are limited in terms of accuracy. With new techniques and advancements in neural network architectures especially Convolutional Neural Networks (CNN's) for computer vision tasks, the deep learning architectures have achieved the high accuracy and low error rate than the previous techniques and have enabled us to perform good in the real world scenarios. In this regard, This paper presents a semi-unsupervised approach to solve the vehicle re-ID problem by training a deep network architecture with a self-paced progressive unsupervised learning technique [7] enabling transfer of deeply learned representation towards unlabeled dataset. Following are the main contributions of the proposed approach.

- Exploiting a trained deep neural network architecture together with the self-paced learning scheme adopting the unsupervised K-means clustering that allows to infer the vehicles IDs in a semi-unsupervised manner.
- The analysis of the developed algorithm has been extensively analyzed over two large available benchmark datasets VeRi [11] and VehicleID [10] for vehicle re-ID with image-to-image and cross-camera searches.

2   Related Work

Due to numerous potential applications e.g., in surveillance and security, the vast amount of literature has framed the problem of re-ID in the domain of person re-ID. In this context, majority of the approaches solving the re-ID problem rely on conventional machine learning techniques [9,16], Weighted Histogram Of Overlapping Stripes (WHOS) [15,16], Bag of Words (BoW) [24] etc. These features have been used to train traditional classifiers like Support Vector Machines (SVM) [1], AdaBoost [17] etc.

Vehicle re-ID is a closely related problem to person re-ID and the techniques developed in person re-ID may not directly applicable for vehicle re-ID domain as most of the feature descriptors (e.g., GOG, LOMO etc.) are specifically designed feature descriptors to re-identify persons and may not be able to handle monotone appearance of vehicles. Among the few existing works, Cheng-Hao *et al.* [8] presented the technique for detection and sub-categorization of vehicles in multiview environments where they used a locally linear embedding and subsequently applied group sampling on the reduced data using k-means and further used the grouped data for training a boosted cascading tree classifier. Feris *et al.* [4] also proposed another technique for multi-view vehicle detection using the motion and shape-based features for training an AdaBoost classifier. Moreover, to overcome the occlusion problem, they adopted the Poisson distribution to synthetically generate the training data. Zapletal *et al.* [22] also presented a 3D bounding box based approach where they employed the color histogram and the histogram oriented gradients (HOG) features with linear regression to perform vehicle re-ID. In the context, of deep learning, Yang *et al.* [21] proposed a dataset COMPCARS for vehicle classification, where they applied the Convolutional Neural Network (CNN) [5] for feature extraction and later trained traditional learning classifiers for classification and attribute predictions. Liu *et al.* [11] also proposed a vehicle re-ID dataset (VeRi-776) and evaluated it using appearance based hybrid model comprising of both low and high level color/texture features extracted through handcrafted (SIFT, Bag-of-words) and CNN models to incorporate vehicle semantics. Liu *et al.* [13] later on proposed Progressive Vehicle re-ID (PROVID) model in which they divided the vehicle re-ID task into coarse-to fine search where the coarse filtering was performed using appearance based features and subsequently utilized Siamese Neural Network (SNN) [2] to match the license plates for accurate searching and later the vehicle re-ID was performed using spatio-temporal near-to-distant search. Liu *et al.* [10] also proposed a Deep Relative Distance Learning (DRDL) technique which uses the two branch CNN with coupled cluster loss for projecting raw vehicle features into Euclidian space and then measured the distance between different vehicles for similarity matching. Zhang *et al.* [23] improved a similarity loss function called triplet method by introducing classification oriented loss triplet sampling of pair wise images to avoid misleading problems. Shen *et al.* [18] proposed a two stage technique where in first stage they used chain Markov random fields (MRF) model to create the spatio-temporal paths for each vehicle and then a Siamese-CNN and Recurrent Neural Network (RNN) with Long Short Term Memory (LSTM) called Path-LSTM model which takes the spatio-temporal path candidates and pair wise queries to perform vehicle re-ID using similarity scores. Liu *et al.* [12] improved their previous work by improving the first stage of coarse-to-fine search where they introduced the metric learning based approach Null-space-based FACT (NuFACT) where they project the multi-level features into a null space where they can use the Euclidean distance for finding the distance between the vehicles.

As supervised algorithms have certain limitations that they require large amount of annotated data for training and limited to the dynamic growth of the data etc. So, using the unsupervised learning we can cope with these issues and in this context, inspired from the unsupervised techniques mentioned above, we have introduced these into vehicle re-ID We have proposed an approach that adopts a person re-ID technique [3] to solve the vehicle re-ID in an unsupervised manner.

3   Methodology

Figure 2 shows the block level diagram of the proposed system architecture highlighting the work flow of the input vehicles to the final output. It essentially formulates the whole vehicle re-ID problem into an unsupervised learning paradigm using a progressive two step approach explained below.

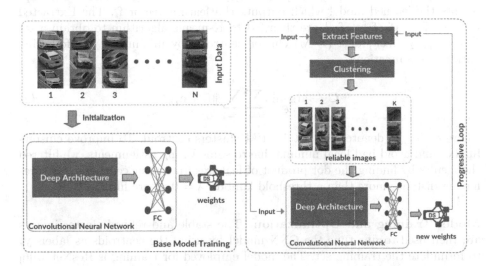

Fig. 2. The framework model for our vehicle re-ID. Irrelevant labeled data is fed into convolutional neural network for training and then trained model is stored in the first phase. Using the saved model features are extracted, clustered and used to find reliable images iteratively, which are then used to fine the base model.

3.1   Base Model Training

Let's suppose that a labeled dataset is given for training, the idea now is to replace the existing labels arbitrarily with unique numbers e.g. sequence number to allow latent space representation of the original labels denoted as $\{y_i\}_{i=1}^{M}$

with M being the total number of vehicles corresponding to $\{x_i\}_{i=1}^N$ where N is the total number of images in the given dataset. Pre-processing using the data augmentation is applied and the data is fed to a deep CNN model (e.g., ResNet50 [6]) for training. The categorical cross entropy loss is used with stochastic gradient descent optimizer. The model is fine tuned till convergence i.e. the loss is not decreasing further and is almost constant.

3.2   Progressive Model Training

The base model is used to initialize and fine tune the progressive training part. This part includes the feature extraction, clustering and reliable feature selection as explained in the following subsections.

Feature Extraction and Clustering. The features are obtained by removing the last classification layer from the deep model and using the average pooling layer as output i.e.

$$\mathbf{f}_i = \varphi(x_i, \theta) \text{ for all } i = 1, ..., N \tag{1}$$

where x_i the denotes the ith input image, θ are the weights and the φ represents the learned model which outputs the feature vector $\mathbf{f}_i$. The Extracted features $\mathbf{F} = \{\mathbf{f}_1, \mathbf{f}_2, ..., \mathbf{f}_N\}$ are then fed to K-means algorithm to obtain a set $\mathbf{C} = \{\mathbf{c}_1, \mathbf{c}_2, ..., \mathbf{c}_k\}$ of k (= M) cluster centroids by minimizing the following optimization function:

$$\mathbf{C} \leftarrow \arg\min_{\mathbf{c}} \sum_{i=1}^{N} \sum_{j=1}^{M} \|\mathbf{f}_i - \mathbf{c}_j\|^2 \tag{2}$$

where $\mathbf{c}_{j=1,...,M}$ denotes the obtained M clusters centroid. To improve clusters further and avoid bad local minima due to some wrong assignments, we filtered the results by finding the dot product of features from their centroids. Features having distance more than a threshold lambda $\lambda = 0.85$ are filtered.

Model Training and Optimization. The stable and refined cluster images are then used to fine tune the CNN model by using the centroids as labels $\mathbf{y}_i$ to formulate the training set. The model employed for training is ResNet50 [6] with some modifications i.e. an additional dropout layer together with a fully connected layer using SoftMax activation are added to the model. The model is initialized with the base model weights θ. The loss function for optimization is categorical cross entropy loss function L with stochastic gradient descent as an optimizer having the learning rate and momentum of 0.001 and 0.9 respectively. The model is thus fine-tuned on the obtained reliable training set of images. The process is iteratively performed where in each iteration, the training sample set is populated with increasingly robust/refined clusters enabling self-progressive and unsupervised learning until convergence i.e. we reach a minima and there is no more improvement. Table 1 depicts the whole algorithm used for training the proposed network architecture.

Algorithm 1. Unsupervised Vehicle Re-Identification

    Input irrelavant labeled data $\{x_i\}_{i=1}^{N}$

         No. of clusters K

         Base model $\varphi(x, \theta_b)$

    Output Model $\varphi(x, \theta_t)$

1: initialize $\theta_o \rightarrow \theta_t$;

2: **while** not convergence **do**

3:     extract features $\mathbf{f}_i = \varphi(x_i, \theta)$ for all $i = 1, ..., N$

4:     **k-means** and select centers $\mathbf{C} \leftarrow \arg\min_{\mathbf{c}} \sum_{i=1}^{N} \sum_{j=1}^{M} \|\mathbf{f}_i - \mathbf{c}_j\|^2$

5:     dot product $\frac{\mathbf{f}_i}{\|\mathbf{f}_i\|} \bullet \frac{\mathbf{c}_j}{\|\mathbf{c}_j\|} > \lambda$

6:     optimize the $\min_{\theta, \mathbf{w}} \sum_{i=1}^{r} L((\mathbf{y}_i, \varphi(\mathbf{x}_i, \theta)), \mathbf{w})$ function with reliable samples

7:     $\rightarrow \theta_t$

8: **end while**

---

4   Experimental Evaluation

There aren't many notable architectures that solves the vehicle re-ID problem using unsupervised deep learning based techniques. However, to analyze and validate the performance of the proposed network architecture, we evaluated and compared the achieved results using state-of-the-art supervised deep learning based vehicle re-ID methods including PROgressive Vehicle re-ID (PROVID) and Deep Relative Deep Learning (DRDL). Before presenting the results, let's just analyze the datasets used.

4.1   Datasets

To validate the performance of the proposed approach, two different datasets VeRi [11] and VehicleID [10] have been used. VeRi is specially designed for the vehicle re-ID purpose having the train set of 576 vehicles and having 37781 images for vehicles and the test set having 200 vehicles and 11579 images with model and color information. VehicleID is a huge dataset as compared to the VeRi in terms of total images and vehicles, it has over 200,000 images and about 26,000 vehicles. Additionally, for about 9000 images and 10319 vehicles the model and color information are also present. The dataset is also divided into the train and test lists where train list has 13164 vehicles and it had multiple test sets based on the difficulty levels.

4.2   Performance Analysis

The performance of the given architecture has been validated using different test sets. The VehicleID dataset does not contain any query set so a query set is created from the test set by random selection from tests sets such that at least two images per vehicle are captured in the query set. In the following subsections, the evaluation techniques metrics of performance of the proposed approach are discussed.

Evaluation Strategy and Metrics. The trained architecture is evaluated on two strategies i.e. cross-camera search strategy where we have multi camera and vehicles information (VeRi dataset only) and image-to-image search strategy where we do not have multi-camera information (i.e., only vehicles information is given). In the first, the search query vehicles are not searched in the same camera but across the other cameras while in the latter, the search for query vehicles are performed in all the images regardless of the camera information. With these two strategies, The CMC curve, Rank@1, Rank@5 (precision at rank 1 and 5) are also used to find the accuracy of the methods along with mean average precision (mAP) to evaluate the comprehensive performance.

Table 1. Image-to-image and cross-camera on VehicleID and VeRi

		Image-to-image		Cross-camera		
		Rank@1	Rank@5	Rank@1	Rank@5	mAP
VehicleID	DRDL	45.41	63.70	-	-	-
	NuFACT	43.72	65.19	-	-	-
	DUPL-VR	**71.45**	**81.69**	-	-	-
VeRi	PROVID	-	-	81.56	**95.11**	**52.42**
	DUPL-VR	100	100	**83.19**	91.12	40.05

Quantitative and Qualitative Results. Table 1 provides the quantitative results obtained over the two employed datasets and the evaluation metrics. As can be seen that the proposed method outperforms the state-of-the-art supervised deep learning DRDL and PROVID methods in Rank@1 accuracy in both image-to-image and cross-camera scenarios. In Rank@5, the algorithm also demonstrates superior performance in image-to-image scenario and also shows competitive results in cross-camera scenarios. Figure 3 represents the CMC curve of the image-to-image search evaluation of the proposed DUPL-VR algorithm using VeRi and VehicleID. The orange line depicts the extra-ordinary performance of the proposed architecture over VeRi dataset. It is due to the reason that from same viewpoint multiple shots of the same vehicle are available at temporally close scales. Figure 4 depicts the CMC curve obtained in a cross-camera search scenario. As can be seen that the curve reaches 90% at Rank@5 meaning which shows that the proposed algorithm finds the correct results in 5 of the best matches.

Figure 4 show the CMC curve in blue shows the DUPL-VR on VeRi for different ranks from 1–50 where the Rank@1 represents the match is found in the first match and so on. VeRi performs quite well as we can see that the curve reaches 90% of the corrects results threshold in the Rank@5 which tell us the high performance of the algorithm. Figures 5 and 6 shows the obtained qualitative results over VehicleID and VeRi datasets using image-to-image and cross-camera search respectively. In Fig. 5 (first row) the results are quite impressing, and the

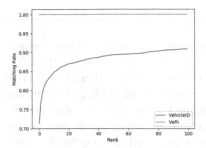

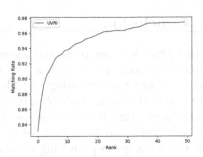

Fig. 3. CMC curve of VehicleID and VeRi in image-to-image strategy.

Fig. 4. CMC curve for the cross-camera search on VeRi only.

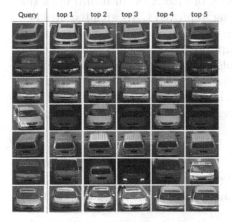

Fig. 5. Top 5 results of image-to-image search.

Fig. 6. Top 5 results of cross-camera search

same car has been found in the top-5 and same is the case with the row 2–5. In 6th row we can see that the top-1 is quite same but is not the same but in top-4 and top-5 same van has been found. In the last row the cars found in top 3 places are the same. In Fig. 6 (first row), we can see that the top-1 image is correctly being recognized while the top-2, top-3 and top-4 results have the same viewpoint but different color. Similarly, in the 2nd row, we can see that retrieved results have strong background appearance similarity (e.g., see the green bushes in top-1, top-2, top-3 and top-5). In third query we can see other cabs but due to same appearance that are hard to distinguish moreover in fourth same bus in appearance but with different license number plate can be seen as well and so on in other queries the results are based on appearance.

5   Conclusion

In this paper we have presented a semi-unsupervised deep learning-based vehicle re-ID technique. This technique uses the deep features extracted using the CNN and then uses the clustering and filtering to group and filter them for reliable selection of the input. Reliable clusters are then used to fine tuning of the model progressively until the convergence. This technique is evaluated on both datasets available VeRi and VehicleID for cross-camera and image-to-image search and it gave us the quite promising results then the supervised techniques. In cross-camera search it performs comparable to the supervised techniques while in image-to-image search it outperforms the supervised work. This technique has no limit on identities as you can train on certain number of identities and later use it on the test set regardless of the number of identities. In future work this technique can be further be improved by using improved CNN architectures better than ResNet50, using other improved clustering algorithms than k-means e.g. mean shift or some deep learning based unsupervised clustering algorithms. Reliable selection based on vehicle model and color will improve the result of reliable image selection and convergence. This does not ensure to optimally discriminate between different models of the vehicles having same color but certainly significantly help in overcoming the wrong and weak cluster assignment problems.

References

1. Bazzani, L., Cristani, M., Perina, A., Murino, V.: Multiple-shot person re-identification by chromatic and epitomic analyses. Pattern Recogn. Lett. **33**(7), 898–903 (2012)
2. Bromley, J., Guyon, I., LeCun, Y., Säckinger, E., Shah, R.: Signature verification using a "siamese" time delay neural network. In: NIPS 1993, pp. 737–744. Morgan Kaufmann Publishers Inc., San Francisco (1993)
3. Fan, H., Zheng, L., Yang, Y.: Unsupervised person re-identification: Clustering and fine-tuning. CoRR abs/1705.10444 (2017)
4. Feris, R., Petterson, J., Siddiquie, B., Brown, L., Pankanti, S.: Large-scale vehicle detection in challenging urban surveillance environments. In: 2011 IEEE Workshop on Applications of Computer Vision (WACV), pp. 527–533, January 2011
5. Feris, R.S., et al.: Large-scale vehicle detection, indexing, and search in urban surveillance videos. IEEE Trans. Multimed. **14**(1), 28–42 (2012)
6. He, K., Zhang, X., Ren, S., Sun, J.: Deep residual learning for image recognition. In: 2016 IEEE Conference on Computer Vision and Pattern Recognition (CVPR) (2016)
7. Jiang, L., Meng, D., Yu, S.I., Lan, Z., Shan, S., Hauptmann, A.G.: Self-paced learning with diversity. In: Proceedings of the 27th International Conference on Neural Information Processing Systems. NIPS 2014, vol. 2, pp. 2078–2086 (2014)
8. Kuo, C.H., Nevatia, R.: Robust multi-view car detection using unsupervised sub-categorization. In: 2009 Workshop on Applications of Computer Vision (WACV), pp. 1–8, December 2009
9. Liao, S., Hu, Y., Zhu, X., Li, S.Z.: Person re-identification by local maximal occurrence representation and metric learning. In: 2015 IEEE Conference on Computer Vision and Pattern Recognition (CVPR), pp. 2197–2206, June 2015

10. Liu, H., Tian, Y., Wang, Y., Pang, L., Huang, T.: Deep relative distance learning: tell the difference between similar vehicles. In: 2016 IEEE Conference on Computer Vision and Pattern Recognition (CVPR), pp. 2167–2175, June 2016

11. Liu, X., Liu, W., Ma, H., Fu, H.: Large-scale vehicle re-identification in urban surveillance videos. In: 2016 IEEE International Conference on Multimedia and Expo (ICME), pp. 1–6, July 2016

12. Liu, X., Liu, W., Mei, T., Ma, H.: Provid: progressive and multimodal vehicle reidentification for large-scale urban surveillance. IEEE Trans. Multimed. **20**(3), 645–658 (2018)

13. Liu, X., Liu, W., Mei, T., Ma, H.: A deep learning-based approach to progressive vehicle re-identification for urban surveillance. In: Leibe, B., Matas, J., Sebe, N., Welling, M. (eds.) ECCV 2016. LNCS, vol. 9906, pp. 869–884. Springer, Cham (2016). https://doi.org/10.1007/978-3-319-46475-6_53

14. Matei, B.C., Sawhney, H.S., Samarasekera, S.: Vehicle tracking across nonoverlapping cameras using joint kinematic and appearance features. CVPR **2011**, 3465–3472 (2011)

15. Mubariz, N., Mumtaz, S., Hamayun, M.M., Fraz, M.M.: Optimization of person re-identification through visual descriptors. In: Proceedings of the 13th International Joint Conference on Computer Vision, Imaging and Computer Graphics Theory and Applications. VISAPP, vol. 4, pp. 348–355 (2018)

16. Mumtaz, S., Mubariz, N., Saleem, S., Fraz, M.M.: Weighted hybrid features for person re-identification. In: 2017 Seventh International Conference on Image Processing Theory, Tools and Applications (IPTA), pp. 1–6, November 2017

17. Prosser, B., Zheng, W.-S., Gong, S., Xiang, T.: Person re-identification by support vector ranking. In: Proceedings of the British Machine Vision Conference, pp. 21.1–11 (2010). ISBN 1-901725-40-5. https://doi.org/10.5244/C.24.21

18. Shen, Y., Xiao, T., Li, H., Yi, S., Wang, X.: Learning deep neural networks for vehicle re-id with visual-spatio-temporal path proposals. In: 2017 IEEE International Conference on Computer Vision (ICCV), pp. 1918–1927, October 2017

19. Sivaraman, S., Trivedi, M.M.: Looking at vehicles on the road: a survey of vision-based vehicle detection, tracking, and behavior analysis. IEEE Trans. Intell. Transp. Syst. **14**(4), 1773–1795 (2013)

20. Watcharapinchai, N., Rujikietgumjorn, S.: Approximate license plate string matching for vehicle re-identification. In: 2017 14th IEEE International Conference on Advanced Video and Signal Based Surveillance (AVSS), pp. 1–6, August 2017

21. Yang, L., Luo, P., Loy, C.C., Tang, X.: A large-scale car dataset for fine-grained categorization and verification. In: 2015 IEEE Conference on Computer Vision and Pattern Recognition (CVPR), pp. 3973–3981, June 2015

22. Zapletal, D., Herout, A.: Vehicle re-identification for automatic video traffic surveillance. In: 2016 IEEE Conference on Computer Vision and Pattern Recognition Workshops (CVPRW), pp. 1568–1574, June 2016

23. Zhang, Y., Liu, D., Zha, Z.J.: Improving triplet-wise training of convolutional neural network for vehicle re-identification. In: 2017 IEEE International Conference on Multimedia and Expo (ICME), pp. 1386–1391, July 2017

24. Zheng, L., Shen, L., Tian, L., Wang, S., Wang, J., Tian, Q.: Scalable person re-identification: a benchmark. In: 2015 IEEE International Conference on Computer Vision (ICCV), pp. 1116–1124, December 2015

Motion and Tracking

Particle Filter Based Tracking and Mapping

Nils Höhner[✉], Anna Katharina Hebborn, and Stefan Müller

Institute for Computational Visualistics, University of Koblenz-Landau,
Koblenz, Germany
{nhoehner,ahebborn,stefanm}@uni-koblenz.de

Abstract. We extended the well known Kinect Fusion approach [11] with a particle filter framework to improve the tracking of abrupt camera movements, while the estimated camera pose is further refined with the ICP algorithm. All performance-critical algorithms were implemented on modern graphics hardware using the CUDA *GPGPU* language and are largely parallelized.

It has been shown that our procedure has only minimal reduced precision compared to known techniques, but provides higher robustness against abrupt camera movements and dynamic occlusions. Furthermore the algorithm runs at a frame-time of approx. 24.6098 ms on modern hardware, hence enabling real time capability.

Keywords: Tracking · Mapping · Particle filter

1 Introduction

A core problem in computer vision research fields such as robotics or augmented reality is the pose estimation of a 6-DoF camera. Typically, this can be done by detecting well-known landmarks such as id-markers in the surrounding area.

SLAM systems (Simultaneous Localization and Mapping) extend the tracking process by simultaneously mapping the environment. Distinctive features such as corners or edges are entered into a global sparse map, enabling mapping of previously unknown environments. The generated map is used in turn by the tracking algorithm to estimate the camera pose, making manual landmark placement obsolete.

Dense-SLAM approaches such as Kinect Fusion [11] go one step further by creating a dense map of the environment. Such dense maps offer many advantages as they allow a complete 3D reconstruction of the environment. Many AR related applications benefit from the resulting possibilities such as the physical interaction of virtual and real objects, the occlusion of virtual elements or realistic, situation-specific lighting. Most Dense-SLAM algorithms rely on the iterative closest point (ICP) technique to determine the cameras pose, since it can be efficiently implemented on modern GPU's and allows a high degree of

© Springer Nature Switzerland AG 2018
G. Bebis et al. (Eds.): ISVC 2018, LNCS 11241, pp. 299–308, 2018.
https://doi.org/10.1007/978-3-030-03801-4_27

precision. Even though the ICP algorithm offers high accuracy, it is prone to abrupt camera movements.

Therefore, we extended the Kinect Fusion approach with a particle filter framework that is able to simulate multiple hypothetical camera movements. This way greater robustness, especially in case of abrupt camera motion, can be achieved.

For each hypothesis the point cloud of a RGB-D sensor is transformed in respect to a particle pose and compared with information that is provided at the corresponding map location. Hypotheses that correspond well are accepted, whereas poor evaluations are rejected. In order to carry out the most precise evaluation possible, the map was supplemented with color, normal and gradient information.

The resulting camera pose is refined with up to three ICP iterations to eliminate jitter that is typically introduced by a particle filter.

The contributions of this work are briefly summarized as follows:

Compressed Dense Map. The distance field map of the Kinect Fusion approach has been enhanced with color, normal and gradient information, compressed in a single 4-channel texture to allow cached read access.

Particle Filter Framework. A particle filter framework has been implemented to handle abrupt camera movements. The likelihood function utilizes all information provided by RGB-D camera and map (point cloud, normals, colors and gradients). Additionally a three step coarse to fine filtering was implemented to increase the maximum trackable movement speed, while simultaneously reducing jitter-effects.

2   Related Work

Tracking and mapping is a fundamental problem in computer vision. Many techniques are well studied throughout different areas. As this work aims to combine particle filter tracking and dense mapping, influential and recent works from both areas are presented.

Particle Filter Tracking. Recent particle filter based tracking techniques focus mainly on *GPGPU* optimization to increase the maximum number of particles and on intelligent likelihood functions to improve overall tracking quality. Typically a given model is rendered for each particle in such a way that the rendered output can be compared with the camera input to estimate a likelihood for each particle. While [2,4,9] focus on a gradient based comparison scheme and intelligent use of the gpu, [5] use a RGB-D camera and extend the likelihood calculation by positional, normal and color information. Poglitsch et al. [13] combined gradient information with texture information and demonstrated the benefit of combining particle filtering with an inertial measurement unit.

Dense Mapping and Tracking. The dense tracking and mapping approaches can be divided into two subgroups. The first one focuses on an implicit surface description which often times resides within a 3D Volume in form of a distance field, while the latter and more recent approaches tend to store their map as a collection of surface elements (hereinafter referred to as surfels). A surfel typically consists of a position, a normal and a radius [12].

Implicit mapping approaches for SLAM systems were introduced by Newcombe *et al.* in their Kinect Fusion paper [11]. The camera pose is obtained via ICP, while the incoming depth data is fused into a 3D volume as a truncated distance field. Every voxel stores the signed distance to the nearest surface as well as a weight which describes the certainty of the measurement. New depth data is integrated by transforming the positions of every volume voxel with the current camera pose, followed by a projection onto the image plane of the depth sensor. The depth value on the corresponding pixel is used to update the current distances by applying a weighted moving average. Most of the later work aims to improve the limited map size and the memory requirements [3,6,15,17].

Unlike implicit approaches, surfel techniques do not rely on grid based data structures, but on an list of surfels. Early approaches used SIFT keypoints and corresponding depth values to align consecutive frames [7]. Later new points were rendered as an index map to associate correspondences and a pyramid-based ICP approach was used for pose estimation [8,16]. Yan *et al.* [18] extend the classic surfel map by introducing a probabilistic view on the surfels position and intensity.

3   Dense-Map

The core of this work's dense map is a truncated distance field that resides within a 3D Textur. Each voxel stores the truncated signed distance T to the nearest surface as well as a weight that describes the certainty of the map entry (similar to [11]). Additionally color, normal and gradient information is encoded into the map to ensure a richer description of the environment. Furthermore texture memory was used to guarantee cached read access for particle weighting, preventing a bottleneck in terms of performance.

Data Structure. The requirements for a data structure that is able to contain the map are twofold. On the one hand fast reading access is desirable to improve the particle weighting performance, while on the other hand as much geometric and photometric information as possible should be covered.

This work utilizes CUDA 3D texture memory which provides a maximum of four 32 bit float values per voxel and offers cached read access for neighboring data. Given that points within a point cloud are usually spatially close to their neighbors, an increase in access times should occur.

To fit as much information as possible in the 128 bit wide texture entry float values are stored using bit shifting without reinterpreting the bit representation. Figure 1 shows the underlying memory layout.

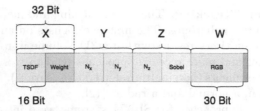

Fig. 1. Encoded map information. The tsdf, weight and sobel take 16 bit each, while the color takes 30 bits, followed by the normal with 48. The last two bits are unused.

Mapping. In order to create and extend the map, new point clouds have to be aligned to the map and corresponding distance measures have to be extracted. To do so we use a similar idea as the Kinect Fusion approach [11]. All map points p are projected onto the sensor plane given a camera matrix K, whereas π performs a perspective projection. The distance metric (Eq. 2) transforms the map position p to the camera coordinate system with the camera pose X_t. In doing so the depth measurements of the RGB-D sensor are aligned to the map. Equation 1 generates the tsdf (*truncated signed distance field*) value T by truncating the calculated distance.

$$T_{X_t} = \Psi(d_t(p)) \tag{1}$$

$$d_t(p) = ||X_t^{-1}p||_2 - pcl_z(p') \tag{2}$$

$$p' = \pi(KX_t^{-1}p) \tag{3}$$

In order to combine multiple depth measurements, we make use of the weight that supplements each map entry. This makes it possible to integrate new depth data into the map as a running average.

4   Particle Tracking

A particle filter is a sequential monte carlo method for dynamic state estimation [1]. The goal is to generate the states probability density function (*PDF*) based on available measurements. In the context of a particle filter the posterior *PDF* at time t is typically described via a set of N weighted samples:

$$S_t = \{\langle s_t^i, w_t^i\rangle | i = 0, ..., N\} \tag{4}$$

Where s_t^i are state hypothesis, while w_t^i are the importance weights. The current state X_t of the system at time t can be evaluated by calculating the weighted average:

$$X_t = \sum_{i=0}^{N} w_t^i s_t^i \tag{5}$$

In the context of camera tracking the state hypothesis of each particle is a possible 6-DoF camera pose. Typically a particle filter approach starts scattering the particles by perturbing the camera poses with normal distributed random values, based on a motion model. Higher standard deviations lead to camera poses that are farther apart and vice versa.

The particle weights are determined by a likelihood function which rates how well the particle state matches sensor inputs. Since there is a limitation in the number of particles that can be simulated, given particles typically drift away from the optimal solution making resampling necessary. There are various resampling strategies [10] of which multinomial resampling was used in this work. The basic idea is to duplicate particles with high weights and replace those with a low rating.

Likelihood Function. The likelihood function is the central part of the particle filter. Incoming sensor data is compared to expected results based on the simulations model.

To guarantee smooth tracking the likelihood function should be able to precisely rate a given camera pose, based on the similarity of the transformed point cloud and the generated map. Therefore each point is evaluated in parallel, based on geometric measurements such as euclidean distances to the nearest surface, surface normal similarities as well as photometric measurements like color and image gradients. The intermediate results are summed up on the gpu by using a parallel reduction scheme, which allows real time performance.

Let w_d, w_n, w_c, w_∇ be the distance, normal, color and gradient weights respectively and $\lambda_d, \lambda_n, \lambda_c, \lambda_\nabla$ user specific parameters to control the importance of the different weight characteristics. Then the likelihood of a given particle i at time t is defined as:

$$Likelihood(X_t^i) = \frac{\lambda_d \cdot w_d + \lambda_n \cdot w_n + \lambda_c \cdot w_c + \lambda_\nabla \cdot w_\nabla}{v} \tag{6}$$

Whereas v is the amount of points that hit a valid volume voxel with a weight greater than zero.

Before the weights are calculated each point pcl_{xyz} of the point cloud is transformed with a particle pose X_t^i, followed by a texture read at it's resulting position to retrieve the corresponding map information.

The distance weight w_d^i of a particle i describes how close the points of a given point cloud are to the surface of the map. Since the tsdf value T is in an interval of -1 and 1, it's absolute value can be used to generate the distance weight.

$$w_d^i = \sum_{x=0}^{N_x} \sum_{y=0}^{N_y} (1 - |T_t(X_t^i \cdot pcl_{xyz}(x,y))|)^2 \tag{7}$$

The normal weight of a particle measures the similarity of the point cloud's normals N_t^* to the corresponding map normal N_t. Therefore the dot product between both is calculated and normalized, such that normals which point in the same direction result in a weight of one.

$$w_n^i = \sum_{x=0}^{N_x} \sum_{y=0}^{N_y} \frac{(\langle N_t^*(x,y), N_t(X_t^i \cdot pcl_{xyz}(x,y)) \rangle + 1)}{2} \tag{8}$$

The color weight evaluates the similarity of the point cloud's color C_t^* to the map's color C_t. To provide invariance to illumination changes the color is first transformed to the HSV color space. The weight of a point is now defined as the inverted angular difference between two hue values (Eq. 10).

$$w_c^i = \sum_{u=0}^{N_u} \sum_{v=0}^{N_v} (1 - hsvDiff(C_t^*(x,y), C_t(X_t^i \cdot pcl_{xyz}(u,v))))^2 \tag{9}$$

$$hsvDiff(c_1, c_2) = \begin{cases} \frac{360 + (c_1 - c_2)}{360} & \text{if } c_2 > c_1 \\ \frac{c_1 - c_2}{360} & \text{otherwise.} \end{cases} \tag{10}$$

The gradient weight w_∇^i rates the overlap of strong image gradients in the point cloud ∇_t^* with previously mapped gradients ∇_t. As gradients are usually sparse in appearance, small camera pose differences have a higher impact, resulting in a likelihood function with a high peak.

$$w_\nabla^i = \sum_{u=0}^{N_u} \sum_{v=0}^{N_v} I(\nabla_t^*(x,y), \nabla_t(X_t^i \cdot pcl_{xyz}(u,v))) \tag{11}$$

The indicator function $I(g_{ij}, s_{ij})$ returns a weight of one if both gradients exceed a user specified threshold ϵ.

$$I(g_{ij}, s_{ij}) = \begin{cases} 1 & \text{if } g_{ij} \geq \epsilon \wedge s_{ij} \geq \epsilon \\ 0 & \text{else} \end{cases} \tag{12}$$

Coarse to Fine Filtering and Refinement. The particle tracking approach is able to track different scenes at acceptable precision. However, the standard deviations for particle scattering have to be compatible with the actual camera movement. If the standard deviation is too high, the system looses precision and suffers from jitter-effects, while a low standard deviation leads to a limitation of the maximum trackable movement speed. In order to meet both requirements, a three-step procedure was developed which starts by estimating a rough camera pose and then gradually reduces the standard deviation. Due to the stochastic nature of a particle filter jitter-effects, especially with a low sample count, cannot be completely avoided. Such occasional inaccuracies have the consequence that a considerable drift can occur with simultaneous mapping. To prevent this the final pose, calculated by the particle filter, is refined using up to three ICP steps. This refining step is essential for the creation of a precise map and allows the advantages of a particle filter to be combined with the precision of the ICP algorithm. Note that only a few iterations are necessary, whereas [11] relies on a pyramid-based calculation with at least 19 iterations.

5   Evaluation

We evaluated the accuracy of the tracking, the quality of the resulting map and
the robustness against sudden camera movements and occlusions. All tests were
carried out with 800 particles, coarse to fine filtering and refinement and are
compared to the ICP algorithm of [11].

Table 1 shows the absolute trajectory errors of two publicly available test
scenes from the RGB-D SLAM benchmark [14]. Both scenes focus on rather
slow translational movements to illustrate the differences of both approaches. In
both scenes the ICP approach is more precise, due to the inherent uncertainty of
particle filtering. Even though the accuracy of the tracking is lower, the resulting
map shows only small differences (Fig. 2).

Table 1. Comparison of particle filtering to ICP. The ICP approach generates
slightly more accurate results, especially in scenes with slow movement speed.

Scene	Algorithm	Absolute Trajectory Error (ATE)		
		rmse	mean	median
freiburg1_xyz	ICP	0.018236 m	0.017932 m	0.016723 m
	PFTaM	0.024530 m	0.021529 m	0.018387 m
freiburg2_xyz	ICP	0.021728 m	0.019372 m	0.018236 m
	PFTaM	0.049084 m	0.035326 m	0.027594 m

Fig. 2. Comparison of the generated maps. Left: Particle filtering. Right: ICP.

In order to demonstrate the robustness towards rapid movement changes the
camera was rotated exclusively around the Y-axis. The camera pans start slowly
at first and become constantly faster. As one can see in Fig. 3 the ICP approach
fails at frame 1108 as the motion blur starts to get visible. The particle filtering,
however, maintains a stable pose until frame 1310 even though heavy motion
blur is present.

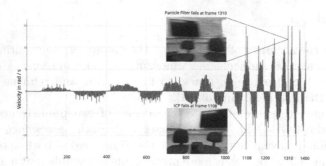

Fig. 3. Visualization of the velocities during the camera pans. Note that the poses are lost during velocity peaks.

We demonstrate the robustness of the particle filter against occlusions on a test scene in which the camera remains static, whereupon an obstacle is moved in front of the sensor. This ranges from slight overlaps at the edge of the image to an almost complete occlusion. To compare the robustness the length of the cameras translation vector was plotted during the tracking process (Fig. 4). Since the camera is stationary, a vector length of zero is equivalent to the ground truth pose.

As one can see the particle filter shows higher uncertainties (jitter-effects) as expected. However, the ICP algorithm fails to continue tracking in case of large occlusions (at frame 530). Here the particle filtering suffers in terms of precision, but is able to regain the camera pose after the occlusion disappeared.

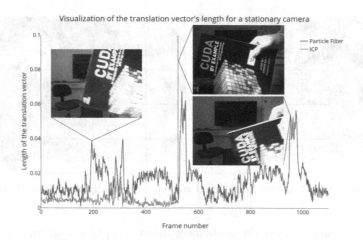

Fig. 4. Visualization of the translation vector's length during different amounts of occlusion. The ICP approach fails at frame 530, while the particle filter is able to regain the camera pose.

Performance and especially real time capability is a crucial factor for tracking and mapping approaches, as user interactions are desirable in many scenarios. Our approach takes 24.6098 ms with 800 particles, coarse to fine filtering and refinement. This settings were chosen, as they provide good results in terms of precision and at the same time ensure real time capability.

All measurements were carried out on an ubuntu 16.04 machine with an Intel Core i7-4770k processor and a NVIDIA GeForce GTX 1080 graphics card (driver version 390.25). The kernel execution times were measured with the NVIDIA visual profiler, while the overall run-time was measured with the C++ Chrono library.

6 Conclusion and Future Work

Within the scope of this work a dense mapping and tracking method was developed and implemented which is capable of mapping a previously unknown area.

The tracking was realized by a particle filter framework which is able to track faster camera movements with a three step coarse to fine filtering procedure. The algorithm is able to simulate 800 particles and takes 24.6098 ms to complete all three coarse to fine iterations.

To keep the performance as high as possible, memory access has been optimized by keeping the three dimensional map exclusively in the texture memory of the graphics card. In addition, all particles are evaluated simultaneously and are independently reduced to a single particle weight by a parallel reduction step.

As demonstrated in the evaluation, the presented method shows slightly less precise results than conventional iterative closest point methods, but offers advantages for abrupt camera pans and dynamic occlusions. Both approaches are able to handle slight sensor occlusions, but suffer from an error increasement in case of a complete concealment. While the ICP approach fails to continue tracking at this stage, the particle filtering is able to regain the camera pose after the occlusion disappears.

An existing problem is the occurring of jitter-effects which, although reduced by coarse to fine filtering, favor an imprecise map and lead to the drift of the camera pose. The presented procedure avoids this problem by additionally refining the final camera pose through the application of an iterative closest point technique. For future work, approaches should attempt to make this refinement obsolete. For example, the scattering of particles should be more targeted. The analysis of the previous camera path as well as the current camera images could help to adjust the standard deviation accordingly.

References

1. Arulampalam, M., Maskell, S., Gordon, N., Clapp, T.: A tutorial on particle filters for online nonlinear/non-Gaussian Bayesian tracking. IEEE Trans. Sig. Process. **50**(2), 174–188 (2002)

2. Brown, J.A., Capson, D.W.: GPU-accelerated 3-D model-based tracking. J. Phys. Conf. Ser. **256** (2010)

3. Chen, J., Bautembach, D., Izadi, S.: Scalable real-time volumetric surface reconstruction. ACM Trans. Graph. **32**(4), 113:1–113:16 (2013)

4. Choi, C., Christensen, H.I.: Robust 3D visual tracking using particle filtering on the special Euclidean group: a combined approach of keypoint and edge features. Int. J. Rob. Res. **31**, 498–519 (2012)

5. Choi, C., Christensen, H.I.: RGB-D object tracking: a particle filter approach on GPU. In: IEEE International Conference on Intelligent Robots and Systems, pp. 1084–1091 (2013)

6. Henry, P., Fox, D., Bhowmik, A., Mongia, R.: Patch volumes: segmentation-based consistent mapping with RGB-D cameras. In: 2013 International Conference on 3D Vision - 3DV 2013, pp. 398–405, June 2013

7. Henry, P., Krainin, M., Herbst, E., Ren, X., Fox, D.: RGB-D mapping: using kinect-style depth cameras for dense 3D modeling of indoor environments. Int. J. Rob. Res. **31**(5), 647–663 (2012)

8. Keller, M., Lefloch, D., Lambers, M., Izadi, S., Weyrich, T., Kolb, A.: Real-time 3D reconstruction in dynamic scenes using point-based fusion. In: 2013 International Conference on 3D Vision - 3DV 2013, pp. 1–8, June 2013

9. Klein, G., Murray, D.: Full-3D edge tracking with a particle filter. In: British Machine Vision Conference (2006)

10. Li, T., Bolic, M., Djuric, P.M.: Resampling methods for particle filtering: classification, implementation, and strategies. IEEE Sig. Process. Mag. **32**(3), 70–86 (2015)

11. Newcombe, R.A., et al.: Kinectfusion: real-time dense surface mapping and tracking. In: 2011 10th IEEE International Symposium on Mixed and Augmented Reality, pp. 127–136, October 2011

12. Pfister, H., Zwicker, M., van Baar, J., Gross, M.: Surfels: surface elements as rendering primitives. In: Proceedings of the 27th Annual Conference on Computer Graphics and Interactive Techniques, SIGGRAPH 2000, pp. 335–342 (2000)

13. Poglitsch, C., Arth, C., Schmalstieg, D., Ventura, J.: [poster] a particle filter approach to outdoor localization using image-based rendering. In: 2015 IEEE International Symposium on Mixed and Augmented Reality, pp. 132–135, September 2015

14. Sturm, J.: RGB-D slam dataset and benchmark. https://vision.in.tum.de/data/datasets/rgbd-dataset. Accessed 07 July 2018

15. Whelan, T., Kaess, M., Fallon, M., Johannsson, H., Leonard, J., McDonald, J.: Kintinuous: spatially extended kinectfusion. In: RSS Workshop on RGB-D: Advanced Reasoning with Depth Cameras, Sydney, Australia, July 2012

16. Whelan, T., Leutenegger, S., Salas-Moreno, R.F., Glocker, B., Davison, A.J.: ElasticFusion: dense SLAM without a pose graph. In: Robotics: Science and Systems (RSS), Rome, Italy, July 2015

17. Whelan, T., Kaess, M., Johannsson, H., Fallon, M., Leonard, J.J., Mcdonald, J.: Real-time large-scale dense RGB-D slam with volumetric fusion. Int. J. Rob. Res. **34**(4–5), 598–626 (2015)

18. Yan, Z., Ye, M., Ren, L.: Dense visual slam with probabilistic surfel map. IEEE Trans. Vis. Comput. Graph. **23**(11), 2389–2398 (2017)

Multi-branch Siamese Networks
with Online Selection for Object Tracking

Zhenxi Li[1]([⊠]), Guillaume-Alexandre Bilodeau[1], and Wassim Bouachir[2]

[1] LITIV Lab, Polytechnique Montreal, Montreal, Canada
{zhenxi.li,guillaume-alexandre.bilodeau}@polymtl.ca
[2] TELUQ University, Montreal, Canada
wassim.bouachir@teluq.ca

Abstract. In this paper, we propose a robust object tracking algorithm based on a branch selection mechanism to choose the most efficient object representations from multi-branch siamese networks. While most deep learning trackers use a single CNN for target representation, the proposed Multi-Branch Siamese Tracker (MBST) employs multiple branches of CNNs pre-trained for different tasks, and used for various target representations in our tracking method. With our branch selection mechanism, the appropriate CNN branch is selected depending on the target characteristics in an online manner. By using the most adequate target representation with respect to the tracked object, our method achieves real-time tracking, while obtaining improved performance compared to standard Siamese network trackers on object tracking benchmarks.

Keywords: Object tracking · Siamese networks
Online branch selection

1 Introduction

Model-free visual object tracking is one of the most fundamental problems in computer vision. Given the object of interest marked in the first video frame, the objective is to localize the target in subsequent frames, despite object motion, changes in viewpoint, lighting variation, among other disturbing factors. One of the most challenging difficulties with model-free tracking is the lack of prior knowledge on the target object appearance. Since any arbitrary object may be tracked, it is impossible to train a fully specialized tracker.

Recently, convolutional neural networks (CNNs) have demonstrated strong power in learning feature representations. To fully exploit the representation power of CNNs in visual tracking, it is desirable to train them on large datasets specialized for visual tracking, and covering a wide range of variations in the combination of target and background. However, it is truly challenging to learn a unified representation based on videos that have completely different characteristics. Some trackers [1] train regression networks for tracking in an entirely offline manner. Other works [2,3,6] propose to train deep CNNs to address the

© Springer Nature Switzerland AG 2018
G. Bebis et al. (Eds.): ISVC 2018, LNCS 11241, pp. 309–319, 2018.
https://doi.org/10.1007/978-3-030-03801-4_28

general similarity learning problem in an offline phase and evaluate the similarity online during tracking. However, since these works have no online adaptation, the representations they learned offline are general but not always discriminative.

Rather than applying a single fixed network for feature extraction, we propose to use multiple network branches with an online branch selection mechanism. It is well known that different networks designed and trained for different tasks have diverse feature representations. With the online branch selection mechanism, our tracker dynamically selects the most efficient and robust branch for target representation, even if the target appearance changes. Our goal is to improve the generalization capability with multiple networks.

The main contributions of our work are summarized as follows. First, we propose a multi-branch framework based on a siamese network for object tracking. The proposed architecture is designed to extract appearance representation robust against target variations and changing contrast with background scene elements. Second, to make the full use of the different branches, we propose an effective and generic branch selection mechanism to dynamically select branches according to their discriminative power. Third, on the basis of multiple branches and branch selection mechanism, we present a novel deep learning tracker achieving real-time and improved tracking performance. Our extensive experiments compare the proposed Multi-Branch Siamese Tracker (MBST) with state-of-the-art trackers on OTB benchmarks [4,5].

2   Related Work

Siamese Network Based Trackers. Object tracking can be addressed using similarity learning. By learning a deep embedding function, we can evaluate the similarity between an exemplar image patch and a candidate patch in a search region. These procedures allow to track the target to the location that obtains the highest similarity score. Inspired by this idea, the pioneering work of SiamFC [2] proposed a fully-convolutional Siamese Network in which the similarity learning with deep CNNs is addressed using a Siamese architecture. Since this approach does not need online training, it can easily achieve real-time tracking. Due to the robustness and real-time performance of the SiamFC [2] approach, several subsequent works proceeded along this direction to address the tracking problem. In this context, EAST [7] employs an early-stopping agent to speed up tracking where easy frames are processed with cheap features, while challenging frames are processed with deep features. CFNet [3] incorporates a Correlation Filter into a shallow siamese network, which can speed up tracking without accuracy drop comparing to a deep Siamese network. TRACA [8] applies context-aware feature compression before tracking to achieve high tracking performance. SA-Siam [6] utilizes the combination of semantic features and appearance features to improve generalization capability. In our work, we use the Siamese Network as embedding function to extract feature representations. All branches use the Siamese architecture to apply identical transformation on target patch and search region.

Multi-branch Tracking Frameworks. The diversity of target representation from a single fixed network is limited. The learned features may not be discriminative in all tracking situations. There are many works using diverse features with context-aware or domain-aware scheme.

TRACA [8] is a multi-branch tracker, which utilizes multiple expert auto-encoders to robustly compress raw deep convolutional features. Since each of expert auto-encoders is trained according to a different context, it performs context-dependent compression. MDNet [9] is composed of shared layers and multiple branches of domain-specific layers. BranchOut [18] employs a CNN for target representation, with a common convolutional layers and multiple branches of fully connected layers. It allows different number of layers in each branch to maintain variable abstraction levels of target appearances.

A common insight of these multi-branch trackers is the possibility to make a robust tracker by utilizing different feature representations. Our method shares some insights and design principles with other multi-branch trackers. Our network architecture is composed of multiple branches separately trained offline and focusing on different types of CNN features. In addition, we use an AlexNet [11] branch in our framework that is designed and pretrained for image classification. In our multi-branch frameworks, the combination of branches trained in different scenarios ensures a better use of diverse feature representations.

Online Branch Selection. Different models produce various feature maps on different tracked targets in different scales, rotations, illumination and other factors. Using all features available for a single object tracking is neither efficient nor effective. BranchOut [18] selects a subset of branches randomly for model update to diversify learned target appearance models. MDNet [9] learns domain-independent representations from pretraining, and identifies branches through online learning.

In our online branch selection mechanism, we analyse the feature representation of each branch to select the most robust branch at every T frames. This allows us to use diverse feature representations and to handle various challenges in the object tracking problem more efficiently.

3   Multi-branch Siamese Tracker

We propose a multi-branch siamese network for tracking. Given that different neural network models produce diverse feature representations, we use many of them as branches in our tracker to produce diverse feature representations and select the most robust branch with our online branch selection mechanism.

3.1   Network Architecture

Using multiple target representations is shown to be beneficial for object tracking [6,10], as different CNNs can provide various feature representations. In our work, we ensemble N_e siamese networks including N_s context-dependent branches and one AlexNet branch as $N_e = N_s + 1$. The context-dependent

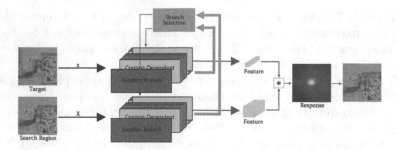

Fig. 1. The architecture of our MBST tracker. Context-dependent branches are indicated by green blocks and AlexNet branch is indicated by purple blocks. (Color figure online)

branches have the same structure as SiamFC [2] and the AlexNet branch has the same structure as AlexNet [11]. Each branch of the tracker is a siamese network applying identical transformation φ_i to both inputs and combining their representation by a cross-correlation layer. The architecture of the proposed tracker is illustrated in Fig. 1.

The input consists of a target patch cropped from the first video frame and another patch containing the search region in the current frame. The target patch z has a size of $W_z \times H_z \times 3$, corresponding to the width, height and color channels of the image patch. The search region X has a size of $W_X \times H_X \times 3$ ($W_z < W_X$ and $H_z < H_X$), representing also the width, height and color channels of the search region. X can be considered as a collection of candidate patches x in the search region with the same dimension as z.

From what we observed, there are two strategies to improve the discriminative ability of the tracking networks. The first one is training the network in different contexts, while the second one is to use multiple networks designed and trained for different tasks. In our approach, we utilize context-dependent branches pretrained in different contexts in addition to another branch pre-trained for image classification task to improve our tracking performance. We note that more branches could be added with other pre-trained networks at the cost of slower performances.

Context-Dependent Branches: We use N_c context-dependent branches and one general branch as $N_s = N_c + 1$. All these branches have the same architecture as the SiamFC network [2]. Context-dependent branches are trained in three steps. Firstly, we train the basic siamese network on the ILSVRC-2015 [12] video dataset (henceforth ImageNet), including 4,000 video sequences and around 1.3 million frames containing about 2 million tracked objects. We keep the basic siamese network as the general branch. Then, we perform contextual clustering on the low level feature map from the ImageNet Video dataset to find N_c ($N_c = 10$) context-dependent clusters. Finally, we use the N_c clusters to train N_c context-dependent branches initialized by the basic siamese network. These branches take (z, X) as input and extract their feature maps. Then, using a cross correlation layer we combine their feature maps to get a response map. The response map of context-dependent branches is calculated as:

$$h_{s_i}(z, X) = corr(f_{s_i}(z), f_{s_i}(X)),\tag{1}$$

where s_i indicates the contextual index including the general branch ($i = 0$), $f(\cdot)$ denotes features generated by the network.

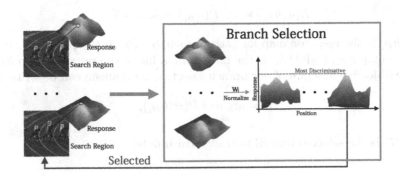

Fig. 2. Online branch selection mechanism and response map example.

The AlexNet Branch: We use AlexNet [11] pretrained on the image classification task as a branch with a network trained for a different task. Small modifications are made on the stride to ensure that the output response map has the same dimension as other branches. Since AlexNet is trained for image classification and the deeper layers encode more semantic information of targets, target representations from this branch are more robust to significant appearance variations. The network output corresponds to (z, X) as input, while the generated features are denoted as $f_a(\cdot)$. The response map is expressed as:

$$h_a(z, X) = corr(f_a(z), f_a(X)).\tag{2}$$

In our implementation, MBST is composed of context-dependent branches and AlexNet branch. The output of each branch is a response map indicating the similarity between target z and candidate patch x within the search region X. The branch selection mechanism compares the maps from each branch to select the most discriminative one. The corresponding branch is then used for $T - 1$ frames.

3.2   Online Branch Selection Mechanism

Different branches trained in different scenarios can be used to diversify the target representation. To ensure the optimal exploitation of the diverse representations from our branches, we designed a branch selection mechanism to monitor the tracking output and automatically select the most discriminative branch as illustrated in Fig. 2.

Given the input image pair, each branch applies identical transformation to both inputs and calculates the response map h using a cross-correlation layer. Since the ranges of feature values from different branches are different, we apply response weights w_i on response map of each branches to normalize their range difference. The discriminative power is then measured based on the weighted response maps from all branches. The heuristic approach we used to measure the discriminative power of branches is formulated as:

$$R(w_i h_{B_i}) = w_i(P(h_{B_i}) - M(h_{B_i})), \tag{3}$$

where h_{B_i} is the response map for each branch B_i, P_{B_i} is the peak value of the response map h_{B_i}, and $M_{h_{B_i}}$ is the minimum value of the response map h_{B_i}.

The objective function of our branch selection mechanism can be written as:

$$B^* = \underset{B_i}{\mathrm{argmax}}\, R(w_i h_{B_i}), \tag{4}$$

where B^* is the selected branch to transform inputs.

4   Experiments

The first aim of our experiments is to investigate the effect of incorporating multiple feature representations with an online branch selection mechanism. For this purpose, we performed ablation analysis on our framework. We then compare our method with state-of-the-art trackers. The experimental results demonstrate that our method achieves improved performance with respect to the basic SiamFC tracker [2].

4.1   Implementation Details

Network Structure: The context-dependent branches have exactly the same structure as the SiamFC network [2]. For the AlexNet branch, we use AlexNet [11] pretrained on ImageNet dataset [12] with a small modification to ensure that the output response map has the same dimension as other branches, which is 17×17. Other branches could also be used based on other network architectures.

Data Dimensions: In our experiment, the target image patch z has a dimension of $127 \times 127 \times 3$, and the search region X has a dimension of $255 \times 255 \times 3$. But since all branches are fully convolution layers, they can also be adapted to any other dimension easily. The embedding output for z and X has a dimension of $6 \times 6 \times 256$ and $22 \times 22 \times 256$ respectively.

Training: We use the ImageNet dataset [12] for training and only consider color images. For simplicity, we randomly pick a pair of images, we crop z in the center and X in the center of another image. Images are scaled such that the bounding box, plus an added margin for context, has a fixed area. The basic siamese branch is trained for 50 epochs with an initial learning rate of 0.01. The learning rate decays after every epoch with a decay factor δ of 0.869. The context-dependent branches are fine-tuned based on the parameters of the general branch with a learning rate 0.00001 for 10 epochs. For the AlexNet branch, we directly use AlexNet [11] pretrained on ImageNet dataset [12].

Our experiments are performed on a PC with a Intel i7-3770 3.40 GHz CPU and a Nvidia Titan X GPU. We evaluated our results using the Python implementation of the OTB toolkit. The average testing speed of MBST is 17 fps.

Table 1. Ablation study of MBST on OTB benchmarks. Various combinations of general siamese branch, context-dependent branches and AlexNet branch are evaluated.

General	Context	AlexNet	OTB-2013		OTB-50		OTB-100		
			AUC	Prec.	AUC	Prec.	AUC	Prec.	FPS
✓			0.600	0.791	0.519	0.698	0.585	0.766	**65.0**
	✓		0.601	0.798	0.523	0.707	0.584	0.768	18.6
		✓	0.581	0.761	0.501	0.678	0.560	0.741	63.6
✓	✓		0.594	0.784	0.535	0.721	0.587	0.770	16.9
✓		✓	0.605	0.796	0.536	0.718	0.599	0.783	42.9
	✓	✓	0.616	0.811	0.570	0.767	0.614	0.806	16.9
✓	✓	✓	**0.620**	**0.816**	**0.573**	**0.773**	**0.617**	**0.811**	16.9

Hyperparameters: The weights w_i for context-dependent branches have the same value of 1.0. For AlexNet branch, we perform a grid search from 8.0 to 12.0 with step 0.5. Evaluation suggests that the best performance is achieved when w_i is 10.5. This value is thus used for all the test sequences. In order to handle scale variations, we rescale the inputs into three different resolutions.

4.2   Dataset and Evaluation Metrics

OTB: We evaluate the proposed tracker on the OTB benchmarks [4,5] with eleven interference attributes for the video sequences. The OTB benchmark uses the precision and success rate for quantitative analysis. For the precision plot, we calculate the average Euclidean distance between the center locations of the tracked targets and the manually labeled ground truth. Then the average center location error over all the frames of one sequences is used to summarize the overall performance. As the representative precision score for each tracker, we use the score for the threshold of 20 pixels. For the success plot, we compute the IoU (intersection over union) between the tracked and ground truth bounding boxes. A success plot is obtained by evaluating the success rate at different IoU thresholds. The area-under-curve (AUC) of the success plot is reported.

4.3   Ablation Analysis

To verify the contribution of each branch and the online branch selection mechanism of our algorithm, we implemented several variations of our approach and evaluated them on the OTB benchmarks.

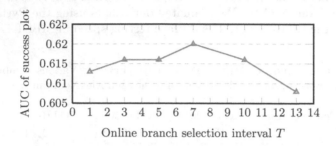

Fig. 3. Curve for the branch selection interval T on OTB2013 benchmark [4].

Multiple Branches Improve the Tracking Result. We compared our full branches algorithm with various combination of branches as illustrated in Table 1. We evaluate the performances of the original branch, context-dependent branches and AlexNet branch alone. Note that branch selection is applied only when we evaluate the context-dependent branches, since many branches are available. For the other experiments in Table 1, we combine these branches with online branch selection for testing. Results clearly demonstrate that the proposed multiple branches architecture allows a better use of diverse feature representations. The best FPS is achieved by the general siamese branch, which is expected since it needs less computations with only one branch.

Online Branch Selection for Every Frame is Not Necessary. As shown in Fig. 3, we conduct experiments on the branch selection interval T by changing the value: $T = 1, 3, 5, 7, 10, 13$. When the value of branch selection interval is less than 7 frames, the tracking performance is reduced. This can be explained by the fact that a frequent execution of the selection mechanism increases the possibility of selecting an inappropriate branch. When the value of branch selection interval is more than 7 frames, the tracking performance is also decreased because we keep for a too long period a branch that is not discriminative anymore. In our experiments, the optimal value of branch selection interval T was 7 frames.

4.4   Comparison with State-of-the Art Trackers

We compare MBST with CFNet [3], SiamFC [2], Staple [13], LCT [14], Struck [15], MEEM [16], SCM [17], LMCF [19], MUSTER [20], TLD [21] on OTB benchmarks. The precision plots and success plots of one path evaluation (OPE) are shown in Fig. 4. Based on precision and success plots, the overall

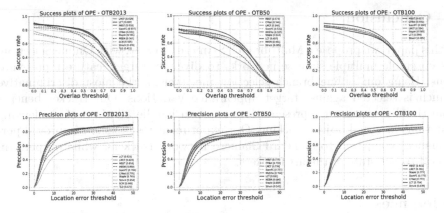

Fig. 4. The success plots and precision plots on OTB benchmarks. Curves and numbers are generated with Python implemented OTB toolkit.

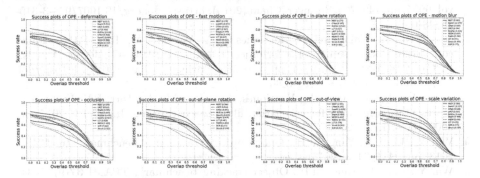

Fig. 5. The Success plot on OTB50 for eight challenge attributes: deformation, fast motion, in-plane rotation, motion blur, occlusion, out-of-plane rotation, out-of-view, scale variation.

comparison suggests that the proposed MBST achieved the best performance among these state-of-the-art trackers on OTB benchmarks. Notably, it outperforms SiamFC [2] as well as its variation CFNet [3] on all datasets. This demonstrates that diverse feature representations are important to improve tracking, as feature maps from various CNNs can be quite different. Figure 5 demonstrates that our tracker effectively handles all kinds of challenging situations that often require high-level semantic understanding. For example, our tracker significantly outperforms SiamFC in the case of deformation, occlusion and out-of-plane rotations because the contrast between the object and the background changes and switching to another feature map may give a better discriminativity. Therefore, our approach is beneficial each time the appearance of the object changes significantly during its tracking.

5   Conclusion

In this paper, we propose a Multi-branch Siamese Network with Online Selection. We ensemble multiple siamese networks to diversify target feature representations. Using our online branch selection mechanism, the most discriminative branch is selected against target appearance variations. Our tracker benefits from the diverse target representation, and can handle all kinds of challenging situations in visual object tracking. Our experiment results show improved performances compared to standard Siamese network trackers, while outperform several recent state-of-the-art trackers.

References

1. Held, D., Thrun, S., Savarese, S.: Learning to track at 100 FPS with deep regression networks. In: Leibe, B., Matas, J., Sebe, N., Welling, M. (eds.) ECCV 2016. LNCS, vol. 9905, pp. 749–765. Springer, Cham (2016). https://doi.org/10.1007/978-3-319-46448-0_45
2. Bertinetto, L., Valmadre, J., Henriques, J.F., Vedaldi, A., Torr, P.H.S.: Fully-convolutional siamese networks for object tracking. In: Hua, G., Jégou, H. (eds.) ECCV 2016. LNCS, vol. 9914, pp. 850–865. Springer, Cham (2016). https://doi.org/10.1007/978-3-319-48881-3_56
3. Valmadre, J., Bertinetto, L., Henriques, J.F., Vedaldi, A., Torr, P.H: End-to-end representation learning for correlation filter based tracking. In: CVPR 2017, pp. 5000–5008. IEEE (2017)
4. Wu, Y., Lim, J., Yang, M.H.: Online object tracking: a benchmark. In: CVPR 2013, pp. 2411–2418 (2013)
5. Wu, Y., Lim, J., Yang, M.H.: Object tracking benchmark. TPAMI **37**(9), 1834–1848 (2015)
6. He, A., Luo, C., Tian, X., Zeng, W.: A twofold siamese network for real-time object tracking. In: CVPR 2018, pp. 4834–4843 (2018)
7. Huang, C., Lucey, S., Ramanan, D.: Learning policies for adaptive tracking with deep feature cascades. In: ICCV 2017, pp. 105–114 (2017)
8. Choi, J., et al.: Context-aware deep feature compression for high-speed visual tracking. In: CVPR 2018, pp. 479–488 (2018)
9. Nam, H., Han, B: Learning multi-domain convolutional neural networks for visual tracking. In: CVPR 2016, pp. 4293–4302 (2016)
10. Nam, H., Baek, M., Han, B.: Modeling and propagating CNNs in a tree structure for visual tracking. arXiv preprint arXiv:1608.07242(2016)
11. Krizhevsky, A., Sutskever, I., Hinton, G.E.: Imagenet classification with deep convolutional neural networks. In: NIPS 2012, pp. 1097–1105 (2012)
12. Russakovsky, O., et al.: Imagenet large scale visual recognition challenge. IJCV **115**(3), 211–252 (2015)
13. Bertinetto, L., Valmadre, J., Golodetz, S., Miksik, O., Torr, P.H.: Staple: Complementary learners for real-time tracking. In: CVPR 2016, pp. 1401–1409 (2016)
14. Ma, C., Yang, X., Zhang, C., Yang, M.H.: Long-term correlation tracking. In: CVPR 2015, pp. 5388–5396 (2015)
15. Hare, S., Saffari, A., Torr, P.H.: Struck: structured output tracking with kernels. In: ICCV 2011, pp. 263–270 (2011)

16. Zhang, J., Ma, S., Sclaroff, S.: MEEM: robust tracking via multiple experts using entropy minimization. In: Fleet, D., Pajdla, T., Schiele, B., Tuytelaars, T. (eds.) ECCV 2014. LNCS, vol. 8694, pp. 188–203. Springer, Cham (2014). https://doi.org/10.1007/978-3-319-10599-4_13
17. Zhong, W., Lu, H., Yang, M.H.: Robust object tracking via sparsity-based collaborative model. In: CVPR 2012, pp. 1838–1845 (2012)
18. Han, B., Sim, J., Adam, H.: BranchOut: regularization for online ensemble tracking with convolutional neural networks. In: ICCV 2017, pp. 2217–2224 (2017)
19. Wang, M., Liu, Y., Huang, Z.: Large margin object tracking with circulant feature maps. In: CVPR 2017, pp. 21–26 (2017)
20. Hong, Z., Chen, Z., Wang, C., Mei, X., Prokhorov, D., Tao, D.: Multi-store tracker (muster): a cognitive psychology inspired approach to object tracking. In: CVPR 2015, pp. 749–758 (2015)
21. Kalal, Z., Mikolajczyk, K., Matas, J., et al.: Tracking-learning-detection. TPAMI **34**(7), 1409 (2012)

Deep Convolutional Correlation Filters for Forward-Backward Visual Tracking

Yong Wang[1], Robert Laganière[1(✉)], Daniel Laroche[2], Ali Osman Ors[2], Xiaoyin Xu[2], and Changyun Zhu[2]

[1] School of Electrical Engineering and Computer Science, University of Ottawa, Ottawa, Canada
ywang6@uottawa.ca, laganier@eecs.uottawa.ca
[2] NXP Semiconductors, Ottawa, ON, Canada
{daniel.laroche,ali.ors,christina.xu,changyun.zhu}@nxp.com

Abstract. In this paper, we exploit convolutional features extracted from multiple layers of a pre-trained deep convolutional neural network. The outputs of the multiple convolutional layers encode both low-level and high-level information about the targets. The earlier convolutional layers provide accurate positional information while the late convolutional layers are invariant to appearance changes and provide more semantic information. Specifically, each convolutional layer locates a target through correlation filter-based tracking and then traces the target backward. By analyzing the forward and backward tracking results, we evaluate the robustness of the tracker in each layer. The final position is determined by fusing the locations from each layer. A region proposal network (RPN) is employed whenever a backward tracker failure occurs. The new position will be chosen from the proposal candidates generated by the RPN. Extensive experiments have been implemented on several benchmark datasets. Our proposed tracking method achieves favorable results compared to state-of-the-art methods.

Keywords: Visual object tracking · Region proposal network
Convolutional features · Correlation filter-based tracking
Forward and backward tracking

1 Introduction

Recently, much attention has been paid to correlation filter-based tracking methods due to their superior performance both in accuracy and speed [1–3]. The key idea behind correlation filter-based trackers is that convolution operation in time domain is equivalent to element-wise multiplication operation in Fourier domain, which leads to compute cyclically shifted candidates very fast. Correlation filter-based tracking methods employ dense sampling as motion model. In the sampling area, a learned filter locates the target in the next frame by searching the location of maximal correlation response. The correlation filter is learned using these samples.

© Springer Nature Switzerland AG 2018
G. Bebis et al. (Eds.): ISVC 2018, LNCS 11241, pp. 320–331, 2018.
https://doi.org/10.1007/978-3-030-03801-4_29

Deep learned features [4–6] have also been adapted to correlation filter-based tracking framework. Tracking performances can also be improved by employing different type of deep features. A certain feature type may fail to track a given target, while multiple trackers using different features can cooperate together to achieve more robust tracking results [4,5]. Furthermore, the tracked positions of multiple feature types can be compared to produce a more robust estimated position. In [5], it is shown that the last convolutional layer represents semantic information of objects and that these representations are robust to appearance changes, while earlier convolutional layers encode localized information. Thus, each convolutional layer can be combined with correlation filters to locate a target. The final position is determined by fusing the prediction from each layer.

As shown in [7–9], the use of a detector can significantly improve the visual tracking results. Since, high-quality candidates are generated, the tracker improves not only the speed but also on the accuracy by reducing the searching window. A detector also helps the tracker when tracker failures occur. Many object detection algorithms have been developed for several decades.

Motivated by the works mentioned above, we propose in this paper a robust tracking framework, in which multiple convolutional layers are employed to encode the appearance of the target. The location of each layer is determined by the maximum correlation filter response. Backward correlation inside each convolutional layer is then carried out. The final position is fused from each layer's prediction. If the backward correlation filter response is below a pre-defined threshold, the new position is searched based on potential candidate locations as generated by a regional proposal network (RPN) [10].

The contribution of our work is as follows. (1) Forward and backward tracking is adapted to our tracking framework. The backward correlation filter response can be used to evaluate the accuracy of the tracking result. In addition, the weighted filter responses are used to fuse the location estimates from each layer. (2) Forward and backward tracking can be used to judge whether tracker failure occurred. Most tracking systems use past information [13–15] to update an appearance model and suppress a good number of tracking errors. (3) In our approach, a RPN is integrated into our tracking system. Whenever a tracking failure occurs, the RPN is employed to generate a new candidate location.

2   Tracking Framework

2.1   Overview

An overview of our proposed tracking algorithm is given in Fig. 1. It consists of four components. First, deep CNN features are extracted from different layers using the pre-trained VGG19-Net [11]. Then each layer from the CNN predicts the new target position based on a correlation filter [5]. Next, backward tracking is employed to compute the overlap score which is used to measure the quality of the tracker. The score is used to fuse the final tracking position from different layers. If the score is higher than a threshold, the final target position is obtained by fusing the tracking positions from the different network layers. Otherwise, a correlation filter is used to locate the final results from candidate proposals which are generate by the RPN. In the following, we give a detailed description of the backward tracking and RPN models.

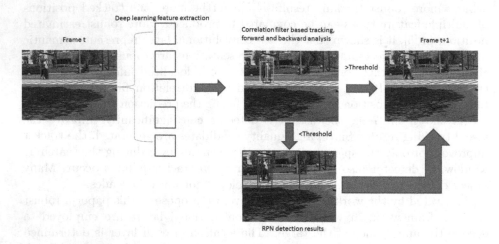

Fig. 1. Illustration of the proposed method. Each layer of the network produces a prediction (blue) that are merged to produce a new target position (red). If this position has a good backward score, it is accepted. Otherwise proposals are used to generate a new target position. (Color figure online)

2.2   Correlation Filter-Based Tracking

We selected the VGG-19 Net [11] which provides very deep features. The VGG-Net is trained on the ImageNet dataset and achieves excellent results on classification tasks. As mentioned previously, in order to obtain a richer description of the target, different layers from the VGG-Net are extracted.

Next, a module based on correlation filters is presented. A deep feature map is extracted from one layer of the VGG-net. The correlation filter-based tracking employ a filter trained on an object appearance in an image patch x of $M * N$ pixels. The training samples are generated by the circular shifts of $x_{m,n} \in \{0, 1, \cdots, M - 1\} * \{0, 1, \cdots, N - 1\}$, i.e.,

$$w = argmin_w \sum_{m,n} |\phi(x_{m,n}) * w - y(m, n)|^2 + \lambda||w||^2 \tag{1}$$

where ϕ denotes a kernel function and λ is a regularization parameter ($\lambda \leq 0$). The fast Fourier transformation (FFT) is used to compute the correlation. Thus, the objective function is $w = \sum_{m,n} a(m, n)\phi(x_{m,n})$, and the coefficient a is computed as

$$A = \mathcal{F}(a) = (\frac{\mathcal{F}(y)}{\mathcal{F}(\phi(x) * \phi(x)) + \lambda}) \tag{2}$$

where $\mathcal{F}$ is the discrete Fourier operator and $y = \{y_{m,n}|(m,n) \in \{0, 1, \cdots, M - 1\} * \{0, 1, \cdots, N - 1\}\}$. In the next new frame, the correlation filter response is carried out on an image patch x and computed as follows

$$\hat{y} = \mathcal{F}^{-1}(A \odot \mathcal{F}(\phi(x) * \phi(\hat{x}))) \tag{3}$$

where $\hat{x}$ is the learned object appearance model and $\odot$ is the element-wise product. The position of the object is determined by searching for the position of maximal $\hat{y}$ value.

2.3 Forward and Backward Tracking

We use a backward tracker which tracks an object in the reverse time direction to measure the robustness of the tracker in each layer of our pre-trained CNN. The backward tracker is initialized at the position given by the forward tracker. By comparing the backward position with the tracked position in the previous frame, we can approximately evaluate the quality of the forward tracking results. Furthermore, multiple features from different layers of the CNN are employed to measure backward tracking quality. Based on the forward and backward trackers, the resulting forward tracking result becomes more accurate and robust.

Figure 2 illustrates five forward and backward trackers from frame t to frame $t + 1$. The red bounding box in frame t is the tracking results. The green, yellow, blue, magenta and cyan bounding boxes in frame t and frame $t + 1$ are the corresponding forward and backward tracking results from five layers of our CNN respectively. The overlap ratio [12] between the red bounding box and the other bounding boxes measure the quality of the tracking results.

$$OL_i = \frac{LB \cap TB}{LB \cup TB}, i = 1, 2, 3, 4, 5. \tag{4}$$

where LB represents the layer backward tracking bounding box and TB represents the final tracked bounding box in frame t. $\cup$ and $\cap$ represent intersection and union of the two regions, respectively. The final result y is computed as follows,

$$y = \alpha_1 y_1^c + \alpha_2 y_2^c + \alpha_3 y_3^c + \alpha_4 y_4^c + \alpha_5 y_5^c \tag{5}$$

where α_1, α_2, α_3, α_4 and α_5 are the normalized overlap ratios (OL) of the five layers, y_1^c, y_2^c, y_3^c, y_4^c and y_5^c are the forward correlation filter tracking results of the five layers.

2.4 Region Proposal Network

A RPN [10] is employed to generate a set of candidate bounding boxes (as shown in Fig. 3). The RPN is a combination of classification and regression layer. It is built on a feature map extracted from a pre-trained VGG network. Whenever the overlap ratio is below a threshold, we use the RPN implemented in [10] to generate candidate bounding boxes. Figure 3(a) shows how our tracking

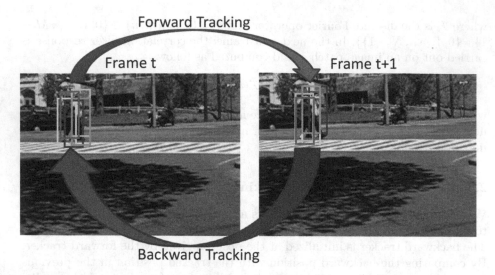

Fig. 2. Forward and backward tracking between two consecutive frames (Color figure online).

method, without RPN, eventually loses the target. The green bounding box is the estimated position. Figure 3(b) shows a tracking failure. The blue bounding boxes are the RPN detection results. Our tracker tracks the candidates in the RPN detection results. And finally the target is relocated. Figure 4 presents our tracking algorithm.

3 Experiment

3.1 Implementation Details

To assess the proposed tracking method, the experiments are performed on OTB100 benchmark dataset [16] which contains 100 challenging videos annotated with 11 attributes.

In the OTB100 dataset, our method is compared with state-of-the-art methods, e.g., Struck [18], SCM [19] adn TLD [20]. Furthermore, two representative deep learning based methods, hedge based tracking (HDT) [4] and CFNet [21], are used in our comparison. Six layers of CNN features are used in HDT. A Siamese network is employed in CFNet.

Two metrics, i.e., center location error and overlapping rate [12], are used in our work to evaluate the performance of the trackers. The center location error measures the difference of the center locations between the trackers and the annotated ground truth. The overlapping rate measures the intersection between the trackers and the ground truth bounding boxes. The one-pass evaluation (OPE) protocol [17] which shows the precision and success plots based on the two metrics is adopted.

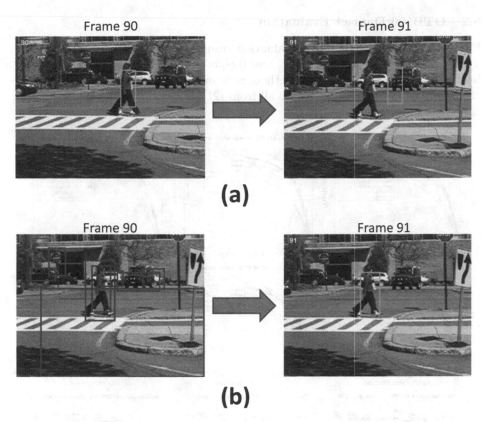

Fig. 3. Two tracking results between consecutive frames. (a) The tracker loosing track of the target. The green bounding box is the tracking result. (b) RPN detection results provide candidate positions. The blue bounding boxes are the detection results. The green bounding box is the tracking result. (Color figure online)

Input: Current position at frame t.
RPN detection result at frame t.
1. Each layer forward tracking via correlation filter-based approach.
2. Each layer backward tracking via correlation filter-based approach.
3. Compute overlap score via equation (4).
4. If overlap score>Threshold
Compute final position by equation (5).
else
RPN detection to obtain candidate positions use correlation filter to recover target from candidates.
Output: Target position at frame t+1.

Fig. 4. The proposed tracking algorithm.

3.2 OTB100 Dataset Evaluation

Figures 5 and 6 show the OPE evaluation results on OTB100 video sequences. The precision and success plot are 0.805 and 0.542 respectively. CNN-backward refers to our proposed method. xc5camera, xc3incf3camera, cf1camera, cf2camera, cf5camera, siamfc3s are all from [21].

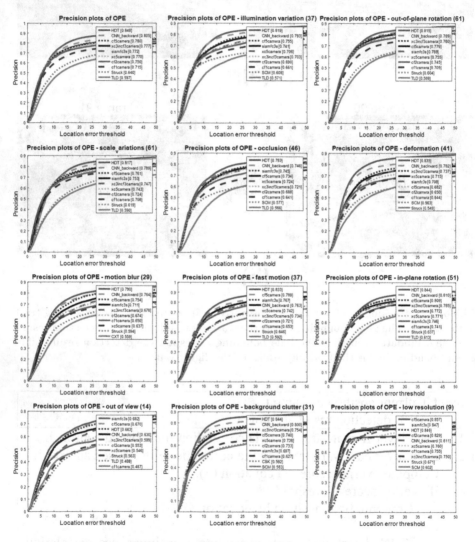

Fig. 5. Distance precision plots with different attributes over OTB100 benchmark sequences in OPE validation schemes.

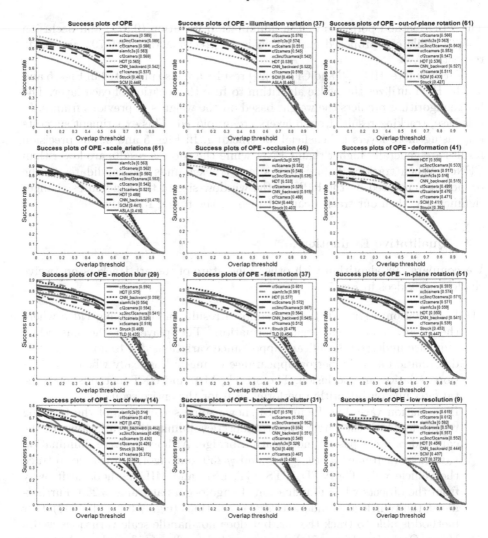

Fig. 6. Success plots with different attributes over OTB100 benchmark sequences in OPE validation schemes.

Attribute-Based Evaluation: 11 attributes are used for analyzing the performance of the trackers in different challenging situations in OTB100. Figure 5 shows experimental results in precision validation schemes with 11 attributes. Figure 6 shows experimental results in success validation schemes with 11 attributes. Among existing methods, the Struck method performs well with overall precision in out-of-plane rotation (0.604), scale variations (0.619), deformation (0.549), motion blur (0.594), fast motion (0.646), out-of-plane (0.637), out of view (0.503) and low resolution (0.671) while our proposed method achieves precision rate of 0.789, 0.789, 0.782, 0.764, 0.763, 0.810, 0.630 and 0.811 respectively.

The TLD method performs well in illumination variation (0.571) and occlusion (0.566) while our proposed method achieves precision rate of 0.793 and 0.746 respectively.

Furthermore, HDT [4] and CFNet [21] results are also presented in Figs. 5 and 6. The HDT utilizes the hedge algorithm to fuse the location of each layer. The hedge algorithm predicts the weight based on the weights in previous frames. In this case, tracking results from 6 layers are employed. This experiment suggests that using more layers is beneficial for tracking. In Figs. 5 and 6, our precision results are generally higher than CFNet while the success results are lower than CFNet. When tracking failure occurs, our tracker finds the candidates in the proposals generated by the RPN. If the window size of the candidates changes significantly, then our tracker can not recover the target robustly.

3.3   Qualitative Evaluation

We compare our algorithm with other nine state-of-the-art trackers on twelve challenging videos in Fig. 7.

(1) Deformation: Figure 7(a) shows sampled results in challenging video where the object undergoes large deformation. The player in the basketball sequence undergoes significant appearance variations due to non-rigid body deformation and the person appearance changes drastically when illumination variation and occlusion. The Struck, MIL and CXT methods loose the target while our algorithm performs well for the entire sequence.

(2) Illumination variation: Figure 7(b) shows some screenshots of the tracking results in which the target object undergoes illumination variations. In the car4 video, a car passes underneath a bridge. Although severe illumination variations at frames #170, #190, and #250, our algorithm is able to track the vehicle well. The VTD, VTS, CT, LSK and MIL methods drift away from the objects when illumination change occurs at frame #250. Furthermore, the vehicle also undergoes scale variations (e.g. #490 and #640). Our method is able to track the car, but does not handle scale variations well.

(3) Heavy Occlusion: Figure 7(c) shows sampled results of video where the target undergoes heavy occlusions. The person in the david3 sequence undergoes significant appearance changes due to body deformation. Furthermore, the person's appearance changes drastically when he walks behind the tree and then turns around. Only our method performs well at all frames.

(4) Fast motion: Figure 7(d) demonstrates some results over challenging video with target undergoes Fast motion. In the Couple sequence, two women walk while their appearance changes much due to fast motion. The VTD, CXT, VTS, CSK, CT, LSK and MIL methods lock on to the background. Our method and TLD method track the couple well.

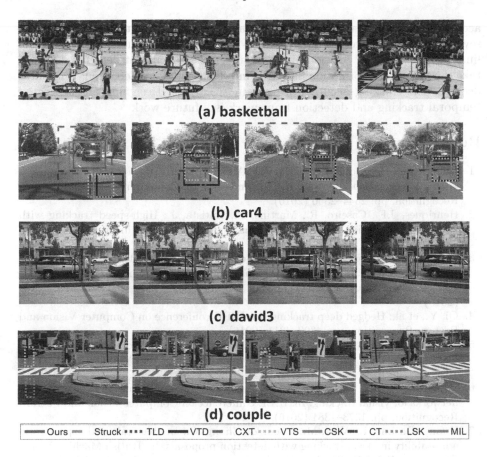

(a) basketball

(b) car4

(c) david3

(d) couple

| Ours | Struck | TLD | VTD | CXT | VTS | CSK | CT | LSK | MIL |

Fig. 7. Qualitative results of the 10 trackers over sequences bolt, david3 and singer2, in which the targets undergo severe deformation.

4 Conclusion

In this paper, we propose a robust tracking method using a pre-trained CNN. Each layer tracks the target based on a correlation filter tracking framework. The forward and backward overlap score between consecutive frames is computed. The accepted results are robustly fused by an overlap score. Furthermore, the quality of the overlap score is an indicator of the reliability of trackers from each layer. RPN is employed whenever a tracking failure is detected. Our method produces competitive results on the OTB100 benchmark dataset.

However, integrating detection into a tracking framework has drawbacks. Indeed, the new target position can suddenly be drifted away as the search area of our RPN detector is applied globally on the image. This searching scheme is effective to situations when the target undergoes heavy occlusion. A better searching scheme should be added in our future work. Similarly the tracker may change the size of the bounding box abruptly, which can degrade the tracking accuracy. The RPN can indeed detect many candidates in one frame and when several bounding boxes of different sizes are proposed around the target, the final target estimated position might be affected. Our current detector does not take the temporal information into account. Therefore false detection candidates decrease the tracking accuracy in certain situations. Designing an integrated temporal tracking and detection framework is a future work.

References

1. Bolme, D.S., Beveridge, J.R., Draper, B.A., Lui, Y.M.: Visual object tracking using adaptive correlation filters. In: IEEE Conference on Computer Vision and Pattern Recognition, pp. 2544–2550 (2010)
2. Henriques, J.F., Caseiro, R., Martins, P., Batista, J.: High-speed tracking with kernelized correlation filters. IEEE Trans. Pattern Anal. Mach. Intell. **37**(3), 583–596 (2015)
3. Montero A.S., Lang, J., Laganiere, R.: Scalable kernel correlation filter with sparse feature integration. In: IEEE International Conference on Computer Vision (ICCV) Workshop on Visual Object Tracking (VOT2015), pp. 24–31, Santiago, Chile (2015)
4. Qi, Y., et al.: Hedged deep tracking. In: IEEE conference on Computer Vision and Pattern Recognition, pp. 4303–4311 (2016)
5. Ma, C., Huang, J.-B., Yang, X., Yang, M.-H.: Hierarchical convolutional features for visual tracking. In: IEEE International Conference on Computer Vision, pp. 3074–3082 (2015)
6. Wang, L., Ouyang, W., Wang, X., Lu, H.: Stct: sequentially training convolutional networks for visual tracking. In: IEEE conference on Computer Vision and Pattern Recognition, pp. 1373–1381 (2016)
7. Huang, D., Luo, L., Wen, M., Chen, Z., Zhang, C.: Enable scale and aspect ratio adaptability in visual tracking with detection proposals. In: British Machine Vision Conference (BMVC) (2015)
8. Ma, C., Yang, X., Zhang, C., Yang, M.-H.: Long-term correlation tracking. In: IEEE conference on Computer Vision and Pattern Recognition (2015)
9. Zhu, G., Porikli, F., Li, H.: Tracking randomly moving objects on edge box proposals. CoRR (2015)
10. Ren, S., He, K., Girshick, R., Sun, J.: Faster R-CNN: towards real-time object detection with region proposal networks. In: Neural Information Processing Systems (NIPS) (2015)
11. Simonyan, K., Zisserman, A.: Very deep convolutional networks for large-scale image recognition. In: ICLR (2015)
12. Everingham, M., Van Gool, L., Williams, C.K.I., Winn, J., Zisserman, A.: The PASCAL visual object classes challenge 2010 (VOC2010) results (2010)
13. Supancic, J., Ramanan, D.: Self-paced learning for longterm tracking. In: IEEE Conference on Computer Vision and Pattern Recognition, pp. 2379–2386 (2013)
14. Zhang, J., Ma, S., Sclaroff, S.: MEEM: robust tracking via multiple experts using entropy minimization. In: Fleet, D., Pajdla, T., Schiele, B., Tuytelaars, T. (eds.) ECCV 2014. LNCS, vol. 8694, pp. 188–203. Springer, Cham (2014). https://doi.org/10.1007/978-3-319-10599-4_13
15. Lee, D.-Y., Sim, J.-Y., Kim, C.-S.: Multihypothesis trajectory analysis for robust visual tracking. In: IEEE Conference on Computer Vision and Pattern Recognition, pp. 5088–5096 (2015)

16. Wu, Y., Lim, J., Yang, M.-H.: Object tracking benchmark. IEEE Trans. Pattern Anal. Mach. Intell. **37**(9), 1834–1848 (2015)
17. Wu, Y., Lim, J., Yang, M.-H.: Online object tracking: a benchmark. In: IEEE conference on Computer Vision and Pattern Recognition, pp. 2411–2418 (2013)
18. Hare, S., Saffari, A., Torr, P.H.S.: Struck: structured output tracking with kernels. In: IEEE International Conference on Computer Vision (2011)
19. Zhong, W., Lu, H., Yang, M.-H.: Robust object tracking via sparsity-based collaborative model. In: IEEE Conference on Computer Vision and Pattern Recognition (2012)
20. Kalal, Z., Mikolajczyk, K., Matas, J.: Tracking-learning-detection. IEEE Trans. Pattern Anal. Mach. Intell. **34**(7), 1409–1422 (2012)
21. Valmadre, J., Bertinetto, L., Henriques, J., Vedaldi, A., Torr, P.: End-to-end representation learning for correlation filter based tracking. In: IEEE Conference on Computer Vision and Pattern Recognition (2017)

The Bird Gets Caught by the WORM: Tracking Multiple Deformable Objects in Noisy Environments Using Weight ORdered Logic Maps

Debajyoti Karmaker[1]([⊠]) [iD], Ingo Schiffner[2] [iD], Michael Wilson[1] [iD], and Mandyam V. Srinivasan[1,3] [iD]

[1] The Queensland Brain Institute, University of Queensland,
St Lucia, QLD, Australia
{d.karmaker,m.wilson,m.srinivasan}@uq.edu.au
[2] Bangor University, Gwynedd, Wales, UK
i.schiffner@bangor.ac.uk
[3] The School of Information Technology and Electrical Engineering,
University of Queensland, St Lucia, Australia

Abstract. Object detection and tracking are active and important research areas in computer vision as well as neuroscience. Of particular interest is the detection and tracking of small, poorly lit, deformable objects in the presence of sensor noise, and large changes in background and foreground illumination. Such conditions are frequently encountered when an animal moves in its natural environment, or in an experimental arena. The problems are exacerbated with the use of high-speed video cameras as the exposure time for high-speed cameras is limited by the frame rate, which limits the SNR. In this paper we present a set of simple algorithms for detecting and tracking multiple, small, poorly lit, deformable objects in environments that feature drastic changes in background and foreground illumination, and poor signal-to-noise ratios. These novel algorithms are shown to exhibit better performance than currently available state-of-the art algorithms.

Keywords: Object detection · Data association · Object tracking
Shortest paths

1 Introduction

The use of Unmanned Aerial Vehicles (UAVs) is becoming more and more pervasive every year, rendering current ground-based control systems inadequate in avoiding mid-air collisions. Most airborne creatures, such as birds or flying insects, are extremely adept at avoiding collisions with their conspecifics or other moving objects in their environments. How they achieve this is largely unknown.

© Springer Nature Switzerland AG 2018
G. Bebis et al. (Eds.): ISVC 2018, LNCS 11241, pp. 332–343, 2018.
https://doi.org/10.1007/978-3-030-03801-4_30

In the past decade, we have started to gain insights into how birds and insects control their flight speed [22], avoid obstacles [27] and perform smooth landings [25]. This has drawn considerable attention from roboticists, who are challenged with similar problems in the design of guidance systems for unmanned aerial vehicles. However, studying bird flight is not simple: firstly one has to be able to collect accurate data from flying animals, with sufficient temporal and spatial resolution. This is best achieved using high-speed cameras and stereo or multi-camera setups. While high-speed cameras are now becoming more and more affordable, algorithms for accurately tracking moving animals in video sequences are scarce; and tracking flying animals, in particular birds, is by no means a trivial task. Flying birds are one of the more challenging "objects" to detect, partly because of their constantly changing shape [8,9]. Tracking multiple birds using high-speed cameras, and dealing with frequent occlusions, is an even more challenging task. However, it is also the most feasible way of measuring the birds' motion states and undertaking a quantitative study of their flight behavior. Conversely, the development of tracking systems that can handle such a challenging task may provide robust techniques for tracking other, less challenging objects.

Robust object tracking is one of the most ubiquitous problems in computer vision science. It has numerous applications, including automatic visual surveillance, traffic monitoring, vehicle navigation, and motion-based object recognition [32]. Despite the continued growth of interest in automated object tracking, the problem continues to be extremely challenging due to factors such as variation of illumination, deformation of non-rigid objects, occlusions, complex motion, and the presence of background clutter. Tracking techniques can be broadly categorized into two approaches [28]: (1) tracking by detection and (2) temporal tracking. In the first approach, objects are detected by spatially processing the image to detect specific points or key features of the object [16,33,34], and then subtracting the background [5,13,15,18,37,38], using various techniques to segment the object from the background [11,23]. In recent years, this approach has been bolstered by using supervised learning [1,14,35], implemented in support vector machines and neural networks [14,31]. The second approach makes use of the temporal information that is available in a video sequence to enhance the accuracy and speed of detection.

In both approaches, the object states from the previous frame and the current frame are usually passed on to either a Kalman filter (KF) [4,10,36] or a particle filter (PF) [3,21] to obtain the best estimate of the object's location in the current frame. However, the KF technique is a recursive process which performs poorly when dealing with complex trajectories [28], and is only suitable for linear state models with Gaussian noise. On the other hand, the PF technique models the process stochastically and can successfully tackle nonlinear and non-Gaussian tracking problems, but is computationally expensive.

Tracking a single object involves locating and tracking the position of the object from frame to frame in the camera's field of view. Tracking multiple birds is more challenging, as it requires the simultaneous prediction of the movement trajectory of each object, as well as correctly identifying each object in each frame. Multiple object tracking (MOT) can be classified into two categories: Offline MOT and Online MOT. Offline MOT takes the entire video as an input, detects the object in each frame, and then constructs the most likely trajectory of each object by associating the data collected over the entire video sequence. Online MOT, on the other hand, can only use information from the video frames that have been acquired up to the current point in time, to predict the location of each object in the current frame.

Most multi-object tracking algorithms are based on the use of an 'appearance' model, specified either in the spatial domain or the frequency domain, to detect the objects in each frame. When dealing with multiple, similar looking objects (e.g. the birds in our case) an appearance model alone is not sufficient to determine the identities of the individual objects accurately and reliably, because the objects (e.g. birds) can have similar sizes and movement patterns, and can frequently occlude one another in the image. Another major issue with tracking live objects is that most tracking algorithms rely on the assumption that the temporal changes are smooth from frame to frame i.e. objects do not change their position significantly between frames. A further problem with tracking multiple objects is that the number of objects can vary from one frame to the next, for example, when one object leaves the camera's field of view, or another object enters it. Thus, a robust MOT system needs to tackle all of the above challenges.

In this paper, we present a technique for detecting and tracking multiple moving objects in environments that feature drastic changes in background and foreground illumination. During long term tracking, moving objects can display abrupt changes in motion, and also be subject to partial or complete occlusion. When birds fly, they produce certain patterns of motion. These patterns often display special spatial properties – for example, their flight path may be restricted to certain regions of the experimental environment, or two birds may strive to achieve a minimum separation when they fly past each other. These structural and motion constraints can be exploited to construct data associations that help preserve and disambiguate the identities of individual objects.

2   Related Works

Most contemporary MOT systems rely on a detection framework for tracking [24], instead of using background subtraction to overcome problems such as cluttered and dynamic backgrounds. In fact, when it comes to tracking one kind of object (e.g. human, bird or car), tracking by detection is more suitable, because it avoids object fragmentation. However, detection frameworks have difficulty with long-term tracking of small flying creatures such as birds or insects from a stationary camera when the object moves well away from the focal plane of the camera. The object then becomes blurry and detection fails due to the inability to track individual features of the object. Moreover, birds are inherently difficult to detect because they are highly articulated, and constitute an extreme example of a nonrigid, deformable object. To tackle this problem, we take a step back and investigate how the background subtraction method can be applied in complex scenarios with dynamic backgrounds and drastic illumination changes.

In motion analysis, background modeling and subtraction play a key role. The concept behind this approach is to construct a probabilistic representation of the scene based on the dynamically changing background over time, which is used to perform the subtraction from the current input image to extract the object. One way to model the static background is to perform image averaging over a certain number of frames, which gives a reasonable portrayal of the mean background image. Ridder [19] proposed a Kalman-filter based approach to model the background, whereas Wren [30] made use of a Gaussian distribution to model the background – which turns out to be too simplistic for modeling real-world scenarios. Stauffer and Grimson [26] proposed a Mixture of Gaussian (MoG) approach to better model multiple background intensity distributions that are generated, for example, by ripples on water surface surfaces, and flickering scene illuminations. However, this requires a decision on how many Gaussians to use. To avoid this difficulty inherent in parametric models Elgamal et al. [7] proposed a non-parametric model that describes background density by extraction of a histogram of pixel intensities at each pixel location. An intensity value that falls outside the range of the histogram at a particular location is taken to belong to the object. Both parametric and non-parametric methods [7,12,13,17] work efficiently only for environments with gradually evolving changes and small variations. They decline in performance when dealing with dynamic background scenes such ocean waves, rain, waving trees, moving clouds, or illumination changes [18].

To overcome the problems with traditional background subtraction methods for describing dynamic scenes, Weng [29] proposed another variation of background subtraction – known as the local dependency histogram (LDH). In this technique, each pixel is modeled as a group of weighted LDHs. Next, the process of labeling the pixel as the foreground or background is performed by comparing the new LDH computed in the current frame against its LDH model. Finally, a fixed threshold value is used to define whether or not a pixel matches its model. Another prominent technique for background subtraction is kernel density estimation [6] to handle scenarios where the background is not completely static but consists of small motion and illumination changes. For each pixel, this technique builds a histogram of background values by accumulating a set of real values sampled from the pixel's recent history. Then, they estimate the probability density function with this histogram to determine whether or not a pixel value of the current frame belongs to the background.

In contrast to all of the above background modeling techniques, which can only deal with slow changes and require constant updating, our method is capable of successfully dealing with a variety of rapid background changes without the need for model updating. Moreover, as will be shown below, this detection method – based on the decomposition of a logical map – has reduced complexity and computational expense. It outperforms all of the background modeling techniques described above and allows more time to be allocated to the data association problem – namely, the problem of connecting the detected locations in a sequence of frames to create an unambiguous track. Approaches that use Kalman filtering make assumptions of constant velocity or acceleration, which are not viable when dealing with objects that are constantly changing their shapes, speeds, and flight directions. As a consequence, Kalman filtering approaches suffer from a greater likelihood of ID swaps when tracking multiple objects in comparison with our data association approach, which exhibits significantly better performance.

3   Proposed Method

In this section, we describe our multiple object tracking method that is based on object detection. Our object detection method is based on computing the inter-frame difference, extraction of a series of intensity levels from the inter-frame difference image, and determining the centroid for each intensity level. The determination of the centroids is highly affected by the level of noise present in the original images that are used to generate the inter-frame difference.

In Sect. 3.1, we describe our object detection method. In Sect. 3.2, we demonstrate how the object locations determined in the sequence of video frames are connected to produce an accurate and unambiguous track(s).

3.1   Object Detection

The method presented here for object detection uses frame-to-frame image differences to detect objects in environments that feature drastic changes in background and foreground illumination, as well as noise (an example video is available at https://www.youtube.com/watch?v=9IE8-82agYc). Unlike traditional background subtraction methods, initial results are not stored in the commonly used format of a logic map. Instead, image frame differences are decomposed into multiple logic maps according to their level of intensity difference. After this step, separate centers of gravity are formed for each individual logic map. Due to this separation into individual maps, regular changes in the background illumination and static noise will automatically be distinguished from the actual target. Using these centers of gravity, one can simply look for a set of n nearest neighbors (pixels around these centers of gravity) and compute their shared center of gravity to define the actual position of the target. As changes in background illumination, unless they are extremely regular, will be represented by centers of gravity that can theoretically lie anywhere on the image, the number of nearest neighbours necessary to successfully track an object is solely dependent on the level of noise present in the video footage. Due to the random nature of noise, most of the centers of gravity will most likely lie in locations very different from that of the image of the object, and noise will, therefore, be effectively suppressed.

The traditional approach of detecting a moving object is to compute the inter-frame difference – that is, to subtract the intensity values of pixels in the current frame (CF) from those in the previous frame (PF). A pixel in the difference image (FD) is considered to belong to the moving object if its value is higher than a prescribed threshold (θ) – assuming that intensity variations in the pixels that constitute the background are small, and below this threshold. If the value of the pixel is lower than the threshold, it is considered to belong to the stationary background. This operation can be expressed as

$$FD\left(x,y\right) = \left|CF\left(x,y\right) - PF(x,y)\right|$$

From this we derive a logic map which defines the motion-associated pixels and stationary background pixels according to

$$logic\,map(x,y) \begin{cases} 1, & FD(x,y) \geq \theta \,\text{Motion region} \\ 0, & FD(x,y) < \theta \end{cases} \tag{1}$$

In our approach, we analyze the logic map at multiple intensity levels in the difference image according to the intensity difference k by using k intensity difference maps:

$$logic\,map_k(x,y) \begin{cases} 1, & FD(x,y) == k \\ 0, & \text{otherwise} \end{cases} \tag{2}$$

(a)   (b)

Fig. 1. (a) Logic map for k=20 on raw frames 79 & 78 (b) Centroids of different logic maps on raw frames 79 & 78.

Next, the centroid is computed for each of these logic maps. The motion of complex objects (in our case birds) will result in a large number of logic maps. Using the centroids of these maps, we look for a set of n nearest neighbors and select their shared center of gravity to best estimate the true position of the moving object. Figure 1a shows an example of the logic map for k = 20 and Fig. 1b shows the centroids for all logic maps.

For detecting multiple objects, after decomposing the logic map at multiple levels, we apply K-means clustering to find the center of gravity of each object. Here in K-means clustering, the value of K is set to the maximum number of objects expected to be present in the video footage. Even if K objects are not present in a particular frame of the video, we can distinguish the false detections by applying a constraint on the maximum number of logic maps (max value of k).

3.2   Data Association

The next challenge is to track the trajectory of the objects reliably, without interchanging their identities. We pose the data association problem as one of finding the shortest path in a graph. Thus, we represent the detection hypotheses from all the frames as a directed acyclic graph (DAG). This graph $G = (V, E)$ consist of a set of nodes (V), which are hypothesized detections, and a set of edges (E), which connect pairs of detections (nodes) and associate each connection with a cost value. The cost of an edge between two nodes is represented as a sum of three sub-costs: (a) appearance dissimilarity, (b) internode separation and (c) change in direction of movement in relation to the previous node pair. Let v and w be nodes in successive frames connected by an edge e. The appearance dissimilarity between v and w is computed by $(1 - v_b.w_b)$ where $v_b.w_b$ denotes the dot product of the detection bounding boxes of v and w respectively. (The greater the overlap between the bounding boxes, the lower the dissimilarity). The cost associated with the change of direction is computed using $\left(\tan^{-1} \frac{v_{by}}{v_{bx}} - \tan^{-1} \frac{w_{by}}{w_{bx}}\right)$ by finding the centroids $(v_b(x, y)$ and $w_b(x, y))$ of the bounding boxes of $v_b and$ w_b. Assigning edge weights in this manner will produce low weights when two successive nodes represent the same object, and large weights when they represent different objects. We also ensure that every edge E points forward in time (as shown in Fig. 2), i.e., the frame number of the detection v is strictly smaller than that of the detection w.

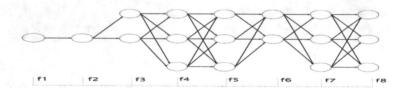

Fig. 2. Initial graph representation of all possible trajectories

Figure 2 shows an example of an initial representation of a graph that represents all of the possible trajectories that can be associated with the detected nodes. The nodes are organized in an ascending order with respect to the frame number. Each node in a frame is connected to every node in the following frame with an edge cost as described above. To tackle situations where nodes are missing, we apply a constraint on the maximum number of frames over which an object can be absent. If the object does not reappear within that range, it is considered to have gone out of the camera's visual field. If it returns within this critical period, it is assumed that the object was temporarily occluded, and a dummy node is added in the location where it was last detected, as shown in Fig. 3. To maintain these criteria, we need to scan the graph from left to right and ensure that at any level of the graph, the number of incoming edges is equal to or lower than the number of outgoing edges. If there are more outgoing edges, this implies that a new object has arrived.

The maximum edge cost for a bird from one frame to next frame is estimated from the ground truth of our dataset. Based on this maximum edge value, we remove all the edges between two nodes - where the cost is greater than the estimated max edge value. This helps to reduce search complexity.

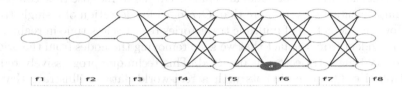

Fig. 3. Dummy node insertion

We then apply Dijkstra's algorithm to find the shortest path for the graph of Fig. 3. Classically, Dijkstra's algorithm works on a single source and a single destination. In our case, no source or destination is defined. Furthermore, if there are multiple objects, we need to determine a different trajectory for each of the objects. For this reason, we represent the graph as a time sequence and consider any node from f1 as the source node. See Fig. 4, orange path. For the destination we do not set any node, rather we continue until the algorithm reaches a node at the last level, or finds a dead end.

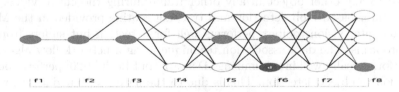

Fig. 4. Selecting the 1st trajectory

Next, we delete all the nodes and every incoming and outgoing edge from these nodes. The remaining graph is shown in Fig. 5. We then select any node which does not have any incoming edge and repeat the process to successively determine the trajectories of each of the other moving objects in the video sequence.

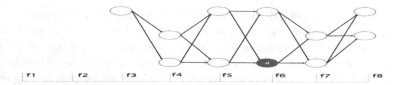

Fig. 5. Removal of nodes and edges

The time complexity of heap implementation of Dijkstra's algorithm is $O(nlogn)$, where n is the number of nodes. As it is guaranteed that our graph is not dense i.e. not all pairs of nodes are connected, the worst-case time complexity of our implementation is no more than $O(nlogn)$ for detection of a single trajectory. However, detection of multiple trajectories requires less time in reality. The reason is evident from the fact that we keep removing the nodes from the original graph every time a trajectory is detected. This technique progressively reduces the graph size. Our experiments with a real-world dataset illustrate that our technique is able to provide results in query time (<1 s) on a standard machine configuration (8 GB RAM, Ubuntu 16, Intel Core-i7 CPU with 3.40 GHz clock speed).

4   Experimental Results

We have compared the method of detection and tracking with four other popular methods available. For this comparison, the ground truth was manually generated for bird locations (bounding boxes) in 10 videos. The same video dataset was used to test all 5 methods. Detection was considered to be correct if successive bounding-boxes overlapped by more than 50%, while tracking multiple objects was deemed incorrect due to misidentification if one object ID was assigned to any other object in any other frame during the entire video. The Kalman-filter based blob detection and tracking routine provided in the MAT-LAB computer vision toolbox performs well for detection but suffers from ID swap problems. The data association technique using a network flow algorithm [20] performs really well in minimizing ID swaps, but both [2, 20] perform poorly in relation to object detection. This is due to the nature of our dataset, where the illumination is poor, and more importantly, whenever the bird flies beyond the camera focus area, it becomes blurry and any feature extraction algorithms such as HoG or Deep learning will be compromised. Table 1 reveals that the proposed method exhibits the best performance with respect to detection accuracy, and the second-best performance with respect to ID swaps.

Table 1. Comparison with other methods

	Detection accuracy	ID swaps
Our method	93%	8%
Blob detection & Kalman Filter-based tracking (Matlab)	86%	37%
Background subtraction & FIR filter [5]	79%	19%
Deep learning & Network flow [20]	67%	3%
HoG & KLT [2]	65%	24%

5 Conclusion

The contributions of this work focus on two distinct aspects of the problem of detection and tracking multiple, deformable moving objects. These are (i) detection using interframe differencing and (ii) trajectory generation using a shortest path algorithm. The main advantage with weight ordered logic map decomposition of our detection method is that it does not need any background model to be updated over time. Thus, it is likely to be computationally much faster than the standard background modeling techniques. Approaches that use Kalman filtering make assumptions of constant velocity or acceleration, which are not viable when dealing with flying birds that are avoiding collisions – they are constantly changing their shapes, speeds, and flight directions. As a consequence, Kalman filtering approaches suffer from a greater likelihood of ID swaps when tracking multiple objects in comparison with our approach, which shows significantly better performance.

References

1. Avidan, S.: Support vector tracking. IEEE Trans. Pattern Anal. Mach. Intell. **26**(8), 1064–1072 (2004)
2. Benfold, B., Reid, I.: Stable multi-target tracking in real-time surveillance video. In: Proceedings of the IEEE Computer Society Conference on Computer Vision and Pattern Recognition, pp. 3457–3464 (2011)
3. Cao, X., Gao, C., Lan, J., Yuan, Y., Yan, P.: Ego motion guided particle filter for vehicle tracking in airborne videos. Neurocomputing **124**, 168–177 (2014)
4. Chan, Y.T., Hu, A.G.C., Plant, J.B.: A Kalman filter based tracking scheme with input estimation. IEEE Trans. Aerosp. Electr. Syst. AES **15**(2), 237–244 (1979)
5. Choi, I.H., Pak, J.M., Ahn, C.K., Lee, S.H., Lim, M.T., Song, M.K.: Arbitration algorithm of FIR filter and optical flow based on ANFIS for visual object tracking. Meas. J. Int. Meas. Confederation **75**(July), 338–353 (2015)
6. Comaniciu, D., Meer, P.: Mean shift: a robust approach toward feature space analysis. IEEE Trans. Pattern Anal. Mach. Intell. **24**(5), 1–37 (2002)
7. Elgammal, A., Harwood, D., Davis, L.: Non-parametric model for background subtraction. In: Vernon, D. (ed.) ECCV 2000. LNCS, vol. 1843, pp. 751–767. Springer, Heidelberg (2000). https://doi.org/10.1007/3-540-45053-X_48

8. Everingham, M., Eslami, S.M.A., Gool, L.V., Williams, C.K.I., Winn, J., Zisserman, A.: Assessing the Significance of Performance Differences on the PASCAL VOC Challenges via Bootstrapping, vol. 1 (2013)

9. Felzenszwalb, P.F., Girshick, R.B., McAllester, D., Ramanan, D.: Object detection with discriminatively trained part-based models. IEEE Trans. Pattern Anal. Mach. Intell. **32**(9), 1627–1645 (2010)

10. Fu, Z., Han, Y.: Centroid weighted Kalman filter for visual object tracking. Meas. J. Int. Meas. Confederation **45**(4), 650–655 (2012)

11. Girshick, R., Donahue, J., Darrell, T., Malik, J.: Rich feature hierarchies for accurate object detection and semantic segmentation. In: Proceedings of the IEEE Computer Society Conference on Computer Vision and Pattern Recognition, pp. 580–587 (2014)

12. Harville, M.: A framework for high-level feedback to adaptive, per-pixel, mixture-of-Gaussian background models. Framework **3**, 543–560 (2002)

13. Javed, O., Shafique, K., Shah, M.: A hierarchical approach to robust background subtraction using color and gradient information. Proc. Workshop Motion Video Comput. MOTION **2002**, 22–27 (2002)

14. Krizhevsky, A., Sutskever, I., Hinton, G.E.: ImageNet classification with deep convolutional neural networks. In: Advances In Neural Information Processing Systems, pp. 1–9 (2012)

15. Lee, D.S.: Effective Gaussian mixture learning for video background subtraction. IEEE Trans. Pattern Anal. Mach. Intell. **27**(5), 827–832 (2005)

16. Lowe, D.G.: Distinctive image features from. Int. J. Comput. Vis. **60**(2), 91–110 (2004)

17. Mittal, A., Huttenlocher, D.: Scene modeling for wide area surveillance and image synthesis. In: Proceedings IEEE Conference on Computer Vision and Pattern Recognition, CVPR 2000 (Cat. No. PR00662), vol. 2, pp. 160–167

18. Monnet, A., Mittal, A., Paragios, N., Ramesh, V.R.V.: Background modeling and subtraction of dynamic scenes. In: Proceedings Ninth IEEE International Conference on Computer Vision (ICCV), vol. 2, pp. 1305–1312 (2003)

19. Ridder, C., Munkelt, O., Kirchner, H.: Adaptive background estimation and foreground detection using Kalman-filtering. In: Proceedings of International Conference on Recent Advances in Mechatronics, pp. 193–199 (1995)

20. Roshan Zamir, A., Dehghan, A., Shah, M.: GMCP-tracker: global multi-object tracking using generalized minimum clique graphs. In: Fitzgibbon, A., Lazebnik, S., Perona, P., Sato, Y., Schmid, C. (eds.) ECCV 2012. LNCS, pp. 343–356. Springer, Heidelberg (2012). https://doi.org/10.1007/978-3-642-33709-3_25

21. Sardari, F., Ebrahimi Moghaddam, M.: A hybrid occlusion free object tracking method using particle filter and modified galaxy based search meta-heuristic algorithm. Appl. Soft Comput. J. **50**, 280–299 (2017)

22. Schiffner, I., Srinivasan, M.V.: Direct evidence for vision-based control of flight speed in Budgerigars. Sci. Rep. **5**, 10992 (2015). https://doi.org/10.1038/srep10992

23. Shi, J., Malik, J.: Normalized cuts and image segmentation normalized cuts and image segmentation. IEEE Trans. Pattern Anal. Mach. Intell. (PAMI) **22**(March), 888–905 (2005)

24. Solera, F., Calderara, S., Cucchiara, R.: Learning to divide and conquer for online multi-target tracking. In: Proceedings of the IEEE International Conference on Computer Vision, pp. 4373–4381, 11–18 December 2016

25. Srinivasan, M.V.: Visual control of navigation in insects and its relevance for robotics. Curr. Opin. Neurobiol. **21**(4), 535–543 (2011)

26. Stauffer, C., Grimson, W.E.L.: Adaptive background mixture models for real-time tracking. In: Proceedings 1999 IEEE Computer Society Conference on Computer Vision and Pattern Recognition Cat No PR00149, vol. 2(c), pp. 246–252 (1999)

27. Vo, H.D., Schiffner, I., Srinivasan, M.V.: Anticipatory manoeuvres in bird flight. Sci. Rep. **6**, 27591 (2016). 27270506[pmid]

28. Watada, J., Musa, Z., Jain, L.C., Fulcher, J.: Human tracking: a state-of-art survey. In: Setchi, R., Jordanov, I., Howlett, R.J., Jain, L.C. (eds.) KES 2010. LNCS (LNAI), vol. 6277, pp. 454–463. Springer, Heidelberg (2010). https://doi.org/10.1007/978-3-642-15390-7_47

29. Weng, J., Zhang, Y., Hwang, W.S.: Candid covariance-free incremental principal component analysis. IEEE Trans. Pattern Anal. Mach. Intell. **25**(8), 1034–1040 (2003)

30. Wren, C., Azarbayejani, A., Darrell, T., Pentland, A.: Pfinder: real-time tracking of the human body. IEEE Trans. Pattern Anal. Mach. Intell. **19**(7), 780–785 (1997)

31. Wu, Y., Lim, J., Yang, M.H.: Object tracking benchmark. IEEE Trans. Pattern Anal. Mach. Intell. **37**(9), 1834–1848 (2015)

32. Yilmaz, A., Javed, O., Shah, M.: Object tracking: a survey. ACM Comput. Surv. **38**(4), 13-es (2006)

33. Yokoi, K.: Probabilistic BPRRC: robust change detection against illumination changes and background movements. IEICE Trans. Inf. Syst. **E93–D**(7), 1700–1707 (2010)

34. Yokoyama, M., Poggio, T.: A contour-based moving object detection and tracking. In: 2005 IEEE International Workshop on Visual Surveillance and Performance Evaluation of Tracking and Surveillance, vol. (1), pp. 271–276 (2005)

35. Zhang, S., Sui, Y., Yu, X., Zhao, S., Zhang, L.: Hybrid support vector machines for robust object tracking. Pattern Recogn. **48**(8), 2474–2488 (2015)

36. Zhong, X., Zhong, X., Peng, X.: Robots visual servo control with features constraint employing Kalman neural network filtering scheme. Neurocomputing **151**(P1), 268–277 (2015)

37. Zivkovic, Z.: Improved adaptive Gaussian mixture model for background subtraction. In: Proceedings of the 17th International Conference on Pattern Recognition, ICPR 2004, vol. 2(2), pp. 28–31 (2004)

38. Zivkovic, Z., Heijden, F.V.D.: Efficient adaptive density estimation per image pixel for the task of background subtraction. Pattern Recogn. Lett. **27**(7), 773–780 (2006)

A Mumford Shah Style Unified Framework for Layering: Pitfalls and Solutions

Fareed ud din Mehmood Jafri[✉], Martin Fritz Mueller, and Anthony Joseph Yezzi[✉]

Georgia Institute of Technology, Atlanta, GA 30332-0250, USA
fjafri3@gatech.edu, martin.fritz.mueller@gmail.com,
anthony.yezzi@ece.gatech.edu

Abstract. Layered models are commonly used in computer vision to estimate the shape, appearance, depth ordering, occlusion structure and motion of objects from a set of images, offering computationally simpler alternatives to full 3D scene models. A unified computational framework for the various modeling elements (shape, appearance, motion and depth ordering), which integrates much of the current and prior work on layered models, would aid our understanding and development of layer extraction algorithms. A notable earlier work by Jackson et al. [2008] sought to provide such a framework in the context of variational methods, neatly cast as a single joint optimization problem. However, it did not perform as anticipated and has not been further developed. As the complexity of their formulation may have hindered its continued exploration, we reformulate their diffeomorphic approach within the much simpler framework of active contours. More importantly, though, we uncover a tricky modeling flaw which poorly extended the classical Mumford-Shah segmentation model to layering, causing unexpected performance degradation of their potentially powerful formulation. We elucidate this flaw and demonstrate its unintended consequences (a shrinking effect on foreground layers). We fix this problem by abandoning their unconstrained joint optimization philosophy and implementing an augmented Lagrangian style optimization process with PDE constraints instead. This new approach, which splits the classical Mumford-Shah appearance and geometric priors into two separate cost functions (one to be minimized with the other as a constraint) fixes the unintended shrinking problem and more properly extends the Mumford-Shah modeling paradigm into the layered framework, yielding far superior results. In doing so, we establish a more solid mathematical foundation for a unified variational approach to layering.

Keywords: Layered models · Active contours · Mumford-Shah · PDEs

This work was supported in part by the National Science Foundation grant No: CCF-1526848 and in part by the Fulbright Association.

G. Bebis et al. (Eds.): ISVC 2018, LNCS 11241, pp. 344–356, 2018.
https://doi.org/10.1007/978-3-030-03801-4_31

1 Introduction

1.1 Related Work

Layered models are a popular and useful way to explain a set of images by a set of moving and overlapping planar regions (ordered depth-wise) that capture 3D scene objects projected onto an imaging plane. Compared to a mere segmentation of an image they allow us to estimate not only the shape and appearance of the objects but also their depth ordering, occlusion structure and motion without estimating a (computationally expensive) full 3D representation of the scene. Layered models on their own are useful for both appearance and motion based segmentation. Several authors [5,9,15,16] utilize the framework of layered models for segmenting images into regions of homogeneous motion and/or appearance. They can also be used to aid the 3D reconstruction of a scene [3,19]. They have also been used for stereo reconstruction [3,7,10] and motion tracking [11,18,23].

The problem of layer extraction from an unlabeled set of input images has been addressed in several ways. Several authors [5,19,23] use an optical flow based approach using flow fields to extract regions of homogeneous motion as layers. Alternatively authors have followed a classification approach in a Bayesian framework for extracting layer information from a set of images [4,14,18,20,23]. Methods using unsupervised learning [8], edge tracking [14], Markov Random Fields and/or graph cuts [7,8,10,15,20,21] and a maximum likelihood estimate (MLE) [12–14] have also been employed for building the layers.

Techniques that target certain attributes of layered models have been developed as well. Works such as [14,15,17,19] focus on an accurate motion description whereas [5,9,15,16] focus on improved region segmentation. Techniques for better estimation of depth ordering and occlusion structure in the layered framework can be found in the works of [10,13,14,16,17,22,23]. Several authors [4,6,16] have also suggested methods to reduce complexity and/or computational cost. Authors have also built layered models with improved resolution and/or appearance [3,20] or having better capabilities of handling large displacement motions in the layers [5,21] and superior motion tracking [18,23].

An attempt to integrate all the modeling elements (shape, motion, appearance and occlusion structure) into a single variational framework was first proposed by Jackson et al. [1]. The advantage of their approach is that the problem is cast into one single joint optimization problem that allows for the fullest generality in modeling these elements and does not assuming any initial knowledge about them. Given the modeling richness, integrated framework, and versatility, the model should have performed at par with many of the other techniques mentioned in Sect. 1.1. However, surprisingly the model showed an unexplained degradation in performance on many data sets where it was designed to excel. It was not further advanced since its proposal in 2008. We anticipate that had this potentially powerful technique performed as expected, it could have comprehensively captured much work done in the context of layering.

1.2   Our Contribution

Our contribution is two-fold. Upon revisiting this earlier work [1] in detail we conjecture two key reasons for its lack of advancement. We address and fix both of these.

First, their diffeomorphic deformation model significantly complicated the numerical implementation and was computationally very expensive. This endowed the model with a level of generality that exceeds what is needed in most applications, and the resulting complexity may have discouraged further development by other researchers. Second, and more importantly, we discovered a subtle modeling flaw that turned out to have serious consequences. Their seemingly natural use of Mumford-Shah style appearance models [2] did not behave as expected when extended to layering and caused an unwanted shrinking effect on occluding (foreground) layer regions.

To obtain a more computationally efficient algorithm we reformulate their model by replacing their diffeomorphic maps with active contours coupled with an affine motion model to capture layer boundaries. This simplified motion model is still adequate for a wide variety of practical applications. To fix the theoretical flaw we illustrate and fix an unnoticed bias in the prior formulation which indirectly penalized layer occlusion that caused the sizes of the occluding layers to shrink. We resolve this problem by replacing their unconstrained joint optimization strategy with a alternative constrained optimization technique using augmented Lagrangian style PDE constraints. We discover that when the Mumford-Shah model is adapted to layering this way it has much more potential than it has in its original framework of segmentation.

1.3   Overview

In Sect. 2 we compare and contrast Mumford-Shah segmentation versus its adaptation to layering for the simplest case (two-layered model of a single image). We show unexpectedly poor results from applying joint appearance and shape optimization in this context. Section 3 gives a mathematical explanation for this problem. In Sect. 4 we show how appearance-constrained shape optimization fixes this problem in the same illustrative simple case of a two-layered model for a single image. Section 5 generalizes the technique to multilayered models of multiple images and accounts for layer motion between images. In Sect. 6 we present our experimental results.

2   Mumford-Shah Segmentation vs. Layering (Some Key Differences)

Individual image segmentation is driven by changes in appearance rather than changes in motion. The Mumford-Shah model Eq. 2.1 was proposed, and has been successfully used, for *appearance* driven segmentation. Its smooth appearance prior was intended to position a contour along unknown appearance boundaries. Comparatively, layering is predominantly driven by changes in *motion.*

One could, however, still leverage a Mumford-Shah style appearance prior for motion segmentation. In this context the appearance prior plays a fundamentally different role. It relaxes the typical (and non realistic) *brightness constancy* assumption that drives many motion segmentation algorithms. This was indeed the philosophy of [1].

Sometimes appearance boundaries and motion boundaries coincide (Fig. 1). Such cases can be segmented equally well based on appearance alone or motion alone. In the central column of Fig. 1(a) we see the results of Mumford-Shah segmentation (which is appearance based) individually applied to each of the images. In the central column of Fig. 1(b) we see its *motion based* adaptation to layering (prior formulation) jointly segmenting both the images (into the *common* and *overlapping* foreground and background layers). The segmenting curve is shown in red. We see that in such cases the earlier adaptation of Mumford-Shah to layering (Fig. 1(b)) worked equally well when compared to individual image segmentations using the original Mumford-Shah segmentation framework (Fig. 1(a)).

$$E(R, f_{in}, f_{out}) = \beta \underbrace{\int_{\partial R} ds}_{\text{Shape prior}}$$

$$+ (1 - \alpha) \underbrace{\int_{R} (I - f_{in})^2 dx}_{\text{Interior fidelity}} + \alpha \underbrace{\int_{R} \|\nabla f_{in}\|^2 dx}_{\text{Interior appearance prior}}$$

$$+ (1 - \alpha) \underbrace{\int_{\Omega \backslash R} (I - f_{out})^2 dx}_{\text{Exterior fidelity}} + \alpha \underbrace{\int_{\Omega \backslash R} \|\nabla f_{out}\|^2 dx}_{\text{Exterior appearance prior}}$$

(2.1)

Mumford-Shah Segmentation

Segmentation model

$$E(R, f_{top}, f_{bottom}) = \beta \underbrace{\int_{\partial R} ds}_{\text{Shape prior}}$$

$$+ (1 - \alpha) \underbrace{\int_{R} (I - f_{top})^2 dx}_{\text{Foreground fidelity}} + \alpha \underbrace{\int_{R} \|\nabla f_{top}\|^2 dx}_{\text{Foreground appearance prior}}$$

$$+ (1 - \alpha) \underbrace{\int_{\Omega \backslash R} (I - f_{bottom})^2 dx}_{\text{Background fidelity}} + \alpha \underbrace{\int_{\Omega = (R + \Omega \backslash R)} \|\nabla f_{bottom}\|^2 dx}_{\text{Background appearance prior}}$$

(2.2)

Mumford-Shah Layering

Synthesized model

On the other hand appearance and motion boundaries might not always coincide (Fig. 2). This is likely to happen when the appearances of the (moving)

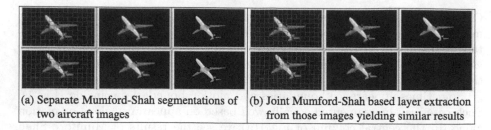

(a) Separate Mumford-Shah segmentations of two aircraft images	(b) Joint Mumford-Shah based layer extraction from those images yielding similar results

Fig. 1. Mumford-Shah segmentation versus layering: initial contour + results (Color figure online)

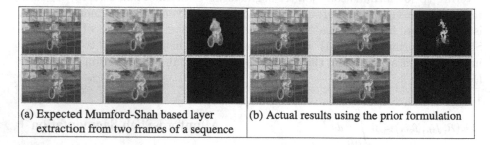

(a) Expected Mumford-Shah based layer extraction from two frames of a sequence	(b) Actual results using the prior formulation

Fig. 2. Revised and prior Mumford-Shah based layer extraction using two frames (Color figure online)

objects (the cyclist) become more heterogeneous. In such cases a pure appearance based segmentation is unlikely to capture the moving object. Motion based layer segmentation on the other hand is *expected* to (jointly) segment according to what we see in the central column of Fig. 2(a). The *desired* segmenting curve is shown in red. Its periphery bounds the moving object (foreground layer) in each image. However the adaptation of the Mumford-Shah model to layering as proposed in [1] instead yields the unexpected results shown in the central column of Fig. 2(b). This happens due to an unintended shrinking effect emanating from a subtle modeling flaw in [1] which we elucidate and fix. Figure 2(a) in reality shows the results obtained using our proposed technique.

The original Mumford-Shah model [2] approximates an image with a piecewise smooth partitioning in which the shapes as well appearances of the partitioning regions are smooth. This was cast as a joint (shape and appearance) optimization problem by minimizing the energy functional in Eq. 2.1. The quantities to be inferred are the shape of the partitioning region R and the functions $f_{in} : x \in R \to \mathbb{R}$ and $f_{out} : x \in \Omega \backslash R \to \mathbb{R}$ representing the smooth appearances of the pieces of the image interior and exterior to the region R respectively. Here Ω is the image plane and $I : x \in \Omega \to \mathbb{R}$ is the intensity function of the image. $\alpha \in [0\ 1]$ and $\beta \in \mathbb{R}$ are the weights on the appearance and shape priors respectively and ds is an infinitesimally small distance along the boundary of R.

Figure 1(a) shows Mumford-Shah style segmentation (Eq. 2.1) applied individually to each of two frames taken from an aircraft sequence with $\alpha = 0.9$ and $\beta = 1000$. The left column in the figure shows (in red) the initial contour (initial shape of R), the central column shows the final contour (final shape of R) and the right column shows the appearance model for R (function f_{in} modeled over R) in each frame.

Figure 1(b) correspondingly shows a layer extraction by now (jointly) segmenting the same frames using the previous adaptation of the Mumford-Shah model to layering. The left column shows the initial contour and the central column shows the final contour in each frame. The right column shows the appearance model of the foreground layer (jointly extracted from the frames). Despite the similar looking results (Fig. 1 (a) and (b)) the two techniques are fundamentally different.

Figure 2(b) (in a way similar to Fig. 1(b)) shows the (unexpected) results using two frames of a cyclist sequence instead. Figure 2(a) correspondingly shows the improved results obtained through our proposed technique.

3 Naive Layer Extension of Mumford-Shah (The Shrinkage Problem)

Let us consider the adaptation of the Mumford-Shah segmentation to layering following the prior work of [1]. Equation 2.2 shows the simplest case which generates a two layered model of a single image. There is a foreground layer that occludes part of a background layer. Ω is the image plane and (in this example only) is also the modeling region of the background layer. $I : x \in \Omega \rightarrow \mathbb{R}$ is the intensity function of the image. The quantities to be inferred are the shape (or boundary) 'C' of the foreground region 'R' and the functions $f_{top} : x \in R \rightarrow \mathbb{R}$ and $f_{bottom} : x \in \Omega \rightarrow \mathbb{R}$ representing the appearances of the foreground and background layer respectively. $\alpha \in [0\ 1]$ and $\beta \in \mathbb{R}$ are weights on the appearance and shape priors respectively and ds is an infinitesimal part of C. The key difference between the simple segmentation Eq. 2.1 and its layered equivalent Eq. 2.2 is that the former incorporates the exterior appearance prior in the exterior region ($\Omega \backslash R$) only but in the latter the corresponding background appearance prior gets incorporated over the entire background domain (Ω). This is necessary because (unlike segmentation) the background is no longer the complement of the foreground but extends *underneath* it. This does not offer any useful purpose for a layered representation of a single image but is crucial when multiple images are used to to *stitch* together the model for each layer with different parts visible in different images. An unintentional outcome is that layer occlusion gets penalized which induces a bias to shrink the regions of any occluding layers. The key contribution here is to present a new formulation that removes this problem.

To get a rudimentary understanding of the problem the background appearance prior in Eq. 2.2 can be decomposed giving Eq. 3.1.

Background appearance prior

$$= \underbrace{\int_{\Omega \backslash R} \|\nabla f_{bottom}\|^2 dx}_{\text{Background exterior (unoccluded)}} + \underbrace{\int_{R} \|\nabla f_{bottom}\|^2 dx}_{\text{Background interior (occluded)}} \quad (3.1)$$

Substituting Eq. 3.1 into Eq. 2.2 will make it look identical to Eq. 2.1 but with an additional term labeled as 'Background interior (occluded)' coming from Eq. 3.1. This additional term can be simply minimized by shrinking the size of the (occluding foreground) region R (that happens when the energy in Eq. 2.2 is minimized) thus producing the shrinking effect. This additional term shows us that the problem tends to worsen as the term $\|\nabla f_{bottom}\|^2$ (inhomogeneity in image appearance) becomes larger.

4   Reformulating Without the Shrinkage Bias

In this section we present our solution to fix the shrinkage problem in (the simplest case of) two-layered models built from a single image. We begin by reformulating the model (Eq. 2.2) as two energies that separate the shape and appearance optimization processes as Eqs. 4.1 and 4.2 respectively. The shape energy (Eq. 4.1) is now optimized with respect to the contour 'C' (boundary of R) subject to the constraint that the appearance energy (Eq. 4.2) remains optimized with respect to f_{top} and f_{bottom} for the current choice of C. The functions f_{top}^* and f_{bottom}^* are optimizers for the appearance energy, Eq. 4.2 (and are not free variables to be jointly optimized with C in the optimization process of Eq. 4.1).

$$E_{shape} = \beta \int_{\partial R} ds + E_d, \quad E_d = (1-\alpha) \left(\int_R (I - f_{top})^2 dx + \int_{\Omega \backslash R} (I - f_{bottom})^2 dx \right) (4.1)$$

$$E_{appearance} = \alpha \left(\int_R \|\nabla f_{top}\|^2 dx + \int_\Omega \|\nabla f_{bottom}\|^2 dx \right) + E_d \quad (4.2)$$

$$\alpha \Delta f_{top}^* + (1-\alpha)(I - f_{top}^*) = 0, \quad \text{over } R \quad (4.3)$$

$$\begin{aligned} \alpha \Delta f_{bottom}^* + (1-\alpha)(I - f_{bottom}^*) = 0, & \quad \text{over } \Omega \backslash R \\ \Delta f_{bottom}^* = 0, & \quad \text{over } R \end{aligned} \quad (4.4)$$

$$E^*_{shape} = E_{shape} + \int_{\Omega \setminus R} \lambda_{bottom} \left(\alpha \Delta f^*_{bottom} + (1 - \alpha)(I - f^*_{bottom}) \right) dx$$
$$+ \int_R \lambda_{top} \left(\alpha \Delta f^*_{top} + (1 - \alpha)(I - f^*_{top}) \right) dx + \int_R \lambda_{bottom} \left(\Delta f^*_{bottom} \right) dx \tag{4.5}$$

$$\frac{\partial C}{\partial t} = - \left(\beta \kappa - \alpha \nabla f^*_{top} \cdot \nabla \lambda_{top} + (1 - \alpha) \left((I - f^*_{top})^2 + \lambda_{top}(I - f^*_{top}) \right) \cdots \right.$$
$$\left. - (1 - \alpha) \left((I - f^*_{bottom})^2 + \lambda_{bottom}(I - f^*_{bottom}) \right) \right) N \tag{4.6}$$

$$\alpha \Delta \lambda_{top} - (1 - \alpha)(\lambda_{top} + 2(I - f^*_{top})) = 0, \quad \text{over } R \tag{4.7}$$

$$\alpha \Delta \lambda_{bottom} - (1 - \alpha)(\lambda_{bottom} + 2(I - f^*_{bottom})) = 0, \quad \text{over } \Omega \setminus R$$
$$\Delta \lambda_{bottom} = 0, \qquad\qquad\qquad\qquad\qquad\qquad\quad \text{over } R \tag{4.8}$$

Through calculus of variations it can be shown that the functions f^*_{top} and f^*_{bottom} satisfy the constraint PDEs (Eqs. 4.3 and 4.4) with vanishing Neumann boundary conditions over R and Ω respectively. Let $\lambda_{top} : x \in R \to \mathbb{R}$ and $\lambda_{bottom} : x \in \Omega \to \mathbb{R}$ be arbitrary twice differentiable functions that act as (pointwise) Lagrange multipliers to impose the constraints obtained in Eqs. 4.3 and 4.4 into Eq. 4.1. We now get a *Lagrangian style* constrained shape energy (Eq. 4.5). From calculus of variations, we obtain Eq. 4.6 (the gradient descent PDE) for optimizing Eq. 4.5 with respect to C where $\kappa : x \in C \to \mathbb{R}$ is the mean curvature of C, $N : x \in C \to \mathbb{R}^2$ gives the unit outward normal to C and λ_{top} and λ_{bottom} satisfy Eqs. 4.7 and 4.8 with vanishing Neumann boundary conditions over R and Ω respectively. To evolve the contour C first the functions f_{top}, f_{bottom}, λ_{top} and λ_{bottom} are computed using Eqs. 4.3, 4.4, 4.7 and 4.8 respectively after which C is evolved by one time step using Eq. 4.6. The process is repeated for further evolution. This fixes the shrinkage problem.

5   Generalization to Multiple Images and Layers with Motion

In this section we extend the revised model (Fig. 3) to multiple layers and multiple images (incorporating motion). There are L layers and N images.

$$E_{shape} = \sum_{l=1}^{L} \beta_l \int_{\partial R_l} ds_l + E_d, \ E_d = \sum_{n=1}^{N} \gamma_n (1 - \alpha) \int_{\Omega_n} (I_n - f^*_{vis_n} \circ g^{-1}_{vis_n,n})^2 dx \tag{5.1}$$

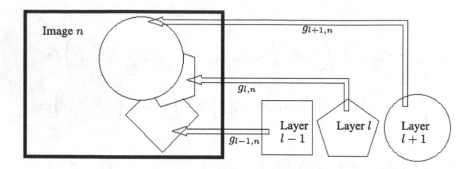

Fig. 3. The multilayered model

$$E_{appearance} = \sum_{l=1}^{L} \alpha \int_{R_l} \|\nabla f_l\|^2 dx + E_d \tag{5.2}$$

$$Constraint_l = (1 - \alpha) \sum_{n=1}^{N} \left(\gamma_n V_{l,n}(D_{l,n}^*)^2 \right) + \alpha \Delta f_l^* = 0, l \in [1\ L] \tag{5.3}$$

$$E_{shape}^* = E_{shape} + \sum_{l=1}^{L} \int_{R_l} \lambda_l Constraint_l\ dx \tag{5.4}$$

There is one background layer (layer 1) and $L - 1$ foreground layers where layer k is allowed to occlude layer l $\forall k > l$. For layer l $R_l \subset \mathbb{R}^2$ is its modeled region $f_l : x \in R_l \rightarrow \mathbb{R}$ is its appearance function, α and β_l are weights on the appearance and shape priors respectively, $C_l \subset R_l$ is the boundary of R_l, ds_l is an infinitesimal part of C_l, $\kappa_l : x \in C_l \rightarrow \mathbb{R}$ is the mean curvature of C_l, $\gamma_n \in [0\ 1]$ is the weightage given to image n, $\Omega_n \subset \mathbb{R}^2$ is the domain of image n, $I_n : x \in \Omega_n \rightarrow \mathbb{R}$ is the intensity function for image n and $g_{l,n} :$ $x \in (R_l \subset \mathbb{R}^2) \rightarrow y \in (\Omega_n \subset \mathbb{R}^2)$ is a parameterized group action containing $K = 6$ parameters $p_{l,n,k}$, $k \in [1\ K]$ (to represent a motion model) which maps every point $x \in R_l$ into a corresponding point in Ω_n (see Eq. 5.9). The functions $vis_n : x \in \Omega_n \rightarrow \mathbb{Z}^+$ and $next_n : x \in \Omega_n \rightarrow \mathbb{Z}^+$ are visibility functions that give the visible (or topmost) layer and the next (visible) layer respectively at a point x in Ω_n. These functions also influence the segmentation process of a particular layer based on the layers that occlude it (Eq. 5.7). We set $\gamma_n = \frac{1}{N}$ $\forall n$.

Corresponding to Eqs. 4.1 and 4.2 we separate the shape and appearance optimization processes for the multilayered model as Eqs. 5.1 and 5.2 respectively. We optimize the shape energy (Eq. 5.1) with respect to the contours C_l, $l \in [2\ L]$ subject to the constraint that the appearance energy (Eq. 5.2) remains optimized with respect to the functions f_l, $l \in [1\ L]$ given a particular set of choices C_l, $l \in [1\ L]$. The optimizers for Eq. 5.2 are f_l^* $l \in [1\ L]$ and it can be shown that they satisfy Eq. 5.3. These equations (Eq. 5.3) are used as constraints to give a Lagrangian style constrained shape energy Eq. 5.4 where $\lambda_l : x \in R_l \to \mathbb{R}$, $l \in [1\ L]$ are a set twice differentiable functions that act as pointwise Lagrange multipliers to impose the constraints. Calculus of variations yields Eqs. 5.5–5.9 where $N_l : x \in C_l \to \mathbb{R}^2$ is the unit outward normal to C_l at x. To evolve the contours first the functions f_l^* and λ_l are computed using Eqs. 5.3 and 5.5 respectively. The contours C_l, $l \in [2\ L]$ and the motion parameters $p_{l,n,k}$ $\forall l, n, k$ are then updated in parallel (by one time step) using Eqs. 5.7 and 5.6 respectively. The process is repeated for further evolution. Figure 2(a) was obtained using the technique outlined here with $N = 2$ and $L = 2$.

$$\alpha \Delta \lambda_l - \lambda_l (1 - \alpha) \left(\sum_{n=1}^{N} \gamma_n V_{l,n} \right) - 2(1 - \alpha) \left(\sum_{n=1}^{N} \gamma_n V_{l,n} D_{l,n}^* \right) = 0, \forall l \quad (5.5)$$

$$\frac{\partial p_{l,n,k}}{\partial t} = -\gamma_n (1 - \alpha) \left(\int_{R_l} V_{l,n} G_{l,n,k} \cdot Q_{l,n} dx + \int_{C_l} V_{l,n} P_{l,n} G_{l,n,k} \cdot N_l ds_l \right) \quad (5.6)$$

$$\frac{\partial C_l}{\partial t} = -\left(\beta_l \kappa_l - \alpha \nabla f_l^* \cdot \nabla \lambda_l (1 - \alpha) \sum_{n=1}^{N} \gamma_n V_{l,n} P_{l,n} \right) N_l \quad (5.7)$$

$$
\begin{aligned}
V_{l,n}(x) &= (\delta_{l,vis_n} \circ g_{l,n}(x)) \det (\text{Jacobian} (g_{l,n}(x))) \\
\overline{\lambda}_{l,n}(x) &= \lambda_{next_n \circ g_{l,n}(x)} \circ g_{next_n \circ g_{l,n}(x),n}^{-1} \circ g_{l,n}(x) \\
P_{l,n} &= (D_{l,n}^*)^2 + \lambda_l D_{l,n}^* - (\overline{D}_{l,n}^*)^2 - \overline{\lambda}_{l,n} \overline{D}_{l,n}^* \\
Q_{l,n} &= (2D_{l,n}^* + \lambda_l) \nabla f_l - D_{l,n}^* \nabla \lambda_l \\
D_{l,n}^*(x) &= (I_n \circ g_{l,n}(x) - f_l^*(x)) \\
\overline{D}_{l,n}^*(x) &= (I_n \circ g_{l,n}(x) - f_{next_n \circ g_{l,n}(x)}^* \circ g_{next_n \circ g_{l,n}(x),n}^{-1} \circ g_{l,n}(x)) \\
G_{l,n,k} &= \left[\text{Jacobian} (g_{l,n}) \right]^{-1} \left[\frac{\partial g_{l,n}}{\partial p_{l,n,k}} \right]
\end{aligned}
\quad (5.8)
$$

$$g_{l,n}(x) = \begin{bmatrix} \cos p_{l,n,5} & -\sin p_{l,n,5} \\ \sin p_{l,n,5} & \cos p_{l,n,5} \end{bmatrix} \begin{bmatrix} p_{l,n,3} & 0 \\ 0 & p_{l,n,4} \end{bmatrix} \begin{bmatrix} 1 & p_{l,n,6} \\ 0 & 1 \end{bmatrix} \begin{bmatrix} x \end{bmatrix} + \begin{bmatrix} p_{l,n,1} \\ p_{l,n,2} \end{bmatrix} \quad (5.9)$$

Table 1. Two layered models built from three frames taking representative examples from the DAVIS dataset using the exact same parameters with the prior and revised formulation. The segmenting curve (red) captures the foreground layer (from all images).

	Best Mumford Shah style two layered models for different examples using the prior joint optimization				Corresponding layered models using the exact same parameters with our revised constrained optimization			
	Frame 1	Frame 2	Frame 3	Foreground Model	Frame 1	Frame 2	Frame 3	Foreground Model
Ex. 1								
Ex. 2								
Ex. 3								
Ex. 4								

$$\text{SF} = \left(\sum_{n=1}^{N} \sum_{l=1}^{L} \left(A_{l,n} \cup \widehat{A_{l,n}} \right) - \left(A_{l,n} \cap \widehat{A_{l,n}} \right) \right) \Big/ \left(\sum_{n=1}^{N} \sum_{l=1}^{L} \left(A_{l,n} \cup \widehat{A_{l,n}} \right) \right) (5.10)$$

6 Experimental Results

In this section we compare results (Tables 1, 2 and 3) using both, the previous adaptation of the Mumford Shah segmentation model to layering as well as our revised formulation with the exact same weightage given to the shape and appearance priors on representative examples from the DAVIS dataset. [1] For each example the weights were adjusted to give (the best results or) the least shrinkage factor (Eq. 5.10) using the prior formulation. Here $Area_{l,n}$ is the ground truth area of layer l in image n and $\widehat{Area_{l,n}}$ is the captured area by layer l in image n. There are L layers and N images. Tables 1 and 2 show visual improvements in the results. The bias to penalize layer occlusion in the prior formulation gets highlighted and comparatively fuller and more complete models for the foreground layers(s) using the revised formulation are observed. Furthermore the shrinkage factor Eq. 5.10 mathematically shows significantly improved values with the revised formulation (Table 3).

---

[1] The contribution here is to show the problem with the prior formulation and to show that we have established the correct theoretical formulation.

Table 2. Three layered models built taking representative examples from the DAVIS dataset using the exact same parameters with the prior and revised formulation. Segmenting curves (red and blue) capture the two foreground layers (from all images). The layer shown in blue can occlude the layer shown in red. The foreground models are shown in the right two columns.

	Best Mumford Shah style two layered models for different examples using the prior joint optimization				Corresponding layered models using the exact same parameters with our revised constrained optimization			
	Initial Frame	Final Frame	Model for Layer 2 (red)	Model for Layer 3 (blue)	Initial Frame	Final Frame	Model for Layer 2 (red)	Model for Layer 3 (blue)
Ex. 5								
Ex. 6								
Ex. 7								
Ex. 8								

Table 3. Shrinkage Factor (SF) for the examples shown in Tables 1 and 2

Example		EX. 1	EX. 2	EX. 3	EX. 4	EX. 5	EX. 6	EX. 7	EX. 8
SF	Previous	0.2822	0.1990	0.4510	0.0252	0.3165	0.2547	0.2396	0.2872
	New	0.011	0.016	0.009	0.005	0.015	0.044	0.017	0.018

References

1. Jackson, J., et al.: Dynamic shape and appearance modelling via moving and deforming layers. Int. J. Comput. Vis. **79**, 71–84 (2008)
2. Mumford, D., Shah, J.: Optimal approximation by piecewise smooth functions and associated variational problems. Comm. Pure Appl. Math. **42**, 577–685 (1989)
3. Baker, S., et al.: A layered approach to stereo reconstruction. In: Proceedings of the IEEE Computer Society Conference on Computer Vision and Pattern Recognition, pp. 434–441 (1998)
4. Criminisi, A., et al.: Bilayer segmentation of live video. In: IEEE Computer Society Conference on Computer Vision and Pattern Recognition, vol. 1, pp. 53–60 (2006)
5. Guillemaut, J., Hilton, A.: Space-time joint multi-layer segmentation and depth estimation. In: International Conference on 3D Imaging, Modeling, Processing, Visualization and Transmission, pp. 440–447 (2012)
6. Ke, Q., Kanade, T.: A subspace approach to layer extraction. In: Proceedings of the IEEE Computer Society Conference on Computer Vision and Pattern Recognition, vol. 1, pp. I-255–I-262 (2001)
7. Kolmogorov, V., et al.: Bi-layer segmentation of binocular stereo video. In: IEEE Computer Society Conference on Computer Vision and Pattern Recognition, vol. 2, pp. 407–414 (2005)

8. Kumar, M., et al.: Learning layered motion segmentations of video. In: International Conference on Computer Vision, vol. 1, pp. 33–40 (2005)
9. Li, Y., Brown, M.: Single image layer separation using relative smoothness. In: IEEE Conference on Computer Vision and Pattern Recognition, pp. 2752–2759 (2014)
10. Lin, M., Tomasi, C.: Surfaces with occlusions from layered stereo. IEEE Trans. Pattern Anal. Mach. Intell. **26**(8), 1073–1078 (2004)
11. Pryor, G., et al.: Layered active contours for tracking. In: BMVC (2007)
12. S., A., H., S.: Layered representation of motion video using robust maximum-likelihood estimation of mixture models and MDL encoding. In: Proceedings of IEEE International Conference on Computer Vision, pp. 777–784 (1995)
13. Schodl, A., Essa, I.: Depth layers from occlusions. In: Proceedings of the IEEE Computer Society Conference on Computer Vision and Pattern Recognition, vol. 1, pp. I-639-I-644 (2001)
14. Smith, P., et al.: Layered motion segmentation and depth ordering by tracking edges. IEEE Trans. Pattern Anal. Mach. Intell. **26**(4), 479–494 (2004)
15. Sun, D., et al.: Layered segmentation and optical flow estimation over time. In: IEEE Conference on Computer Vision and Pattern Recognition, pp. 1768–1775 (2012)
16. Sun, D., et al.: A fully-connected layered model of foreground and background flow. In: IEEE Conference on Computer Vision and Pattern Recognition, pp. 2451–2458 (2013)
17. Sun, D., et al.: Local layering for joint motion estimation and occlusion detection. In: IEEE Conference on Computer Vision and Pattern Recognition, pp. 1098–1105 (2014)
18. Tao, H., et al.: Dynamic layer representation with applications to tracking. In: Proceedings of the IEEE Conference on Computer Vision and Pattern Recognition, vol. 2, pp. 134–141 (2000)
19. Wang, J., Adelson, E.: Representing moving images with layers. IEEE Trans. Image Process. **3**(5), 625–638 (1994)
20. Xiao, J., Shah, M.: Accurate motion layer segmentation and matting. In: IEEE Computer Society Conference on Computer Vision and Pattern Recognition, vol. 2, pp. 698–703 (2005)
21. Xu, F., Dai, Q.: Occlusion-aware motion layer extraction under large interframe motions. IEEE Trans. Image Process. **20**(9), 2615–2626 (2011)
22. Zhao, L., et al.: Layered scene models from single hazy images. IEEE Trans. Vis. Comput. Graph. **PP**(99), 1 (2017)
23. Zhou, Y., Tao, H.: A background layer model for object tracking through occlusion. In: Proceedings of IEEE International Conference on Computer Vision, vol. 2, pp. 1079–1085 (2003)

Visualization

Visualization of Parameter Sensitivity of 2D Time-Dependent Flow

Karsten Hanser[1]([✉]), Ole Klein[1], Bastian Rieck[2], Bettina Wiebe[3], Tobias Selz[4], Marian Piatkowski[1], Antoni Sagristà[1], Boyan Zheng[1], Mária Lukácová-Medvidová[3], George Craig[4], Heike Leitte[5], and Filip Sadlo[1]

[1] Heidelberg University, Heidelberg, Germany
karsten.hanser@iwr.uni-heidelberg.de
[2] ETH Zurich, Zürich, Switzerland
[3] Johannes Gutenberg University Mainz, Mainz, Germany
[4] Ludwig Maximilian University of Munich, Munich, Germany
[5] University of Kaiserslautern, Kaiserslautern, Germany

Abstract. In this paper, we present an approach to analyze 1D parameter spaces of time-dependent flow simulation ensembles. By extending the concept of the finite-time Lyapunov exponent to the ensemble domain, i.e., to the parameter that gives rise to the ensemble, we obtain a tool for quantitative analysis of parameter sensitivity both in space and time. We exemplify our approach using 2D synthetic examples and computational fluid dynamics ensembles.

Keywords: Visualization of flow ensembles · Parameter sensitivity

1 Introduction

There are many problems in science and engineering that exhibit parameter dependency. A prominent type of such dependency is regarding simulation parameters, such as initial and boundary conditions, model properties, and configuration of the numerical methods. In such cases, individual simulation results cannot provide a basis for reliable investigation of the underlying problem. By contrast, ensemble-based analysis, i.e., the investigation of the respective parameter spaces by means of sets of simulations, has proven successful in such situations. That is, such ensembles consist of a set of members, with each member being an individual simulation for the respective parameter value.

One intensely researched difficulty with ensemble-based analysis, is the interpretation of the results. For example, there is an increasing body of visualization literature on the analysis of ensembles, often employing clustering techniques and techniques based on distributions. The traditional approach to conduct ensemble-based analysis is to choose some interval in the respective parameter space, sample this range using a regular sampling—each sample representing a respective member—followed by (visual) analysis of the resulting ensemble.

© Springer Nature Switzerland AG 2018
G. Bebis et al. (Eds.): ISVC 2018, LNCS 11241, pp. 359–370, 2018.
https://doi.org/10.1007/978-3-030-03801-4_32

A difficulty with traditional ensemble visualization approaches is, however, that they focus on the data. That is, they focus on the members, and do not relate these data to the ensemble domain, i.e., they do not relate them to the parameter space that gave rise to the ensemble. In this paper, in contrast, we focus on the variation of flow ensembles with respect to 1D parameter spaces.

The main contributions of this paper are:

- extension of the Lyapunov exponent concept to ensemble variation, and
- its decomposition into parameter sensitivity and spatial error growth.

2   Related Work

Closely related work groups into two main fields, which we address in the following: visualization of ensembles and uncertainty, and sensitivity analysis.

Ensemble visualization is currently one of the intensely researched topics in visualization research. Ferstl et al. [4] present streamline variability plots, and a technique for contour analysis based on correlation [5], similar to Sanyal et al. [10]. Contour distribution is addressed by Pfaffelmoser and Westermann [9]. Whitaker et al. [13] introduce contour boxplots. For related work regarding uncertainty visualization, we to refer to Bonneau et al. [1].

In the field of comparative ensemble visualization with respect to Lagrangian transport, the most closely related work is that by Hummel et al. [7]. In their work, they investigate the spatial spread of trajectories for each ensemble member individually, based on principal component analysis, and the variance of the spread of the respective spatial distribution means over all members. This enables Hummel et al. to investigate the spread of any type of ensembles, i.e., also discrete ones originating from different simulation models. On the other hand, their method cannot provide insight into the structure of the dependence with respect to parameter variation. Our approach, in contrast, provides this insight in the structure of parameter dependency, but requires ensembles that originate from variation of such a parameter. Due to our parametric representation, our approach also enables visualization of the spread over all members. Thus, our approach is somewhat complementary to the one by Hummel et al.

Concerning sensitivity analysis, Chen et al. [3] provide analysis with respect to errors stemming from interpolation in time-varying data. McLoughlin et al. [8] focus on visualizing the effects of parameter perturbations by means of the geometry of pathlines. In a similar vein, Chandler et al. [2] analyze errors that arise from different pathline tracing methods. Nevertheless, none of these techniques addresses sensitivity in ensemble parameter space.

3   Method

The subject of our analysis are time-dependent flow ensembles, where each member j of the ensemble is a continuous vector field

$$\mathbf{u}^j(\mathbf{x}, t) = \left(u_1^j(\mathbf{x}, t), \dots, u_n^j(\mathbf{x}, t) \right)^\top, \tag{1}$$

with position $\mathbf{x} := (x_1, \ldots, x_n)^\top \in \Omega \subseteq \mathbb{R}^n$, time t, and vector component u_i^j of member j along axis of x_i, i.e., $j \in \mathbb{R}$ also represents the ensemble parameter. This leads to the *ensemble domain* $\overline{\Omega} \subseteq \mathbb{R}^n \times \mathbb{R}$, *space-parameter position*

$$\overline{\mathbf{x}} = (\mathbf{x}^\top, j)^\top := (x_1, \ldots, x_n, j)^\top \in \overline{\Omega}, \tag{2}$$

and the continuous *ensemble vector field*

$$\overline{\mathbf{u}}(\overline{\mathbf{x}}, t) := \left(u_1^j(\mathbf{x}, t), \ldots, u_n^j(\mathbf{x}, t), 0 \right)^\top \in \overline{\Omega}. \tag{3}$$

Following the finite-time Lyapunov exponent (FTLE) approach by Haller [6], we base our approach on the flow map $\boldsymbol{\phi}_{t_0}^T(\mathbf{x})$, which maps the seed $\mathbf{x}$ of a pathline $\boldsymbol{\xi}_{t_0}^\mathbf{x}(t)$ started at time t_0 to its endpoint after advection for time T, i.e.,

$$\boldsymbol{\phi}_{t_0}^T(\mathbf{x}) = \left(\phi_{t_0,1}^T(\mathbf{x}), \ldots, \phi_{t_0,n}^T(\mathbf{x}) \right)^\top := \boldsymbol{\xi}_{t_0}^\mathbf{x}(t_0 + T), \tag{4}$$

with $\boldsymbol{\xi}_{t_0}^\mathbf{x}(t_0) := \mathbf{x}$, and $\phi_{t_0,i}^T$ being the ith component of the flow map. For traditional vector fields, the FTLE is defined from this by

$$\sigma_{t_0}^T(\mathbf{x}) := \frac{1}{|T|} \ln \left\| \nabla \boldsymbol{\phi}_{t_0}^T(\mathbf{x}) \right\|_2, \tag{5}$$

with $\| \cdot \|_2$ being the spectral matrix norm, i.e., for a matrix A, the square root of the largest eigenvalue of $A^\top A$.

In our ensemble field setting, this leads to the *ensemble flow map* $\overline{\boldsymbol{\phi}}_{t_0}^T(\overline{\mathbf{x}})$ that maps a space-parameter start point $\overline{\mathbf{x}}$ of a (purely spatial) pathline seeded at $\mathbf{x}$ and time t_0 in member j to its space-parameter endpoint

$$\overline{\boldsymbol{\phi}}_{t_0}^T(\overline{\mathbf{x}}) := \left(\boldsymbol{\phi}_{t_0}^T(\mathbf{x})^\top, j \right)^\top \tag{6}$$

after advection for time T. The mapping from ② to ②' in Fig. 1(a) is an example of such a trajectory within a member, and for the resulting entry in the ensemble flow map $\overline{\boldsymbol{\phi}}_{t_0}^T(\overline{\mathbf{x}})$.

3.1 Ensemble Spread

Following Eq. 5, it would be straightforward to derive an ensemble finite-time Lyapunov exponent field $\overline{\sigma}_{t_0}^T(\overline{\mathbf{x}})$ from the ensemble flow map via

$$\overline{\sigma}_{t_0}^T(\overline{\mathbf{x}}) := \frac{1}{|T|} \ln \left\| \nabla \overline{\boldsymbol{\phi}}_{t_0}^T(\overline{\mathbf{x}}) \right\|_2. \tag{7}$$

However, taking a look at the Jacobian $\nabla \overline{\boldsymbol{\phi}}_{t_0}^T(\overline{\mathbf{x}})$ reveals the following structure:

$$\nabla \overline{\boldsymbol{\phi}}_{t_0}^T := \begin{pmatrix} \frac{\partial}{\partial x_1} \phi_{t_0,1}^T & \cdots & \frac{\partial}{\partial x_n} \phi_{t_0,1}^T & \frac{\partial}{\partial j} \phi_{t_0,1}^T \\ \vdots & \ddots & \vdots & \vdots \\ \frac{\partial}{\partial x_1} \phi_{t_0,n}^T & \cdots & \frac{\partial}{\partial x_n} \phi_{t_0,n}^T & \frac{\partial}{\partial j} \phi_{t_0,n}^T \\ \frac{\partial j}{\partial x_1} = 0 & \cdots & \frac{\partial j}{\partial x_n} = 0 & \frac{\partial j}{\partial j} = 1 \end{pmatrix} = \begin{pmatrix} \nabla \boldsymbol{\phi}_{t_0}^T & \frac{\partial}{\partial j} \boldsymbol{\phi}_{t_0}^T \\ \mathbf{0}^\top & 1 \end{pmatrix}. \tag{8}$$

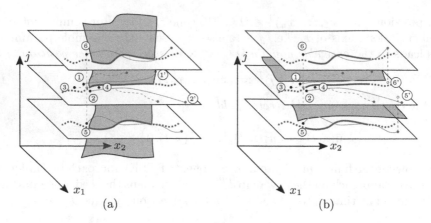

Fig. 1. Ensemble vector field of 2D members in 3D ensemble domain ($x_1 \times x_2 \times j$). (a) ES-FTLE ${}^s\sigma_{t_0}^T(\overline{\mathbf{x}})$ measures spatial separation ((①'-②')) with respect to spatial perturbation (in x_i, ①-②), and thus predictability and topology of trajectories (red manifold). (b) EP-FTLE ${}^p\sigma_{t_0}^T(\overline{\mathbf{x}})$ measures spatial separation ((⑤'-⑥')) with respect to parametric perturbation (in j, ⑤-⑥), and thus parameter sensitivity (red manifold).

We identify an upper left block, which has unit 1 because the flow map is derived with respect to the input coordinate, and an upper right block, which has generally a different unit: the unit of the coordinates x_i divided by the unit of j. Thus, $\overline{\sigma}_{t_0}^T$ has no direct utility/interpretation, and is influenced by the "scaling" between the different units, which could be, in general, chosen arbitrarily. Additionally, it would measure the combined spread in x_i and j with respect to x_i and j, meaning that the Euclidean distance factor for the respective endpoints in the ensemble domain $\overline{\Omega}$ would be larger or equal than 1 (since, as can be seen from Eq. 3, trajectories cannot approach or deviate in j-direction). These circumstances motivate us to decompose $\nabla\overline{\phi}_{t_0}^T$ into these two blocks.

3.2 Ensemble-Space Finite-Time Lyapunov Exponent

The upper left block in Eq. 8 represents the traditional (purely spatial) flow map gradient, as used for traditional FTLE computation (Eq. 5), although with the difference that it is now a field in the entire $(n+1)$-dimensional ensemble domain $\overline{\Omega}$, i.e., we have $\nabla\phi_{t_0}^T(\overline{\mathbf{x}})$ instead of $\nabla\phi_{t_0}^T(\mathbf{x})$, leading to the ensemble-space finite-time Lyapunov exponent (ES-FTLE) field

$$
{}^s\sigma_{t_0}^T(\overline{\mathbf{x}}) := \frac{1}{|T|} \ln \left\| \nabla\phi_{t_0}^T(\overline{\mathbf{x}}) \right\|_2 \tag{9}
$$

in the ensemble domain. This field captures, for each space-parameter point $\overline{\mathbf{x}}$, the amount of *spatial* separation of trajectories started in the *spatial* vicinity of $\mathbf{x}$ in member j. In Fig. 1(a), the increase of the distance between ① and ② before advection to the distance between ①' and ②' after advection illustrates this. On the one hand, this traditional (spatial) FTLE in the ensemble domain enables us to analyze predictability, i.e., error growth with respect to the seed *position* of a trajectory. On the other hand, it also enables us to reveal the spatial time-dependent topology [12] by extracting Lagrangian coherent structures (LCS) in terms of height ridges therefrom [11], which separate spatial regions of qualitatively different spatial behavior. Since our ensemble domain is $(n+1)$-dimensional, the respective $(n-1)$-dimensional ridges (lines in case of $n=2$) in Ω are present as n-dimensional ridges (surfaces in case of $n=2$) in $\overline{\Omega}$. Since in our work the focus is on parameter sensitivity and not topology, we visualize the resulting fields with volume rendering instead of extracting ridges.

3.3   Ensemble-Parameter Finite-Time Lyapunov Exponent

The upper right block in Eq. 8 represents the partial derivative of the flow map with respect to the ensemble parameter j. We use it to derive the ensemble-parameter finite-time Lyapunov exponent (EP-FTLE) field

$$ {}^{p}\sigma_{t_0}^{T}(\overline{\mathbf{x}}) := \frac{1}{|T|} \ln \left\| \frac{\partial}{\partial j} \boldsymbol{\phi}_{t_0}^{T}(\overline{\mathbf{x}}) \right\|_2 . \tag{10} $$

Since $\partial\boldsymbol{\phi}_{t_0}^{T}/\partial j$ is a $n \times 1$ matrix, we may interpret it as a vector that linearizes the flow map. Hence, its spectral norm is simply the Euclidean norm. The EP-FTLE represents, for each position $\overline{\mathbf{x}} \in \overline{\Omega}$, the amount of *spatial* separation of trajectories started at position $\mathbf{x}$ in the *parametric* vicinity of member j. In Fig. 1(b), the growth of the distance between ⑤ and ⑥ before advection to the distance between ⑤' and ⑥' (the spatial projection of the endpoints after advection) represents this quantity (note that the distance between ⑤ and ⑥ is illustrated too large for clarity, it is intrinsically identical to the distance between ① and ②). The EP-FTLE represents the Lagrangian parameter sensitivity of the ensemble j at position $\mathbf{x}$ and time t_0 with respect to perturbation of j. Thus, regions in $\overline{\Omega}$, where the EP-FTLE is low, are not subject to substantial change if j is varied. A possible consequence is that such regions do not need to be explored at higher resolution with respect to j. On the other hand, in regions with a high EP-FTLE, the choice of j has large impact on the result and thus needs to be carefully investigated.

Notice that the (ES-)FTLE is a logarithmic measure representing a rate of particle separation. Since it is widely used for qualitative (topological) analysis, the logarithm is not an issue in visualization. However, we present our EP-FTLE for quantitative analysis of parameter sensitivity. Therefore, in our visualizations, we omit the logarithm in Eq. 10.

Notice also that our approach is basically applicable to *any* number of ensemble parameters, i.e., it supports an m-dimensional vector $\mathbf{j}$ instead of a scalar parameter j. In this case, the upper right block in Eq. 8 is a matrix $\nabla_{\mathbf{j}} \boldsymbol{\phi}_{t_0}^{T}$, which can be evaluated in Eq. 10 with the spectral matrix norm. In cases where all m parameters have the same unit, the result is well-defined and directly interpretable. Nevertheless, we do not exemplify such cases for two main reasons:

First, direct visualizations of $\overline{\Omega}$ are infeasible in general because they exceed three dimensions. The more important reason is, however, that different parameters typically have different units. As we argue in this paper, mixing those units may lead to interpretation difficulties. Our technique would be able to visualize the impact of each parameter individually, though. We leave the problem of handling multiple parameters as future work.

4   Results

We employ our technique to a set of synthetic and simulated 2D flow ensembles of increasing complexity. The first synthetic ensembles serve for an introduction and illustration of the properties of our technique. The remaining examples include cases from computational fluid dynamics (CFD) and meteorology—a field in which ensemble simulation plays a predominant role.

4.1   Saddle

We start with a simple synthetic stationary (time-independent) 2D flow ensemble that exhibits trajectory separation:

$$\overline{\mathbf{u}}(\overline{\mathbf{x}}) = \begin{pmatrix} -\sin(x)\cos(y) \\ \sin(y)\cos(x) \\ 0 \end{pmatrix} \tag{11}$$

in the domain $\overline{\Omega} = [-0.5, 0.5] \times [-0.5, 0.5] \times [-0.5, 0.5]$. This vector field represents the region around the origin of the Double Gyre example [11] in standard configuration. As can be seen, this ensemble does not vary in (is not a function of) j, i.e., all members are identical. It exhibits saddle-type nonlinear dynamics, which are captured by the traditional FTLE.

Figure 2(a) illustrates the ensemble and provides the respective ES-FTLE result with $T = 100$, sampled within $\overline{\Omega}$ at a resolution of $400 \times 400 \times 200$ nodes. One can nicely observe the high ES-FTLE values representing a ridge surface in $\overline{\Omega}$ (yellow in Fig. 2(a)). This ridge surface represents a spatial (traditional) LCS that illustrates the bifurcation due to the saddle-type flow, i.e., it separates the two regions of $\overline{\Omega}$. Since there is no variation of $\overline{\mathbf{u}}(\overline{\mathbf{x}})$ in j-direction, the EP-FTLE field is constant zero in this case and thus not investigated.

4.2   Rotation

As a complement to the Saddle example, we now investigate a stationary field that does not exhibit variation in space Ω within the members j, but instead exhibits variation across the members, i.e., in j-direction:

$$\overline{\mathbf{u}}(\overline{\mathbf{x}}) = \begin{pmatrix} \cos\left(\frac{\pi}{4}\left(\tanh(5\pi j) + 1\right)\right) \\ \sin\left(\frac{\pi}{4}\left(\tanh(5\pi j) + 1\right)\right) \\ 0 \end{pmatrix} \tag{12}$$

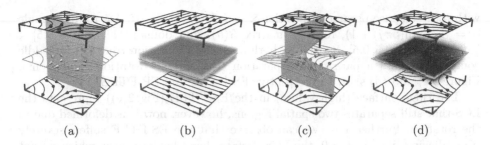

(a)   (b)   (c)   (d)

Fig. 2. Synthetic steady flow examples (here, and in all figures: x-axis red, y-axis green, j-axis blue, and ES/EP-FTLE low value blue and high value yellow). Saddle (a) exhibits ridge (yellow) in ES-FTLE ${}^s\sigma_{t_0}^T(\overline{\mathbf{x}})$ but zero EP-FTLE ${}^p\sigma_{t_0}^T(\overline{\mathbf{x}})$. Rotation (b) exhibits zero ES-FTLE but our EP-FTLE clearly shows high parametric variation (yellow ridge) at the center of the parameter interval. In the Rotating Saddle example, ${}^s\sigma_{t_0}^T(\overline{\mathbf{x}})$ (c) shows spatial separation but fails to capture parametric variation (see separated orange lines at the center of the parameter interval). In contrast, our ${}^p\sigma_{t_0}^T(\overline{\mathbf{x}})$ (d) captures ensemble variation well, but does not capture spatial separation. Thus, ES-FTLE provides qualitative insight into the (topological) organization of flow ensembles, while the EP-FTLE is a quantitative measure for ensemble variation, i.e., parameter sensitivity.

in the domain $\overline{\Omega} = [-0.5, 0.5] \times [-0.5, 0.5] \times [-0.5, 0.5]$. Each member of this ensemble is a uniform 2D vector field with magnitude one. The direction, however, varies with member parameter j according to the hyperbolic tangent, i.e., the angle does vary very slowly at $j = -0.5$ and $j = 0.5$ and most of the range, except for $j \approx 0$, where it changes fast. As a result, the parameter sensitivity of the members is overall low with a peak at $j = 0$.

Figure 2(b) illustrates the ensemble and depicts the EP-FTLE result with $T = 100$. One can see that in this case, the EP-FTLE exhibits a ridge surface in $\overline{\Omega}$ at $j = 0$. This visualizes that the strongest member variation, i.e., largest parameter sensitivity, is at $j = 0$, and that the high EP-FTLE values separate the two regions that are qualitatively similar and exhibit small parameter sensitivity. Since the individual members represent uniform flow, the ES-FTLE is trivially constant in this case and thus not investigated.

4.3   Rotating Saddle

The third and last simple example for introducing our approach, consists of a combination of the Saddle (Sect. 4.1) and Rotation (Sect. 4.2) examples. That is, we have the flow from the Saddle example, but in this case the members undergo the same rotation as they did in the Rotation example:

$$\overline{\mathbf{u}}(\overline{\mathbf{x}}) = R(-\alpha) \begin{pmatrix} -\sin(x')\cos(y') \\ \sin(y')\cos(x') \\ 0 \end{pmatrix}, \quad R(\theta) = \begin{pmatrix} \cos(\theta) & -\sin(\theta) & 0 \\ \sin(\theta) & \cos(\theta) & 0 \\ 0 & 0 & 1 \end{pmatrix}, \quad (13)$$

with rotated space-parameter position $\overline{\mathbf{x}}' = (x', y', j)^\top := R(\alpha)\,\overline{\mathbf{x}}$, rotation angle $\alpha = \frac{\pi}{4}(\tanh(5\pi j) + 1)$, rotation matrix $R(\theta)$, and domain $\overline{\Omega} = [-0.5, 0.5] \times [-0.5, 0.5] \times [-0.5, 0.5]$. It exhibits both a spatial separation (due to the Saddle component), and a parametric separation (due to the Rotation component). Figure 2(c) and (d) show the respective ES-FTLE and EP-FTLE.

The ridge surface (high values) in the ES-FTLE (Fig. 2(c)) represents the LCS that still separates two spatial regions, however, now it is deformed due to the rotation. Furthermore, we can observe that the ES-FTLE suffers severely from aliasing, i.e., at $j \approx 0$, the LCS surface degrades into lines, which do not partition $\overline{\Omega}$. In contrast, the EP-FTLE field (Fig. 2(d)) does not indicate the spatial sensitivity, but instead depicts very well (without aliasing issues) the high parameter sensitivity around $j = 0$, i.e., the high EP-FTLE values separate the two regions of $\overline{\Omega}$ with low parameter sensitivity.

4.4 Pulsating Injector

This CFD example brings us now to time-dependent simulation ensembles. It examines the injection of pulsating flow, e.g., in the context of gas injection for combustion, and consists of a 2D channel, with inflow on the left, outflow on the right, no-slip boundaries on top and bottom, and an injector inlet at the bottom left with time-dependent inflow behavior. The injector's velocity magnitude pulsates with a temporal sine. In this study, the pulsation frequency is the ensemble parameter to be examined, and is investigated in the interval $[0, 7]$, resulting in the domain $\overline{\Omega} = [0, 0.2] \times [0, 0.1] \times [0, 7]$, sampled on a grid of $800 \times 400 \times 568$.

Computing the space-parameter flow map with reverse advection time $T = -0.1$ reveals that parameter sensitivity is particularly high for low frequencies (Fig. 3(a)). We select a fixed position (curve in parameter space) and start a pathline at this position in every 9th member, resulting in a "parameter pathline rake". Additionally, we map the EP-FTLE to the parameter curve, revealing that high EP-FTLE values separate parameter ranges with qualitatively different pathline behavior. In contrast, the ES-FTLE (Fig. 3(b)), which captures the spatial separation, does not provide such a quantitative property: it tends to be lower than the EP-FTLE at low frequencies but higher than the EP-FTLE at higher frequencies, although the pathlines do not exhibit high separation with respect to parameter variation there.

4.5 Rising Bubble

This example represents a simulation of free convection of a smooth warm air bubble surrounded by cold air, from a meteorological study, based on the Euler equations of gas dynamics. In this example, the potential temperature variation was examined by ensemble simulation. The potential temperature variation represents the deviation of the air bubble potential temperature from background equilibrium, and in this ensemble it was sampled at 31 equidistant

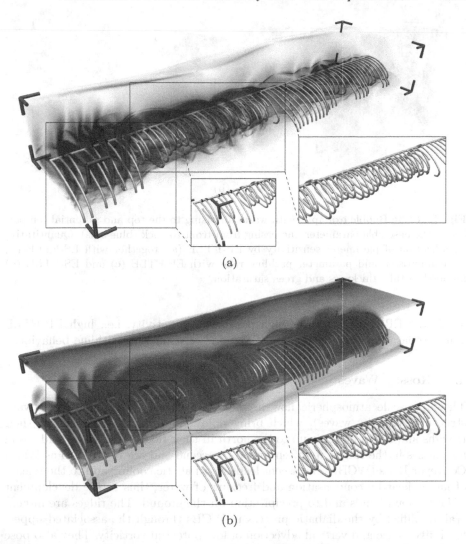

(a)

(b)

Fig. 3. Pulsating Injector example, with injection frequency increasing from left to right (blue axis). (a) EP-FTLE reveals regions of high parameter sensitivity. EP-FTLE mapped to radius and green saturation along the pathline seed "rake" reveals that large EP-FTLE quantitatively separates parameter regions with different pathline behavior. ES-FTLE (b) does not provide such quantitative view on parameter sensitivity, i.e., it is not consistent with pathline behavior (here, ES-FTLE mapped to pathline rake).

points in the interval [0.401, 0.599]. We discretized the computational domain $\overline{\Omega} = [0, 1500]^2 \times [0.401, 0.599]$ to a grid of $1500 \times 1500 \times 31$ nodes for our analysis.

We seeded the flow map trajectories at time $t_0 = 1000$ and integrated them in reverse direction for $T = -400$. Figure 4 shows our EP-FTLE result, together with a pathline rake, and the ES-FTLE. As can be seen from the pathline vari-

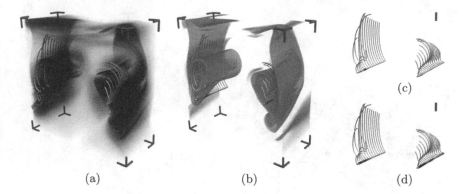

(a)   (b)   (d)

(c)

Fig. 4. Rising Bubble example, with warm air rising to the top and potential temperature, the ensemble parameter, increasing from front to back (blue axis). Quantitative visualization of parameter sensitivity by EP-FTLE (a), together with ES-FTLE (b) for comparison, and parameter pathline rake with EP-FTLE (c) and ES-FTLE (d) mapped to tube thickness and green saturation.

ation, the EP-FTLE captures high parameter sensitivity, i.e., high EP-FTLE values separate parameter regions of qualitatively different pathline behavior.

4.6   Rossby Waves

The large-scale atmospheric flow in the mid-latitudes is dominated by wave structures (Rossby waves), which bring polar air down to the south in their troughs and subtropical air up to the north in their ridges. The moist and warm air masses in the ridges are often forced to ascend and are referred to as Warm Conveyor Belts (WCB). The ascent leads to adiabatic cooling and to the release of latent heat by condensation and freezing of water, thus to the development of large cloud bands and to precipitation on the ground. The ridges are in general amplified by the diabatic process in WCBs through the associated upper-level divergence and vertical advection of low potential vorticity. They also pose challenges to numerical weather prediction, since the relevant quantities and processes are difficult to measure and to model. The global model ICON from Deutscher Wetterdienst (DWD) has been used to conduct a series of experiments, where the amount of the latent heat release has been modified by using different values for the enthalpy of condensation and freezing in the model. The enthalpy has been varied from 80% up to 120% of its true value in steps of 1% in this ensemble, which should lead to a damped or increased WCB activity and associated ridge amplification.

For visualization by our technique, we discretized the computational domain $\overline{\Omega} = [-\pi, \pi] \times [0, 17/36\pi] \times [0.8, 1.2]$, representing the northern hemisphere in terms of longitude and latitude times the ensemble dimension, to a grid of $2000 \times 500 \times 41$ nodes. The flow map trajectories are seeded at $t_0 = 3.6 \cdot 10^5 \, \text{s} = 100 \, \text{h}$ and advected for $T = 1.8 \cdot 10^5 \, \text{s} = 50 \, \text{h}$.

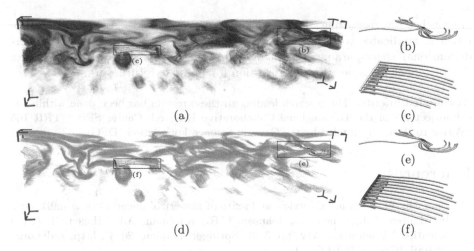

Fig. 5. Rossby Waves example, with enthalpy, the ensemble parameter, increasing from front to back (blue axis). Quantitative visualization by means of EP-FTLE (a) reveals only few regions with strong parameter sensitivity. The ES-FTLE (d), in contrast, reveals strong coherent structures also toward the equator (bottom). Parameter pathline rakes with EP-FTLE and ES-FTLE mapped to seed curve thickness and green saturation. EP-FTLE captures separation due to parameter perturbation (b), (c), whereas ES-FTLE separation only due to spatial perturbation (e), (f).

For analysis, we again conduct the same steps as in the previous examples. Whereas predictability/topology by means of ES-FTLE shows many strong coherent vortex structures (Fig. 5(d)), the EP-FTLE has only a few peaks. This shows that although there is a large number of topological structures identified by means of the ES-FTLE (Fig. 5(d)), the sensitivity with respect to enthalpy in the ensemble parameter space is constrained to small subregions (orange/yellow in Fig. 5(a)). This reveals that the structures closer to the equator are less parameter-sensitive than those at the polar regions. A closer investigation of the reasons and implications is, however, beyond the scope of this paper and subject to future work in meteorology.

4.7 Conclusion

We presented an approach to quantify and visualize parameter sensitivity for 2D time-dependent flow ensembles. We extended the concept of the finite-time Lyapunov exponent to the parameter space of ensembles, and presented a decomposition, providing a "stacked" version of the traditional finite-time Lyapunov exponent which measures predictability and which we denote ES-FTLE, and providing its counterpart, the EP-FTLE, which measures parameter sensitivity of ensembles with respect to the space-time behavior of pathlines integrated over a finite time interval.

As future work, we would like to investigate parameter sampling approaches for efficient and effective ensemble computation, and investigate related

approaches for visualizing 3D time-dependent vector fields. Although our approach is applicable to multi-parameter ensembles, this would lead to higher-
dimensional space-parameter domains, involving visual representation issues.
Addressing these issues is also a direction for possible future work.

Acknowledgments. The research leading to these results has been done within the
subproject A7 of the Transregional Collaborative Research Center SFB / TRR 165
"Waves to Weather" funded by the German Science Foundation (DFG).

References

1. Bonneau, G.-P., et al.: Overview and state-of-the-art of uncertainty visualization.
   In: Hansen, C.D., Chen, M., Johnson, C.R., Kaufman, A.E., Hagen, H. (eds.)
   Scientific Visualization. MV, pp. 3–27. Springer, London (2014). https://doi.org/
   10.1007/978-1-4471-6497-5_1
2. Chandler, J., Bujack, R., Joy, K.I.: Analysis of error in interpolation-based pathline
   tracing. In: EuroVis Short Paper Proceeedings (2016)
3. Chen, C., Biswas, A., Shen, H.W.: Uncertainty modeling and error reduction for
   pathline computation in time-varying flow fields. In: IEEE Pacific Visualization
   Symposium (PacificVis), pp. 215–222, April 2015
4. Ferstl, F., Bürger, K., Westermann, R.: Streamline variability plots for characterizing the uncertainty in vector field ensembles. IEEE Trans. Vis. Comput. Graph.
   22(1), 767–776 (2016)
5. Ferstl, F., Kanzler, M., Rautenhaus, M., Westermann, R.: Visual analysis of spatial
   variability and global correlations in ensembles of iso-contours. Comput. Graph.
   Forum **35**(3), 221–230 (2016)
6. Haller, G.: Distinguished material surfaces and coherent structures in three-
   dimensional fluid flows. Physica D **149**, 248–277 (2001)
7. Hummel, M., Obermaier, H., Garth, C., Joy, K.I.: Comparative visual analysis
   of Lagrangian transport in CFD ensembles. IEEE Trans. Vis. Comput. Graph.
   19(12), 2743–2752 (2013)
8. McLoughlin, T., et al.: Visualization of input parameters for stream and pathline
   seeding. Int. J. Adv. Comput. Sci. Appl. (IJACSA) **6**(4), 124–135 (2015)
9. Pfaffelmoser, T., Westermann, R.: Visualizing contour distributions in 2D ensemble
   data. In: EuroVis Short Paper Proceedings, pp. 55–59 (2013)
10. Sanyal, J., Zhang, S., Dyer, J., Mercer, A., Amburn, P., Moorhead, R.: Noodles:
    a tool for visualization of numerical weather model ensemble uncertainty. IEEE
    Trans. Vis. Comput. Graph. **16**(6), 1421–1430 (2010)
11. Shadden, S., Lekien, F., Marsden, J.: Definition and properties of Lagrangian coher-
    ent structures from finite-time Lyapunov exponents in two-dimensional aperiodic
    flows. Physica D: Nonlinear Phenom. **212**(3–4), 271–304 (2005)
12. Üffinger, M., Sadlo, F., Ertl, T.: A time-dependent vector field topology based on
    streak surfaces. IEEE Trans. Vis. Comput. Graph. **19**(3), 379–392 (2013)
13. Whitaker, R.T., Mirzargar, M., Kirby, R.M.: Contour boxplots: a method for char-
    acterizing uncertainty in feature sets from simulation ensembles. IEEE Trans. Vis.
    Comput. Graph. **19**(12), 2713–2722 (2013)

Non-stationary Generalized Wishart Processes for Enhancing Resolution over Diffusion Tensor Fields

Jhon F. Cuellar-Fierro[1]([✉]), Hernán Darío Vargas-Cardona[1],
Andrés M. Álvarez[1], Álvaro A. Orozco[1], and Mauricio A. Álvarez[2]

[1] Automatic Researh Group, Universidad Tecnológica de Pereira, Pereira, Colombia
{jfcuellar,hernan.vargas,andres.alvarez1,aaog}@utp.edu.co
[2] University of Sheffield, Sheffield, UK
mauricio.alvarez@sheffield.ac.uk

Abstract. Low spatial resolution of diffusion resonance magnetic imaging (dMRI) restricts its clinical applications. Usually, the measures are obtained in a range from 1 to $2\,\text{mm}^3$ per voxel, and some structures cannot be studied in detail. Due to clinical acquisition protocols (exposure time, field strength, among others) and technological limitations, it is not possible to acquire images with high resolution. In this work, we present a methodology for enhancing the spatial resolution of diffusion tensor (DT) fields obtained from dMRI. The proposed methodology assumes that a DT field follows a generalized Wishart process (GWP), which is a stochastic process defined over symmetric and positive definite matrices indexed by spatial coordinates. A GWP is modulated by a set of Gaussian processes (GPs). Therefore, the kernel hyperparameters of the GPs control the spatial dynamic of a GWP. Following this notion, we employ a non-stationary kernel for describing DT fields whose statistical properties are not constant over the space. We test our proposed method in synthetic and real dMRI data. Results show that non-stationary GWP can describe complex DT fields (i.e. crossing fibers where the shape, size and orientation properties change abruptly), and it is a competitive methodology for interpolation of DT fields, when we compare with methods established in literature evaluating Frobenius and Riemann distances.

1 Introduction

Diffusion magnetic resonance imaging (dMRI) is an advanced technique of medical imaging based on magnetic resonance. dMRI describes the diffusion of water particles in biological tissues. The basic mathematical description of the diffusion is through a second order tensor $\mathbf{D} \in \mathbb{R}^{3 \times 3}$ represented by a 3×3 symmetric and positive definite (SPD) matrix, whose elements D_{ii} (where $i = x, y, z$) represent the diffusion in the main directions and D_{ij} the correlation between them. Also, it allows to describe internal structures of living organisms through estimation of derived scalar measures obtained from $\mathbf{D}$, such as fractional anisotropy maps

© Springer Nature Switzerland AG 2018
G. Bebis et al. (Eds.): ISVC 2018, LNCS 11241, pp. 371–381, 2018.
https://doi.org/10.1007/978-3-030-03801-4_33

[1]. The clinical applications of this type of images include: diagnosis of neurological diseases, e.g., Parkinson and Epilepsy, fiber tracking [2], detection of brain tumors [3], among others. The collection of diffusion tensors spatially related is known as diffusion tensor (DT) field or diffusion tensor imaging (DTI). A DT field is obtained from a dMRI study solving the Stejskal-Tanner formulation [4]. However, the use of DT fields estimated from dMRI is limited due to the images are acquired with low spatial resolution. Technological limitations and clinical acquisition protocols restrict the dMRI to a poor spatial resolution: from 1 to $2\,\text{mm}^3$. In some clinical applications, it is necessary to analyze in detail the studied structures (i.e. gray mater, tumors, tissues fiber) for performing a medical procedure. At these scenarios, the low spatial resolution becomes in a considerable difficulty. For this reason, researchers have proposed methodologies for enhancing the spatial resolution of dMRI studies as the presented by [5–8].

Interpolation of diffusion tensors is a feasible solution to obtain images with high resolution. Nevertheless, given that the tensors of a field have different characteristics the interpolation is challenging. Moreover, a DT has mandatory restrictions. For example, tensors must be SPD matrices; and the determinants of neighboring tensors must change monotonically for avoiding the swelling effect [7]. Another relevant factor is the spatial correlation among nearing tensors. Specifically, some DT fields have smooth spatial transitions, on the contrary, there are fields where the shape, size, and orientation of tensors change strongly. This type of fields are complex to interpolate. Regarding this, several methodologies for interpolation of diffusion tensors have been proposed. A straightforward methodology is the Euclidean interpolation [5], where each component of the tensor is interpolated linearly and independently. This Euclidean method has a drawback consisting of a swelling effect in interpolated tensors [7]. For solving this issue, it was implemented a logarithmic transformation to the tensor components for ensuring a monotonic variation of determinants, avoiding the swelling effect and preserving the SPD constraint. An important limitation of this technique is the modification of relevant clinical information extracted from DTI, i.e. fractional anisotropy (FA) and mean diffusivity (MD). Additionally, a framework based in Riemannian geometry was proposed by [6]. Here, the authors propose two methods: the rotational and geodesic interpolation. However, the methods are computationally expensive and modify the FA and MD information. Alternative approaches based on interpolation of tensor features were proposed. Basically, the tensors are decomposed in shape and orientation features (eigenvalues and Euler angles). The first attempt was presented in [7], here the features are linearly and separately interpolated. Also, in [8] a probabilistic method based on multi-output Gaussian processes is applied, unlike the method of [7], the features are jointly interpolated. The mentioned tensor decomposition is not unique, for this reason, there is an ambiguity with the tensor reconstruction. A recent probabilistic technique proposed by [9] interpolates the tensors using generalized Wishart processes (GWP). This method keeps the properties and constraints of diffusion tensors, but it has a low performance over fields with strong transitions (non-stationary fields). Hence, according to the previously mentioned, there are unsolved problems related to the low spatial resolution of DT fields, and some drawbacks and limitations of proposed methods for interpolation.

In this work, we are interested in characterizing, describing and representing non-stationary DT fields, to do this, we introduce a non-stationary GWP (NGWP) combining different kernels. The introduction of a non-stationary function implies that statistical properties of a DT field: mean, variance and covariance, are not modeled constantly into the space coordinates. For validation, we test the performance of the proposed model over three different datasets. We compare against log-Euclidean (LogEu) [5], feature based linear interpolation (FBLI) [7] and GWP [9], evaluating two metrics defined over SPD matrices: the Frobenius (Frob) and Riemann (Riem) distance. Finally, we evaluate morphological properties computing the mean squared error (MSE) for FA and MD.

The paper is arranged as follows: Sect. 2 presents the mathematical formulation of the NGWP model, and the procedure for parameters estimation. The Sect. 3 describe the databases and experimental setup. In the Sect. 4 we show interpolation results for three different datasets. In Sect. 5, we present the main conclusions about the significance of obtained results. Finally, in acknowledgments we thank to organizations funded this work.

2   Non-stationary Generalized Wishart Processes

A generalized Wishart process (GWP) is a collection of symmetric and positive definite random matrices $\{\mathbf{D}_n(\mathbf{z})\}_{n=1}^N$ where $\mathbf{D} \in \mathbb{R}^{P \times P}$, indexed by an arbitrary dependent variable $\mathbf{z} \in \mathbb{R}^M$ [10]. The idea is to assume a GWP as a prior over a DT field. Thus, $P = 3$ is the dimensionality and $\mathbf{z} = [x, y]^\top$ corresponds to the coordinates of each voxel in an image. A GWP is constructed through a superposition of outer products of Gaussian processes (GPs), weighted by a $P \times P$ scale matrix $\mathbf{V} = \mathbf{L}\mathbf{L}^\top$,

$$\mathbf{D}(\mathbf{z}) = \sum_{i=1}^{\nu} \mathbf{L}\hat{\mathbf{u}}_i(\mathbf{z})\hat{\mathbf{u}}_i^\top(\mathbf{z})\mathbf{L}^\top \sim \mathcal{GWP}_P(\nu, \mathbf{V}, k(\mathbf{z}, \mathbf{z}')), \tag{1}$$

where $\hat{\mathbf{u}}_i = (u_{i1}(\mathbf{z}), u_{i2}(\mathbf{z}), u_{i3}(\mathbf{z}))^\top$, with $u_{ip}(\mathbf{z}) \sim \mathcal{GP}(0, k)$, $i = 1, ..., \nu$ and $p = 1, 2, 3$, $k(\mathbf{z}, \mathbf{z}')$ is the kernel function for the GPs and $\mathbf{L}$ is the lower Cholesky decomposition from $\mathbf{V}$. The joint distribution for all $u_{id}(\mathbf{z})$ functions evaluated in a set of input data $\{\mathbf{z}_n\}_{n=1}^N$, $(u_{id}(\mathbf{z}_1), u_{id}(\mathbf{z}_2), ..., u_{id}(\mathbf{z}_N))^\top \sim \mathcal{N}(\mathbf{0}, \mathbf{K})$ follows a Gaussian distribution, where $\mathbf{K}$ is a $N \times N$ Gram matrix, with entries $K_{i,j} = k(\mathbf{z}_i, \mathbf{z}_j)$. This parametrization separates the contributions between the shape parameters ($\mathbf{L}$) and spatial dynamic parameters ($\hat{\mathbf{u}}_i$). In particular, the parameter $\mathbf{L}$ describes the expected tensor of $\mathbf{D}(\mathbf{z})$, the degrees of freedom ν controls the model flexibility, and the kernel parameters $\boldsymbol{\theta}$ in $k(\mathbf{z}, \mathbf{z}')$ determine how the matrices change over the spatial coordinates $\mathbf{z}$. Unlike of the work proposed in [9], where the diffusion tensors are modeled using a GWP with a stationary kernel, we introduce a non-stationary kernel function. The purpose is spatially modeling the statistical properties (mean, variance, covariance) of a

DT field. The kernel function applied in this approach was proposed by [11] and it allows to describe changes of multidimensional surfaces. We call to this model: Non-stationary generalized Wishart process (NGWP).

The non-stationary kernel is constructed by combining a set of different kernels $\{k_i(\mathbf{z}, \mathbf{z}')\}_{i=1}^{r}$, or the same kernel with different hyper-parameters [11]:

$$k(\mathbf{z}, \mathbf{z}') = \sum_{i=1}^{r} \sigma(w_i(\mathbf{z})) k_i(\mathbf{z}, \mathbf{z}') \sigma(w_i(\mathbf{z}')), \tag{2}$$

where $w_i(\mathbf{z}) : \mathbb{R}^M \rightarrow \mathbb{R}^1$ is the weighting function, with $M = 3$ the dimensional input, $w_i(\mathbf{z}) = \sum_{j=1}^{v} a_j \cos(\boldsymbol{\omega}_j^\top \mathbf{z} + b_j)$. $\sigma(z) : \mathbb{R}^1 \rightarrow [0,1]$, is the warping function, that is computed as a convex combination over the weighting function $\sigma(w_i(\mathbf{z})) = \exp(w_i(\mathbf{z}))/\sum_{i=1}^{r} \exp(w_i(\mathbf{z}))$, $\sum_{i=1}^{r} \sigma(w_i(\mathbf{z})) = 1$, inducing a partial discretization over each kernel. This function induces non-stationarity, since it does not depend of the distance between input variables $(\mathbf{z}, \mathbf{z}')$. In the context of DT interpolation, we employ $r = 3$ squared exponential (RBF) kernels with different inverse width (γ) hyper-parameters.

2.1   Parameters Estimation

The scheme for parameters estimation is similar to the one used in previous works [9,10], which is based on Bayesian inference employing Markov chain Monte Carlo (MCMC) algorithms. The aim is to compute the posterior distribution for the variables in the model: a vector $\mathbf{u}$ whose elements are the values of the GPs functions, and the kernel parameters $\boldsymbol{\theta} = \{a_j, \boldsymbol{\omega}_j, b_j, \gamma_i\}$, where $j = 1, ..., \nu$ and $i = 1, ..., r$ given a set of data $\mathcal{D} = (\mathbf{S}(\mathbf{z}_1), ..., \mathbf{S}(\mathbf{z}_N))$. As we pointed out before, we assume that a DT field follows a NGWP prior, where the likelihood function is given by

$$p(\mathcal{D}|\mathbf{u}, \boldsymbol{\theta}, \mathbf{L}, \nu) \propto \prod_{i=1}^{N} \exp\left\{ -\frac{1}{2\beta^2} \|\mathbf{S}(\mathbf{z}_i) - \mathbf{D}(\mathbf{z}_i)\|_f^2 \right\}, \tag{3}$$

being the $\mathbf{S}(\mathbf{z}_i)$ the tensors from the training set, $\mathbf{D}(\mathbf{z}_i)$ are the estimated tensors, $\|\cdot\|_f$ is the Frobenius norm, and β^2 is a variance parameter. Previous works [9,10] show that inference over the values $\mathbf{L}$ and degree of freedom ν increases the computational cost and does not contribute significantly to the model performance. Moreover, they suggest to fix $\mathbf{L}$ as the average tensor of the training data, and to set $\nu = P + 1$. According to the above, we sample from posterior distribution of parameters ($\mathbf{u}$ and $\boldsymbol{\theta}$) with an iterative procedure based on Gibbs sampling. Thus, the full conditional equations are given by,

$$p(\mathbf{u}|\boldsymbol{\theta}, \mathbf{L}, \nu, \mathcal{D}) \propto p(\mathcal{D}|\mathbf{u}, \boldsymbol{\theta}, \mathbf{L}, \nu) p(\mathbf{u}|\boldsymbol{\theta}), \tag{4}$$

$$p(\boldsymbol{\theta}|\mathbf{u}, \mathbf{L}, \nu, \mathcal{D}) \propto p(\mathbf{u}|\boldsymbol{\theta}) p(\boldsymbol{\theta}), \tag{5}$$

where $p(\mathbf{u}|\boldsymbol{\theta}) = \mathcal{N}(\mathbf{0}, \mathbf{K}_B)$, $\mathbf{K}_B$ is a $NP\nu \times NP\nu$ block diagonal covariance matrix, formed by $P\nu$ blocks of N-dimensional $\mathbf{K}$ matrices, and $p(\boldsymbol{\theta})$ is the prior for the kernel hyper-parameters. For sampling from (4) and (5) we employ elliptical slice sampling [12] and Metropolis-Hastings algorithm, respectively. Finally, we set the variance parameter β as the median of quadratic Frobenius norm computed from the training data.

2.2 DTI Field Interpolation

The aim is to estimate a matrix $\mathbf{D}(\mathbf{z}_*)$ in a test point $\mathbf{z}_*$, employing the learned parameters during the training stage. We compute the conditional distribution for $\mathbf{u}_*$ given $\mathbf{u}$ from the jointly distribution of $[\mathbf{u}, \mathbf{u}_*]^\top$. This distribution is given by [10],

$$\mathbf{u}_*|\mathbf{u} \sim \mathcal{N}(\mathbf{A}\mathbf{K}_B^{-1}\mathbf{u}, \mathbf{I} - \mathbf{A}\mathbf{K}_B^{-1}\mathbf{A}^\top), \qquad (6)$$

where $\mathbf{A}$ is the covariance matrix between the spatial coordinates $\mathbf{z}_*$ and $\mathbf{z}$ of training and test data, respectively. Once we obtain the values of $\mathbf{u}_*$ from Eq. (6), we compute the matrix $\mathbf{D}(\mathbf{z}_*)$ using the Eq. (1).

3 Datasets and Experimental Procedure

We test the proposed model over three datasets: First, a 2D toy DT field of 41×41 voxels obtained from a generative NGWP. Second, a synthetic field of 29×29 tensors computed from a simulation of crossing fibers using the FanDTasia Toolbox [13]. Third, a real dMRI study acquired from the head of a healthy male subject with an age between 20 and 30 years, on a General Electrical Signa HDxt 3.0T MR scanner using a body coil for excitation, employing 25 gradient directions with a value of b equal to $1000 \, \text{S/mm}^2$. The DT field is a region of interest with 41×41 voxels from a slice centered in the corpus callosum. We downsample in a factor of two the original datasets for obtaining the training sets. The rest of the data are used as ground truth (gold standard). For validation, we compare against log-Euclidean (LogEu) [5], feature based linear interpolation (FBLI) [7] and GWP [9]. We compute two error metrics: the Frobenius norm (Frob) and Riemann norm (Riem) [5],

$$\text{Fr}(\mathbf{D}_1, \mathbf{D}_2) = \sqrt{\text{trace}\left[(\mathbf{D}_1 - \mathbf{D}_2)^\top (\mathbf{D}_1 - \mathbf{D}_2)\right]}, \qquad (7)$$

$$\text{Ri}(\mathbf{D}_1, \mathbf{D}_2) = \sqrt{\text{trace}\left[\log(\mathbf{D}_1^{-1/2}\mathbf{D}_2\mathbf{D}_1^{-1/2})^\top \log(\mathbf{D}_1^{-1/2}\mathbf{D}_2\mathbf{D}_1^{-1/2})\right]}, \qquad (8)$$

where $\mathbf{D}_1$ and $\mathbf{D}_2$ are the interpolated and the ground-truth tensors, respectively. Additionally, we evaluated morphological properties of the estimated tensors using fractional anisotropy (FA) errors maps and computing the mean square error (MSE) for the FA and mean diffusion (MD). The reader can find detailed information about FA and MD in [7].

4   Results and Discussion

4.1   Synthetic Crossing Fibers Data

We test the proposed model and the comparison methods: LogEu, FBLI, GWP, and NGWP over a simulation of crossing fibers. Graphical results of interpolation are illustrated in the Fig. 1. Where (a) Ground-truth, (b) training data, (c) LogEu, (d)FBLI, (e) GWP, and (f) NGWP. Also, we report the MSE map of MD in the Fig. 2. Finally, in the Table 1 we report numerical results of errors.

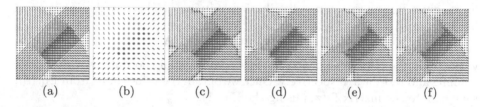

Fig. 1. Crossing fibers interpolation for the comparison methods: (a) Ground-truth, (b) Training data, (c) LogEu, (d) FBLI, (e) GWP, and (f) NGWP.

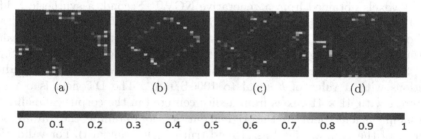

Fig. 2. MSE maps of MD of the interpolated crossing fibers DT field, (a) LogEu, (b) FBLI, (c) GWP and (d) NGWP. (Color figure online)

The crossing fibers is a challenging interpolation problem, because the properties of the tensors vary abruptly across the space. The MSE maps of MD showed in the Fig. 2 show that the proposed method preserves the clinical information of the diffusion tensors with less error (color blue) than the comparison methods, mainly over the abrupt transition regions. We explain the above in the sense that the non-stationary kernel used in the NGWP model is constructed by combining different kernels, where each kernel can describe a particular region in the whole field. Finally, in Table 1, we report the mean and standard deviation of the Frob distance, Riem distance, and the MSE of the FA and MD. Statistically, there are no significant differences among all compared methods. However, our proposal is a suitable methodology for describing, representing, and interpolating complex tensor data, such as crossing fibers. Also, the NGWP preserves the clinical information (FA and MD) high accuracy.

Table 1. Error metrics for the interpolation methods: Frobenius distance (Frob), Riemann distances (Rem) and MSE of the FA and MD.

Model	Frob	Riem	FA	MD
LogEu	0.5687 ± 0.2190	0.5208 ± 0.2014	0.1616 ± 0.2438	0.1826 ± 0.3308
FBLI	0.6340 ± 0.2053	0.6295 ± 0.2213	0.1575 ± 0.2412	0.1764 ± 0.2745
GWP	0.5325 ± 0.2094	0.4520 ± 0.1431	0.1569 ± 0.1540	0.1437 ± 0.1415
NGWP	$\mathbf{0.5126 \pm 0.1859}$	$\mathbf{0.4159 \pm 0.1072}$	$\mathbf{0.1451 \pm 0.1776}$	$\mathbf{0.1428 \pm 0.1469}$

4.2 Toy Data

Second, we evaluate the performance over a toy DT field obtained from sampling the NGWP model. This field has smooth regions and abrupt changes. The Fig. 3(a), (b) correspond to the ground-truth and training data. Figure 3(c), (d), (e), (f) show the interpolated fields with LogEu, FBLI, GWP and NGWP, respectively.

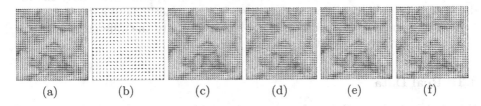

(a)   (b)   (c)   (d)   (e)   (f)

Fig. 3. Interpolation of a toy DT field, (a) Ground truth, (b) Training data. Interpolated fields: (c) LogEu, (d) FBLI, (e) GWP, and (f) NGWP.

The Fig. 4 shows the MSE maps of the MD for each interpolation method. Also, we evaluate the error metrics of the interpolated fields and their clinical information. These results are showed in the Table 2.

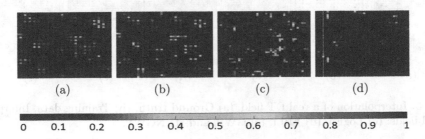

(a)   (b)   (c)   (d)

0   0.1   0.2   0.3   0.4   0.5   0.6   0.7   0.8   0.9   1

Fig. 4. MSE map of MD of the interpolated toy DT field, (a) LogEu, (b) FBLI, (c) GWP and (d) NGWP.

Table 2. Error metrics of the interpolation methods, Frobenius distance (Frob), Riemann distances (Rem) and MSE of the FA and MD properties.

Model	Frob	Riem	FA	MD
LogEu	0.5112 ± 0.1093	0.5539 ± 0.1698	0.1622 ± 0.1772	0.1444 ± 0.1053
FBLI	0.5306 ± 0.1356	0.5390 ± 0.1470	0.1573 ± 0.1532	0.1565 ± 0.1411
GWP	0.5311 ± 0.1189	0.5113 ± 0.1166	0.1426 ± 0.1274	0.1329 ± 0.1286
NGWP	**0.5080 ± 0.1472**	**0.5161 ± 0.1303**	**0.1416 ± 0.1402**	**0.1308 ± 0.1368**

The toy DT field has regions where the tensors properties (size, shape and orientation) change slowly. Also, there are other areas where the changes are abrupt. The proposed NGWP demonstrates that it is possible to adapt a model to different type of tensors, whether soft or complex fields, as we show in Fig. 3. Additionally, the proposed method has the ability of preserving the clinical information when a DT field is interpolated. If we give a closer look to Fig. 4, the MD is preserved with higher accuracy than the comparison methods. The metric errors reported in Table 2 show that NGWP can interpolate accurately the toy data, with a similar precision to the state of the art methods. We think the nonstationary kernel of our model, provides adaptability to the different transitions (smooth or strong) inherent to diffusion tensor data.

4.3   Real Data

Finally, we evaluate the performance of the interpolation methods in a real DT field. The Fig. 5(a) corresponds to a region of interest of 41×41 tensors from a slice centered in the corpus callosum. The Fig. 5(b) is the training data. Figures 5(c), (d), (e), (f) are the interpolated fields with the LogEu, FBLI, GWP and NGWP. Also, the Fig. 6 shows the MSE maps of MD for each method. In the Table 3, we report numerical results of the error metrics.

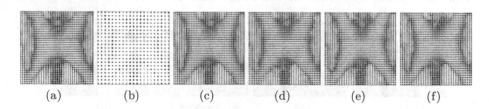

(a)   (b)   (c)   (d)   (e)   (f)

Fig. 5. Interpolation of a real DT field, (a) Ground truth, (b) Training data. Interpolated fields: (c) LogEu, (d) FBLI, (e) GWP, and (f) NGWP.

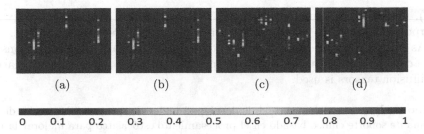

Fig. 6. MSE maps of MD of the interpolated a real DT field, (a) LogEu, (b) FBLI, (c) GWP and (d) NGWP.

Table 3. Error metrics of the interpolation methods, Frobenius distance (Frob), Riemann distances (Rem) and MSE of the FA and MD properties.

Model	Frob	Riem	FA	MD
LogEu	0.4179 ± 0.1413	0.5266 ± 0.2130	0.4204 ± 0.1659	0.5422 ± 0.2161
FBLI	0.4214 ± 0.1386	0.5236 ± 0.2081	0.4579 ± 0.1738	0.5389 ± 0.2170
GWP	0.4145 ± 0.1089	0.5238 ± 0.2095	0.5095 ± 0.1890	0.4854 ± 0.2081
NGWP	$\mathbf{0.4098 \pm 0.1250}$	$\mathbf{0.5046 \pm 0.2159}$	$\mathbf{0.4690 \pm 0.1730}$	$\mathbf{0.4813 \pm 0.1673}$

A Real DT field has tensors with different sizes, forms, and orientations. These properties make difficult an accurate interpolation. Graphical results of Figs. 5 and 6, and error metrics of Table 3 show that NGWP can describe, represent and interpolate non-stationary tensors fields obtained from real dMRI studies. The proposed method reaches a performance similar to LogEu, FBL, and GWP. Again, the NGWP preserves the clinical information derived form the dMRI, as we show in Fig. 6 where we computed the MSE maps of MD. Moreover, error metrics are reported in the Table 3. From these results, we can establish that NGWP is a competitive methodology for interpolation of DT fields.

5 Conclusions and Future Work

In this work, we presented a probabilistic methodology for interpolation of diffusion tensor fields. Specifically, we model a DT field as a stochastic process defined over SPD matrices called Non-stationary generalized Wishart process (NGWP). The idea is to describe non-stationary properties of DT fields. To do this, we introduce a non-stationary kernel by combining different functions. Particularly, we combine $r = 3$ squared exponential kernels (RBF) with different length-scale hyper-parameters. We evaluated the performance of the proposed method using the Frobenius and Riemman distance over synthetic and real DT fields. Also, we evaluate the clinical information using errors maps of mean diffusivity (MD) and reporting the mean and standard deviation of the MSE of Fractional Anisotropy

(FA). Outcomes demonstrated that NGWP is a competitive methodology for interpolating DT fields in comparison with methods of the state-of-the-art.

As future work, we would like to extend non-stationary kernel functions to more complex models such as tractography procedures where the interpolation of diffusion tensors is used.

Acknowledgments. This research is developed under the project "Desarrollo de un sistema de soporte clínico basado en el procesamiento estócasitco para mejorar la resolución espacial de la resonancia magnética estructural y de difusión con aplicación al procedimiento de la ablación de tumores" financed by COLCIENCIAS with code 111074455860. H.D. Vargas is funded by Colciencias under the program: Convocatoria 617 de 2013. J.F. Cuellar is funded by Colciencias under program: *Jóvenes investigadores e innovadores-Convocatoria 761 de 2016*. We thank to the program of master in electrical engineering of the Universidad Tecnológica de Pereira.

References

1. Le Bihan, D., et al.: Diffusion tensor imaging: concepts and applications. J. Magn. Reson. Imaging **13**(4), 534–546 (2001)
2. Sasiadek, M.J., Szewczyk, P., Bladowska, J.: Application of diffusion tensor imaging (DTI) in pathological changes of the spinal cord. Med. Sci. Monit. **18**(6), 73–79 (2012)
3. Chenevert, T.L., et al.: Diffusion magnetic resonance imaging: an early surrogate marker of therapeutic efficacy in brain tumors. J. Natl. Cancer Inst. **92**(24), 2029–2036 (2000)
4. Stejskal, E.O., Tanner, J.E.: Spin diffusion measurements: spin echoes in the presence of a time-dependent field gradient. J. Chem. Phys. **42**(1), 288–292 (1965)
5. Arsigny, V., Fillard, P., Pennec, X., Ayache, N.: Log-Euclidean metrics for fast and simple calculus on diffusion tensors. Magn. Reson. Med. **56**(2), 411–421 (2006)
6. Batchelor, P., Moakher, M., Atkinson, D., Calamante, F., Connelly, A.: A rigorous framework for diffusion tensor calculus. Magn. Reson. Med. **53**(1), 221–225 (2005)
7. Yang, F., Zhu, Y.-M., Magnin, I.E., Luo, J.-H., Croisille, P., Kingsley, P.B.: Feature-based interpolation of diffusion tensor fields and application to human cardiac DT-MRI. Med. Image Anal. **16**(2), 459–481 (2012)
8. Cardona, H.D.V., Orozco, Á.A., Álvarez, M.A.: Multi-output Gaussian processes for enhancing resolution of diffusion tensor fields. In: 2016 IEEE 38th Annual International Conference of the EMBC, pp. 1111–1114. IEEE (2016)
9. Cardona, H.D.V., Álvarez, M.A., Orozco, Á.A.: Generalized Wishart processes for interpolation over diffusion tensor fields. In: Bebis, G., et al. (eds.) ISVC 2015. LNCS, vol. 9475, pp. 499–508. Springer, Cham (2015). https://doi.org/10.1007/978-3-319-27863-6_46
10. Wilson, A.G., Ghahramani, Z.: Generalised Wishart processes. In: UAI 2011, Proceedings of the Twenty-Seventh Conference on Uncertainty in Artificial Intelligence, Barcelona, Spain, 14–17 July 2011, pp. 736–744 (2011). https://dslpitt.org/uai/displayArticleDetails.jsp?mmnu=1&smnu=2&article_id=2184&proceeding_id=27
11. Herlands, W., et al.: Scalable Gaussian processes for characterizing multidimensional change surfaces. arXiv preprint arXiv:1511.04408 (2015)

12. Murray, I., Adams, R.P., MacKay, D.J.C.: Elliptical slice sampling. In: Proceedings of the Thirteenth International Conference on Artificial Intelligence and Statistics, AISTATS 2010, Chia Laguna Resort, Sardinia, Italy, 13–15 May 2010, pp. 541–548 (2010). http://www.jmlr.org/proceedings/papers/v9/murray10a.html
13. Barmpoutis, A., Vemuri, B.C.: A unified framework for estimating diffusion tensors of any order with symmetric positive-definite constraints. In: Biomedical Imaging: From Nano to Macro, pp. 1385–1388. IEEE (2010)

Reduced-Reference Image Quality Assessment Based on Improved Local Binary Pattern

Xi-kui Miao[1,2(✉)], Dah-Jye Lee[2], Xiang-zheng Cheng[1], and Xiao-yu Yang[1]

[1] School of Information Engineering, Henan University of Science and Technology, Luoyang City 471000, Henan Province, China
miaoxikui@gmail.com
[2] Department of Electrical and Computer Engineering, Brigham Young University, Provo, UT 84602, USA

Abstract. The structure of image consists of two aspects: intensity of structure and distribution of structure. Image distortions that degrade image quality potentially affect both the intensity and distribution of image structure. Yet most structure-based image quality assessment methods focus only on the change of the intensity of structure. In this paper, we propose an improved structure-based image quality assessment method that takes both into account. First, we employ image gradients magnitude to describe the intensity of structure and attempt to explore the distribution of structure with local binary pattern (LBP) and newly designed center-surrounding pixels pattern (CSPP, complementary pattern for LBP). LBP and CSPP features are mapped into a combined histogram weighted by the intensity of structure to represent the image structure. Finally, the change of structure which can gauge image quality is measured by calculating the similarity of the histograms of the reference and distorted images. Support vector regression (SVR) is employed to pool structure features to predict an image quality score. Experimental results on three benchmark databases demonstrate that the proposed structure pattern can effectively represent the intensity and distribution of the structure of the image. The proposed method achieves high consistency with subjective perception with 17 reference values, performing better than the existing methods.

Keywords: Reduced-reference · Image quality assessment
Intensity of structure · Distribution of structure

1 Introduction

With the exponential growth of image and video data, there is a need to assess the image quality for any system that processes images and videos for human viewing [1, 2], and the performance of image quality assessment (IQA) has become a critical metric for these systems [3]. How to effectively and efficiently assess image quality has gained tremendous attention as a research field over the past several years.

Subjective quality assessment is the most reliable way to assess image quality, but it is labor-intensive and time-consuming. Automatic objective quality assessment methods are in great demand. According to the availability of reference data, the

© Springer Nature Switzerland AG 2018
G. Bebis et al. (Eds.): ISVC 2018, LNCS 11241, pp. 382–394, 2018.
https://doi.org/10.1007/978-3-030-03801-4_34

objective IQA methods can be classified into three categories: Full-Reference (FR), Reduced-Reference (RR), and No-Reference (NR) [4]. FR methods require the whole reference image for quality assessment [5]. However, the reference image is not always available in practice. NR methods are expected to predict quality without using any external information [6], making NR IQA an extremely difficult task. RR methods are designed to predict the quality by using partial information of the reference image [7]. In this work, we focus on developing an effective RR IQA method.

Wang proposed a wavelet-domain natural image statistic metric (WNISM) for RR IQA based on change of marginal distribution of wavelet coefficients of image [7]. The quality is measured based on the error between wavelet coefficients and that of the reference image. Li adopted a divisive normalization transform procedure to improve the RR IQA [8]. Gao suggested to measure the quality based on the statistical correlations of wavelet coefficients in different sub-bands, and proposed a multiscale geometric analysis based RR IQA method [9]. Soundararajan suggested to measure the quality degradation according to the scaled entropies of wavelet coefficients, and proposed a Reduced Reference Entropic Differences (RRED) method [10]. Ma reorganized the DCT coefficients into several representative sub-bands and evaluated the perceptual quality based on their city-block distance (ROCB) [11]. Zhai developed a RR free-energy-based distortion metric (FEDM) [12]. The premise of the method is that visual cognition is an active inference process, fitting brain model to visual sensory data, and the quality of image is quantified using the free energy. Wu decomposed image into orderly and disorderly portion according to internal generative mechanism and measured the energy changes of the visual contents caused by distortion (RRVIF) [13]. With only 2 reference data, RRVIF cannot get high quality prediction accuracy. Redi proposed a double-layer RR IQA method, mapping color distribution information into a numerical expression for the perceived quality, and used support vector machine in identification of the distortions and quality prediction [14].

Image scene is comprised of spatially distributed structure features, and human vision system (HVS) is sensitive to these structure features which consist of two aspects: intensity of structure and distribution of structure. The pixels belonging to a structure are related to each other with a specifically relative intensity relationship, making the structure of the visual content a distinctive spatial distribution. The visual information that the structure contains is hidden behind the intensity and distribution of the structure. When an image is deteriorated, we believe that the intensity and distribution of its structure would vary as a function of distortions. A good IQA should consider the distribution of structure which most existing methods ignore. We suggest that IQA should take both intensity of the structure and distribution of structure into account.

The above analysis suggests that image distortions will not only lead to changes of intensity, but also alter the spatial distribution of structure. Measuring the differences of the intensity of structure and distribution of structure between reference and distorted image can provide a clue to developing a good IQA method. However, how to effectively measure the changes of distribution of structure is still an open problem. Here, we employ the image gradients magnitude to describe the intensity of structure and attempt to represent distribution of structure with LBP and especially-designed CSPP (a complementary pattern for LBP). Based on this theory, a new IQA method is devised by comparing the changes of intensity of structure and spatial distribution of structure. First, a combined histogram, concatenating LBP histogram and CSPP histogram is built and weighted by intensity of structure. Next, histogram similarity between reference and distorted images is calculated to measure the changes of the distribution of structure. Finally, quality score is predicted by learning a support vector regression model. Experimental results on three benchmark databases demonstrate that the proposed method is highly consistent with the human perception.

The rest of this paper is organized as follows. In Sect. 2, LBP is introduced and CSPP is designed to represent distribution of structure. In Sect. 3, IQA method based on intensity and distribution of structure is detailed. Experimental results and analysis are presented in Sect. 4. Finally, conclusions are drawn in Sect. 5.

2 Structure Based on LBP and CSPP

Structure represents the main visual contents of image, which includes intensity of structure and distribution of structure behind which the visual information hides. Although LBP can represent the distribution of structure with the spatial correlations between the central pixel and its neighbors, it cannot represent the spatial correlations among the neighborhood pixels. In order to capture the relative intensity relationship among the center-surrounding pixels, the center-surrounding pixels pattern (CSPP) is introduced as a complementary pattern for LBP to represent image structure.

2.1 Local Binary Pattern (LBP)

Local binary pattern (LBP) is designed for structure description. The spatial correlations between the central pixel and its neighbors are analyzed with the relative intensity relationship [15]. Here, we employ the LBP to describe the distribution of structure. For the central pixel x_c and its neighbors x_i, the LBP is defined as follows.

$$LBP(x_c) = \sum_{i=0}^{P-1} s(I_i - I_c)2^i \tag{1}$$

$$s(I_i - I_c) = \begin{cases} 1, & I_i - I_c \geq 0 \\ 0, & I_i - I_c < 0 \end{cases} \tag{2}$$

Where I_i and I_c are the gray values of the central pixel x_c and the neighbor x_i, P is the number of neighbors, and R is the radius of the neighborhood. Ojala also investigated the uniform LBP [15], which provides majority structural information (almost 90%), and the rotation invariant uniform pattern is defined as:

$$LBP^{ur}(x_i) = \begin{cases} \sum_{i=0}^{P-1} s(I_i - I_c), & if \quad \mu(LBP(x_i)) \leq 2 \\ P+1, & else \end{cases} \tag{3}$$

Where $\mu(LBP(x_i)) = |s(I_{P-1} - I_c) - s(I_0 - I_c)| + \sum_{i=1}^{P-1} |s(I_i - I_c) - s(I_{i-1} - I_c)|$.

For R = 1, P = 8, there are 10 types of rotation invariant uniform LBPs. After obtaining LBPs, a LBP histogram is built to represent image structure distribution. In the experiments, we found that for greater values of P and R, the computational complexity significantly increases, and only make little contribution to the performance of IQA. In this paper, R and P are set to 1 and 8.

With image distortions, the LBP of a pixel can change from one type to another (as to be elaborated next). Moreover, different kinds of distortions result in different changes to the structure with the accompanying changes to its LBPs. For example, Gaussian blur mainly degrades the edge of an image. As a result, an edge pattern may be distorted into a flat one. On the other hand, JPEG compression mainly causes blockiness artifact. A flat pattern may be distorted into an edge one. Specifically, the LBP '00001111' of a pixel may represent an edge feature, as shown in Fig. 1. When distortion is present, the LBP pattern will be altered, resulting in '00011111', which represents the corner feature or '00111111', which represents the end-of-line feature.

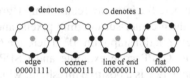

Fig. 1. Illustration of changes of LBPs

2.2 Center-Surrounding Pixels Pattern (CSPP)

As defined in Eq. (1), the LBP considers only the relative intensity relationship between the center pixel and its center-surrounding pixels. It neglects the relative intensity relationship among the center-surrounding pixels and cannot describe image structure fully. In order to handle this shortcoming, we investigate the relative intensity relationship among the center-surrounding pixels by a ranking mechanism which captures the intensity relationship among the center-surrounding pixels while maintains controllable feature dimension. This new center-surrounding pixels pattern (CSPP) is designed specifically to compensate for the shortcoming of LBP.

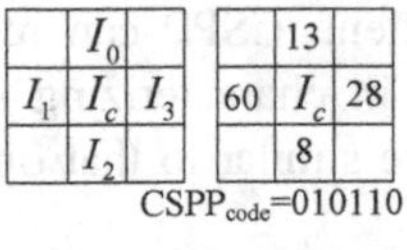

			13	
I_1	I_c	I_3	60	I_c	28
	I_2		8	

I_0

CSPP$_{code}$=010110

Fig. 2. An example CSPP

Table 1. CSPP encoding algorithm

Input: values of center and 4 center-surrounding pixels
If ($I_0 \geq I_1 + T$) : encode Bit 5 to 1, else: encode Bit 5 to 0
If ($I_0 \geq I_2 + T$) : encode Bit 4 to 1, else: encode Bit 4 to 0
If ($I_0 \geq I_3 + T$) : encode Bit 3 to 1, else: encode Bit 3 to 0
If ($I_1 \geq I_2 + T$) : encode Bit 2 to 1, else: encode Bit 2 to 0
If ($I_1 \geq I_3 + T$) : encode Bit 1 to 1, else: encode Bit 1 to 0
If ($I_2 \geq I_3 + T$) : encode Bit 0 to 1, else: encode Bit 0 to 0

For simplicity, we consider only the intensity order of 4 center-surrounding pixels, as shown in Fig. 2. We compare the intensity relationship ('greater or equal' and 'less') between any two pixels of the 4 center-surrounding pixels, and encode greater or equal relationship with '1' and less relationship with '0'. There are 6 comparisons among the 4 center-surrounding pixels. CSPP code example and CSPP encoding algorithm are illustrated in Fig. 2 and Table 1. T is a positive threshold, which discriminates intensity dissimilarities among the 4 center-surrounding pixels, according to the experiments in Sect. 4, T is set to 3 for a high performance IQA. Following the encoding algorithm in Table 1 and using the values in Fig. 2 as an example, $13 < 60 + T$ (set Bit 5 to 0), $13 \geq 8 + T$ (set Bit 4 to 1), $13 < 28 + T$ (set Bit 3 to 0), $60 \geq 8 + T$ (set Bit 2 to 1), $60 \geq 28 + T$ (set Bit 1 to 1), and $8 < 28 + T$ (set Bit 0 to 0), which generates a CSPP code of '010110'.

In order to reduce the number of CSPPs, we explore the relationships among CSPPs for further combination. During experiment we have found that the CSPPs with same number of '1' are more likely to present similar structure. There are 7 types of CSPPs after combination, Combination can reduce the dimensionality of CSPPs, and improve the accuracy of quality prediction. After getting CSPPs of the image, a CSPP based structural histogram is built to represent image structure distribution.

The reason why CSPP can be used for IQA is that distortion would alter local intensity order relationship of center-surrounding pixels, resulting in the changes of image structure. And to some extent, CSPP can represent image structure, playing complementary roles to the LBP in characterizing structure. The effects that image distortions impact on the CSPP are similar to that on LBP.

3   IQA Based on Intensity and Distribution of Structure

In this section, image gradients magnitude is used to describe the intensity of structure. Then two histograms are mapped based on LBP and CSPP. Finally, we learn a SVR model to return the quality score using histogram similarity vectors.

3.1 IQA on Intensity of Structure

According to HVS, human vision is sensitive to low-level features such as edges, lines, and corners, etc. These low-level features represent intensity of structure and often attract attention at first sight. Image distortions would alter these low-level features. In order to measure intensity of structure of image, we employ image gradients magnitude to characterize the intensity of structure. A complex image gradients computation method is used. It is defined as follows.

$$G^t = \max\left(\frac{1}{16}I^t * F_{n=1,2,3,4}\right) \tag{4}$$

$F_{n=1,2,3,4}$ are four gradient filters, as shown in Fig. 3. The star sign (*) denotes the convolution. I^t denotes the image and G^t denotes the gradient map. $t \in r, d$ denotes reference (r) and distorted images (d). Here, small filters such as Sobel or Prewitt are not used. They are small and only have two directions, resulting insufficient structure information in the neighborhood. Instead, we use 4 directions, larger size filters to obtain a better image gradients map which is more consistent with HVS.

0	0	0	0	0	0	0	1	0	0	0	0	1	0	0	0	1	0	-1	0
1	3	8	3	1	0	8	3	0	0	0	0	3	8	0	0	3	0	-3	0
0	0	0	0	0	1	3	0	-3	-1	-1	-3	0	3	1	0	8	0	-8	0
-1	-3	-8	-3	-1	0	0	-3	-8	0	0	-8	-3	0	0	0	3	0	-3	0
0	0	0	0	0	0	0	-1	0	0	0	0	-1	0	0	0	1	0	-1	0
F_1					F_2					F_3					F_4				

Fig. 3. Image gradient filters

3.2 IQA on Spatial Distribution of Structure

Image gradient is sensitive to image distortions. In order to highlight the pixels with severe degradations on intensity of structure while weaken the pixels with little degradation on the intensity of structure, we employ image gradient magnitude as weighting factors for LBP histogram and CSPP histogram creations.

$$H_t^{LBP}(b) = \frac{1}{MN}\sum_{i=0}^{M-1}\sum_{j=0}^{N-1}\omega\left(LBP^{ur}(x_{ij}), b-1\right), b \in [1, 10] \tag{5}$$

$$H_t^{CSPP}(b) = \frac{1}{MN}\sum_{i=0}^{M-1}\sum_{j=0}^{N-1}\omega\left(CSPP_{P,R}^{ur}(x_{ij}), b-1\right), b \in [1, 7] \tag{6}$$

$$\omega\left(LBP^{ur}(x_{ij}), b-1\right) = \begin{cases} G_{ij}^t, & \text{if } \left(LBP_{P,R}^{ur}(x_{ij})\right) = b-1 \\ 0, & \text{else} \end{cases} \tag{7}$$

$$\omega\big(CSPP(x_{ij}), b-1\big) = \begin{cases} G_{ij}^t, & if \ (CSPP(x_{ij})) = b-1 \\ 0, & else \end{cases} \tag{8}$$

Where $t \in r, d$, $H_r^{LBP}(b)$, $H_d^{LBP}(b)$ denote LBP histogram of reference and distorted images, and $H_r^{CSPP}(b), H_d^{CSPP}(b)$ denote CSPP histogram of reference and distorted images. The number of bins of LBP histogram and CSPP histogram is 10 and 7, respectively. We concatenate the two histograms as a joint 17-bin histogram, getting 17 features to characterize the distributions of structure.

$$H(I_t) = concatenation\big(H_t^{LBP}(b), H_t^{CSPP}(b)\big) b \in 1, 17 \tag{9}$$

Where, $t \in r, d$ denotes the reference and distorted images.

3.3   Image Quality Prediction

Distortions alter both intensity of structure and distribution of structure, resulting in quality degradation. Based on above analysis, a 17-bin histogram based LBP and CSPP weighted by image gradients is constructed to represent the image structure. In order to measure the changes of structural features, the similarity formulation [7] is adopted to compute the changes of histograms of the reference and distorted images.

$$S_h(I_r, I_d) = \frac{2 \times H(I_r) \cdot H(I_d)}{H(I_r)^2 + H(I_t)^2} \tag{10}$$

A 17-dimension histogram-based similarity vector can be obtained using Eq. (10) to measure the similarity between the reference and distorted images. However, how to effectively pool features to get a quality score with high consistency with the subjective perception is an open problem. Since each LBP histogram and CSPP histogram represent different structure, different histogram-based similarity vectors represent different levels of degradation on the intensity and distribution of the structure, leading to different quality scores. Support vector regression (SVR) based pooling features method is a good choice for quality prediction. We learn a SVR model using histogram-based similarity vectors extracted from image datasets to predict a quality score. In the experiments, we adopt the LibSVM package [16] with a radial basis function (RBF) kernel to train a SVR model.

$$SVR_{model} = SVR_{train}\big(S_{h,train}(I_r, I_d), Gtrue\big) \tag{11}$$

Where $S_{h,train}(I_r, I_d)$ denotes histogram-based similarity vectors extracted from the training dataset, Gtrue denotes the ground true of the quality score, and SVR_{model} denotes the trained model. Quality scores can be calculated using the trained model.

$$Q(I_r, I_d) = SVR_{model}\big(S_{h,test}(I_r, I_d)\big) \tag{12}$$

Where, $S_{h,test}(I_r, I_d)$ denotes histogram-based similarity vectors extracted from the test dataset and $Q(I_r, I_d)$ denotes the predicted quality score.

4   Experimental Results and Analysis

The LBP and CSPP histograms are analyzed to demonstrate the effectiveness of the proposed method. Then, we compared the proposed method with existing RR IQA methods. The source code is available online at https://github.com/miaoxikui.

4.1   Effectiveness of the Proposed IQA

The proposed method uses both the intensity of structure and distribution of structure to gauge the changes of structure with the LBP and CSPP histograms. In order to visualize how two structural histograms vary as a function of distortions, Figs. 4 and 5 show an example of histogram changes on the painted house (from TID2013 database). Figure 4 shows the reference and the distorted images which are distorted by four types of distortions (additive white Gaussian noise (AWGN), Gaussian blur (GBLUR), JPEG (JPG) compression noise, and JPEG2000 (J2K) compression noise). The distortion energies (measured as MSE, Mean-Square Error) of these four distorted images are 258.21, 235.21, 213.44 and 251.82, respectively. Their image qualities (measured as MOS, Mean Opinion Score) are 4.14, 3.17, 3.28 and 2.57, respectively. Though the distortion energies on the four distorted images are similar, the qualities of these images are quite different.

(a) reference image   (b) AWGN   (c) GBLUR   (d) JPG   (e) J2K

Fig. 4. Reference image and four types of distorted images. (a) reference image (b) AWGN (c) GBLUR (d) JPG (e) J2K

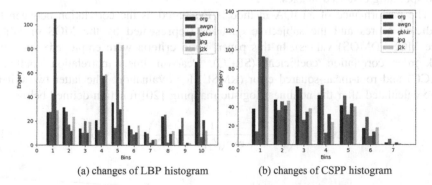

(a) changes of LBP histogram   (b) changes of CSPP histogram

Fig. 5. Structure changes distorted by four different distortions.

As shown in Fig. 5, different types of distortion result in significantly different histogram changes. Specifically, as shown in Fig. 4(b), AWGN adds lots of random disturbances to the image. Intuitively, the energy in every bin of LBP histogram should increase. As the red bars shown in Fig. 5(a), the energy increment for AWGN is actually small except the 10th bin and the energy of 6 bins decrease slightly. As complementary structure features, AWGN also alters the intensity ordering relationship of the center-surrounding pixels. The energy of most CSPP bins increased significantly compared to the reference image, as the red bars indicate in Fig. 5(b). The significant increase in the histogram indicates that CSPP is a better discriminator for IQA than LPB. On the contrary, GBLUR smooths image visual content, degrading image structure as shown in Fig. 4(c). As a result, the energies in all bins of both histograms should decrease. However, only 3 bins (1, 4, and 5) of LBP histogram increased, as the green bars indicate in Fig. 5(a). The bin energies of CSPP histogram decreased dramatically except for the 1st bin, as the green bars show in Fig. 5(b). This character makes CSPP a good measure for IQA.

The changes in LBP histogram and CSPP histogram caused by JPG and J2K are more complex than the changes caused by AWGN or GBLUR. As shown in Fig. 4(d), (e), JPG and J2K compressions not only discard high frequency information resulting in the distortion of the original edges, but also cause image blockiness and artifacts, leading to some new structure such as edges in smooth region. JPG and J2K randomly increase and decrease of some bins of LBP and CSPP histograms.

Based on the analysis, we can summarize that different types of distortions can cause different structural degradations. LBP and CSPP histograms can effectively capture the changes of intensity of structure and distribution of structure when image is distorted. The proposed method can effectively represent visual degradation from different types of distortions.

4.2 Performance Comparison on Databases

In order to perform a comprehensive analysis on the performance, we compared the proposed method with three existing RR IQA methods (WNISM [7], RRED [10], FEDM [12], RRVIF [13]) on three large databases. LIVE [17] has 29 reference images and 779 corresponding distorted images. CSIQ [18] has 30 reference images and 866 corresponding distorted images. TID2013 [19] has 25 reference images and 3000 corresponding distorted images.

The performance of an IQA method is evaluated as the correlation between the predicted scores and the subjective qualities (represented by the MOS or Difference MOS (DMOS) values). In this paper, three criteria were employed: Spearman rank-order correlation coefficient (SRCC), Pearson linear correlation coefficient (PLCC) and root-mean-squared error (RMSE) for evaluation. The latter two criteria were calculated after the nonlinear logistic mapping [20] function defined below.

$$q(x) = \beta_1 \left(\frac{1}{2} - \frac{1}{1 + \exp(\beta_2(x - \beta_3))} \right) + \beta_4 x + \beta_5 \tag{13}$$

Where $\beta_1, \beta_2, \beta_3, \beta_4, \beta_5$ are five parameters to be fitted. A good IQA returns high PLCC/SRCC values and a low RMSE value. And better RR IQA algorithm should use very little data from the reference images and achieve high prediction accuracy.

In the experiments, we randomly selected 80% reference images and corresponding distorted images for training the SVR model and used the rest of images for testing. In order to eliminate the performance bias, training-testing procedure is repeated 100 times, and the average performance is calculated for the final result. Since the range of RMSE on LIVE and the range of RMSE on CSIQ and TID2013 are quite different, for convenience, we firstly performed comparison on the LIVE database, and then performed comparisons on the CSIQ database and TID2013 database.

The performance and the number of reference data of the proposed method and compared methods on the LIVE database are listed in Table 2. The number of reference data in RRED can be set from 1-N (N is the number of pixels of the reference image). We mainly focus on the accuracy of IQA, and set the number of reference data as 20 due to the convenience of accessing the RRED results.

Table 2. Compared performance LIVE database (779 images)

Distortions	Ref. data	Criteria	AWGN	GBLUR	JPEG	J2K	FF	Overall
Proposed	17 scalars	PLCC	**0.972**	**0.968**	0.908	**0.960**	**0.954**	**0.941**
		SRCC	**0.964**	**0.960**	0.867	**0.953**	**0.933**	**0.938**
		RMSE	**3.250**	**4.130**	6.780	**3.260**	**4.720**	**9.490**
RRVIF	30 bits	PLCC	0.957	0.955	0.895	0.932	0.944	0.725
		SRCC	0.946	0.961	0.885	0.950	0.941	0.732
		RMSE	4.658	4.660	7.148	5.881	5.424	17.60
RRED	20 scalars	PLCC	0.938	0.956	**0.962**	0.956	0.892	0.831
		SRCC	0.950	0.951	**0.956**	0.951	0.920	0.834
		RMSE	9.710	5.430	**4.700**	3.280	12.86	15.20
WNISM	18 scalars	PLCC	0.892	0.888	0.876	0.924	0.925	0.710
		SRCC	0.872	0.915	0.851	0.920	0.923	0.703
		RMSE	7.290	7.220	7.710	6.180	6.250	18.40
FEDM	32 bits	PLCC	0.925	0.902	0.875	0.921	0.875	0.893
		SRCC	0.915	0.931	0.854	0.915	0.852	0.887
		RMSE	6.065	6.783	7.733	6.316	7.961	**7.132**

From Table 2, the proposed method used only 17 reference data, fewer than WNISM and REED, and outperformed the other RR IQA methods on AWGN, GBLUR, J2K and FF distortions. The performance of the proposed method on distortions of JPG is very similar to the best IQA metric, RRED. However, the number of reference data used was smaller than the RRED. The overall performance of the proposed method was much better than others.

Table 3 shows the comparison results on the CSIQ and TID2013 databases. The comparison of FEDM on CSIQ and TID2013 are not available and are not included. For each database, 80% of reference and distorted images were randomly chosen for training and the remaining 20% of images were used for testing. Table 3 shows that the proposed method outperformed the other three methods in terms of PLCC, SRCC, and RMSE.

Table 3. Compared performance on CSIQ and TID2013

Database	Criteria	Proposed	RRVIF	RRED	WNISM
CSIQ (866)	PLCC	**0.879**	0.689	0.780	0.696
	SRCC	**0.876**	0.733	0.780	0.705
	RMSE	**0.130**	0.182	0.164	0.189
TID2013 (3000)	PLCC	**0.821**	0.535	0.725	0.572
	SRCC	**0.825**	0.500	0.709	0.495
	RMSE	**0.725**	1.134	0.924	1.101

4.3 Computational Cost

The computational cost of each competing IQA method was also evaluated. Experiments were performed on a HP desktop with Intel(R) i7-4790 CPU@3.6 GHz and 6G RAM. The software platform was Matlab R2017b. The time cost consumed of compared methods is averaged out by 100 distorted images (768×512 from LIVE), and listed in Table 4. The proposed method has the least computational complexity.

Table 4. Time cost of each compared RR IQA method

Methods	Proposed	RRVIF	RRED	WNISM	FEDM
Runtime(s)	0.8164	3.7017	2.1192	1.7654	3.5801

5   Conclusions

Image structure conveys the main visual contents, to which HVS is highly sensitive. Most existing structure-based IQA metrics only consider the intensity of structure. Image distortions alter image structure, which include intensity of structure and spatial distribution of structure. Based on this observation, this paper proposes an improved structure-based IQA method via measuring the changes of intensity of structure and spatial distribution of structure. In order to measure changes of structure, gradient magnitude is employed to describe the intensity of structure. LBP and the proposed CSPP are used to capture the distribution of structure. CSPP plays a complementary role in characterizing the image structure. A combined histogram is mapped by weighting factor of the gradient magnitude based on LBP and CSPP. Histogram similarity is calculated between the histograms of the reference and distorted images.

Finally, a quality score is calculated by learning a support vector regression model. Experimental results on three public datasets have demonstrated that the proposed method achieved high consistency with subjective perception and per-formed better than the existing methods.

Acknowledgements. This work is sponsored by China Scholarship Council (CSC) program and the Robotic Vision Lab (RVL) at Brigham Young University.

References

1. Liu, L., Hua, Y., Zhao, Q., Huang, H., Bovik, A.C.: Blind image quality assessment by relative gradient statistics and Adaboosting neural network. Sig. Process. Image Commun. **40**(1), 1–15 (2016)
2. Bampis, C., Li, Z., Moorthy, A.K., Katsavounidis, I., Aaron, A., Bovik, A.C.: Study of temporal effects on subjective video quality of experience. IEEE Trans. Image Process. **26**(11), 5217–5231 (2017)
3. Xie, F., Lu, Y., Bovik, A.C., Jiang, Z., Meng, R.: Application-driven no reference quality assessment for dermoscopy images with multiple distortions. IEEE Trans. Biomed. Eng. **63**(6), 1248–1256 (2016)
4. Lin, W., Kuo, C.-C.J.: Perceptual visual quality metrics: a survey. J. Vis. Commun. Image Represent. **22**(4), 297–312 (2011)
5. Shao, F., Li, K., Lin, W., Jiang, G., Yu, M., Dai, Q.: Full-reference quality assessment of stereoscopic images by learning binocular receptive field properties. IEEE Trans. Image Process. **24**(10), 2971–2983 (2015)
6. Li, Q., Lin, W., Fang, Y.: No-reference quality assessment for multiply-distorted images in gradient domain. IEEE Signal Process. Lett. **23**(4), 541–545 (2016)
7. Wang, Z., Simoncelli, E.P.: Reduced-reference image quality assessment using a wavelet-domain natural image statistic model. In: Proceedings of the Human Vision and Electronic Imaging X, vol. 5666, pp. 149–159. SPIE, California, United States (2005)
8. Li, Q., Wang, Z.: Reduced-reference image quality assessment using divisive normalization-based image representation. IEEE J. Sel. Top. Signal Process. **3**(2), 202–211 (2009)
9. Gao, X., Lu, W., Tao, D., Li, X.: Image quality assessment based on multiscale geometric analysis. IEEE Trans. Image Process. **18**(7), 1409–1423 (2009)
10. Soundararajan, R., Bovik, A.C.: RRED indices: reduced reference entropic differencing for image quality assessment. IEEE Trans. Image Process. **21**(2), 517–526 (2012)
11. Ma, L., Li, S., Zhang, F., Ngan, K.N.: Reduced-reference imagequality assessment using reorganized DCT-based image representation. IEEE Trans. Multimed. **13**(4), 824–829 (2011)
12. Zhai, G., Wu, X., Yang, X., Lin, W., Zhang, W.: A psychovisual quality metric in free energy principle. IEEE Trans. Image Process. **21**(1), 41–52 (2012)
13. Wu, J., Lin, W., Shi, G., Liu, A.: Reduced-reference image quality assessment with visual information fidelity. IEEE Trans. Multimed. **15**(7), 1700–1705 (2013)
14. Redi, J., Gastaldo, P., Heynderickx, I., Zunino, R.: Color distribution information for the reduced-reference assessment of perceived image quality. IEEE Trans. Circuits Syst. Video Technol. **20**(12), 1757–1769 (2010)
15. Ojala, T., Valkealahti, K., Oja, E.: Texture discrimination with multidimensional distributions of signed gray-level differences. Pattern Recogn. **34**(3), 727–739 (2001)

16. Chang, C.C., Lin, C.J.: LIBSVM: a library for support vector machines. ACM Trans. Intell. Syst. Technol. **2**(27), 1–27 (2011)
17. Sheikh, H.R., Wang, Z., Cormack, L., Bovik, A.C.: LIVE Image Quality Assessment Database Release 2. http://live.ece.utexas.edu/research/quality,last. Accessed 21 June 2018
18. Larson, E.C., Chandler, D.M.: Categorical image quality (CSIQ) database. http://vision. okstate.edu/csiq. Accessed 21 June 2018
19. Ponomarenko, N., Jin, L., Ieremeiev, O., Lukin, V.: Image database TID2013: peculiarities, results and perspectives. Sig. Process. Image Commun. **30**, 57–77 (2015)
20. Sheikh, H.R., Sabir, M.F., Bovik, A.C.: A statistical evaluation of recent full reference image quality assessment algorithms. IEEE Trans. Image Process. **15**(11), 3440–3451 (2006)

Web System for Visualization of Weather Data of the Hydrometeorological Network of Tungurahua, Ecuador

Jaime Santana[✉], Fernando A. Chicaiza, Víctor H. Andaluz,
and Patrick Reuter

Universidad de las Fuerzas Armadas ESPE, Latacunga, Ecuador
sistemas@santana.ec, fernandochicaizal37@gmail.com,
patrickreuter@gmail.com, vhandaluz@espe.edu.ec

Abstract. The information provided by hydrometeorological stations can propose predictive solutions to adverse changes caused by weather in different regions. In this aspect, the publication of this type of information can help common users, farmers or populations at high risk of flooding or propose solutions to droughts. This work presents a hydrometeorological visualization system published in http://rrnn.tungurahua.gob.ec/red, including wind parameters, wind direction, precipitation, and temperature, in a graphic and documented way. The structure of the system presents the whole information required prior to the programming of the two-dimensional and three-dimensional interfaces, detailing all the tools used for the generation of graphics layers. Additionally, all the required files are presented to show the necessary graphic details, such as elevations, boundaries between cantons, roads, water bodies, and so on. Finally, a quick navigation of the bi-dimensional and three-dimensional interface is presented, where all options contained in the developed system are quickly displayed.

Keywords: Hydrometereological stations · Webpage · MapServer
Ortophotography

1 Introduction

The use of meteorological stations located in the field for the collection of climatic information can propose solutions to several problems cause by different economic activities [1, 2]. Problems related to droughts, excessive rainfall, frost, very high temperatures, and so on, can be partially mitigated through the information provided by the historical hydrometeorological data, allowing to find solutions to possible affections of important economies such as agriculture, livestock, aquaculture, and so forth [3]. For instance, a common case is a drought, known as a growing phenomenon which affects aspects such as food security, the environment, and the people's health. A 38-year record (1970–2007) [4] indicates that in Asia alone the drought has caused around $ 30 billion in damages, information which corroborates the impact of the drought in different regions and keeps changing under different climate change scenarios.

G. Bebis et al. (Eds.): ISVC 2018, LNCS 11241, pp. 395–406, 2018.
https://doi.org/10.1007/978-3-030-03801-4_35

However, the information obtained by this kind of stations requires big data processing, reliable communication between the data collection station and the processing station, information validators, and storage methods [5]. The difficulty in access to this type of information limits the farmers to rely on empirical knowledge, which many times is misguided given the recent climatic changes. By means of the proposed web system linked to the hydrometeorological observance network, a coordinated and climate-sensitive effort in agricultural and livestock farming can be carried out [6]. Especially in developing countries, the usage of this type of information could have a positive effect on food production and investment recovery [7].

In Ecuador, hydrometeorological monitoring networks are usually composed of rain gauges, radars, and sensors, which collect meteorological and hydrometric data in order to obtain information and produce guidelines for the sustainable management of water resources and decision making processes linked to early warning systems [8]. Companies, as well as government entities, have implemented computer applications to carry out their processes effectively, safely, and quickly. In this way, several meteorological and hydrometric data monitoring networks that are regulated by the National Institute of Meteorology and Hydrology [9] (INAMHI) have been strategically located in the central region of Ecuador. These networks or monitoring stations are located in the different provinces of the country, for instance in Azuay, Chimborazo, and Carchi, many of which are difficult to access due to their strategic positioning. The information generated by the hydrometeorological networks passes a complete process of verification and control until it is stored in a database, so that the variables acquired can be easily interpreted by an end user [10, 11].

This work presents the implementation of a web system with a standardized method to process hydrometeorological data, which is published in the Geoportal of the Honorable Provincial Government of Tungurahua, Ecuador. The implemented web page shows both updated and historical information on wind variables, wind direction, precipitation, and temperature. The objective of the implementation of this system is to provide hydrometeorological information to sectors of production which can take advantage of these data to foresee losses in food production, the activation of early warnings in populations close to water dams, water resource management and so on. Compared with other similar works, the system allows integrating new types of hydrometeorological stations and thus expand the data collection area without complicated and expensive configurations, providing more information for a better analysis. The process of validating data according to the World Meteorological Organization (WMO) standards is also something new in the country. This process allows the quick detection of a malfunction of a measuring instrument and, therefore, a quick replacement or calibration of the affected instrument.

2 System Structure

The general structure of the System is shown in Fig. 1 and is split into five main groups, which directly show the workflow to achieve the solution to the problems encountered. The data upload considers the methods of acquiring information from each of the meteorological stations, information that can be collected in two different ways. On the other hand, the storage methods are shown in the second block, where the pre-processing of information is considered to validate the data before saving them.

The (i) *data load* consists of the collection of information, either manually (collected station by station and uploaded to the system in *.csv format) or automatically through a series of scripts that access via stations to TELNET and downloaded the data to a local FTP server for further processing. The data collected manually or automatically have the structure of Fig. 2, where the label A represents the date on which the sample was taken, B is the time at which the reading of the data corresponds, C corresponds to the type of parameter and D is the value of the hydrometeorological parameter. This received structure (ii) *is mapped* using PHP *and stored* in the MongoDB database, creating an index for each group of 50000 data.

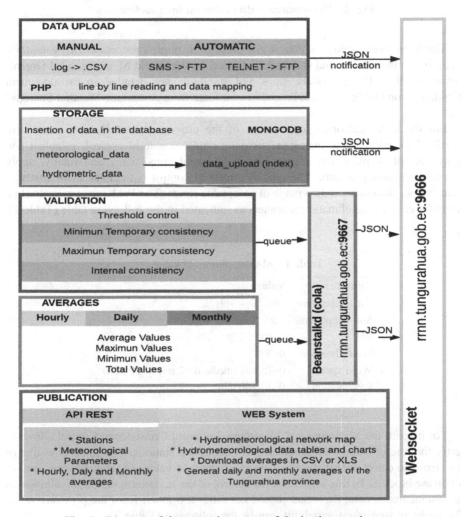

Fig. 1. Diagram of the general structure of the implemented system

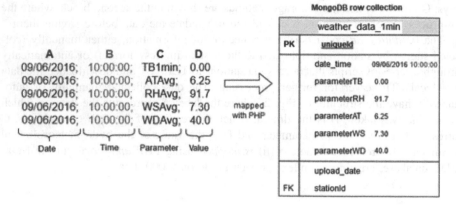

Fig. 2. The structure of data collected from each station

The hydro-meteorological data stored must go through a process of (iii) *validation* according to the models and standards indicated by the World Meteorological Organization (WMO). These models, steps and standards are detailed in the document "Guidelines on Quality Control Procedures for Data from Automatic Weather Stations" [4].

For the hydrometeorological stations of the province, the following steps were identified to validate the instantaneous data: apply threshold control, establish and apply control of minimum and maximum temporal consistency and finally, apply internal consistency control. The goal of threshold control is to check if the instantaneous values fluctuate within a range of acceptable limits. The WMO proposes absolute limits for each of the climatic parameters as indicated in the following table (Table 1).

Table 1. Absolute threshold values

Parameter	Value
Air temperature	−80 °C – +60 °C
Soil temperature	−50 °C – +50 °C
RH	0–100%
Wind direction	0–360°
Wind speed	0–75 m/s (media de 2 min o 10 min)
Precipitation	0–40 mm/min

For its part, the Minimum and Maximum Temporal Consistency Control allows to verify the rate of change of instantaneous data of the stations. The main objective of this step is to detect unrealistic spontaneous changes of values or repetitions by sensors which are blocked. In this aspect, for the control of the maximum variability allowed in the instantaneous data, the value should not differ too much from the previous value. The limits of maximum variability can be the following (Table 2):

Table 2. Limits of maximum variability imposed by WMO

Parameter	Value
Air temperature	3 °C
RH	10%
Atmospheric pressure	0,5 hPa
Wind speed	20 m/s
Solar radiation	1000 W/m²

To check the maximum variability, the instantaneous value must be compared with the previous and following ones, and if the data exceeds the established limits, it is marked as incorrect:

$$|V_i - V_{i-1}| + |V_i - V_{i+1}| \leq 4 \cdot \sigma_V \qquad (1)$$

V_i: Instantaneous value of the climate parameter,
V_{i-1}: Previous instantaneous value of the climate parameter,
V_{i+1}: Next instantaneous value of the climate parameter,
σ_V: Standard deviation of the climatic parameter calculated from the last 60 min.

Remark 1: In the event that the previous or next value does not exist, the corresponding part of the formula is omitted and the comparative term is $2 \cdot \sigma_V$.

Furthermore, a control of minimum variability is required to consider the cases in which the instantaneous value of one minute does not change for more than a specific limit during one hour, being marked as doubtful the group of values acquired. The possible limits of minimum variability required for a period of 60 min are (Table 3):

Table 3. Limits of minimum variability imposed by WMO

Parameter	Value
Air temperature	0.1 °C
RH	1%
Atmospheric pressure	0,1 hPa
Wind speed	0,5 m/s
Wind direction	10°

Finally, the control of the internal consistency of data is made based on the relationship between two climatic parameters, that is, if the wind speed is 0, the wind direction must also be 0. According to the WMO, the parameters have to comply with the following conditions to approve the internal consistency control:

Wind speed = 00 *and wind direction* = 00
Wind speed ≠ 00 *and wind direction* ≠ 00

Likewise, the (iv) *Generation of Averages* calculates values that represent a period of time that summarizes the capture of information to simplify the interpretation of acquired values. This measure is applied in order to offer a more of hydrometeorological data, which can be downloaded in the Geoportal of the HGPT. It was observed that data with intervals of less than one hour are usually not requested by users of the Geoportal. In addition, the reduction of information is necessary to facilitate the sending of data to INAMHI, which is responsible for a second phase of validation. Finally, the (v) *publication results* phase details the methods used to generate the interface with which the end user interacts. In this study, two visualization methods are considered: 2D and 3D. These measures are meant to improve the interaction between system and user, providing a downloading option of historical climate data, the location of each station in map that includes surfaces and altitudes, boundaries between cantons and useful information with respect to the maintenance of the station.

3   Web System Construction

The construction of the web system requires basic information to reach the level of detail of the maps, as well as the adequate presentation of the data received by the primary stations. Figure 3 presents all the information necessary to achieve the proposed interface, detailing the format in which the data is imported. In this way, the geospatial information of the Tungurahua province is stored in Raster and vector files. The *(i) raster files* generated for the web system are the georeferenced aerial shots of the province, where isotherms and isohyets maps, digital terrain models, and orthophotos are included.

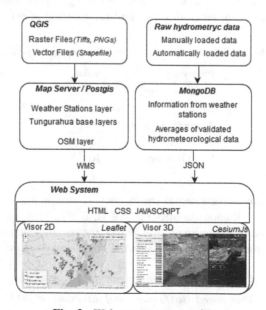

Fig. 3. Web system construction

The most representative raster files are the orthophotos of the whole province, purchased from the Geophysical Institute of Ecuador by the HGPT. The Raster (*.tiff) files for the orthophoto has a size of approximately 260 GB; in these satellite images the terrain is displayed with a relatively low percentage of cloudiness. The information obtained by the HGPT is captured in vector files (Shapefiles), which are formed by points, lines or polygons and are used to represent locations of places or objects, relevant areas, towns, routes, rivers, boundaries and other elements which can be represented through geometric figures. The vector files are generated manually using the software QGIS, based on consultancies or surveys of the authors of this work.

In order for geospatial information to be presented in a web environment, it is necessary to publish it through a Web Map Service (WMS), being MapServer and GeoServer the most used open source map servers. The proposed structure uses Mapserver, since most of the system is programmed over PHP and the support presented for this programming language is adequate, unlike GeoServer, which has greater support for systems developed in Java. MapServer allows to generate web services of maps (WMSs) from vector or raster information, where a WMS represents a map that can be made up of several layers, each layer corresponding to a single shapefile or *.tiff file. To generate the WMS to publish the orthophoto it is necessary to make an image arrangement and process them so that the 260 GB of images are reduced to 90% using tools from the GDAL library. Figure 4 presents a working diagram of MapServer, showing the files and services that are required inputs and the result of internal processing.

The construction of the web system interface uses HTML and CSS, which allow presenting the information in a structured and stylized way in a web page javascript, on the other hand, allows to include the interaction and the animation which is displayed on the web. Javascript has several libraries to present maps using the WMSs, of which Leaflet and CesiumJS are used. With Leaflet it is possible to present maps in 2D (using WMSs), add markers and popups to the map so that the user can interact with the interface by increasing or decreasing the zoom, dragging it or clicking on the maps to obtain information of a specific point or consulting the historical of each month, day or year.

Remark 2: The exclusive use of open source programs provides an excellent opportunity for the dissemination of the process and thus the system can be replicated elsewhere.

The 2D viewer made with leaflet includes the base layer of OpenStreetMaps (Fig. 5) used as a background on which are added the cantonal division layers and the markers which indicate the position of each hydrometeorological station within the province.

The climatological information that is shown when interacting with the map and opening the file of each hydrometeorological station is obtained from the non-relational MongoDB database in JSON format. The database contains the average, minimum and maximum values of the hydrometeorological parameters that were manually or automatically loaded and that later passed the validation and averaging process to be included in the 2D or 3D viewer.

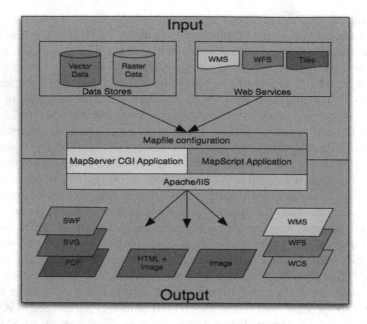

Fig. 4. MapServer operation diagram

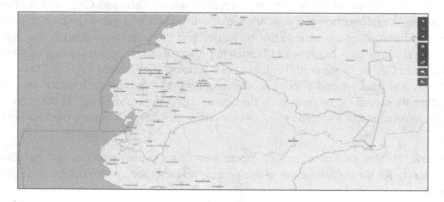

Fig. 5. Base layer provided by OpenStreetMaps

Furthermore, the 3D viewer made with CesiumJS includes the WMSs with the most relevant layers to be displayed in a three-dimensional way. In this case, the layers with hydrometeorological stations, the base layers of orthophotos, height, relief and cantons of Tungurahua are included to have a broader perspective of the location of the stations or the acquired measurements, including roads, rivers, water bodies, provincial and parish divisions, cities and isothermal maps (Fig. 6).

Fig. 6. Display showing the base layers of orthophotos and height

4 Results

The results presented in this section show the 2D and 3D displays implemented with Leaflet and CesiumJS respectively, which obtain the maps from MapServer through the pre-configured WMS and the weather information validated and averaged from MongoDB. The results are completely interactive, with data and measured parameters entered intuitively, as shown in the figures presented in this section.

4.1 2D Display

The main window (Fig. 7) shows the interface of the 2D viewer that allows to see the location of the meteorological and hydrometric stations distributed in the 8 cantons of the province of Tungurahua. When interacting with the map the client can filter the stations by region, type of station or measured parameters. Additionally, the user can access the climatic information of each station or region and see the historical data available, by clicking on the area that he wishes to consult (Fig. 8).

Fig. 7. A. 2D Viewer of the Tungurahua's Hydrometeorological network

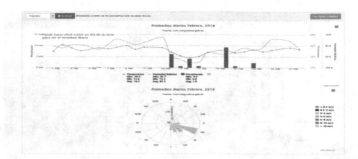

Fig. 8. Historical climate information of a hydrometeorological station

The result shown allows access to a detailed view of each station, which consists of its geographical location, basic data (Fig. 9), a section with the climatic history of each hydrometeorological parameter and a section to download the hydrometeorological data in csv or excel format.

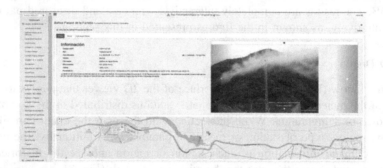

Fig. 9. Complete display of hydro meteorological station and geographical location

4.2   Visor 3D

The 3D viewer consists of 3 main sections. The first contains a list of the layers loaded through the WMS of the Weather Stations and base layers of Tungurahua. These layers have the characteristic of modification of opacity and allow to be added on the second section containing the 3D map and the markers of the climatic stations (Fig. 10).

The third section of the 3D display shows a table with information about the selected station and allows you to position and orient the map to obtain a panoramic view of the area where each station is located. Additionally, you can set the heading, pitch and roll values of the camera to change the orientation of the viewfinder manually (Fig. 11).

Fig. 10. 3D display of hydrometeorological network and base layers available

Fig. 11. Location of weather station on 3D map and base information.

5 Conclusions

A system for presenting data collected from hydrometeorological stations is easy to interpret and use when they are processed and displayed graphically. In this context, the implemented system collects manual or automatic information for the plotting of climate parameters, such as wind speed, wind direction, precipitation, and temperature, in order to show summarized information. Through this system, a common user can have access to graphical information of the received data, as well as the historical information of each of the stations. By means of the user-friendly and interactive webpage, the acquired, processed and stored information can be used, for instance, in agricultural and livestock planning, water resource management, and disaster prevention. This facility of interaction is achieved through the representation of two-dimensional and three-dimensional maps, which show the location of each of the stations on a map including altitudes, populations, water bodies, flora and fauna, and so on.

Acknowledgment. The authors would like to thank the Corporación Ecuatoriana para el Desarrollo de la Investigación y Academia – CEDIA for the financing given to research, development, and innovation, through the Grupos de Trabajo, GT, especially to the GTeTURISMO; as well as the Department of Water Resources and Environmental Conservation of the Honorable Provincial Government of Tungurahua-HGPT for the information provided for this investigation, and Grupo de Investigación en Automatización, Robótica y Sistemas Inteligentes, GI-ARSI, for the support to develop this work.

References

1. Iizumi, T., Ramankutty, N.: How do weather and climate influence cropping area and intensity? Glob. Food Secur. **4**, 46–50 (2015)
2. Lipper, L., Thornton, P., Campbell, B.M., et al.: Climate-smart agriculture for food security. Nat. Clim. Change **4**, 1068–1072 (2014)
3. Leng, G., Tang, Q., Rayburg, S.: Climate change impacts on meteorological, agricultural and hydrological droughts in China. Glob. Planet. Change **126**, 23–34 (2015)
4. World Meteorological Organization: Guidelines on Quality Control Procedures for Data from Automatic Weather Stations. WMO, Geneva (2004)
5. Fang, W., Sheng, V.S., Wen, X., Pan, W.: Meteorological data analysis using MapReduce. Sci. World J. **2014**, 1–11 (2014)
6. Wang, Y.Q.: MeteoInfo: GIS software for meteorological data visualization and analysis. Meteorol. Appl. **21**, 360–368 (2014)
7. Shock, D.A., et al.: Studying the relationship between on-farm environmental conditions and local meteorological station data during the summer. Am. Dairy Sci. Assoc. **99**, 1–11 (2016)
8. Golian, S., Mazdiyasni, O., AghaKouchak, A.: Trends in meteorological and agricultural droughts in Iran. Theor. Appl. Climatol. **119**(3–4), 679–688 (2015)
9. Mase, A.S., Prokopy, L.S.: Unrealized potential: a review of perceptions and use of weather and climate information in agricultural decision making. Am. Metereol. Soc. **2014**, 1–10 (2014)
10. INAMHI: Meteorological instruments. INAMHI (2018). [En línea]. http://www.serviciometeorologico.gob.ec/. Último acceso 03 July 2018
11. Campozano, L., Tenelanda, D., Sanchez, E., Samaniego, E., Feyen, J.: Comparison of statistical downscaling methods for monthly total precipitation: case study for the Paute River Basin in Southern Ecuador. Adv. Meteorol. **2016**(1), 1–13 (2016)

Analysis and Visualization of Sports Performance Anxiety in Tennis Matches

Shiraj Pokharel[✉] and Ying Zhu[✉]

Department of Computer Science and Creative Media Industries Institute,
Georgia State University, Atlanta, GA 30303, USA
spokharel3@student.gsu.edu, yzhu@gsu.edu

Abstract. According to sports psychology, anxiety has a big impact on an athlete's performance in a sport event. Although much work has been done in sports data analysis and visualization, analysis of anxiety has rarely been included in previous work. In this paper, we propose a method to analyze a tennis player's anxiety level during a tennis match. This method is based on the psychological theories of anxiety and a database of over 4,000 professional tennis matches. In our model, an athlete's anxiety level is based on three factors: uncertainty, anticipation, and threat. We have also developed data visualizations to help users study the potential correlation between a tennis player's anxiety level and his/her skilled performance, such as unforced errors, forced errors, winners, serve directions, first-serve faults, and double faults.

Keywords: Visual analytics · Visualization
Visual knowledge discovery · Visual knowledge representation
Sports analytics

1 Introduction

Anxiety can have a great impact on human performance, particularly when the stake is huge, the competition is strong, or the time pressure is high. Perhaps the most visible cases of anxiety influencing performance is in sports events. Sports psychologists have long studied anxiety and considered it the most important factor that influences an athlete's performance. However, the relationship between anxiety and skilled performance in a competitive event is still not well understood. Such analysis is traditionally done by human with relatively small samples.

In recent years, data-driven sports analysis have become a rapidly growing area because of the availability of large amount of sports performance data. However, anxiety has rarely been included in sports data analysis and visualizations. Our work is an attempt to address this issue.

In this paper, we describe a method to computationally build a tennis player's anxiety model based on detailed performance data. In our model, a player's anxiety is influenced by three main factors: uncertainty, anticipation, and threat. Our

© Springer Nature Switzerland AG 2018
G. Bebis et al. (Eds.): ISVC 2018, LNCS 11241, pp. 407–419, 2018.
https://doi.org/10.1007/978-3-030-03801-4_36

model can estimate the anxiety level of a tennis player as the tennis match progresses. We have also developed data visualizations to help correlate anxiety with various performance measures, such as unforced errors, forced errors, winners, serve directions, first-serve faults, and double faults. This visual anxiety-performance analytics tool can help sports psychologists, tennis players, coaches, analysts, and fans better understand the relationship between anxiety and performance. For example, is there a correlation between high anxiety level and increased unforced errors? Does a player prefer certain types of serves or shots when the anxiety level is high? Although We choose to study sports performance anxiety because of the aboundance of sports performance data, the proposed anxiety-performance analysis methods and tools can be adapted to other fields if similar data sets are available.

2   Related Work

He and Zhu [1] proposed a data visualization that shows the progression of a tennis match. Users can highlight various performance data on the visualization, such as unforced errors, shot types, etc. Some researchers [2–7] have done statistical analysis of tennis matches. However, none of the above works have included anxiety in their analysis. Kovalchik, et al. [8] analyzed the win-lose rate of different players at critical moments (e.g. break-points, set-points, etc.) and identified mental characteristics of these players. However, compared to our work, they did not build an explicit anxiety profile. Their performance measure is winning or losing a point, without the specific performance data use in our study (such as unforced error, winners, and serve faults). Their work also did not provide data visualizations.

3   Data

Our analysis is based on the tennis match data from Tennis Abstract [9], an open source project that, as of the summer of 2018, provides point-by-point, shot-by-shot statistics of over 4000 professional tennis matches. The data includes the type of shot, direction of shot, types of serves, direction of serves, depth of returns, types of errors, etc. This data set is more detailed (and more useful) than the data retrieved from any tennis video analysis, which can identify the players' movements but cannot yet identify the type of shots and type of errors.

4   Basic Performance Anxiety Model

Anxiety is a type of fear reaction. Based on psychological and neuroscience studies [12], we have identified three factors that influence the level of anxiety: uncertainty, anticipation, and threat. These three factors not only apply to sports but also to other fields.

4.1   Uncertainty

We define uncertainty as a function of the gap in scores. The bigger the gap in scores, the lower the uncertainty. Uncertainty is at the highest when the score is tied. In our model, the uncertainty level (integer) ranges from 1 to 4, with 4 being the highest. (We do not include a 0 level uncertainty because in competitive sports there is always some uncertainty until the game is over.) For example, if a tennis game progresses as 0-0, 15-0, 15-15, 30-15, 40-15, the corresponding uncertainty levels would be 4, 3, 4, 3, 2 respectively.

4.2   Anticipation

We define anticipation as how close a player is to win a game. The closer to the end of the game, the higher the anticipation level. Specifically, the anticipation level is a function of the number of points a player needs to win in order to win the game. In our model, the anticipation index (integer) ranges from 0 to 3, with 3 being the highest. If the game goes to deuce, the anticipation index can increase to 4. For example, if a game runs 0-0, 15-0, 30-0, 30-15, and 40-15, the corresponding anticipation levels for the winning player would be 0, 1, 2, 2, and 3. At the start of the game, the anticipation is 0. At 30-0, the leading player is 2 points away from winning the game, the corresponding anticipation level is 2. At 40-15, the leading player is one point away from winning, therefore the anticipation level is 3.

4.3   Threat

We define threat as how close a player is to lose a game. If the opponent is closer to winning a game, a player perceives a higher level of threat and, as a result, a higher level of anxiety. In our model, threat index (integer) ranges from 0 to 3, with 3 being the highest. If the game goes to deuce, the threat index can increase to 4. The threat level is a function of how many points the opponent needs to win a game. For example, if a game goes 0-0, 15-0, 30-0, 30-15, 40-15, the corresponding threat levels for the winning player would be 0, 0, 0, 1, 1. One player's anticipation is the opposing player's threat.

5   Performance Anxiety Model for Tennis

In our model, the Anxiety score is a combination of Uncertainty, Anticipation, and Threat.

$$Anxiety = Uncertainty + Anticipation + Threat \qquad (1)$$

Additionally a few minor factors influence a player's anxiety level in a complicated game like tennis. Statistics indicates that professional tennis players have a high probability to win their service games. For example, ATP players usually win 70% to 90% of their service games, while WTA players usually win 60%

to 80% of their service games. This means a slightly higher expectation (and higher anxiety) for the server to win the current game because the server knows the opponent will likely win the next game (the opponent's service game). If the player has a weak serve, then the anxiety level should be even higher. For the same reason, a player is slightly less anxious when returning serves. If the player has a higher return game won percentage, the anxiety level should be even lower.

Therefore, in our model the anxiety score from Equation (1) is multiplied by a serve anxiety index. The serve anxiety index for the server is larger than 1 and is calculated based on the winning percentage of a player's service games. For example, if a player has a 75% service game won percentage, then the serve anxiety index is $100/75 = 1.33$. (If a player's statistics is unknown, the average percentage is used.) On the other hand, When a player is returning serve, the serve anxiety index is smaller than 1 and is calculated based on the winning percentage of the player's return game. For example, if a player has a 25% return game won rate, then the serve anxiety index is $(1 - 0.25) = 0.75$.

6   Case Studies

In this section we demonstrate our method and visualization output (Figs. 1, 2, 3, 4, 5 and 6) using the Tennis Abstract match data for the 2017 US Open semifinal between ATP players Kevin Anderson and Pablo Carreno Busta (henceforth referred to as KA and PCB respectively), where KA defeated PCB 4-6, 7-5, 6-3, 6-4. Each row in the visualization represents a set. The top row represents the first set, the second row the second set, and so on. Each individual chart represents a game. Based on the ATP tour stats [10], KA and PCB's service game won percentages are 86% and 76% respectively. Their return games won percentages are 17% and 25% respectively.

The programs are implemented with Python. The data visualizations are implemented with Python library Bokeh [11]. The game-by-game anxiety indexes are plotted as individual line charts, with performance data such as first serve fault, double fault, serve directions plotted as colored markers on the anxiety score lines. Compared with pure statistical analysis, these visualizations can help users correlate anxiety with various performance measures and conduct in-depth analysis on point-by-point, game-by-game basis.

6.1   Uncertainty

Figure 1 shows the correlation between uncertainty and unforced errors, forced errors, and winners for player PCB. In tennis, every point ends with one of the three outcomes: unforced error, forced error, or winner. An unforced error is an error made when a player is balanced and has enough time to make the shot, indicating poor performance. For top professional players, most of the unforced errors are attributed to nervousness, which is directly related to anxiety. A forced error is an error made by a player who is either out of balance (e.g. stretching to reach the ball) or has very little time to react. A forced error may not be directly related to anxiety but it may indicate that the player's previous shot is weak. A winner is a winning shot that the opponent is unable to reach, indicating excellent level of performance. Our analysis and visualization show a strong correlation between uncertainty and unforced errors and winners. Out of 83 unforced errors, 59% of them were made when uncertainty index is 3, and 30% of them were made when the uncertainty index is 4. Nine unforced errors were made when the uncertainty index is 2, and no unforced error was made when the uncertainty index is 1 (lowest). Out of 49 winners, 54% of them were made when the uncertainty index is 3, and 29% of them were made when the uncertainty index is 4. This shows both the negative and positive impact of uncertainty on the performance: when the scores are close, the player made more unforced errors but also made more winning shots.

6.2 Anticipation

Figure 2 shows the correlation between anticipation and the performance for PCB. Overall, this analysis suggests a weak correlation between anticipation and performance. The unforced errors are more or less evenly distributed at different anticipation levels. However, there are more winners when the anticipation level is low. For all the winners, about 35% of them were made when the anticipation index is 0, compared to 24% for the anticipation index 1, 20% for the anticipation index 2, and 20% for the anticipation index 3. This suggests that PCB was more aggressive when the anticipation level is low (e.g. early in the game).

6.3 Threat

Figure 3 shows the correlation between threat and PCB's performance. There is a strong correlation between low threat level and unforced errors. Among the unforced errors, 36% of them were made at the threat index of 0, 35% made at the threat index of 1, 16% were made at the threat index of 2, and only 12% were made at the threat index of 3. This suggests that PCB was a little careless when the threat level is low but made a conscious effort to avoid unforced errors when the threat level is high (close to losing). There is also a correlation between low threat level and winners. Among the winners, 31% of them were at the threat index 0 and 1 respectively, 18% were made at the threat index 2, and 20% were made at the threat index 3. This suggests that PCB was slightly but noticeably more cautious when the threat level is high.

6.4 Anxiety Score

Figure 4 shows the correlation between the combined anxiety index and performance for PCB. Our analysis shows that unforced errors exhibit a normal distribution with regards to the anxiety index. Among unforced errors, 64% of them occur in the anxiety index range 5 to 10 (medium), 25% of them occur in the anxiety index range 0 to 5 (low), and 11% occur in the anxiety index range

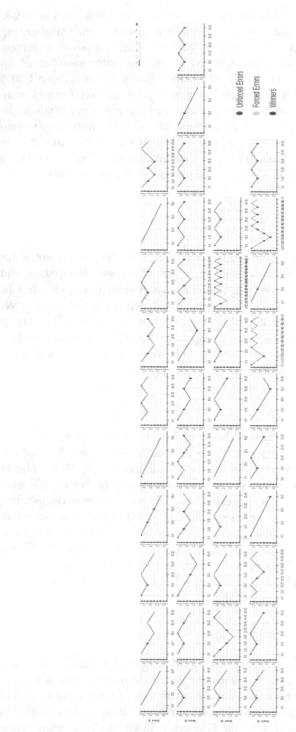

Fig. 1. Correlating uncertainty with unforced errors, forced errors and winners for PCB.

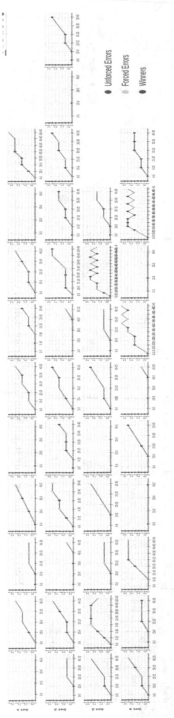

Fig. 2. Correlating anticipation with unforced errors, forced errors and winners for PCB.

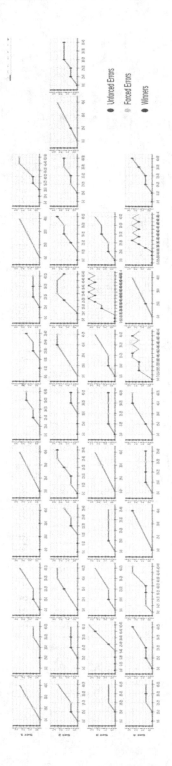

Fig. 3. Correlating threat with unforced errors, forced errors and winners for PCB.

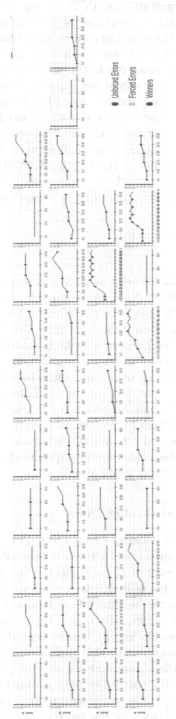

Fig. 4. Correlating (combined) anxiety with unforced errors, forced errors and winners for PCB.

10 and above (high). This suggests that PCB managed to reduce his unforced errors at high pressure situations, perhaps by playing more cautiously. Most unforced errors occur in medium anxiety situations. Our analysis shows that most of the winners were produced in low to medium anxiety situations. Among all winners, 38% of them were produced in the anxiety index range 0 to 5 (low), 44% of them produced in the anxiety index range 5 to 10 (medium), and only 18% were produced in the anxiety index range 10 or higher. This suggests that PCB was more aggressive in low anxiety situations but took less risk in high anxiety situations. However, our data visualizations show there are exceptions to this general pattern, thus allowing more nuanced analysis. In the eighth game of the third set and the ninth game of the fourth set, PCB produced 13 winners, with 8 of them in high anxiety situations (anxiety index of 10 or higher). This indicates that PCB decided to be more aggressive and took more risk when he was close to losing a set.

6.5   Serve Direction

Figure 5 shows the correlation between anxiety and serve directions. There are three directions in a tennis serve: Wide, Body, and Down-the-T. In high anxiety situations, a player tends to use his/her most effective serve. Our analysis shows that PCB's favorite serve direction in high anxiety situations (anxiety index of 10 or higher) is wide - 44% of his serves in high anxiety situations are wide. Our data visualizations also show an interesting pattern. PCB did not use any Down-the-T serve in high anxiety situations until the 8th game in the 3rd set and the 7th and 9th games in the last set, in which he suddenly served seven times Down-the-T at critical moments. Similarly, he only served 7 times to the Body in the first 29 games in high anxiety situations, but served 9 times to the Body in the 8th game of the 3rd set and the 9th game of the 4th set in high anxiety situations. This may be a calculated decision to change his serve patterns to surprise his opponent at critical moments.

6.6   First Serve Fault and Double Fault

Figure 6 shows the correlation between first serve faults and double faults with anxiety index. Our analysis shows that PCB made only 4 first serve faults in high anxiety situations (anxiety index of 10 or higher) in the first 14 service games. Then he made 12 first serve faults in the last 6 service games in high anxiety situations. This suggests that the heightened anxiety near the end of the match might cause these errors. Or perhaps PCB decided to serve more aggressively later in the match when he was losing. PCB made two double faults, both near the end of the games, perhaps indicating that high level of threats or anticipation led to the errors. Based on the above analysis, we can give a brief summary of current world number 21 PCB's pattern of play in this match. In high anxiety situations, he was cautious and able to reduce unforced errors and serve faults. In medium to low anxiety situations, he was more aggressive but also made many

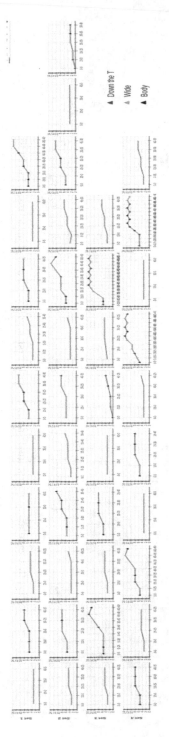

Fig. 5. Correlating (combined) anxiety with serve direction for PCB.

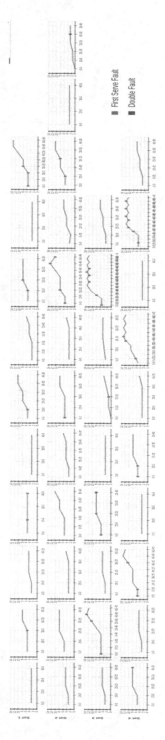

Fig. 6. Correlating (combined) anxiety with first serve fault and double fault for PCB.

unforced errors. However, when close to losing the match, he could become very aggressive in high anxiety situations.

7   Conclusion

In this paper, we described a method to computationally analyze and visualize the relationship between a player's anxiety and performance in a tennis match. Our case study shows that we are able to discover useful patterns through these analysis and visualizations. Our method has its limitations. It is an indirect estimate of an athlete's anxiety status, not a direct measurement of the athlete's physiological state (which is usually difficult to do in a professional match). Our methods do not include factors outside of the match, such as physical condition, environment, etc. In the future, we plan to expand our data analysis and visualizations to other factors such as confidence, while also planning to expand our methods to other fields where anxiety-performance analysis is useful.

References

1. He, X., Zhu, Y.: TennisMatchViz: a tennis match visualization. In: Proceedings of International Conference on Visualization and Data Analysis (VDA) (2016)
2. Madurska, M.: A set-by-set analysis method for predicting the outcome of professional singles tennis matches. Master's thesis, Imperial College London (2012)
3. O'Malley, A.J.: Probability formulas and statistical analysis in tennis. J. Quant. Anal. Sport. **4**(2), 1–23 (2008)
4. Newton, P., Keller, J.: Probability of winning at tennis I. Stud. Appl. Math. Theory Data Stud. Appl. Math. **114**(3), 241–269 (2005)
5. Riddle, L.: Probability models for tennis scoring systems. J. R. Stat. Society. Ser. C (Appl. Stat.) **37**(1), 63–75 (1988)
6. Jackson, D., Mosurski, K.: Heavy defeats in tennis: psychological momentum or random effect? CHANCE **10**(2), 27–34 (1997)
7. MacPhee, I., Rougier, J., Pollard, G.: Server advantage in tennis matches. J. Appl. Probab. **41**(4), 1182–1186 (2004)
8. Kovalchik, S., Ingram, M.: Hot heads, cool heads, and tacticians: measuring the mental game in tennis. In: MIT Sloan Sports Analytics Conference (2016)
9. Tennis Match Charting Project. https://github.com/JeffSackmann/tennis_MatchChartingProject
10. ATP Stats. https://www.atpworldtour.com/en/stats
11. Bokeh. http://www.bokeh.pydata.org
12. Grupe, D.W., Nitschke, J.B.: Uncertainty and anticipation in anxiety: an integral neurobiological and psychological perspective. Nat. Rev. Neurosci. **14**(7), 488–501 (2013)

Object Detection and Recognition

Detailed Sentence Generation Architecture for Image Semantics Description

Imran Khurram[1(✉)], Muhammad Moazam Fraz[1,2,3], and Muhammad Shahzad[1]

[1] School of Electrical Engineering and Computer Science,
National University of Sciences and Technology, Islamabad, Pakistan
{ikhurram.mscs16seecs,moazam.fraz,muhammad.shehzad}@seecs.edu.pk
[2] The Alan Turing Institute, London NW1 2DB, UK
[3] Department of Computer Science, University of Warwick, Coventry CV47AL, UK

Abstract. Automatic image captioning deals with the objective of describing an image in human understandable natural language. Majority of the existing approaches aiming to solve this problem are based on holistic techniques which translate the whole image into a single sentence description rendering the possibility of losing important aspects of the scene. To enable better and more detailed caption generations, we propose a dense captioning architecture which first extracts and describes the objects of the image which in turn is helpful in generating dense and detailed image captions. The proposed architecture has two modules where the first one generates the region descriptions that describe the objects and their relationships while the other generates object attributes which are helpful to produce object details. Both of these outputs are concatenated and given as input to another sentence generation that is based on an encoder-decoder formulation to generate a single meaningful and grammatically detailed sentence. The results achieved with the proposed architecture shows superior performance when compared with current state-of-the-art image captioning techniques e.g., Neural Talk and Show, Attend and Tell, using standard evaluation metrics.

Keywords: Image captioning · Scene understanding
Visual captioning · Recurrent neural networks
Convolution neural networks

1 Introduction

Automatic image captioning is a task to describe an image in human understandable language that helps to interpret the details of the scene. Image captioning has numerous applications e.g., robotics where the image based captioning may help in semantic scene analysis [23], in security where the image captioning system may be fused with an alarming system to help in anomaly detection [21], in assisting visually impaired people [17] and many others.

© Springer Nature Switzerland AG 2018
G. Bebis et al. (Eds.): ISVC 2018, LNCS 11241, pp. 423–432, 2018.
https://doi.org/10.1007/978-3-030-03801-4_37

Traditionally, image captioning has been done using sentence templates [12] which uses hard-coded visual concepts to fill the templates. The problem with such methods is that they generate simple sentences for complex scenes and limits the text variations.

With recent advancements in artificial neural networks, deep architectures have shown promising results in diverse computer vision applications. Considering this fact, there has been a paradigm shift in techniques solving the image captioning problem. Most of the existing techniques [6,7,15,22] now focus on employing deep learning to cope with the challenges in image captioning problem. A big contribution was made by NeuralTalk [6] and Neural Image Caption (NIC) [22], which typically work by learning certain alignments between image features and language sequences. These alignments help the system to determine the semantics of various objects/actions and subsequently translate the recognized semantics into textual form. Commonly, these techniques employ Convolutional Neural Networks (CNNs) as an encoder to convert image to feature representation and Recurrent Neural Network (RNN) as a sentence generation module or a decoder to decode the feature representation into a proper sentence. These techniques do not have any mechanism to validate that the words correspond to objects which are truly present in the image. Such a validation mechanism has been employed by Kelvin *et al.* [7] which uses attention mechanism to focus on image regions for generating next word. The problem with such attention-based approach is that it takes too much extra computations by generating attention for all unnecessary words like "to", "from". To overcome this, an adaptive attention mechanism has been proposed in [15] which uses visual sentinel vector to decide whether to generate attention for the generated word or not.

Existing architectures do not extract the object level semantic information and therefore lacks in generating the dense descriptions because a real-life image may contain many objects in the scene. Incorporating object detection module in image captioning may help in obtaining detailed captions as e.g., done in [5] where the object regions are extracted out using a region proposal network [19] and later the descriptions are generated for all the extracted regions instead of producing a single caption of the whole image. Although the presented approach works well in generating the individual text for each detected object but it is insufficient to semantically describe the image as a whole in one complete sentence.

In the above context, this paper presents a novel modular image captioning approach that focuses on generating image captions by individually detecting and describing the objects. Following are the main contributions proposed in this paper:

- An object-based architecture for automatic image captioning is proposed which overcomes the limitations of existing methodologies by first detecting and describing the objects present in the image. Subsequently, using those object descriptions to form single image caption.
- A separate sentence generation module is proposed that is used to join region descriptions and object attributes to form a single line caption. The basic

task of this module is to join small sentences and words into a single detailed sentence.
- The developed architecture has been validated over the IAPR TC-12 dataset [2] which provides detailed descriptions with real life images. The quantitative results show that the proposed system performs better than the state-of-the-art image captioning architectures in all the standard evaluation metrics.

The organization of this paper is as follow. Section 2 explains the proposed methodology consisting of region extraction using RPN, RNN based region description and attribute generation and the sentence generation based on RNN encoder-decoder with attention mechanism. Section 3 then presents the results obtained on available/generated datasets and the performance analysis of the proposed framework. Finally, the Sect. 4 concludes and presents the future research directions.

2   Methodology

This paper provides an architecture (shown in Fig. 1) which localizes and describes each region separately to give a complete and more detailed description of the image.

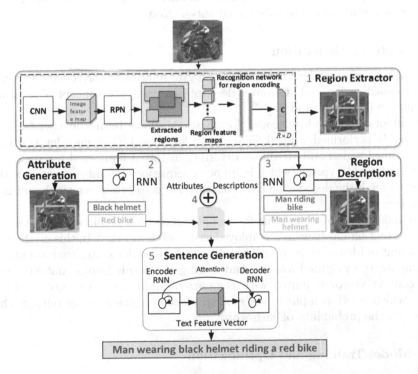

Fig. 1. Model overview. Region extraction module extracts object regions. These regions are converted into region descriptions and object attributes. Sentence Generation block then joins all region descriptions and attributes to form a detailed sentence

First the regions of interest are extracted using region extraction module. The region extraction module consists of a sequential CNN layer followed by an adapted RPN [19] architecture and a two-layer recognition network as proposed in [5]. Sequential CNN layer first extracts the features of the whole input image which are then converted into regional feature maps by an adapted RPN. Later, these feature maps of the individual regions are encoded into a compact representation for further efficient processing by a fully connected recognition network. The proposed system then uses two modules to describe the image objects. The first one generates the region descriptions including object relationships and the second one generates the object attributes i.e., the region and attribute description includes the text formulations such as "trees on the road" and "tall trees" respectively. Typically, RNNs are employed in text and sequence generation tasks to incorporate contextual information. Moreover, to cope with the vanishing gradient problems, the LSTMs (Long short-term memory) [3] — variant of RNNs — are commonly used for caption generation e.g., [5,7,22]. These two types of textual descriptions are then concatenated and given as input to the sentence generation module which adopts an encoder-decoder framework that incorporates the grammatical context ensuring syntactical correctness to generate a single meaningful and detailed sentence describing the whole scene. The approach is modular and consists of following building blocks: (1) Region extraction, (2) RNN for language generation and (3) Sentence Generation which is described in detail in the subsequent sub-section.

2.1 Sentence Generation

This module forms a single meaningful and grammatically correct sentence from the combined region and attributes descriptions using the concept of sequence-to-sequence (seq2seq) models [16–18].

It adopts an encoder-decoder formulation where both the encoding and decoding is performed using LSTM networks. The LSTM encoder translates the combined region and attributes descriptions into a numbered representation called a "thought" vector (which is simply a sequence of numbers) which is then passed through the decoder LSTM that converts it to produce a single but more descriptive sentence.

To make the module feasible for complex scenarios consisting of larger sentences, attention mechanism is employed as depicted in Fig. 2. In this mechanism, the current hidden state is compared with all the encoder states that are utilized to compute the weighted average and storing the result into a context vector. This context vector is united with the current hidden state to give attention vector which is fed as input to the next time step to give a vector output which represents the probability of each word.

2.2 Model Training and Optimization

The proposed region extraction and attribute generation models are trained as encoder-decoder framework for 50,000 iterations having 512 units at each

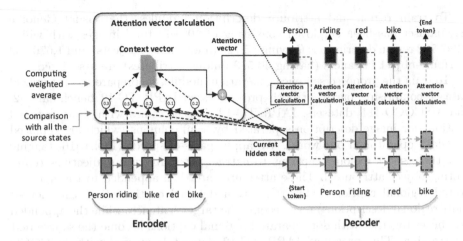

Fig. 2. RNN based encoder decoder framework with attention mechanism.

layer of LSTM. The dropout of 0.5 is used for regularization to reduce any overfitting. For the training of CNN, the conventional stochastic gradient descent (SGD) has been used with learning rate of 1×10^{-6} while the training of the region and attribute descriptions modules has been performed using adaptive moment estimation [8]. The network architecture of the sentence generation module includes 2 hidden layers each with 200 LSTM units (of both encoder and decoder). The network is trained for 20,000 iterations (with dropout of 0.2 for regularization) using the stochastic gradient descent as an optimization strategy with learning rate of 1.0. High learning rate for sentence generation depicts that text training do not require as much low learning rate as required for feature training.

3   Experimental Results and Validation

To validate and analyse the performance of the proposed network architecture, we compared the obtained results outcome with existing state-of-the-art methods in generating dense image descriptions e.g., Neural Talk [6] and Show, Attend and Tell [7]. Before presenting the results, we first emphasize on the employed datasets used in this research.

3.1   Datasets

To assess the performance of the proposed approach, two different datasets have been used. The first dataset is utilized to train the network for region description and attributes generation while the other is employed for training the network to learn the process of fusing small descriptions and attributes to form one complete sentence.

To train region and attribute description modules, the Visual Genome [11] dataset has been employed consisting of 108,077 total images with which 4,297,502 region descriptions (having 75,729 unique image objects) and 1,670,182 attribute-object instances (having 40,513 unique attributes) are associated.

To train the proposed sentence generation module, we prepared a customized dataset comprising partly of both pre-processed IAPR TC-12 benchmark [2] and MSCOCO [14] datasets. IAPR TC-12 dataset comes with short regional captions for image description separated by semi columns (which are replaced by "dot" operator in our work). We apply parts-of-speech (POS) [16] tagging over these short regional captions to extract attributes (i.e., adjectives representing object attributes). These attributes are then appended to the dot separated regional captions. Thus, the given detailed captions (i.e., the merged short regional descriptions) now become the target sentences while the appended attributes together with dot separated regional captions become the source text for training. This processed IAPR TC-12 dataset is merged with MSCOCO dataset after some pre-processing. MSCOCO dataset comes with 5 descriptions per image. To find the most related target sentence, these 5 descriptions are compared with off-the-shelf region descriptions by employing distributionally related words using co-occurrences (DISCO) similarity measure [9]. The off-shelf region descriptions are obtained by feeding the MSCOCO images to DenseCap (dense regional captioning algorithm) [5]. DISCO is a Java library which uses cosine similarity measure to compute semantic similarity between the words/phrases. Similar to IAPR TC-12, the attributes from MSCOCO dataset are also extracted using POS tagging the target sentence and extracting the adjectives. The unique words in both source and target sentences make huge vocabularies. To improve the training accuracy and time, the adjective in the sentences are further POS tagged to reduce vocaublary size. Thus, the total vocabulary of source and target training sets reduces to 4,829 and 7,817 (words, numbers, characters) respectively. For both the source and target, the total captions for training, validation and testing contains 58,702, 14,675 and 18,344 respectively.

3.2   Qualitative and Quantitative Results

The evaluation of the proposed architecture for automatic image captioning has been carried out at dense level by comparing its performance (both qualitatively and quantitatively) with the existing state of the art techniques.

A subset of IAPR TC-12 dataset is used for training while the rest (6802 images obtained after some pruning i.e., removing captions containing non-English characters) is used for evaluation of the developed approach as it is probably the only dataset containing dense and detailed image captions.

The quantitative results using the standard evaluation metrics (BLEU [18], ROUGE-L [13] and METEOR [1]) obtained on 6,802 images are shown in the Table 1. As depicted, the proposed network has outperformed the other two state-of-the-art techniques in all the performance measures showing that the network is capable of describing complex scenes in a more detailed way.

Table 1. Comparison of quantitative results (obtained using 6,802 images) with state-of-the-art techniques. Higher values depict better results.

Evaluation metric	Network models		
	NeuralTalk [6]	Show, attend and tell [7]	Our system
BLEU-1	0.091	0.080	**0.128**
BLEU-2	0.047	0.041	**0.064**
BLEU-3	0.025	0.022	**0.031**
BLEU-4	0.013	0.011	**0.016**
METEOR	0.624	0.600	**0.686**
ROUGE-L	0.215	0.207	**0.216**

Table 2. Qualitative Results - Comparison with state-of-the-art techniques. Second column shows the results obtained on NeuralTalk, third column shows the results obtained on Show, Attend and Tell and fourth column shows the results obtained on proposed architecture.

Images	NeuralTalk [6]	Show, Attend and Tell [7]	Our system
	a large body of water with a bridge in the background.	a view of a city with a city.	the buildings are in the background, a large ship in the water, a large white building and a white boat in the water.
	a woman riding a bike down a street.	a person riding a bike down a street.	a man wearing a shirt and a black helmet is riding a bicycle.
	a black and white photo of a bird in the woods.	a black and white photo of a person on a surfboard.	a large rock in a large body of water.
	a bedroom with a bed and a table	a bedroom with a bed and a bed.	a bed with a comforter and a wooden headboard.
	a group of people sitting on a bench.	a view of a large body of water.	a body of water with blue water, white clouds in a blue sky in the background.

Table 2 (4th column) shows the visual results of the descriptions produced by the proposed network. Specifically, we compared the results with NeuralTalk [6] (2nd column) and Show, Attend and tell [7] (3rd column) so that both types of mechanisms can be compared i.e. with attention and without attention. As can be seen, the network has successfully described the region details of the image and the overall description is dense and more descriptive in comparison to existing state-of-the-art methods. For instance, in Table 2 (1st row), one can easily note that the overall network has successfully recognized buildings and white boat. Similarly, in all other examples, the network has included most of the object details in the image description clearly highlighting that the proposed architecture describes the scenes in a more detailed and dense manner.

3.3   Discussion

The proposed architecture performs better than the existing state-of-the-art methods in describing the scenes having complex nature or many objects. The reason behind this is that instead of describing image as a whole, it breaks the image into objects and generates their individual descriptions before generating full image caption.

Our system can detect parts of the objects e.g. "headboard" of bed shown Table 2 (4th row and 4th column). Similarly, it can detect attributes e.g. "wooden", relationships between objects e.g. "with" in the sentence "a bed with a comforter" etc. Other examples can be seen in Table 2. This type of in-depth description helps to explain minor details of the scene.

The datasets used for training the system contains generic images and natural scenes. The system can be made specific by training on different types of datasets e.g. cars dataset [10]. If the system is trained on cars dataset, then it will start generating descriptions which will include car models and years. Similarly, it can be trained on garments dataset [20] for more detailed attribute detection of the clothes. Capability of the system to generate more descriptive statements in a specific area can be increased by using these kinds of category specific datasets.

Although the approach works very well, a situation needs to be discussed here is when there can be some repeated object descriptions in the full caption. This is because one object can be detected at different box sizes and with high objectness scores, the system will always pick top scoring objects which is why one object can be selected multiple times. This problem cannot be easily minimized because there can be some real scenarios when same kind of objects appear multiple times in the scene, for instance, there can be an image having multiple large buildings. Considering this fact, the repeated objects cannot be completely eliminated from the descriptions.

4   Conclusion

In this research, we propose a modular dense captioning architecture for detailed image caption generation. Our approach localizes individual objects of the input image to extract object attributes and region descriptions prior to generate full image caption. Exploiting this regional information helps to incorporate important aspects of the image in the final description. The proposed architecture contains a region extraction module to detect the object regions using adapted RPN network. These regions are translated into region descriptions and object attributes using RNNs. Finally, the sentence generation module joins these two types of text descriptions using encoder-decoder framework to form single line syntactically and grammatically correct image caption. The system is evaluated on IAPR TC-12 dataset consisting of detailed descriptions against real life images. Our proposed architecture has out-performed existing state-of-the-art methodologies as depicted by both qualitative and quantitative results. For future work, extraction of rectangular regions can be altered to detect morphed regions [4]. Furthermore, the sentence generation module can be trained to join region descriptions and object attributes to form a sentence in another language giving an inherited translation effect.

References

1. Banerjee, S., Lavie, A.: METEOR: an automatic metric for MT evaluation with improved correlation with human judgments. In: Proceedings of the ACL Workshop on Intrinsic and Extrinsic Evaluation Measures for Machine Translation and/or Summarization, pp. 65–72 (2005)
2. Grubinger, M., Clough, P., Müller, H., Deselaers, T.: The IAPR TC-12 benchmark: A new evaluation resource for visual information systems. In: International workshop ontoImage. vol. 5, p. 10 (2006)
3. Hochreiter, S., Schmidhuber, J.: Long short-term memory. Neural Comput. **9**(8), 1735–1780 (1997)
4. Jaderberg, M., Simonyan, K., Zisserman, A.: Spatial transformer networks. In: Advances in Neural Information Processing Systems, pp. 2017–2025 (2015)
5. Johnson, J., Karpathy, A., Fei-Fei, L.: Densecap: fully convolutional localization networks for dense captioning. In: 2016 IEEE Conference on Computer Vision and Pattern Recognition (CVPR), pp. 4565–4574 (2016)
6. Karpathy, A., Fei-Fei, L.: Deep visual-semantic alignments for generating image descriptions. In: 2015 IEEE Conference on Computer Vision and Pattern Recognition (CVPR), pp. 3128–3137 (2015)
7. Kelvin, X., et al.: Show, attend and tell: neural image caption generation with visual attention, 1 June 2015
8. Kingma, D.P., Ba, J.: Adam: A method for stochastic optimization. arXiv preprint arXiv:1412.6980 (2014)
9. Kolb, P.: DISCO: A multilingual database of distributionally similar words. In: In Proceedings of KONVENS (2008)
10. Krause, J., Stark, M., Deng, J., Fei-Fei, L.: 3D object representations for fine-grained categorization. In: 2013 IEEE International Conference on Computer Vision Workshops (ICCVW), pp. 554–561. IEEE (2013)
11. Krishna, R., et al.: Visual genome: connecting language and vision using crowd-sourced dense image annotations. Int. J. Comput. Vis. **123**(1), 32–73 (2017)
12. Kulkarni, G., et al.: Baby talk: understanding and generating image descriptions. In: Proceedings of the 24th CVPR. Citeseer (2011)

13. Lin, C.Y.: ROUGE: A package for automatic evaluation of summaries. Text Summarization Branches Out (2004)

14. Lin, T.-Y., et al.: Microsoft COCO: common objects in context. In: Fleet, D., Pajdla, T., Schiele, B., Tuytelaars, T. (eds.) ECCV 2014. LNCS, vol. 8693, pp. 740–755. Springer, Cham (2014). https://doi.org/10.1007/978-3-319-10602-1_48

15. Lu, J., Xiong, C., Parikh, D., Socher, R.: Knowing when to look: adaptive attention via a visual sentinel for image captioning. In: Proceedings of the IEEE Conference on Computer Vision and Pattern Recognition (CVPR), vol. 6 (2017)

16. Manning, C.D.: Part-of-speech tagging from 97% to 100%: is it time for some linguistics? In: Gelbukh, A.F. (ed.) CICLing 2011. LNCS, vol. 6608, pp. 171–189. Springer, Heidelberg (2011). https://doi.org/10.1007/978-3-642-19400-9_14

17. Nganji, J.T., Brayshaw, M., Tompsett, B.: Describing and assessing image descriptions for visually impaired web users with IDAT. In: Proceedings of the Third International Conference on Intelligent Human Computer Interaction (IHCI 2011), Prague, Czech Republic, August 2011, pp. 27–37. Springer, Heidelberg (2013). https://doi.org/10.1007/978-3-642-31603-6_3

18. Papineni, K., Roukos, S., Ward, T., Zhu, W.J.: BLEU: a method for automatic evaluation of machine translation. In: Proceedings of the 40th Annual Meeting on Association for Computational Linguistics, pp. 311–318. Association for Computational Linguistics (2002)

19. Ren, S., He, K., Girshick, R., Sun, J.: Faster R-CNN: towards real-time object detection with region proposal networks, pp. 91–99 (2015)

20. Shen, J., et al.: Unified structured learning for simultaneous human pose estimation and garment attribute classification. IEEE Trans. Image Process. 23(11), 4786–4798 (2014)

21. Trundle, S.S., McCarthy, R.J., Martin, J.P., Slavin, A.J., Hutz, D.J.: Image surveillance and reporting technology (2015)

22. Vinyals, O., Toshev, A., Bengio, S., Erhan, D.: Show and tell: a neural image caption generator. In: 2015 IEEE Conference on Computer Vision and Pattern Recognition (CVPR), pp. 3156–3164. IEEE (2015)

23. Ye, C., Yang, Y., Mao, R., Fermüller, C., Aloimonos, Y.: What can i do around here? Deep functional scene understanding for cognitive robots. In: 2017 IEEE International Conference on Robotics and Automation (ICRA), pp. 4604–4611. IEEE (2017)

Pupil Localization Using Geodesic Distance

Radovan Fusek[(✉)]

FEECS, Department of Computer Science, Technical University of Ostrava,
17. listopadu 15, 708 33 Ostrava-Poruba, Czech Republic
radovan.fusek@vsb.cz

Abstract. The main contributions of the presented paper can be summarized as follows. Firstly, we introduce a unique and robust dataset of human eyes that can be used in many detection and recognition scenarios, especially for the recognition of driver drowsiness, gaze direction, or eye-blinking frequency. The dataset consists of approximately 85,000 different eye regions that were captured using various near-infrared cameras, various resolutions, and various lighting conditions. The images are annotated into many categories. Secondly, we present a new method for pupil localization that is based on the geodesic distance. The presented experiments show that the proposed method outperforms the state-of-the-art methods in this area.

Keywords: Pupil detection · Object detection · Shape analysis
Geodesic distance

1 Introduction

In this paper, we focus on the eye detection and pupil localization, especially for recognition of driver behavior inside the car cockpit (e.g. driver fatigue, drowsiness, gaze direction, or eye-blinking frequency). Driving safety is a very important topic and a robust drowsiness detection system can save a lot of human lives. Similar systems can be used for controlling various devices using the eyes as well. Many of the micro-sleep or drowsiness scenarios occur during late-night driving, and it is difficult to recognize them using classical RGB images and sensors which have big problems in low-light conditions. The use of the near-infrared cameras and images may represent an appropriate solution. These images are not so sensitive to different lighting conditions as the day and night images looks relatively similar thanks to IR illuminator, which is part of many IR cameras. Therefore, the quality of night images can be relatively good. However, lots of the state-of-the-art recognition approaches have to be tested or trained on a large number of different eye regions captured by infrared sensors. Obtaining such a large number images is difficult.

Therefore, we believe that the contribution of the paper is twofold. We offer the big dataset that was created using the images of various people using various

© Springer Nature Switzerland AG 2018
G. Bebis et al. (Eds.): ISVC 2018, LNCS 11241, pp. 433–444, 2018.
https://doi.org/10.1007/978-3-030-03801-4_38

IR cameras under many different lighting conditions. We proposed a new method for localization of pupil based on the geodesic distance. We tested the method on the two datasets (dataset [5] proposed by us and BioID dataset [9]).

The rest of the paper is organized as follows. The proposed dataset is described in Sect. 2. The previously presented papers from the area of eye analysis and pupil localization are mentioned in Sect. 3. In Sect. 4, the main ideas of proposed method are described. In Sect. 5, the results of experiments are presented showing the properties of the new method.

Fig. 1. Examples of images captured by an in-car infra-red camera.

Fig. 2. Examples of eye detection using the HOG-SVM detector that we created for automatic eye region detection. The images were obtained using different camera settings (e.g. different distances of the person). The eye images presented in the proposed dataset can be used to train the eye detector.

2   Proposed Dataset

Many datasets that contain eye images have been introduced in recent years. These datasets are usually recorded in good conditions and contain images in a high resolution, which makes them suitable for pupil detection, iris detection, eye tracking, or gaze detection. For the tasks such as pupil detection, high-resolution images are required to achieve precise detection. For example, the dataset focused on pupil tracking and the gaze detection was introduced in [12]. This dataset contains 720 × 480 eye images recorded by an infrared camera placed very close to the eye. The dataset presented in [14] is designed for the iris detection and contains the color and infra-red eye images of the size of 900 × 800 pixels, and the iris images of the size of 400 × 300 pixels. In [1], the authors introduced the dataset for eye tracking. This dataset contains videos of various people recorded in the resolution of 1280 × 720 by an RGB camera placed approximately 80 cm in front of the person. This setup makes the detection more challenging since the eye images have lower resolution, but it contains only the color images in which no IR reflections occur. The Closed Eyes In The Wild (CEW) dataset is mentioned in [15]. This dataset consists of approximately 5,000 eye images that are obtained from the Labeled Face in the Wild database [7]. However, the images are without IR reflections. In [13], the authors proposed the ZJU eyeblink database that contains indoor images (also without IR reflections). The eye images can also be obtained from the BioID Face database [9] (1521 gray level images), or the GI4E database [17] (1236 images acquired by a usual camera).

The quality of images that are included in the majority of the mentioned datasets usually does not correspond to the conditions that occur in the real environment when the ambient light or the distance of the person from camera is changing. We can suppose that (in near future) a lot of vehicles will be equipped with in-car cameras that watch the driver. Driver's fatigue or the gaze direction can be determined from these cameras. To reduce the cost of such equipments, low-cost cameras are often used; sample images are presented in Fig. 1. It is seen that the eye covers only a small region of the image. Unfortunately, the extracted eye images are usually of a lower quality, which makes the eye state estimation or the eye parts more difficult than it would be in the previously mentioned eye datasets. Hoverer, many detection methods are based on the training and testing process and it is difficult to acquire a big training dataset that consists of suitable images. Therefore, in this paper, we propose a new big dataset of human eye images captured by various near-infrared (NIR) cameras (e.g. Intel Realsense, IDS Imaging cameras).

2.1   The Eye Regions

To obtain eye images, we manually cropped many thousands of eye regions from several NIR images at the first stage; the sample input images are presented in Fig. 1. At the second stage, we used the manually cropped images to train the eye detector based on the histogram of oriented gradients combined with the SVM classifier. This detector was used to automatically extract the eye regions. The example of eye region detection is shown in Fig. 2. After the detection step, we thoroughly checked each detected region and we removed the false positives. We created and checked 85,000 eye images of various people (37 different persons) captured in various lighting conditions and situations; the dataset contains images of different quality with different properties. In the following paragraphs, we will show the examples of eyes that can be found in the proposed dataset.

For example, the eyes of persons with eye glasses are shown in the first row in Fig. 3. The problems that often occur with the glasses are reflections.

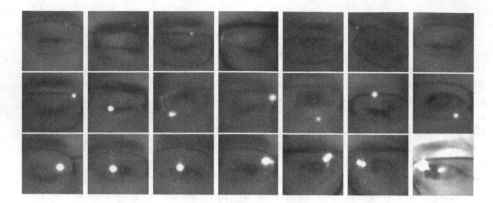

Fig. 3. Examples of eyes with glasses and reflections that are included in the proposed dataset.

Fig. 4. Examples of eye reflections without glasses that are included in the proposed dataset.

In the dataset, we focused on this problem and we provide lots of images with reflections. Moreover, for each eye image, we provide three state of reflections based on the size of reflections areas in each image; no reflections (the first row in Fig. 3), small reflections (Fig. 3), and big reflections (the third row in Fig. 3). In Fig. 4, the dataset examples show that the reflections can also occur without glasses (e.g. in sclera and pupil).

In general, a lot of women use synthetic eyelash and eyebrow, which can cause the problem for the recognizers of gaze direction and eye state. Therefore, in the dataset, we also provide the information about the gender of each person. The examples of open and closed eyes of woman with a tinted eyelash or eyebrow are shown in Fig. 5.

2.2 Annotation and Statistics of Dataset

In order to simplify the comparison of algorithms, the images are divided into several categories, which also makes the dataset suitable for training and testing classifiers. We annotated the following properties:

- subject ID; in the dataset, we collected the data of 37 different persons (33 men and 4 women)
- image ID; the dataset consists of 84, 898 images
- gender [0 - man, 1 - woman]; the dataset contains the information about gender of the person in each image (man, woman)

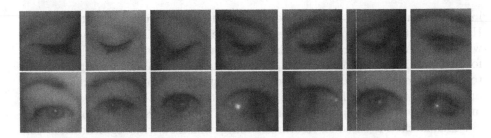

Fig. 5. Examples of women eyes with a tinted eyelash or eyebrow that are included in the proposed dataset.

- glasses [0 - no, 1 - yes]; the information if the eye image contains glasses is also provided for each image (with and without the glasses); 24,001 images with glasses
- eye state [0 - closed, 1 - open]; this property contains the information about two eye states (41,945 closed and 42,953 open);
- reflections [0 - none, 1 - small, 2 - big]; we annotated three reflection states based on the size of reflections (66,060 none, 6,129 small, and 12,709 big reflections)
- lighting conditions [0 - bad, 1 - good]; based on the amount of light during capturing the videos (53,630 bad, 31,268 good)
- sensor ID [01 - RealSense, 02 - IDS, 03 - Aptina]; at this moment, the dataset contains the images captured by three different sensors (Intel RealSense RS 300 sensor with 640 × 480 resolution, IDS Imaging sensor with 1280 × 1024 resolution, and Aptina sensor with 752 × 480 resolution)
- aside from the previous properties, we also provide the annotation for approximately 15,000 pupil points (images)

In summary, the dataset contains eye images in low resolutions, images with reflections in the eyes, or with reflections on glasses that are caused by the IR illuminator placed in front of the person. Some eye images in which the head is not aiming at the camera are also included. All these types of images in this dataset make detection of eye parts more difficult than it would be in the previously mentioned eye datasets. The collection is available for the public [5].

3   Related Work

In the area of eye analysis and pupil localization, many methods were proposed in recent years. A head-mounted eye-tracking system (starburst) was presented in [11]. The starburst method combines feature-based and model-based approaches. In the first step, the corneal reflection is removed. In the next step, the pupil edge points are located using feature-based method. Finally, the detected edge points are used for ellipse fitting using RANSAC. Another pupil localization method that used RANSAC (for ellipse fitting) was proposed by Swirsky et al.

in [16]. In this method, the approximate position of pupil is estimated using a Haar-like feature detector. In the next step, the k-means histogram segmentation with RANSAC is performed. An Exclusive Curve Selector (ExCuSe) algorithm for eye-tracking was proposed in [3]. The method uses the Canny edge detector to filter the edges that cannot correspond to the pupil, followed by the straight line removal technique. Finally, the ellipse is fitted using the direct least squares method. A low cost pupil detection method (known as SET) was proposed in [8]. This method is based on the thresholding combined with segmentation. The pupil border is then extracted using the convex hull method and the best segment is selected.

Another pupil detection method named Ellipse Selector (known as ElSe) was presented in [4]. The first step of ElSE is based on the Canny edge detector. In the second step, edge thinning (using the morphologic approach) and deletion of edges with too many neighbors are performed. In the next steps, straight lines are removed, and ellipse evaluation combined with pupil validation is realized. If the approach cannot find a suitable pupil edge, a next way for pupil localization is chosen. In this case, the authors used two different convolution filters (surface difference filter and mean filter) to find the best position of the pupil. The authors reported that the ElSe achieved high detection rates and a fast runtime in comparison to state-of-the-art algorithms (ExCuse, SET, Starburst, Swirsky).

The method for localization of iris center position was proposed in [6]. In this approach, the selected candidates of boundary points of iris are used to fit an ellipse using the RANSAC algorithm. In [10], the pupil localization method based on the training process (supervised) was presented. This approach uses the Hough regression forest. Evaluation of the state-of-the-art pupil detection algorithms was presented in [2].

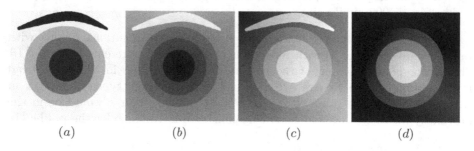

(a) (b) (c) (d)

Fig. 6. An ideal eye model and the first steps of the proposed method for localization of the approximate (potential) regions of the eyeball. The input image (a). The visualization of the distance function from the centroid (b) and the left corner (c). The difference (d) (only non-zero distances are shown) between (c) and (b). The values of distance function are depicted by the level of brightness; in the input image, minimum amount of noise is added for more realistic visualization of distances.

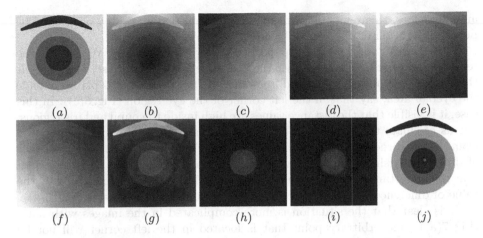

Fig. 7. A noisy eye model and the main steps of the proposed method. The input image (a). The visualization of the distance function from the centroid (b) and from the particular corners (c, d, e, f). The mean of all corner distances (g). The difference (h) between (g) and (b) (only non-zero distances are shown). The convolution step (i). The final position of pupil center (j). The values of distance function are depicted by the level of brightness.

4   Proposed Method

The main idea of the proposed method for the localization of pupil center is based on the fact that the pupil center can be localized using the geodesic distances in the image. Since the approach also takes into account physiological properties of eyes, let us consider the following ideal case of eye model in Fig. 6(a); we suppose that the position of eye region is obtained beforehand (e.g. using facial landmarks or classical eye or face detectors). In this model, the pupil is represented by the black circle area that is surrounded by a slightly brighter area of iris, and the iris area is surrounded by brighter sclera. The goal of the pupil localization methods is to find the black circular pupil area only. The location of the pupil center is crucial information for gaze direction recognition.

In the first step of the proposed method, the approximate (potential) regions of the pupil are localized. In general, the pupil can be located arbitrarily in the eye region, however (for simplicity), we consider that the position of pupil is close to the center of the eye region in our theoretical model. Therefore, suppose a point (centroid) that is placed in the center of this eye region. Let us compute the geodesic distance function from the centroid to all other points inside the image. The visualization of the distance function values is shown in Fig. 6(b). In general, the geodesic distance between two points computes the shortest curve that connects both points along the image manifold. Therefore, the values of distance function are low inside the eyeball area; especially in the pupil and iris (Fig. 6(b)). This step is also important for the removal of eyebrow. It can be observed that the values of distance function are high in the area of eyebrow and, therefore, this region is not expected to be a potential area of pupil. The potential location of pupil is in the areas with low distances.

In the next step, the area of pupil is detected more reliably. We finalize the removal of the eyebrow and sclera in the ideal case. For this purpose, suppose that the geodesic distance is calculated from an arbitrary point that is placed outside the eyeball area; say that in the left corner of the eye region (Fig. 6(c)). In this case, it is visible that the distance values are high inside the pupil and iris regions. Let us calculate the difference between the distance function values computed from the left corner (Fig. 6(c)) and the centroid (Fig. 6(b)). In Fig. 6(d), the result of difference is shown; only non-zero distance values are shown. It can be seen that the important areas of eyeball (iris and pupil) are correctly indicated by the value of difference without the sclera and other unwanted eye parts (Fig. 6(d)).

It is clear that the situation is more complicated in the images with noise (Fig. 7(a)). One arbitrary point that is located in the left corner will not be enough to equally cover the whole image. Therefore, we suggest to calculate the geodesic distance from each image corner separately (Fig. 7(c–f)) and use the mean of four distance matrices (Fig. 7(g)) for the difference with the distance function values from the centroid (Fig. 7(b)). Again, it can be seen that the eyebrow and sclera are removed using this difference step. In Fig. 7(h), it can be observed that the mentioned difference gives the highest values in the pupil area in this case.

In the final step, the pupil center is localized by the convolution operation applied to image in Fig. 7(h). Since we consider that a real center of pupil is the location with the maximum distance value in the previously calculated difference matrix (Fig. 7(h)), we suggest the use of the Gaussian kernel. The center of the pupil is then determined as the location with the maximal value after the convolution step (Fig. 7(j)). In Fig. 7(i), the result of convolution operation is shown.

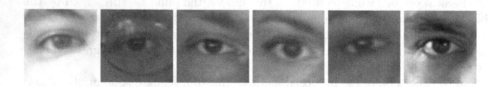

Fig. 8. Examples of BioID eye images.

5   Experiments

To evaluate the results of the presented method, we used two datasets; BioID [9] and the proposed dataset [5]. The BioID dataset contains 1521 gray level images with the resolution of 384×286 pixels in different indoor environments. We extracted the eye images based on the eye corner positions provided by the authors of the dataset. In Fig. 8, examples of BioID eye images that are used for experiments are shown. It is important to note that the eye images from BioID dataset were purposely extracted with the eyebrow to test the methods in complicated conditions. The size of each extracted eye image (from both datasets) is 100 × 100 pixels in the following experiments.

In Fig. 9, the detection process of the proposed method can be seen in an image taken from the proposed dataset. In Fig. 10, the detection process of the proposed method can be seen in the image taken from the BioID dataset.

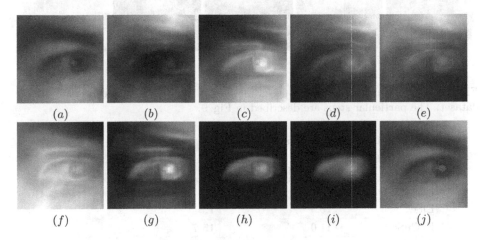

Fig. 9. The main steps of the proposed method in the image taken from the proposed dataset. The input image (a). The visualization of the distance function from the centroid (b) and from the particular corners (c, d, e, f). The mean of all corner distances (g). The difference (h) between (g) and (b) (only non-zero distances are shown). The convolution step (i). The final position of pupil center (j). The values of distance function are depicted by the level of brightness.

For comparison with the state-of-the-art methods, we used two renowned methods: ElSe and ExCuSe. For ElSe, we used the setting for remotely acquired images published by the authors of the algorithm in [2]. In Table 1, the detection results of methods are shown. The provided (absolute) error is calculated as the Euclidean distance between the ground truth of pupil center and the center provided by the particular detection method. From the results, it can be seen that the proposed detector based on the geodesic distance is the best performing approach. Especially on the BioID dataset, the proposed method has a very small error 5.5 pixels. The achieved results reflect that the proposed method is developed to work also in the images with eyebrows; in contrast to the other tested methods. In the case of the proposed dataset, our method also achieved a lower error (6.2 pixels) than the state-of-the-art methods. However, it is important to note that ElSe achieved relatively good results (7.5 pixels) on the proposed dataset. Examples of images in which our method works better compared to

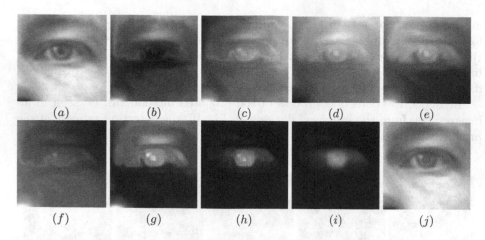

Fig. 10. The main steps of the proposed method in the image taken from the BioID dataset. The particular steps are described in Fig. 9.

Table 1. A comparison of average absolute errors.

	Error BioID (pixels)	Error Prop. Dataset (pixels)
Proposed method	5.5	6.2
ElSe	10.5	7.5
ExCuSe	11.0	15.7

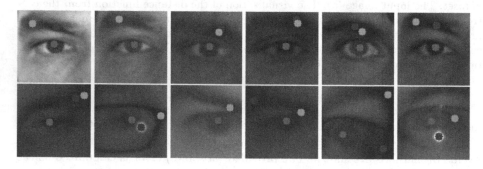

Fig. 11. Examples of comparison of the methods for pupil center localization (the first row: BioID dataset, the second row: proposed dataset); proposed method - red, ElSe - green, ExCuSe - blue. (Color figure online)

other tested methods are shown in Fig. 11. In this figure, it is visible that the typical cause of errors is the presence of eyebrow.

As was mentioned in the previous section, the final step of the presented method is based on convolution with the Gaussian kernel. In our experiments, the kernel size was set to 7×7 pixels, and the standard deviation was 3. We note that the average time needed for processing one eye region on an Intel core i3 processor (3.7 GHz) took approximately 9.0 milliseconds.

6 Conclusion

We believe that the contribution of the paper is twofold. We present a new method for localization of the pupil center. We offer the big dataset [5] used for evaluating the new method (together with the BioID dataset [9]).

Based on the experiment results, we can conclude that the proposed method based on the geodesic distance achieved very promising detection score. It is worth mentioning that various other distances can be used as well. We leave the experiments with various types of distance for future work.

Acknowledgments. This work was partially supported by Grant of SGS No. SP2018/42, VŠB - Technical University of Ostrava, Czech Republic.

References

1. Ferhat, O., Vilarino, F., Sanchez, F.J.: A cheap portable eye-tracker solution for common setups. J. Eye Mov. Res. **7**(3) (2014)
2. Fuhl, W., Geisler, D., Santini, T., Rosenstiel, W., Kasneci, E.: Evaluation of state-of-the-art pupil detection algorithms on remote eye images. In: Proceedings of the 2016 ACM International Joint Conference on Pervasive and Ubiquitous Computing: Adjunct, UbiComp 2016, pp. 1716–1725. ACM, New York (2016). https://doi.org/10.1145/2968219.2968340
3. Fuhl, W., Kübler, T., Sippel, K., Rosenstiel, W., Kasneci, E.: ExCuSe: robust pupil detection in real-world scenarios. In: Azzopardi, G., Petkov, N. (eds.) CAIP 2015. LNCS, vol. 9256, pp. 39–51. Springer, Cham (2015). https://doi.org/10.1007/978-3-319-23192-1_4
4. Fuhl, W., Santini, T.C., Kübler, T.C., Kasneci, E.: Else: Ellipse selection for robust pupil detection in real-world environments. CoRR abs/1511.06575 (2015). http://arxiv.org/abs/1511.06575
5. Fusek, R.: MRL eye dataset. http://mrl.cs.vsb.cz/eyedataset (Jan 2018)
6. George, A., Routray, A.: Fast and accurate algorithm for eye localisation for gaze tracking in low-resolution images. IET Comput. Vis. **10**(7), 660–669 (2016)
7. Huang, G.B., Ramesh, M., Berg, T., Learned-Miller, E.: Labeled faces in the wild: a database for studying face recognition in unconstrained environments. Technical report 07–49, University of Massachusetts, Amherst, October 2007
8. Javadi, A.H., Hakimi, Z., Barati, M., Walsh, V., Tcheang, L.: Set: a pupil detection method using sinusoidal approximation. Front. Neuroeng. **8**, 4 (2015). https://www.frontiersin.org/article/10.3389/fneng.2015.00004
9. Jesorsky, O., Kirchberg, K.J., Frischholz, R.W.: Robust face detection using the hausdorff distance. In: Bigun, J., Smeraldi, F. (eds.) AVBPA 2001. LNCS, vol. 2091, pp. 90–95. Springer, Heidelberg (2001). https://doi.org/10.1007/3-540-45344-X_14
10. Kacete, A., Royan, J., Seguier, R., Collobert, M., Soladie, C.: Real-time eye pupil localization using hough regression forest. In: 2016 IEEE Winter Conference on Applications of Computer Vision (WACV), pp. 1–8, March 2016

11. Li, D., Winfield, D., Parkhurst, D.J.: Starburst: a hybrid algorithm for video-based eye tracking combining feature-based and model-based approaches. In: 2005 IEEE Computer Society Conference on Computer Vision and Pattern Recognition (CVPR 2005) - Workshops, pp. 79–79, June 2005
12. McMurrough, C.D., Metsis, V., Rich, J., Makedon, F.: An eye tracking dataset for point of gaze detection. In: Proceedings of the Symposium on Eye Tracking Research and Applications, ETRA 2012, pp. 305–308. ACM, New York (2012)
13. Pan, G., Sun, L., Wu, Z., Lao, S.: Eyeblink-based anti-spoofing in face recognition from a generic webcamera. In: 2007 IEEE 11th International Conference on Computer Vision, pp. 1–8, October 2007
14. Sequeira, A., et al.: Cross-eyed - cross-spectral iris/periocular recognition database and competition. In: 2016 International Conference of the Biometrics Special Interest Group (BIOSIG), pp. 1–5, September 2016
15. Song, F., Tan, X., Liu, X., Chen, S.: Eyes closeness detection from still images with multi-scale histograms of principal oriented gradients. Pattern Recognit. **47**(9), 2825–2838 (2014)
16. Świrski, L., Bulling, A., Dodgson, N.: Robust real-time pupil tracking in highly off-axis images. In: Proceedings of the Symposium on Eye Tracking Research and Applications, ETRA 2012, pp. 173–176. ACM, New York (2012). https://doi.org/10.1145/2168556.2168585
17. Villanueva, A., Ponz, V., Sesma-Sanchez, L., Ariz, M., Porta, S., Cabeza, R.: Hybrid method based on topography for robust detection of iris center and eye corners. ACM Trans. Multimedia Comput. Commun. Appl. **9**(4), 25:1–25:20 (2013). https://doi.org/10.1145/2501643.2501647

Parallel Curves Detection Using Multi-agent System

Shengzhi Du[1(✉)] and Chunling Tu[2]

[1] Department of Electrical Engineering, Tshwane University of Technology,
Pretoria 0001, South Africa
dushengzhi@gmail.com
[2] Department of Computer Systems Engineering,
Tshwane University of Technology, Pretoria 0001, South Africa
tclchunling@gmail.com

Abstract. This paper addresses the possibility of modelling pixel spacial relationship of curves in images using the movement of second order dynamic systems. A multi-agent system is then considered to control the 'movement' of pixels in a single image to detect parallel curves. The music scripts are used as example to demonstrate the performance of the proposed method. The experiment results show that it is reliable to model the pixel spatial chain (pixels positioned adjacently or nearly connected in sequence) by the dynamics of a second order system, and the proposed multi-agent method has potential to detect parallel curves in images.

Keywords: Dynamic systems · Multi-agent consensus
Coupling systems · Line detection · Curve detection
Image pixel modelling

1 Introduction

Since the beginning of 20th century, the control systems theory has been developed to a complete theory framework. Benefitting from the mechanism of feedback, state observation, and performance analysis, control systems have been successful in numerous applications in engineering across almost all fields. The concepts and tools developed in control systems can be easily embedded to other fields.

As an important component of computer vision, basic object/shape detection determines the success of subsequent operations. Various algorithms were proposed to detect geometric shapes, such as straight lines, circles, ellipse, rectangles, and even arbitrary irregular shapes. These algorithms can be categorized to the analytic methods such as Hough Transform and its varieties, and statistical methods such as artificial neural network.

With the advances of complete concepts and tools in control systems theory, however, there were few ideas reported to embed these ideas in image processing. One reason might be the fact that control systems theory usually needs

© Springer Nature Switzerland AG 2018
G. Bebis et al. (Eds.): ISVC 2018, LNCS 11241, pp. 445–454, 2018.
https://doi.org/10.1007/978-3-030-03801-4_39

a model to present the physical systems to be studied, however, the pixel-wise image processing does not explicitly provide this convenience. For instance, the pixels are basically assumed to be able to appear at any position in the 2D space regardless of physical possibility. However, when physical objects are contained in images, the pixels appearing either on the boundaries or inside of the contour have to be constrained by some geometric principles, i.e. not just being 'irrationally' positioned but somehow determined or rational. The exceptions might be random noise, which are usually supposed to be removed. So it is possible to model these 'meaningful' pixels by physical or mathematical models.

This paper prompts to model the most common pattern existing in images, that is the pixel clusters connected or nearly positioned in a spatial chain (or a curve), using second order dynamic systems. The states(or their observations) are used to present the position of the pixels, i.e., presenting the spatial pixel chain by the trajectory of the dynamic systems. To demonstrate this idea, a multi-agent system is then proposed to detect the parallel curves in distorted music scripts as example. The application of the proposed method is not only limited to parallel curves detection. By extend the coupling relationship of agents, it is possible to detect other geometry shapes or curves.

The rest of the paper is organized as follows: Sect. 2 introduces the relevant works that the paper establishes its idea on; Sect. 3 describes the second order dynamic systems and a multi-agent system presenting the pixel spatial chain(s); Sect. 4 demonstrate some experiments and results; Sect. 5 concludes the paper and shows future work.

2   Related Works

With the development of computer vision, varieties of object detection applications were developed, such as vehicle detection [1], human detection [2], wildlife detection [3] etc. All of object detection methods need the basic patterns, such as straight lines, boundaries, edges, contours, area, etc. Most of the these basic patterns can be considered as spatial pixel chains or curves. This section will focus on the existing curve detection methods and control systems which can be considered to present these curves using their trajectories (states or their observations).

2.1   Straight Line and Curve Detection

Straight lines are basic and most common pattern forming geometric shapes. Hough transform [4] and its varieties are widely considered to detect straight lines or its components [5].

With the assumption of the existence of a straight line supported by a group of pixels, some statistical methods such as regression or fitting methods were also reported [6].

When arbitrary irregular shapes are considered, curve detection gets the advantages, such as parametric [7] or non-parametric [8–11] methods.

2.2   Second Order Dynamic Systems

In control theory, second order systems are most common objects to be studied because of the following facts: (1) the state dynamics of such system can be easily analyzed with accurate results, (2) most high order dynamic systems can be approximated by second order systems with acceptable 'error', (3) many algorithms are available for the performance analysis and control of second order systems. A basic state representation of a second order dynamic system is shown in Eq. (1).

$$\begin{cases} \dot{X} = AX + Bu \\ Y = CX + Du \end{cases} \tag{1}$$

where $X = [x_1, x_2]^T$ is the state vector, $A = \begin{bmatrix} a_{11} & a_{12} \\ a_{21} & a_{22} \end{bmatrix}$ is the state transition matrix, $B = [0, 1]^T$ is the control input gain, u is the control variable or reference, Y is the system output (which is ignored with the whole output equation in this paper, because only the system state X is considered to present the spatial pixel chain).

2.3   Multi-agent Systems

Multi-agent systems consist of multiple subsystems (agents) which can communicate to some of other subsystems (agents) towards some common goals, i.e. consensus, for example the formation of states (such as relative positions) of agents. Various forms of multi-agent system were developed [12,13]. In control theory, the coupling dynamic systems shown in Eq. (2) is a typical multi-agent system.

$$\dot{X}_i = A_i X_i + B_i u_i \tag{2}$$

where X_i, A_i, B_i, u_i are the state, transition matrix, input gain, and input variable of the ith agent respectively. u_i is usually coupled with some other agents (containing information of other agents) in the form of

$$u_i = K(Cf(X_1, ..., X_{i-1}, X_{i+1}, ..., X_N) - X_i) \tag{3}$$

where K is the control gain, C is the coupling factor, N is the number of agents that coupled with agent i, f is a linear or nonlinear function of other agents' states.

3   The Proposed Method

This research aims to model the spatial pixel chain by the state trajectory of dynamic systems, and build multi-agent system to detect parallel curves in music scripts.

3.1 Potentials of Modeling Spatial Pixel Chain by the State Trajectory of Second Order Dynamic Systems

Noise exists commonly in digital images, which makes errors influencing the performance of various computer vision tasks. Generally, noise can be grouped into structural and nonstructural categories. Nonstructural noise usually demonstrate some random properties, which might not abide determinable principles. These random noise is more common, but with relatively less influences.

Considering the physical dynamic systems usually have some 'mass' therefore 'inertia', so their state trajectories are 'smooth' in a small time span. This property can be used to describe some 'smooth' edges/curves commonly existing on the boundaries of geometric shapes. Because of the 'inertia', the state trajectory abides some physical or mathematical principles, therefore, conquer influences from the 'irrational' nonstructural noise.

This section aims to demonstrate the potential of modelling the pixel spatial chain by the state trajectory of second order dynamic systems.

Considering the state transition equation of the system in Eq. (1)

$$\dot{X} = AX + Bu \tag{4}$$

where $X = [x_p, x_v]^T$, x_p and x_v are the position and velocity of the object described by the system, and $\dot{X} = [x_v, x_a]^T$ with x_a the acceleration of the object. If

$$\begin{cases} A = \begin{bmatrix} 0 & 1 \\ 0 & 0 \end{bmatrix} \\ B = [0, 1]^T \end{cases} \tag{5}$$

then the object acceleration is controlled only by the control input u.

To consider the 'internal' dynamics of the system, one can simply set

$$\begin{cases} A = \begin{bmatrix} 0 & 1 \\ a_{21} & a_{22} \end{bmatrix} \\ B = [0, 1]^T \end{cases} \tag{6}$$

where a_{21} and a_{22} are typically selected as negative values to maintain the stability of dynamic systems. Then the system acceleration will be determined by both the internal dynamics X and external control input u.

When a single system or uncoupled systems are considered, u is relevant to the reference signal obtained from images and the system states. For the sake of simplicity of explanation, when the curve is a single valued function, u is determined by the difference of reference signal p (vertical positions of pixels locating on a spatial chain) and the system state X_i, as shown in Eq. (7).

$$u_i = BK([p_{i,t} \ \ 0]^T - X_i) \tag{7}$$

where K is the control gain. In this case, the horizontal position of pixels is considered as time t.

For the curves formed by multi-valued functions (for instance, a circle in an image might have two points on a horizontal coordinate), the 2D coordinates can be represented by two second order dynamic systems with implicit time t.

The 'inertia' will make the trajectory smooth according to its internal dynamics, therefore, depress the irrational noises.

3.2   Multi-agent System for Parallel Curves Detection

Considering the boundaries of geometric shapes usually consist of multiple components of curves, and their properties, such as the position, the orientation, and the length, are strongly relative to each other to form the object contour. These clues are important sources of human vision system to recognize objects. These strongly coupled curves can be modelled by the state trajectories of the agents in a multi-agent system as shown in Eq. (2) and the control u as shown in Eq. (8).

$$u_i = B_i K(p_{i,t} - X_i) + B_i C(f(X_1, ..., X_{i-1}, X_{i+1}, ..., X_N) - X_i) \qquad (8)$$

where K is the control gain, C is the coupling factor, N is the number of agents that coupled with agent i, f is a linear or nonlinear function of other agents' states. Figure 1 demonstrates the system diagram.

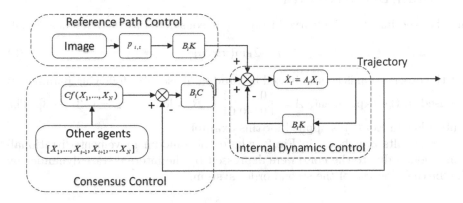

Fig. 1. The control diagram of the proposed multiagent system

4   Experiments and Results

To demonstrate the performance of the proposed method, both synthetic and real images are used to setup experiments.

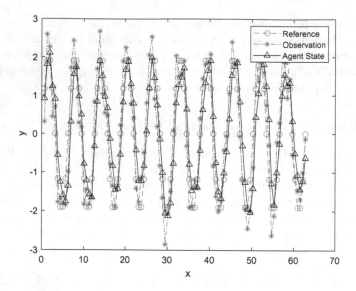

Fig. 2. The single curve detection using the proposed dynamic control system

4.1 Modelling Single Curve Using the State Trajectory of a Second Order Dynamic System

In this experiment, a sine curve in Eq. (9) is considered as the reference signal,

$$y = 2\sin(\pi x/5) \tag{9}$$

but the observation is contaminated by random noise. The following parameters are used in the experiment, $A = \begin{bmatrix} 0 & 1 \\ 0 & -0.01 \end{bmatrix}, B = [0 \ 1]^T, K = [-3 \ -3]$. The control law in Eq. (7) is applied for this example.

The results are shown in Fig. 2, where the random movements('irrational' components) due to the noise were depressed by the internal state dynamics by the 'instinct inertia' of the second order system.

4.2 Modelling Parallel Curves Using the State Trajectory of a Multiagent System

In this experiment, a set of parallel sine curves in Eq. (10) are considered as the reference signals for the agents respectively,

$$y_i = 2\sin(\pi x_i/5) + 10(i - 1), \quad i = 1, ..., 5 \tag{10}$$

The observations are contaminated by random noise $n = N(0, 4)$. The following parameters are used in the experiment, $A = \begin{bmatrix} 0 & 1 \\ 0 & -0.01 \end{bmatrix}, B = [0 \ 1]^T, K = [-3 \ -3]$,

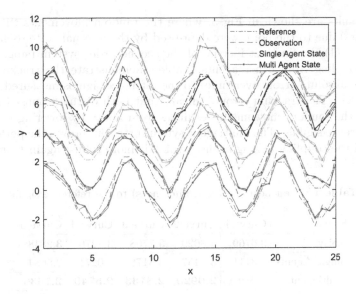

Fig. 3. Parallel curves detections using the proposed multiagent system

To implement the coupling of other agents in the control law in Eq. (8), the Kronecker tensor product is applied to A and BK as follows.

$$A_1 = \text{kron}(I_N, A) \tag{11}$$

where N is the number of agents (5 for this example), and I_N is N-by-N unity.

$$B_1 = \text{kron}(NI_N - 1_N, BK) \tag{12}$$

where 1_N is the N-by-N matrix will all elements equal to 1. Then the state transition equation becomes

$$\dot{X} = A_1 X + B_1(X - h) + K(r - X) \tag{13}$$

where

$$X = [x_p^1 \ x_v^1, ..., x_p^N \ x_v^N]^T \tag{14}$$

$$h = \begin{bmatrix} 2 & 0 \\ 4 & 0 \\ 6 & 0 \\ 8 & 0 \\ 10 & 0 \end{bmatrix} \tag{15}$$

and $[y1(t) \ 0 \ y2(t) \ 0 \ y3(t) \ 0 \ y4(t) \ 0 \ y5(t) \ 0]'$

$$X = [x_p^1 \ x_v^1, ..., x_p^N \ x_v^N]^T \tag{16}$$

$$r = [y_1 \ 0, ..., y_N \ 0]^T \tag{17}$$

The results are shown in Fig. 3, where the random movements ('irrational' components) due to the noise were depressed by the internal state dynamics by two factors: (1) the 'instinct inertia' of the second order system (single agent), and (2) coupling from other agents. Table 1 demonstrate the tracking errors (average of absolute errors over time) to the reference signals measured with the unit of pixels. The tracking errors indicate that both of the proposed methods depressed the random movements resulting from noise, by lowering differences to the reference signals. The multiagent sytem further improves the performance because of the coupling among agents, which is more robust against 'irrational' dynamics.

Table 1. The tracking errors (differences) to the reference signal

Signal	Curve 1	Curve 2	Curve 3	Curve 4	Curve 5
Noisy	3.6769	4.0629	3.7708	3.4270	3.2848
Single Agents	3.3111	3.5457	3.3178	3.0271	2.5684
Multiagent	**2.8081**	**2.9920**	**2.8133**	**2.5749**	**2.1636**

4.3   Evaluation of the Proposed Methods in Real World Image

This experiment aims to validate the proposed methods in real images. The deformed music scripts are considered with the objective to detected the distorted parallel lines. Because of the script book pages are not flat, the picture captured got deformation, therefore, the parallel straight lines becomes parallel curves. To obtain the reference signals, a starting section, the green straight lines denoted in Fig. 5 is obtained using the improved Hough Transform [5]. These straight line segments are considered as the reference signals at the initial stage. Then each initial reference signal was extrapolated to establish a box which is validated by the pixels iteratively. The detection results (red curves in Fig. 5) show some robustness against random noise and structural disturbances (the music elements in the scripts, such as the notes, connection lines, slur curves, and bar lines, etc) (Fig. 4).

Fig. 4. Music scripts with distorted parallel curves

For the case of wide curves (multiple pixel width), the reference signal can be obtained by averaging the pixel positions for a given horizontal coordinate. Therefore, the proposed method tracks the central line of the curves.

Fig. 5. Detected parallel curves (Color figure online)

4.4   Discussion on Parameter Selection and Running Time of the Proposed System

The selection of A, B, K, and N in the proposed method is based on the following two aspects of the multi-agent system: (1) stability; (2) response speed (time constant). According to the dynamics of the curves (reference signals), these parameters should be selected considering both of these two aspects.

The running time of the proposed method depends on the agent number N (the number of curves to be detected). Given N, the running time is determined by solving of differential equations in Eq. (16). Fast differential equation solvers are available to cater this need.

5   Conclusion

In this paper, we proposed the idea of modelling curves in images using the state trajectory of second order dynamic systems. A multi-agent system, in the form of a set of strongly coupled dynamics systems, is then used to detect the parallel curves of music scripts. The proposed method has the following advantages: (1) the internal dynamics depresses the noises and makes the curves more rational, (2) not only irrational noise but also structural noise can be depressed by the proposed methods, (3) the proposed is a non-parametric method so no curve equations are needed, (4) the intrinsic coupling boundaries among the curves forming geometric shapes become the clue guiding multi-agent system states evolution, and as return these properties are kept and enhanced.

The experiments based on synthetic and real images demonstrated that the proposed method is suitable to model and detect curves from digital images. The future work includes how to contain reference generating in the multiagent system, therefore, the multiagent system can detect parallel curves independently(without the need of other methods to generate the reference signal). To detect unparallel curves, such as the curves forming closed geometric shapes, is another future work to be done.

References

1. Tu, C.-L., Du, S.-Z.: Moving vehicle detection in dynamic traffic contexts. In: Hussain, A. (ed.) Electronics, Communications and Networks V. LNEE, vol. 382, pp. 263–269. Springer, Singapore (2016). https://doi.org/10.1007/978-981-10-0740-8_30
2. Santoso, P.S., Hang, H.-M.: Learning-based human detection applied to RGB-D images. In: IEEE International Conference on Image Processing (ICIP) (2017)
3. Du, S., Du, C., Abdoola, R., van Wyk, B.J.: A gaussian mixture model feature for wildlife detection. In: Bebis, G., et al. (eds.) ISVC 2016. LNCS, vol. 10072, pp. 757–765. Springer, Cham (2016). https://doi.org/10.1007/978-3-319-50835-1_68
4. Hough Paul, V.C.: Method and means for recognizing complex patterns. U.S. Patent 3,069,654, issued December 18 (1962)
5. Du, S., Tu, C., van Wyk, B.J., Chen, Z.: Collinear segment detection using HT neighborhoods. IEEE Trans. Image Process. **20**(12), 3912–3920 (2011)
6. Xu, Z., Shin, B.-S., Klette, R.: A statistical method for line segment detection. Comput. Vis. Image Underst. **138**, 61–73 (2015)
7. Levashov, A.E., Yurin, D.V.: Fast parametric curves detection based on statistical hypotheses estimation. Pattern Recognit. Image Anal. **23**(4), 445–454 (2013)
8. Sandberg, K.: The curve filter transform – a robust method for curve enhancement. In: Bebis, G., et al. (eds.) ISVC 2010. LNCS, vol. 6454, pp. 107–116. Springer, Heidelberg (2010). https://doi.org/10.1007/978-3-642-17274-8_11
9. Sandberg, K.: Curve enhancement using orientation fields. In: Bebis, G., et al. (eds.) ISVC 2009. LNCS, vol. 5875, pp. 564–575. Springer, Heidelberg (2009). https://doi.org/10.1007/978-3-642-10331-5_53
10. Sandberg, K., Brega, M.: Segmentation of thin structures in electron micrographs using orientation fields. J. Struct. Biol. **157**(2), 403–415 (2007)
11. Bowman, A.W., Pope, A., Ismail, B.: Detecting discontinuities in nonparametric regression curves and surfaces. Stat. Comput. **16**(4), 377–390 (2006)
12. Hou, J., Zheng, R.: Hierarchical consensus problem via group information exchange. IEEE Trans. Cybern. **PP**(99), 1–7 (2018)
13. Abraham, I., Murphey, T.D.: Decentralized ergodic control: distribution-driven sensing and exploration for multiagent systems. IEEE Robot. Autom. Lett. **3**(4) (2018)

Can Deep Learning Learn the Principle of Closed Contour Detection?

Xinhua Zhang[1,2], Yijing Watkins[2], and Garrett T. Kenyon[2(✉)]

[1] Department of Computer Science, University of New Mexico,
Albuquerque, NM 87131, USA
xinhua@unm.edu
[2] Computer and Computational Science Division,
CCS-3, Los Alamos National Laboratory, Los Alamos, NM 87544, USA
{twatkins,gkenyon}@lanl.gov

Abstract. Learning the principle of a task should always be the primary goal of a learning system. Otherwise it reduces to a memorizing system and there always exists edge cases. In spite of its recent success in visual recognition tasks, convolutional neural networks' (CNNs) ability to learn principles is still questionable. While CNNs exhibit a certain degree of generalization, they eventually break when the variability exceeds their capacity, indicating a failure to learn the underlying principles. We use edge cases of a closed contour detection task to support our arguments. We argue that lateral interactions, which are not a part of pure feedforward CNNs but common in biological vision, are essential to this task.

1 Introduction

The perception of closed contours plays a fundamental role in the rapid detection of objects [1]. It is believed that such perception is achieved in the early stages of visual processing. Psychophysical experiments have shown that human subjects can detect closed contours in less than 200 ms [3] (Fig. 1). In order to perceive a closed contour, it is first necessary to perceive smooth curvature, following the Gestalt law of *good continuation*. Association fields, a grouping strategy that integrates information across neighboring, similarly oriented filters, was proposed in [2] to describe how lateral interactions could mediate such principles. By matching many aspects of the time course and detection accuracy of human subjects, [3] showed that lateral interactions are likely essential to the perception of closed contours, in additional to feed-forward connections, confirming the idea of association fields. A more sophisticated computational model, based on stochastic completion fields, was proposed in [13], which describes the relationship between neighboring oriented filters as a Markov chain in $R^2 \times S^1$ space (its index has the form (x, y, θ), where (x, y) is the location of the oriented filter and θ is the orientation of it). Given an affine matrix in $(R^2 \times S^1) \times (R^2 \times S^1)$, the closed contour is the eigenvector which corresponds the largest eigenvalue of the matrix [14]. A recurrent network is necessary for solving the eigenvalue problem.

© Springer Nature Switzerland AG 2018
G. Bebis et al. (Eds.): ISVC 2018, LNCS 11241, pp. 455–460, 2018.
https://doi.org/10.1007/978-3-030-03801-4_40

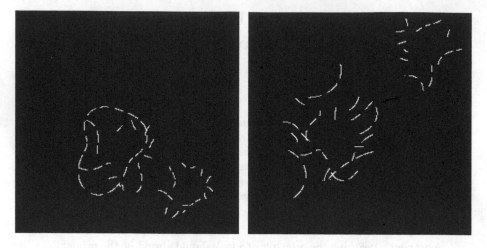

Fig. 1. The figure on the left contains a closed contour whereas the one on the right does not. Human subjects can detect the closed contour within 200 ms [3].

Feed-forward CNNs have shown success in beating traditional feature engineering methods on large-scale image classification datasets [9], such as CIFAR10 [8] and ImageNet [6]. Moreover, the performance of CNNs continues to improve [4,5]. Because of its black box nature, however, whether or not CNNs can learn the abstract principles underlying a given task has been questioned in recent years. [7] shows that CNNs tend to learn surface statistical regularities in the dataset rather than higher-level abstract concepts. [11] shows decreases in accuracy by creating a new test set of truly unseen images, suggesting the possibility of over-fitting. Moreover, [12] shows that CNNs fail to learn visual relations even if they are able to achieve 100% training accuracy.

In this paper, we investigate a similar question regarding the capability to learn abstract principles by applying CNNs to a closed contour detection task. We show that CNNs fail to learn the principle, i.e. association field or stochastic completion field, and what they learn are very likely to be a set of fixed patterns or templates.

2   Problem Formation

We design two tasks: a classification task and a clustering task. In the former, every image is assigned an label. When there is a closed contour, the label is 1, otherwise it is 0, thus defining a binary classification problem. In the latter, the position, where corresponding pixel value is 0, is labeled as 0, the clutter background is labeled as 1 and the closed contour is label as 2. This pixel-wise labeling task requires the learning system to be able to predict a label for every single position, thus defining a clustering problem.

3   Experiments

3.1   Dataset

We follow the rules for creating amoeba/no-amoeba images in [3] (Fig. 1). Amoebas are radial frequency patterns constructed around a circle. The training set consists of 4 different radial frequencies: 2, 4, 8 and 16. There are 1,000 amoeba images for each frequency. For a training (testing) set, there are 1,000 mixed-frequency amoeba images and 1,000 no-amoeba images, 2,000 images in total. The size of each image is 256 × 256.

The radius of an amoeba is the key to the experiment, because the principle is about solving an eigenvalue problem in $R^2 \times S^1$ space, thus the solution should not be affected by the radius of an amoeba. Let α be the ratio between the maximum radius of an amoeba and the size of the image where the amoeba is located. The maximum radius of an amoeba is randomly drawn within a range of α. We created three training/testing sets with amoebas of different sizes: (1) Full: $\alpha \in (0.15, 0.85)$; (2) Small-Large: $\alpha \in (0.15, 0.25)$ or $\alpha \in (0.75, 0.85)$; (3) Medium: $\alpha \in (0.35, 0.65)$. There is no overlap between the Small-Large and the Medium sets.

3.2   Convolutional Neural Networks

For classification task, we use the AlexNet [9] and a 40-layer DenseNet [5]. For clustering task, we use a deconvolution network which is used for semantic segmentation [10]. It is also reported being used in the contour detection task [15]. We choose these networks because they all achieved state-of-the-art performance at the time when they were published.

4   Results

The classification accuracies are shown in Tables 1 and 2. Results in each row use the same training set and ones in each column use the same testing set. These results show that when the sizes of amoebas in the training set are not overlapped with the ones in the testing set, accuracies drop, compared to cases where sizes in training and testing sets are overlapped. Although DenseNet has

Table 1. Classification accuracy (%) from AlexNet. The rows stand for training sets and the columns stand for testing set.

	Full	Small large	Medium
Full	85.90	86.95	84.50
Small large	78.20	90.25	72.45
Medium	81.80	75.80	87.10

Table 2. Classification accuracy (%) from DenseNet. The rows stand for training sets and the columns stand for testing set.

	Full	Small large	Medium
Full	92.85	93.50	93.00
Small large	80.05	87.35	78.95
Medium	83.33	80.00	88.85

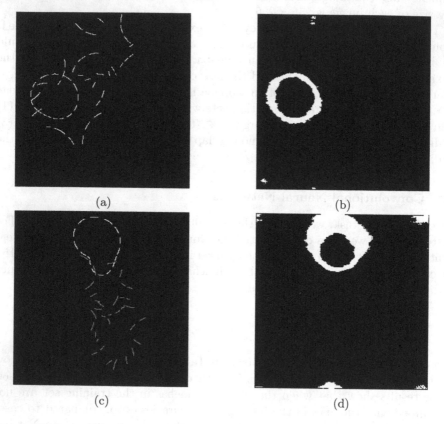

     (a)   (b)

     (c)   (d)

Fig. 2. Cluttering results: (a) and (c) are amoeba images, (b) and (d) are amoeba labels predicted by deconvolution network [10].

an overall better performance than AlexNet does, this phenomenon holds. Similar trend has been observed in [11]. The fact that accuracies don't drop to chance (50%) indicates that there is still a certain degree of generalization. If the size variation, however, exceeds the capability of generalization, CNNs will fail to detect amoebas correctly. The result of clustering task supports this conclusion as well. The prediction of the deconvolution network looks like a mask (Fig. 2).

It is not hard to imagine if an amoeba varies with the mask, it is recognizable to CNNs. What CNNs have learned are probably not principles of this task but a set of circle patterns.

5 Conclusion

In this paper, we use the amoeba/no-amoeba experiment to support the suspicion that instead of learning principles of tasks, CNNs memorize patterns. While better CNN achieves better performance, the decrease in accuracy is inevitable. To solve a problem like amoeba/no-amoeba task, a network with different architecture, such as recurrent network and top-down feedback network, may be needed, but what is more important is about understanding the theory of a problem. We cannot expect the pure feed-forward networks to solve everything. Although they look promising on many changeling datasets, the impressive performances achieved by CNNs could be deceiving.

References

1. Elder, J.H., Velisavljevi, L.: Cue dynamics underlying rapid detection of animals in natural scenes. J. Vis. (2018)
2. Field, D., Hayes, A., Hess, R.: Contour integration by the human visual system: evidence for a local "association field". Vis. Res. **33**, 173–193 (1993)
3. Gintautas, V., et al.: Model cortical association fields account for the time course and dependence on target complexity of human contour perception. PLoS Comput. Biol. **7**, e1002162 (2011)
4. He, K., Zhang, X., Ren, S., Sun, J.: Deep residual learning for image recognition. In: CVPR (2016)
5. Huang, G., Liu, Z., van der Maaten, L., Weinberger, K.Q.: Densely connected convolutional networks. In: CVPR (2017)
6. Deng, J., Dong, W., Socher, R., Li, L.-J., Li, K., Fei-Fei, L.: ImageNet: a large-scale hierarchical image database. In: CVPR (2009)
7. Jo, J., Bengio, Y.: Measuring the tendency of CNNs to Learn Surface Statistical Regularities. ArXiv e-prints (2017)
8. Krizhevsky, A.: Learning Multiple Layers of Features from Tiny Images. Technical report (2009)
9. Krizhevsky, A., Sutskever, I., Hinton, G.E.: ImageNet classification with deep convolutional neural networks. In: NIPS (2012)
10. Noh, H., Hong, S., Han, B.: Learning deconvolution network for semantic segmentation. In: ICCV (2015)
11. Recht, B., Roelofs, R., Schmidt, L.: Do CIFAR-10 Classifiers Generalize to CIFAR-10? ArXiv e-prints (2018)
12. Ricci, M., Kim, J., Serre, T.: Not-So-CLEVR: Visual Relations Strain Feedforward Neural Networks. ArXiv e-prints (2018)
13. Williams, L.R., Jacobs, D.W.: Stochastic completion fields; a neural model of illusory contour shape and salience. Neural Comput. **9**, 837–858 (1997)

14. Williams, L.R., Thornber, K.K.: A comparison of measures for detecting natural shapes in cluttered backgrounds. In: Burkhardt, H., Neumann, B. (eds.) ECCV 1998. LNCS, vol. 1407, pp. 432–448. Springer, Heidelberg (1998). https://doi.org/10.1007/BFb0054757
15. Yang, J., Price, B., Cohen, S., Lee, H., Yang, M.H.: Object contour detection with a fully convolutional encoder-decoder network. In: CVPR (2016)

Deep Learning II

DensSiam: End-to-End Densely-Siamese Network with Self-Attention Model for Object Tracking

Mohamed H. Abdelpakey[1(✉)], Mohamed S. Shehata[1], and Mostafa M. Mohamed[2,3]

[1] Faculty of Engineering and Applied Science, Memorial University of Newfoundland, St. John's, NL A1B 3X5, Canada
mha241@mun.ca
[2] Electrical and Computer Engineering Department, University of Calgary, Calgary, Canada
[3] Biomedical Engineering Department, Helwan University, Helwan, Egypt

Abstract. Convolutional Siamese neural networks have been recently used to track objects using deep features. Siamese architecture can achieve real time speed, however it is still difficult to find a Siamese architecture that maintains the generalization capability, high accuracy and speed while decreasing the number of shared parameters especially when it is very deep. Furthermore, a conventional Siamese architecture usually processes one local neighborhood at a time, which makes the appearance model local and non-robust to appearance changes.

To overcome these two problems, this paper proposes DensSiam, a novel convolutional Siamese architecture, which uses the concept of dense layers and connects each dense layer to all layers in a feed-forward fashion with a similarity-learning function. DensSiam also includes a Self-Attention mechanism to force the network to pay more attention to the non-local features during offline training. Extensive experiments are performed on four tracking benchmarks: OTB2013 and OTB2015 for validation set; and VOT2015, VOT2016 and VOT2017 for testing set. The obtained results show that DensSiam achieves superior results on these benchmarks compared to other current state-of-the-art methods.

Keywords: Object tracking · Siamese-network · Densely-Siamese Self-attention

1 Introduction

Visual object tracking is an important task in many computer vision applications such as image understanding [19], surveillance [17], human-computer interactions [24] and autonomous driving [5]. One of the main challenges in object tracking is how to represent the appearance model in such a way that the model is robust to appearance changes such as motion blur, occlusions, background clutter [2,36].

© Springer Nature Switzerland AG 2018
G. Bebis et al. (Eds.): ISVC 2018, LNCS 11241, pp. 463–473, 2018.
https://doi.org/10.1007/978-3-030-03801-4_41

Many trackers use handcrafted features such as CACF [25], SRDCF [9], KCF [14] and SAMF [21] which have inferior accuracy and/or robustness compared to deep features.

In recent years, deep convolutional neural networks (CNNs) have shown superior performance in various vision tasks. They also increased the performance of object tracking methods. Many trackers have been developed using the strength of CNN features and significantly improved their accuracy and robustness. Deep trackers include SiamFC [4], CFNet [31], DeepSRDCF [8], HCF [23]. However, these trackers exploit the deep features which originally designed for object recognition and neither consider the temporal information such as SiamFC [4] nor non-local features such as the rest of the trackers. The key to design a high-performance tracker is to find the best deep architecture that captures the non-local features while maintaining the real-time speed. Non-local features allow the tracker to be well-generalized from one domain to another domain (e.g. from ImageNet videos domain to OTB/VOT videos domain).

In this paper, we present a novel network design for robust visual object tracking to improve the generalization capability of Siamese architecture. DensSiam network solves these issues and produces a non-local response map. DensSiam has two branches, the target branch that takes the input target patch from the first frame and the search branch that takes later images in the whole sequence. The target branch consists of dense blocks separated by a transition layer, each block has many convolutional layers and each transition layer has a convolutional layer with an average pool layer. Each dense layer is connected to every other layer in a feed-forward fashion. The target response map is fed into the Self-Attention module to calculate response at a position as a weighted sum of the features at all positions. The search branch is the same architecture as the target branch except that it does not have the Self-Attention module since we calculate the similarity function between the target patch with non-local features and the candidate patches. Both target and search branches share the same network parameters across channels extracted from the same dense layers. To the best of our knowledge, this is the first densely Siamese network with a Self-Attention model.

To summarize, the main contributions of this work are three-fold.

- A novel end-to-end deep Densely-Siamese architecture is proposed for object tracking. The new architecture can capture the non-local features which are robust to appearance changes. Additionally, it reduces the number of shared parameters between layers while building up deeper network compared to other existing Siamese-based architectures commonly used in current state-of-the-art trackers.
- An effective response map based on Self-Attention module that boosts the DensSiam tracker performance. The response map has no-local features and captures the semantic information about the target object.
- The proposed architecture tackles the vanishing-gradient problem, leverages feature reuse and improves the generalization capability.

The rest of the paper is organized as follows. We first introduce related work in Sect. 2. Section 3 details the proposed approach. We present the experimental results in Sect. 4. Finally, Sect. 5 concludes the paper.

2 Related Work

There are extensive surveys on visual object tracking in the literatures [20]. Recently, deep features have demonstrated breakthrough accuracies compared to handcrafted features. DeepSRDCF [8] uses deep features of a pretrained CNN (e.g. VGG [28]) from different layers and integrate them into a correlation filter. Visual object tracking can be modeled as a similarity learning function in an offline training phase. Siamese architecture consists of two branches, the target object branch and the search image branch. Siamese architecture takes the advantage of end-to-end learning. Consequently, the learned function can be evaluated online during tracking.

The pioneering work for object tracking is the SiamFC [4]. SiamFC has two branches, the target branch and the appearance branch, a correlation layer is used to calculate the correlation between the target patch and the candidate patches in the search image. The search image is usually larger than the target patch to calculate the similarities in a single evaluation. CFNet [31] improved SiamFC by introducing a differentiable correlation filter layer to the target branch to adapt the target model online. DSiam [12] uses a fast transfer motion to update the leaned model online. Significantly improved performance as it captures some information about the object's context.

SINT [30] uses optical flow and formulates the visual object tracking as a verification problem within Siamese architecture, it has a better performance however, the speed dropped down from 86 to 4 frames per second. SA-Siam [13] uses two Siamese networks based on the original Siamese architecture [4]. The first network for semantic information and the other one for appearance model. This architecture supranationally improved the tracker performance as it allows the semantic information of the appearance model representation to incorporate into the response map. However these trackers use the features taken directly from CNN which processes the information in a local neighborhood. Consequently the output features are local and do not have a lot information about the neighbourhood. Thus using convolutional layers alone is not effective to capture the generic appearance model.

3 Proposed Approach

We propose effective and efficient deep architecture for visual tracking named Densely-Siamese network (DensSiam). Figure 1 shows the DensSiam architecture of the proposed tracker. The core idea behind this design is that, using densely blocks separated by transition layers to build up Siamese network with Self-Attention model to capture non-local features.

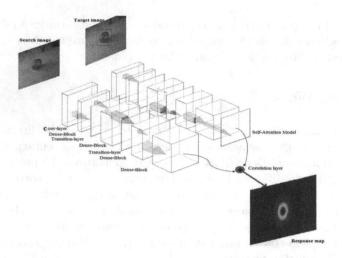

Fig. 1. The architecture of DensSiam tracker. The target branch has the Self-Attention model to capture the semantic information during offline training.

3.1   Densely-Siamese Architecture

DensSiam architecture consists of two branches, the target branch and the appearance branch. The target branch architecture as follows: input-ConvNet-DenseBlock-TransitionLayer-DenseBlock-TransitionLayer-DenseBlock-DenseBlock-SelfAttention.

Dense Block: Consists of Batch Normalization (BN) [16], Rectified Linear Units (ReLU), pooling and Convolution layers, all dimensions are shown in Table 1. Each layer in dense block takes all preceding feature maps as input and concatenate them. These connections ensure that the network will preserve the information needed from all preceding feature maps and improve the information flow between layers, and thus improves the generalization capability as shown in Fig. 2. In traditional Siamese the output of lth layer is fed in as input to the $(l + 1)^{th}$ layer we denote the output of lth layer as x_l. To formulate the information flow between layers in dense block lets assume that the input tensor is $x_0 \in \Re^{C \times N \times D}$. Consequently, l^{th} layer receives all feature maps according to this equation:

$$x_l = H_l([x_0, x_1, ..., x_{l-1}]), \tag{1}$$

Where H_l is a three consecutive operations, batch normalization, ReLU and a 3×3 convolution and $[x_0, x_1, ..., x_{l-1}]$ is a feature map concatenation.

Transition Layer: Consists of convolutional operation, average pooling and dropout [29]. Adding dropout to dense block and transition layer decreases the risk that DensSiam overfits to negative classes. DensSiam does not use padding operation since it is a fully-convolutional and padding violates this property. Consequently, the size of feature maps in dense blocks varies and can not be concatenated. Therefore, transition layers are used to match up the size of dense blocks and concatenate them properly.

Fig. 2. The internal structure of dense block without BN, ReLU, 1×1 conv and Pooling layers shows the connections between convolutional layers in $DenseBlock_2$

3.2 Self-Attention Model

Attention mechanism was used in image classification [33], multi-object tracking [6], pose estimation [10] and *etc.* In addition to the new architecture of DensSiam and inspired by [32,35] that use the attention mechanism in object detection, DensSiam architecture integrates the Self-Attention model to target branch as shown in Fig. 3.

Given the input tensor $x \in \Re^{W \times H \times D}$ which is the output feature map of the target branch, Self-Attention model divides the feature map into three maps through 1×1 convolutional operation to capture the attention, $f(x)$ and $g(x)$ can be calculated as follows:

$$f(x) = W_f \times x, \tag{2}$$

$$g(x) = W_g \times x, \tag{3}$$

Where W_f, W_g are the offline learned parameters. Attention feature map can be calculated as follows:

$$\phi = \frac{\exp(m)}{\sum\limits_{i=1}^{N} \exp(m)}, \tag{4}$$

Where ϕ is the attention map weights and $m = f(x_i)^T \times g(x_i)$. Self-Attention feature map can be calculated as follows:

$$\sum\limits_{i=1}^{N} (\phi \times h(x_i)), \tag{5}$$

Where $h(x) = W_h \times x$ and W_h is the offline learned parameter. We use logistic loss for both dense block and Self-Attention model to calculate the weights using Stochastic Gradient Descent (SGD) as follows:

$$l(y, v) = log(1 + \exp(-yv)), \tag{6}$$

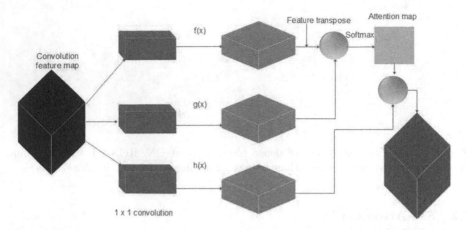

Fig. 3. Self-Attention Model, the feature map is divided into three maps, blue circles are matrix multiplication. The input and the output tensors are the same size. (Color figure online)

Where v is the single score value of target-candidate pair and $y \in [-1, +1]$ its ground truth label. To calculate the loss function for the feature map we use the mean of the loss over the whole map as follows:

$$L(y, v) = \frac{1}{N} \sum_{n \in N} l(y[n], v[n]), \tag{7}$$

Finally, the search branch has the same architecture as target branch except the search branch does not have the Self-Attention model. The output of Self-Attention map and the output of the search branch are fed into correlation layer to learn the similarity function.

4   Experimental Results

We divided the benchmarks to two sets, the validation set which includes OTB2013, OTB2015 and the testing set which includes VOT2015 VOT2016 and VOT2017. We provide the implementation details and hyper-parameters in the next subsection.

4.1   Implementation Details

DensSiam is pre-trained offline from scratch on the video object detection dataset of the ImageNet Large Scale Visual Recognition Challenge (ILSVRC15) [27]. ILSVRC15 contains 1.3 million labelled frames in 4000 sequences and it has a wide variety of objects which contribute to the generalization of the DensSiam network.

Table 1. Data dimensions in DensSiam.

Layers	Output size	Target branch	Search branch
Convolution	Tensor (8, 61, 61, 72)	7 × 7 conv, stride 2	7 × 7 conv, stride 2
$DenseBlock_1$	Tensor(8, 61, 61, 144)	[1 × 1 conv] ×2 [3 × 3 conv] ×2	[1 × 1 conv] ×2 [3 × 3 conv] ×2
$TransitionLayer$	Tensor (8, 30, 30, 36)	1 × 1 conv , average pool	1 × 1 conv , average pool
$DenseBlock_2$	Tensor(8, 30, 30, 180)	[1 × 1 conv] ×4 [3 × 3 conv] ×4	[1 × 1 conv] ×4 [3 × 3 conv] ×4
$TransitionLayer$	Tensor(8, 15, 15, 36)	1 × 1 conv , average pool	1 × 1 conv , average pool
$DenseBlock_3$	Tensor (8, 15, 15, 252)	[1 × 1 conv] ×6 [3 × 3 conv] ×6	[1 × 1 conv] ×6 [3 × 3 conv] ×6
$DenseBlock_4$	Tensor(8, 9, 9, 128)	[7 × 7 conv] × 3	[7 × 7 conv] × 3
$Self - Attention$	Tensor(8, 9, 9, 128)	[1 × 1 conv] ×3	–

Table 2. Comparison with the state-of-the-art trackers including the top four non-realtime for VOT2015.

Tracker	A	R	EAO	FPS
MDNet	0.60	0.69	0.38	1
DeepSRDCF	0.56	1.05	0.32	<1
EBT	0.47	1.02	0.31	4.4
SRDCF	0.56	1.24	0.2	5
BACF	0.59	1.56	–	35
EAST	0.57	1.03	0.34	159
Staple	0.57	1.39	0.30	80
SamFC	0.55	1.58	0.29	86
DensSiam(ours)	0.619	1.24	0.34	60

Table 3. Comparison with the state-of-the-art trackers on VOT2016.

Tracker	A	R	EAO	FPS
ECOhc	0.54	1.19	0.3221	60
Staple	0.54	1.42	0.2952	80
STAPLE+	0.55	1.31	0.2862	>25
SiamRN	0.55	1.36	0.2766	>25
GCF	0.51	1.57	0.2179	>25
DensSiam(ours)	0.56	1.08	0.3310	60

Network Architecture. We adopt this architecture $input - ConvNet - DenseBlock_1 - TransitionLayer - DenseBlock_2 - TransitionLayer - DenseBlock_3 - DenseBlock_4 - SelfAttention$ as shown in Table 1.

Hyper-Parameters Settings. Training is performed over 100 epochs, each with 53,200 sampled pairs. Stochastic gradient descent (SGD) is applied with momentum of 0.9 to train the network. We adopt the mini-batches of size 8 and the learning rate is annealed geometrically at each epoch from 10^{-3} to 10^{-8}. We implement DensSiam in TensorFlow [1] 1.8 framework. The experiments are performed on a PC with a Xeon E5 2.20 GHz CPU and a Titan XP GPU. The testing speed of DensSiam is 60 fps.

Tracking Settings. We adapt the scale variations by searching for the object on three scales O^s where $O = 1.0375$ and $s = \{-2, 0, 2\}$. The input target image size is 127×127 and the search image size is 255×255. We use the linear interpolation to update the scale with a factor 0.764.

4.2   Comparison with the State-of-the-Arts

In this section we use VOT toolkit standard metrics [18], accuracy (A), robustness (R) and expected average overlap (EAO). Table 2 shows the comparison of DensSaim with MDNet [26], DeepSRDCF [8], EBT [37], BACF [11], EAST [15], Staple [3] and SiamFC [4]. The four top trackers are non-realtime trackers and we still outperform them. In terms of accuracy, DensSiam is about 2% higher than MDNet while it is the best second after MDNet in terms of expected average overlap. DensSiam is the highest in terms of robustness score in real-time trackers. We also report the results of our tracker on VOT2016 and VOT2017 as shown in Tables 3 and 4. The comparison includes ECOhc [7], SiamFC [4], SiamDCF [34], Staple [3], CSRDCF++ [22]. DensSiam outperforms all trackers in terms of accuracy, robustness score and expected average overlap.

Table 4. Comparison with the state-of-the-art trackers on VOT2017.

Tracker	A	R	EAO	FPS
SiamDCF	0.500	0.473	0.249	60
ECOhc	0.494	0.435	0.238	60
CSRDCF++	0.453	0.370	0.229	>25
SiamFC	0.502	0.585	0.188	86
SAPKLTF	0.482	0.581	0.184	>25
Staple	0.530	0.688	0.169	>80
ASMS	0.494	0.623	0.169	>25
DensSiam(ours)	0.540	0.350	0.250	60

5   Conclusions and Future Work

This paper proposed DensSiam, a new Siamese architecture for object tracking. DensSiam uses non-local features to represent the appearance model in such a way that allows the deep feature map to be robust to appearance changes. DenSaim allows different feature levels (e.g. low level and high level features) to flow through the network layers without vanishing gradients and improves the generalization capability. The resulting tracker greatly benefits from the Densely-Siamese architecture with Self-Attention model and substantially increases the accuracy and robustness while decreasing the number of shared network parameters. The architecture of DensSiam can be extended to other tasks of computer vision such as object verification, recognition and detection since it is general Siamese framework.

References

1. Abadi, M., et al.: TensorFlow: large-scale machine learning on heterogeneous distributed systems. arxiv preprint (2016). arXiv preprint arXiv:1603.04467
2. Alahari, K., et al.: The thermal infrared visual object tracking VOT-TIR2015 challenge results. In: 2015 IEEE International Conference on Computer Vision Workshop (ICCVW), pp. 639–651. IEEE (2015)
3. Bertinetto, L., Valmadre, J., Golodetz, S., Miksik, O., Torr, P.H.: Staple: complementary learners for real-time tracking. In: Proceedings of the IEEE Conference on Computer Vision and Pattern Recognition, pp. 1401–1409 (2016)
4. Bertinetto, L., Valmadre, J., Henriques, J.F., Vedaldi, A., Torr, P.H.S.: Fully-convolutional Siamese networks for object tracking. In: Hua, G., Jégou, H. (eds.) ECCV 2016. LNCS, vol. 9914, pp. 850–865. Springer, Cham (2016). https://doi.org/10.1007/978-3-319-48881-3_56
5. Chen, C., Seff, A., Kornhauser, A., Xiao, J.: DeepDriving: learning affordance for direct perception in autonomous driving. In: 2015 IEEE International Conference on Computer Vision (ICCV), pp. 2722–2730. IEEE (2015)
6. Chu, Q., Ouyang, W., Li, H., Wang, X., Liu, B., Yu, N.: Online multi-object tracking using CNN-based single object tracker with spatial-temporal attention mechanism. In: 2017 IEEE International Conference on Computer Vision (ICCV), pp. 4846–4855, October 2017
7. Danelljan, M., Bhat, G., Khan, F.S., Felsberg, M.: ECO: efficient convolution operators for tracking. In: Proceedings of the 2017 IEEE Conference on Computer Vision and Pattern Recognition (CVPR), Honolulu, HI, USA, pp. 21–26 (2017)
8. Danelljan, M., Hager, G., Shahbaz Khan, F., Felsberg, M.: Convolutional features for correlation filter based visual tracking. In: Proceedings of the IEEE International Conference on Computer Vision Workshops, pp. 58–66 (2015)
9. Danelljan, M., Hager, G., Shahbaz Khan, F., Felsberg, M.: Learning spatially regularized correlation filters for visual tracking. In: Proceedings of the IEEE International Conference on Computer Vision, pp. 4310–4318 (2015)
10. Du, W., Wang, Y., Qiao, Y.: RPAN: an end-to-end recurrent pose-attention network for action recognition in videos. In: IEEE International Conference on Computer Vision, vol. 2 (2017)
11. Galoogahi, H.K., Fagg, A., Lucey, S.: Learning background-aware correlation filters for visual tracking. In: Proceedings of the 2017 IEEE Conference on Computer Vision and Pattern Recognition (CVPR), Honolulu, HI, USA, pp. 21–26 (2017)
12. Guo, Q., Feng, W., Zhou, C., Huang, R., Wan, L., Wang, S.: Learning dynamic Siamese network for visual object tracking. In: Proceedings of IEEE International Conference on Computer Vision, pp. 1–9 (2017)
13. He, A., Luo, C., Tian, X., Zeng, W.: A twofold Siamese network for real-time object tracking. In: Proceedings of the IEEE Conference on Computer Vision and Pattern Recognition, pp. 4834–4843 (2018)
14. Henriques, J.F., Caseiro, R., Martins, P., Batista, J.: High-speed tracking with kernelized correlation filters. IEEE Trans. Patt. Anal. Mach. Intell. 37(3), 583–596 (2015)
15. Huang, C., Lucey, S., Ramanan, D.: Learning policies for adaptive tracking with deep feature cascades. In: IEEE International Conference on Computer Vision (ICCV), pp. 105–114 (2017)
16. Ioffe, S., Szegedy, C.: Batch normalization: accelerating deep network training by reducing internal covariate shift. In: ICML, vol. 37, pp. 448–456 (2015)

17. Kendall, A., Grimes, M., Cipolla, R.: PoseNet: a convolutional network for real-time 6-DOF camera relocalization. In: 2015 IEEE International Conference on Computer Vision (ICCV), pp. 2938–2946. IEEE (2015)
18. Kristan, M., et al.: The visual object tracking VOT2016 challenge results. In: Hua, G., Jégou, H. (eds.) ECCV 2016. LNCS, vol. 9914, pp. 777–823. Springer, Cham (2016). https://doi.org/10.1007/978-3-319-48881-3_54
19. Lenc, K., Vedaldi, A.: Understanding image representations by measuring their equivariance and equivalence. In: Proceedings of the IEEE Conference on Computer Vision and Pattern Recognition (CVPR) (2015)
20. Li, X., Hu, W., Shen, C., Zhang, Z., Dick, A., Hengel, A.V.D.: A survey of appearance models in visual object tracking. ACM Trans. Intell. Syst. Technol. (TIST) 4(4), 58 (2013)
21. Li, Y., Zhu, J.: A scale adaptive kernel correlation filter tracker with feature integration. In: Agapito, L., Bronstein, M.M., Rother, C. (eds.) ECCV 2014. LNCS, vol. 8926, pp. 254–265. Springer, Cham (2015). https://doi.org/10.1007/978-3-319-16181-5_18
22. Lukezic, A., Vojir, T., Zajc, L.C., Matas, J., Kristan, M.: Discriminative correlation filter with channel and spatial reliability. In: Proceedings of the IEEE Conference on Computer Vision and Pattern Recognition, vol. 2 (2017)
23. Ma, C., Huang, J.B., Yang, X., Yang, M.H.: Hierarchical convolutional features for visual tracking. In: Proceedings of the IEEE International Conference on Computer Vision, pp. 3074–3082 (2015)
24. Molchanov, P., Yang, X., Gupta, S., Kim, K., Tyree, S., Kautz, J.: Online detection and classification of dynamic hand gestures with recurrent 3D convolutional neural network. In: Proceedings of the IEEE Conference on Computer Vision and Pattern Recognition, pp. 4207–4215 (2016)
25. Mueller, M., Smith, N., Ghanem, B.: Context-aware correlation filter tracking. In: Proceedings of IEEE Conference on Computer Vision and Pattern Recognition (CVPR), pp. 1396–1404 (2017)
26. Nam, H., Han, B.: Learning multi-domain convolutional neural networks for visual tracking. In: Proceedings of the IEEE Conference on Computer Vision and Pattern Recognition, pp. 4293–4302 (2016)
27. Russakovsky, O., et al.: Imagenet large scale visual recognition challenge. Int. J. Comput. Vis. 115(3), 211–252 (2015)
28. Simonyan, K., Zisserman, A.: Very deep convolutional networks for large-scale image recognition. In: International Conference on Learning Representations (2015)
29. Srivastava, N., Hinton, G., Krizhevsky, A., Sutskever, I., Salakhutdinov, R.: Dropout: a simple way to prevent neural networks from overfitting. J. Mach. Learn. Res. 15(1), 1929–1958 (2014)
30. Tao, R., Gavves, E., Smeulders, A.W.: Siamese instance search for tracking. In: 2016 IEEE Conference on Computer Vision and Pattern Recognition (CVPR), pp. 1420–1429. IEEE (2016)
31. Valmadre, J., Bertinetto, L., Henriques, J., Vedaldi, A., Torr, P.H.: End-to-end representation learning for correlation filter based tracking. In: 2017 IEEE Conference on Computer Vision and Pattern Recognition (CVPR), pp. 5000–5008. IEEE (2017)
32. Vaswani, A., et al.: Attention is all you need. In: Advances in Neural Information Processing Systems, pp. 6000–6010 (2017)
33. Wang, F., et al.: Residual attention network for image classification. arXiv preprint arXiv:1704.06904 (2017)

34. Wang, Q., Gao, J., Xing, J., Zhang, M., Hu, W.: DCFNet: discriminant correlation filters network for visual tracking. arXiv preprint arXiv:1704.04057 (2017)
35. Wang, X., Girshick, R., Gupta, A., He, K.: Non-local neural networks. In: CVPR (2018)
36. Wu, Y., Lim, J., Yang, M.H.: Object tracking benchmark. IEEE Trans. Patt. Anal. Mach. Intell. **37**(9), 1834–1848 (2015)
37. Zhu, G., Porikli, F., Li, H.: Beyond local search: tracking objects everywhere with instance-specific proposals. In: Proceedings of the IEEE Conference on Computer Vision and Pattern Recognition, pp. 943–951 (2016)

Convolutional Adaptive Particle Filter with Multiple Models for Visual Tracking

Reza Jalil Mozhdehi[✉], Yevgeniy Reznichenko, Abubakar Siddique,
and Henry Medeiros

Electrical and Computer Engineering Department, Marquette University,
Milwaukee, WI, USA
{reza.jalilmozhdehi,yevgeniy.reznichenko,abubakar.siddique,
henry.medeiros}@marquette.edu

Abstract. Although particle filters improve the performance of convolutional-correlation trackers, especially in challenging scenarios such as occlusion and deformation, they considerably increase the computational cost. We present an adaptive particle filter to decrease the number of particles in simple frames in which there is no challenging scenario and the target model closely reflects the current appearance of the target. In this method, we consider the estimated position of each particle in the current frame as a particle in the next frame. These refined particles are more reliable than sampling new particles in every frame. In simple frames, target estimation is easier, therefore many particles may converge together. Consequently, the number of particles decreases in these frames. We implement resampling when the number of particles or the weight of the selected particle is too small. We use the weight computed in the first frame as a threshold for resampling because that weight is calculated by the ground truth model. Another contribution of this article is the generation of several target models by applying different adjusting rates to each of the high-likelihood particles. Thus, we create multiple models; some are useful in challenging frames because they are more influenced by the previous model, while other models are suitable for simple frames because they are less affected by the previous model. Experimental results on the Visual Tracker Benchmark v1.1 beta (OTB100) demonstrate that our proposed framework significantly outperforms state-of-the-art methods.

Keywords: Adaptive particle filter
Deep convolutional neural network
Correlation models · Adjusting rate · Visual tracking

1 Introduction

Tracking a specific target in challenging scenarios such as occlusion and deformation has attracted the attention of computer vision researchers for decades. Recently, deep convolutional neural networks (CNN) have been used to extract

© Springer Nature Switzerland AG 2018
G. Bebis et al. (Eds.): ISVC 2018, LNCS 11241, pp. 474–486, 2018.
https://doi.org/10.1007/978-3-030-03801-4_42

the target's features. One particularly effective mechanism to determine the similarity between an image patch and the target is the correlation filter tracking framework [1–3]. Trackers based on correlation filters measure the correlation between the target model and an image patch in the frequency domain and are agnostic to the features used to represent the targets. As a consequence, most state-of-the art CNN-based trackers integrate convolutional features and correlation filters [4]. The Hierarchical Convolutional Feature Tracker (HCFT) proposed by Ma et al. [5] uses the hierarchical convolutional features generated by multiple layers of a deep CNN in a coarse-to-fine manner in conjunction with the correlation filter proposed in [6]. HCFT shows substantial performance improvement in comparison with other visual trackers such as MEEM [7], Struck [8], SCM [9] and TLD [10]. Thus, the idea of employing features generated using CNNs with different filtering mechanisms is becoming increasingly more popular. However, the main limitation of these correlation filters is to generate only one model in each frame, which leads to high dependency on the estimated target size and position. Incorrectly updating the model causes inaccuracies in the determination of the target size and position in subsequent frames.

In this article, we extend our previous visual tracker named Deep Convolutional Particle Filter with Adaptive Correlation Maps (DCPF2) [11]. Similar to DCPF [12], DCPF2 employs a particle filter in conjunction with a CNN and an adaptive correlation filter. However, DCPF considers the target size to be fixed while DCFP2 also estimates the target size in each frame. In our new tracker named Deep Convolutional Adaptive Particle Filter with Multiple Correlation Models (CAP-mc), we replace the particle filter proposed in DCPF2 with an adaptive particle filter. Adaptive particle filters can improve the results of object tracking [13]. However, they have not been used in conjunction with CNNs and correlation filters yet. Our adaptive particle filter decreases the number of particles and the computation cost in simple frames in which there is no challenging scenario and the target model closely reflects the current appearance of the target. Additionally, our adaptive particle filter can refine the particles' locations to be used in the next frame. This method is more reliable than sampling new particles in every frame which was employed in DCPF2. We use the weight calculated in the first frame as one of the resampling thresholds because it is based on the ground truth target model, and hence serve as a reference for the quality of subsequent models. Another threshold for resampling is the number of particles.

Additionally, we determined that the adjusting rate is a critical parameter in correlation-based trackers. The adaptive correlation filter proposed in DCPF2 generates several target models based on all the high-likelihood particles to cover probable errors instead of generating one model based on the selected particle. In our new tracker, we apply different adjusting rates to generate several target models for each high-likelihood particle. Thus, we create multiple models; some are less affected by the previous model, such models are useful in simple frames, while other models, more affected by the previous model, are suitable for challenging frames. We tested our tracker on The Visual Tracker Benchmark v1.1 beta (OTB100) [14], and the results show outstanding performance of our tracker against state-of-the-art methods.

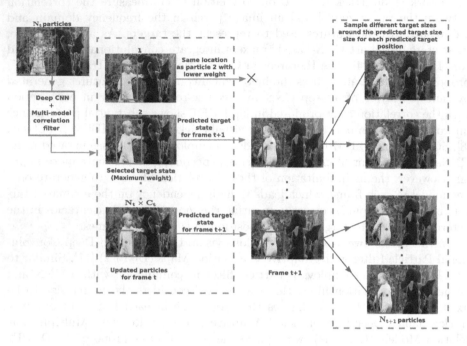

Fig. 1. Our proposed adaptive particle filter (when resampling is not needed).

2 Deep Convolutional Adaptive Particle Filter with Multiple Correlation Models

In this section, we present our adaptive particle filter illustrated in Fig. 1. We then discuss our new adaptive correlation filter based on employing different adjusting rates.

2.1 Adaptive Particle Filter

Algorithm 1 explains our adaptive particle filter. In visual tracking, the ground truth target position and size are used for initialization. Let z_1 be the ground truth target position and size in the first frame

$$z_1 = \begin{bmatrix} u_1, v_1, h_1, w_1 \end{bmatrix}^T, \tag{1}$$

where u_1 and v_1 are the ground truth locations of the target and h_1 and w_1 are its ground truth width and height. The target state is defined by

$$x_1 = \begin{bmatrix} z_1, \dot{z}_1 \end{bmatrix}^T, \tag{2}$$

where $\dot{z}_1$ is the velocity of z_1 and is assumed to be zero in the first frame. After extracting a patch from the first frame based on based on z_1, we feed this patch to a CNN [15] to calculate its convolutional features. the ground truth target model is then generated by applying the Fourier transform to the convolutional features as explained in [5]. The ground truth target model is used in calculating a threshold for the resampling process as explained later in this section. Additionally, this model is updated during the next frames as discussed in the next section.

In the next step, we generate and evaluate the initial particles as explained in Algorithm 2. Considering x_{t-1} as the previous target state, the predicted target state is calculated by [11]

$$\hat{x}_t = Ax_{t-1}, \tag{3}$$

where t is the frame number and A is a standard constant velocity process matrix defined by

$$A = \begin{bmatrix} I_4 & | & I_4 \\ 0_{(4,4)} & | & I_4 \end{bmatrix}, \tag{4}$$

where I_y is an $y \times y$ identity matrix and $0_{(u,z)}$ is a $u \times v$ zero matrix. It is clear that $\hat{x}_2 = x_1$ because of $\dot{z}_1 = 0$. As discussed in [11], by sampling from a zero-mean normal distribution and adding those samples $\zeta_t \in \mathbb{R}^8$ to $\hat{x}_t$, the particles are generated according to

$$x_t^{(i)} = \hat{x}_t + \zeta_t^{(i)}, \tag{5}$$

where

$$x_t^{(i)} = \left[z_t^{(i)}, \dot{z}_t^{(i)} \right]^T, \tag{6}$$

where $i = 1, \ldots, N_t$ and N_t is the number of initial particles.

Algorithm 1. Adaptive particle filter

Input: Current frame, previous target state x_{t-1} and C_{t-1} target models $\mho_{t-1}^{(j)}$

Output: Current target state x_t, particles $x_{t+1}^{(i)}$ for the next frame

1: Generate initial particles to determine the target state x_t according to Algorithm 2
2: **if** t = 1 **then**
3:     Calculate T_w
4: **end if**
5: Update particles and remove redundant ones using Algorithm 3
6: Examine the resampling conditions according to Eq. 15 and Eq. 16
7: **if** resampling is needed **then**
8:     Generate particles $x_{t+1}^{(i)}$ for the next frame based on Algorithm 2
9: **else**
10:     Calculate the predicted particles $\hat{x}_{(t+1)}^{(p)}$ for frame $t + 1$ using Eq. 17
11:     **for** each $\hat{x}_{(t+1)}^{(p)}$ **do**
12:         Generate β samples of the target size
13:         Calculate the particles for the next frame $t + 1$ according to Eq. 18
14:     **end for**
15: **end if**

Algorithm 2. Generate and evaluate initial particles

Input: Current frame, previous target state x_{t-1} and C_{t-1} target models $\mho_{t-1}^{(j)}$

Output: Current target state x_t, N_t particles $x_t^{(i)}$, their correlation
response maps $R^{(i)(j)}$, their weights $\omega^{(i)(j)}$, maximum weight $\omega^{(i^*)(j^*)}$ and the
best target model $\mho_{t-1}^*$

1: Calculate the predicted target state $\hat{x}_t$ according to Eq. 3 and Eq. 4
2: Generate N_t particles $x_t^{(i)}$ around the predicted target state according to Eq. 5 and Eq. 6
3: **for** each particle $x_t^{(i)}$ **do**
4:     **for** each of the C_{t-1} target models $\mho_{t-1}^{(j)}$ **do**
5:         Generate the correlation response map $R^{(i)(j)}$
6:         Calculate its weight $\omega^{(i)(j)}$ according to Eq. 7
7:     **end for**
8: **end for**
9: Find the maximum weight $\omega^{(i^*)(j^*)}$ based on Eq. 8
10: Consider the particle corresponding to $\omega^{(i^*)(j^*)}$ as the final target state x_t
11: Consider the target model corresponding to $\omega^{(i^*)(j^*)}$ as the best model $\mho_{t-1}^*$

In the next step, different patches from frame t are generated based on $z_t^{(i)}$. For each patch, a convolutional feature map is calculated using the CNN. Let $R^{(i)(j)} \in \mathbb{R}^{M \times Q}$ be the final correlation response map for particle i and target model $j, j = 1, \ldots, C_{t-1}$ (the generation of different target models in the previous frame is explained in the next section). M and Q are the length and width of the final correlation response map. These correlation response maps are computed by comparing the target models and the convolutional feature maps [5]. For each correlation response map, the likelihood or weight is calculated by [11]

$$\omega^{(i)(j)} = \sum_{m=1}^{M} \sum_{q=1}^{Q} R_{(m,q)}^{(i)(j)}, \tag{7}$$

Algorithm 3. Update particles and remove redundant ones

Input: N_t particles $x_t^{(i)}$, their correlation response maps $R^{(i)(j)}$, their weights $\omega^{(i)(j)}$

Output: Remaining updated particles $\bar{x}_t^{(i)(j)}$

1: **for** each $R^{(i)(j)}$ **do**
2:     Calculate its peak according to Eq. 9
3:     Update its state $x_t^{(i)}$ to find $\bar{x}_t^{(i)(j)}$ using Eq. 10 to Eq. 12
4: **end for**
5: **for** every pair of particles **do**
6:     **if** Eq. 13 is satisfied **then**
7:         Remove the particle with lower weight
8:     **end if**
9: **end for**

In the first frame, after comparing the convolutional features with the ground truth model , we save the weight calculated from the correlation response map as a threshold T_w which is a reliable representative of the target because it is calculated based on the ground truth model. The location of the particle with the maximum weight is [11]

$$[i^*, j^*] = \arg\max_{i,j} \omega^{(i)(j)}. \tag{8}$$

Algorithm 4. Generate multiple target models

Input: Current frame, maximum weight $\omega^{(i^*)(j^*)}$, updated states $\bar{x}_t^{(i)(j)}$, their weights $\omega^{(i)(j)}$
and the best target model $\mho_{t-1}^*$

Output: C_t target models $\mho_t^{(j)}$ for the next frame $t+1$
1: Examine Eq. 20 to determine the high-likelihood states
2: Generate K_t current target models $\breve{\mho}_t^{(j)}$ based on the high-likelihood states
3: **for** Each $\breve{\mho}_t^{(j)}$ **do**
4:     **if** Eq. 15 is correct **then**
5:         Select the set with higher adjusting rates S_1
6:     **else**
7:         Select the set with lower adjusting rates S_2
8:     **end if**
9:     Generate Γ final target models $\mho_t^{(j)}$ for the next frame based on Eq. 21
10: **end for**

The maximum weight is therefore $\omega^{(i^*)(j^*)}$, i.e., the weight corresponding to $[i^*, j^*]$. The target size corresponding to the maximum weight is then selected as the size of the bounding box for the current frame [11]. For the target position, the peak of the correlation response map with maximum weight is added to the corresponding particle location as discussed in [11]. Thus, the final target state x_t is calculated by comparing the convolutional features of particle i^* (the best particle) and the j^*th target model (the best target model). We define the best model as $\mho_{t-1}^*$, which is one of the C_{t-1} target models generated in frame $t-1$.

We then use the positions estimated in frame t as the locations of the new particles for frame $t+1$ as explained in Algorithm 3. The peak of the correlation response map of particle i compared with target model j is given by [11]

$$[\delta_u^{(i)(j)}, \delta_v^{(i)(j)}] = \underset{m,q}{\arg\max} \, R_{(m,q)}^{(i)(j)}. \tag{9}$$

The target position corresponding to that particle and target model is then given by [11]

$$[\tilde{u}_t^{(i)(j)}, \tilde{v}_t^{(i)(j)}] = [u_t^{(i)} + \delta_u^{(i)(j)}, v_t^{(i)} + \delta_v^{(i)(j)}], \tag{10}$$

where $[u_t^{(i)}, v_t^{(i)}]$ corresponds to the location of particle i according to Eq. 5. As seen in Eq. 9, for the location of each particle $x_t^{(i)}$, we estimate C_{t-1} target positions. The updated particle i compared with target model j in frame t is

$$\bar{x}_t^{(i)(j)} = \left[\bar{z}_t^{(i)(j)}, \dot{\bar{z}}_t^{(i)(j)}\right]^T, \tag{11}$$

where $\dot{\bar{z}}_t^{(i)(j)}$ is the updated version of $\dot{z}_t^{(i)}$ based on $[\tilde{u}_t^{(i)(j)}, \tilde{v}_t^{(i)(j)}]$ and

$$\bar{z}_t^{(i)(j)} = \left[\tilde{u}_t^{(i)(j)}, \tilde{v}_t^{(i)(j)}, h_t^{(i)}, w_t^{(i)}\right]^T. \tag{12}$$

$\bar{z}_t^{(i)(j)}$ is rounded because target positions and sizes are discrete quantities measured in pixels. After rounding, several $\bar{z}_t^{(i)(j)}$ may map to the same location. Since the initial particles can refine their locations for subsequent frames, these refined particles perform better than newly sampled particles in every frame.

Fig. 2. Decreasing the number of the particles in simple frames and implementing resampling in difficult frames.

Their locations can also merge especially in simple frames to decrease the number of particles. Thus, the number of particles in simple frames is lower. For the target size, our tracker samples around each remaining particle based on its velocity. Consider two particles $\bar{x}_t^{(i')(j')}$ and $\bar{x}_t^{(i'')(j'')}$, if

$$[\tilde{u}_t^{(i')(j')}, \tilde{v}_t^{(i')(j')}] = [\tilde{u}_t^{(i'')(j'')}, \tilde{v}_t^{(i'')(j'')}], \tag{13}$$

and

$$\omega^{(i')(j')} > \omega^{(i'')(j'')}, \tag{14}$$

$\bar{x}_t^{(i')(j')}$ is selected and $\bar{x}_t^{(i'')(j'')}$ is removed, that is, if two particles converge to the same target position, the one with highest weight is selected and the other is removed. In the next step, the C_t target models are generated as discussed in the following section.

Two resampling conditions are then examined for frame $t + 1$. The first condition is

$$\omega^{(i^*)(j^*)} > \varphi \times T_w. \tag{15}$$

As explained earlier, T_w is the maximum particle weight in the first frame. This maximum weight is calculated based on the comparison with the model generated by the ground truth in the same frame. When the maximum weight in frame t is less than T_w, it means our tracker could not produce a reliable correlation response map because of challenging scenarios such as occlusion. Therefore, the particles cannot properly refine their locations based on these weak correlation response maps. In these scenarios, we resample new particles. The second resampling condition is

$$N_t \cdot C_{t-1} - Z > T_t, \tag{16}$$

where T_t is the minimum number of particles to transfer to the next frame, and Z is the number of $\bar{x}_t$ which are removed. When too many particles converge to the same location and Z is too high, we increase the number of particles by resampling.

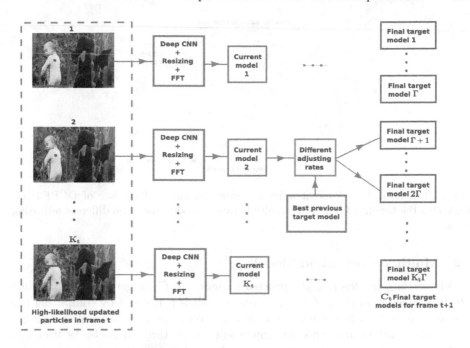

Fig. 3. Our proposed multiple models with different adjusting rates.

If resampling is not needed, we should predict new particles for the next frame based on the remaining particles in the current frame. Let $P = N_t \cdot C_{t-1} - Z$ be the number of remaining particles. We then predict the new particles for frame $t + 1$ according to

$$\hat{x}_{t+1}^{(p)} = A\bar{x}_t^{(p)}, \tag{17}$$

where $p = 1, \ldots, (N_t \cdot C_{t-1} - Z)$ is the index of the remaining particles. We generate β samples to be added to the target size of each $\hat{x}_{(t+1)}^{(p)}$ according to

$$x_{t+1}^{(f)} = \hat{x}_{t+1}^{(p)} + [0_{(1,4)}, \zeta_{t+1}^{(f)}], \tag{18}$$

where $\zeta_{t+1}^{(f)} \in \mathbb{R}^4$ is drawn from a zero-mean normal distribution and $f = 1, \ldots, \beta$. Thus, the number of particles for frame $t + 1$ is

$$N_{t+1} = \beta \cdot (N_t \cdot C_{t-1} - Z). \tag{19}$$

If the resampling conditions are not met, the selected target state x_t for frame t is applied in Eq. 3 to Eq. 6 to generate the new particles. Figure 2 illustrates how the number of the particles decrease in simple frames. Additionally, the figure shows when the maximum weight significantly decreases comparing with T_w, resampling is implemented.

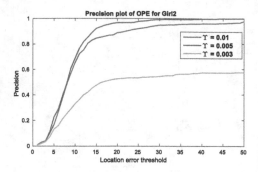

Fig. 4. The impact of different adjusting rates on the performance of DCPF2 [11] illustrates the benefit of generating multiple target models based on different adjusting rates

2.2 Multiple Correlation Models

In this section, we describe the process to generate C_t target models for frame t to be employed in frame $t + 1$. A target model is generated by computing the Fourier transform of the convolutional features corresponding to an image patch. Figure 3 illustrates our method for generating several target models. As discussed in [11], a comparison between the best model and the most accurate target size and position results in higher weights. Similar to [11], we select all high-likelihood target states by examining the following relation over all $N_t \times C_{t-1}$ weights

$$\omega^{(i)(j)} > \alpha \omega^*, \tag{20}$$

where we set α to 0.8. The particles that satisfy Eq. 20 are considered high-likelihood candidates [11]. A target model is generated based on each of the K_t selected high-likelihood particles in frame t, as discussed in [11]. Let $\breve{\mho}_t^{(j)}$ represent one of the K_t target models generated from the current frame. The final target models to be used in frame $t + 1$ are a combination of the current target models and the previous selected target model according to [5]

$$\mho_t^{(j)} = (1 - \Upsilon)\mho_{t-1}^* + \Upsilon\breve{\mho}_t^{(j)}, \tag{21}$$

where Υ is the adjusting rate. As seen in Fig. 4, the adjusting rate has a significant influence on the performance of correlation trackers. In our tracker, we consider different adjusting rates and then apply them to Eq. 21. Thus, the number of target models becomes

$$C_t = \Gamma K_t, \tag{22}$$

where Γ is the number of adjusting rates. We define two sets of adjusting rates S_1 and S_2. Equation 15, determines which set should be used at each frame. When the tracker does not satisfy Eq. 15, the correlation response maps are not reliable because of challenging scenarios, and we should use lower adjusting rates to increase the effect of the previous target model and decrease the current one. When Eq. 15 is satisfied, we can use higher adjusting rates. Algorithm 4 explains the method of generating multiple target models.

Fig. 5. Qualitative evaluation of our tracker, *DCPF2*, *SINT* and *HCFT* on three challenging sequences (from top to bottom *Human3*, *Car1* and *Freeman4*, respectively).

3   Results and Discussion

We used the Visual Tracker Benchmark v1.1 beta (OTB100) to test our tracker performance. This benchmark contains 100 data sequences and considers 11 challenging scenarios. Results are based on a one-pass evaluation, which means the ground truth target size and position are used in the first frame to initialize the tracker. We select $N_t = 300$, $\varphi = 0.7$, $Tr2 = 4$, $\beta = 5$, $\Gamma = 3$, $S_1 = [0.0075, 0.01, 0.015]$ and $S_2 = [0.0075, 0.005, 0.001]$. The number of adjusting rates in each set is limited to three because of the computation costs. However, these sets are defined based on experiments. The precision and success criteria are explained in [14].

Figure 5 illustrates the qualitative evaluation of our tracker compared to DCPF2, SINT [16] and HCFT. In the first data sequence *Human3*, the lower adjusting rate helps our tracker to rely more on the previous target model. In the second data sequence *Car1*, Our tracker improves the estimated target position. Additionally, it is able to better handle the occlusion in the third data sequence *Freeman4*.

We compared our tracker with eight state of the art trackers including: CFNet-conv3 [17], SiameseFC [18], SINT, LCT [19] and CNN-SVM [20], HDT, HCFT and DCPF2. As illustrated in Fig. 6, our overall performance in terms of precision and success are improved by 3.5% and 5.5% in comparison with DCPF2, which is the second and fourth-best tracker in the precision and success plots, respectively. Our tracker outperforms SINT, the second-best tracker in the success plot, by around 4.5%. On deformation and occlusion, our performance is better because we employ different adjusting rates and decrease the updating rate of the model in challenging frames. As seen in Fig. 6, for deformation and occlusion, our performance is improved around 4.5% in precision and 6% in success in comparison with the second-best tracker. For other challenging scenarios such as motion blur, background clutter and out of plane rotation, our tracker shows improvements of approximately 5%, 3.5% and 3%, respectively, in comparison to the second-best tracker.

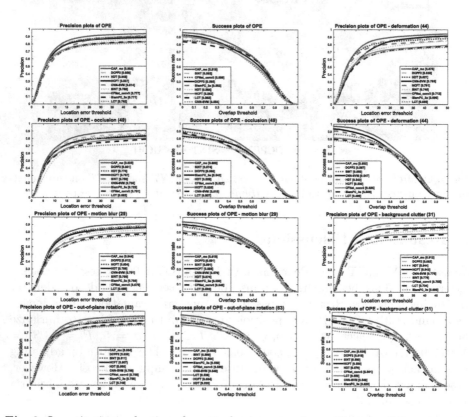

Fig. 6. Quantitative evaluation of our tracker in comparison with state-of-the-art trackers on OPE.

4   Conclusion

This article proposes a novel framework for visual tracking based on the integration of an adaptive particle filter, a deep CNN, and a correlation filter. In our adaptive particle filter, the locations of the updated particle in the current frame are used as particles for the next frame, which provides more reliable particles than sampling around the final estimated target state in every frame.

Our adaptive particle filter can decrease the number of particles especially in simple frames because the particles can converge together. If the number of particles is too small or the maximum weight in the current frame is significantly lower than the weight in the first frame, resampling is performed. The reason for using the weight in the first frame as a threshold for resampling is that it is computed based on the ground truth target model, and hence serves as an upper bound on the weight of subsequent particles. Additionally, we generate multiple target models in each frame by applying different adjusting rates to the models created by the high-likelihood particles. For challenging frames, we use lower adjusting rates, which means we rely more on previous target models. The Visual Tracker Benchmark v1.1 beta (OTB100) is used for evaluating the proposed tracker's performance. The results show that our tracker outperforms several state-of-the-art methods.

References

1. Choi, J., Chang, H.J., Jeong, J., Demiris, Y., Choi, J.Y.: Visual tracking using attention-modulated disintegration and integration. In: IEEE Conference on Computer Vision and Pattern Recognition (CVPR), June 2016
2. Tang, M., Feng, J.: Multi-kernel correlation filter for visual tracking. In: IEEE International Conference on Computer Vision (ICCV), pp. 3038–3046 (2015)
3. Danelljan, M., Hager, G., Khan, F.S., Felsberg, M.: Learning spatially regularized correlation filters for visual tracking. In: IEEE International Conference on Computer Vision (ICCV), December 2015
4. Danelljan, M., Hager, G., Shahbaz Khan, F., Felsberg, M.: Convolutional features for correlation filter based visual tracking. In: IEEE International Conference on Computer Vision (ICCV) Workshops, December 2015
5. Ma, C., Huang, J.-B., Yang, X., Yang, M.-H.: Hierarchical convolutional features for visual tracking. In: IEEE International Conference on Computer Vision (ICCV), December 2015
6. Henriques, J.F., Caseiro, R., Martins, P., Batista, J.: High-speed tracking with kernelized correlation filters. IEEE Trans. Pattern Anal. Mach. Intell. **37**(3), 583–596 (2015)
7. Zhang, J., Ma, S., Sclaroff, S.: MEEM: robust tracking via multiple experts using entropy minimization. In: Fleet, D., Pajdla, T., Schiele, B., Tuytelaars, T. (eds.) ECCV 2014. LNCS, vol. 8694, pp. 188–203. Springer, Cham (2014). https://doi.org/10.1007/978-3-319-10599-4_13
8. Hare, S., Saffari, A., Torr, P.H.S.: Struck: structured output tracking with kernels. In: IEEE International Conference on Computer Vision (ICCV), pp. 263–270. IEEE Computer Society (2011)
9. Zhong, W., Lu, H., Yang, M.H.: Robust object tracking via sparse collaborative appearance model. IEEE Trans. Image Process. **23**(5), 2356–2368 (2014)
10. Kalal, Z., Mikolajczyk, K., Matas, J.: Tracking-learning-detection. IEEE Trans. Pattern Anal. Mach. Intell. **34**(7), 1409–1422 (2012)
11. Mozhdehi, R.J., Reznichenko, Y., Siddique, A., Medeiros, H.: Deep convolutional particle filter with adaptive correlation maps for visual tracking. In: IEEE International Conference on Image Processing (ICIP) (2018)

12. Mozhdehi, R.J., Medeiros, H.: Deep convolutional particle filter for visual tracking. In: IEEE International Conference on Image Processing (ICIP) (2017)
13. Cheng, H.Y., Hwang, J.N.: Adaptive particle sampling and adaptive appearance for multiple video object tracking. Signal Process. **89**(9), 1844–1849 (2009)
14. Wu, Y., Lim, J., Yang, M.-H.: Online object tracking: a benchmark. In: IEEE Conference on Computer Vision and Pattern Recognition (CVPR) (2013)
15. Simonyan, K., Zisserman, A.: Very deep convolutional networks for large-scale image recognition. In: International Conference on Learning Representations (ICLR) (2015)
16. Tao, R., Gavves, E., Smeulders, A.W.M.: Siamese instance search for tracking. In: IEEE Conference on Computer Vision and Pattern Recognition (CVPR) (2016)
17. Valmadre, J., Bertinetto, L., Henriques, J., Vedaldi, A., Torr, P.H.S.: End-to-end representation learning for correlation filter based tracking. In: IEEE Conference on Computer Vision and Pattern Recognition (CVPR), July 2017
18. Bertinetto, L., Valmadre, J., Henriques, J.F., Vedaldi, A., Torr, P.H.S.: Fully-convolutional siamese networks for object tracking. In: Hua, G., Jégou, H. (eds.) ECCV 2016. LNCS, vol. 9914, pp. 850–865. Springer, Cham (2016). https://doi.org/10.1007/978-3-319-48881-3_56
19. Ma, C., Yang, X., Zhang, C., Yang, M.-H.: Long-term correlation tracking. In: IEEE Conference on Computer Vision and Pattern Recognition (CVPR), pp. 5388–5396 (2015)
20. Hong, S., You, T., Kwak, S., Han, B.: Online tracking by learning discriminative saliency map with convolutional neural network. In: 32nd International Conference on Machine Learning (2015)

Scale-Aware RPN for Vehicle Detection

Lu Ding[1], Yong Wang[2], Robert Laganière[2(✉)], Xinbin Luo[3], and Shan Fu[3]

[1] School of Aeronautics and Astronautics, Shanghai Jiao Tong University,
Shanghai, China
{dinglu,losinbin,sfu}@sjtu.edu.cn
[2] School of Electrical Engineering and Computer Science, University of Ottawa,
Ottawa, Canada
ywang6@uottawa.ca,laganier@eecs.uottawa.ca
[3] School of Electronic Information and Electrical Engineering,
Shanghai Jiao Tong University,
Shanghai, China

Abstract. In this paper, we develop a scale-aware Region Proposal
Network (RPN) model to address the problem of vehicle detection in
challenging situations. Our model introduces two built in sub-networks
which detect vehicles with scales from disjoint ranges. Therefore, the
model is capable of training the specialized sub-networks for large-scale
and small-scale vehicles in order to capture their unique characteristics.
Meanwhile, high resolution of feature maps for handling small vehicle
instances is obtained. The network model is followed by two XGBoost
classifiers with bootstrapping strategy for mining hard negative examples. The method is evaluated on the challenging KITTI dataset and
achieves comparable results against the state-of-the-art methods.

Keywords: Vehicle detection · Region proposal network
XGBoost classifiers

1 Introduction

The problem of vehicle detection has been studied for years with the aim of
ensuring the robust vehicle detection algorithm to unseen images. However, the
detection results in recent vehicle detection methods are still far away from the
demands in practice due to a number of challenges. Figure 1 illustrates the various factors that need to be considered, e.g., heavy occlusion, lighting conditions,
low resolution, etc.

Faster R-CNN [1] is a successful method for object detection. It consists
of two components: a Region Proposal Network (RPN) for proposing candidate
regions, and a Fast R-CNN [2] classifier. Although it's appealing performance on
several multi-category benchmarks, Faster R-CNN has not presented competitive
results on popular vehicle detection datasets (e.g., the KITTI dataset [3]). We
argue that such unsatisfactory performance is attributed to the following two
reasons.

© Springer Nature Switzerland AG 2018
G. Bebis et al. (Eds.): ISVC 2018, LNCS 11241, pp. 487–499, 2018.
https://doi.org/10.1007/978-3-030-03801-4_43

Fig. 1. Some examples of vehicle detection results using our proposed method on KITTI dataset [3].

First, the convolutional feature maps of the Faster R-CNN and RPN are of low solution for detecting small objects. Typical scenarios of vehicle detection generally present vehicles of small sizes as shown in Fig. 1. Therefore, low resolution feature map which is generated by the Region of Interest (RoI) pooling layer can lead to "plain" features due to collapsing bins. These features are not discriminative enough on small targets, and degrade the performance of the following classifier. We note that in the KITTI dataset, the perspective geometry information can be employed. We address this problem by designing a scale-aware RPN model which consists of two sub-networks to detect vehicles with different scales ranges.

Second, in vehicle detection the false predictions are mainly caused by confusions of hard background instances. To address hard negative examples, we adopt XGBoost [4] to classify the RPN proposals. We exploit the deeply learned features by using the deep convolutional features of RPN to train the XGBoost classifier.

In this paper, we present a scale-aware RPN model to deal with the problem of vehicle detection under various challenging factors. Our method extends the framework of RPN with the significant modification in both the training and detection procedure to address challenging conditions to provide a robust vehicle detection algorithm in the wild. The method takes advantages of RPN to introduce a number of region proposals and extract the RoIs. A confidence score is assigned to each RoI. The convolution feature map and proposal are fed to XGBoost classifiers to produce detection results.

To sum up, this paper makes the following contributions. Firstly, we propose a novel scale-aware RPN model for object proposal generation by incorporating a large-size sub-network and a small-size sub-network into a unified architecture. Secondly, XGBoost boosting mechanism is proposed to lift the contribution of the sub-network specialized for the current input scales and improve the final detection performance. Thirdly, we present compelling results on KITTI dataset.

Specifically, our approach has substantially better localization accuracy on the dataset under an Intersection-over-Union (IoU) threshold of 0.7 for evaluation.

2   Related Work

2.1   Object Proposal

Object proposal can be mainly categorized to scoring methods and grouping methods. Object proposal is first proposed in [5] by sampling a group of proposals according to a saliency map. The proposals are ranked by using several factors, e.g., saliency, superpixel, contrast, edge density, etc. The structured output ranking and cascaded ranking SVM are employed to generate object proposals in [7] and [8] respectively. BING is proposed in [9] which uses a linear classifier with the learned gradient features to rank proposals that generated from sliding windows. The work is then extended in [10] and [11]. EdgeBoxes is introduced in [12] which scores thousands of windows by evaluating the relationship between the contours enclosed within the box and those overlapping the box's boundary. It is extended in [13] by proposing Contour Box to reject proposals which do not have explicit closed contours. DeepBox is introduced in [14] which ranks proposals generated by Edgeboxes by using convolutional neural network (CNN). In summary, the main drawback of these scoring methods is their localization bias [15]. That is, high recall is only achieved at an IoU threshold. The bias is reduced in [16] by using multi-thresholding strategy. However, the localization bias issue was not completely resolved.

Grouping methods usually achieve better localization compared to scoring methods. A constrained parametric min-cuts (CPMC) problem is solved with several foreground and background seeds to generate proposals [17]. The CPMC is accelerated in [19] by reusing computation across multiple min-cuts. Selective Search [20] is one of the most well-known grouping methods and has been widely adopted in object detectors [2,22]. More specifically, hierarchical segmentations are performed in multiple color spaces by using graph-based segmentation algorithm [23]. And adjacent superpixels are greedily merged to generate proposals according to low-level features. Different features are used for superpixel merging and graph-cuts are employed to generate proposals [24]. Geodesic distance transforms are computed from foreground-background masks to identify level sets as proposals [25]. In summary, some grouping methods do not provide ranked proposals or only provide random scores which leads to ineffectiveness in preserving proposal recall when handling a small set of proposals.

2.2   CNN Based Object Detection

CNN has been used to object detection and achieved good results. In [26], object detection is considered as a regression problem to bounding box masks. A CNN is learned to generate and predict object bounding boxes. A CNN is designed in [27] to propose class-agnostic bounding boxes for object detection. A regression network which is pre-trained for classification tasks is used to localize object bounding boxes in [28]. Each bounding box is assigned a confidence score indicating the probability of an object class. The R-CNN framework is proposed in [22]. Selective search is used to generate object proposals to fine-tune a CNN for detection task. The work is extended in [29] by gradually generating bounding boxes within a search window and imposing a loss function to penalize localization errors. Fast R-CNN [2] is proposed to reduce the cost of forward pass for each proposal in R-CNN by sharing convolutional features and pooling object proposals only from the last convolutional layer. Faster R-CNN [1] is proposed to replace the generation of object proposals by a RPN and achieves further speed-up. RPN followed by boost forests is employed for pedestrian detection [18]. A two sub-networks model is proposed in [6] to handle the small size pedestrian instances and large size pedestrian instances separately since the features of two instances are significantly different. In addition, the CNN based object detection method is used in embedded systems [21].

Motivated by the work mentioned above, we develop a novel scale-aware RPN network model, which combines the RPN and XGBoost pipeline. The proposed network model integrates a large-size sub-network and a small-size sub-network into a unified architecture. Given an input image, the model first passes the raw image through the bottom shared convolutional layers and the sub-networks to extract its whole feature maps. Different object proposals are generated by the two sub-networks. Taking these feature maps and the locations of object proposals as inputs, two sub-networks provide different confidence scores and bounding box for each proposal. The proposals are fed to XGBoost classifiers to generate the final detection results.

3 Our Algorithm

Our approach consists of two components, and the overall architecture is illustrated in Fig. 2. The scale-aware RPN model aims at better detecting small scale objects around the vanishing point by exploiting the image inherent perspective geometry. We propose one sub-network to detect the object in the region around the vanishing point. Another one sub-network is used to detect the object in the entire image. The region around vanishing point is then re-scaled and receives finer processing by the sub-network. In this way, small distant objects are untangled from large near objects for detecting. Two XGBoost classifiers apply to these proposals using these convolutional features which are generated by the RPN.

3.1 Architecture of Our Model

The proposed scale-aware RPN model which is an ensemble of two scale specific sub-networks detects the vehicles of large and small scales, respectively. Figure 3 demonstrates the architecture of our model. Such collaboration of two sub-networks enables the proposed method to accurately capture unique characteristics of objects at different sizes, and meanwhile the shared convolutional

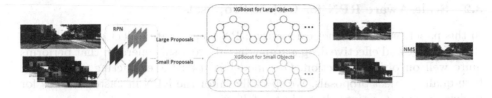

Fig. 2. Our pipeline. Our scale-aware RPN is used to compute candidate bounding boxes, scores, and convolutional feature maps. The candidate boxes are fed into XGBoost for classification, using the features pooled from the convolutional feature maps computed by the scale-aware RPN model.

filters in its early layers also incorporate the common characteristics shared by all instances. The architecture of our network is developed based on the popular RPN framework [1] due to its superior performance and computation efficiency in detecting general objects. Our model takes the whole image as input, and then outputs the object proposals.

The features of the input image are first extracted by a sequence of convolutional layers and max pooling layers, and then fed into two sub-networks. Each sub-network first utilizes several convolutional layers to further extract scale-specific features. Then, a RoI pooling layer pools the produced feature maps into a fixed-length feature vector and then a sequence of fully connected layers ending up with two output layers are performed to generate scale-specific detection results: one outputs classification scores over vehicle object classes plus a "background" class and the other outputs refined bounding-box positions for each of the vehicle classes. Finally, the object proposals are obtained via the outputs of the two sub-networks.

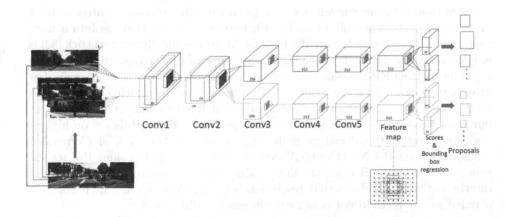

Fig. 3. The architecture of our scale-aware RPN model.

3.2   Scale-Aware RPN for Object Proposals

In this paper, we utilize the scale-aware RPN to generate object proposals. The RPN is a fast and effective deep learning based proposal generator that performs quite well on object detection. Our model is used for extracting and mining high-quality object proposals. We specially tailor the RPN in Faster R-CNN for vehicle detection, as introduced in the following.

We apply anchors of three aspect ratio of 0.5, 1, 2 (width to height), starting from 32 pixels height with a scaling stride of 2. We apply the multi-scale anchors to waive the requirement of using feature pyramids to detect multi-scale vehicles. Following [1], VGG-16 net [30] pre-trained on the ImageNet dataset [31] is adopted as the backbone network. The RPN is built on top of the $Conv5\_3$ layer, which is followed by a 3 * 3 convolutional layer and two 1 * 1 convolutional layers for classification and bounding box regression. In this way, our scale-aware RPN regresses boxes with a stride of 16 pixels ($Conv5\_3$). The outputs of the classification layer are confidence scores of the estimated bounding boxes, which can be employed as the initial scores of the XGBoost classifiers that follow.

3.3   Feature Extraction

With the proposals generated by the scale-aware RPN model, we adopt RoI pooling [2] to extract fixed-length features from regions. These features will be used to train XGBoost classifiers as introduced in the next section. Unlike Faster R-CNN which requires to feed these features into the original fully-connected (fc) layers and thus limits their dimensions, the XGBoost classifiers imposes no constraint on the dimensions of features.

For example, features can be extracted from RoIs on $Conv3\_3$ (of a stride = 4 pixels) and $Conv4\_3$ (of a stride = 4 pixels). The features are pooled into a fixed resolution of 7 * 7. Due to the flexibility of the XGBoost classifiers, these features from different convolutional maps can be simply concatenated without normalization. It is flexible for us to utilize features of rescaled resolution since there is no constraint to feature dimensions. More specifically, à trous trick [33] is employed to calculate convolutional feature maps of higher resolution when the input layers from RPN (stride = 4 on $Conv3$, 8 on $Conv4$, and 16 on $Conv5$). For example, we can reduce the stride of $Conv4$ from 8 to 4 by dilating $Conv4$ filters by 2. Different from previous works [33,34] that fine-tune the dilated filters, in our work we only utilize them for feature generation. These RoIs are on higher-resolution convolutional feature maps (e.g., $Conv3\_3$, $Conv4\_3$, or $Conv4\_3$ à trous) than Fast R-CNN ($Conv5\_3$) despite of the usage of the same RoI resolution (7 * 7) as Faster R-CNN [2]. The pooling bins collapse and the features lost discriminative if a RoI's output resolution is bigger than input. The problem is avoided as our method not constrains the feature dimension.

Figure 3 shows the architecture of our model in details. The whole image and the center cropped region are passed into several convolutional layers and max pooling layers to extract feature maps. Then the network branches into two sub-networks, which are trained specifically to detect large-size and small-size vehicles respectively. The feature maps generated from the previous convolutional layers are treated as input to the sub-networks. Then the feature maps which are specialized for a specific range of input size are produced through several convolutional layers. The RoI pooling layer as proposed in [2] is employed to pool the feature maps of each input object proposal into a fixed-length feature vector which is fed into XGBoost classifier.

Each sub-network has two output layers which generate two output vectors for each object proposal. Specifically, one layer outputs classification scores over vehicle class and background class. Another one is the bounding box. The classification scores are sent into a softmax layer to generate softmax probabilities over 2 classes per object proposal.

3.4   XGBoost Classifier

The scale-aware RPN generates the region proposals, confidence scores, and features, all of which are utilized to train the followed XGBoost classifiers which are fast implementation of gradient boosting trees [35]. We adopt the XGBoost algorithm [4], and mainly follow the hyper-parameters in [18]. Many successful solutions in Kaggle competitions are developed with this additional tree boosting method. Formally, the training is bootstrapped by 6 times, and the forest in each stage has $\{64, 128, 256, 512, 1024, 1536\}$ trees. Initially, the training set includes all positive samples (20009 on the KITTI set) which the overlap with ground truth is above 0.8. And the same number (15000) of sampled negative examples from the proposals which the overlap with ground truth is above 0 and below 0.5. After each stage, additional hard negative examples (whose number is 10% of the positives, 5k on KITTI) are mined and added into the training set. Finally, a forest of 2048 trees is trained after all bootstrapping steps. This final classifier is utilized for classification. Our implementation is based on [36]. Figure 4 illustrates the XGBoost classifier processing steps.

4   Experiment

4.1   Experiment Setup

Dataset. We evaluate our model on KITTI detection benchmark [3]. The KITTI dataset is composed of 7481 images for training, and 7518 images for testing. The training dataset contains 28742 number of car annotations. For the KITTI train and validation experiment, all the training and testing images are resized to 500 pixel height. Following the standard setting on the KITTI dataset, we train our scale-aware RPN on the KITTI training set and apply the model on training and testing images with a low detection threshold of 0.7 to generate object proposals. The images are resized as 500 pixels on the shortest side during the training and testing time.

Since there are no ground truth labels in the testing set, the training sets is used to train and evaluate the performance of the proposed method. Specifically,

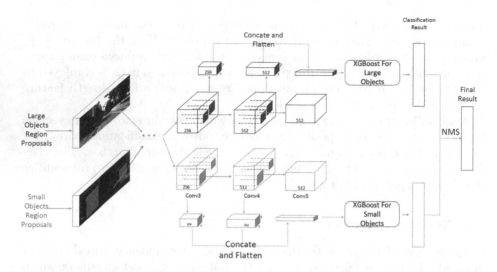

Fig. 4. Our XGBoost classifier processing steps.

the training set includes 5000 images, the testing set includes 2480 images. And there is no overlap between the two sets in terms of images extracted from the same video sequence.

Implementation Detail. For scale-aware RPN training stage, if an anchor has an IoU ratio greater than 0.5 with one ground truth box, it is considered as a positive example. Otherwise, it is a negative example. The image-centric training strategy [1,2] is adopted. And each mini-batch includes 1 image and 120 randomly exampled anchors for calculating the loss. The ratio of positive and negative examples is 1:5 in a mini-batch. We follow the parameters of RPN as in [2]. The publicly available code of [2] is used to fine-tune the RPN. Non-maximum suppression (NMS) with a threshold of 0.7 is employed to filter the proposal regions. Next the proposal regions are ranked by their scores.

We use the pre-trained VGG16 network [30] to initialize our scale-aware RPN network, which is employed in the most recent state-of-the-art method. The first four convolutional layers and two max pooling layers of the VGG16 network are utilized as the shared convolutional layers before the two sub-networks to generate feature maps from the input image. The rest layers of the VGG16 network are employed to initialize the two sub-networks. Following RPN [18], the last max pooling layer of the VGG16 network is replaced by a 3 * 3 convolutional layer. The fully connected layer and softmax are replaced with two sibling fully convolutional layers. Our scale-aware RPN network is trained with Stochastic Gradient Descent (SGD) with momentum of 0.9, and weight decay of 0.0005. Our algorithm is implemented based on the publicly available Caffe platform [37]. The whole network is trained on a single NVIDIA GeForce GTX TITAN X GPU with 12 GB memory.

We discard the features from Conv5 since the resolution of the feature maps is small. The features from Conv3 and Conv4 are put into ROI pooling and concatenated to produce a feature vector. The feature vectors are sent to the XGBoost classifiers for training and testing. For XGBoost classifiers training, the training set is constructed by selecting the top-ranked 1000 proposals and ground truths of each image. The tree depth is set as 5 for the KITTI dataset. For XGBoost classifiers testing, the top-ranked 100 proposals in an image are used, which are classified by the XGBoost classifiers.

Evaluation Metric. To evaluate the performance on KITTI dataset, we compute the average precision (AP). AP is the area under the Precision-Recall curve. A detected vehicle is considered positive or negative according to its overlap with the ground truth bounding box. A detected box is true if the overlap score is more than 0.7. The overlap score between two boxes is computed as $\frac{GT \cap DET}{GT \cup DET}$, where GT is area of ground truth bounding box and DET is area of detected bounding box. KITTI evaluates the AP under three difficulty levels: "Easy", "Moderate", and "Hard", where the difficulty is measured by the minimal scale of the vehicles to be considered and the occlusion and truncation of the vehicles.

4.2   Experiment Results

Figure 5 shows the performance comparisons on KITTI dataset. Our method has competitive accuracy. We compare the result of our method (SA RPN + XGBoost) with Faster R-CNN method, RPN with XGBoost method (denoted with RPN + XGBoost) and scale-aware RPN method (denoted with SA RPN

method	AP on Easy	AP on Moderate	AP on Hard	Times
Faster R-CNN	0.6411	0.5746	0.4568	0.107
RPN+xgboost	0.6941	0.6243	0.5395	0.268
SA RPN no bootstrapping	0.7287	0.6912	0.6015	0.900
SA RPN+xgboost	0.8958	0.8481	0.7084	0.900

Fig. 5. The comparison of our method on vehicle detection with other compared methods on the KITTI dataset. Our approach has a test-time speed of 0.9 second per image.

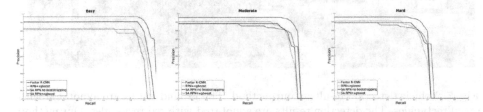

Fig. 6. ROC curves of vehicle detection on AP measure obtained by Faster R-CNN, RPN+xgboost, SA RPN without bootstrapping, and our method. Our method achieves the state-of-the-art results on this dataset.

Fig. 7. Vehicle detection results of our method. The ground-truths are annotated with green rectangles. The detection results are annotated with red rectangles. Our method can successfully detect most small-size vehicles. For better viewing, please see original PDF file.

no bootstrapping). It can be observed that SA RPN with XGBoost method outperform other methods. Faster R-CNN is the state-of-the-art object detection method. The detection results are representative. Since there is only one RPN in the RPN with XGBoost method, the detection results illustrate the effect of our two sub-networks model. The detection results of SA RPN no bootstrapping indicates that the 6 stages of bootstrapping improves the performance.

4.3   Visualization of Detection Results

Several detection results of our method are visualized in Fig. 7 to further illustrate the superiority of our method in detecting small-size vehicles. The ground-truths are annotated with green rectangles. The detection results are annotated with red rectangles. One can observe that our method can successfully detect most small-size vehicles. More details can be found in the supplementary file (Fig. 6).

5   Conclusion

In this paper, we present an effective scale-aware RPN and XGBoost based approach to handle the problems of vehicle detection in images collected in vehicles under challenging situations. The proposed method employs a scale-aware RPN and XGBoost classifier to provide a robust vehicle detection system. The system is flexible for (1) combining features of small vehicle instances and large vehicle instances. (2) Incorporating effective bootstrapping for vehicle detection. These nice properties overcome the limitation of tradition method for vehicle detection. The method is evaluated on the challenging vehicle detection KITTI dataset. Our proposed method is able to achieve the state-of-the-art performance on KITTI dataset.

References

1. Ren, S., He, K., et al.: Faster R-CNN: towards real-time object detection with region proposal networks. In: NIPS (2015)
2. Girshick, R.: Fast R-CNN. In: ICCV (2015)
3. Geiger, A., Lenz, P., Urtasun, R.: Are we ready for autonomous driving? The kitti vision benchmark suite. In: CVPR (2012)
4. Chen, T., Guestrin, C.: XGBoost: a scalable tree boosting system. In: ACM SIGKDD, pp. 785–794. ACM (2016)
5. Alexe, B., Deselaers, T., Ferrari, V.: What is an object? In: CVPR, pp. 73–80 (2010)
6. Li, J., Liang, X., et al.: Scale-aware fast R-CNN for pedestrian detection. IEEE Trans. Multimedia **20**, 985–996 (2017)
7. Rahtu, E., Kannala, J., Blaschko, M.B.: Learning a category independent object detection cascade. In: ICCV (2011)
8. Zhang, Z., Warrell, J., Torr, P.H.S.: Proposal generation for object detection using cascaded ranking SVMs. In: CVPR, pp. 1497–1504 (2011)

9. Cheng, M.-M., Zhang, Z., et al.: BING: Binarized normed gradients for objectness estimation at 300fps. In: CVPR, pp. 3286–3293 (2014)
10. Zhao, Q., Liu, Z., Yin, B.: Cracking BING and beyond. In: BMVC (2014)
11. Zhang, Z., Liu, Y., et al.: BING++: a fast high quality object proposal generator at 100 fps. arXiv:1511.04511
12. Zitnick, C.L., Dollár, P.: Edge boxes: locating object proposals from edges. In: Fleet, D., Pajdla, T., Schiele, B., Tuytelaars, T. (eds.) ECCV 2014. LNCS, vol. 8693, pp. 391–405. Springer, Cham (2014). https://doi.org/10.1007/978-3-319-10602-1_26
13. Lu, C., Liu, S., Jia, J., Tang, C.K.: Contour box: rejecting object proposals without explicit closed contours. In: ICCV (2015)
14. Kuo, W., Hariharan, B., Malik, J.: DeepBox: learning objectness with convolutional networks. In: ICCV, pp. 2479–2487 (2015)
15. Hosang, J., Benenson, R., Dollar, P., Schiele, B.: What makes for effective detection proposals? IEEE TPAMI 38(4), 814–830 (2016)
16. Chen, X., Ma, H., Wang, X., Zhao, Z.: Improving object proposals with multi-thresholding straddling expansion. In: CVPR, pp. 2587–2595 (2015)
17. Carreira, J., Sminchisescu, C.: Constrained parametric min-cuts for automatic object segmentation. In: CVPR, pp. 3241–3248 (2010)
18. Zhang, L., Lin, L., Liang, X., He, K.: Is faster R-CNN doing well for pedestrian detection? In: ECCV, pp. 443–457 (2016)
19. Humayun, A., Li, F., Rehg, J.M.: RIGOR: reusing inference in graph cuts for generating object regions. In: CVPR, pp. 336–343 (2014)
20. van de Sande, K.E.A., Uijlings, J.R., Gevers, T., Smeulders, A.W.M.: Segmentation as selective search for object recognition. In: ICCV (2011)
21. Verbickas, R., Laganiere, R., et al.: SqueezeMap: fast pedestrian detection on a low-power automotive processor using efficient convolutional neural networks. In: CVPRW, pp. 146–154 (2017)
22. Girshick, R., Donahue, J., Darrell, T., Malik, J.: Rich feature hierarchies for accurate object detection and semantic segmentation. In: CVPR, pp. 580–587 (2014)
23. Felzenszwalb, P.F., Huttenlocher, D.P.: Efficient graph-based image segmentation. IJCV 59(2), 167–181 (2004)
24. Arbeláez, P., Pont-Tuset, J., Barron, J.T., Marques, F., Malik, J.: Multiscale combinatorial grouping. In: CVPR, pp. 328–335 (2014)
25. Krähenbühl, P., Koltun, V.: Geodesic object proposals. In: Fleet, D., Pajdla, T., Schiele, B., Tuytelaars, T. (eds.) ECCV 2014. LNCS, vol. 8693, pp. 725–739. Springer, Cham (2014). https://doi.org/10.1007/978-3-319-10602-1_47
26. Szegedy, C., Toshev, A., Erhan, D.: Deep neural networks for object detection. In: NIPS, pp. 2553–2561 (2013)
27. Erhan, D., Szegedy, C., Toshev, A., Anguelov, D.: Scalable object detection using deep neural networks. In: CVPR, pp. 2155–2162 (2014)
28. Sermanet, P., Eigen, D., et al.: Overfeat: integrated recognition, localization and detection using convolutional networks, CoRR, abs/1312.6229 (2013)
29. Zhang, Y., Sohn, K., Villegas, R., Pan, G., Lee, H.: Improving object detection with deep convolutional networks via Bayesian optimization and structured prediction. In: CVPR, pp. 249–258 (2015)
30. Simonyan, K., Zisserman, A.: Very deep convolutional networks for large-scale image recognition, arXiv:1409.1556 (2014)
31. Russakovsky, O., Deng, J., et al.: ImageNet large scale visual recognition challenge. IJCV 115(3), 211–252 (2015)

32. Liu, W., Rabinovich, A., Berg, A.C.: Parsenet: Looking wider to see better, arXiv:1506.04579 (2015)
33. Chen, L.C., Papandreou, G., et al.: Semantic image segmentation with deep convolutional nets and fully connected crfs, arXiv:1412.7062 (2014)
34. Long, J., Shelhamer, E., Darrell, T.: Fully convolutional networks for semantic segmentation. In: CVPR (2015)
35. Friedman, J.H.: Greedy function approximation: a gradient boosting machine. Ann. Stat. **29**, 1189–1232 (2001)
36. http://xgboost.readthedocs.io/en/latest/
37. Jia, Y., Shelhamer, E., Donahue, J., Karayev, S., et al.: Caffe: convolutional architecture for fast feature embedding. In: ACMMM, pp. 675–678 (2014)

Object Detection to Assist Visually Impaired People: A Deep Neural Network Adventure

Fereshteh S. Bashiri[1,2(✉)], Eric LaRose[1], Jonathan C. Badger[1],
Roshan M. D'Souza[2], Zeyun Yu[2], and Peggy Peissig[1]

[1] Marshfield Clinic Research Institute, Marshfield, USA
bashiri.fereshteh@marshfieldresearch.org
[2] University of Wisconsin-Milwaukee, Milwaukee, USA

Abstract. Blindness or vision impairment, one of the top ten disabilities among men and women, targets more than 7 million Americans of all ages. Accessible visual information is of paramount importance to improve independence and safety of blind and visually impaired people, and there is a pressing need to develop smart automated systems to assist their navigation, specifically in unfamiliar healthcare environments, such as clinics, hospitals, and urgent cares. This contribution focused on developing computer vision algorithms composed with a deep neural network to assist visually impaired individual's mobility in clinical environments by accurately detecting doors, stairs, and signages, the most remarkable landmarks. Quantitative experiments demonstrate that with enough number of training samples, the network recognizes the objects of interest with an accuracy of over 98% within a fraction of a second.

Keywords: Machine learning and predictive modeling
Mobile health and wearable devices
Data mining and knowledge discovery
Assistive technology for visually impaired people

1 Introduction

Worldwide prevalence statistics show 216.6 million people with moderate to severe visual impairment, almost 188.5 million with mild visual impairment [5], and among those more than 7 million Americans across all ages are either blind or visually impaired [6]. The metadata analysis, recently established by Bourne et al. [5], estimates 38.5 million completely blind people by 2020 increasing to 115 million by 2050, emphasizing the degree of the challenge we will face. Accessible visual information is of vital importance to improve independence and safety of blind or visually impaired people. In addition to all common mobility equipment and facilities used in support (e.g., canes or dog guides), there is crucial need to develop smart automated systems to assist visually impaired

© Springer Nature Switzerland AG 2018
G. Bebis et al. (Eds.): ISVC 2018, LNCS 11241, pp. 500–510, 2018.
https://doi.org/10.1007/978-3-030-03801-4_44

individuals in day-to-day life in detecting, recognizing, reading, and even feeling objects surrounding them. In recent years, the advances in machine intelligence, Internet of Things (IoT), and telecommunication systems led to the implementation of efficient computational methods to tackle different challenges existing in the literature. Utilizing computer vision algorithms, Tekin et al. [23,24] developed barcode and LED/LCD reader for visually impaired people. Combining embedded systems with an optical character recognition algorithm, Gaudissart et al. [7] implemented an automatic text reading system, called SYPOLE. Additionally, and with the use of machine intelligence strategies, several research projects [1,3,11,18,19] have also been conducted to detect indoor objects for the blind, helping individuals to walk, move, and find desired objects independently.

Daily navigation for blind and visually impaired people, particularly in unfamiliar environments, could be an intimidating task without the help of machine intelligence systems. The primary objective of the current contribution is to investigate the possibility of expanding the support given to visually impaired people during mobility in hospitals, clinics, and urgent cares. To this aim, we mainly focus on the problem of detecting doors, stairs, and signs, the very remarkable landmarks for indoor navigation, specifically in unfamiliar healthcare environments. We briefly summarize our *main contributions* as follows:

- Inspired by recent advances in deep learning, we developed a machine intelligence assistive mechanism to detect doors, stairs, and hospital signs accurately. While computer vision methods have been widely utilized in the literature, the development of deep learning components to support those who are suffering from visual impairment has been insufficient so far. To the best of our knowledge, our work is one of the first to investigate a convolutional neural network (CNN) model combined with a very large-scale dataset to predict notable landmarks for visually impaired people, assisting their indoor mobility in healthcare environments.
- Employing different machine learning classifiers, we present a set of predictive models that obtained a very promising accuracy, precision, and recall. We trained these models with a massive image dataset collected in Marshfield Clinic. Although there are several components available in our proposed model (Fig. 1), in the present paper, and for experimental validation purposes, we limited ourselves to analyze the performance of only the proposed predictive models. The qualitative and quantitative analyses of the user interface, network latency, usability, and the general performance of the proposed software architectural model are beyond the scope of the current work.
- We established a comparative study over different CNN-based predictive models combined with widely used machine learning classifiers, such as naïve Bayes (NB), support vector machine (SVM), and k-nearest neighbor (KNN).
- With the present contribution, a fully-labeled image dataset is available freely and publicly to the research community. The dataset covers several variations (e.g., viewpoint variation, intra-class variation, and noisy conditions) to every object model, including doors, stairs, and hospital signs in favor of boosting

object detection research. The dataset is fully documented and available at [4] for any academic, research, and educational purposes.

The organization of the paper is as follows. We start by describing the materials and methods. Next, we describe the experimental validations, including the test bed, dataset, performance analysis of the predictive model, and a comparative study. We then further discuss the future applications and research avenues and conclude the work in the very last section.

2   Materials and Methods

The proposed method is fully described in this section. Figure 1 presents the proposed software architectural model, which includes three tiers as (1) Client tier, (2) Communication tier, and (3) Deep Learning tier. In the client tier, due to the high volume of computing and network communication, an Enterprise Edition of a Google glass device is recommended to support a visually impaired person during his/her mobility. It assists the person to take an image and sends it to the predictive model. The communication between the Google glass device and the predictive model is feasible through the existing Wi-Fi system. The last tier, learning tier, employs a deep CNN trained by a large-scale fully-labeled dataset to make a predictive model that annotates the given image and will guide the person by converting the predicted label to voice.

The practical solution shall incorporate several software/hardware components, such as user interface, computer network platform, and an electronic device to integrate all parts into a single and comprehensive assistive device. Development of the entire proposed software architectural model is beyond the scope of the present contribution. Therefore, we limited this study to develop and validate only the proposed predictive models. To make the current contribution self-contained, we shall start with a brief introduction to the CNN network.

2.1   A CNN-Based Deep Learning Model

Traditionally, computer vision techniques were the primary approach for coping with image recognition problems [20]. In 2012, Alex Krizhevsky from the University of Toronto won the ImageNet Large Scale Visual Recognition Challenge (ILSVRC 2012) by a large margin by taking CNN network into account [12]. The network, popularly called AlexNet, proved its efficiency by nearly halving the error rate [10]. As a result, it gained the attention of scientists and since then has been employed in various vision problems [20].

A CNN model is a deep-learning feed-forward neural network, which its structure consists of a stack of multiple convolutional, pooling, and fully connected layers [15]. A convolutional layer detects specific features in the image while it preserves the spatial information of features by convolving the input image with a set of independent filter kernels. The role of a pooling layer is to reduce the image size by merging semantically similar features while it retains the information. The last few layers of a CNN model are composed of fully connected layers,

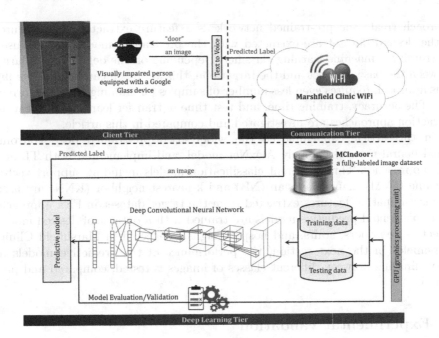

Fig. 1. The entire software architectural model of the proposed system, which spreads across three tiers: (1) Client tier, (2) Communication tier, and (3) Deep Learning tier. The Deep Learning tier employs a deep CNN composed of a large-scale fully-labeled dataset to build a predictive model. A visually impaired person is equipped with a Google glass device (The Enterprise Edition) and the photo taken by the device would be sent to the predictive model via the existing Wi-Fi system. The predictive model annotates the image and guides the person by converting the predicted label to voice.

known as neural networks. They are fed by an extracted feature map from the image and learn the underlying nature of the image, in our case the class of the image [8,15]. The basic architecture of a deep CNN and its applications are fully explained in the literature. Interested readers are referred to works accomplished by LeCun et al. [15–17], Krizhevsky et al. [12], Zeiler and Fergus [25], Szegedy et al. [22], Sutskever et al. [21], Lawrence et al. [14], Kruthiventi et al. [13], and Havaei et al. [9].

Instead of designing and training a CNN model from scratch, which requires an extensive dataset and takes a very long time, e.g., days, it is more efficient to take advantage of a pre-trained model for a new task. There are two approaches for this purpose: (1) Transfer Learning (TL), (2) Feature Extraction (FEx). The TL approach preserves the network architecture that has already been trained, perhaps with thousands of images from each class as in AlexNet, and weights of the neural network have been configured. By fine-tuning the network and retraining the model with the target dataset, we attain a stable and accurate predictive model. Compared with training a model from scratch, this approach requires a smaller dataset and takes less time to train. On the other hand, FEx approach treats the pre-trained network as a feature extractor. The features of the desired dataset are extracted with the pre-trained model and are used for training a machine learning classifier. Depending on the degree of similarity between the base data set and the target one, this approach can be effective [9]. This approach requires even less number of samples for training than the former one. The accuracy, training time, and test time of transfer learning and feature extraction approaches are investigated and compared in this article.

In this article, we employed the widely-used pre-trained deep convolutional neural network, namely AlexNet model, and implemented both TL and FEx approaches. Three different classification models including support vector machine (SVM), naïve Bayesian (NB) and k-nearest neighbor (KNN) are used for discriminating features extracted from the target dataset in FEx approach. All implemented predictive models are trained with a dataset of desired indoor objects - i.e., doors, stairs, and hospital signs - collected in Marshfield Clinic, Marshfield. In the next section, the performance of the predictive models in discriminating between different classes of images is tested, compared and presented.

3 Experimental Validation

In this section, several experimental validations were performed to analyze the quality and quantity attributes of the proposed predictive model. In this section, we utilize real indoor image data to examine the system performance in object classification. We begin by introducing the test bed and the proposed datasets.

3.1 Experimental Setup

From the computational perspective, a high-performance computer with 64-bit MS Windows 7 operating system, 3.6 GHz Intel Core i7-4790 CPU, 8 MB cache and 32 GB of RAM were used to run the present experimental study. The current system is equipped with an NVIDIA Quadro M5000 GPU.

Table 1. Dataset attributes are shown in this table. The table presents the total number of images along with the number of images in every single class.

Dataset ID	Name	Total number of instances	Doors	Stairs	Signs
DS#1	MCIndoor2000	2055	754	599	702
DS#2	MCIndoor6000	6165	2262	1797	2106

To analyze the reliability and accuracy of the proposed predictive model a set of image classification dataset was acquired [2]. Table 1 illustrates the proposed datasets. The first dataset, namely MCIndoor2000 includes 2055 original images collected in Marshfield Clinic. There are several ways to increase the accuracy and stability of an image classification model. One way is to utilize a more extensive training set. The other way is to generate an augmented set by adding variations to the existing dataset [9,12]. Inspired by that, our second dataset, namely MCIndoor6000, carries multiple variations, including Gaussian and Poisson noise models of the original images. Regarding the Gaussian noise model, a rotationally symmetric Gaussian low-pass filter of size 250 with the standard deviation of 10 was applied to the original images. To provide the Poisson noise model, we generated Poisson noise with the use of given original images. All original images were taken using a 4 MP Compact Digital Camera and a smartphone with a 5 MP camera.

3.2   Experimental Results

To assess the performance of the implemented deep CNN predictive models on discriminating 2D images of indoor objects in the clinical environment, and to analyze the time spent to train each model and classify a sample image, several extensive experiments are carried out.

Each experimental procedure contains the following steps. First, the desired dataset from Table 1, e.g., DS#1, is split into two sub-datasets as training and test sets. The training dataset contains P percentage of images selected randomly from each class, and the test dataset contains the remaining images. The label of each image is stored for further training and performance evaluation. Then, each predictive model explained in the previous section is trained with the same training dataset separately. The models' configuration setup is fully explained later in this section. Next, the performance of each predictive model is evaluated using the test dataset by measuring the accuracy, recall, and precision of prediction. Finally, the running time of both training and testing stages are recorded. This experiment is repeated with several P percentage values for every dataset of Table 1 for every predictive model.

The TL-based model is fine-tuned by adding an extra fully connected layer with an initial learning rate of 0.0001, maximum Epochs number of 20, and a minimum batch size of 128, selected based on previous experiences. Each FEx-based model extracts features of an image and utilizes them for training the specified classifier with 5-fold cross-validation.

The performance of the presented predictive models is investigated (Fig. 2). These results suggest that the FEx-based learning model tends to be more accurate (statistically significant at $p = .05$) than the TL-based model.

The TL-based model requires a more extensive training set to achieve accuracy comparable to the FEx-based models. When a large dataset is not available, data augmentation by adding slight noise or other types of non-rigid deformation transformation is widely used in the machine learning community [9,12]. Comparing the accuracy of the TL-based model using DS#1 and DS#2 provides empirical proof to this claim. Among the presented FEx-based models, the NB classifier is slightly less successful in the classification of desired subjects. In the presence of a large-scale dataset, the result illustrates that the TL-based model can exceed the FEx-based model with NB classifier.

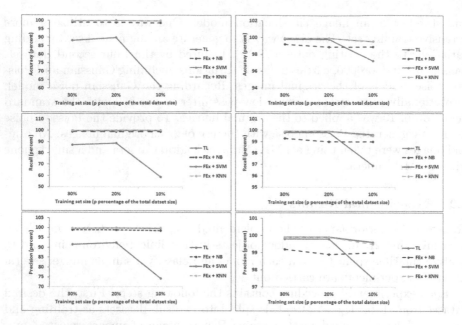

Fig. 2. (Top row) Accuracy, (Middle row) Recall, and (Bottom row) Precision of presented predictive CNN models including TL- and FEx-based models with NB, SVM, and KNN classifiers obtained with respect to the size of the training set sampled from (Left column) MCIndoor2000 and (Right column) MCIndoor6000 datasets.

The training time of each predictive model is recorded in seconds with respect to the size of the training set as a P percentage of the dataset and is demonstrated in Fig. 3. One can see the TL-based learning model requires more time to be trained given the neural network architectural model.

Since each image is individually processed when evaluating the functionality of the predictive models, the average time required for image labeling is recorded and presented in Fig. 4. Considering the testbed specifications mentioned earlier,

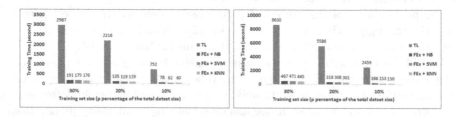

Fig. 3. Elapsed time (in seconds) of training four different deep CNN predictive models including TL and FEx approaches with NB, SVM and KNN classifiers versus different training set size as a P percentage of the dataset size using (Left) MCIndoor2000 and (Right) MCIndoor6000 datasets.

the average time for labeling each image from DS#1 and DS#2 is 290 and 240 milliseconds respectively, regardless of the training size. The main takeaway from Fig. 4 is that the time required for classifying each image is less than 300ms, regardless of the type of the predictive model. It indicates that either TL-based or FEx-based deep CNN predictive models are beneficial in real-time applications.

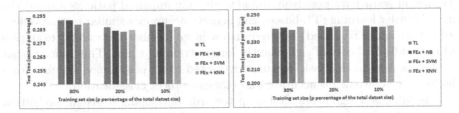

Fig. 4. The average time (in seconds) for classifying one image with four different deep CNN predictive models including TL and FEx approaches with NB, SVM and KNN classifiers versus different training set size as a P percentage of the dataset size using (Left)MCIndoor2000 and (Right)MCIndoor6000 datasets.

In the long run, to investigate the necessity of using high-throughput processors, e.g., Graphics Processing Unit (GPU), we arranged another experiment. In this one, we split the DS#1 into 30% as training and 70% as testing sub-datasets. Then, while the aforementioned predictive models were being trained and tested, the elapsed time of each stage was recorded and reported in Table 2. While the GPU speeds up training/testing stages of FEx-based models as well as the testing stage of the TL-based model by more than 250%, it expedites the training of the TL-based model by almost 20 times, and results are statistically significant at $p = 0.05$.

Table 2. Elapsed time (in seconds) of training and testing TL-based and FEx-based deep CNN predictive models using GPU and CPU processing units.

Processor	TL		FEx+NB		FEx+SVM		FEx+kNN	
	Train	Test	Train	Test	Train	Test	Train	Test
GPU	2913	419	193	414	183	412	179	419
CPU	57153	1083	476	1090	463	1094	466	1086

4   Discussion and Outlook

The future of modern medicine is pointed in a direction that runs parallel with advances in information technology, artificial intelligence, and personalized medicine. Investments in modern healthcare systems should include accessibility features geared toward patients with visual disabilities, harnessing new technologies to improve their independence and safety. Combining a variety of advanced computational technologies, our preliminary work indicates that features extracted utilizing weights from AlexNet, and trained using classifiers such as SVM and KNN, can achieve not only accuracy but precision and recall (key parameters in developing a lucrative model), higher than 98% for three types of objects familiar to any healthcare facility. Even a tiny increase in specificity, accuracy, or sensitivity positively impacts visually impaired patients around the clinic. Transfer learning (TL-based) can achieve accuracies similar to that of feature extraction (FEx-based) but requires a large number of training examples and the additional cost of significantly longer training times. Thus, for at least the objects used in this task, features extracted using pre-trained weights from AlexNet are sufficient for accurate and efficient object classification.

This work is a significant first step towards developing a visual navigation system for the interior of healthcare facilities; although some limitations exist. Indeed, the current work detected hospital signs, but there is much more to signage than to detect and recognize. Next step would be converting a hospital sign to a more meaningful term. There are more opportunities to explore in the research area. For example, stairs and escalators have a similar shape and structure but perform a different function. We plan to extend our list of objects to include escalators, obstacles, and elevators in order to tackle the problem of real-time multi-object detection, that is to say, detecting multiple objects in a single image. Future work would also include image-text to audio translation and development of communication and client tier technologies.

Detection of objects could transform smartphones, tablets, and electronic glasses into indispensable aids for visually impaired, partially-blind, and blind people. The present work is expected to stimulate more interest and draw attention from the deep learning and computer vision community to improve life for visually impaired people.

Acknowledgements. The authors greatly appreciate and acknowledge the contributions of Dr. Ahmad Pahlavan Tafti for his contributions on study design, data collection and drafting the manuscript. Our special thanks goes to Daniel Wall and Anne Nikolai at Marshfield Clinic Research Institute (MCRI) for their help and contributions in collecting the dataset and preparing the current paper. F.S. Bashiri would like to thank the Summer Research Internship Program (SRIP) at MCRI for financial support. Furthermore, we gratefully acknowledge the support of NVIDIA Corporation with the donation of the Quadro M5000 GPU used for this research.

References

1. Ahmetovic, D., et al.: Achieving practical and accurate indoor navigation for people with visual impairments. In: Proceedings of the 14th Web for All Conference on The Future of Accessible Work, p. 31. ACM (2017)
2. Bashiri, F.S., LaRose, E., Peissig, P., Tafti, A.P.: Mcindoor20000: a fully-labeled image dataset to advance indoor objects detection. Data Brief **17**, 71–75 (2018)

3. Berger, A., Vokalova, A., Maly, F., Poulova, P.: Google glass used as assistive technology its utilization for blind and visually impaired people. In: Younas, M., Awan, I., Holubova, I. (eds.) MobiWIS 2017. LNCS, vol. 10486, pp. 70–82. Springer, Cham (2017). https://doi.org/10.1007/978-3-319-65515-4_6

4. BIRCatMCRI: Mcindoor20000. GitHub repository (2017)

5. Bourne, R.R., et al.: Magnitude, temporal trends, and projections of the global prevalence of blindness and distance and near vision impairment: a systematic review and meta-analysis. Lancet Glob. Health 5(9), e888–e897 (2017)

6. Erickson, W., Lee, C.G., von Schrader, S.: 2016 disability status reports: United states (2018)

7. Gaudissart, V., Ferreira, S., Thillou, C., Gosselin, B.: Sypole: mobile reading assistant for blind people. In: 9th Conference Speech and Computer (2004)

8. Gupta, D.S.: Architecture of convolutional neural networks (CNNs) demystified (2017)

9. Havaei, M., Guizard, N., Larochelle, H., Jodoin, P.-M.: Deep learning trends for focal brain pathology segmentation in MRI. In: Holzinger, A. (ed.) Machine Learning for Health Informatics. LNCS (LNAI), vol. 9605, pp. 125–148. Springer, Cham (2016). https://doi.org/10.1007/978-3-319-50478-0_6

10. Huang, J.: Accelerating AI with GPUs: A New Computing Model (2016)

11. Jabnoun, H., Benzarti, F., Amiri, H.: A new method for text detection and recognition in indoor scene for assisting blind people. In: Ninth International Conference on Machine Vision (ICMV 2016), vol. 10341, p. 1034123. International Society for Optics and Photonics (2017)

12. Krizhevsky, A., Sutskever, I., Hinton, G.E.: Imagenet classification with deep convolutional neural networks. In: Advances in Neural Information Processing Systems, pp. 1097–1105 (2012)

13. Kruthiventi, S.S., Ayush, K., Babu, R.V.: Deepfix: a fully convolutional neural network for predicting human eye fixations. arXiv preprint arXiv:1510.02927 (2015)

14. Lawrence, S., Giles, C.L., Tsoi, A.C., Back, A.D.: Face recognition: a convolutional neural-network approach. IEEE Trans. Neural Netw. 8(1), 98–113 (1997)

15. LeCun, Y., Bengio, Y., Hinton, G.: Deep learning. Nature 521(7553), 436 (2015)

16. LeCun, Y., et al.: Handwritten digit recognition with a back-propagation network. In: Advances in Neural Information Processing Systems, pp. 396–404 (1990)

17. LeCun, Y., Bottou, L., Bengio, Y., Haffner, P.: Gradient-based learning applied to document recognition. Proc. IEEE 86(11), 2278–2324 (1998)

18. Manoj, B., Rohini, V.: A novel approach to object detection and distance measurement for visually impaired people. Int. J. Comput. Intell. Res. 13(4), 479–484 (2017)

19. Mekhalfi, M.L., Melgani, F., Bazi, Y., Alajlan, N.: Fast indoor scene description for blind people with multiresolution random projections. J. Vis. Commun. Image Represent. 44, 95–105 (2017)

20. Srinivas, S., Sarvadevabhatla, R.K., Mopuri, K.R., Prabhu, N., Kruthiventi, S.S., Babu, R.V.: A taxonomy of deep convolutional neural nets for computer vision. Front. Robot. AI 2, 36 (2016)

21. Sutskever, I., Vinyals, O., Le, Q.V.: Sequence to sequence learning with neural networks. In: Advances in Neural Information Processing Systems, pp. 3104–3112 (2014)

22. Szegedy, C., et al.: Going deeper with convolutions. In: Proceedings of the IEEE Conference on Computer Vision and Pattern Recognition, pp. 1–9 (2015)

23. Tekin, E., Coughlan, J.M., Shen, H.: Real-time detection and reading of LED/LCD displays for visually impaired persons. In: Proceedings/IEEE Workshop on Applications of Computer Vision. IEEE Workshop on Applications of Computer Vision, p. 491. NIH Public Access (2011)
24. Tekin, E., Vásquez, D., Coughlan, J.M.: SK smartphone barcode reader for the blind. In: Journal on technology and persons with disabilities:... Annual International Technology and Persons with Disabilities Conference, vol. 28, p. 230. NIH Public Access (2013)
25. Zeiler, M.D., Fergus, R.: Visualizing and understanding convolutional networks. In: Fleet, D., Pajdla, T., Schiele, B., Tuytelaars, T. (eds.) ECCV 2014. LNCS, vol. 8689, pp. 818–833. Springer, Cham (2014). https://doi.org/10.1007/978-3-319-10590-1_53

Large Scale Application Response Time Measurement Using Image Recognition and Deep Learning

Lan Vu$^{(\boxtimes)}$ [iD], Uday Kurkure [iD], Hari Sivaraman [iD], and Aravind Bappanadu [iD]

VMware, Palo Alto, CA 94304, USA
{lanv,ukurkure,hsivaraman,abappanadu}@vmware.com

Abstract. Application response time is a critical performance metric to assess the quality of software products. It is also an objective metric for user experience evaluation. In this paper, we present a novel method named CVART (Computer Vision–based Application Response Time measurement) for measuring the response time (latency) of an application. In our solution, we use image recognition and deep learning techniques to capture visible changes in the display of the device running the application to compute the application response time of an operation that triggers these visual changes. Appling CVART can bring multiple benefits compared to traditional methods. First, it allows measuring the response time that reflects a real user experience. Second, the solution enables the measurement of operations that are extremely hard or impossible to measure when using traditional methods. Third, it does not require application instrumentation, which is infeasible in many use cases. Finally, the method does not depend on any specific application or software platform, which allows building performance measurement and application monitoring tools that work on multiple platforms and on multiple devices. For demonstration, we present one use case of applying CVART to measure the application response time of virtual desktops hosted in the cloud or datacenter, and we evaluate its efficiency on measurement at large scale.

Keywords: Application response time · Deep learning
Performance benchmarking · Image recognition · Application monitoring

1 Introduction

Computer vision has recently achieved significant progress thanks to the evolution in deep learning, including novel deep convolutional neural network architectures [1–4]. Its applications have been pervasive in many aspects of our life like security cameras, traffic monitoring, robotic surgery, self-driving cars, photo classification, cancer detection in medical imaging, automated product-categorizing machines in manufacturing or agriculture, and face or fingerprint detection for authentication [5]. In the retail area, Amazon has recently introduced Amazon Go, which transforms shopping by applying computer vision and deep learning algorithms to allow shoppers to buy products without having to go through checkout lines [6]. The potential of computer

© Springer Nature Switzerland AG 2018
G. Bebis et al. (Eds.): ISVC 2018, LNCS 11241, pp. 511–526, 2018.
https://doi.org/10.1007/978-3-030-03801-4_45

vision is huge because it provides computers the capability to perceive the real world the way humans do to help us make better decisions and build more intelligent applications and products. In this paper, we present a novel method that applies computer vision and deep learning to build application performance monitoring and benchmarking tools that capture latency data closely reflecting real user experience. This solution is inspired by a real-world need for performance information and the challenges in collecting this information at scale from very complex and continuously evolving software.

For software applications involving user interactions—like end-user computing products; management software; and desktop, mobile, and web applications—responsiveness is one of the key metrics for users to evaluate product quality in order to decide whether or not to use that product [7]. Accurately measuring end-to-end response time reflecting a real user experience is important, especially in the virtualization environment. It is, however, also extremely challenging [8].

Four traditional approaches for programmatically measuring the end-to-end responsiveness of these software systems include: (1) *Application instrumentation*: modifying the application at the source code level to collect performance data; (2) *Client instrumentation*: inserting hooks into the client environment to collect data on activities such as operating system interrupts and/or messages. (3) *Wire Sniffing*: monitoring, decoding, and analyzing either raw network traffic or server network packets (i.e., TCP/IP); (4) *Benchmarking*: application scripts periodically executed and measured [9]. These methods usually do not follow the same approach as the end user does (i.e., interacting with the software system and tracking visible changes to user interface (UI)), so they create proxy measures of responsiveness that are frequently unreliable. Using these methods requires deep knowledge of the software system being monitored. Further complicating matters, the software systems use asynchronous subprocesses and external services to achieve functionality. These challenges lead to highly sophisticated monitoring systems with low confidence in the measured responsiveness of products, requiring extensive manual verification. In many cases, the traditional measurements can lead to the latency results not reflecting accurately how application behaviors are visually perceived by the end users.

In contrast, users without knowledge of the complicated software system are able to judge its responsiveness since they rely on visible screen updates. Upon this observation, we developed a new method for measuring application response time that mimics the human in the performance assessment. Highlight contributions of our research include:

- CVART: a new method that applies computer vision to measure application response time. We base this method on image recognition and deep learning to track visible changes of the application to the screen and use it to extract the response time of the application similar to the way humans do. (Sect. 2).
- An application of CVART for application monitoring and performance benchmarking remote desktops from the cloud at large scale (Sect. 3). Applying this solution, we are able to measure performance of applications running on remote desktops in many use cases that are extremely hard or impossible to do previously. We also evaluate the accuracy, scalability, and efficiency of CVART.

Sections 4 and 5 are about related works and our conclusion.

2   CVART: A Method for Measuring Application Response Time Using Image Recognition and Deep Learning

In this section, we describe CVART, which applies image recognition and deep learning to measure the response time of application operations with visible UI changes. Each operation is a specific task that a user performs when using the application. It includes a series of interactions between users and the application system, the operation execution, and the changes in UI (e.g., loading a web page, opening a dialog, running an application, moving windows and other objects around the screen, opening a file, etc.). The start and end points are usually observed with human vision. In our solution, the application response time of an operation is measured by automatically monitoring screen changes (e.g., UI updates) from the beginning to the end of the operation, and by computing its latency using the elapsed time. Deep learning, in this approach, is used for image recognition to detect application user interface updates. Some advantages of CVART include

(1) Measuring application responsiveness in the way humans assess the performance of an application to provide a more accurate measure of user experience.
(2) Neither modification to application program source code nor in-depth understanding of the internal processes of the applications is required in this method. In real use cases, modifying the application program is infeasible (e.g., benchmarking customer applications running on cloud environment).
(3) This approach is generic, and can be applied in different types of applications with UI interactions like desktop, mobile, and web applications.
(4) Image recognition is used for detecting UI updates. This helps to overcome challenges coming from UI differences in themes, colors, and screen solutions as well as other UI component variations (illustrated in Fig. 4) that most regular UI-based techniques may have.
(5) Deep learning, specifically deep neural networks, can provide higher accuracy in image recognition task compared to the traditional machine learning solutions like traditional networks, K-nearest neighbor, or principal component analysis when the data size grows [22]. For measuring application response with high accuracy, the datasets for training recognition models include an extremely large number of images to simulate all real use cases. Therefore, the use of deep learning is essential and extremely important for this measurement to be practical in real world use. For example, our dataset used to train each operation can have up to ten thousands or more UI object images with various themes, backgrounds, and sizes generated by a data generator.

CVART includes two separate modules: one for building recognition models and the other for using built models that measure application response time.

2.1   Building Recognition Models for Response Time Measurement

Prior to application response time measurement, CVART builds recognition models used to detect UI updates from the relevant operation. This process is depicted in Fig. 1.

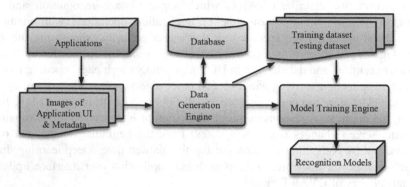

Fig. 1. Recognition models to measure response time

There are two main components in the model-building module: the data generator engine and the model training engine. The snapshots of UI objects and relevant metadata are collected for each operation. For example, the operation of opening Microsoft Word by clicking the application icon on the desktop initiates the following data:

- A screenshot of the display device where the Word icon is located, including information about the icon's location and dimension. Alternatively, the pre-existing images of the Word icon are provided.
- A screenshot of the display device where the Word application is activated. Alternatively, the pre-existing images of the Word UI when it is first opened is used.

Data Generation Engine. This engine provides data for training and testing recognition models. It extracts sub-images from the raw input images and metadata. It also queries relevant pre-existing images of the same type of UI from the database. It then performs multiple image processing techniques like resizing, adding noise, changing object backgrounds, and creating new images with different qualities in order to generate a larger set of images that are used for training recognition models. Newly generated datasets derived from raw data and pre-existing data help to improve the accuracy of the object recognition task.

Model Training Engine. This component is responsible for training recognition models, which are used in the response time measurement. It takes datasets created by the data generator engine and applies deep learning (e.g., deep neutral network [1–4], deep support vector machine [10], etc.) to train one or multiple recognition models.

Each model is used to recognize different UI objects of one or multiple operations, which come with some metadata as the operations' inputs and outputs.

2.2 Measuring Response Time Using Image Recognition

The response time of an operation is measured in three main tasks. Figure 2 shows the components and the workflow of measuring application response time based on image recognition.

(1) Periodically capturing images of the application UI during the time the operation executes. The operation is driven by either human user or computer program.
(2) Applying the recognition engine to detect the beginning and end points of that operation from the captured images.
(3) Computing application response time.

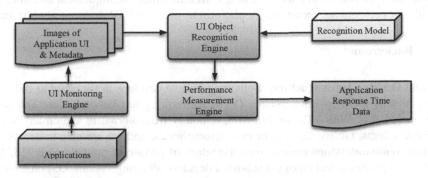

Fig. 2. Measuring response time using image recognition

User Interface Monitoring Engine. This engine continuously monitors application UI, capturing application screenshots to extract the portions or the entire UI of the running application. Timestamps of these screenshots are also recorded. Depending on the captured images of screenshots, additional image processing techniques can be applied to make appropriate the image quality and dimension to enhance the efficiency of the recognition task. This engine also keeps track of the overhead of the monitoring process for latency computation.

User Interface Object Recognition Engine. This engine identifies the beginning, intermediate, and end points of operations and their timestamps. To do that, it loads the recognition model and metadata of the operation, fetches the images captured by the User Interface Monitoring Engine, and searches for the UI objects that help to identify the UI changes and keep track of their timestamps. The process is completed when the end point of the operation is found. This engine also keeps track of the overhead of the monitoring process for later latency computation.

Performance Measurement Engine. This engine computes the application latency of the operation being measured by computing the elapsed time between the beginning and end points found in previous steps. The final latency is adjusted with all overheads of previous steps to ensure the accuracy of the result. Optionally, the elapsed times between the intermediate points of the operation (i.e., the operation with multiple UI changes) are also computed as the latencies of sub-operations using the timestamp values and the overhead times. The outputs are the operation latency, latency breakdown, timestamps, screenshots of UI changes, and metadata, all of which can be used for later performance analysis.

3 Using CVART for the Large Scale Performance Measurement of VDI Remote Desktops

CVART can be used to measure the performance of different types of applications. In this section, we present one use case of CVART in which we implement and integrate it with our performance measurement platform to measure VDI desktops at large scale.

3.1 Background

Virtual Desktop Infrastructure. Delivering remote desktops in the cloud to end users using Virtual Desktop Infrastructure (VDI) technology has become more and more popular [11–14]. With VDI, we can work remotely from anywhere and on any device like thin clients, tablets, laptops, or even smartphones, and we are able to access virtualized remote desktops running on datacenters of private or public clouds [15, 16]. VDI is virtualization technology that hosts a desktop operating system (OS) on a virtual machine (VM) on a centralized server of a datacenter. These virtualized desktops may have moderate computing power for regular users or high performance computing power with GPUs for special types of users like designers, scientists, etc. VDI employs a client-server computing model where users use a client, like a web browser, to connect to remote desktops running inside the datacenter to load its display content using a remote display protocol and to interact with the desktop [19]. Several popular VDI solutions include VMware Horizon, Citrix XenDesktop, and Microsoft VDI [16–18].

Figure 3 depicts an overview of VDI. Its software infrastructure can include multiple components like a VDI connection broker, VDI composer, load balancer, VDI agents, hypervisor, hypervisor manager, etc. VDI requires infrastructure with high network bandwidth, fast storage systems, servers with large CPU, memory resources, etc. To support 3D graphics applications, the servers can be equipped with multiple high-end GPUs. Each server can host hundreds of Windows/Linux desktop virtual machines and the total number of servers scale based on the number of real users. For large organizations like banks, hospitals, and higher education institutes, the scale of VDI deployment can go up to hundreds of thousands of remote desktops [16].

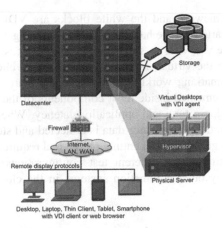

Fig. 3. A simplified architecture of VDI

Remote Display Protocol. Remote display protocol is a critical component of VDI. It connects an end-user device to a remote desktop or an application running remotely in a datacenter. The choice of remote display protocol has a huge impact on end-user experience and resource utilization in the datacenter. High quality user experience implies low latency, lossless images, high frame rates for videos, and requires higher network bandwidth and higher CPU utilization per user. VDI needs to strike a balance between resource consumption and end-user experience. Some remote display protocols include VMware Blast Extreme [19], Teradici PCoIP, and Microsoft RemoteFX, which are supported by VMware VDI and other VDI products.

VDI Performance Measurement. A key requirement for successful VDI adoption is ensuring the best end-user experience when deploying it at scale. A realistic performance benchmarking tool for VDI must accurately capture user experience metrics to evaluate if the VDI solution brings an end-user experience as seamless as on a physical desktop. In some cases, we expect VDI to deliver better user experience than the physical desktops (e.g., 3D graphics, machine learning, etc.) because the remote desktop has access to powerful computing resources in the datacenter. Depending on the type of applications running inside the desktop, the user experience metrics may include application response time, login time, frames per second, or total execution time, and measuring them accurately in a large scale distributed computing model of VDI is nontrivial. Scalability is another capability that a VDI performance benchmarking tool must support. An efficient VDI solution needs to optimize the resource usage to achieve a high consolidation ratio (i.e., number of desktops per physical server) and scale well with the number of users. Frequently, performance issues are found only when the VDI deployment is tested at large scale.

Performance Measurement Framework. For VDI performance monitoring and benchmarking, VMware View Planner is used as an automation framework that allows measuring VDI remote desktops performance at large scale [20]. The working mechanism of this framework is demonstrated in Fig. 4, in which the green blocks are the components in our framework and the white blocks are VDI software components. A benchmarking job starts with the harness controller booting VMs at the desktop side and the client side. We use VMs to simulate end-user devices. Then, the client VMs automatically log in to the virtual desktops using the VDI client or a web browser. After login, the benchmarking workloads automatically start. At the same time, the performance tools implemented inside most components of the framework collect the performance data like login time and application latency. When the workloads in all desktop VMs complete, the performance data is collected and stored in a database, and a performance report is generated. Depending on the real requirements, this process can be repeated multiple times with different test configurations specified by users or automatically created by other automation systems in the cloud for continuous performance monitoring.

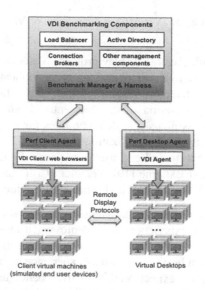

Fig. 4. Remote desktop benchmarking

3.2   Measuring VDI Performance Using Image Recognition and Deep Learning

In this section, we present a use case where we apply the proposed method to measure and benchmark the login time and application latency of Horizon View desktops, a VDI software solution provided by VMware [21]. These performance metrics play an important role in identifying the best practices and evaluating the efficiency of the VDI deployment with many software and hardware components like VMware Horizon View, VMware App Volumes (application management solution), VMware vSphere (hypervisor), VMware vSAN (hyper-converged infrastructure solution), VMware vCenter (hypervisor manager), Active Directory, high performance computing, and storage systems, GPUs, etc. The users expect the remote desktop experience—including logging into desktops, opening and using the applications, playing videos, and mouse and keyboard events—to be as seamless and quick as that of a physical desktop. Accurately measuring the response times of these interactions is challenging, especially from the client side, because of the network latency in transferring the image data of screen updates and the interaction of events between the View client and the View desktop in the datacenter.

Previously, the application latency of VDI desktops was measured by driving the benchmarking workloads at the desktop side to passively measure the screen updates at the client using a watermarking technique. For each operation, a watermark is drawn on the desktop encoding the operation ID and its start or end point ID. The client reads the watermarking information to compute the application latency. This method ignores the interactions between the user and the virtual desktop through the View client [12, 20]. By applying the image recognition–based method as presented in Sect. 2, we are able to measure the application response time more accurately.

To measure the response time of different user interactions in VDI, we specify the key objects identifying the UI changes of an interaction, collect their UI images, and use a convolutional neural network to train recognition models, as described in Sect. 2.1. For example, the login time operation is computed from the time a user enters credentials in login box of the View client to the time Windows is fully loaded, which is identified by the occurrence of a start button in the remote desktop screen. The recognition model is trained to recognize the start button of the Windows screen using a dataset of start button images. Figure 5-a illustrates some images with different forms of the button and different resolutions used for training. In the performance tool, these models are used for recognizing the objects and measuring the response time as described in Sect. 2.2. Figure 5-b shows an example of the recognition model, and its

(a) Example dataset of a UI object (Start button)

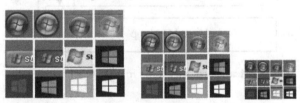

(b) Example of recognition model for UI object detection

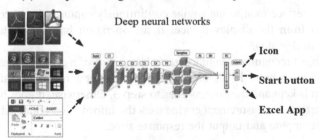

Fig. 5. Examples of training data and recognition model

inputs and outputs. We chose deep neural networks like Inception V3 [2] and MobileNet [3] for our recognition engine because they are among the most advanced solutions for image recognition these days, compared to other traditional machine learning methods like k-nearest neighbors, principal component analysis, and traditional artificial neural networks [22].

To illustrate the efficiency of our new solution, we implement CVART and integrate it into VMware View Planner, the framework for performance measurement and optimization of VDI desktops at scale described Sect. 3.2. Figure 6 shows a performance agent integrated with CVART. View Planner uses two groups of VMs; one for client VMs simulating end-user devices and the other for VDI desktops.

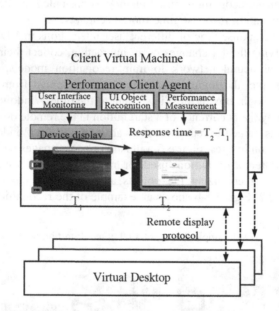

Fig. 6. Measure response time in VDI benchmarking

The response time measurement involves these steps:

(1) The user interface monitoring engine continuously captures the screenshot and its timestamp from the display device. If an operation has not started, it can be triggered in this step.
(2) The UI object recognition engine detects UI objects of a certain operation from the captured screenshots. If UI objects specify the end of an operation, the end timestamp is kept and the process goes to step 3. Otherwise, it goes back to step 1.
(3) The performance measurement engine uses the information collected in step 1 and step 2 to compute and output the response time.

Experimental Setup. We used TensorFlow [23] as the framework to train the models and to build the recognition engine. VDI performance was benchmarked at different scales ranging from 1 to 100 virtual desktops. View desktop login time was also measured as part of the assessment. The software components in our experiments included Horizon View 7.2, App Volume 2.13, vSphere 6.5, vCenter 6.5, and View Planner 4.0. The client and desktop VMs ran Windows 10. We used three Dell R730 servers (each had dual 12-core E5-2690 processors, 24 cores @ 2.6 GHz, 256 GB memory, and 2.91 TB storage) connected via LAN, in which one server was for the View desktop VMs, one was used for the View client VMs, and one was used for the other management components.

Measuring Response Time of Different Operations. Applying CVART, we are able to measure the response time of operations that are difficult or unable to be measured previously like "drag and drop" (i.e., drag a file or an icon from one location and drop it at another location) or "dragging an application" (i.e., drag an application window around the device display). It is because these operations require the capability of seeing things on the display of the device to perform the operations. In our experiments, we implemented the measurement of some operations including login, open application, drag and drop, and drag an application. Response time of these operations when testing with 1 VM is shown in Fig. 7.

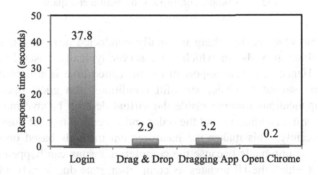

Fig. 7. Response time of different operations

Accuracy. The important reason for adopting this new measurement approach is the ability to capture the response time that accurately reflects a real user experience and does not requiring the modification of the application. For evaluation, we measured the login time process from the time users entered a username and password at the View client agent to the time the Windows desktops were fully loaded. Figure 8 presents the average login time in one desktop run using two different techniques: (1) image recognition as described in this paper and (2) the watermarking technique that has been used previously. Our manual human measurement with stopwatch shows that the image recognition–based solution provides accurate results, while the watermarking technique gives ~ 12 s (37.8 s with image recognition vs. 49.8 s with watermarking before adjustment), more than 33% of what can be assessed by human eyes. This is because the watermarking technique is based on the application startup event of Windows, which is usually trigged right after other startup services on Windows 10, and this can cause some delay. Previously, using the watermarking technique, we had to subtract the measured time with this delay time to obtain a more precise response time (watermarking after adjustment is shown in Fig. 8). However, the delay time can vary for different Windows versions and benchmarking conditions, making it hard to derive the correct measured time for all test cases.

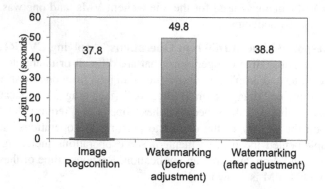

Fig. 8. Comparison of two different techniques

Scalability. Our VDI benchmarking is usually conducted at scale from hundreds to thousands of desktop VMs, in which each server typically hosts 100–200 virtual desktop VMs. Hence, it is also important the measured time is still correct when the system is being saturated. Under stressful conditions, the guest operating system (OS) and its applications running inside the virtual desktop behave much differently than those of normal conditions, and the order and execution time of guest OS services changes significantly. This makes the measurement methods based on events, mentioned above, less unreliable because the completion events can happen much sooner than the time at which the UI updates its completion state due to network delay. This also happens in many different software systems other than VDI. The image recognition–based solution shows its advantage in such scenarios as compared to other

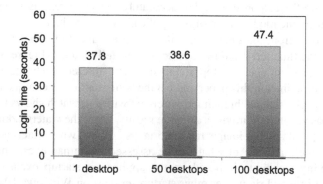

Fig. 9. The average login time at scale

methods because it relies only on the visual behaviors of the software. Figure 9 presents the average login time for different numbers of concurrent users.

Figure 10 shows the login time of each individual user in the cases of 100 concurrent users. In this experiment, 100 clients randomly logged into the remote desktops with an average of one login for every 10 s. So, during the login time frame, the loads of each virtual desktop and of the entire server hosting 100 desktops vary, and they impact the login time of each client.

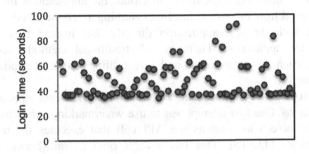

Fig. 10. The login time of each of 100 desktops

Efficiency. Applying the image recognition for latency measurement gives a better performance metric in many cases, but this solution also requires more computing resource because both image processing and neural network inference are computationally intensive. Therefore, for practical use, we tried several deep neural network architectures to evaluate their efficiency in terms of resource utilization because of our need for large scale benchmarking with many recognition tasks concurrently executed at the same time on the same server.

In Table 1, we compare the resource utilization in three cases: cases 1 and 2 with login time measurement using two well-known deep neural network architectures Inception V3 [2] and MobileNet [3] and case 3 without log time measurement while logging in. We do not use GPU in this test case. These results are collected on the server of the View client VMs where the recognition engine was activated. It can be seen that using Inception V3 gave higher CPU utilization and memory because its architecture with 48 layers requires more memory to present more nodes and weights as well as more computations (i.e. 5713 million multiply–accumulate operations (MACs) per inference). MobileNet with 28 layers has much less overhead on CPU (183 million MACs) and memory compared to case 3 because it is designed for efficient use on

Table 1. Resource utilization of server hosting 50 concurrent desktops

Test cases	CPU utilization (%)	Memory usage (GB)
Measurement uses Inception V3	40	90.8
Measurement uses MobileNet	25	37.6
Without time measurement	17	37.2

mobile devices. Inception V3 helps to encapsulate more information for complex recognition tasks like real world photo classification. In our use case, MobileNet gives a better practical use because our UI screenshot images are as less variant as real world images and do not need complex neural networks to archive high recognition accuracy.

4 Related Works

In the context of remote desktops from the cloud, the applications run on end user devices are streamed from the virtual machines running at remote datacenters and users do not interact with the real application directly, but instead they interact with screenshots of the application. Therefore, all traditional methods like application instrumentation, client instrumentation, and wire sniffing cannot be applied to measure the response time [9].

In the context of a VDI environment, we have made several attempts to measure the latency of operations. One first attempt was to use watermarking, whereby a watermark is applied to the screen as soon as the API call that executes the user-originated operation completes [13, 15]. This has several obvious drawbacks. First, use of watermarking merely measures the time to execute the API call, which is just a part of the entire operation that starts when the user clicks the mouse or taps a key, and only ends when the corresponding screen update is completed. This drawback can be mitigated somewhat by intercepting mouse clicks and keyboard events but that is impractical in a real-world environment. Second, it requires the monitored application to make the calls to do the watermarking, or the API calls to be intercepted and augmented with a call to do watermarking. Both are impractical for generic applications in a non-benchmark environment. Third, the time at which an API call completes may not in any way indicate that the screen update that signals completion of the operation that was instigated by the API call has completed. It may merely be the case that the API call has completed, while the corresponding screen update is still in progress. A second attempt to measure latency involved accessing VMware SVGA driver and inserting watermarks using the VMware BLAST protocol [19]. This attempt requires that the code to measure latency be tied to the VDI protocol, requiring maintenance and updates as the protocol is changed, and this works only in a VDI environment. It is not a generalized approach. A third attempt involved using statistical analysis to correlate screen updates with mouse and keyboard events. This is too complicated because it requires taking into account many parameters and variables. Hence, conventional approaches, while viable in a benchmark environment, do not work effectively in a real-world production environment.

5 Conclusion

We present a novel solution that applies computer vision for measuring application response time. Our solution provides a more reliable way to compute end-to-end response time for interactive operations that involve visual changes in a user interface. This approach does not require application modification and in-depth knowledge of the software system like the traditional methods. The measured time can be used as an alternative or in combination with other performance measures for assessing and improving the quality of software products or monitoring application performance in real time.

Acknowledgements. The authors would like to thank Juan Garcia-Rovetta and Bruce Herndon, Julie Brodeur for their support of this work.

References

1. LeCun, Y., Bottou, L., Bengio, Haffner, P.: Gradient-based learning applied to document recognition. Proc. IEEE **86**(11), 2278–2324 (1998)
2. Szegedy, C., Vanhoucke, V., Ioffe, S., Shlens, J., Wojna, Z.: Rethinking the inception architecture for computer vision. In: Proceedings of Computer Vision and Pattern Recognition Conference, pp. 2818–2826 (2016)
3. Howard, A.G., et al.: MobileNets: efficient convolutional neural networks for mobile vision applications. arXiv:1704.04861 (2017)
4. Zaremba, W., Sutskever, I., Vinyals, O.: Recurrent Neural Network Regularization. arXiv: 1409.2329 (2014)
5. Szeliski, R.: Computer Vision: Algorithms and Applications. Springer, New York (2010). https://doi.org/10.1007/978-1-84882-935-0
6. Carroll, J.: Computer vision and deep learning technology at the heart of Amazon Go. www.vision-systems.com
7. Zeldovich, N., Chandra, R.: Interactive performance measurement with VNCplay. In: Proceedings of the FREENIX Track: 2005 USENIX Annual Technical Conference, Anaheim, CA, USA, 10–15 April 2005 (2005)
8. Friston, S., Steed, A.: Measuring latency in virtual environments. IEEE Trans. Vis. Comput. Graphics **20**(4), 616–625 (2014)
9. Norton, T.R.: End-to-end response time: where to measure? In: Proceedings of the 1999 Computer Measurement Group Conference (1999)
10. Tang, Y.: Deep learning using linear support vector machines. In: Proceedings of International Conference on Machine Learning, Challenges in Representation Learning Workshop, Atlanta, Georgia, USA (2013)
11. Berryman, A., Calyam, P., Honigford, M., Lai, A.: VDBench: a benchmarking toolkit for thin-client based virtual desktop environments. In: Proceedings of 2nd IEEE International Conference on Cloud Computing Technology and Science, pp. 480–481 (2010)
12. Agrawal, B., et al.: VMware view planner: measuring true virtual desktop experience at scale. VMware Tech. J. (2009)
13. Wang, S.Y., Wang, W.J.: Benchmarking the performance of XenDesktop Virtual DeskTop Infrastructure (VDI) platform. In: Proceedings of the 14th International Conference on Networks, pp. 37–43 (2015)
14. Casas, P., Seufert, M., Egger, S., Schatz, R.: Quality of experience in remote virtual desktop services. In: Proceedings of 2013 IFIP/IEEE International Symposium on Integrated Network Management, pp. 1352–1357 (2013)
15. Top 5 Use Cases for VDI. http://www.gomindsight.com/blog/top-5-use-cases-vdi
16. VMware Always On Point of Care Solution Reference Implementation Case Study for European Healthcare Provider, Technical White Paper (2012)

17. Young, R., Laing, D.: IDC MarketScape: Worldwide Virtual Client Computing Software 2015 Vendor Assessment. IDC MarketScape (2015)
18. Young, R., Laing, D.: IDC MarketScape: Worldwide Virtual Client Computing Software 2016 Vendor Assessment. IDC MarketScape (2016)
19. Arakelian, C., Halstead, C.: Blast extreme display protocol in Horizon 7. In: VMware Technical White Paper (2016)
20. Pandey, A., Vu, L., Puthiyaveettil, V., Sivaraman, H., Kurkure, U., Bappanadu, A.: An automation framework for benchmarking and optimizing performance of remote desktops in the cloud. In: The Proceedings of the 2017 International Conference for High Performance Computing & Simulation (2017)
21. Horizon 7. https://www.vmware.com/products/horizon.html
22. Hastie, T., Tibshirani, R., Friedman, J.: The Elements of Statistical Learning. Data Mining, Inference, and Prediction, 2nd edn. Springer, Berlin (2009). https://doi.org/10.1007/978-0-387-84858-7
23. TensoreFlow. https://www.tensorflow.org
24. Kurkure, U., Sivaraman, H., Vu, L.: Machine learning using virtualized GPU in cloud environment. In: Proceedings of the 12th Workshop on Virtualization in High-Performance Cloud Computing (2017)

Applications I

Vision-Depth Landmarks and Inertial Fusion for Navigation in Degraded Visual Environments

Shehryar Khattak$^{(\boxtimes)}$, Christos Papachristos, and Kostas Alexis

Autonomous Robots Lab, University of Nevada, Reno, NV, USA
shehryar@nevada.unr.edu
http://www.autonomousrobotslab.com

Abstract. This paper proposes a method for tight fusion of visual, depth and inertial data in order to extend robotic capabilities for navigation in GPS-denied, poorly illuminated, and textureless environments. Visual and depth information are fused at the feature detection and descriptor extraction levels to augment one sensing modality with the other. These multimodal features are then further integrated with inertial sensor cues using an extended Kalman filter to estimate the robot pose, sensor bias terms, and landmark positions simultaneously as part of the filter state. As demonstrated through a set of hand-held and Micro Aerial Vehicle experiments, the proposed algorithm is shown to perform reliably in challenging visually-degraded environments using RGB-D information from a lightweight and low-cost sensor and data from an IMU.

Keywords: Robot · Depth · Sensor degradation · Localization

1 Introduction

Robotic systems are being integrated in an increasingly large variety of applications such as infrastructure inspection [1–5], monitoring and surveillance [6], search and rescue [7] and more. However, in many critical tasks robots have to be able to cope with difficult conditions that challenge their autonomy. Of particular interest are cases involving GPS-denied Degraded Visual Environments (DVEs) that stress the abilities of onboard perception especially for Simultaneous Localization And Mapping (SLAM). Examples of relevant applications include navigating, mapping and characterization of underground settings, as well as search and rescue missions.

The focus of this work is on enabling reliable robotic autonomy in poorly illuminated, textureless and GPS-denied environments through the use of lightweight and ubiquitous sensing technology; specifically, miniaturized RGB-D sensors and Inertial Measurement Units (IMU). For this purpose we first develop a methodology for fusion of visual and depth information at the feature detection and descriptor extraction levels followed by the integration of these multimodal

© Springer Nature Switzerland AG 2018
G. Bebis et al. (Eds.): ISVC 2018, LNCS 11241, pp. 529–540, 2018.
https://doi.org/10.1007/978-3-030-03801-4_46

features with inertial sensor information in an Extended Kalman Filter (EKF) fashion. This approach reflects the fact that small RGB-D sensors have limited range, and is different from (a) methods that fuse LiDAR and visual camera data in a loosely-coupled manner, (b) RGB-D SLAM algorithms that depend on vision as prime sensing modality, or (c) technological approaches that integrate onboard illumination or night vision.

Fig. 1. Aerial robotic operation in low-light GPS-denied conditions. An Intel Realsense D435 Depth Camera is integrated onboard a Micro Aerial Vehicle of the F450 class.

To verify the proposed solution, a set of experimental studies were conducted including (a) a proof-of-concept hand-held validation test inside a dark room where visual information is extremely limited, and (b) an aerial robot trajectory in very low-light conditions. Comparison with ground truth and reconstructed maps are presented to demonstrate the reliability of the proposed localization system and its performance in such visually-degraded conditions.

The remainder of the paper is structured as follows: Sect. 2 provides an overview of related work. The proposed approach for common visual and depth features alongside fusion with IMU is presented in Sect. 3, followed by experimental evaluation in Sect. 4. Finally, conclusions are drawn in Sect. 5.

2   Related Work

Methods for odometry estimation and SLAM have seen rapid growth in the recent years and employ a multitude of sensing modalities. For camera-based systems a set of feature-based [8–10], and semi-direct [11] visual odometry algorithms have been proposed. Furthermore, visual-inertial fusion approaches have presented increased robustness and reliability especially when dynamic motion is considered [12,13]. Although visual odometry techniques have seen great growth in variety and robustness, yet the fact remains that all these techniques rely on proper scene illumination and availability of texture for their operation. On the other hand, direct depth sensors such as Light Detection And Ranging (LiDAR) and dense depth sensor are robust against illumination changes or lack of texture. Light Detection And Ranging (LiDAR) units can produce depth measurements at long ranges and return data in the form of sparse point clouds. Techniques using LiDAR along with IMU integration to generate odometry estimates have shown very robust results over long ranges [14] but tend to suffer when matched with short-range sensors and/or when they operate in structure-less environments where geometric constraints are not enough to constrain the underlying optimization process [15]. Similarly, dense depth sensors produce dense depth data at short ranges and can be easily combined with RGB images. Techniques such as [16–18], have shown good odometry estimation results when using RGB-D data. However, despite the fact that these methods take advantage of the availability of direct depth estimates, on closer inspection it can be noted that handling of depth and visual data is done separately. In [16,17] feature detection and matching is done solely on the visual image for odometry estimation and depth data is utilized for scale estimation and mapping purposes. Similarly, visual approaches that deal with cases of poor illumination usually do not integrate any other type of information and require an external light source [3,19]. Due to this separate handling of the two sensing modalities, the overall odometry estimation remains prone to illumination changes and lack of texture. To remedy these problems, recent work [20,21] proposes to encode visual and depth information on the feature detection and descriptor level. Although these approaches improve the robustness in large illumination changes, they are sensitive to the quality of depth data and can become computationally burdensome for real time operations.

Motivated by the discussion above, in this work we present an EKF framework that fuses inertial, visual and depth information for odometry estimation. We use a robot-centric formulation and use inertial measurements to predict feature pixel positions between frames and use the re-projection error as an innovation term for the update step. Visual and depth information are encoded at the feature detector and descriptor level making them more robust in certain DVEs, i.e. low illumination and texture-less conditions. Only a small number of features are tracked as part of the filter state making the whole odometry computationally tractable for real time on-board robot navigation tasks. To the best of our knowledge this tightly integrated multimodal framework has no precedent in the robot odometry estimation literature.

3   Proposed Approach

Our proposed approach consists of three main components, namely (a) Visual-Depth Feature generation, (b) Descriptor Extraction and (c) inertial fusion using an EKF, as shown in Fig. 2.

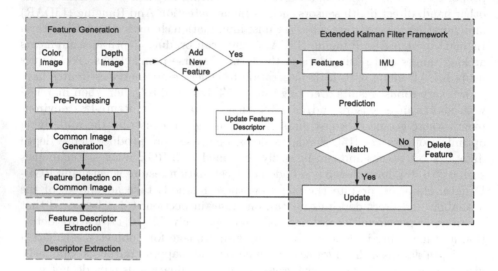

Fig. 2. An overview of the proposed approach.

3.1   Feature Detection

Upon receiving a pair of visual and depth images our method generates a combined score image that identifies keypoints in both sensing modalities by making use of the intuition that edges in both domains often lie along same image coordinates [22]. For this purpose we perform registration between the two images using the intrinsic and extrinsic calibration parameters of the cameras. For detection of features in the visual image we make use of the ORB feature detector [23] due to its robustness to image noise and scale invariant properties. We threshold detected ORB points by imposing a quality metric λ, representing the minimum acceptable Harris corner score, to ensure repeatable detection in low light conditions. We normalize the scores of the remaining visual keypoints and annotate them to create a visual score map $\mathcal{V}_s(x)$ which represents the score of a visual keypoint at pixel location x. For identification of key points in the depth image we calculate the second derivative at each pixel location by applying the Laplacian operator to the image. This allows us to identify edges in the depth domain, as well as to differentiate between points that lie near object edges as part of background or foreground since points in the background take a negative value. Next, we filter out noisy edge points by comparing the score at the pixel location to the depth error of the neighbouring pixels used in the calculation, which is a quadratic function of depth as mentioned in [24]. This operation is defined as:

$$\mathcal{D}_s(x) = \max\left(\mathcal{L}(x) - \sum_{i=1}^{n}\mathcal{N}(i), 0\right) \tag{1}$$

where $\mathcal{D}_s(x)$ is the score at depth pixel location x, $\mathcal{L}(x)$ is the result of applying Laplacian operation at the pixel location and $\mathcal{N}(i)$ is the depth error at pixel location i among the n neighboring pixels used in the calculation. Furthermore, to reduce the number of points along the edges and to identify corner points, we apply non-maxima suppression and only keep points with a gradient direction in the range of $30° \leq \theta \leq 60°$ in each quadrant. We normalize the scores to get our final depth score map $\mathcal{D}_s(x)$. The visual and depth score maps are then combined into a single score map which allows the method to identify multimodal keypoints and also maintain the best keypoints from each modality. This is given as:

$$\mathcal{C}_s(x) = \min(\gamma\mathcal{V}_s(x) + (1 - \gamma)\,\mathcal{D}_s(x), s_{\text{sat}}) \tag{2}$$

where $\mathcal{C}_s(x)$ represents the combined score at every pixel location, γ defines the contribution factor of each sensing modality, and s_{sat} is a fixed value used to saturate the value of $\mathcal{C}_s(x)$. The best keypoints from the combined score map are selected using an adaptive Euclidean distance constraint to ensure the method balances having enough features tracked in the filter while maintaining a distribution of features across the image frame. Figure 3 illustrates an example of this process for common feature detection.

3.2   Descriptor Extraction

Given a set of multimodal keypoints we extract a descriptor that utilizes both visual and depth information. For this purpose we chose to use the binary descriptor BRAND [20] because of its ability to encode visual and depth information, while maintaining fast performance during the descriptor extraction and matching processes. BRAND generates two binary strings that encode the visual and depth neighborhood information of keypoints individually, by performing pair-wise intensity and geometric tests on visual and depth images respectively. These bit strings are then combined using a bit-wise OR operation to create a combined descriptor. To generate the visual part of the descriptor, for a pair of pixel locations P_1 and P_2 with intensities I_1 and I_2, BRAND performs the following visual comparison V:

$$V(P_1, P_2) = \begin{cases} 1, & \text{if } I_1 < I_2 \\ 0, & \text{otherwise} \end{cases} \tag{3}$$

However, differing from the original work, our method modifies the above comparison for two reasons. First, comparing pixel intensities directly is susceptible

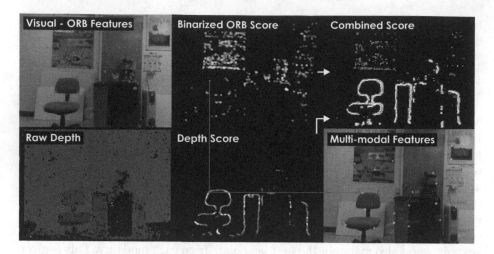

Fig. 3. Indicative example with steps of the process for common visual and depth feature detection. With red line, the case of one of the multimodal features is presented. (Color figure online).

to pixel noise and can cause erroneous bit switching in the descriptor. Secondly, in poorly illuminated conditions, visual camera sensors are susceptible to dark noise which can generate false intensity values that can introduce noise in the visual part of the descriptor. To reduce the sensitivity of the descriptor to pixel noise, instead of comparing pixel intensity values we compare mean intensity values using patches of size 9×9 created around sampled pair locations. Secondly, to reduce the effect of dark noise we subtract a small intensity value, representing dark noise, from the mean intensity values of the patches before performing the pair-wise comparison. This intensity representation of dark noise (I_{DN}) can be calculated by collecting images in a very dark environment where we expect the intensity value to be zero and deriving the mean intensity value across these images. The modified intensity comparison function for a pair of pixel locations P_1 and P_2 with mean patch intensities $\bar{I}_1$ and $\bar{I}_2$ takes the form:

$$V(P_1, P_2) = \begin{cases} 1, & \text{if } \max\left(0, \bar{I}_1 - I_{\mathrm{DN}}\right) < \max\left(0, \bar{I}_2 - I_{\mathrm{DN}}\right) \\ 0, & \text{otherwise} \end{cases} \quad (4)$$

The max function in the above equation ensures that the minimum allowed intensity value is 0. The depth part of the descriptor is maintained as describe in [20].

3.3 Extended Kalman Filter for IMU Fusion

We fuse inertial information with our multimodal features (landmarks) by tracking them as part of the state of an EKF, where state propagation is done by using proper acceleration $\hat{\mathbf{f}}$ and rotational rate measurements $\hat{\omega}$ provided by an IMU. This formulation allows us to predict the feature locations between successive frames hence reducing the search space for feature matching without the need for feature mismatch pruning. As features are part of the filter state we have an estimate of their uncertainty which we utilize to dynamically scale the search patch for every feature individually for feature matching purposes. Our filter structure is similar to the one proposed in [12]. In our formulation, three coordinate frames namely, IMU fixed coordinate frame ($\mathcal{B}$), the camera fixed frame $\mathcal{V}$, and the world inertial frame $\mathcal{W}$, are used. As we register our depth image with respect to the visual image, all the depth data is expressed in the camera fixed frame $\mathcal{V}$. Our multimodal features are expressed in $\mathcal{V}$ and are parameterized using a landmark approach which models 3D feature locations by using a 2D bearing vector $\boldsymbol{\mu}$, parametrized with azimuth and elevation angles, and a depth parameter $\boldsymbol{d}$. By using this parameterization, feature locations in the camera frame and their depth estimates are decoupled which allows us to use multimodal, vision-only and depth-only features interchangeably as part of the state vector. Hence, the employed state vector with dimension l and associated covariance matrix $\boldsymbol{\Sigma}_l$ is:

$$
\mathbf{x} = [\ \underbrace{\overbrace{\mathbf{r}\ \mathbf{q}}^{\text{pose, } l_p}\ \boldsymbol{v}\ \mathbf{b}_f\ \mathbf{b}_\omega}_{\text{robot states, } l_s}\ \ \underbrace{\boldsymbol{\mu}_0,\ \cdots\ \boldsymbol{\mu}_J\ \rho_0\ \cdots\ \rho_J}_{\text{multimodal features states, } l_f}\ ]^T \tag{5}
$$

where l_p, l_s, l_f are dimensions, $\mathbf{r}$ and $\boldsymbol{v}$ are the robot-centric position and velocity of the IMU respectively, expressed in $\mathcal{B}$, $\mathbf{q}$ is the IMU attitude represented as a map from $\mathcal{B} \to \mathcal{W}$, $\mathbf{b}_f$ and $\mathbf{b}_\omega$ represents the additive accelerometer and gyroscope biases respectively expressed in $\mathcal{B}$, while $\boldsymbol{\mu}_j$ is the bearing vector to feature j expressed in $\mathcal{V}$ and ρ_j is the depth parameter of the jth feature such that the feature distance d_j is $d(\rho_j) = 1/\rho_j$. Given the estimation of the robot pose, this is then expressed on the world frame $\mathcal{W}$ and the relevant pose transformations are available. This enables state feedback control and allows autonomy in difficult DVE cases of darkness and broadly poor illumination and lack of texture.

4   Experimental Evaluation

To evaluate the proposed solution for multimodal sensor fusion, a visual-depth-inertial perception unit consisting of a lightweight and low-cost Intel Realsense D435 Depth Camera, and a software synchronized VN-100 IMU from VectorNav was employed. Intel Realsense D435 provides RGB images as well as reliable depth information in the range from 0.75 m to 6.0 m. Beyond intrinsics calibration, camera-to-IMU extrinsics are identified based on the work in [25]. A set of experimental studies were conducted, in particular (a) a hand-held evaluation study inside a dark room, alongside (b) an experiment using a small aerial robot operating in low-light conditions. For both studies, the method processes Realsense D435 data at 10 Hz, while IMU updates are received at 200 Hz.

4.1 Hand-Held Evaluation

The first experimental evaluation refers to the localization and mapping inside a $7.6 \times 5 \times 2.3$ m dark room. Utilizing the Intel Realsense D435 Depth Camera and the VN-100 IMU, the method was found to be able to reliably estimate the motion trajectory and therefore allow consistent reconstruction of the 3D map. Most notably, the method maintains robustness even in very dark subsets of the environment, where visual camera data is non-informative and therefore traditional visual or visual-inertial odometry pipelines cannot cope with in a reliable manner. In these areas, furniture provides depth information that allows the framework to work. Figure 4 presents results from this study.

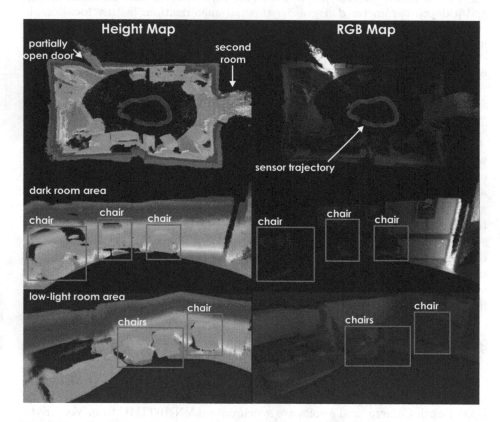

Fig. 4. Hand-held results regarding the localization inside a dark room. The mapping result indicates the consistency of the estimated trajectory which remains robust even in the most dark and low-light subsets of the environment.

4.2 Micro Aerial Vehicle Flight Test

For the flight experiment, a custom-built hexarotor Micro Aerial Vehicle (MAV) is employed and has a weight of 2.6 kg. The system relies on a Pixhawk-autopilot for its attitude control, while integrating an Intel NUC5i7RYH and executing a complete set of high-level tasks on-board with the support of the Robot Operating System (ROS). For the purposes of position control, a Linear Model Predictive Control strategy has been deployed following previous work in [26]. The robot integrates the same perception unit, i.e., the Intel Realsense D435 Depth Camera and the VN-100 IMU. An instance of the robot during the flight experiment is shown in Fig. 1.

The conducted experimental study relates to that of tracking a prescribed rectangle trajectory (length = 4.8 m, width = 1.95 m) in a low-light environment. The real-time estimated trajectory is compared against ground-truth

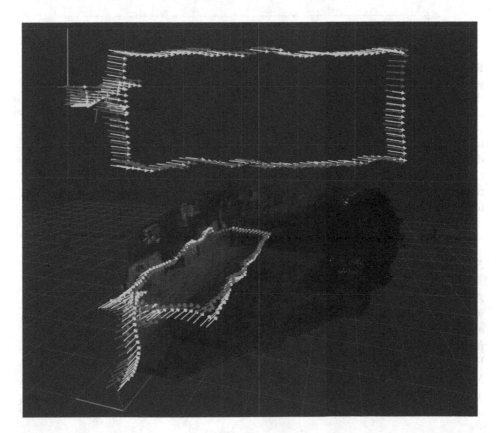

Fig. 5. Upper plot: The estimated robot trajectory (red) versus ground-truth information using a VICON motion capture system (yellow). As shown, the proposed method provides consistent localization results in dark visually-degraded conditions based on the fusion of visual-depth and inertial data. Bottom plot: reconstructed map of the environment based on the trajectory conducted by the robot. As shown, a major part of the environment presents very low-light conditions. In all plots, it can be identified that the motion capture system presented partial loss of data for segments of the conducted trajectory. A video of this experiment is uploaded at (Color figure online).

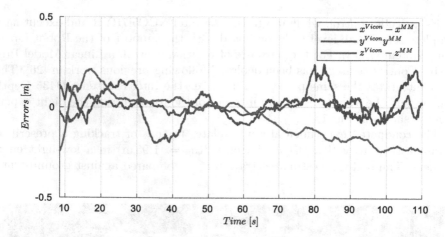

Fig. 6. Error plot between the onboard estimated trajectory $(\cdot)^{MM}$ and ground-truth provided by a VICON motion capture system. As shown, very small error is achieved despite the operation in dark visually-degraded conditions.

information provided by a VICON Motion Capture system. Figure 5 presents the derived results with the proposed method running on-board the MAV, alongside the reconstructed map of the environment. As shown, the derived trajectory is mostly on par with the ground-truth data and therefore reliable mapping is also achieved. Figure 6 presents an error plot for each axis of the robot trajectory. The video of the experiment can be seen at (https://tinyurl.com/DVEResults).

5   Conclusions

A method for common visual and depth data features alongside their fusion with IMU cues in order to enable autonomous localization in degraded visual environments and specifically low-light, dark, and textureless conditions was proposed. The focus is on an approach that exploits lightweight and ubiquitous RGB-D sensors and therefore can be integrated onboard small systems such as Micro Aerial Vehicles. A set of experimental evaluation studies are presented and demonstrate the ability of the system to provide reliable localization and mapping data in sensing-degraded conditions of darkness and low-light flight.

References

1. Papachristos, C., Khattak, S., Alexis, K.: Autonomous exploration of visually-degraded environments using aerial robots. In: 2017 International Conference on Unmanned Aircraft Systems. IEEE (2017)
2. Papachristos, C., Khattak, S., Alexis, K.: Uncertainty-aware receding horizon exploration and mapping using aerial robots. In: IEEE International Conference on Robotics and Automation, May 2017

3. Mascarich, F., Khattak, S., Papachristos, C., Alexis, K.: A multi-modal mapping unit for autonomous exploration and mapping of underground tunnels. In: 2018 IEEE Aerospace Conference, pp. 1–7. IEEE (2018)
4. Papachristos, C., et al.: Autonomous exploration and inspection path planning for aerial robots using the robot operating system. In: Koubaa, A. (ed.) Robot Operating System (ROS). SCI, vol. 778, pp. 67–111. Springer, Cham (2019). https://doi.org/10.1007/978-3-319-91590-6_3
5. Dang, T., Papachristos, T., Alexis, K.: Visual saliency-aware receding horizon autonomous exploration with application to aerial robotics. In: IEEE International Conference on Robotics and Automation (ICRA), May 2018
6. Grocholsky, B., Keller, J., Kumar, V., Pappas, G.: Cooperative air and ground surveillance. IEEE Robot. Autom. Mag. **13**(3), 16–25 (2006)
7. Balta, H., et al.: Integrated data management for a fleet of search-and-rescue robots. J. Field Robot. **34** (2017)
8. Mur-Artal, R., Montiel, J.M.M., Tardos, J.D.: ORB-SLAM: a versatile and accurate monocular SLAM system. IEEE Trans. Robot. **31**(5), 1147–1163 (2015)
9. Kitt, B., et al.: Visual odometry based on stereo image sequences with RANSAC-based outlier rejection scheme. In: Intelligent Vehicles Symposium (IV) (2010)
10. Scaramuzza, D., Fraundorfer, F.: Visual odometry: part I: the first 30 years and fundamentals. IEEE Robot. Autom. Mag. **18**(4), 80–92 (2011)
11. Forster, C., Pizzoli, M., Scaramuzza, D.: SVO: fast semi-direct monocular visual odometry. In: International Conference on Robotics and Automation (2014)
12. Bloesch, M., Omari, S., Hutter, M., Siegwart, R.: Robust visual inertial odometry using a direct EKF-based approach. In: Intelligent Robots and Systems (IROS), pp. 298–304. IEEE (2015)
13. Leutenegger, S., Lynen, S., Bosse, M., Siegwart, R., Furgale, P.: Keyframe-based visual-inertial odometry using nonlinear optimization. Int. J. Robot. Res. **34**(3), 314–334 (2015)
14. Zhang, J., Singh, S.: LOAM: LiDAR odometry and mapping in real-time. In: Robotics: Science and Systems Conference, Pittsburgh, PA (2014)
15. Zhang, J., et al.: On degeneracy of optimization-based state estimation problems. In: IEEE International Conference on Robotics and Automation (2016)
16. Kerl, C., Sturm, J., Cremers, D.: Robust odometry estimation for RGB-D cameras. In: International Conference on Robotics and Automation (2013)
17. Labbe, M., Michaud, F.: Appearance-based loop closure detection for online large-scale and long-term operation. IEEE Trans. Robot. **29**(3), 734–745 (2013)
18. Endres, F., Hess, J., Sturm, J., Cremers, D., Burgard, W.: 3-D mapping with an RGB-D camera. IEEE Trans. Robot. **30**(1), 177–187 (2014)
19. Alismail, H., Kaess, M., Browning, B., Lucey, S.: Direct visual odometry in low light using binary descriptors. IEEE Robot. Autom. Lett. **2**(2), 444–451 (2017)
20. Nascimento, E.R., et al.: BRAND: a robust appearance and depth descriptor for RGB-D images. In: International Conference on Intelligent Robots and Systems (2012)
21. Wu, K., et al.: RISAS: a novel rotation, illumination, scale invariant appearance and shape feature. In: International Conference on Robotics and Automation (2017)
22. Levinson, J., Thrun, S.: Automatic online calibration of cameras and lasers. In: Robotics: Science and Systems, vol. 2 (2013)
23. Rublee, E., Rabaud, V., Konolige, K., Bradski, G.: ORB: an efficient alternative to sift or surf. In: International conference on Computer Vision (ICCV) (2011)

24. Keselman, L., et al.: Intel (R) realsense (TM) stereoscopic depth cameras. In: Computer Vision and Pattern Recognition Workshops (CVPRW). IEEE (2017)
25. Furgale, P., Maye, J., Rehder, J., Schneider, T., Oth, L.: Kalibr (2014). https://github.com/ethz-asl/kalibr
26. Kamel, M., Stastny, T., Alexis, K., Siegwart, R.: Model predictive control for trajectory tracking of unmanned aerial vehicles using Robot Operating System. In: Koubaa, A. (ed.) Robot Operating System (ROS). SCI, vol. 707, pp. 3–39. Springer, Cham (2017). https://doi.org/10.1007/978-3-319-54927-9_1

Efficient Nearest Neighbors Search
for Large-Scale Landmark Recognition

Federico Magliani[✉], Tomaso Fontanini, and Andrea Prati

IMP Lab, University of Parma, 43124 Parma, Italy
federico.magliani@studenti.unipr.it
http://implab.ce.unipr.it/

Abstract. The problem of landmark recognition has achieved excellent results in small-scale datasets. Instead, when dealing with large-scale retrieval, issues that were irrelevant with small amount of data, quickly become fundamental for an efficient retrieval phase. In particular, computational time needs to be kept as low as possible, whilst the retrieval accuracy has to be preserved as much as possible. In this paper we propose a novel multi-index hashing method called Bag of Indexes (BoI) for Approximate Nearest Neighbors (ANN) search. It allows to drastically reduce the query time and outperforms the accuracy results compared to the state-of-the-art methods for large-scale landmark recognition. It has been demonstrated that this family of algorithms can be applied on different embedding techniques like VLAD and R-MAC obtaining excellent results in very short times on different public datasets: Holidays+Flickr1M, Oxford105k and Paris106k.

Keywords: Landmark recognition · Nearest neighbors search
Large-scale image retrieval · Approximate search

1 Introduction

Landmark recognition is an emerging field of research in computer vision. In a nutshell, starting from an image dataset divided into classes, with each image represented by a feature vector, the objective is to correctly identify to which class a query image belongs. This task presents several challenges: reaching high accuracy in the recognition phase, fast research time during the retrieval phase and reduced memory occupancy when working with a large amount of data. The large-scale retrieval has recently become interesting because the results obtained in the majority of small-scale datasets are over the 90% of the accuracy retrieval (*e.g.* to Gordo *et al.* [6]). Searching the correct k nearest neighbors of each query is the crucial problem of large-scale retrieval because, due to the great dimension of data, a lot of distractors are present and should not be considered as possible query neighbors. In order to deal with large-scale datasets, an efficient search algorithm, that retrieves query results faster than näive brute force approach, while keeping a high accuracy, is crucial. With an approximate search not all

© Springer Nature Switzerland AG 2018
G. Bebis et al. (Eds.): ISVC 2018, LNCS 11241, pp. 541–551, 2018.
https://doi.org/10.1007/978-3-030-03801-4_47

the returned neighbors are correct, but they are typically still close to the exact neighbors. Usually, obtaining good results in the image retrieval task is strictly correlated with the high dimensionality of the global image descriptors, but on a large-scale version of the same problem is not advisable to use the same approach, due to the large amount of memory that would be needed. A possible solution is to first reduce the dimensionality of the descriptors, for example through PCA, and, then, apply techniques based on hashing functions for an efficient retrieval.

Following this strategy, this paper introduces a new multi-index hashing method called *Bag of Indexes* (BoI) for large-scale landmark recognition based on Locality-Sensitive Hashing (LSH) and its variants, which allows to minimize the accuracy reduction with the growth of the data. The proposed method is tested on different public benchmarks using different embeddings in order to prove that is not an ad-hoc solution.

This paper is organized as follows. Section 2 introduces the general techniques used in the state of the art. Next, Sect. 3 describes the proposed *Bag of Indexes* (BoI) algorithm. Finally, Sect. 4 reports the experimental results on three public datasets: Holidays+Flickr1M, Oxford105k and Paris106k. Finally, concluding remarks are reported.

2   Related Work

In the last years, the problem of landmark recognition was addressed in many different ways [12,19,22]. Recently, with the development of new powerful GPUs, the deep learning approach has shown its superior performance in many tasks of image retrieval [1,5,24,26].

Whenever the number of images in the dataset becomes too large, a Nearest Neighbor (NN) search approach to the landmark recognition task becomes infeasible, due to the well-known problem of the curse of dimensionality. Therefore, Approximate Nearest Neighbors (ANN) becomes useful, since it consists in returning a point that has a distance from the query equals to at most c times the distance from the query to its nearest points, where $c > 1$.

One of the proposed techniques that allows to efficiently treat the ANN search problem is the Locality-Sensitive Hashing (LSH [9]), where the index of the descriptor is created through hash functions. LSH projects points that are close to each other into the same bucket with high probability. There are many different variants of LSH, such as E2LSH [3], multi-probe LSH [15], and many others.

While LSH is a data-independent hashing method, there exist also data-dependent methods like Spectral Hashing [25], which, however, is slower than LSH and therefore not appropriate for large-scale retrieval. In Permutation-Pivots index [2], data objects and queries are represented as appropriate permutations of a set of randomly selected reference objects, and their similarity is approximated by comparing their representation in terms of permutations. Product Quantization (PQ) [10] is used for searching local descriptors. It divides the feature space in disjoint subspaces and then quantizes each subspace separately.

It pre-computes the distances and saves them in look-up tables for speeding up the search. Locally Optimized Product Quantization (LOPQ) [13] is an optimization of PQ that tries to locally optimize an individual product quantizer per cell and uses it to encode residuals. Instead, FLANN [17] is an open source library for ANN and one of the most popular for nearest neighbor matching. It includes different algorithms and has an automated configuration procedure for finding the best algorithm to search in a particular data set.

3   Bag of Indexes

The proposed Bag of Indexes (BoI) borrows concepts from the well-known Bag of Words (BoW) approach. It is a form of multi-index hashing method [7,18] for the resolution of ANN search problem.

Firstly, following the LSH approach, L hash tables composed by 2^δ buckets, that will contain the indexes of the database descriptors, are created. The parameter δ represents the hash dimension in bits. The list of parameters of BoI and chosen values are reported in Table 1 in Sect. 3.2. Secondly, the descriptors are projected L times using hashing functions. It is worth to note that this approach can be used in combination with different projection functions, not only hashing and LSH functions. Finally, each index of the descriptors is saved in the corresponding bucket that is the one matching the projection result.

At query time, for each query, a BoI structure is created, that is a vector of n weights (each corresponding to one image of the database) initiliazed to zero. Every element of the vector will be filled based on the weighing method explained in Sect. 3.1. So, at the end of the projection phase, it is possible to make a coarse-grain evaluation of the similarity between the query image and the other images without calculating the Euclidean distance between them, but considering only their frequencies in the query buckets. Subsequently, at the end of the retrieval phase, the ε elements of the vector with the highest weights are re-ranked according to their Euclidean distance from the query. The nearest neighbor is then searched only in this short re-ranked list. By computing the Euclidean distances only at the end of the retrieval phase and only on this short list (instead of computing them on each hash table like in standard LSH), the computational time is greatly reduced. Furthermore, this approach, unlike LSH, does not require to maintain a ranking list without duplicates for all the L hash tables. The detailed analysis of the memory occupation of BoI is reported in Sect. 4.

3.1   Weighing Metric

As previously reported, BoI can be used in combination with different hashing functions. When used with baseline LSH, the corresponding bucket of the query image will be checked. In this case, even thought it is faster than LSH, the accuracy suffers a significant loss. Conversely, when BoI is combined with multi-probe LSH, also the l-neighboring buckets are considered.

The l-neighbors are the buckets that have a Hamming distance less than or equal to l from the hashed value of the query, which corresponds to the query bucket. The weights for the any value of l are chosen as follows:

$$w(i,q,l) = \begin{cases} \frac{1}{2^{H(i,q)}} & \text{if } H(i,q) \leq l \\ 0 & \text{otherwise} \end{cases} \tag{1}$$

where i is a generic bucket, q is the query bucket and $H(i,q)$ is the Hamming distance between i and q. The BoI multi-probe LSH approach increases the number of buckets considered during the retrieval and, thus, the probability of retrieving the correct result, by exploiting the main principle of LSH that similar objects should fall in the same bucket or in the ones that are close to it. However, even if we want to account for some uncertainty in the selection of the correct bucket, we also want to weight less as soon as we move farther from the "central" bucket.

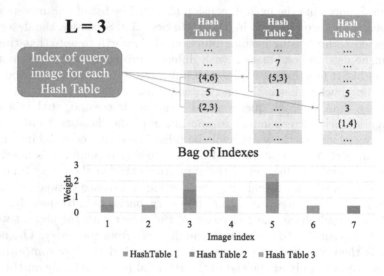

Fig. 1. Overview figure of the retrieval through BoI multi-probe LSH.

Figure 1 shows an exemplar overview of the BoI computation. With $L = 3$ hash tables and 1-neighbours (i.e., $l = 1$), a query can be projected in different buckets. The corresponding weights (see Eq. 1) are accumulated in the BoI (see the graph on the bottom of the image). Only the ϵ images with the highest weights are considered for the last step (re-ranking) for improving the recall.

3.2   BoI Adaptive Multi-probe LSH

This BoI multi-probe LSH approach has the drawback of increasing the computational time since it also needs to search in neighboring buckets (which are

$\sum_{i=0}^{l} \binom{\log_2 \delta}{i}$, being δ the hash dimension). To mitigate this drawback, we introduce a further variant, called *BoI adaptive multi-probe LSH*. The main idea of this approach is to iteratively refine the search bucket space, by starting with a large number of neighboring buckets γ_0 (e.g., 10) and slowly reduce γ when the number of hash tables increases. This adaptive increase of focus can, on the one hand, reduce the computational time and, on the other hand, reduce the noise. In fact, at each iteration, the retrieval results are supposed to be more likely correct and the last iterations are meant to just confirm them, so there is no need to search on a large number of buckets. In order to avoid checking the same neighbors during different experiments, the list of neighbors to check is shuffled randomly at each experiment.

Two different techniques for the reduction of the number of hash tables are evaluated:

- *linear*: the number of neighboring buckets γ is reduced by 2 every 40 hash tables, i.e.:

$$\gamma_i = \begin{cases} \gamma_{i-1} - 2 & \text{if } i = \{\Delta_1, \ldots, k_1 \Delta_1\} \\ \gamma_{i-1} & \text{otherwise} \end{cases} \tag{2}$$

  with $i = \{1, \ldots, L\}$, $\Delta_1 = 40$ and $k_1 : k_1 \Delta_1 \leq L$

- *sublinear*: the number of neighboring buckets γ is reduced by 2 every 25 hash tables, but only after the first half of hash tables, i.e.:

$$\gamma_i = \begin{cases} \gamma_{i-1} & \text{if } i \leq L/2 \\ \gamma_{i-1} - 2 & \text{if } i = \{L/2, L/2 + \Delta_2, \ldots, L/2 + k_2 \Delta_2\} \\ \gamma_{i-1} & \text{otherwise} \end{cases} \tag{3}$$

  with $i = \{1, \ldots, L\}$, $\Delta_2 = 25$ and $k_2 : L/2 + k_2 \Delta_2 \leq L$

The parameters has been chosen through fine tuning after the execution of many test.

The proposed approach contains several parameters. Their values were chosen after an extensive parameter analysis (out of the scope of this paper) and

Table 1. Summary of notation.

Symbol	Definition	Chosen value
n	Number of images	-
δ	Hash dimension	$2^8 = 256$
L	Number of hash tables	100
γ_0	Initial gap	10
l	Neighbors bucket	1-neighbors
ε	Elements in the re-ranking list	250
-	Reduction	Sublinear

summary of notation is reported in Table 1. L, δ and l should be as low as possible since they directly affect the number of buckets $\mathcal{N}_q^l$ to be checked and therefore the computational time at each query q, as follows:

$$\mathcal{N}_q^l = L \sum_{i=0}^{l} \binom{\gamma_i}{i} = L \sum_{i=0}^{l} \frac{(\gamma_i)!}{i!\,(\gamma_i - i)!} \tag{4}$$

where $\gamma_i = \gamma_0 = \log_2 \delta, \forall i$ for standard BoI multi-probe LSH, whereas, in the case of BoI adaptive multi-probe LSH, γ_i can be computed using the Eqs. 2 or 3.

4 Experimental Results

The proposed approach has been extensively tested on public datasets in order to evaluate the accuracy against the state of the art.

4.1 Datasets and Evaluation Metrics

The performance is measured on three public image datasets: Holidays+Flickr1M, Oxford105k and Paris106k as shown in Table 2.

Table 2. Datasets used in the experiments

Dataset	Size	Query images
Holidays [11] + Flickr1M	1 001 491	500
Oxford105k [20]	105 063	55
Paris106k [21]	106 392	55

Holidays [11] is composed by 1491 images representing the holidays photos of different locations, subdivided in 500 classes. The database images are 991 and the query images are 500, one for every class.

Oxford5k [20] is composed by 5062 images of Oxford landmarks. The classes are 11 and the queries are 55 (5 for each class).

Paris [21] is composed by 6412 images of landmarks of Paris, France. The classes are 11 and the queries are 55 (5 for each class).

Flickr1M [8] contains 1 million Flickr images used as distractors for Holidays, Oxford5k and Paris6k generating Holidays +Flickr1M, Oxford105k and Paris106k datasets.

Evaluation. Mean Average Precision (mAP) was used as metrics for accuracy.

Distance. L_2 distance was employed to compare query images with the database.

Implementation. All experiments have been run on 4 separate threads. The CNN features used for the creation of locVLAD [16] descriptors are calculated on a NVIDIA GeForce GTX 1070 GPU mounted on a computer with 8-core and 3.40GHz CPU.

4.2   Results on Holidays+Flickr1M Datasets

This section reports the results of our approach, by adding to the Holidays dataset a different number of distractors, obtained from the Flickr1M dataset. All the experiments have been conducted several times and a mean has been computed in order to eliminate the randomness of the Gaussian distribution used in the hashing function. The embeddings used are locVLAD descriptors [16], while the features are extracted from the layer mixed8 of Inception V3 network [23] that is a CNN pre-trained on the ImageNet [4] dataset. The vocabulary used for the creation of locVLAD descriptors is calculated on Paris6k.

Table 3. Results in terms of mAP and average retrieval time in msec on Holidays+Flickr1M. * indicates our re-implementation.

Method	ϵ	Holidays+Flickr1M	
		mAP	avg retrieval time (msec)
LSH*	250	86.03%	3 103
Multi-probe LSH* (L = 50)	250	86.10%	16 706
PP-index* [2]	250	82.70%	2 844
LOPQ [13]	250	36.37%	4
FLANN [17]	250	83.97%	995
BoI LSH	250	78.10%	5
BoI multi-probe LSH	250	85.16%	12
BoI adaptive multi-probe LSH	250	85.35%	8
PP-index* [2]	10k	85.51%	15 640
LOPQ [13]	10k	67.22%	72
FLANN [17]	10k	85.66%	1 004
BoI adaptive multi-probe LSH	10k	**86.09%**	**16**

Table 3 summarizes the results on Holidays+Flickr1M dataset in terms of mAP and average retrieval time (msec). The first experiments evaluated only the top $\epsilon = 250$ nearest neighbors.

LSH and multi-probe LSH achieve excellent results, but with an huge retrieval time. Also PP-index [2] needs more than 3 seconds for a query to retrieve the results. LOPQ [13] reaches poor results on large-scale retrieval with an accuracy equals to 36.37%, while FLANN [17] achieved a better result of 83.97%. However, while query time for LOPQ is pretty low compared to the other test cases, FLANN is not able to keep the query time low. It is worth saying that both LOPQ and FLANN has been tested using the available codes from authors and reported results correspond to the best found configuration of parameters. Given the significantly low (especially for LOPQ) performance in accuracy, further experiments have been conducted for LOPQ, FLANN, as well as PP-index and our method by increasing ϵ from 250 to 10k. As foreseeable, all the accuracy results improved with respect to $\epsilon = 250$ (LOPQ increases from 36.37%

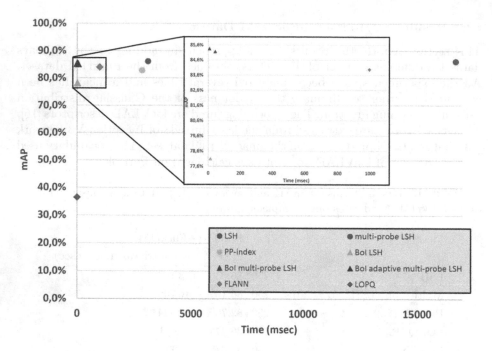

Fig. 2. Relationship between time and accuracy on Holidays+Flickr1M with different approaches.

to 67.22%), but the proposed BoI adaptive multi-probe LSH method still out-performs all the others. Moreover, our method still results to be faster than the others (LOPQ is fast like ours, but with lower accuracy, while PP-index and FLANN are slightly lower in accuracy, but much slower).

Overall speaking, our proposal outperforms all the compared methods in the trade-off between accuracy and efficiency. To better highlight this, Fig. 2 shows jointly the mAP (on y-axis) and the average query time (on x-axis). The best trade-off has to be found in the upper left corner of this graph, i.e. corresponding to high accuracy and low query time. All the BoI-based methods clearly outperform the other methods.

Regarding the memory footprint of the algorithm for 1M images with 1M descriptors of 128D (float = 4 bytes), brute-force approach requires 0.5 Gb (1M × 128 × 4). LSH needs only 100 Mb: 1M indexes for each of the L = 100 hash tables, because each indexes is represented by a byte (8 bit) and so 1M indexes × 100 hash tables × 1 byte = 100 Mb. The proposed BoI only requires additional 4 Mb to store 1M weights.

4.3   Results on Oxford105k and Paris106k Datasets

Since our goal is to execute large-scale retrieval for landmark recognition, we have also used the Oxford105k and Paris106k datasets. In this case, all the methods are tested using R-MAC descriptors, fine-tuned by Gordo *et al.* [6], since VLAD descriptors are demonstrated to be not suited for these datasets [14].

Table 4. Results in terms of mAP and average retrieval time (msec) on Oxford105k and Paris106k. * indicates our re-implementation of the method.

Method	ϵ	Oxford105k		Paris106k	
		mAP	avg ret. time (msec)	mAP	avg ret. time (msec)
LSH*	2500	80.83%	610	86.50%	607
PP-index* [2]	2500	81.89%	240	88.14%	140
LOPQ [13]	2500	71.90%	346	87.47%	295
FLANN [17]	2500	70.33%	2118	68.93%	2132
BoI adaptive multi-probe LSH	2500	81.44%	12	87.90%	13
PP-index* [2]	10k	82.82%	250	89.04%	164
LOPQ [13]	10k	69.94%	1153	88.00%	841
FLANN [17]	10k	69.37%	2135	70.73%	2156
BoI adaptive multi-probe LSH	10k	**84.38%**	**25**	**92.31%**	**27**

Table 4 show the mAP and the average retrieval time. Using $\epsilon = 2500$, the proposed approach obtained slightly worse results than PP-index, but resulted one order of magnitude faster in both datasets. When more top-ranked images are used ($\epsilon = 10k$), BoI adaptive multi-probe LSH obtained the best results and with lower query time. Furthermore, LOPQ [13] works better on Paris106k than Oxford105k, while FLANN [17] performs poorly on both datasets.

5 Conclusions

In this paper, a novel multi-index hashing methods called Bag of Indexes (BoI) for approximate nearest neighbor search problem is proposed. This method demonstrated an overall better trade-off between accuracy and speed w.r.t. state-of-the-art methods on several large-scale landmark recognition datasets. Also, it works well with different embedding types (VLAD and R-MAC). The main future directions of our work will be related to reduce the dimension of the descriptor in order to speed the creation of bucket structure and to adapt the proposed method for dataset with billions of elements.

Acknowledgments. This work is partially funded by Regione Emilia Romagna under the "Piano triennale alte competenze per la ricerca, il trasferimento tecnologico e l'imprenditorialità".

References

1. Babenko, A., Slesarev, A., Chigorin, A., Lempitsky, V.: Neural codes for image retrieval. In: Fleet, D., Pajdla, T., Schiele, B., Tuytelaars, T. (eds.) ECCV 2014. LNCS, vol. 8689, pp. 584–599. Springer, Cham (2014). https://doi.org/10.1007/978-3-319-10590-1_38
2. Chavez, E., Figueroa, K., Navarro, G.: Effective proximity retrieval by ordering permutations. IEEE Trans. Pattern Anal. Mach. Intell. **30**, 1647–1658 (2008)
3. Datar, M., Immorlica, N., Indyk, P., Mirrokni, V.S.: Locality-sensitive hashing scheme based on p-stable distributions. In: Proceedings of the Twentieth Annual Symposium on Computational Geometry, pp. 253–262. ACM (2004)
4. Deng, J., Dong, W., Socher, R., Li, L.J., Li, K., Fei-Fei, L.: ImageNet: a large-scale hierarchical image database. In: IEEE Conference on Computer Vision and Pattern Recognition, CVPR 2009, pp. 248–255. IEEE (2009)
5. Gordo, A., Almazán, J., Revaud, J., Larlus, D.: Deep image retrieval: learning global representations for image search. In: Leibe, B., Matas, J., Sebe, N., Welling, M. (eds.) ECCV 2016. LNCS, vol. 9910, pp. 241–257. Springer, Cham (2016). https://doi.org/10.1007/978-3-319-46466-4_15
6. Gordo, A., Almazan, J., Revaud, J., Larlus, D.: End-to-end learning of deep visual representations for image retrieval. Int. J. Comput. Vis. **124**(2), 237–254 (2017)
7. Greene, D., Parnas, M., Yao, F.: Multi-index hashing for information retrieval. In: 1994 Proceedings of the 35th Annual Symposium on Foundations of Computer Science, pp. 722–731. IEEE (1994)
8. Huiskes, M.J., Lew, M.S.: The MIR flickr retrieval evaluation. In: Proceedings of the 1st ACM International Conference on Multimedia Information Retrieval, pp. 39–43. ACM (2008)
9. Indyk, P., Motwani, R.: Approximate nearest neighbors: towards removing the curse of dimensionality. In: Proceedings of the Thirtieth Annual ACM Symposium on Theory of Computing, pp. 604–613. ACM (1998)
10. Jegou, H., Douze, M., Schmid, C.: Product quantization for nearest neighbor search. IEEE Trans. Pattern Anal. Mach. Intell. **33**(1), 117–128 (2011)
11. Jégou, H., Douze, M., Schmid, C.: Hamming embedding and weak geometry consistency for large scale image search-extended version (2008)
12. Jégou, H., Douze, M., Schmid, C., Pérez, P.: Aggregating local descriptors into a compact image representation. In: CVPR, pp. 3304–3311 (2010)
13. Kalantidis, Y., Avrithis, Y.: Locally optimized product quantization for approximate nearest neighbor search. In: Proceedings of the IEEE Conference on Computer Vision and Pattern Recognition, pp. 2321–2328 (2014)
14. Liu, Y., Zhang, D., Lu, G., Ma, W.Y.: A survey of content-based image retrieval with high-level semantics. Pattern Recognit. **40**(1), 262–282 (2007)
15. Lv, Q., Josephson, W., Wang, Z., Charikar, M., Li, K.: Multi-probe LSH: efficient indexing for high-dimensional similarity search. In: Proceedings of the 33rd International Conference on Very Large Data Bases, pp. 950–961. VLDB Endowment (2007)
16. Magliani, F., Bidgoli, N.M., Prati, A.: A location-aware embedding technique for accurate landmark recognition. In: ICDSC (2017)
17. Muja, M., Lowe, D.G.: Scalable nearest neighbor algorithms for high dimensional data. IEEE Trans. Pattern Anal. Mach. Intell. **36**(11), 2227–2240 (2014)
18. Norouzi, M., Punjani, A., Fleet, D.J.: Fast search in hamming space with multi-index hashing. In: 2012 IEEE Conference on Computer Vision and Pattern Recognition (CVPR), pp. 3108–3115. IEEE (2012)

19. Perronnin, F., Liu, Y., Sánchez, J., Poirier, H.: Large-scale image retrieval with compressed fisher vectors. In: 2010 IEEE Conference on Computer Vision and Pattern Recognition (CVPR), pp. 3384–3391. IEEE (2010)

20. Philbin, J., Chum, O., Isard, M., Sivic, J., Zisserman, A.: Object retrieval with large vocabularies and fast spatial matching. In: Proceedings of the IEEE Conference on Computer Vision and Pattern Recognition (2007)

21. Philbin, J., Chum, O., Isard, M., Sivic, J., Zisserman, A.: Lost in quantization: improving particular object retrieval in large scale image databases. In: CVPR (2008)

22. Sivic, J., Zisserman, A.: Video Google: a text retrieval approach to object matching in videos. ICCV **2**, 1470–1477 (2003)

23. Szegedy, C., Vanhoucke, V., Ioffe, S., Shlens, J., Wojna, Z.: Rethinking the inception architecture for computer vision. In: Proceedings of the IEEE Conference on Computer Vision and Pattern Recognition, pp. 2818–2826 (2016)

24. Tolias, G., Sicre, R., Jégou, H.: Particular object retrieval with integral max-pooling of CNN activations. arXiv preprint arXiv:1511.05879 (2015)

25. Weiss, Y., Torralba, A., Fergus, R.: Spectral hashing. In: Advances in Neural Information Processing Systems, pp. 1753–1760 (2009)

26. Yue-Hei Ng, J., Yang, F., Davis, L.S.: Exploiting local features from deep networks for image retrieval. In: Proceedings of the IEEE Conference on Computer Vision and Pattern Recognition Workshops, pp. 53–61 (2015)

Patient's Body Motion Study Using Multimodal RGBDT Videos

Mohammad A. Haque[1(✉)], Simon S. Kjeldsen[2], Federico G. Arguissain[3], Iris Brunner[2], Kamal Nasrollahi[1], Ole Kæseler Andersen[3], Jørgen F. Nielsen[2], Thomas B. Moeslund[1], and Anders Jørgensen[1]

[1] Visual Analysis of People Lab, Aalborg University, Aalborg, Denmark
mah@create.aau.dk
[2] Regionshospitalet Hammel Neurocenter, Hammel, Denmark
[3] SMI®, Department of Health Science and Technology, Aalborg University, Aalborg, Denmark

Abstract. Automatic analysis of body movement to identify physical activity of patients who are at bed rest is crucial for treatment or rehabilitation purposes. Existing methods of physical activity analysis mostly focused on the detection of primitive motion/non-motion states in unimodal video data captured by either RGB or depth or thermal sensor. In this paper, we propose a multimodal vision-based approach to classify body motion of a person lying on a bed. We mimicked a real scenario of 'patient on bed' by recording multimodal video data from healthy volunteers in a hospital room in a neurorehabilitation center. We first defined a taxonomy of possible physical activities based on observations of patients with acquired brain injuries. We then investigated different motion analysis and machine learning approaches to classify physical activities automatically. A multimodal database including RGB, depth and thermal videos was collected and annotated with eight predefined physical activities. Experimental results show that we can achieve moderately high accuracy (77.68%) to classify physical activities by tracking the body motion using an optical flow-based approach. To the best of our knowledge this is the first multimodal RGBDT video analysis for such application.

Keywords: Physical activity · Multimodal · RGBDT · Video Rest activity · Patient on bed

1 Introduction

Tracking of physical activity (PA) or body motion has received great interest and use in the health care sector, mainly because of the importance of assessing the amount of PA that is performed by healthy individuals and by patients with different conditions [1–3]. The information provided by PA tracking is regularly used to develop recommendations and guidelines for promoting a healthy lifestyle, and to improve the outcome of rehabilitation therapies. Particularly, tracking PA

© Springer Nature Switzerland AG 2018
G. Bebis et al. (Eds.): ISVC 2018, LNCS 11241, pp. 552–564, 2018.
https://doi.org/10.1007/978-3-030-03801-4_48

while subjects are lying on the bed has been widely used in sleep analysis and also in many other health care applications like breathing, epilepsy, vital signs and activity monitoring [4,5]. Technological modalities such as actigraphy and global positioning systems are emerging tools in the health care sector that provide objective measurements of PA [6]. Particularly, actigraphy is an accelerometer-based method which is widely used to track PA [7,8]. Actigraphy has also been used to quantify rest activity-cycles and to monitor sleep in recumbent persons, in patients with severe traumatic brain injury and in intensive care patients [9]. These studies show that actigraphy is a useful tool in these situations. However, it is very likely that wakefulness is underestimated in these bedridden, inactive awake patients possibly due to the low specificity of actigraphy in detecting wakefulness and the poor agreement between actigraphy devices placed in different positions of the body [10]. Besides the use of actigraphy, video-based analysis of PA or body motion has drawn notable interest over the last three decades due to inherent unobtrusiveness, low cost and ubiquity [11,12].

When a subject is lying on a bed, tracking PA or body motion has been mostly focused on detecting the presence of motion and non-motion states in temporal dimension [13–15]. However, certain health care applications would benefit from detecting more than just motion and non-motion states. In fact, human body motion is a broad concept that includes as many different movements as the human body can exhibit [12]. While some of these motions mostly represent the primitive configuration change of the body parts over time (e.g. movement of fingers or head), some motions can be interpreted as different perceptual classes like pose, gesture and expression. This concept suggests that meaningful body motion information could be extracted by analyzing perceptual physical activity classes in situations where patients are lying on hospital beds. For example, neurorehabilitation institutions that monitor patients with Acquired Brain Injury (ABI) would take advantage of an automatic detection and identification of spontaneous motor activity in an otherwise paralytic extremity. This information could be crucial for the prognosis of these patients [16,17]. In such a scenario, different PAs associated with motor activity need to be classified in order to document patient's activity level and variation of activities. However, there are two categories of challenges associated with this kind of application: (a) methodological challenges and (b) resource-related challenges.

Methodological challenges are associated to the procedure of tracking body motion or PA in videos. Three popular methods have been previously used in the literature: frame differencing, optical flow, and block matching [14]. Frame differencing is used to identify areas with motion, and optical flow and block matching are used to estimate local displacement. While considering video data, the differences in choices between different video sensors such as RGB, thermal and depth were also observed [4]. Resource-related challenges are mostly associated with lack of availability of databases to evaluate the performance of a methodological proposal for tracking PA [5].

In this paper, we envision to develop a system that will facilitate patient monitoring in a "patient in bed" scenario of a neurorehabilitation or care-giving institution. Thus, as a preliminary step, we propose here a multimodal vision-based approach to detect and classify body motion in an experimental setting with healthy volunteers that mimicked a real scenario of "patient on bed". Unlike the traditional methods that mostly focused on detecting primitive motion/non-motion states in unimodal video data captured by either of RGB or depth or thermal sensors, our contributions are:

- Recognize the scenario of "patient on bed" to categorize relevant PAs.
- Assess different motion analysis and machine learning approaches to detect and classify PAs.
- Collect a multimodal RGBDT video database with healthy volunteers and exploit its multi-modality to achieve better classification accuracy.

To the best of our knowledge this is the first multimodal RGBDT video analysis for such applications.

The rest of the paper is organized as follows. Section 2 explains the relevant scenario and categories of PAs considered in this study. Section 3 describes the database along with acquisition and processing challenges. Section 4 illustrates the proposed methodology of detecting and classifying PAs and Sect. 5 shows the performance of the system on the collected database. Finally, Sect. 6 concludes the paper.

2   Scenario and Categorization of the PAs

The main motivation for this study is to develop a tool to monitor patients with ABI who are admitted to Hammel Neurorehabilitation and Research Center (HNRC), Denmark. This is a specialized neurorehabilitation hospital, which is responsible for rehabilitation of patients with ABI from Western Denmark. The developed tool could potentially be used to help HNRC health workers in neurorehabilitation to automatically identify spontaneous motor activity during hours without direct monitoring. It could also be used to document and monitor the overall 24-h motor activity of bedridden patients with disorders of consciousness. This information would be not only very useful in the prognosis of these patients [17], but also with regard to providing the right intervention at the right time.

To initiate the process of developing a video-based, body motion analysis tool that could be implemented in a hospital setting, we first performed the present experimental study on healthy subjects. We first categorized the possible body movement events, that are typically observed by the clinical staff in patients lying in a hospital bed. We then divided them into two categories, based on the presence or absence of a blanket that covered the subject's lower body (Fig. 1). In each category we put five different movements based on the following body segments: foot, wrist, head, leg and arm. Two movements of the whole body were also considered: body turning and moving from 'lying down' in the bed to 'sitting on the edge of the bed'. These movements cover different possible small, moderate and large body movements performed by patients in a real scenario (Fig. 1). Employing healthy volunteers and a predefined sequence of movements allowed us to evaluate the performance of the computer vision-based data processing methodology in a controlled-fashion.

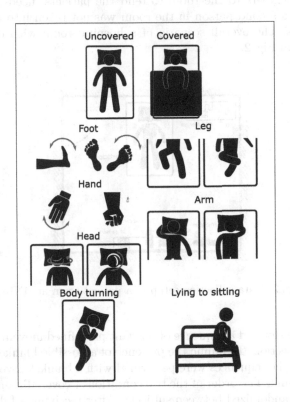

Fig. 1. Different PA performed by healthy volunteers in a hospital setting while mimicking the "patient on bed" scenario

3 The Database

The database was collected from healthy volunteers including both men and women. All volunteers gave written informed consent before participating. To mimic a genuine hospital setting, a patient room at HNRC was outfitted with a hospital bed and relevant monitoring equipment. Volunteers were asked to lie in the bed in a supine position. The recordings were performed under regular lighting conditions, and the room temperature was that of the hospital. In order to replicate the hospital setting in the best possible way, we took into account some of the common challenges that are observed at the HNRC ward in terms of standard video monitoring of the rooms. First, it was noticed that cameras are generally located in the ceiling or up in the walls, so they do not interfere with the work of the staff members. Other challenging aspects that have to be taken into account are the positioning of the body relative to the field of view of the camera, the presence of monitoring and life-support equipment, the furniture and the lighting conditions of the room. Other practical challenges are the regular visits of staff members to the room to tend the patients' needs. Nevertheless, the presence of a second person in the room was not taken into account in the present analysis. The overall scenario of a hospital room with data collection setup is shown in Fig. 2.

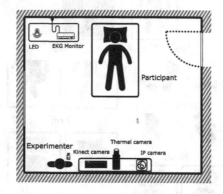

Fig. 2. Data collection setup in a patient room at HNRC

Volunteers performed a sequence of relevant predefined movements described in the previous section. To mimic the presence of a possible blanket covering the patients, half of the sequences were performed with a blanket covering the lower body and the trunk. The order of the two conditions ('covered', 'uncovered') was alternated and randomized between subjects. After receiving a full explanation, the subjects were instructed to lie in the bed still and wait for the instructions of the experimenter. Each movement of the sequence was pre-announced verbally by the experimenter, who gave the verbal command 'go' to cue the subject to perform the movement. It was emphasized that the subjects could choose to move relatively free, only constraining their movement to the body segment that was announced before. Subjects were also asked to make movements that resembled those that they would do while resting in bed e.g. scratching hair, crossing legs, putting arm behind their head, etc. Participants performed 70 movements in total (2 conditions, each repeated in 5 sequences of 7 movements). As baseline measurements (non-motion data), we used the frames from the pause between two consecutive movements.

Video cameras were mounted in a wall shelf, in front of the patient and facing the foot-board of the bed. Three video cameras were set to record simultaneously: a Microsoft Kinect V2 for depth, an axis 214 PTZ RGB camera [18], and an axis Q1922 thermal camera. The final database contained the videos (one video contains one event of PA) annotated with eight PA categories (including a non-motion category). RGB and thermal video resolution was 640×480 with fps $= 30$, and depth video resolution was 512×424 with fps < 30. The database contained 1127 annotated videos (duration 1–7 s) from 9 subjects. Each video contained one motion event.

4   The Methodology of Body Motion Analysis

In this section, we describe the step-by-step procedure to identify perceptual PA from the body motions in a "patient in bed" scenario.

4.1   Data Preprocessing

The multimodal video data was captured by different cameras with different video frame rates. In order to synchronize the video data across modalities, we followed the time-stamps of the depth frames and kept only the corresponding frames from the other modalities by following [19]. Before going to motion tracking we needed to reduce the search space in the video frames. This was possible since the patient was lying on the bed while performing PA and the remaining area of the room was not our concern while tracking. We assumed that the bed area in the hospital room is fixed in a specific room setting. Therefore, we cropped the whole bed area as the Region of Interest (ROI). Figure 3 shows the cropped bed region in each modality while a subject is lying on the bed.

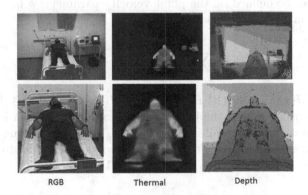

Fig. 3. Original video frames (top row) and the cropped bed area as the ROI (bottom row) in different modalities

4.2   Body Motion Tracking

While detecting motion/non-motion states, the body motion exhibited globally in the ROI could be used as total surface motion. Any presence of surface motion after noise elimination could be considered as a trigger to the presence of body motion [14]. However, as we were considering the classification of 8 perceptual PA categories, global surface motion was not sufficient. Instead, we needed to find the local motions within the ROI and the intensity of motion as well. This was needed because in some situations the movements of different body segments might fall in the same region. For example, a movement of the wrist may occur in a similar region as a movement of the arm. However, the intensities of movement are not same, as the range of movement for the wrist is significantly lower than that of the whole arm. Thus, in order to track the movement and its intensity, we employed a point-based motion tracking approach which uses a method called 'Good Features to Track (GFT)' to detect appropriate pixels in the ROI and a method called Lucas-Kanade-Tomasi (LKT) feature tracker to track those points [20,21]. The process is described below.

The pattern of pixel intensities changes due to body movement in consecutive video frames. This intensity change can be expressed by an affine motion model in order to form a tracking algorithm. Let I and J be two consecutive video frames. The two quantities $I(\mathbf{x}) = I(x,y)$ and $J(\mathbf{x}) = J(x,y)$ present the intensity values of the two images at the coordinate $\mathbf{x} = [x,y]^T$. If $\mathbf{p} = [p_x, p_y]^T$ is an image point on the first frame I, tracking this point in the next frame J is a feature tracking problem. The goal of feature tracking is to find the location $\mathbf{q} = \mathbf{p} + \delta = [p_x + \delta_x, p_y + \delta_y]^T$ on the second frame J, such as $I(\mathbf{p})$ and $J(\mathbf{q})$ are similar. The vector $\delta = [\delta_x, \delta_y]^T$ is called optical flow or image velocity at the point $\mathbf{x} = [x,y]^T$. In a practical scenario the notion of similarity between two points in two frames are defined by using the so-called 'neighborhood sense' or window of pixels. Thus, tracking a window of size $w_x \times w_y$ in the frame I to the frame J can be defined on the point velocity parameter δ by minimizing a residual function f_{GFT} as follows:

$$f_{GFT}(\delta) = \sum_{x=p_x}^{p_x+w_x} \sum_{y=p_y}^{p_y+w_y} (I(\mathbf{x}) - J(\mathbf{x}+\delta))^2 \tag{1}$$

where $(I(\mathbf{x}) - J(\mathbf{x}+\delta))$ stands for $(I(x,y) - J(x+\delta_x, y+\delta_y))$. The velocity parameter δ is a function of the image position $\mathbf{x}$, and variation in δ are often noticeable even within the small window $w_x \times w_y$ used for tracking. Thus, there can be different displacements within the same window. In order to address this matter an affine motion field was proposed in [21] as follows:

$$\delta = \vartheta \mathbf{x} + \alpha \tag{2}$$

where $\vartheta = \begin{bmatrix} \vartheta_{xx} & \vartheta_{xy} \\ \vartheta_{yx} & \vartheta_{yy} \end{bmatrix}$ is a deformation matrix and $\alpha = [\alpha_x, \alpha_y]^T$ is the translation of the feature window's center in video frames. Thus, tracking a point (or window) from image I to image J means determining the 6 parameters of ϑ and α. Bouguet [20] proposed a minimization scheme of f_{GFT} by using a LKT feature tracker [22]. According to the observation in [23,24], the quality of estimate by this tracker depends on three factors: the size of the window, the texturedness of the image frame, and the amount of motion between frames.

When the ROI is detected after preprocessing, we first detected the appropriate feature points (pixels) in the ROI including body region by GFT. However, tracking only the best few points selected globally over the whole ROI by GFT exhibits the problem of having no points to track on some of the body-parts. This happens due to low-texturedness in some portion of the body in the video frames, which the GFT automatically discard as bad feature points in comparison to high-textured areas. In order to solve this problem, we divided the whole ROI into a grid of certain size (20×20 in the experiment) and then employed the GFT to each of the grid cells separately. Thus, we got certain number of feature points to track in each of the grid cells representing certain body-parts. As a measure of tracking the body motion, we then tracked those pixels in the subsequent video frames by LKT tracker. The tracks provided a motion map in the ROI where the motion of a specific part of the body was reflected by higher intensity level. The motion map has three dimensions: first axis contains the video frame index, second axis contains the tracked feature points' index, and the third axis show the intensity of motion of the feature points over consecutive video frames. However, instead of putting the difference of the location of feature points to represent intensity of body motion, we simply kept the locations of feature points over time in the original map. Thus, among these three dimensions, first axis implied temporal dimension over video, second axis implied spatial dimensions over feature points in the frames, and the third axis implied intensity.

4.3   Feature Extraction for Activity Type Classification

The motion maps for the PA events were different in size, because of the varying length of the individual videos representing individual PA events. Furthermore, the numbers of feature points tracked in the videos by GFT varied also from video to video. Thus, if we consider a two dimensional grid of feature points vs video frames with the intensity of movement in the third dimension, the resulting motion map is not only varying in the intensities in the third dimension, but also in other two dimensions. Keeping this in mind, we extracted the following three categories of features from the motion map to discriminate between the PA categories.

First Difference of the Motion Map (FDiff). This feature is extracted by calculating the first difference of feature map over third dimensions. As the third dimension kept the location of the feature points over time, the first difference gave us the true intensity of the body motion. We employed Euclidean distance metric to calculate the difference between locations. However, this intensity map had a varying size in the first two dimensions as discussed before. So, we employed a grid of 50×50 along with bicubic interpolation in the third dimension to augment the map and obtain our first feature $FDiff$.

Principal Components (PCA). Principal component analysis is widely used to reduce the size of data (or feature) by employing an orthogonal transformation [5]. While reducing the feature size one can effectively select the most discriminative features based on the energy represented by each feature. We started from the $FDiff$ features to extract PCA features from the motion map. We then employed the transformation on the spatial dimension and obtained the features that kept 90% of the discriminative energy.

Primitive Radon Features (PRadon). Radon transform is an integral transform that computes projections of an image matrix along specified directions and that is widely used to reconstruct images from medical computed tomography scan [25]. As our motion map was similar to a two-dimensional image and our focus is to discriminate in the motion map by the location and intensity of PA events, we employed Radon transform on the first difference of the feature map as we did for $FDiff$. The resulting Radon image had 180 line-directions in the spatial dimension, while keeping the original temporal dimension of the motion map. We then resized the temporal dimension with a grid of 180×50 along with bicubic interpolation in the third dimension and obtained the $PRadon$ features.

Radon Distance Features (DiffRadon). We have previously showed that the point-to-point distance of a Radon image also has an effective discriminating property [25]. Thus, we employed a pairwise-distance method between every possible pairs of pixels in the PRadon feature vector. The resulting matrix produced a $DiffRadon$ feature vector.

4.4   Classification of Activities

The obtained feature vectors were then fed into a classification framework to identify the PA categories from which each specific video event belonged to. In this paper, we examined 6 well-known shallow learning classifiers to evaluate the discrimination performance: K-Nearest Neighbor with $k = 3$ (KNN), Linear Discriminant Analysis (LDA), Support Vector Machines with linear kernel (SVM), Decision Tree (DT), Naive Bayes (NB), and Generalized Linear Model (GLM) [5].

5   Experimental Environment and Results

The proposed methodology was implemented in MATLAB 2017. We extracted all four categories of features and classifiers described before to find the best performing scenario. The experiment was conducted on individual video modalities first, and then on a feature level concatenation for early fusion of video modalities. We used 80/20 percent train/test ratio of the data.

From the track of the feature points over video, we obtained a motion map, which kept the location of feature points in the consecutive video frames. When we took the first difference of this motion map, we got the intensity of movement in the motion map. Figure 4 shows the example motion maps for 7-categories of PAs of a subject. It can be observed that the location and intensity of motion varies in different PA occurrences. In fact, this constitutes the rationale of generating such motion maps to find discriminatory features for different PAs.

Table 1 shows the performance of the different extracted features with different classifiers for individual video modalities. Furthermore, Table 2 shows the results when different modalities are fused at the feature level. It can be observed

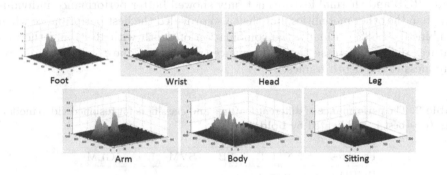

Fig. 4. Example motion intensity map for different PA from a subject's RGB videos

Table 1. The performance of different features and classifiers for video modalities (row-best is highlighted by **bold**).

Features	KNN	DT	NB	SVM	LDA	GLM
RGB (accuracy in %)						
FDiff	35.82	42.47	**49.68**	49.29	30.14	45.96
PCA	55.51	43.94	59.51	**60.00**	56.82	57.47
PRadon	68.25	61.45	12.50	**72.66**	66.74	71.57
DiffRadon	65.76	63.72	61.90	58.63	63.09	**68.02**
Thermal (accuracy in %)						
FDiff	36.21	32.65	**47.49**	44.83	33.38	45.56
PCA	**56.57**	33.29	12.50	46.49	46.40	48.73
PRadon	58.52	63.34	12.50	63.18	41.37	**64.10**
DiffRadon	63.11	58.13	49.43	32.72	59.05	**64.95**
Depth (accuracy in %)						
FDiff	18.22	24.51	**29.19**	28.54	21.68	26.70
PCA	28.26	22.97	32.20	**37.83**	32.21	34.31
PRadon	38.38	42.32	12.50	46.19	**50.81**	46.67
DiffRadon	41.37	37.65	33.67	**47.12**	44.26	45.24

that Radon transform-based features (*PRadon* and *DiffRadon*) showed better discriminating performance than *FDiff* and *PCA* both in individual and
fusioned cases. On the other hand, both *FDiff* and *PCA* showed relatively better performance than the other features when considering the NB and SVM classifiers performance. Notably, a moderately high classification performance was
achieved by the GLM classifier using the PRadon features (77.68%). When comparing the different video modalities, we observed that depth features showed
lower discriminating ability than the other two modalities (Table 1). Furthermore, RGB and thermal features not only showed better performance individually than the other modalities, but they also provided the best performance when
combined (77.68%). Finally, the combination of depth with RGB and thermal
features did not increase the performance, which may due to the lack of texturedness in the depth frames.

Table 2. The performance of different features and classifiers for fusioned video modalities (row-best is highlighted by **bold**).

Features	KNN	DT	NB	SVM	LDA	GLM
RGBD (accuracy in %)						
FDiff	30.73	**53.13**	49.30	50.02	34.28	47.72
PCA	52.33	48.28	**63.01**	51.83	48.99	53.77
PRadon	59.20	59.34	12.50	**72.29**	70.30	70.26
DiffRadon	60.40	60.90	61.39	55.84	65.89	**70.20**
RGBT (accuracy in %)						
FDiff	39.70	44.22	**54.97**	49.29	40.32	50.10
PCA	61.19	45.48	12.50	60.82	57.48	**62.62**
PRadon	69.38	60.39	12.50	74.93	71.24	**77.68**
DiffRadon	61.81	67.89	66.04	55.74	68.72	**72.41**
DT (accuracy in %)						
FDiff	27.81	37.33	42.81	**48.08**	31.17	42.62
PCA	42.16	35.19	12.50	46.17	40.61	**47.03**
PRadon	50.50	54.17	12.50	59.40	51.95	**61.12**
DiffRadon	53.91	52.91	49.18	40.98	59.25	**63.96**
RGBDT (accuracy in %)						
FDiff	32.62	46.68	**52.56**	48.24	38.43	47.49
PCA	53.57	41.67	12.50	57.29	52.03	**57.75**
PRadon	61.31	66.60	12.50	**75.28**	72.62	74.58
DiffRadon	69.53	66.25	67.18	51.40	**73.10**	71.46

6 Conclusions

Body motion analysis of a subject lying on a bed may have important applications for diagnostic and rehabilitation purposes. In this paper, we investigated that notion by first defining the taxonomy of some physical activities commonly exhibited by patients while lying on a bed. We collected a multimodal RGBDT video database of those activities from healthy subjects by mimicking a hospital room scenario in a neurorehabilitation center. Relevant feature extraction and machine learning methods were also investigated. The presented work is the first step towards the development of a multimodal video-based tool to assess patient movements in a "patient on bed" scenario. From the obtained results, new questions for the future work arise. E.g.: can we improve the accuracy of the PA classification by, e.g., employing a human body shape model? Will the system work in real-time, and/or is it possible to make an automated PA log over time by video sensing? The present work is just the beginning of the quest to find the solutions to these challenges.

References

1. Hamer, M., Kivimaki, M., Steptoe, A.: Longitudinal patterns in physical activity and sedentary behaviour from mid-life to early old age: a substudy of the Whitehall II cohort. J. Epidemiol. Community Health **66**, 1110–1115 (2012)
2. Telama, R.: Tracking of physical activity from childhood to adulthood: a review. Obes Facts **2**, 187–195 (2009)
3. Talkowski, J.B., Lenze, E.J., Munin, M.C., Harrison, C., Brach, J.S.: Patient participation and physical activity during rehabilitation and future functional outcomes in patients after hip fracture. Arch. Phys. Med. Rehabil. **90**, 618–622 (2009)
4. Sathyanarayana, S., Satzoda, R.K., Sathyanarayana, S., Thambipillai, S.: Vision-based patient monitoring: a comprehensive review of algorithms and technologies. J. Ambient. Intell. Hum. Comput. (2015)
5. Klonovs, J., et al.: Distributed Computing and Monitoring Technologies for Older Patients. SCS. Springer, Cham (2016). https://doi.org/10.1007/978-3-319-27024-1
6. Gluck, S., Chapple, L.S., Chapman, M.J., Iwashyna, T.J., Deane, A.M.: A scoping review of use of wearable devices to evaluate outcomes in survivors of critical illness. Crit. Care Resusc. **19**, 197–204 (2017)
7. Martin, J.L., Hakim, A.D.: Wrist actigraphy. Chest **139**, 1514–1527 (2011)
8. Sadeh, A.: The role and validity of actigraphy in sleep medicine: an update. Sleep Med. Rev. **15**, 259–267 (2011)
9. Beecroft, J.M., Ward, M., Younes, M., Crombach, S., Smith, O., Hanly, P.J.: Sleep monitoring in the intensive care unit: comparison of nurse assessment, actigraphy and polysomnography. Intensive Care Med. **34**, 2076–2083 (2008)
10. Kamdar, B.B., et al.: Feasibility of continuous actigraphy in patients in a medical intensive care unit. Am. J. Crit. Care **26**, 329–335 (2017)
11. Roebuck, A., et al.: A review of signals used in sleep analysis. Physiol. Meas. **35**, 1–57 (2014)
12. Poppe, R.: Vision-based human motion analysis: an overview. Comput. Vis. Image Underst. **108**(1), 4–18 (2007). Special Issue on Vision for Human-Computer Interaction

13. Heinrich, A., Geng, D., Znamenskiy, D., Vink, J.P., de Haan, G.: Robust and sensitive video motion detection for sleep analysis. IEEE J. Biomed. Health Inform. **18**, 790–798 (2014)
14. Cabon, S., et al.: Motion estimation and characterization in premature newborns using long duration video recordings. IRBM **38**(4), 207–213 (2017)
15. Heinrich, A., van Heesch, F., Puvvula, B., Rocque, M.: Video based actigraphy and breathing monitoring from the bedside table of shared beds. J. Ambient. Intell. Hum. Comput. **6**, 107–120 (2015)
16. Ilyas, C., Nasrollahi, K., Moeslund, T., Rehm, M., Haque, M.: Facial expression recognition for traumatic brain injured patients, vol. 4, 1. SCITEPRESS Digital Library (2018)
17. Duclos, C., et al.: Rest-activity cycle disturbances in the acute phase of moderate to severe traumatic brain injury. Neurorehabil. Neural Repair **28**, 472–482 (2014)
18. Haque, M.A., Nasrollahi, K., Moeslund, T.B.: Real-time acquisition of high quality face sequences from an active pan-tilt-zoom camera. In: 2013 10th IEEE International Conference on Advanced Video and Signal Based Surveillance, pp. 443–448, August 2013
19. Haque, M.A., et al.: Deep multimodal pain recognition: a database and comparison of spatio-temporal visual modalities. In: 2018 13th IEEE International Conference on Automatic Face Gesture Recognition (FG 2018), pp. 250–257, May 2018
20. Bouguet, J.: Pyramidal implementation of the Lucas Kanade feature tracker. Intel Corporation, Microprocessor Research Labs (2000)
21. Shi, J., Tomasi, C.: Good features to track. In: 1994 Proceedings of IEEE Conference on Computer Vision and Pattern Recognition, pp. 593–600, June 1994
22. Baker, S., Matthews, I.: Lucas-Kanade 20 years on: a unifying framework. Int. J. Comput. Vis. **56**, 221–255 (2004)
23. Haque, M.A., Irani, R., Nasrollahi, K., Moeslund, T.B.: Heartbeat rate measurement from facial video. IEEE Intell. Syst. **31**, 40–48 (2016)
24. Haque, M.A., Irani, R., Nasrollahi, K., Moeslund, T.B.: Facial video-based detection of physical fatigue for maximal muscle activity. IET Comput. Vis. **10**(4), 323–329 (2016)
25. Haque, M.A., Nasrollahi, K., Moeslund, T.B.: Heartbeat signal from facial video for biometric recognition. In: Paulsen, R.R., Pedersen, K.S. (eds.) SCIA 2015. LNCS, vol. 9127, pp. 165–174. Springer, Cham (2015). https://doi.org/10.1007/978-3-319-19665-7_14

Marker Based Thermal-Inertial Localization for Aerial Robots in Obscurant Filled Environments

Shehryar Khattak$^{(\boxtimes)}$, Christos Papachristos, and Kostas Alexis

Autonomous Robots Lab, University of Nevada, Reno, NV, USA
shehryar@nevada.unr.edu
http://www.autonomousrobotslab.com

Abstract. For robotic inspection tasks in known environments fiducial markers provide a reliable and low-cost solution for robot localization. However, detection of such markers relies on the quality of RGB camera data, which degrades significantly in the presence of visual obscurants such as fog and smoke. The ability to navigate known environments in the presence of obscurants can be critical for inspection tasks especially, in the aftermath of a disaster. Addressing such a scenario, this work proposes a method for the design of fiducial markers to be used with thermal cameras for the pose estimation of aerial robots. Our low cost markers are designed to work in the long wave infrared spectrum, which is not affected by the presence of obscurants, and can be affixed to any object that has measurable temperature difference with respect to its surroundings. Furthermore, the estimated pose from the fiducial markers is fused with inertial measurements in an extended Kalman filter to remove high frequency noise and error present in the fiducial pose estimates. The proposed markers and the pose estimation method are experimentally evaluated in an obscurant filled environment using an aerial robot carrying a thermal camera.

Keywords: Thermal · Marker · Sensor degradation · Robot

1 Introduction

Robotic inspection of infrastructure has seen an increasing interest over the past decade as it promises to mitigate risk to human life, minimize costs and reduce other disruptions frequently encountered during structural inspection tasks [1]. In particular, aerial robots, because of their advanced agility and flexibility have been applied to a variety of such inspection tasks [2–7]. To navigate in known and unknown environments robots rely on reliable pose estimation information. Such information can be provided externally or estimated on-board using the data provided by sensors carried by the robot. External pose estimation is typically provided by Global Positioning System (GPS) in outdoor environments and by motion capture systems such as VICON or OptiTrack in indoor operations.

© Springer Nature Switzerland AG 2018
G. Bebis et al. (Eds.): ISVC 2018, LNCS 11241, pp. 565–575, 2018.
https://doi.org/10.1007/978-3-030-03801-4_49

However, GPS is limited to outdoor operations and suffers from multi-path inaccuracies in close vicinity to structures. Similarly, motion capture systems limit the work space of operation and require repetitive calibration for providing accurate pose estimates. Motion capture system can be also be very cost prohibitive. On-board a robot, pose can be estimated by utilizing sensors such as RGB camera systems, which due to their low weight and affordable cost are a popular choice. Using RGB camera images, visual odometry can be estimated reliably for local estimates, but tends to drift over time and relies on the quality of camera data. In addition, visual odometry estimates are local to robot's frame and do not provide any correspondence to a global map. Hybrid approaches, utilizing on-board sensing and the presence of previously known objects in the environment, such as fiducial markers, provide a low cost and reliable navigation solution to obtain global localization information. However, such methods still require quality camera data to localize the known markers [8,9]. As noted in [1,10], not uncommon instances of inspection tasks are carried out in previously known environments in post-disaster conditions such as in the aftermath of a fire. These environments present a challenge for robot operations as they can be GPS-denied in nature and contain visual obscurants such as smoke. Although previously known environments provide the opportunity to have known markers placed in the environment for providing global positioning, yet in the presence of obscurants these disaster scenarios degrade RGB camera data significantly.

Motivated by the challenging nature of such scenarios, in this paper we propose to extend the design and usage of fiducial markers into the Long Wave Infrared (LWIR) spectrum using thermal cameras for robot operation in obscurant filled environments. As opposed to the typical RGB cameras operating in the visible part of the electromagnetic spectrum, the selected thermal cameras operate in the LWIR part of spectrum and as a result, do not suffer from the same data degradation in the presence of certain obscurants, such as smoke and fog [11]. Similarly, utilizing the different optical properties of materials in the LWIR spectrum as compared to visible spectrum we extend the design of fiducial markers for LWIR spectrum usage while remaining unobtrusive in the visible spectrum. Furthermore, we augment marker based pose estimation by integrating inertial measurements for improved accuracy, higher update rate and accounting for frames with unreliable or missing marker detection. To verify the feasibility of the designed markers, detection of the designed markers with a thermal camera and inertial measurements fused pose estimation, an experimental study was conducted using an aerial robot in an obscurant filled environment. An instance of this study is shown in Fig. 1.

The remainder of the paper is structured as follows: Sect. 2 details the design of thermal fiducial markers, the mapping algorithm and the pose estimation solution. Section 3 presents the results of experimental study. Finally, conclusions are drawn in Sect. 4.

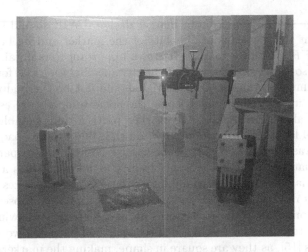

Fig. 1. Instance of an experiment during which an aerial robot equipped with a thermal camera navigates a fog filled room using thermal fiducial markers mounted on space heaters. Thermal fiducial markers are transparent in visible domain and only their corner foam mounting points can be seen in the image.

2 Proposed Method

The proposed approach can be broadly divided into three sections, namely: (i) Marker Design (ii) Map Building and (iii) Robot Pose Estimation, each of which are detailed below:

2.1 Marker Design

In the field of computer vision a wide variety of fiducial markers have been proposed for robust camera pose estimation [12–14]. These markers are binary in nature and contain an internal coding of ON/OFF bits represented by white and black colors respectively making the marker pattern unique and easy to identify. Although these markers can be in different shapes, square markers have the advantage of providing enough correspondences i.e. four corners from detection of a single marker to estimate the pose of the camera by solving the perspective-n-point problem. Similarly, knowing the dimension of one side of a square marker is enough for the accurate estimation of scale. For computer vision applications these markers are usually printed on a piece of white paper and affixed to a flat surface with the white paper providing the ON bits and black printer ink providing OFF bits. However this approach cannot be directly used in the presence of obscurants or with a thermal camera (responding to LWIR) without re-designing the fiducial marker. For the implementation of fiducial markers in the LWIR spectrum, we exploit the fact that thermal images respond and measure based on the emitted infrared radiation from objects of different temperatures and different material properties and encode this information on the grayscale image space. Hence in our marker design, LWIR should be allowed to pass through at the locations of ON bits of the marker and be blocked at the locations of OFF bits of the marker. It is also important to maintain the flatness of the marker so it does not warp and the distance between the four corners is maintained. Similarly, the marker material should not be thermally conductive as to not heat up over time and become the same temperature as the surface to which it is affixed to making the marker pattern undetectable. Given the requirements of low thermal conductivity and the ability to be opaque to LWIR, *acrylic* sheet was chosen as it is lightweight, low-cost, and transparent, making it a suitable material for such an application. Furthermore, it is a high tensile strength material enabling it to maintain its flatness and vaporizes during laser cutting process resulting in clean and precise cuts, similar to those obtained by printing commonly used fiducial patterns on paper, thereby allowing the use of those same patterns in the thermal domain. For our purposes we chose to use ArUco markers [15], as they are square in shape, making the marker cutting process less complex. ArUco markers also allow us to create dictionaries of varying sizes and adjusting their intra-marker distances for better detection. A marker dictionary was created using the OpenCV implementation of the ArUco library and marker designs were exported as images. These images were first converted into vector graphics and then into CAD drawings for laser cutting. The process of marker creation as well its detection in thermal domain is shown in Fig. 2. It should be noted that our thermal fiducial marker design is very low cost and unobtrusive in visible spectrum. Our marker design can be accessed at (https://tinyurl.com/LWIRMarkers).

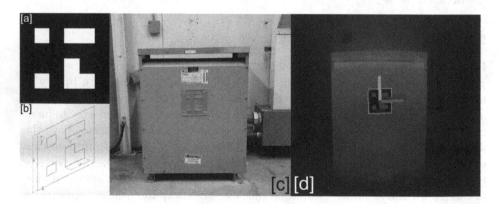

Fig. 2. The proposed marker design for thermal fiducial markers. [a] shows the original ArUco marker, [b] shows the generated CAD model for the marker, [c] shows the clear acrylic laser cut marker affixed to a transformer unit in a machine shop and [d] shows the detection of marker in the thermal image of the same scene.

2.2   Map Building

For robot localization in a known environment, a map is built by detecting markers attached to fixed objects in the environment. For map building we follow an approach is similar to [16]. The constructed map is represented in the world coordinate frame ($\mathcal{W}$). This map is built in an incremental manner and adds new markers positions to the map only when they are mutually observed with markers previously defined in the map. When a set of markers is detected in a thermal image, first, we check which among the detected markers already exist in the map and then use them to estimate the camera pose in $\mathcal{W}$. Next, we estimate the pose of markers which do not exist in the map with respect to the camera coordinate frame ($\mathcal{C}$). Finally, we calculate the pose of the new markers in $\mathcal{W}$ and add them to the map using their pose defined in $\mathcal{C}$ and the calculated camera pose defined in $\mathcal{W}$. We make two assumptions to build the map. First, the pose of at least one marker is known in $\mathcal{W}$ and this marker is used to start building the map. Second, at least two markers are visible in each thermal image as the environment is being mapped and new markers are being added. The first assumption allows for the building of a global map and estimate all marker positions in $\mathcal{W}$. The second assumption only needs to be held true during the process of incrementally creating a map as adding new markers to the map requires calculation of the camera pose in $\mathcal{W}$. Once markers have been added to the map, the camera pose can be estimated by observing a single marker afterwards. Before adding a new marker to the map, we compute its re-projection error as a measure of its quality. This error is updated with each observation of the marker and is used as a weight when multiple known markers are observed in a single thermal image and used to determine camera pose in $\mathcal{W}$. Our marker map can be combined with other map representations as shown in Sect. 3, where we combine our marker map to a previously generated volumetric map. Such combinations can be used for other applications beyond the motivation of this paper e.g. offline path planning for inspection tasks using a volumetric map for collision avoidance and a marker map for viewpoint selection to improve localization [17]. The steps of the map building process are summarized in Algorithm 1.

2.3   Robot Pose Estimation

Once we obtain the camera pose against a known map in $\mathcal{W}$, we can then calculate the pose of the robot by knowing the transformation between the camera coordinate frame ($\mathcal{C}$) and the robot coordinate frame ($\mathcal{R}$). As shown in [8,9,18] pose estimation from fiducial markers alone is sufficient to estimate the robot trajectory, however the accuracy of the estimated pose is subject to multiple factors such as the reliability of marker detection, the resolution of the camera, and the angle of marker observation. Also, as mentioned in [15], the locations of the detected marker corners are prone to jitter if a corner is detected at lower resolution or from a large distance. This unreliable detection of corners causes the pose estimates of the robot to be noisy and less reliable which can then greatly impact onboard control. This is especially problematic for thermal cameras, as

---

Algorithm 1. Map Building

1: $\mathcal{MAP} \leftarrow$ Read Map
2: $\mathcal{I} \leftarrow$ Acquire New Thermal Image
3: $\mathcal{D} \leftarrow$ **DetectFidcuialMarkers**$(\mathcal{I})$
4: $\mathcal{M}_{known}, \mathcal{M}_{new} \leftarrow$ **CheckKnownMarkers**$(\mathcal{D}, \mathcal{MAP})$
5: $\mathcal{C}_{pose} \leftarrow$ **CalculateCameraPose**$(\mathcal{M}_{known})$
6: $\mathcal{E}_{reprojection} \leftarrow$ **ComputeReprojectionError**$(\mathcal{M}_{known})$
7: $\mathcal{E}_{previous} \leftarrow$ **GetPreviousError**$(\mathcal{M}_{known}, \mathcal{MAP})$
8: $\mathcal{C}_{refined} \leftarrow$ **RefineCameraPose**$(\mathcal{M}_{known}, \mathcal{E}_{reprojection}, \mathcal{E}_{previous})$
9: $\mathcal{MAP} \leftarrow$ **UpdateError**$(\mathcal{E}_{reprojection}, \mathcal{E}_{previous})$
10: **for all** $\mathcal{M}_{new}$ **do**
11:     $\mathcal{M}_{pose} \leftarrow$ **CalculateMarkerPose**$(\mathcal{M}_{new}, \mathcal{C}_{refined})$
12:     $\mathcal{M}_{error} \leftarrow$ **ComputeReprojectionError**$(\mathcal{M}_{pose})$
13:     $\mathcal{MAP} \leftarrow$ **AddMarkertoMap**$(\mathcal{M}_{pose}, \mathcal{M}_{error})$
14: **end for**

---

the commercially available and lightweight units operate at much lower resolution than their visible domain counterparts. Similarly, in some frames, marker detection can fail which causes jumps between pose estimates from fiducial. To make the robot's pose estimation robust, the estimated camera pose from the fiducial markers is fused with inertial measurements, obtained from the Inertial Measurement Unit (IMU) of the autopilot onboard the robot, using an extended Kalman filter (EKF). We use a formulation similar to [19], for our filter design where inertial measurements are used to propagate the state of the robot and pose estimates from the fiducial markers are used in the correction step of the filter. The state of our filter can be written as:

$$\mathbf{x} = [\mathbf{p} \ \mathbf{v} \ \mathbf{q} \ \mathbf{b}_f \ \mathbf{b}_\omega]^T \tag{1}$$

In our formulation, the robot coordinate frame $\mathcal{R}$ is aligned and centered with the IMU of the robot hence, $\mathbf{p}$ and $\mathbf{v}$ are the robot-centric position and velocity of the robot expressed in $\mathcal{R}$, $\mathbf{q}$ is the robot attitude represented as a map from $\mathcal{R} \rightarrow \mathcal{W}$, $\mathbf{b}_f$, $\mathbf{b}_f$ represents the additive accelerometer bias expressed in $\mathcal{R}$, $\mathbf{b}_\omega$ stands for the additive gyroscope bias expressed in $\mathcal{R}$. Proper IMU measurements i.e. the bias corrected, but noise affected accelerometer and gyroscope measurements are used to propagate the filter state. Camera pose measurements from the fiducial markers are then used in the correction step, where the differences between predicted and measured position ($\mathbf{p}$) and rotation ($\mathbf{q}$) states are used as an innovation term. This formulation helps in the reduction of noise and makes the pose estimation smooth, as well as enables the generation of robot pose estimates at the higher update rate of the IMU, making it suitable to be used for robot control tasks.

3   Experimental Evaluation

For the testing of the proposed markers and pose estimation method an experimental evaluation was conducted using an aerial robot carrying a thermal camera in an obscurant filled environment. The system and the experiment are detailed below:

3.1   System Overview

For the purpose of experimental studies a DJI Matrice 100 quadrotor was used. An Intel NUC i7 computer (NUC7i7BNH) was carried on-board the robot for performing all the high-level processing tasks including marker detection, map building and pose estimation. A FLIR Tau 2 thermal camera was mounted on the robot to provide thermal images of 640×512 resolution at 30 frames per second. The intrinsic calibration parameters of the thermal camera were calculated using our custom designed thermal checker board pattern [20]. The robot autopilot IMU was used for providing inertial measurements. All algorithms were implemented as Robot Operating System (ROS) nodes and run in real-time fully on-board the robot. Figure 3 provides the system overview of the robot system.

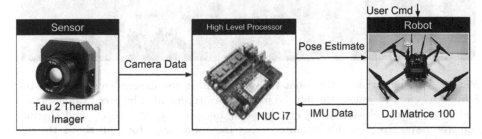

Fig. 3. High-level processor (Intel NUCi7) receives thermal images from Tau 2 camera and inertial measurements from the robot. The thermal images are processed for fiducial marker detection and initial pose estimation. The pose estimate is then integrated with inertial measurement using an Extended-Kalman Filter.

3.2   Robotic Experiment

To evaluate the real-time on-board performance of the proposed approach, a test was conducted in an obscurant filled environment. In an industrial environment thermal markers are to be affixed to objects with a higher thermal signature with respect to their environment, an example is shown in Fig. 2 where a thermal marker is affixed to a transformer unit. For the experiment, the designed thermal markers were affixed to space heaters in order to simulate an industrial setting. Our markers were cut from an 5 mm thick acrylic sheet. A fog generator was used to fill the testing environment with fog to serve as an obscurant. An instance of the experiment showing the transparent thermal markers mounted on a space heater and the obscurant filled environment is shown in Fig. 1. A map for the fixed thermal markers was built and stored on-board the robot. To validate the accuracy of marker positions, a volumetric map of the environment was built separately in good visibility conditions using a pointcloud obtained from a visible light stereo camera along with localization provided by visual inertial solution ROVIO [21]. The two independently built maps align accurately as shown in Fig. 4. A robot trajectory was executed with the same take-off and landing points, the mid-point of this trajectory is shown in Fig. 4.

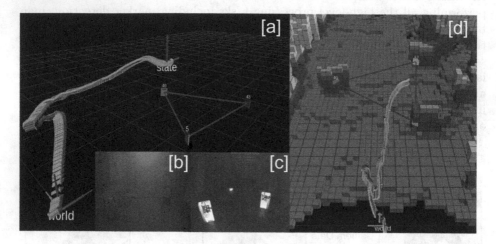

Fig. 4. A visualization of the robot trajectory during the experiment. [a] shows the robot trajectory in yellow, the fiducial markers are represented by green (unobserved) and red squares (observed). [b] and [c] show images from the visible and thermal cameras respectively at this instance during the robot trajectory. [d] shows the top view of the same trajectory with the fiducial marker map and volumetric map shown. On visual inspection it can be noted that the two marker maps are accurately aligned. (Color figure online)

To understand the improvement in pose estimation due to fusion of inertial measurements, the pose estimation from fiducial markers alone was compared to pose estimates generated by the implemented EKF described in Sect. 2.3. As shown in Fig. 5 the pose estimation from fiducial markers alone is subject to jitter because of distorted marker observations and low resolution at long ranges. This jitter is filtered out after fusion with inertial measurements. A video of experimental results can be found at (https://tinyurl.com/ObscuranctResults).

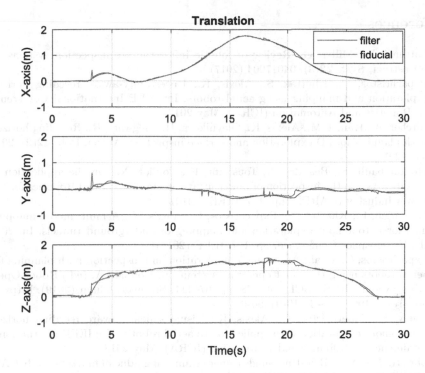

Fig. 5. The plot compares position estimation from the fiducial markers alone (red) and its integration with IMU measurement using an EKF (blue). The fiducial only position estimation is subject to jitters depending on the quality of observation. This is filtered out by fusion with inertial data. (Color figure online)

4   Conclusions

In this paper we demostrated a method to design and extend fiducial markers from the visible spectrum to the LWIR spectrum to work with thermal cameras. Fiducial markers were designed and manufactured at very low cost and are minimally intrusive visually. The use of the designed markers was demonstrated by estimating the pose of an aerial robot in an obscurant filled environment. The pose estimation from the fiducial markers was made robust by fusion with inertial measurements using an EKF. Future work would consist of integrating the current solution with thermal-inertial navigation solutions for the robot to operate seamlessly between environments both containing and not containing markers. Similarly, in the future using visible and thermal markers in conjunction would be explored to make the solution more robust and generalizable to a variety of operating conditions and environments.

References

1. Lattanzi, D., Miller, G.: Review of robotic infrastructure inspection systems. J. Infrastruct. Syst. **23**(3), 04017004 (2017)
2. Papachristos, C., Khattak, S., Alexis, K.: Uncertainty-aware receding horizon exploration and mapping using aerial robots. In: IEEE International Conference on Robotics and Automation (ICRA), May 2017
3. Bircher, A., Kamel, M., Alexis, K., Oleynikova, H., Siegwart, R.: Receding horizon path planning for 3D exploration and surface inspection. Auton. Rob. **42**(2), 291–306 (2018)
4. Montambault, S., Beaudry, J., Toussaint, K., Pouliot, N.: On the application of VTOL UAVs to the inspection of power utility assets. In: Applied Robotics for the Power Industry (CARPI), pp. 1–7. IEEE (2010)
5. Mascarich, F., Khattak, S., Papachristos, C., Alexis, K.: A multi-modal mapping unit for autonomous exploration and mapping of underground tunnels. In: 2018 IEEE Aerospace Conference, pp. 1–7. IEEE (2018)
6. Papachristos, C., et al.: Autonomous exploration and inspection path planning for aerial robots using the robot operating system. In: Koubaa, A. (ed.) Robot Operating System (ROS). SCI, vol. 778, pp. 67–111. Springer, Cham (2019). https://doi.org/10.1007/978-3-319-91590-6_3
7. Dang, T., Papachristos, C., Alexis, K.: Visual saliency-aware receding horizon autonomous exploration with application to aerial robotics. In: IEEE International Conference on Robotics and Automation (ICRA), May 2018
8. Lim, H., Lee, Y.S.: Real-time single camera slam using fiducial markers. In: ICCAS-SICE 2009, pp. 177–182. IEEE (2009)
9. Davison, A.J., Reid, I.D., Molton, N.D., Stasse, O.: MonoSLAM: real-time single camera SLAM. IEEE Trans. Pattern Anal. Mach. Intell. **6**, 1052–1067 (2007)
10. Balta, H., et al.: Integrated data management for a fleet of search-and-rescue robots. J. Field Rob. (2016)
11. Brunner, C., Peynot, T.: Perception quality evaluation with visual and infrared cameras in challenging environmental conditions. In: Khatib, O., Kumar, V., Sukhatme, G. (eds.) Experimental Robotics. Springer Tracts in Advanced Robotics, vol. 79, pp. 711–725. Springer, Heidelberg (2014). https://doi.org/10.1007/978-3-642-28572-1_49
12. Olson, E.: AprilTag: a robust and flexible visual fiducial system. In: Proceedings of the IEEE International Conference on Robotics and Automation (ICRA), pp. 3400–3407. IEEE, May 2011
13. Fiala, M.: ARTag, a fiducial marker system using digital techniques. In: 2005 IEEE Computer Society Conference on Computer Vision and Pattern Recognition, CVPR 2005, vol. 2, pp. 590–596. IEEE (2005)
14. Fiala, M.: Designing highly reliable fiducial markers. IEEE Trans. Pattern Anal. Mach. Intell. **7**, 1317–1324 (2009)
15. Garrido-Jurado, S., et al.: Automatic generation and detection of highly reliable fiducial markers under occlusion. Pattern Recogn. **47**, 2280–92 (2014)
16. Vaughan, J., Agrawal, R.: Fiducial slam software (2018)
17. Bircher, A., et al.: Structural inspection path planning via iterative viewpoint resampling with application to aerial robotics, pp. 6423–6430 (2015)
18. Breitenmoser, A., Kneip, L., Siegwart, R.Y.: A monocular vision-based system for 6D relative robot localization. In: IEEE International Conference on Intelligent Robots and Systems, pp. 79–85. IEEE (2011)

19. Lynen, S., et al.: A robust and modular multi-sensor fusion approach applied to MAV navigation. In: IEEE Conference on Intelligent Robots and Systems (2013)
20. Papachristos, C., Mascarich, F., Alexis, K.: Thermal-inertial localization for autonomous navigation of aerial robots through obscurants. In: 2018 International Conference on Unmanned Aircraft Systems (ICUAS). IEEE (2018)
21. Bloesch, M., Omari, S., Hutter, M., Siegwart, R.: Robust visual inertial odometry using a direct EKF-based approach. In: Intelligent Robots and Systems (IROS), pp. 298–304. IEEE (2015)

Shape-Based Smoothing of Binary Digital Objects Using Signed Distance Transform

Xiaoliu Zhang[1(✉)], Cheng Chen[1(✉)], Gregory Chang[2(✉)], and Punam K. Saha[1(✉)]

[1] Electrical and Computer Engineering, University of Iowa,
Iowa City, IA 52242, USA
{xiaoliu-zhang, cheng-chen}@uiowa.edu,
pksaha@healthcare.uiowa.edu
[2] School of Medicine, New York University, New York, NY 10016, USA
gregory.chang@nyumc.org

Abstract. Digital staircase effects and noisy protrusions and dents on object boundaries add major challenges for quantitative structural analysis and visual assessment. In this paper, we present a shape-based smoothing algorithm for binary digital objects to eliminate digital staircase artifacts and remove boundary noise. The method uses a signed distance transform image, where the zero level set defines the object boundary. The key idea of our algorithm is to smooth this zero level set by applying a smoothing filter on the signed distance transform image. The method has been applied on slice-by-slice segmentation results of human proximal femur bone volumes from hip MR imaging. The observed results are encouraging, which suggest that the new method is capable of successfully eliminating digital staircase effects, while preserving the basic geometry of the target object. Quantitative analysis of a phantom experiment results reveals that a notion of "optimum scale" of smoothing exists for the new algorithm, and it is related to the scale of noisy protrusions and dents. The quantitative experiments have shown that, at the optimum smoothing scale, the new method can achieve 98.5% to 99.6% Dice similarity coefficient for noisy protrusions and dents of different sizes.

Keywords: Shape-based smoothing · Signed distance transform
Hip MR imaging · Staircase effects · Binary objects · Zero level set

1 Introduction

Quantitative structural analysis and/or expert observer evaluation of objects are needed in many real-life applications including those involving three-dimensional (3-D) medical imaging. Often, medical imaging devices produce images with large voxels and significantly greater length in the imaging slice direction. Also, in many *in vivo* imaging applications [1, 2], acquired signal-to-noise ratio is limited. Such limitations of imaging devices together with additional artifacts incurred during image segmentation [3–5] introduce digital staircase artifacts as well as boundary surface noise in segmented object volumes. Such artifacts and noise add further challenges during computerized structural analysis or visual assessment of objects. In this paper, we present a

© Springer Nature Switzerland AG 2018
G. Bebis et al. (Eds.): ISVC 2018, LNCS 11241, pp. 576–584, 2018.
https://doi.org/10.1007/978-3-030-03801-4_50

new algorithm for shape-based smoothing of segmented binary digital objects to remove staircase artifacts and boundary noise, while preserving the overall object geometry and shape.

The new shape-based smoothing algorithm is based on smoothing a signed distance transform field. Distance transform (DT) [6, 7] can be applied on binary or fuzzy objects, which assigned the shortest distance value at an object point from its boundary. Signed DT [8] is primarily applied on binary objects, where the distances are computed in both directions from a boundary, and positive and negative values are assigned to object and background points, respectively, or the vice versa. Udupa and Raya [9] used signed DT to develop a novel shape-based interpolation algorithm that used the signed distance transform to track the deformation of a binary object region in between two successive image slices and generating its representation at an intermediate image slice location. Shape based interpolation method was further studied and improved by other research groups [10, 11]. Grevera and Udupa [12] generalized the shape-based interpolation algorithm for gray-scale input images. DeCoro et al. [13] used 2-D signed DT and Gaussian smoothing to simulate dilation and shrinking of shadows.

Here, we present a new application of signed DT for smoothing object boundaries, while eliminating digital staircase effects and removing noisy protrusions and dents. The zero level set [14] of a signed DT image defines the object boundary. The key idea of our shape-based smoothing algorithm is to smooth the zero level set of the signed distance transform by applying a smoothing filter on the signed DT image. The theory and algorithm of our shape-based smoothing approach is presented in Sect. 2 and the experiments and results of application of the new method are discussed in Sect. 3. The relationship between the scale of granular noise and the optimum scale of smoothing kernel is also studied and the results are presented. Finally, the conclusions and future research directions are presented in Sect. 4.

2 Theory and Algorithm

Our method uses signed DT where object points get positive values, while the background points are assigned with negative values. Although, the method is described in a three-dimensional (3-D) cubic grid, it's generalizable in any dimension as well as for other digital grids [15]. A 3-D cubic grid is often represented using the set Z^3, where Z denotes the set of integers. An element of Z^3 is referred to as a *voxel*. In most *in vivo* applications, the voxel resolution in scanned images is non-isotropic, and, often slice spacing is significantly larger than in-plane resolution. Let $\rho = \begin{bmatrix} \rho_x & \rho_y & \rho_z \end{bmatrix}$ denote a resolution vector, where ρ_x, ρ_y, and ρ_z represent the voxel size or image resolution along the three grid co-ordinate directions. Commonly, $\rho_x = \rho_y$ denote the in-plane resolution while $\rho_z > \rho_x$ or ρ_y represents the slice spacing.

The conventional definitions of 6-, 18-, and 26-adjacencies [16] of a cubic grid are adopted in this paper. Our algorithms work for binary images. An *object* in a binary image is a non-empty set $O \subset Z^3$ of finitely many points or voxels [17]. The *background* of an object O is the set $\bar{O} = Z^3 - O$ of voxels. The *boundary* of an object, denoted by ∂O, is the set of ordered voxel pairs (p, q) such that $p \in O$, $q \in \bar{O}$, and p, q

are 26-adjacent. Note that the use of a pair of adjacent voxels, one from object and the other from background, allows to avoid the bias of using object (or, background) voxels in defining the boundary. Rather, it uses the simplicial interface separating object and background voxels to define the boundary.

An α-*path* π, where $\alpha \in \{6, 18, 26\}$, is a nonempty sequence $p_0, \cdots, p_{l-1}$ of voxels and every two successive voxels p_{i-1} and p_i are α-adjacent. Although, for connectivity analysis in digital images, different adjacency relations are used for object and background voxels [18], a single path-adjacency is used for both object and background voxels, while performing distance analysis. Therefore, we use 26-paths for computing the distance between any two voxels. In other words, the distance metric is an image grid property independent of object and background configuration. A *26-link* is a 26-path p, q of exactly two voxels, and the *length of a link* p, q is defined as follows:

$$L(\langle p, q \rangle) = \sqrt{|p_x - q_x|^2 \rho_x^2 + |p_y - q_y|^2 \rho_y^2 + |p_z - q_z|^2 \rho_z^2}, \qquad (1)$$

where $p = (p_x, p_y, p_z)$, $q = (q_x, q_y, q_z)$, and ρ_x, ρ_y, ρ_z represent the image resolution. For images with isotropic resolution, i.e., $\rho_x = \rho_y = \rho_z$, it is recommended to use the $\langle 3, 4, 5 \rangle$ chamfer DT [6] originally proposed by Borgefors. The length of a path $\pi = \langle p_0, \ldots, p_{l-1} \rangle$ is the sum of the lengths of all links on the path, i.e., $L(\pi) = \sum_{i=0}^{l-2} L(\langle p_i, p_{i+1} \rangle)$. The distance $D(p, q)$ between two voxels $p, q \in Z^3$ is the length of the shortest path between p and q, i.e., $D(p, q) = \min_{\pi \in \mathcal{P}_{pq}} L(\pi)$, where $\mathcal{P}_{pq}$ denote the set of all possible paths between the two voxels p and q. The distance $D^*(p, S)$ between a voxel $p \in Z^3$ and a non-empty set of voxels $S \subset Z^3$ is the distance between p and a nearest voxel in S, i.e., $D^*(p, S) = \min_{q \in S} D(p, q)$. Finally, for a given object $O \subset Z^3$, the signed DT is a function of image $SDT_O(p)$ defined as follows:

$$SDT_O(p) = \begin{cases} D^*(p, \bar{O}) & \text{if } p \in O, \\ -D^*(p, O) & \text{otherwise.} \end{cases} \qquad (2)$$

It can be shown that a simple thresholding at '0' on the $SDT_O(\cdot)$ image allows us to retrieve the original object O.

To explain the basic idea of our method, let us consider the example of Fig. 1, where (a) shows segmented human femur of an image slice using manual outlining, and (b) presents a 3-D surface rendition of segmented femur volume where digital staircase effects are clearly visible. These staircase effects are also visible on an axial image slice shown in (c). A color-coded display of SDT of the segmented femur volume on the axial image slice of (c) is shown in (d). The digital staircase effect of segmentation is clearly visible in the SDT image of (d). The idea of shape-based smoothing is to apply a smoothing filter on the SDT image to eliminate these staircase effects and, thus, smooth different level set boundaries including the zero level set.

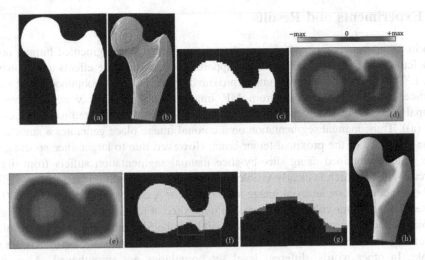

Fig. 1. Intermediate steps of shape-based smoothing for digital shapes. (a) Manual outline of a human proximal femur bone boundary on a coronal image plane from hip MRI. (b) 3-D surface rendition of the segmented human proximal femur bone. (c) Representation of the proximal femur bone on an axial slice. Digital staircase effects due to large slice spacing are visible in both (b) and (c). (d) Color-coded signed DT image of the segmented femur volume on the axial slice of (c). (e) Results of smoothing on the signed DT field on the same axial slice of (d); the same color-coding of (d) was used. (f) Results of shape-based smoothing of the proximal femur bone using a simple thresholding of (e) at '0'. (g) A zoomed in display of the region marked in (f). (h) 3-D surface rendition of the human proximal femur bone after shape-based smoothing. (Color figure online)

Let $o = (0,0,0)$ denote the origin and d_0 be a constant distance value. A smoothing kernel may be denoted as $K(p) | \forall p s.t. D(p,o) \le d_0$, where K is a monotonically non-increasing radial basis function, i.e., $K(p) = f_0(D(p,o))$ such that $d < d'$ implies $f_0(d) \ge f_0(d')$. Two popular smoothing kernels are simple averaging and Gaussian smoothing kernels. In this paper, we have used Gaussian smoothing kernels, where the standard deviation parameter σ_s represents scale parameter. A smooth SDT image $SDT^*_{O,K}$ is computed by convolving the original SDT image SDT_O with the smoothing kernel K, i.e.,

$$SDT^*_{O,K}(p) = (SDT_O * K)(p). \qquad (3)$$

Finally, the shape-based smoothing of a digital object O using a kernel K is defined as follow:

$$M(O,K) = \left\{ p | p \in Z^3 \text{ and } SDT^*_{O,K}(p) > 0 \right\}. \qquad (4)$$

3 Experiments and Results

Results of intermediate steps of shape-based smoothing of a segmented human proximal femur bone volume with visually apparent digital staircase effects are shown in Fig. 1. The digital volume of a human proximal femur bone was obtained using slice-by-slice manual segmentation from MR images. These images were acquired on coronal planes with relatively higher in-plane resolution as compared to slice spacing (see (a)). Thus, manual segmentation on a coronal image place generates a smooth in-plane boundary of the proximal femur bone. However, due to larger slice spacing, the bone volume obtained using slice-by-slice manual segmentation suffers from digital staircase effects which is clearly visible in its 3-D surface rendition (see (b)) as well as the bone boundary on an axial image slice (see (c)). A color-coded display of SDT of the segmented femur volume on the axial image slice of (c) is shown in (d). The digital staircase effect of segmentation is clearly visible in the SDT image of (d). The result of smoothing on the SDT image is shown in (e), where the digital staircase effects are not visible. In other words, different level set boundaries are smoothened. Also, it is important to note that, although a local smoothing filter smooths out the level set boundaries, it does not shift the level set boundaries. (f) shows the bone region (cyan) obtained by segmenting the smooth SDT image, which is superimposed on original bone region. As, observed in (f), the bone boundary after shape-based smoothing is significantly smoother than the original boundary, while avoiding any local shift in the bone boundary. The overall effect of shape-based smoothing is shown in (g). As visually apparent, the shape-based smoothing algorithms removes digital staircase effects, while preserving the overall shape of the original proximal femur bone.

The new shape-based smoothing algorithm was applied on five proximal femur bone volumes generated from MR imaging of postmenopausal women collected at the New York University. Written informed consent was obtained from all subjects. Results of application on one bone volume is presented in Fig. 1, while the results for other four bone volumes are presented in Fig. 2. These proximal femur bone boundaries were manually outlined on individual MR image slices. MR images were acquired in feet-first supine position on a 3-T MR imager (Skyra; Siemens, Erlangen, Germany) by using a 26-element radiofrequency coil setup (three rows of six elements from the Siemens commercial flexible array coil, two rows of four elements from the Siemens commercial spine coil) to detect the MR signal [19]. MR images of the entire proximal femur in a slightly oblique coronal plane parallel to the femoral neck by using a three-dimensional fast low-angle shot sequence (repetition time msec/echo time msec, 31/4.92; flip angle, 25°; matrix, 512×512; field of view, 120 mm; in-plane voxel size, 0.234×0.234 mm; section thickness, 1.5 mm; 60 coronal sections; acquisition time 25 min 30 s; bandwidth, 200 Hz/pixel) similar to that used in prior studies [20]. This study had institutional review board approval and was Health Insurance Portability and Accountability Act (HIPAA) compliant. Written informed consent was obtained from all subjects. It is visually apparent for 3-D surface renditions in Figs. 1 and 2 that manual segmentation results of proximal femur bone volumes from MRI suffer from digital staircase artifacts. These staircase artifacts were primarily contributed by two factors – (1) large slice-spacing as compared to in-plane resolution and (2) the slice-by-slice

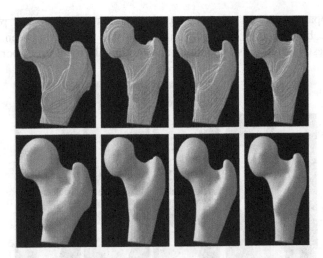

Fig. 2. Results of application of shape-based smoothing on manually segmented proximal femur bone volumes from hip MRI of postmenopausal women. Top row: 3-D surface rendition of the original slice-by-slice manual segmentation results. Bottom row: 3-D rendition of proximal femur bone surfaces after shape-based smoothing.

manual outlining approach used for segmentation. It is encouraging to observe from the 3-D rendition of smooth femur volumes in Figs. 1 and 2 the shape-based smoothing successfully generates smooth bone volume eliminating staircase artifacts, while preserving the basic shape and geometry of individual bone objects.

To quantitatively evaluate the performance of the new shape based smoothing algorithm, we generated phantom images with noisy granular protrusions and dents on the surface of known smooth objects. Specifically, the results of shape-based smoothing of the five proximal femur bone volumes described in Figs. 1 and 2 were used as the ground truth. To generate noisy granular protrusions and dents, we started with a white Gaussian noise image with zero mean and standard deviation of one. The initial noise image was blurred with a Gaussian smoothing kernel with the standard deviation σ_N. The parameter σ_N was varied to control the size of noisy dents and protrusions. The image of positive noise granules was generated by thresholding the blurred noise image strictly above zero and then applying a shape-based opening operation to break connected paths of noisy granules. The image of negative noise granules was generated similarly except the thresholding step, where blur noise values strictly below zero were used. Finally, the noisy protrusions and dents were generated by adding positive noise granules and subtracting negative noise granules, which intersect with the object-boundary interface ∂O. For our experiments, we generated three phantoms from each ground truth bone volume at granule size $\sigma_N = 1, 2, 3$. Thus, for each granule size, we generated five phantoms, and altogether, fifteen phantom images were used. Three test phantoms from a ground truth bone volume with different noise granule sizes are illustrated in Fig. 3. The difference in the size of noise granules is visually apparent. Results of shape-based smoothing on these test phantoms are shown on the bottom row. No visual difference was noticed between shape-based smoothened results from noisy phantoms and the initial ground truth bone volume.

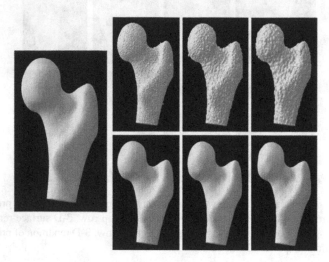

Fig. 3. Results of application of shape-based smoothing on phantom images with different noisy granular protrusions and dents on object boundaries. Left column: The ground truth representation of a human proximal femur bone for the phantom experiment. Top row for right three columns: Test phantoms generated from the ground truth proximal femur bone after adding noisy granular protrusions and dents on the object boundary. Size of noise granules increases from left to right. Bottom row for right three columns: Results of shape-based smoothing on the test phantoms shown in the top row. See text for further details.

For quantitative assessment of the performance of our shape-based smoothing, we analyzed the Dice similarity coefficient (DSC) between the ground truth and the result of shape-based smoothing. Let $O_T \subset Z^3$ denote a true object and $O_{\sigma_N} \subset Z^3$ be a phantom generated from a O_T at the granular noise size σ_N. The performance of shape-based smoothing of O_{σ_N} using a Gaussian smoothing kernel K_{σ_s} with the scale σ_s is computed as follows:

$$DSC(O_T, M(O_{\sigma_N}, K_{\sigma_s})) = \frac{2|O_T \cap M(O_{\sigma_N}, K_{\sigma_s})|}{|O_T| + |M(O_{\sigma_N}, K_{\sigma_s})|}, \tag{5}$$

where $|\cdot|$ represents the cardinality of a set. Note that, similar to O_T and O_{σ_N}, $M(O_{\sigma_N}, K_{\sigma_s})$ is a set of voxels, i.e., $M(O_{\sigma_N}, K_{\sigma_s}) \subset Z^3$. For a given granular noise size of σ_N and a scale σ_s of smoothing kernels, we obtained five DSC measure values corresponding to the five ground truth proximal femur bone objects; let DSC_{σ_N, σ_s} denote the mean of these five DSC values. For a given noise granule size σ_N, Fig. 4 presents the mean DSC values DSC_{σ_N, σ_s} as a function of the smoothing kernel scale σ_s. As observed from the figure, for each granule size, there is an optimum smoothing kernel scale producing the highest mean DSC value. Also, the optimum smoothing kernel scale is monotonically related to the noise granule size. Specifically, phantoms

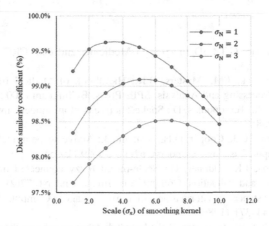

Fig. 4. Dice similarity coefficient (DSC) between the ground truth and the result of shape-based smoothing at different noise granule sizes and smoothing kernel scales. Each data point represents mean of the DSC values obtained from different phantoms at a given value of granule size σ_N and smoothing scale σ_s. For each noise granule size, the mean DSC values are shown as a function of σ_s. See the text.

with smaller noise granules yield smaller optimum scale of smoothing kernel. Finally, the optimum mean DSC value is inversely related to the noise granule size. In other words, the optimum DSC value for phantoms with larger noise granules is lower as compared to those for phantoms with smaller noise granules. The mean of DSC values at optimum smoothing scale were 99.6%, 99.1%, and 98.5% for the noise granule size $\sigma_N = 1, 2, 3$, respectively.

4   Conclusions

A new shape-based smoothing algorithm using signed DT has been presented that removes digital staircase artifacts as well as noisy protrusions and dents on object boundaries, while preserving the shape and geometric features. The performance of the method has been demonstrated on MRI-based manual segmentation of human proximal femur bones with ample digital staircase artifacts primarily contributed by large slice-spacing of MRI and slice-by-slice manual outlining. A quantitative experiment evaluating the performance of the new algorithm on phantoms with different sizes of noise granules has validated the method's effectiveness, also, it has demonstrated the relationship between the size of noise granules and the optimum smoothing kernel scale.

The current algorithm uses a constant value for the smoothing kernel scale and may fail to spatially adopt the kernel scale based on local object features as well as noise. Currently, we are working to develop a space variant strategy of optimizing local smoothing kernel scales based on local features.

Acknowledgement. This work was supported by the NIH grants NIH R01 AR066008 and NIH R01 AR070131.

References

1. Udupa, J.K., Herman, G.T.: 3D Imaging in Medicine, 2nd edn. CRC Press, Boca Raton (1999)
2. Sonka, M., Fitzpatrick, J.M., Masters, B.R.: Handbook of Medical Imaging, Volume 2: Medical Image Processing and Analysis. SPIE Press, Bellingham (2002)
3. Kass, M., Witkin, A., Terzopoulos, D.: Snakes: active contour models. Int. J. Comput. Vis. **1**(4), 321–331 (1988)
4. Cootes, T.F., Taylor, C.J., Cooper, D.H., Graham, J.: Active shape models-their training and application. Comput. Vis. Image Underst. **61**(1), 38–59 (1995)
5. Saha, P.K., Udupa, J.K., Odhner, D.: Scale-based fuzzy connected image segmentation: theory, algorithms, and validation. Comput. Vis. Image Underst. **77**(2), 145–174 (2000)
6. Borgefors, G.: Distance transformations in digital images. Comput. Vis. Graph. Image Process. **34**(3), 344–371 (1986)
7. Saha, P.K., Wehrli, F.W., Gomberg, B.R.: Fuzzy distance transform: theory, algorithms, and applications. Comput. Vis. Image Underst. **86**(3), 171–190 (2002)
8. Ye, Q.-Z.: The signed Euclidean distance transform and its applications. In: Proceedings of the 9th International Conference on Pattern Recognition, pp. 495–499. IEEE (1988)
9. Raya, S.P., Udupa, J.K.: Shape-based interpolation of multidimensional objects. IEEE Trans. Med. Imaging **9**(1), 32–42 (1990)
10. Herman, G.T., Zheng, J., Bucholtz, C.A.: Shape-based interpolation. IEEE Comput. Graph. Appl. **12**(3), 69–79 (1992)
11. Higgins, W.E., Morice, C., Ritman, E.L.: Shape-based interpolation of tree-like structures in three-dimensional images. IEEE Trans. Med. Imaging **12**(3), 439–450 (1993)
12. Grevera, G.J., Udupa, J.K.: Shape-based interpolation of multidimensional grey-level images. IEEE Trans. Med. Imaging **15**(6), 881–892 (1996)
13. DeCoro, C., Cole, F., Finkelstein, A., Rusinkiewicz, S.: Stylized shadows. In: Proceedings of the 5th International Symposium on Non-Photorealistic Animation and Rendering, pp. 77–83 (2007)
14. Malladi, R., Sethian, J.A., Vemuri, B.C.: Shape modeling with front propagation: a level set approach. IEEE Trans. Pattern Anal. Mach. Intell. **17**(2), 158–175 (1995)
15. Saha, P.K., Strand, R., Borgefors, G.: Digital topology and geometry in medical imaging: a survey. IEEE Trans. Med. Imaging **34**(9), 1940–1964 (2015)
16. Saha, P.K., Borgefors, G., Sanniti di Baja, G.: A survey on skeletonization algorithms and their applications. Pattern Recognit. Lett. **76**, 3–12 (2016)
17. Saha, P.K., Chaudhuri, B.B.: 3D digital topology under binary transformation with applications. Comput. Vis. Image Underst. **63**(3), 418–429 (1996)
18. Kong, T.Y., Rosenfeld, A.: Digital topology: introduction and survey. Comput. Vis. Graph. Image Process. **48**(3), 357–393 (1989)
19. Chang, G., Deniz, C.M., Honig, S., Rajapakse, C.S., Egol, K., Regatte, R.R., Brown, R.: Feasibility of three-dimensional MRI of proximal femur microarchitecture at 3 Tesla using 26 receive elements without and with parallel imaging. Magn. Reson. Imaging **40**(1), 229–238 (2014)
20. Chang, G., Honig, S., Brown, R., Deniz, C.M., Egol, K.A., Babb, J.S., Regatte, R.R., Rajapakse, C.S.: Finite element analysis applied to 3-T MR imaging of proximal femur microarchitecture: lower bone strength in patients with fragility fractures compared with control subjects. Radiology **272**(2), 464–474 (2014)

Segmentation

Patch-Based Potentials for Interactive Contour Extraction

Thoraya Ben Chattah[1,2], Sébastien Bougleux[1(✉)], Olivier Lézoray[1], and Atef Hamouda[2]

[1] Normandie Univ, UNICAEN, ENSICAEN, CNRS, GREYC, 14000 Caen, France
{bougleux,olivier.lezoray}@unicaen.fr
[2] University of Tunis El Manar, Faculty of Siences of Tunis, LIPAH-LR11ES14, 2092 Tunis, Tunisia

Abstract. The problem of interactive contour extraction of targeted objects of interest in images is challenging and finds many applications in image editing tasks. Several methods have been proposed to address this problem with a common objective: performing an accurate contour extraction with minimum user effort. For minimal paths techniques, achieving this goal depends critically on the ability of the so-called potential map to capture edges. In this context we propose new patch-based potentials designed to have small values at the boundary of the targeted object. To evaluate these potentials, we consider the livewire framework and quantify their abilities in terms of number of needed seed points. Both visual and quantitative results demonstrated the strong capability of our proposed potentials in reducing the user's interaction while preserving a good accuracy of extraction.

Keywords: Contour extraction · Patch · Minimal paths

1 Introduction

Despite the high number of research works in image segmentation, interactive contour extraction is still a very challenging image processing problem. In contrast to the traditional image segmentation problem, many real-world applications focus on identifying the pixels belonging to a specific object. Their aim is to precisely delineate the contour of a targeted object. This is at the core of many image editing tasks in photography or medical image analysis: using a selection tool, an object is extracted and the background is removed. This process can be very difficult to do cleanly manually because of the presence of structures with ill-defined borders, and assistive tools can be very beneficial for end-users. For that, it is necessary for the user to provide inputs to ease the object extraction. These inputs can take different forms that are then incorporated into the segmentation process as hard or soft constraints. Since this requires an interaction with the user, all methods try to obtain accurate segmentation results while reducing the user's effort. There are essentially three methods in the literature to allow the user to specify the targeted object. The first is to label

G. Bebis et al. (Eds.): ISVC 2018, LNCS 11241, pp. 587–597, 2018.
https://doi.org/10.1007/978-3-030-03801-4_51

some pixels inside/outside the object [10] and to use a labeling process such as graph-cut based-methods [8]. The second method is to provide a sub-region within the image that contains the object. Bounding boxes have often been considered for that, see [1], and have been popularized by the GrabCut method [15]. The third method is to provide a curve close to the boundary or seed points on the boundary. Providing curves has been extensively employed in level sets and snakes methods [4]. Providing points has been mainly employed with minimal path approaches [5]. In the sequel we will focus on that last type of interaction that we call seed-based interactive contour extraction methods.

The paper is organized as follows. Section 2 provides a review of the minimal paths approach for interactive contour extraction and describes the livewire framework. Section 3 describes our patch-based potentials. They are compared in Sect. 4 through experiments on ISEG dataset.

2   Seed-Based Interactive Contour Extraction Methods

2.1   Minimal Paths

Most seed-based interactive contour extraction methods rely on minimal paths. Given an image $f : \Omega \subset \mathbb{R}^2 \to \mathbb{R}^n_+$ and two seeds $p_s, p_e \in \Omega$ located on the contour of an object, the objective is to find a path from p_s to p_e that represents a piece of contour. In this paper, we consider the classical model presented in [5]. A path from p_s to p_e is defined as a parametric curve $\gamma : [0,1] \to \Omega$ so that $\gamma(0) = p_s$ and $\gamma(1) = p_e$, and its length as the cost:

$$L(\gamma) = \int_0^1 P(\gamma(s)) \|\gamma'(s)\| ds. \tag{1}$$

γ' is the derivative of γ. $P : \Omega \to R^*_+$ is a potential function derived from image f that has low values for edges. The length $L(\gamma)$ is smaller when it goes through low values of P and one can search for curves that minimize $L(\gamma)$ given a pair of starting and ending points. The goal is therefore to capture the minimal path γ^*, also called the geodesic path, that globally minimizes the cost function defined in (1):

$$L(\gamma^*) = \min_{\gamma \in \mathcal{A}(p_s, p_e)} L(\gamma) \tag{2}$$

with $\mathcal{A}(p_s, p_e)$ the set of all possible paths joining p_s to p_e. The optimal cost defines the geodesic distance $d(p_s, p_e) = L(\gamma^*)$.

To tackle the minimization problem (2), the geodesic distance map $\mathcal{U}_{\{p_s\}} : \Omega \to \mathbb{R}_+$ from a point p_s to any other point $p \in \Omega$ is considered: $\mathcal{U}_{\{p_s\}}(p) = d(p_s, p) = \min_{\gamma \in \mathcal{A}(p_s, p)} L(\gamma)$. The distance map is solution of the Eikonal equation:

$$\begin{cases} \|\nabla \mathcal{U}_{\{p_s\}}(p)\| = P(p), & \forall p \in \Omega \\ \mathcal{U}_{\{p_s\}}(p_s) = 0 \end{cases} \tag{3}$$

The value $\mathcal{U}_{\{p_s\}}(p)$ can be interpreted as the arrival time at p of a front propagating from a point p_s with speed $1/P$. Fast marching method [5,16] and Dijkstra's algorithm [6] are often used to compute the values of $U_{\{p_s\}}$ in increasing order, so that the process can be stopped when the end point p_e is reached. Then the minimal path between p_s and p_e can be constructed by applying a back-propagation procedure (gradient descent) starting from p_e along the gradient of the map $\mathcal{U}_{p_s}$ until arriving at p_s. See [14] for more details.

An interesting thing to note is that the result curve γ^* depends strongly on the potential functional P which is usually built such as it takes lower values at the desired structure of interest and higher values elsewhere. Some works have suggested the use of new potential functionals or path cost functions in order to better discriminate the discontinuities between objects and background. To this end, and to go beyond classical edge-based energies, some authors have considered more evolved information such as texture, curvature [3], or orientation [2]. We focus on this track of research in this paper.

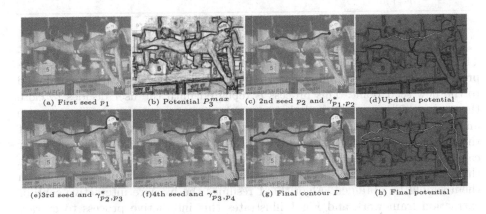

(a) First seed p_1 (b) Potential P_3^{max} (c) 2nd seed p_2 and $\gamma^*_{p_1,p_2}$ (d)Updated potential

(e)3rd seed and $\gamma^*_{p_2,p_3}$ (f)4th seed and $\gamma^*_{p_3,p_4}$ (g) Final contour Γ (h) Final potential

Fig. 1. A livewire interactive contour extraction.

2.2   Livewire Interactive Contour Extraction Framework

Before entering into the details of our proposed potentials, we focus on how interaction can be considered in seed-based minimal paths interactive contour extraction. When points are provided as seeds in minimal path approaches for contour extraction, the employed methods all adopt the same strategy. The user places *seed points* that provides an initial labelling for some pixels of the image. Then, an algorithm is performed to propagate the labels of seeds to unlabeled regions until an optimum criterion is reached. If this strategy is similar from one method to another, the interaction with the user for the providing of seeds differs. A first way to proceed consists in iteratively minimizing an energy functional for a given set of seed points on a contour [5,11]. The main drawback of this type of user interaction is that the user cannot easily add new boundary points on the contour segments that were poorly extracted: this requires a complete re-computation of the solution. A second more popular way to proceed is to let the user place new seed points after each label propagation step.

Algorithm 1. Livewire contour extraction framework

Potential function P, Seed set $\mathcal{S} = \emptyset$, extracted contour Γ
Select seed point p_1
Compute geodesic distance map $\mathcal{U}_{\{p_1\}}$ with P
$p_s \leftarrow p_1$, $\mathcal{S} \leftarrow \mathcal{S} \cup \{p_s\}$
repeat
    Select p_e
    Backtrack to determine the shortest curve $\gamma^*_{p_s,p_e}$ from $\mathcal{U}_{\{p_s\}}$
    $\mathcal{S} \leftarrow \mathcal{S} \cup \{p_e\}$, $\Gamma \leftarrow \Gamma \cup \gamma^*_{p_s,p_e}$
    Update Potential $P(q) \leftarrow +\infty$, $\forall q \in \gamma^*_{p_s,p_e} \setminus \{p_s, p_e\}$
    Compute geodesic distance map $\mathcal{U}_{\{p_e\}}$ with P
    Backtrack to determine the shortest curve $\gamma^*_{p_e,p_1}$ from $\mathcal{U}_{\{p_e\}}$
    $p_s \leftarrow p_e$
until The user is satisfied with the extracted contour
$\Gamma = \Gamma \cup \gamma^*_{p_{i+1},p_1}$

The user provides starting seed points and the optimal boundary is extracted. Then, the user can add another seed point if he is not satisfied. In that case, the previously extracted boundary is frozen and a new optimal path is computed to the new seed point. This process is repeated until the user decides to close the contour. These methods do belong to the livewire framework. They require an ordered sequence of seed points (provided one after the other) to extract the object's contour. The advantage of this type of interaction is that the user can control and predict the final result. The interaction should be minimal in the sense that few seeds should be used and the largest optimum path between them should be obtained. Algorithm 1 resumes the livewire interactive contour extraction framework and Fig. 1 illustrates this interactive process to extract one contour with one of the potentials (P_3^{max}) we propose thereafter. Significant examples of the livewire framework include intelligent scissors methods [13], their variations with the on-the-fly extension [7], the G-wire extension [9] and the riverbed algorithm [12].

3 Patch-Based Potentials

In this section, we introduce new patch-based potentials for livewire contour extraction. Generally speaking, a contour is a curve Γ that separates optimally two regions $\mathcal{R}^+$ and $\mathcal{R}^-$ that have different features (e.g., color, texture). Our proposal consists in using patches as texture descriptors to build a potential map that has small values especially for edges pixels.

3.1 Notations

For a color image f, the color at a pixel $p_i = (x_i, y_i)^T$ is given by $f(p_i) \in \mathbb{R}^3$. A patch is a rectangular region of size $(2w+1)^2$ around a pixel and is defined by the vector $\mathcal{P}(p_i) = (f(p_i + t), \forall t \in [-w, w]^2)^T \in \mathbb{R}^{3(2w+1)^2}$. The difference between two patches is provided by the L_2-norm $d(\mathcal{P}(p_i), \mathcal{P}(p_j)) = \|\mathcal{P}(p_i) - \mathcal{P}(p_j)\|_2$.

Given $t_{\theta,\delta}$ a vector of translation δ according to the angle θ with the horizontal line, we can define the left and right pixels at a distance δ of a pixel p_i on a line of angle θ with the horizon as: $p_i^{l,\theta,\delta} = p_i + t_{\theta,\delta}$ and $p_i^{r,\theta,\delta} = p_i - t_{\theta,\delta}$. In the sequel, we will consider lines of angle $\theta \in \{0°, 45°, 90°, 135°\}$.

3.2   Pixel-Surround Potentials

We propose two first potentials that consider only the pixels surrounding a current pixel p_i in a 8-neighborhood. A pixel can be considered as lying on an edge if the patch at its left is different from the patch at its right. If we compute distances between these left and right patches, a high value means a high probability of contour. We therefore define a patch difference centered on p_i as: $d_c^{\theta,\delta}(p_i) = d\left(\mathcal{P}(p_i^{l,\theta,\delta}), \mathcal{P}(p_i^{r,\theta,\delta})\right)$. However, the edge is not necessarily oriented along the y axis and we have to test all the possible orientations in a 8-neighborhood to define the potential: $P_1(p_i) = \max_\theta d_c^{\theta,1}(p_i)$ with $\delta = 1$ since we consider only the surrounding pixels. This first potential is illustrated in Fig. 2 (first row, first column). Since a pixel on an edge is also not supposed to be similar to its surrounding pixels, we can enhance this potential by computing upwind left or right differences between the pixel and its neighbors. We define $d_l^{\theta,\delta}(p_i) = d\left(\mathcal{P}(p_i), \mathcal{P}(p_i^{l,\theta,\delta})\right)$ and $d_r^{\theta,\delta}(p_i) = d\left(\mathcal{P}(p_i), \mathcal{P}(p_i^{r,\theta,\delta})\right)$. Then, we can aggregate all these distances along a direction and take the maximum on all directions:

$$P_2^{AF}(p_i) = \max_\theta AF(d_s^{\theta,1}(p_i)) \tag{4}$$

with $d_s^{\theta,1}(p_i) = \{d_l^{\theta,1}(p_i), d_c^{\theta,1}(p_i), d_r^{\theta,1}(p_i)\}$ and AF an aggregation function among the min, the max and the mean. This second potential is illustrated in Fig. 2 (first row, second column) and Fig. 3.

3.3   Band-Based Potentials

The drawback of the previous potentials is that they are operating on a small neighborhood to discriminate edge from non-edge pixels. It might be much more beneficial to study a larger neighborhood. Indeed if there is a texture edge at pixel p_i it is natural to expect that shifted patches to the left are different from shifted patches to the right. To take this into account we generalize the previous potential P_2 to operate on a longer line and to consider pixels that are much farther than a distance $\delta = 1$. To that aim, we consider a band of ns patches on a side of the line and to avoid an overlap between the patch at p_i and its left and right patches, we consider pixels at a distance $\delta \in [\epsilon, \epsilon + ns]$. For each possible set of distances (left d_l, right d_r or center d_c), we keep only the minimum on a side. Then we can aggregate all these distances between the band of patches along a direction and take the maximum on all directions:

$$P_3^{AF}(p_i) = \max_\theta AF\left(\left\{\min_{\delta \in [\epsilon, \epsilon + ns]}, d_s^{\theta,\delta}(p_i), \forall s \in \{l, c, r\}\right\}\right) \tag{5}$$

This third potential is illustrated in Fig. 2 (second row, first column) and Fig. 3.

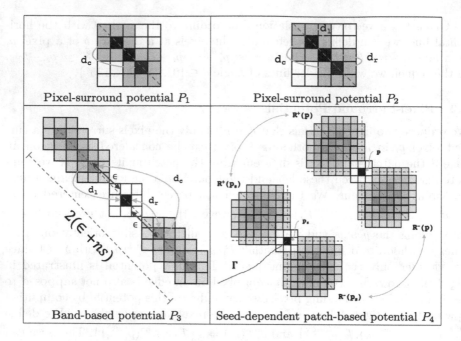

Fig. 2. Computation principles of the proposed potentials.

3.4 Seed-Dependent Patch-Based Potential

All the previous potentials we proposed can be considered as blind as they do
not take into account the previously positioned seeds to compute the potential.
To overcome this, we design a seed-dependent patch-based potential. Given a
seed p_s, it is expected that the regions $\mathcal{R}^+(p_s)$ and $\mathcal{R}^-(p_s)$ on its both sides will
be similar to the other regions for the next points of the contour. However, for
the first seed $p_s = p_1$ (Algorithm 1), we have no exact idea of the orientation to
define the regions it separates. To cope with this, we search for the angle θ_s that
maximizes the differences between the set of patches of the two regions. These
set of patches are contained within $45°$ to the band defined by the angle θ to
the horizon. We consider only 5 patches of size 5×5 with minimum overlap for
each region. Finally for p_1,

$$\theta_1 = \arg\max_\theta \max_{\substack{q_1 \times q_2 \\ q_1 \in \mathcal{R}_\theta^+(p_1) \\ q_2 \in \mathcal{R}_\theta^-(p_1)}} d(\mathcal{P}(q_1), \mathcal{P}(q_2)) \tag{6}$$

This provides two regions $\mathcal{R}_{\theta_1}^+(p_1)$ and $\mathcal{R}_{\theta_1}^-(p_1)$ according to the retained orientation θ_1. For any other seed $p_s \neq p_1$, the regions $\mathcal{R}_{\theta_s}^+(p_s)$ and $\mathcal{R}_{\theta_s}^-(p_s)$ are
defined from the normal $N_s = (\gamma_{s-1,s}^{*\prime}(p_s))^\perp / \|\gamma_{s-1,s}^{*\prime}(p_s)\|$ to the shortest path
$\gamma_{s-1,s}^*$ at p_s by the angle $\theta_s = \arg\min_\theta \angle(N_s, p_s p_s^{l,\theta,1})$.

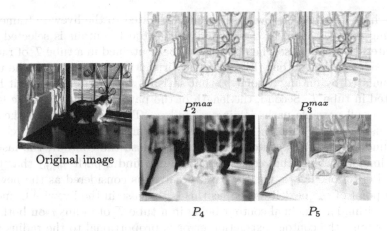

Fig. 3. Potentials maps with 5×5 patches, $AF = \max$ for P_2 and P_3, $\epsilon = 2$ and $ns = 5$ for P_3, and $\alpha = 0.3$ for P_5. (Color figure online)

Then, for each point p_i of the image, we compute all the pairwise distances between the regions $\mathcal{R}_{\theta_s}^{+}(p_s)$ and $\mathcal{R}_{\theta}^{+}(p_i)$ (and similarly for $\mathcal{R}^{-}$) for different orientations θ around p_i. We retain only the minimum value that accounts for a very similar configuration between p_s and p_i. This can be formulated by:

$$P_4(p_i) = \min_{\theta} \left(\min_{\substack{q_1 \times q_2 \\ q_1 \in \mathcal{R}_{\theta}^{+}(p_i) \\ q_2 \in \mathcal{R}_{\theta_s}^{+}(p_s)}} d(\mathcal{P}(q_1), \mathcal{P}(q_2)) + \min_{\substack{q_1 \times q_2 \\ q_1 \in \mathcal{R}_{\theta}^{-}(p_i) \\ q_2 \in \mathcal{R}_{\theta_s}^{-}(p_s)}} d(\mathcal{P}(q_1), \mathcal{P}(q_2)) \right) \quad (7)$$

This potential is illustrated in Fig. 2 (second row, second column) and Fig. 3 (the red point shows the seed p_s). Contrary to the other potentials, it must be computed at each iteration of Algorithm 1.

4   Experiments

4.1   User Simulation for Contour Extraction Evaluation

As introduced in [17], to reliably evaluate the effectiveness of approaches for contour extraction, one should ideally eliminate the user bias, while obtaining quality measures of the result. To cope with this, user agents have to be considered. These agents should be able to simulate the human user behavior through the addition of seeds close to the object's boundary. To do so, they have to evaluate the optimum-boundary segment being computed from a previously selected seed point to a virtual mouse position, seeking for the longest possible segment with minimum acceptable error. A new seed is then added when the error is too high and the agents iterate until closing the contour, just like real users. To achieve that, we have designed our own user agent dedicated to the livewire framework. A starting point p_s close to the ground truth object contour is selected using some criterion. In our case, the point has to be contained in a tube $\mathcal{T}$ of radius r on both sides of the contour (Fig. 5b). The virtual mouse position of the user is then simulated by finding a point p_e that satisfies three criteria. First it has to be located in tube $\mathcal{T}$. Second, the length of the path γ_{p_s,p_e} must be the largest one among all possible paths joining p_s and p_e. Third, all points of the curve γ_{p_s,p_e} must be in the tube $\mathcal{T}$. To do so, we perform a dichotomous search along the ground truth object contour (Fig. 5b). To close the contour, the last step of our simulation algorithm consists of trying to find a path γ_{p_s,p_e} that fulfills the third criterion. If it is not the case, point p_e is considered as the new seed starting point of the next iteration, as this is the case in the livewire framework (see Algorithm 1). The final contour being in a tube $\mathcal{T}$ of radius r on both sides of the contour, the contour extraction error is proportional to the radius of the tube: the larger r, the higher the contour extraction error.

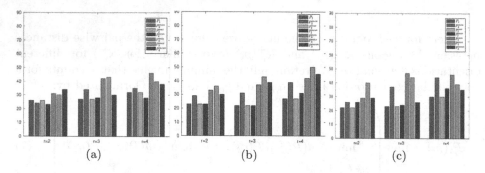

Fig. 4. Number of times where a potential gives the minimum % of seeds (a) $w = 1$; (b) $w = 2$; (c) $w = 3$.

4.2 Results

To demonstrate the ability of the proposed potentials to recover closed boundaries of objects in color images, we have carried out experiments on ISEG [8]. We ran Algorithm 1 for all the potentials with the user agent behavior. To have a fair comparison between the compared potentials, the first starting point is always the same on a given image. The criteria used to compare two potentials will be: (i) the average of the ratio between the number of seeds and the length of the ground truth contour (the lesser the better, this will be denoted by % of seeds), (ii) the Jaccard index that measures the similarity between the extracted contour and the ground truth. Since we use patch-based potentials, the first question that we can ask is what is the best patch size. We have considered three different patch sizes $w \in \{1, 2, 3\}$ that correspond to 3×3, 5×5 and 7×7 patches. For band-based potentials (i.e., P_3), the length of the band is set to $ns = 5$. For potentials that rely on an aggregation function (P_2 and P_3), we consider the min, max and mean aggregation functions. This means that we have three different configurations for each one of these potentials and this will be specified with an upperscript. Figure 4 shows an histogram that counts, on the ISEG dataset, the number of times that a potential gives the minimum % of seeds for different patch sizes. We do not show the Jaccard index since its average values are very close for all potentials (this was attended since we use simulated user agents). From these results, we can see that the best results are mostly always obtained with band-based potentials (with P_3^{max}). This shows the interest of going farther than the pixel surround and the proposed patch-based potentials have the ability to better delineate the object contour with less seeds when considering 5×5 patches. In the sequel we have retained this size.

Potential	Radius	Mean % seeds	Mean Jaccard index
P_E	2	4.58	0.96
	3	2.96	0.95
	4	2.31	0.94
P_3^{max}	2	3.93	0.97
	3	2.67	0.95
	4	2.12	0.94
P_4	2	4.42	0.95
	3	3.13	0.93
	4	2.52	0.91
P_5	2	3.67	0.97
	3	2.38	0.95
	4	1.86	0.94

(a)

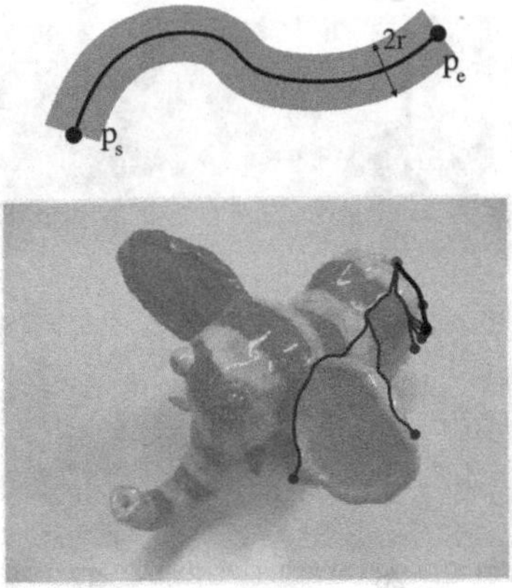

(b)

Fig. 5. (a) Quantitative comparison between potentials. (b) Tube of radius r surrounding a ground truth curve and process to find the next seed from the current one (red dot). The black curve is finally retained. (Color figure online)

Once this best patch size has been fixed, we compare the best potential we have proposed and tested so far, namely P_3^{max}, with the classical pixel-edge potential map [11] based on gradient magnitude and defined as $P_E = \mu + \max\left(0, \frac{\|\nabla f(p_i)\|}{\max \|\nabla f(p)\|}\right)$ with $\mu = 0.2$. Whatever the agent configuration (different values of r), the potential P_3^{max} performs always better than the baseline P_E potential in terms of both criteria (% of seeds and Jaccard index). It is important to note that a difference of 0.1% on the average % of seeds corresponds to 1.5 points). This is shown in Fig. 5a. However, if the results are in favor of potential P_3^{max}, this is not the case for potential P_4. But for some images, P_4 performs better. This is illustrated in Fig. 6 where less seeds are needed for the first image. Since no general rule can be devised to choose between potentials P_3^{max} and P_4, we choose to combine them with $P_5 = \alpha P_3^{max} + (1 - \alpha)P_4$. To choose the best

α, we have tested values within $[0, 1]$ and retained the one that minimizes the % of seeds. We obtained a value of $\alpha = 0.3$. With this new potential P_5, one can see that we overpass by far the classical pixel-edge potential as well as all the patch-based potential we considered. In addition, this is true whatever the considered radius r of the user agent, which enforces the robustness of our proposed seed-dependent patch-based potential P_5.

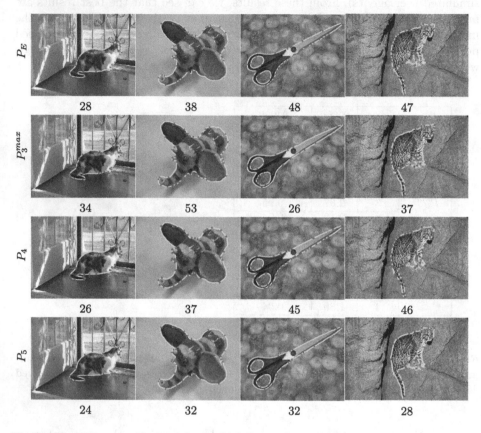

Fig. 6. Contour extraction results with different potentials (the number of required seed points is provided below each result).

5   Conclusion

In this paper new patch-based potentials have been proposed for minimal path contour extraction. Their interest has been assessed in terms of the number points needed to perform the contour extraction, so that the user interaction is potentially minimized. To eliminate the user bias in the interactive process, a dedicated user agent has been conceived. Results have shown that patch-based potentials can overcome the classical pixel-based ones and improve object contour extraction.

References

1. Blake, A., Rother, C., Brown, M., Perez, P., Torr, P.: Interactive image segmentation using an adaptive GMMRF model. In: Pajdla, T., Matas, J. (eds.) ECCV 2004. LNCS, vol. 3021, pp. 428–441. Springer, Heidelberg (2004). https://doi.org/10.1007/978-3-540-24670-1_33
2. Bougleux, S., Peyré, G., Cohen, L.: Anisotropic geodesics for perceptual grouping and domain meshing. In: Forsyth, D., Torr, P., Zisserman, A. (eds.) ECCV 2008. LNCS, vol. 5303, pp. 129–142. Springer, Heidelberg (2008). https://doi.org/10.1007/978-3-540-88688-4_10
3. Chen, D., Mirebeau, J.M., Cohen, L.D.: Global minimum for curvature penalized minimal path method. In: BMVC, pp. 86–86 (2015)
4. Cohen, L.D.: On active contour models and balloons. CVGIP Image Underst. 53(2), 211–218 (1991)
5. Cohen, L.D., Kimmel, R.: Global minimum for active contour models: a minimal path approach. IJCV 24(1), 57–78 (1997)
6. Dijkstra, E.W.: A note on two problems in connexion with graphs. Numer. Math 1(1), 269–271 (1959)
7. Falcão, A.X., Udupa, J.K., Miyazawa, F.K.: An ultra-fast user-steered image segmentation paradigm: live wire on the fly. IEEE Trans. Med. Imag. 19(1), 55–62 (2000)
8. Gulshan, V., Rother, C., Criminisi, A., Blake, A., Zisserman, A.: Geodesic star convexity for interactive image segmentation. In: CVPR, pp. 3129–3136 (2010)
9. Kang, H.W.: G-wire: a livewire segmentation algorithm based on a generalized graph formulation. Pattern Recogn. Lett. 26(13), 2042–2051 (2005)
10. Liu, D., Xiong, Y., Shapiro, L., Pulli, K.: Robust interactive image segmentation with automatic boundary refinement. In: ICIP, pp. 225–228 (2010)
11. Mille, J., Bougleux, S., Cohen, L.D.: Combination of piecewise-geodesic paths for interactive segmentation. IJCV 112(1), 1–22 (2015)
12. Miranda, P.A.V., Falcão, A.X., Spina, T.V.: Riverbed: a novel user-steered image segmentation method based on optimum boundary tracking. IEEE Trans. Image Process. 21(6), 3042–3052 (2012)
13. Mortensen, E.N., Barrett, W.A.: Intelligent scissors for image composition. In: Proceedings of the 22nd Annual Conference on Computer Graphics and Interactive Techniques, pp. 191–198 (1995)
14. Peyré, G., Pechaud, M., Keriven, R., Cohen, L.: Geodesic methods in computer vision and graphics. Found. Trends Comput. Graph. Vis. 5(3–4), 197–397 (2010)
15. Rother, C., Kolmogorov, V., Blake, A.: Grabcut: interactive foreground extraction using iterated graph cuts. ACM Trans. Graph. 23(3), 309–314 (2004)
16. Sethian, J.A.: A fast marching level set method for monotonically advancing fronts. Proc. Natl. Acad. Sci. 93(4), 1591–1595 (1996)
17. Spina, T.V., Falcão, A.X.: Robot users for the evaluation of boundary-tracking approaches in interactive image segmentation. In: ICIP, pp. 3248–3252 (2014)

A New Algorithm for Local Blur-Scale Computation and Edge Detection

Indranil Guha$^{(\boxtimes)}$ and Punam K. Saha

Electrical and Computer Engineering, University of Iowa,
Iowa City, IA 52242, USA
indranil-guha@uiowa.edu, pksaha@healthcare.uiowa.edu

Abstract. Precise and efficient object boundary detection is the key for successful accomplishment of many imaging applications involving object segmentation or recognition. Blur-scale at a given image location represents the transition-width of the local object interface. Hence, the knowledge of blur-scale is crucial for accurate edge detection and object segmentation. In this paper, we present new theory and algorithms for computing local blur-scales and apply it for scale-based gradient computation and edge detection. The new blur-scale computation method is based on our observation that gradients inside a blur-scale region follow a Gaussian distribution with non-zero mean. New statistical criteria using maximal likelihood functions are established and applied for local blur-scale computation. Gradient vectors over a blur-scale region are summed to enhance gradients at blurred object interfaces while leaving gradients at sharp transitions unaffected. Finally, a blur-scale based non-maxima suppression method is developed for edge detection. The method has been applied to both natural and phantom images. Experimental results show that computed blur-scales capture true blur extents at individual image locations. Also, the new scale-based gradient computation and edge detection algorithms successfully detect gradients and edges, especially at the blurred object interfaces.

Keywords: Scale · Intensity gradient · Blur-scale
Maximum likelihood function · Mahalanobis distance · Edge detection

1 Introduction

Computerized image analysis and understanding [1, 2] has drawn major attention over the last two decades inspired by the rapid growth in image data generated from different sections of human society including medical imaging and social networking. Object segmentation, quantitative structural analysis, and recognition are key challenges in many imaging applications [3–8]. The performance of most object segmentation methods is largely dependent on accurate definition and detection of object interfaces and edges [9, 10]. Often, object interfaces or boundaries are defined by sudden or gradual shifts in single or multiple image properties. For example, in a grayscale image, object interfaces are distinguished by changes in image intensity values [11]. Such shifts in image properties at object interfaces may be sudden or gradual, and the notion of blur-scale [10, 12] is used to express transition-widths of object interfaces. Blur-

© Springer Nature Switzerland AG 2018
G. Bebis et al. (Eds.): ISVC 2018, LNCS 11241, pp. 598–606, 2018.
https://doi.org/10.1007/978-3-030-03801-4_52

scales may be different for different images; also, it may be space-variant within the same image.

In general, image segmentation algorithms [13–20] use high intensity gradients to define object boundaries. However, difficulties emerge at object interfaces with large blur-scales, where intensity changes from one object to the other are gradual, and a condition of high intensity gradients may fail causing leakages. Thus, it is essential to determine blur-scales to capture the total intensity shift across a full transition of intensities between two objects for accurate and robust detection of edges. Several theories and methods have been proposed in the literature to compute space-variant blur-scales and their applications for edge detection [9, 12]. To the best of our knowledge, Marr and Hildreth [12] first introduced the notion of blur-scale and used the second derivative of multi-scale Gaussian kernels and zero crossing segments of different scales for edge detection. Canny [9] presented a multi-scale edge detection algorithm using novel approaches of non-maximal suppression generating single pixel thick edges and hysteresis allowing two threshold values for improved discrimination among noisy and true edge segments. Canny's edge detection algorithm has been widely used, and it has been further studied and improved by others. Bao et al. [21] improved Canny's method and suggested to combine gradient responses at different scales by multiplication and use the combined gradient response for edge detection. Bergholm [22], proposed an edge detection algorithm that tracks events important to edge detection from the coarse to finer scale to localize the edges accurately. There are several methods in the literature, which explicitly compute local blur-scales [10, 23, 24]. Jeong and Kim [23] developed an adaptive scale based edge detection algorithm where local optimum scale is defined by the size of the Gaussian filter that minimizes a predefined energy function. As reported by the authors, the scale computation results are sensitive to local minima issues of the energy function. Lindeberg [24] presented a similar local scale computation algorithm for edge detection, where optimal scale at a pixel is determined at the maxima of a local edge strength function. Elder and Zucker [10] proposed a local blur-scale computation based edge detection algorithm, where the intensity profile across an object transition is modeled using a pre-defined sigmoid function.

Most of the above algorithms use a pre-defined model for edge transition functions and suffer from local optima related problems. In this paper, we present a model-independent local blur-scale computation algorithm and apply it for edge detection. Our method is based on a simple observation that intensity gradients over a blur-scale region follow a Gaussian distribution with a non-zero mean. A blur-scale based gradient computation method has been presented that enhances gradients at blurred edges while leaving gradients at sharp edges unaffected. Finally, a scale-based edge detection algorithm is developed using scale-based gradients.

2 Theory and Algorithms

In this section, we describe new theory and algorithms to compute local blur-scale and present its application to edge detection. In general, in a true scene, object interfaces form sharp transition in illumination or material density. Finite image resolution or other artifacts, add blur at such interfaces. Specifically, in a grayscale image, blur-scale of an object interface at a given location is the transition-width of the interface at that location. The premise of our blur-scale computation algorithm is based on a simple observation that intensity gradients inside a local blur-scale region follow a Gaussian distribution with nonzero mean. In the following paragraphs, we formulate new test criteria and present a new algorithm for blur-scale computation guided by this obser-vation, and finally describe its application in edge detection.

Let I denote an image intensity function and ∇x_i denote the gradient vector at a given location x_i. The blur-scale computation algorithm is developed based on the evaluation of two hypotheses. Our first hypothesis is that observed gradient vectors $\nabla x_1, \nabla x_2, \ldots, \nabla x_n$ inside a blur-scale region are random samples from a population with an expected probability density function (pdf) $G(\cdot|\mu_e, \Sigma_e)$, where μ_e and Σ_e are the mean and covariance matrix of gradient vectors. Let X_o denote the set $\{\nabla x_1, \nabla x_2, \ldots, \nabla x_n\}$. We formulate a test criterion to evaluate the first hypothesis based on the ratio of two likelihood estimators [25]. Let $\mathcal{P}_n$ denote the set of all possible sets of n gradient vectors. Let $L(\mu_e, \Sigma_e|X)$ denote the likelihood measure that the gradient vectors in a set $X \in \mathcal{P}_n$ are random samples from a population with the pdf $G(\cdot|\mu_e, \Sigma_e)$. Thus, the following likelihood ratio estimator evaluates whether gradient vectors in X_o are random samples from a known population:

$$\lambda_1(X_o|\mu_e, \Sigma_e) = \frac{L(\mu_e, \Sigma_e|X_o)}{\sup\limits_{X \in \mathcal{P}_n} L(\mu_e, \Sigma_e|X)}. \tag{1}$$

To test our hypothesis, we define a rejection region of the form $\lambda_1(X_o|\mu_e, \Sigma_e) \leq c_1$, where $c_1|0 \leq c_1 \leq 1$ is the rejection confidence. Using the fact that the largest value of $L(\mu_e, \Sigma_e|X)$ occurs when all gradient vectors in X equates to μ_e, it can be shown that $\lambda_1(X_o|\mu_e, \Sigma_e) \leq c_1$ is equivalent to the following test criterion:

$$\sqrt{\frac{\sum_{i=1}^n d_M^2(\nabla x_i, \mu_e, \Sigma_e)}{n}} > \sqrt{\frac{-2 \log c_1}{n}}, \tag{2}$$

where $d_M(\nabla x_i, \mu_e, \Sigma_e)$ is the Mahalanobis distance [26] of x_i from the mean μ_e using the covariance matrix Σ_e.

Our second hypothesis is that the mean of the gradient vectors $\nabla x_1, \nabla x_2, \ldots, \nabla x_n$ is non-zero. In other words, we examine whether the Mahalanobis distances from the set $D_o = \{d_M(\nabla x_i, 0, \Sigma_N)|i = 1 \text{ to } n\}$ are random samples from a standard normal distribution, where Σ_N represents image noise derived from homogeneous regions. Note that $d_M(\nabla x_i, 0, \Sigma_N)$ is the Mahalanobis distance of a gradient vector ∇x_i from the null vector 0. Hence, the rejection region for the second hypothesis is formulated as:

$$\lambda_2(D_o) = \frac{L(0, 1|D_o)}{\sup\limits_{\mu} L(\mu, 1|D_o)} \leq c_2, \tag{3}$$

where $c_2|0 \leq c_2 \leq 1$ is the rejection confidence. It can be shown that the maximum value of the likelihood estimation $L(\mu, 1|D_o)$ happens when μ equates to the mean μ_o of Mahalanobis distances in D_o. Using the optimality criterion and a few algebraic operations, we can rewrite (3) as follows:

$$\frac{\sum_{i=1}^n d_M(\nabla \mathbf{x}_i, \mathbf{0}, \Sigma_N)}{n} > \sqrt{\frac{-2 \log c_2}{n}}. \tag{4}$$

2.1   Algorithms

The new blur-scale computation algorithm starts with the computation of gradient vectors at all image pixels using a derivative of Gaussian (DoG) kernel. The method computes the blur-scale at each image pixel using a star line approach and an iterative method. A blur-scale region at a pixel p is a circular disk centered at p, and its diameter $2r$ represents the corresponding blur-scale. At a given pixel, the scale computation starts with $r = 0.5$, and after each iteration, the value of r is incremented by 0.5 until both hypotheses are rejected or a maximum scale value occurs. At a given pixel p and a scale $2r$, we verify the test criteria defined in Eqs. (2) and (4) as follows. First, we compute the set $X_o = \{\nabla \mathbf{x}_1, \nabla \mathbf{x}_2, \ldots, \nabla \mathbf{x}_n\}$ of gradient vectors at uniformly distributed sample points along the circle $C_r(p)$ centered at p with radius r. To make the sample density independent of r, we sample $6r$ number of gradient vectors on $C_r(p)$. The gradient vector at a sample point is computed using linear interpolation [27] of gradient vectors at the four nearest pixels. The expected mean gradient vector μ_e is computed as the vector mean of the gradient vectors at all pixels inside the circular disk representing the immediate smaller scale, i.e., $2r - 1$. A constant 2-by-2 matrix is used for Σ_e, which is defined in terms of image noise. Image noise is represented by a covariance matrix Σ_N, which is computed over homogeneous regions. Assuming that noise is isotropic and uncorrelated, the matrix $\Sigma_N[1, 1] = \Sigma_N[2, 2] = \frac{\sigma^2}{2}$ and $\Sigma_N[1, 2] = \Sigma_N[2, 1] = 0$ is used, where σ^2 is the variance of the intensity gradients computed over homogenous regions. Finally, the covariance matrix Σ_e is defined as $\Sigma_e = 9\Sigma_N$.

Scale-based gradient at a pixel p is computed as the vector sum of the gradients over the circular disk $C_{I_s(p)/2}(p)$ centered at p, where $I_s(p)$ represents the computed blur-scale at p; note that blur-scale denotes the diameter of the local blur region, which is divided by two to get the value of radius. Our edge detection algorithm is applied on the scale-based gradient image, which is accomplished using the following steps similar to the algorithm by Canny [9] – (1) non-maximal suppression, (2) hysteresis, and (3) skeletonization [28, 29] and removing noisy branches [8, 30–32]. During non-maximal suppression, a pixel p with a blur-scale $2r$ is a local maxima if and only if there is no point q on the diameter of $C_r(p)$ along the gradient direction of p such that the scale-based gradient at q is greater than that of p. In the next step, hysteresis thresholding is applied using two threshold values t_{low} and t_{high} to select meaningful edge segments, while suppressing noisy edges [9]. The use of two thresholds allows to apply a high threshold value t_{high} for isolated noisy edge points and a low threshold value t_{low} for edge segments containing contextual information. Finally, the edge map obtained after hysteresis is skeletonized and noisy branches are pruned to get single pixel-thick edges.

3 Experiments and Results

In this section, we will discuss our experiments and results using the new blur-scale computation and edge detection algorithms. The algorithms are applied on both real and computer generated phantom images. For all experiments, a constant value of 0.002 was used for both c_1 and c_2 to ensure that, for the test criterion $\lambda_1(X_o|\mu_e, \Sigma_e) > c_1$, at least three observed gradients have a Mahalanobis distance of two from their expected mean.

Results of blur-scale computation and edge detection for a grayscale image are shown in Fig. 1. Figure (a) shows a grayscale image of a plant and its shadow, and (b) represents the result of non-scale based gradient computation using a location invariant DoG kernel. Figure (c) presents the result of the blur-scale computation, where the intensity brightness is proportional to the local blur-scale. It may be noted from the blur-scale image that blur-scales along the shadow boundary form ridges that represent optimal edge locations. Also, the ridges along the shadow boundary are brighter than the ridges along the sharp edges of the plant, which implies that blur-scales along the boundary of the shadow are higher as compared to blur-scales along the boundary of the plant. Finally, it is worthy to note that blur-scales at homogeneous regions far from an edge are large. In figure (d), computed blur-scales along different boundary regions are shown by circles centered at manually selected pixels along edges. Specifically, the diameter of each circle represents the value of the blur-scale at its center. It may be visually noted that individual circles fully cover local object interface transition-widths at respective locations. Also, along the shadow boundary, circles are larger indicating greater blur. The result of blur-scale based gradient computation is presented in figure (e). Following our algorithm, the computed blur-scale based gradient captures the total intensity difference across the full width of the object transition, which is visually notable along blurred regions of the shadow boundary. In general, gradient values at blurred locations on the shadow boundary are enhanced, while those near the sharp edges remain unchanged. This improvement in gradient computation will be helpful for precise detection of edges near highly blurred regions. In figure (f), edges detected by our blur-scale based edge detection algorithm are shown in green. It is encouraging to note that the sharp edges along the plant as well as blurred edges along the shadow boundary are fully recovered.

Figure 2 presents the performance of our edge detection algorithm on a computer-generated noisy phantom. A phantom was generated from a binary image of a bird, shown in Fig. 2(a). A slow-varying blur field, as shown in (b), was applied on the binary phantom image in the form of Gaussian smoothing to generate a blurred grayscale image. This blurred image was further degenerated by a correlated white Gaussian noise at the contrast-to-noise ratio of 12 to get the final test phantom image shown in (c). Results of local gradient and blur-scale computation on the phantom image of (c) are presented in (d,e), respectively. An illustration of the local blur-scale values using circles at quasi-regular sample points along the object boundary is

Fig. 1. Results of application of the new blur-scale computation and edge detection algorithms. (a) A grayscale image. (b) Color-coded representation of non-scale based gradient computation results using a constant DoG kernel. The color-coding scheme follows the color-disk, where the hue and intensity components of color represent the gradient orientation and magnitude, respectively. (c) Results of local blur-scale computation. (d) Illustration of blur-scales using circles centered at manually selected pixels along different edges. Diameters of individual circles represent blur-scales at respective pixels. (e) Color-coded display of scale-based gradient computation results using the same color-coding shown in (b). (f) Results of edge detection using blur-scale based gradients. Edge locations are shown in green. (Color figure online)

presented in (f). The displayed blur-scales in (f) are satisfactory with visual blur at individual edge locations. Finally, the result of blur-scale based gradient computation is shown in (g), which is displayed using the exact same color coding used for (d). The blur-scale based gradient successfully captures the slow-varying edges, which are hardly visible in the non-scale based gradient image in (d). Figure (h) shows the detected edges in green which is completely aligned to the boundary of the test phantom despite such high noise.

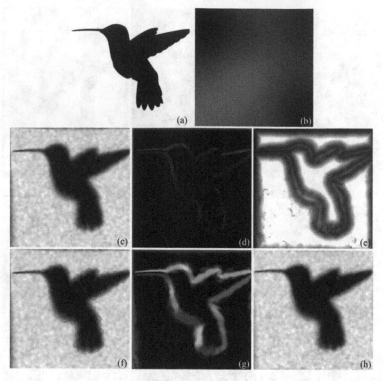

Fig. 2. Results of the new blur-scale computation and edge detection algorithms for a computer-generated phantom image. (a) Original binary image. (b) A slow varying computer-generated blur field used to apply a space-varying blur on the binary image. (c) Test phantom, generated by applying the blur field of (b) and a correlated white Gaussian noise at a contrast-to-noise ratio of 12 on (a). (d–h) same as Fig. 1(b–f) but for the phantom image shown in (c).

4   Conclusions

A new theory and algorithms for local blur-scale computation have been presented and their applications to edge-detection have been demonstrated. The performance of the new algorithms on both natural and phantom images has been examined and the results are presented. New statistical test criteria examining whether a set of observed gradient vectors follow an expected Gaussian distribution with a non-zero mean have been introduced and applied to compute blur-scale at individual image pixels. It has been experimentally observed that blur-scales capture the extent of blur along the object boundary. Computed blur-scales have been applied to develop a scale-based gradient computation algorithm, where the gradient vectors over the local blur-scale region are summed. Results of scale-based gradient computation provide effective edge detection by enhancing gradient magnitudes along the blurred edges, while gradients at the sharp edges remain unchanged and noise in homogenous regions is suppressed. Also, computed blur-scale has been used to formulate a scale-based non-maxima suppression algorithm for edge detection. It has been experimentally shown that the new blur-scale based edge detection algorithm successfully detects edges even at blurred object regions. In the phantom experiment, it has been demonstrated that, despite the presence of significant noise and blur in the image, the algorithm successfully detects the boundary of the image. These initial results of blur-scale computation and edge detection are encouraging, which validates our new theory and algorithms for blur-scale computation and its applications.

References

1. Sonka, M., Hlavac, V., Boyle, R.: Image Processing, Analysis and Machine Vision. Cengage Learning, Boston (2014)
2. Udupa, J.K., Herman, G.T.: 3D Imaging in Medicine. CRC Press, Boca Raton (1991)
3. Müller, R., et al.: Morphometric analysis of human bone biopsies: a quantitative structural comparison of histological sections and micro-computed tomography. Bone 23, 59–66 (1998)
4. Saetta, M., Di Stefano, A., Rosina, C., Thiene, G., Fabbri, L.M.: Quantitative structural analysis of peripheral airways and arteries in sudden fatal asthma. Am. Rev. Respir. Dis. 143, 138–143 (1991)
5. Saha, P.K., Gomberg, B.R., Wehrli, F.W.: Three-dimensional digital topological characterization of cancellous bone architecture. Int. J. Imaging Syst. Technol. 11, 81–90 (2000)
6. Chen, C., et al.: Quantitative imaging of peripheral trabecular bone microarchitecture using MDCT. Med. Phys. 45, 236–249 (2018)
7. Chang, G., et al.: 3-T MR Imaging of proximal femur microarchitecture in subjects with and without fragility fracture and nonosteoporotic proximal femur bone mineral density. Radiology 287, 608–619 (2018)
8. Saha, P.K., Xu, Y., Duan, H., Heiner, A., Liang, G.: Volumetric topological analysis: a novel approach for trabecular bone classification on the continuum between plates and rods. IEEE Trans. Med. Imaging 29, 1821–1838 (2010)
9. Canny, J.: A computational approach to edge detection. IEEE Trans. Pattern Anal. Mach. Intell. 6, 679–698 (1986)
10. Elder, J.H., Zucker, S.W.: Local scale control for edge detection and blur estimation. IEEE Trans. Pattern Anal. Mach. Intell. 20, 699–716 (1998)
11. Saha, P.K., Udupa, J.K.: Optimum image thresholding via class uncertainty and region homogeneity. IEEE Trans. Pattern Anal. Mach. Intell. 6, 689–706 (2001)
12. Marr, D., Hildretch, E.: Theory of edge detection. Proc. R. Soc. Lond. B 207, 187–217 (1980)
13. Kass, M., Witkin, A., Terzopoulos, D.: Snakes: active contour models. Int. J. Comput. Vis. 1, 321–331 (1988)
14. Otsu, N.: A threshold selection method from gray-level histograms. IEEE Trans. Syst. Man Cybern. 9, 62–66 (1979)
15. Saha, P.K., Udupa, J.K., Odhner, D.: Scale-based fuzzy connected image segmentation: theory, algorithms, and validation. Comput. Vis. Image Underst. 77, 145–174 (2000)
16. Saha, P.K., Strand, R., Borgefors, G.: Digital topology and geometry in medical imaging: a survey. IEEE Trans. Med. Imaging 34, 1940–1964 (2015)
17. Strand, R., Ciesielski, K.C., Malmberg, F., Saha, P.K.: The minimum barrier distance. Comput. Vis. Image Underst. 117, 429–437 (2013)
18. Udupa, J.K., Saha, P.K.: Fuzzy connectedness and image segmentation. Proc. IEEE 91, 1649–1669 (2003)

19. Udupa, J.K., Saha, P.K., Lotufo, R.D.A.: Relative fuzzy connectedness and object definition: theory, algorithms, and applications in image segmentation. IEEE Trans. Pattern Anal. Mach. Intell. **24**, 1-1500 (2002)

20. Saha, P.K., Udupa, J.K.: Iterative relative fuzzy connectedness and object definition: theory, algorithms, and applications in image segmentation. In: Proceedings of IEEE Workshop on Mathematical Methods in Biomedical Image Analysis, pp. 28–35. IEEE (2000)

21. Bao, P., Zhang, L., Wu, X.: Canny edge detection enhancement by scale multiplication. IEEE Trans. Pattern Anal. Mach. Intell. **27**, 1485–1490 (2005)

22. Bergholm, F.: Edge focusing. IEEE Trans. Pattern Anal. Mach. Intell. **6**, 726–741 (1987)

23. Jeong, H., Kim, C.: Adaptive determination of filter scales for edge detection. IEEE Trans. Pattern Anal. Mach. Intell. **5**, 579–585 (1992)

24. Lindeberg, T.: Edge detection and ridge detection with automatic scale selection. Int. J. Comput. Vis. **30**, 117–156 (1998)

25. Casella, G., Berger, R.L.: Statistical Inference. Duxbury Pacific Grove, CA (2002)

26. Mahalanobis, P.C.: On the Generalized Distance in Statistics. National Institute of Science of India (1936)

27. Meijering, E.H., Niessen, W.J., Viergever, M.A.: Quantitative evaluation of convolution-based methods for medical image interpolation. Med. Image Anal. **5**, 111–126 (2001)

28. Saha, P.K., Borgefors, G., Sanniti di Baja, G.: A survey on skeletonization algorithms and their applications. Pattern Recogn. Lett. **76**, 3–12 (2016)

29. Saha, P.K., Chaudhuri, B.B.: Detection of 3-D simple points for topology preserving transformations with application to thinning. IEEE Trans. Pattern Anal. Mach. Intell. **16**, 1028–1032 (1994)

30. Németh, G., Kardos, P., Palágyi, K.: Thinning combined with iteration-by-iteration smoothing for 3D binary images. Graph. Models **73**, 335–345 (2011)

31. Borgefors, G., Ramella, G., Sanniti di Baja, G.: Hierarchical decomposition of multiscale skeletons. IEEE Trans. Pattern Anal. Mach. Intell. **11**, 1296–1312 (2001)

32. Attali, D., Sanniti di Baja, G., Thiel, E.: Skeleton simplification through non significant branch removal. Image Process. Commun. **3**, 63–72 (1997)

Semantic Segmentation by Integrating Classifiers for Different Difficulty Levels

Daisuke Matsuzuki[✉] and Kazuhiro Hotta

Meijo University, 1-501 Shiogamaguchi, Tempaku-ku, Nagoya 468-8502, Japan
140442123@ccalumni.meijo-u.ac.jp,
kazuhotta@meijo-u.ac.jp

Abstract. Semantic segmentation assigns class labels to all pixels in an input image. In general, when the number of classes is large or when the appearance of each class frequency changes, the segmentation accuracy decreases drastically. In this paper, we propose to divide a classification task into sub-tasks according to the difficulty of classes. Our proposed method consists of 2 parts; training a network for each sub-task and training an integration network. Difficulty level depends on the number of pixels. By training the network for each difficulty level, we obtain probability maps for each sub-task. Then we train the integration network from those maps. In experiments, we evaluate the segmentation accuracy on the CamVid dataset which contains 11 classes. We divide all classes to 3 classes; easy, normal, and difficult classes. We compared our method with conventional method using all classes. We confirmed that the proposed method outperformed the conventional method.

Keywords: Semantic segmentation · U-net · Sub-tasks
Integration of classifiers and difficulty level

1 Introduction

In recent years, many researchers are doing research on semantic segmentation because it can be applied to CT segmentation, cancer segmentation and automatic driving. Famous semantic segmentation methods are Fully Convolutional Networks (FCN) [1] and encoder-decoder CNN. FCN consists of convolution layers and upsampling layers to recover the spatial information. Famous encoder-decoder CNN is the SegNet [2]. However, small objects and correct location of objects are vanished in encoder part. Thus, U-net [3] used skip connections between encoder and decoder to compensate for the information.

The state-of-the-art semantic segmentation methods are based on deeper CNN [4–8]. ResNet [5] which is state-of-the-art network for image classification is frequently used as feature extractor for segmentation. ResNet used residual block with the shortcut connection enabled deeper feature extraction.

Deeper CNN is effective to extract features but is not tackle multi-scale. Thus, there are some methods using multi-scale [9–14]. Dilated convolution [9] is one of the most mainstream examples to tackle the multi-scale problem by wide range feature extraction. PSPNet [10] achieved high accuracy by using the dilated convolution for semantic

© Springer Nature Switzerland AG 2018
G. Bebis et al. (Eds.): ISVC 2018, LNCS 11241, pp. 607–615, 2018.
https://doi.org/10.1007/978-3-030-03801-4_53

segmentation. However those methods tackle multi-scale problems from single image but they did not pay attention the difficulty levels of classes.

In general, when the number of classes is large or when the appearance of objects frequency changes, the segmentation accuracy decreases. However, there are some methods to address the problem [15–17]. Curriculum learning [15] is the method which trains from easy task to difficult task. Deep layer cascade [16] used cascade IRNet (extended ResNet architecture) [17], and segmentation is carried out step by step according to difficulty levels. Dividing a task into sub-tasks is applicable to various methods and datasets because many datasets include easy and difficult classes for classification.

In this paper, we propose to divide the classification problem of all classes into sub-classification problems according to difficulty level. We define difficult classes as follows. Difficult class consists of small number of pixels in an image. In addition, the frequency of appearance of the difficult class is low in dataset. When we divide all classes into some difficulty levels, we use the number of pixels of each class in dataset.

We train deep neural network for each difficulty level. Probability maps obtained from each network are fed into an integration network, and final segmentation result is obtained. Of course, all networks are trained by end-to-end manner.

In this paper, we used the CamVid dataset [18] which contains 11 classes. We divide 11 classes into 3 difficulty levels according to the number of pixels in each class; easy, normal and difficult classes. Easy class includes 4 classes with large number of pixels and difficult class includes 3 classes with small number of pixels. Remaining classes are included into normal class. Our method outperformed the conventional method using only one CNN with all classes.

This paper is organized as follows. In Sect. 2, we explain the details of the proposed method. Section 3 shows experimental results. We compare our method with conventional method without difficulty levels. In Sect. 4, we describe conclusion and future works.

2 Proposed Method

Figure 1 shows that our proposed method consists of 2 parts; training a network for each sub-task and training an integration network. By training the network for each difficulty level, we obtain probability maps for each sub-task. Then we train the integration network from those maps. Of course, we train all network by end-to-end manner.

In Sect. 2.1, we explain how to train each difficulty level. Section 2.2 shows the details of an integration network. Finally, Sect. 2.3 describes implementation details.

2.1 Training Each Difficulty Level

Our method divides all classes into some difficulty levels. In generally, if the number of pixels of a certain class is large, the class is easy to segment. On the other hand, if the number of pixels is small, segmentation of the class is difficult. Thus, we divide all classes into some difficulty levels according to the number of pixels in each class.

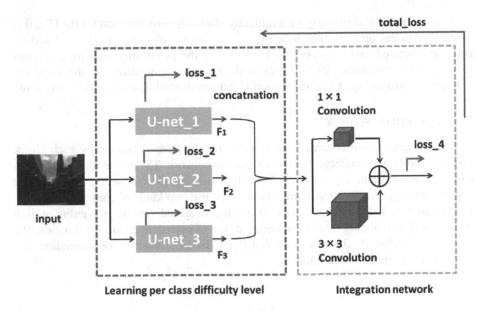

Fig. 1. Overview of the proposed method using some difficulty levels. The network consists of two parts; training each difficulty level and integration network.

Figure 2 is the example of the CamVid dataset which contains 11 classes. In this experiment, since the memory of GPU is only 8 GB, we divide 11 classes into 3 categories; easy, normal and difficult classes. Easy class has the top 4 number of pixels. Difficult class has the least 3 number of pixels. The remaining 4 classes are included into normal class. When we divide all classes into some difficulty levels, each category must be constructed from the classes with similar number of pixels. If the number of pixels is quite different in one difficulty level, easy and difficult classes are generated in one category.

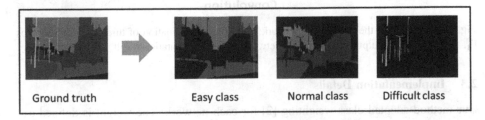

Fig. 2. Example of the CamVid dataset. From left to right images show ground truth, easy class, normal class, and difficult class. Easy class includes *Sky, Building, Road and Tree*. Normal class includes *Pavement, Sign, Fence and Car*. Difficult class includes *Pole, Pedestrian and Bicyclist*.

U-net is used for classifying each difficulty class. The loss function for the U-nets is softmax-cross-entropy. As shown in Fig. 1, the outputs of U-net_1, U-net_2 and U-net_3 are denoted as F_1, F_2 and F_3. F represents the probability map by a softmax function. The input image for all U-nets is the same but annotations are different. The red squared area in Fig. 1 optimizes each U-net corresponding to each difficulty level.

2.2   Integration Network

Semantic segmentation is carried out from probability maps obtained by each U-net. Figure 3 shows the architecture of the integration network. The probability maps F_1, F_2 and F_3 are concatenated, and they fed into the integration network. We optimize convolution layer in the integration network. We use two kinds of convolution layers; 1×1 and 3×3. 1×1 convolution means the weighted sum of probability at each pixel. 3×3 convolution means the weighted sum of probabilities in a local region. We obtain final probability by a softmax function. The loss function for integration networks is also softmax-cross-entropy.

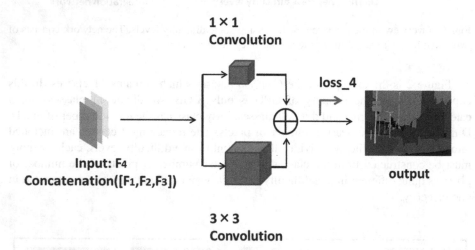

Fig. 3. Overview of the integration network. F_4 is the concatenation of three probability maps F_1, F_2 and F_3. The output of integration network is the segmentation result.

2.3   Implementation Details

Our method adopted class weighting [2] for each network. The weight is defined as

$$w_c = median\,frequency/frequency\,(c) \tag{1}$$

where median frequency is the median of frequencies of all classes. The frequency(c) represents the number of pixels of class c in training images. Class weighting sets the weight by the ratio of the total amount number of pixels. When we train the whole network, we minimize total loss function as follows.

$$total\_loss = loss\_1 + loss\_2 + loss\_3 + loss\_4 \tag{2}$$

where total_loss is the sum of loss of each network. Thus, our method enables to train each difficulty level. Table 1 shows the architecture, difficulty level, class weighting and loss function. In Table 1, Class_weight_1, Class_weight_2 and Class_weight_3 are class weighting calculated from the annotation of each difficulty level.

Table 1. Details of architecture, difficulty level, class weighting and loss.

Architecture	Difficulty level	Class weighting	loss
U-net_1	Easy	Class_weight_1	loss_1
U-net_2	Normal	Class_weight_2	loss_2
U-net_3	Difficult	Class_weight_3	loss_3
Integration network	All classes	Class_weight	loss_4

3 Experiments

In this section, we compared our method with conventional method without class difficulty level. We evaluate the accuracy by mean Intersection over Union (IoU). IoU which is computed as

$$IoU = TP/TP + FN + FP \tag{3}$$

where TP, FN, and FP denote true positive, false negative, and false positive. Thus, IoU represents the overlap ratio between semantic segmentation result and ground truth annotation. In Sect. 3.1, we explain experimental setting and dataset. In Sect. 3.2, we show experimental results.

3.1 Experimental Setting

We evaluate our method on the CamVid dataset for urban scene understanding. CamVid dataset contains 11 classes and 701 images (367 training, 101 validation and 233 test images) and image size is 360×480 pixels. We set batch size to 2 due to the memory of GPU and learning rate is set to 1e-3.

Our method divides all classes into some difficulty levels according to the number of pixels in each class. Table 2 shows total number of pixels in training set. In this experiment, since the memory of GPU is 8 GB, we tried only two and three difficulty levels. In the case of two difficulty levels, easy class includes *Sky, Building, Road, Tree* and *Car. D*ifficult class includes *Pole, Pavement, Sign, Pedestrian* and *Bicyclist*. When we used three difficulty levels, easy class includes *Sky, Building, Road and Tree*, normal class includes *Pavement, Sign, Fence and Car* and difficult class includes *Pole, Pedestrian and Bicyclist*.

Table 2. Total number of pixels in each class of training dataset.

Class	Sky	Building	Pole	Road	Pavement
Number of pixels	21,365,534	29,500,158	1,246,698	40,153,760	5,690,170

Tree	Sign	Fence	Car	Pedestrian	Bicyclist
12,333,524	1,487,718	1,429,190	7,439,754	810,770	369,934

3.2 Evaluation Results

Table 3 shows the accuracy of the proposed method and conventional method on IoU. U-net, Our(2) and Our(3) denote only one U-net, our method using two difficulty levels and the proposed method using three difficulty levels. The IoU in Table 3 is the average of three times evaluations because the accuracy of deep learning changes according to the initial weight. As shown in Table 3, the proposed method improved mean IoU over 2% in comparison with the U-net without difficulty levels. Especially, *Fence, Pedestrian* and *Bicyclist* improved more than 5%. Those classes belong to difficult class or normal class. The result shows that our method is effective for relatively difficult classes.

Table 3. Result on CamVid datset.

	Sky	Building	Pole	Road	Pavement	Tree	Sign	Fence	Car	Pedestrian	Bicyclist	Mean IoU
U-net	91.2	76.1	**29.4**	88.5	71.0	68.5	32.9	32.2	66.4	41.9	32.2	57.4
Our(2)	**91.5**	**76.3**	28.4	89.4	71.5	70.2	**35.3**	33.2	**69.6**	45.2	**39.6**	59.1
Our(3)	90.9	**76.3**	29.2	**89.5**	**72.7**	**70.4**	33.0	**38.2**	69.3	**47.0**	39.5	**59.6**

When we compare Our(2) with Our(3), *Sign* class of Our(2) is especially higher than Our(3). *Sign* class belongs to difficult class in Our(3) but the number of pixels of *Sign* class is the least in the difficulty class. Thus, the class weight was small and the accuracy may decrease. In Our(2), *Sign* class also belongs to difficulty level but the number of pixels is middle in the level, and the class weight is not so small. We consider that this is the reason why Sign class in Our(3) is worse than that in Our(2).

Figure 4 shows segmentation results by Our(3) and single U-net. Figure shows that proposed method can reduce noise in comparison with conventional U-net. For example, we see that the noise in *Car* class decreased and the accuracy of difficult class such as *Pedestrian* and *Fence* is improved.

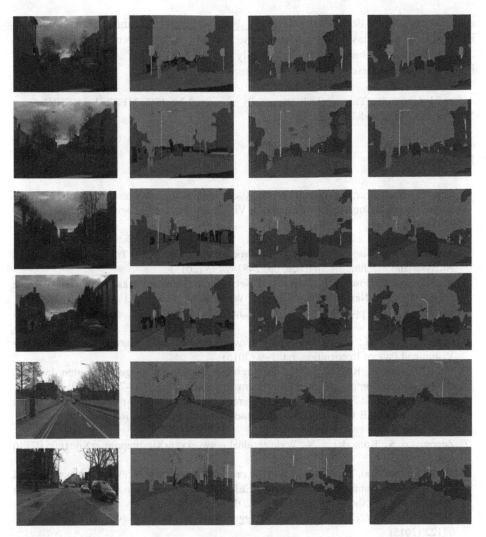

Fig. 4. Segmentation results on the CamVid dataset. From left to right images show input image, ground truth, single U-net and our proposed method using three difficulty levels.

4   Conclusion

In this paper, we proposed semantic segmentation by integrating classifiers for different difficulty levels. The proposed method improved the accuracy in comparison with conventional method without difficulty levels. The effectiveness of division of difficulty levels is demonstrated by experiments.

However, the mean IoU score of our method was not the state of the art because the network for each difficulty level is not so deep. We should use deeper baseline network such as ResNet [5]. In addition, although we used the U-net with the same structure for each difficulty level, deeper network is suitable to difficult class and shallower network is suitable to easy class. We should use the network with different structure for each difficulty level. Furthermore, we will apply our method to the segmentation of cell images [14, 19]. These are subjects for future works.

Acknowledgements. This research is partially supported by JSPS/MEXT KAKENHI Grant Number 18K11382 and 18H04746.

References

1. Long, J., Shelhamer, E., Darrell, T.: Fully convolutional networks for semantic segmentation. In: IEEE Conference on Computer Vision and Pattern Recognition, pp. 3431–3440 (2015)
2. Badrinarayanan, V., Kendall, A., Cipolla, R.: SegNet: a deep convolutional encoder-decoder architecture for image segmentation. In: Proceedings of the IEEE Transactions on Pattern Analysis and Machine Intelligence, pp. 2481–2495 (2017)
3. Ronneberger, O., Fischer, P., Brox, T.: U-Net: convolutional networks for biomedical image segmentation. In: Navab, N., Hornegger, J., Wells, W.M., Frangi, A.F. (eds.) MICCAI 2015. LNCS, vol. 9351, pp. 234–241. Springer, Cham (2015). https://doi.org/10.1007/978-3-319-24574-4_28
4. Szegedy, C., et al.: Going deeper with convolutions. In: IEEE Conference on Computer Vision and Pattern Recognition, pp. 1–9 (2015)
5. He, K., Zhang, X., Ren, S., Sun, J.: Deep residual learning for image recognition. In: IEEE Conference on Computer Vision and Pattern Recognition, pp. 770–778 (2016)
6. Xie, S., Girshick, R., Dollár, P., Tu, Z.: Aggregated residual transformations for deep neural networks. In: IEEE Conference on Computer Vision and Pattern Recognition, pp. 5987–5995 (2017)
7. Zagoruyko, S., Komodakis, N.: Wide residual networks. arXiv preprint arXiv:1605.07146 (2016)
8. Jégou, S., Drozdzal, M., Vazquez, D.: The one hundred layers tiramisu: fully convolutional densenets for semantic segmentation. In: IEEE Conference on Computer Vision and Pattern Recognition Workshops, pp. 1175–1183 (2017)
9. Yu, F., Koltun, V.: Multi-scale context aggregation by dilated convolutions. arXiv:1511.07122 (2015)
10. Zhao, H., Shi, J., Qi, X., Wang, X.: Pyramid scene parsing network. In: IEEE Conference on Computer Vision and Pattern Recognition, pp. 2881–2890 (2017)
11. Chen, L.C., Papandreou, G., Kokkinos, I., Murphy, K., Yuille, A.-L.: DeepLab: semantic image segmentation with deep convolutional nets, atrous convolution, and fully connected CRFs. IEEE Trans. Pattern Anal. Mach. Intell. **40**, 834–848 (2018)
12. Chen, L.C., Papandreou, G., Schroff, F., Adam, H.: Rethinking atrous convolution for semantic image segmentation. arXiv preprint arXiv:1706.05587 (2017)
13. Lin, G., Milan, A., Shen, C., Reid, I.: RefineNet: multi-path refinement networks for high-resolution semantic segmentation. In: IEEE Conference on Computer Vision and Pattern Recognition, vol. 1, no. 2, p. 5 (2017)
14. Hiramatsu, Y., Hotta, K., Matsuda, M., Terai, K., Imanishi, A.: Cell image segmentation by integrating multiple CNNs. In: IEEE Conference on Computer Vision and Pattern Recognition Workshops, pp. 2205–2211 (2018)

15. Bengio, Y., Louradour, J., Collobert, R., Weston, J.: Curriculum learning. In: International Conference on Machine Learning, pp. 1–127. ACM (2009)
16. Li, X., Liu, Z., Luo, P., Loy, C.C., Tang, X.: Not all pixels are equal: difficulty-aware semantic segmentation via deep layer cascade. In: IEEE Conference on Computer Vision and Pattern Recognition, p. 2 (2017)
17. Szegedy, C., Ioffe, S., Vanhoucke, V., Alemi, A.A.: Inception-v4, Inception-ResNet and the impact of residual connections on learning. In: AAAI Conference on Artificial Intelligence, p. 12 (2017)
18. Brostow, G.J., Shotton, J., Fauqueur, J., Cipolla, R.: Segmentation and recognition using structure from motion point clouds. In: Forsyth, D., Torr, P., Zisserman, A. (eds.) ECCV 2008. LNCS, vol. 5302, pp. 44–57. Springer, Heidelberg (2008). https://doi.org/10.1007/978-3-540-88682-2_5
19. Hayashi, Y., et al.: Automated adherent cell elimination by a high-speed laser mediated by a light-responsive polymer. bioRxiv 280487 (2018)

Applications II

Fast Image Dehazing Methods for Real-Time Video Processing

Yang Chen and Deepak Khosla$^{(\boxtimes)}$

HRL Laboratories, LLC, Malibu, CA 90265, USA
dkhosla@hrl.com

Abstract. Images of outdoor scenes are usually degraded by atmospheric particles, such as haze, fog and smoke, which fade the color and reduce the contrast of objects in the scene. This reduces image quality for manual or automated analysis in a variety of outdoor video surveillance applications, for example threat or anomaly detection. Current dehazing techniques, based on atmospheric models and frame-by-frame approaches, perform reasonably well, but are slow and unsuitable for real-time processing. This paper addresses the need for an online robust and fast dehazing algorithm that can improve video quality for a variety of surveillance applications. We build upon and expand state of the art dehazing techniques to develop a robust real-time dehazing algorithm with the following key characteristics and advantages: (1) We leverage temporal correlations and exploit special haze models to achieve 4× speed-up over the baseline algorithm [1] with no loss in detection performance, (2) We develop a pixel-by-pixel approach that allows us to retain sharp detail near object boundaries, which is essential for both manual and automated object detection and recognition applications, (3) We introduce a method for estimating global atmospheric lighting which makes it very robust for a variety of outdoor applications, and (4) We introduce a simple and effective sky segmentation method for improving the global atmospheric light estimation which has the effect of mitigating color distortion. We evaluate our approach on video data from multiple test locations, demonstrate both qualitative and quantitative improvements in image quality, and object detection accuracy.

Keywords: Dehazing · Surveillance · Threat detection · Real-time surveillance
Atmospheric model · Sky segmentation

1 Introduction

Images of outdoor scenes are usually degraded by atmospheric particles, such as haze, fog and smoke, which fade the color and reduce the contrast of the objects, depending on the distances of the scene points from the camera. Poor visibility and image quality is a major problem for outdoor video surveillance applications.

Haze removal is difficult because the amount of visible haze is dependent on the scene depth. The depth information is unknown given only a single image, making the dehazing problem ill-posed. Even when the depth information can be estimated, noise can be a major problem when restoring hazy images. Standard image enhancement algorithms such as histogram equalization, linear mapping, and gamma correction

© Springer Nature Switzerland AG 2018
G. Bebis et al. (Eds.): ISVC 2018, LNCS 11241, pp. 619–628, 2018.
https://doi.org/10.1007/978-3-030-03801-4_54

introduce halo artifacts and color distortion. Existing dehazing approaches rely on sophisticated numerical optimization algorithms, which result in high computational cost and cannot satisfy real-time application requirements, especially for a high-resolution video surveillance system.

There have been several attempts to remove haze and enhance the visibility of images. Some researchers rely on additional information, including multiple images of the same scene taken under various atmospheric conditions or under different polarization angles, and depth-map or a 3D model obtained by user assistance. These kinds of methods are very constraining for data acquisition and are unable to deal with dynamic scenes limiting their practicality for outdoor applications.

Recent work on single image dehazing has made significant progress. He et al. [2] proposes dark channel prior for single image haze removal. A coarse estimation of the transmission map is obtained by dark pixels in local windows and then refined by an image soft-matting technique. Fattal [4] obtains the transmission map through independent component analysis by assuming that transmission and surface shading are locally uncorrelated. Tan [3] aims to maximize the local contrast by developing a cost function in the framework of Markov random fields (MRFs). The common problem of above methods is that they are too slow for real-time applications. For example, the method of He et al. [2] takes approximately 250 s for a 3000 by 400 image on modern computer (CPU is Intel core i7 2.67 GHz). Besides, the method of Fattal [4] is reported to have bad performance for heavy haze images and the method of Tan [3] suffers from very saturated scene.

Tarel et al. [1] propose a very simple and elegant median filter-based algorithm to solve the single image dehazing problem. It is much faster compared to [2–4] since its complexity is only a linear function of the number of input image pixels. However, it still takes 0.6 s on the same CPU for an image of 3000 by 400 pixels. In addition, Tarel's method estimates the global atmospheric light from the pixels with high intensity, which may lead to incorrect global atmospheric light estimation due to white objects in the scene. There has been a flurry of recent work in deep learning for image dehazing, but the best methods still need training data or semantic information about objects in the scene.

This paper is based on estimating the atmospheric model, and provides a fast dehazing approach for video sequences suitable for real-time applications with high resolution videos. The basic idea is based on a state of the art algorithm that uses a median-filter-based single image dehazing algorithm [1]. The atmospheric veil is first roughly estimated by the minimal component of color channel and then refined by median filter to smooth and preserve sharp edge discontinuities. In addition, we propose a simple and effective sky segmentation to improve the global atmospheric light estimation and prevent color distortion. We exploit temporal correlations between successive image frames in a video sequence to reduce redundant calculations and improve processing speed. We also exploit the special imaging condition of landscape scene to simplify the estimation of atmospheric model; therefore further improving processing speed.

The main advantage of our method is its speed and no reliance on training data. We apply the single-image based de-haze algorithm periodically to estimate the key parameters, which will be re-used for subsequent frames, reducing re-calculation.

In addition, temporal correlation is applied to determine the differences of pixels in sub-sequences. If the region in the current frame is similar to the co-located region in the previous frame, the stored corresponding result can be re-used. By applying a rough sky segmentation step to estimate the global atmospheric lighting, our method can achieve similar or better quality results as the original algorithm with 4× speed-ups, making it suitable for real-time applications. Moreover, our approach works on a per pixel basis. This allows us to retain sharp details near object boundaries.

2 Approach

In the following sections, we first describe the basic steps in Tarel et al. [1]. Then we introduce our optimized approaches for real-time video processing. Figure 1 shows a high-level flowchart of the proposed approach.

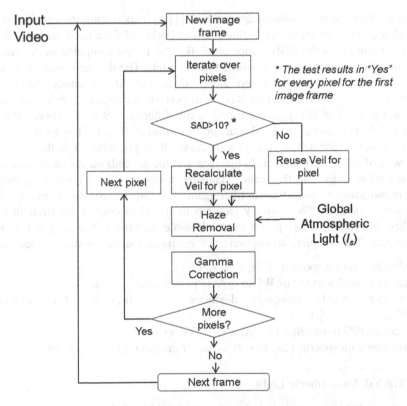

Fig. 1. High-level flowchart of the proposed dehazing algorithm.

2.1 Atmospheric Scattering Model

The atmospheric scattering model [5] is used to describe a hazy image, as shown in Eq. (1).

$$I(x,y) = R(x,y)\left(1 - \frac{V(x,y)}{I_s}\right) + V(x,y) \tag{1}$$

where $I(x, y)$ is the input hazy image at (x, y); $R(x, y)$ is the dehazed (or restored) image; I_s is the global atmospheric light; and $V(x, y)$ is the atmospheric veil, also called the transmission map. I_s is usually set to (1, 1, 1) assuming that the input image $I(x, y)$ is normalized between 0 and 1. Since the accuracy of the global atmospheric light I_s plays an important role in the restoration process, we propose a simple but more robust method for its estimation, which will be discussed later.

2.2 Atmospheric Veil

We adopt the median filter-based approach of [1] by maximizing the contrast to infer atmospheric veil from input image. Since atmospheric veil for a pixel cannot be higher than the minimum of the RGB components, $W(x,y)$ is first computed as the image of the minimal component of $I(x, y)$ over RGB channels. The dehazed image is assumed to be smooth in most regions except along edges with large intensity discontinuity. Therefore, median filter is used on $W(x, y)$ to perform an edge preserving smoothing. The atmospheric veil $V(x, y)$ is computed as the difference, $B(x, y)$, between the local average of $W(x, y)$ and of the local standard deviation of $W(x, y)$. The local average of $W(x, y)$ is thus computed as $A(x, y) = \text{median}_s (W(x, y))$, where s is the size of the window used in the median filter. In practice, s value depends on the maximum size of assumed white objects in the scene. Standard deviation $|W(x,y) - A(x,y)|$ must be robustly estimated by using median filter again. The last step consists of multiplying B $(x, y) = A - \text{median}_s (|W - A|)$ by factor p in [0, 1] to control the strength of the visibility restoration, where p is a user selectable parameter. We set p = 0.7 in our experiments. The complete atmospheric veil estimation steps are summarized below:

1. Calculate min component, $W(x,y) = \min(I(x,y))$.
2. Calculate local average of $W(x,y)$, $A(x, y) = \text{median}_s (W(x, y))$.
3. Calculate local standard deviation of $W(x,y)$, $S(x,y) = \text{median}_s (|W(x,y) - A(x,y)|)$.
4. Calculate difference, $B(x,y) = A(x,y) - S(x,y)$.
5. Calculate atmospheric veil, $V(x,y) = \max(\min(pB(x,y), W(x,y)), 0)$.

2.3 Global Atmospheric Light

In [1], the global atmospheric light is estimated by white (bright) regions in the image, which are usually part of the sky. To avoid any undesired effect on bright objects in the scene, this method relies on choosing a suitable window size for the median filter. However, this is not a robust approach since incorrect estimation of global atmospheric light could distort colors in dehazed images.

We adopt a simple approach to roughly estimate the sky region. We assume the sky is free of larger gradients and at the top of image. We search regions which have small gradients in image intensity and border the upper portions of the image. The global atmospheric light is then selected as the average of K% of the brightest pixels in these regions. Typically K is chosen to be 5%.

2.4 Recovery of Hazy Image

Since the global atmospheric light I_s and the atmospheric veil V(x, y) are inferred, according to Eq. (1), we can recover hazy image by

$$R(x,y) = \frac{I(x,y) - V(x,y)}{1 - \frac{V(x,y)}{I_s}} \tag{2}$$

The image after haze removal looks dim and therefore gamma correction can be applied for contrast enhancement.

2.5 Optimized Dehazing with Acceleration

In surveillance applications with a fixed video camera operating at a nominal 30 Hz rate, background mostly does not change between successive frames. This makes it possible to accelerate dehazing by re-using computed results between neighboring frames. If the pixels in the current frame are similar to the co-located pixels in the previous frame, the stored results computed from previous frame are re-used for the corresponding pixels in the current frame, therefore bypassing the calculation for the background region of the current frame. We use Sum of Absolute Differences (SAD) with a 5 by 5 window size to determine if a pixel is similar to its co-located corresponding pixel in the previous frame. We use luminance channel to calculate SAD. If the SAD is less than pre-defined threshold (e.g., chosen as a value of 10 in all of our experiments), the entire 5 by 5 block is considered "similar". The calculation for this block is skipped and the previous results of corresponding block are filled in. Moreover, since illumination is almost similar between temporal successive frames, the parameters of gamma correction can also be re-used for other frames. In order to deal with illumination changes over time for long-term surveillance, the parameters of gamma correction are updated every N frames, where typically $N \sim 200$ frames.

2.6 Optimization Using Scene Constraints

A second way to apply dehazing to video sequences for improved object detection uses information about expected certain scene conditions. Figure 2 shows a frame of the high-resolution video collected from stationary camera in our surveillance application. This is an example of scene of a large landscape of mostly flat ground with or without mountain in the far distance. The horizontal axis of the image runs parallel to the horizon line. In this situation, the haze caused by the atmosphere, or light fog, is uniform across the horizon, and decreases monotonically (or at least non-increasingly) with the increase in image row coordinates (counting rows from the top of the image).

Given this assumption, we can bypass veil estimation approach described in Atmospheric Veil, and use a single value to represent the veil for each row of the image. Furthermore, the veil value for each row can be estimated based on the minimal value of the image color components of that row (see Atmospheric Veil for discussion). This is a huge saving in computation compared with the approach described in [1]. We can achieve further computational savings by estimating the veil using only a single image frame, and applying it to subsequent image frames, and only updating the veil map infrequently (e.g., every 200 frames) to adapt to slow change in haze/fog conditions.

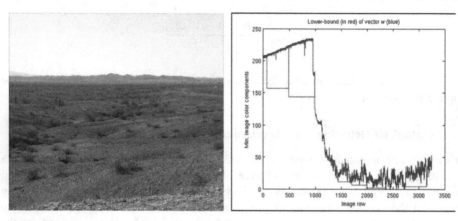

Fig. 2. The original image (left), and the "lower-bound" as the estimates for the veil from the values of vector w (right), which represents the minimum of image color components across each row of the image on the left. The curve in blue represents w, and the curve in red is the "lower-bound". (Color figure online)

Based on the above discussion, we outline below the steps for the dehazing using this specific scene constraint:

1. Take one input image from the input video (e.g., first frame) of size N (row) by M (column). First find the minimal value of all 3 color components and across each image row. Each image row gives one such minimal value. This gives a vector w of size N.
2. Find the lower bound of w, which is a conservative estimate of the monotonically decreasing veil value as a function of image row, let the result vector be z. It has the same size, N, as w (see more details below).
3. Use z as a column, and duplicate horizontally to form an image of N (row) by M (column). This is our veil map of the image, V (see Eqs. (1) and (2)).
4. Recover the input image and each subsequent image in the video sequence according to Eq. (2) using veil map V from Step 3; re-estimate V every 200 frames according Steps 1–3.

In Step 2 above, an approach for finding the "lower-bound" of w is needed. Recall that w is the minimal value of three color components across each row. It is also a non-increasing function of its index, i.e., image row. In real images, w has a "bowl" shape (Fig. 2) with several small ripples that violate our "non-increasing" assumption. We can adopt the same approach as described in the Atmospheric Veil section to filter w to obtain veil.

Here we describe an alternative "lower-bound" process that creates a rough approximation of veil with a "non-increasing" function based on the values of w. An example of this lower-bound can be seen in Fig. 2. The curve in blue represents w, and the curve in red is the "lower-bound". As can be seen, w not only contains ripples, but also some big errors due to sensor defects (e.g., the big downward spike on the left side of curve plot). Our current "lower-bound" algorithm is very simplistic, and can be improved. For example, we can apply smoothing to w to remove small ripples and sensor defects. Furthermore, the "lower-bound" curve beyond rows corresponding to the minimum of w (e.g., near row 2400 in Fig. 2) should stay near zero rather than go back up as shown. Nevertheless, the region in the image to which we apply object detection algorithm is limited to within rows 800 to 2000. Therefore, these improvements will not have much effect on the results shown in the next section.

3 Results

In this section, we describe results of applying our methods for video quality improvement as well as object and threat detection in streaming video applications.

3.1 Optimized Dehazing with Acceleration

We test our algorithm on a video sequence consisting of 200 frames captured by a high-resolution camera. Each frame is 3200×400 pixels. Figure 3 shows a sample of a hazy image (top) and its corresponding dehazed result (bottom).

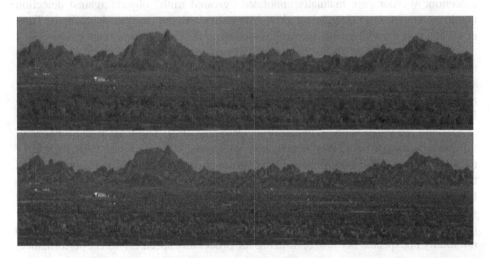

Fig. 3. Image dehazing. Top: Original image extracted from a high-resolution video sequence. Bottom: dehazed image.

Our method implemented on a desktop CPU (Intel core i7 2.67 GHz) processes this sequence in 13.6 s or at about 15 frames/s. In comparison, the technique of Tarel et al. [1] processes frame by frame in 60.6 s or at about 3.3 frames/s. However, as can be observed in Fig. 4, the baseline method [1] tends to introduce artifacts and distorts the color. These problems are mitigated by applying our sky detection to provide a more robust estimate for the global atmospheric light. The result is presented in panel (b) of Fig. 4.

(a)   (b)   (c)

Fig. 4. Comparison between [1] and our algorithm. (a) Original image (b) Dehazed image with our approach, (c) Dehazed image with approach of Tarel et al. [1]. Notice that artifacts are introduced and color distorted in the sky for (c).

We also evaluated the impact of running our dehazing algorithm as a pre-processing step on automated object detection. Since dehazing removes the "veil" due to fog, smoke or atmospheric scatter, we expect that the object detection algorithm will result in improvement in detection performance at the expense of higher computations. We run a deterministic object detection algorithm [6] on video sequences. This detection algorithm is based on modeling the background and using that for change detection. We compare manually annotated "ground truth" objects against detection results generated from the original video, the video with the baseline dehazing of Tarel et al. [1], and the video with accelerated dehazing described in this paper.

We expect that the baseline dehazing will perform the best, but that dehazing with acceleration will generate cases where there is an increase in detection over the original video input, while benefitting from a speed increase over the baseline dehazing, by removing reoccurring costs. Figure 5 presents these results in the form of detection ROC (Receiver Operating Characteristics) curves. The x-axis is the False Alarm Rate (FAR) and the y-axis is the probability of Detection (Pd). The FAR is the number of false detections per hour. We are primarily concerned with the lower FAR regions of the ROC curves. In all experiments, global atmosphere light estimation is not used, and the light source is simply assumed to be white (255,255,255) for 8-bit color images. Figure 5 presents two interesting cases. In the first case, both dehazing and dehazing with optimization improve performance. This is the expected behavior for a hazy image. In the second case, dehazing helps but not dehazing with optimization. This is not totally unexpected because optimizing for processing speed can affect performance.

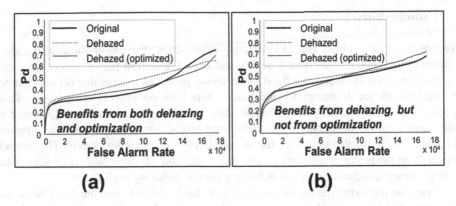

(a)   **(b)**

Fig. 5. Performance comparisons of dehazing algorithms optimized for acceleration of computation. Example sequences where dehazing helps, but optimization may or may not help.

3.2 Optimization Using Scene Constraints

We applied this algorithm to 19 video sequences collected during field test for an object detection application developed under the DARPA Cognitive Technology Threat Warning System (CT2WS). These videos contain static and moving vehicles and dismounts at a range of up to 10 km. An independent evaluation team manually annotated the location of each object in all frames as the ground truth.

The goal of this project was to develop and evaluate automatic visual saliency algorithms to accurately detect and localize all objects. The object detection results are compared against the manually annotated ground truth to compute Pd and FAR. The original and dehazed videos undergo the exact same object detection algorithm. We plot the ROC curves for the original and dehazed videos (Fig. 6). These results show that dehazing achieved approximately 5% increase in Pd at the same FAR compared to the unprocessed video.

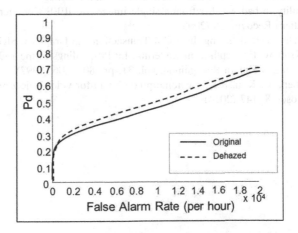

Fig. 6. ROCs of baseline object detection algorithm using original videos vs. dehazed videos. The ROC for dehazed videos has appreciably higher Pd (by 5%) for most of the operating regime.

4 Conclusions

We presented two robust and fast dehazing approaches that are applicable to video sequences to achieve better visual quality and object detection performance. The first approach exploits the fact that a fixed video sensor produces images that do not change in pixel values much except for locations where moving objects are present. This approach is computationally very efficient compared to baseline methods [1] because it infrequently applies dehazing on full-frame images (e.g., every 200 frames) and applies dehazing only to pixels in these frames that are likely to be moving objects. The second approach exploits the constraints of imaging condition of large landscape scenes to further reduce computation, while achieving robust dehazing performance.

Based on our experiments we conclude that the decision to use the first optimized dehazing algorithm should be scene dependent, and only apply to scenes that have visible haze. The performance of the second optimized dehazing algorithm is more robust and does not suffer from this restriction, due to a more conservative estimation of the veil in the image.

Acknowledgement. This material is based upon work supported by DARPA under Contract No. W31P4Q-08-C-0264. The views, opinions and/or findings expressed are those of the author and should not be interpreted as representing the official views or policies of the Department of Defense or the U.S. Government (Distribution Statement "A"-Approved for Public Release, Distribution Unlimited).

References

1. Tarel, J., Hautiere, N.: Fast visibility restoration from a single color or gray level image. In: IEEE 12th International Conference on Computer Vision (2009)
2. He, K., Sun, J., Tang, X.: Single image haze removal using dark channel prior. In: IEEE Conference on Computer Vision and Pattern Recognition (2009)
3. Tan, R.: Visibility in bad weather from a single image. In: IEEE Conference on Computer Vision and Pattern Recognition (2008)
4. Fattal, R.: Single image dehazing. In: ACM Transactions on Graphics, SIGGRAPH (2008)
5. Cozman, F., Krotkov, E.: Depth from scattering. In: Proceedings of the 1997 Conference on Computer Vision and Pattern Recognition, vol. 31, pp. 801–806 (1997)
6. Khosla, D., Chen, Y., Kim, K.: A neuromorphic system for video object recognition. Front. Comput. Neurosci. **8**, 147 (2014)

GPU Accelerated Non-Parametric Background Subtraction

William Porr[1], James Easton[2], Alireza Tavakkoli[3(✉)], Donald Loffredo[4],
and Sean Simmons[4]

[1] University of California-Berkeley, Berkeley, CA 94720, USA
porrliam@gmail.com
[2] University of Texas, Austin, TX 78712, USA
jweaston99@gmail.com
[3] University of Nevada, Reno, Reno, NV 89557, USA
tavakkol@unr.edu
[4] University of Houston-Victoria, Victoria, TX 77901, USA
{LoffredoD,SimmonsS}@uhv.edu

Abstract. Accurate background subtraction is an essential tool for high
level computer vision applications. However, as research continues to
increase the accuracy of background subtraction algorithms, computational efficiency has often suffered as a result of increased complexity.
Consequentially, many sophisticated algorithms are unable to maintain
real-time speeds with increasingly high resolution video inputs. To com-
bat this unfortunate reality, we propose to exploit the inherently parallelizable nature of background subtraction algorithms by making use
of NVIDIA's parallel computing platform known as CUDA. By using
the CUDA interface to execute parallel tasks in the Graphics Processing
Unit (GPU), we are able to achieve up to a two orders of magnitude
speed up over traditional techniques. Moreover, the proposed GPU algorithm achieves over 8x speed over its CPU-based background subtraction
implementation proposed in our previous work [1].

Keywords: Graphics Processing Unit (GPU)
Non-parametric · Background subtraction · CUDA · NVIDIA
Parallel programming

1 Introduction

Accurate separation of foreground from background is essential for many computer vision and video surveillance applications. The separation serves as a basis
from which other, higher level applications can be conducted more efficiently.
Such higher-level applications include tasks such as object tracking or, as what
was done in [5], the segmentation of body parts. The general approach is to create
a statistical model of the background at either each pixel or a larger surrounding region using the known values from the video feed. Then for each incoming

© Springer Nature Switzerland AG 2018
G. Bebis et al. (Eds.): ISVC 2018, LNCS 11241, pp. 629–639, 2018.
https://doi.org/10.1007/978-3-030-03801-4_55

frame, the pixel or region models are referenced using the incoming values. This "referencing" will then return a value which reflects how closely the incoming value corresponds to the background model. Those values with low probabilities of belonging to the background model are to be designated as foreground.

There are more simplistic approaches to background subtraction which result in incredibly fast execution times such as [10], yet these methods often yield segmentation results which cannot be relied upon for higher level applications. On the other hand, there are extremely accurate algorithms, such as [9], that are extremely complex and consequentially suffer from high computational load. One method researchers have used to accelerate the speed of these more sophisticated algorithms is to push some portion of the computation to the GPU. The GPU is designed to handle massively parallel tasks, making it a useful tool in background subtraction processing since each pixel location in a video feed is often able to be processed independently.

The chief innovation of [1] is its ability to strike a crucial balance between speed and accuracy. Here we intend to show the true extent of that balance by incorporating the GPU. The speed and accuracy we are able to achieve make real time video processing more practical for more modern video hardware with higher resolutions and framerates. In this paper we will explain the methods we used to integrate GPU processing into the background subtraction implementation proposed in [1,14]. This scheme develops a pixel-wise non parametric probability density function. This model is then updated by applying dynamic learning weights to observed values in the density function. The rest of the paper is outlined as follows. Section 2 will explain the theory behind the implementation used. Section 3 will explain in detail the construction of the GPU and the CUDA interface. Section 4 will explain the methods used to implement the GPU processing and the strategies used to maximize efficiency. And finally we will have our experimental results in Sect. 5 followed by a conclusion.

2   Non-parametric Background Detection

The scheme used in our previous work [1] creates pixel-wise non-parametric density functions using observed values from the various frames of a video feed. Each function represents the probability density function for one channel of one pixel in the video frame, and this model is updated as new intensities are observed at the pixel location. A model for one channel of location $\mathbf{x}$ can be represented at time t by:

$$\overset{\sim t}{\theta}(\mathbf{x}) = \alpha \overset{\sim t-1}{\theta}(\mathbf{x}^t) - \beta \overset{\sim t-1}{\theta}(\sim \mathbf{x}^t) \tag{1}$$

such that

$$\sum_{i=0}^{D} \overset{\sim t}{\theta}(\mathbf{x}_i) = 1 \tag{2}$$

Where $\mathbf{x}^t$ is the most recently observed channel intensity at location $\mathbf{x}$, $\sim \mathbf{x}^t$ reflects all values in the function that are not $\mathbf{x}^t$, and D is the size of the domain of the function. α is the value by which $\overset{\sim t-1}{\theta}(\mathbf{x^t})$ is updated at time t, and β is the value by which all unobserved values of the function are forgotten. In this sense, α reflects the learning rate of the function, and β the forgetting rate. For our purposes, α and β can be substituted by linear functions, such that:

$$\alpha = \frac{N^{t-1} - (\overset{\sim t-1}{\theta}(\mathbf{x^t}) \cdot N^{t-1})}{(N^{t-1})^2 + N^{t-1}} \tag{3}$$

And

$$\beta = \frac{\overset{\sim t-1}{\theta}(\mathbf{x^t}) \cdot N^{t-1}}{(N^{t-1})^2 + N^{t-1}} \tag{4}$$

Where N^t is the number of samples in the function with relation to time t. These functions reflect decreasing values of α and β which approach 0 as $N \to \infty$. We chose these dynamic values of α and β for the computational efficiency and accuracy it provides. A decreasing learning and forgetting rate allows for the formation of a general model quickly in the beginning of the video sequence since earlier frames will have the largest influence. This rough model is then finely tuned during latter frames of the sequence using the lowered rates.

One may desire for a learning rate which approaches a constant value rather than zero as $N \to \infty$. In that case, the Eq. 1 could be reworked as:

$$\overset{\sim t}{\theta}(\mathbf{x}) = \frac{\alpha \overset{\sim t-1}{\theta}(\mathbf{x^t})}{1+\alpha} + \frac{\overset{\sim t-1}{\theta}(\sim \mathbf{x^t})}{1+\alpha} \tag{5}$$

Where

$$\alpha = \frac{1 + Z \cdot N^{t-1}}{N^{t-1}} \tag{6}$$

Where Z is the constant α will approach as $N \to \infty$. This approach would have the benefit of increased adaptability at later frames.

In order to determine if location $\mathbf{x}$ is a background pixel, the process used in Eq. 1 to model the function at time t is then repeated for the other two channels of pixel $\mathbf{x}$. In order to calculate the probability of $\mathbf{x}$ being a part of the background using the three probabilistic values gathered from Eq. 1, we use the following equation:

$$P(BG|\mathbf{x}) = \overset{\sim t}{\theta}(\mathbf{x_B^t}) \cdot \overset{\sim t}{\theta}(\mathbf{x_G^t}) \cdot \overset{\sim t}{\theta}(\mathbf{x_R^t}) \tag{7}$$

By multiplying these probabilities, we are able to acquire a probabilistic value which assumes a statistical independence at each channel. To decide which values are associated with the background and which are to be considered foreground, we establish a global threshold value th. Now, we determine that pixel $\mathbf{x}$ is a background pixel only if its probability as gathered from Eq. 7 is greater than th. Also, for the purposes of computational efficiency and improving end results, we adopted a parameter σ to serve as a bandwidth for the probability density function. This bandwidth should be chosen in such a way that the effect of random noise in the video sequence is diminished, while avoiding the effects of oversmoothing.

3   Graphics Processing Unit

In an attempt to satiate the market demand for high quality consumer and professional graphics, GPUs have developed into a highly parallel manycore processing unit with high memory bandwidth. In order to leverage this device with such immense parallel computing capabilities, NVIDIA introduced CUDA as a general purpose parallel computing platform which comes with a built in software environment, effectively integrating GPU instruction capabilities into popular programming languages such as C [11]. CUDA allows developers to create and call CUDA functions, known as *kernels*, which are individually executed on the GPU by a specified number of threads in parallel. The number of threads specified is expressed as a number of uniform blocks within a grid, each block containing a chosen number of threads, and a two-dimensional grid containing a number of blocks [11].

The NVIDIA architecture is built around an array of multiprocessors. When a kernel grid is called by a host program, all the threads of an individual block are executed concurrently on one multiprocessor, and each multiprocessor is able to execute one or more blocks depending on the availability of computational resources. In order to manage hundreds of concurrently executing processing threads, NVIDIA incorporates Single-Instruction, Multiple-Thread architecture (SIMT). This architecture manages and instructs groups of 32 threads known as *warps* [11].

The two major pools of memory on a device are the global and shared memory spaces. Global memory is the larger pool accessable by all threads of the device. In contrast, shared memory is only accessable by all the threads within a single block. The reason this distinction is important is because global memory access is much slower than shared memory access, prompting a developer to replace global memory access with shared memory access wherever possible [11].

4   GPU Implementation

As was stated previously, background subtraction inherently possesses an extremely parallelizable processing structure. A simple and popular method commonly used, such as in [2,7,12], is to process an entire frame concurrently by assigning a single thread to each pixel location. In addition to this however, other optimization methods must be used in order to maximize computational efficiency.

4.1   Page-Locked Memory and Cuda Streams

By far the most pressing issue in using both CPU and GPU processing for a single program is memory transfer. More specifically, copying from the host memory to the device memory or vice-versa can have a latency large enough to even *slow down* the processing speed of a single program. For this reason, the proposed method makes use of pinned, or page-locked, memory. Using page-locked memory on the host side ensures that any memory being copied from the host to the device is not swapped out of host memory [13]. The benefit of using this memory is that systems will often have more memory bandwith in host-device transfers and it allows for memory transfers to be executed concurrently with kernel execution [11]. CUDA streams are objects used to manage the concurrent execution of CUDA code, which in this case is concurrent memory transfers and kernel executions. In the proposed method, streams are used such that as the kernel for frame F_t is being executed, the information corresponding following frame F_{t+1} is being sent to the GPU simultaneously. Around the time that the kernel for frame F_t completes, the memory transfer from the device back to the host is executed concurrently with the kernel execution for frame F_{t+1}. The result of this is a partial masking of the latency caused by memory transfers from the host to the device [15].

4.2 Global Memory Accessing

Another major bottleneck in GPU execution is global memory access. Global memory can only be accessed in 32, 64, or 128 byte transactions. Warps coalesce the global memory access of their corresponding threads into one or more of these transactions, the ideal being one transaction per warp [11]. For this reason, the proposed method converts each frame into a four channel image, (BGRR), so that each thread requests for four bytes of information in global memory, resulting in a single 128 byte transaction for each warp and an increase in computational efficiency [7].

5 Experimental Results

For the results, we used two different video sequences from the Changedetection.net 2012 dataset, the PETS2006 video and the smaller highway video [6]. This dataset provides a convenient benchmarking standard that is widely used and closely resembles situations encountered in real life situations, an overview can be found in [6]. We also gathered an HD video for benchmarking purposes. We tested both the original CPU implementation and the GPU implementation together and compared the results. The benchmarks were taken using a 6 core Intel i7-5820k CPU @ 3.30 GHz and a GTX 980 GPU on Windows 10 64-bit. Each test was taken using a single CPU thread (Table 1).

5.1 Our Parameters

We included accuracy results in this paper, but these results were expected to be the same as in [1] because the core algorithm is the same. We chose to include them however because we felt that it would help the reader's understanding when we speak of the algorithm's ability to perform in terms of accuracy. The parameters we used for our core algorithm are as follows. We set our bandwidth

Table 1. Method results

Video	CPU implementation	GPU implementation	Speedup
Highway (320×240)	882.82 FPS	3834.93 FPS	4.34x
PETS2006 (720×576)	155.44 FPS	849.26 FPS	5.46x
HD video (1920×1080)	21.94 FPS	179.20 FPS	8.17x

to 42.67 and $th = 0.03$, which proved to provide the speed and accuracy required. We updated each probability density function at every interval of 8 frames. We found that this combination produced the best results in all of our test cases, as it strikes a balance between speed and accuracy.

5.2 Choice of Other Methods

We used the top three state-of-the-art algorithms from the Change Detection workshop at CVPR 2014, to test against our program in terms of accuracy, SOBS [9], ViBe [4], and the Zipfian method [10]. The purpose of this comparison is to show how our algorithm performs relative to established methods, facilitating the process of judging our method's value in the field of computer vision. SOBS was chosen to serve as an example of the relative upper boundary in segmentation precision possible today, which is coupled by its often slow computational times. On the other end of the spectrum, the Zipfian method was chosen as an example of the relative upper boundary in computational time. ViBe was chosen as one of the better-established methods which seeks to strike the same balance between computational speed and precision as we do in this paper.

5.3 Parameters of Other Methods and Specifications

The parameters of SOBS are $e1 = 1.0$, $e2 = 0.008$, $c1 = 1.0$, $c2 = 0.05$; any parameters not listed were left at default as given in [8]. For ViBe, the opencv C++ implementation was used to gather the results. We acquired the source code from [3] and left the parameters at their default values. The parameters of the C implementation of the ZipFian method were left at the default values set by the author who kindly provided the source code. The raw TP, FP, FN, and TN numbers were computed using the C++ comparator program provided by changedetection.net. The ViBe and Zipfian methods were built from source and tested on Linux Mint 18 Cinnamon 64-Bit with Linux Kernel version 4.4.0-21-generic, while the SOBS method was tested on Windows 10 using the executable found on the author's website [8].

5.4 Qualitative Comparisons

Figures 1, 2, and 3 show the comparison between the qualitative results on frames for each method in each category, in the order of GroundTruth, SOBS, Our Method, ViBe, and ZipFian. As it can be seen, our proposed method produces competitive results with much faster frame rates in all categories.

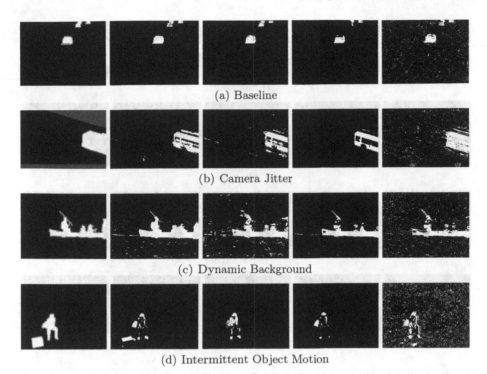

(a) Baseline

(b) Camera Jitter

(c) Dynamic Background

(d) Intermittent Object Motion

Fig. 1. Qualitative Results Comparison between methods. From left, GroundTruth, SOBS, Our Method, ViBe, and ZipFian.

5.5   Quantitative Comparisons

Table 2 shows the comparison of various measurements from our proposed technique with those of the top 4 performing methods from the Change Detection Competition. We observed that the sequences where our method struggled the most are those which incorporate camera jittering or turbulence, which are also categories that algorithms like ViBe excel at. The ViBe implementation randomly incorporates spatial information from the surrounding area when processing pixels, which allows it to excel in sequences where there are small camera displacements or poor image quality. That being said however, our algorithm produces competitive results in other categories, especially in terms of F-Measure. Also, the CPU to GPU speedup of our implementation at higher resolutions still exceeds those reported by ViBe. It is likely that the ViBe algorithm does not scale as well to higher resolutions using the GPU because of the extra processing and memory transfer required to incorporate spatial information. Our algorithm however does not suffer from this burden.

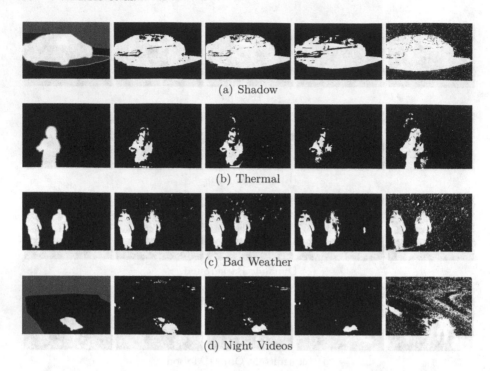

(a) Shadow

(b) Thermal

(c) Bad Weather

(d) Night Videos

Fig. 2. Qualitative Results Comparison between methods. From left, GroundTruth, SOBS, Our Method, ViBe, and ZipFian.

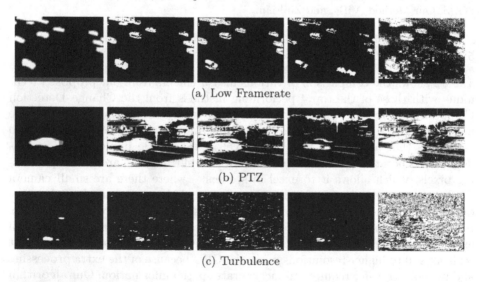

(a) Low Framerate

(b) PTZ

(c) Turbulence

Fig. 3. Qualitative Results Comparison between methods. From left, GroundTruth, SOBS, Our Method, ViBe, and ZipFian.

Table 2. Method results

		Results					Results		
		SOBS	Our	ViBe	ZipFian		SOBS	Our	ViBe	ZipFian
Baseline	Recall	0.771	0.609	0.534	0.648	**Bad Weather**	0.569	0.643	0.434	0.787
	Specificity	0.998	0.996	0.998	0.856		0.997	0.993	0.996	0.855
	FPR	0.001	0.003	0.001	0.143		—	0.006	—	0.144
	FNR	0.228	0.390	0.465	0.351		0.430	0.356	0.565	0.212
	PWC	0.902	1.989	1.954	15.278		0.872	1.277	1.287	14.630
	F-Measure	0.839	0.709	0.680	0.296		0.666	0.609	0.555	0.236
	Precision	0.920	0.868	0.994	0.23		0.835	0.618	0.857	0.166
Jitter	Recall	0.717	0.594	0.452	0.604	**Low Framerate**	0.550	0.419	0.263	0.486
	Specificity	0.972	0.960	0.998	0.869		0.955	0.988	0.982	0.928
	FPR	0.027	0.039	0.011	0.130		0.044	0.011	—	0.071
	FNR	0.282	0.405	0.547	0.359		0.449	0.580	0.736	0.513
	PWC	3.737	5.323	3.311	13.951		5.779	2.873	6.905	8.238
	F-Measure	0.616	0.492	0.521	0.267		0.472	0.379	0.330	0.248
	Precision	0.545	0.429	0.638	0.174		0.548	0.451	0.674	0.184
Dynamic	Recall	0.726	0.636	0.443	0.524	**Night Video**	0.603	0.491	0.283	0.638
	Specificity	0.985	0.979	0.997	0.966		0.958	0.967	0.993	0.862
	FPR	0.014	0.020	—	0.033		0.041	0.032	0.006	0.137
	FNR	0.273	0.363	0.556	0.475		0.396	0.508	0.716	0.361
	PWC	1.643	2.448	0.822	3.840		4.944	4.326	2.147	14.225
	F-Measure	0.528	0.443	0.504	0.215		0.363	0.308	0.331	0.179
	Precision	0.467	0.402	0.671	0.153		0.301	0.267	0.483	0.115
Obj. Motion	Recall	0.549	0.365	0.263	0.357	**PTZ**	0.699	0.582	0.313	0.483
	Specificity	0.901	0.984	0.982	0.946		0.682	0.866	0.904	0.722
	FPR	0.098	0.015	—	0.053		0.317	0.133	0.095	0.277
	FNR	0.450	0.634	0.736	0.642		0.300	0.417	0.686	0.516
	PWC	11.012	6.136	6.905	9.638		31.780	13.681	10.152	28.103
	F-Measure	0.495	0.379	0.330	0.272		0.040	0.195	0.089	0.033
	Precision	0.554	0.691	0.674	0.269		0.021	0.170	0.059	0.018
Shadow	Recall	0.729	0.665	0.545	0.650	**Turbulence**	0.631	0.672	0.578	0.696
	Specificity	0.988	0.975	0.994	0.932		0.994	0.971	0.999	0.898
	FPR	0.011	0.024	0.005	0.067		0.005	0.028	—	0.101
	FNR	0.270	0.334	0.454	0.349		0.368	0.327	0.421	0.303
	PWC	2.234	3.737	2.399	7.912		0.750	3.013	0.269	10.248
	F-Measure	0.731	0.588	0.659	0.407		0.463	0.234	0.674	0.062
	Precision	0.740	0.581	0.874	0.305		0.438	0.163	0.822	0.034
Thermal	Recall	0.482	0.439	0.296	0.639					
	Specificity	0.996	0.990	0.999	0.882					
	FPR	0.003	0.009	—	0.117					
	FNR	0.517	0.560	0.703	0.360					
	PWC	2.641	5.071	4.591	13.570					
	F-Measure	0.594	0.519	0.434	0.391					
	Precision	0.862	0.699	0.984	0.317					

6 Final Thoughts

From the testing results, we can see that our GPU implementation is able to significantly improve the performance of the original CPU implementation. The speedup is not as significant at lower resolution videos, which can be attributed to the latency caused by the transfer of data from the host to the device and vice-versa. The computational power of the gpu is more readily seen in higher resolution videos, where the memory transfer latency is less prominent relative to the increased computational demand provided by the extra pixels. In addition, one could easily take the parallelization further by utilizing multiple CPU cores, all of which would run concurrent kernels relative to eachother. The high processing speeds allowed by the algorithm proposed in [1], coupled with the added computational power provided by the GPU allow for a much more practical solution to modern day background subtraction. Real time background subtraction has become more difficult as video sequences have grown in both frame-rate and pixel resolution, which would often require expensive state-of-the-art hardware to run in a reasonable time if one wanted decent accuracy. However, this implementation could process high definition video sequences in real time with fair accuracy while only running on a minimal system. This makes it more applicable to a wider audience of users than other techniques.

7 Conclusions

Here we have proposed a GPU implementation of the background subtraction algorithm proposed in our previous work [1]. In order to make use of the inherently parallelizable nature of background subtraction algorithms, we incorporated GPU processing using NVIDIA's CUDA computing platform. This method significantly improves upon the original cpu implementation, especially in high resolution video sequences. The proposed method also implements many memory optimization methods in order to prevent common bottlenecks caused by latency in memory transfers, including adjustments for memory coalescing and CUDA Streams. The utilization of GPU processing as done here will allow background subtraction algorithms to remain applicable as the consumer and professional markets continue to demand higher quality videos.

Acknowledgments. This material is based upon work supported in part by the U. S. Army Research Laboratory and the U. S. Department of Defense under grant number W911NF-15-1-0024, W911NF-15-1-0455, and W911NF-16-1-0473. This support does not necessarily imply endorsement by the DoD or ARL.

References

1. Non-parametric background detection for video surveillance (2017)
2. Amamra, A., Mouats, T., Aouf, N.: GPU based GMM segmentation of kinect data. In: Proceedings ELMAR-2014, pp. 1–4, September 2014. https://doi.org/10.1109/ELMAR.2014.6923325

3. Barnich, O., Droogenbroeck, M.V.: Vibe source code, original implementation
4. Barnich, O., Droogenbroeck, M.V.: ViBe: a universal background subtraction algorithm for video sequences. IEEE Trans. Image Process. **20**(6), 1709–1724 (2011). https://doi.org/10.1109/TIP.2010.2101613
5. Elgammal, A., Duraiswami, R., Harwood, D., Davis, L.S.: Background and foreground modeling using nonparametric kernel density estimation for visual surveillance. Proc. IEEE **90**(7), 1151–1163 (2002). https://doi.org/10.1109/JPROC.2002.801448
6. Goyette, N., Jodoin, P.M., Porikli, F., Konrad, J., Ishwar, P.: Changedetection.net: a new change detection benchmark dataset. In: 2012 IEEE Computer Society Conference on Computer Vision and Pattern Recognition Workshops, pp. 1–8, June 2012. https://doi.org/10.1109/CVPRW.2012.6238919
7. Liu, D.: GPU accelerated background subtraction. In: 2015 IEEE 16th International Conference on Communication Technology (ICCT), pp. 372–375, October 2015. https://doi.org/10.1109/ICCT.2015.7399860
8. Maddalena, L., Petrosino, A.: Sobs executable for windows
9. Maddalena, L., Petrosino, A.: A self-organizing approach to background subtraction for visual surveillance applications. IEEE Trans. Image Process. **17**(7), 1168–1177 (2008). https://doi.org/10.1109/TIP.2008.924285
10. Manzanera, A.: Σ-Δ background subtraction and the Zipf law. In: Rueda, L., Mery, D., Kittler, J. (eds.) CIARP 2007. LNCS, vol. 4756, pp. 42–51. Springer, Heidelberg (2007). https://doi.org/10.1007/978-3-540-76725-1_5
11. NVIDIA Corporation: CUDA C Programming Guide, 8.0 edn. (2017)
12. Pham, V., Vo, P., Hung, V.T., Bac, L.H.: GPU implementation of extended Gaussian mixture model for background subtraction. In: 2010 IEEE RIVF International Conference on Computing Communication Technologies, Research, Innovation, and Vision for the Future (RIVF), pp. 1–4, November 2010. https://doi.org/10.1109/RIVF.2010.5634007
13. University of Virginia: Choosing Between Pinned and Non-Pinned Memory
14. Wilson, B., Tavakkoli., A.: An efficient non-parametric background modeling technique with CUDA heterogeneous parallel architecture. In: Proceedings of 11th International Symposium on Visual Computing, pp. 210–220, December 2016
15. Zhang, C., Tabkhi, H., Schirner, G.: A GPU-based algorithm-specific optimization for high-performance background subtraction. In: 2014 43rd International Conference on Parallel Processing, pp. 182–191, September 2014. https://doi.org/10.1109/ICPP.2014.27

Budget-Constrained Online Video Summarisation of Egocentric Video Using Control Charts

Paria Yousefi[(✉)] [iD], Clare E. Matthews[iD], and Ludmila I. Kuncheva[iD]

School of Computer Science, Bangor University, Bangor, UK
paria.yousefi@bangor.ac.uk,
http://pages.bangor.ac.uk/~mas00a/activities/Leverhulme/
project_RPG_2015_188.html

Abstract. Despite the existence of a large number of approaches for generating summaries from egocentric video, online video summarisation has not been fully explored yet. We present an online video summarisation algorithm to generate keyframe summaries during video capture. Event boundaries are identified using control charts and a keyframe is subsequently selected for each event. The number of keyframes is restricted from above which requires a constant review and possible reduction of the cumulatively built summary. The new method was compared against a baseline and a state-of-the-art online video summarisation methods. The evaluation was done on an egocentric video database (Activity of Daily Living (ADL)). Semantic content of the frames in the video was used to evaluate matches with ground truth. The summaries generated by the proposed method outperform those generated by the two competitors.

Keywords: Egocentric · Summarisation · Control chart

1 Introduction

Wearable camcorders provide consumers with the ability to record their daily activities all day long. Having a voluminous and at the same time largely redundant stream of frames makes browsing the videos a disagreeable task. A fast-speed, user-friendly system would be required to replace the multitude of video images with a concise set of frames containing valuable information [12]. The system must be capable of generating keyframes from forthcoming data streams. Online video summarisation addresses the issue of generating summary on-the-fly from a video stream, in which the algorithm performs under the constraints of low computational processing time and a limited amount of memory. Such an approach could be useful in applications including monitoring the daily routines

Supported by project RPG-2015-188 funded by The Leverhulme Trust, UK.

G. Bebis et al. (Eds.): ISVC 2018, LNCS 11241, pp. 640–649, 2018.
https://doi.org/10.1007/978-3-030-03801-4_56

of elderly people [14], memory support [9,10,23], and health behavior monitoring such as sedentary behavior [8] or dietary analysis [15].

Nine online video summarisation methods were described and experimentally compared on non-egocentric video in our previous study [11]. While these methods work reasonably well for non-egocentric videos, it is reasonable to expect that loosely defined event boundaries in egocentric videos will render their performance inadequate. Therefore, this paper proposes a new online summarisation method suitable for egocentric video (Fig. 1).

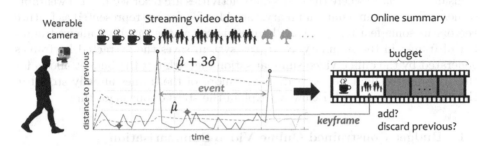

Fig. 1. A sketch of the proposed online video summarisation method for egocentric video. The plot shows the Shewhart chart of the distance between consecutive frames, with the mean μ and the 3σ event-detection boundary, both calculated from the streaming data.

At any moment of the recording video, a valid summary is accessible up to that moment. We required that the new method has low computational complexity and is robust with respect to the feature representation of the video frames. We compare our method against the top-performing online method from our previous study (called 'submodular convex optimisation' [6]) and a baseline method of uniform sampling of events (named 'uniform events').

The rest of the paper is organised as follows: Sect. 2 reviews related works. Our new summarisation method is introduced in Sect. 3, followed by its quantitative evaluation and summarisation examples in Sect. 4. Finally, Sect. 5 offers the conclusions.

2 Related Work

Application-specific surveys provide comprehensive comparisons among existing video summarisation methods on egocentric videos [5] and traditional videos (third-person view) [22]. We recently carried out a survey on online video summarisation for traditional videos [11].

For online applications, typically the video is segmented into smaller units of interest (shots, scenes, events) following two strategies: detecting changes of the content information [1,2,19,22]; or grouping frames into clusters using distribution model [16,21], connectivity model [6,13] or centroid model [3]. Subsequently, keyframes are selected based on their temporal positions [2,19,22]; central positions in clusters [3,6,21] or the relative values of the metric measuring content information [1,13].

The number of keyframes can be either determined by the algorithm itself [1, 2,6,13,16,19,21,22] or defined by some cardinality constraint [3,5,18].

3   Online Video Summarisation

Consider a scenario where the user's daily activities are recorded using a wearable camera. To create an online summary, the video frames are represented as feature vectors in some feature space. A 'budget' is set as the maximal allowed number of frames in the summary. Next, the system saves the extracted keyframes generated by the online video summarisation algorithm if the budget allows for this. Should the limit be reached, one or more of the frames already stored in the summary is removed. Below we explain the steps of our algorithm.

3.1   Budget-Constrained Online Video Summarisation

In statistics, control charts have been used to monitor and control ongoing processes over time. Previously [12], we introduced the use of control charts to identify event boundaries from a streaming video. The closest frame to the center of each event, represented as a cluster in the feature space, is selected as a keyframe. Here, we additionally, impose a constraint on the number of keyframes, hence the term 'budget-constrained' video summarisation. We also introduce a dynamic, similarity threshold into the algorithm that varies the probability of selecting new keyframes according to the number of existing keyframes and total budget. The pseudo-code of the algorithm is given in Algorithm 1[1].

Given an integer constant β, the purpose is to select a set of no more than β keyframes which describe the video as fully and accurately as possible. Unlike the classical summarisation approaches, we derive the summary on-the-go by processing each frame as it comes and selecting keyframes before the full video content is available. The algorithm requires only a limited memory to keep the frames selected thus far, and the frames belonging to the current event.

A control chart is used to detect the event boundaries [20]. The quantity being monitored is the difference between consecutive frames, defined by the distance between the frames in some chosen feature space $\mathbb{R}^L$. Assuming that the frames are represented as points $\mathbb{R}^L$, the hypothesis is that different events in the video are represented by relatively distant clusters. Then transition from one event to the next will be associated with large distance between consecutive frames. As both outlier and transition frames may be detected as an event boundary, we observe a minimum event size, m. If the number of frames in an event is less than m, the algorithm ignores the candidate-event without extracting a

---

[1] Matlab code is available at: https://github.com/pariay/Budget-constrained-Online-Video-Summarisation-of-Egocentric-Video.

Algorithm 1. Budget-constrained online video summarisation

Input: Data stream $F = \{f_1, \ldots, f_N\}, f_i \in \mathbb{R}^L$, initial buffer size b, minimum event length m, threshold parameter for keyframe difference θ, desired number of keyframes β.
Output: Selected set of keyframes $K \subset F, |K| \leq \beta$.

   INITIALISATION
1:   $K \leftarrow \emptyset$
2:   $E \leftarrow \{f_1, \ldots, f_b\}$ $\triangleright$ initial buffer
3:   Calculate the $b - 1$ distances between the consecutive frames in E.
4:   $\mu \leftarrow$ average distance.
5:   $\sigma \leftarrow$ standard deviation.

   PROCESSING OF THE VIDEO
6:   **for** frame number $i = b + 1, \ldots, N$ **do**
7:      $d_i \leftarrow d(f_i, f_{i-1})$ $\triangleright$ calculate distance to previous frame
8:      **if** $d_i <= \mu + 3\sigma$ **then** $\triangleright$ - - - - - - - - - - - - - - - - - - - **same event**
9:         $[\mu, \sigma] \leftarrow$ update μ & σ with d_i
10:       $E \leftarrow E \cup f_i$ $\triangleright$ store the frame
11:      **else if** $|E| < m$ **then** $\triangleright$ - - - - - - - - - - - - - - - - **event too short**
12:         $E \leftarrow f_i$ $\triangleright$ remove frames in E and start a new event
13:      **else** $\triangleright$ - - - - - - - - - - - - **event sufficiently long**
14:         $k \leftarrow$ SELECT-KEYFRAME(E)
15:         **if** K empty **then** $\triangleright$ - - - - - - - - - - - - - - - - - **first keyframe**
16:           $K \leftarrow k$
17:         **else** $\triangleright$ - - k **included if sufficiently different to K**
18:           $k_{last} \leftarrow$ last keyframe in K
19:           $\delta \leftarrow$ KEYFRAME-DIFF(k, k_{last})
20:           $\delta_{min} \leftarrow$ smallest distance among consecutive keyframes in K
21:           **if** $|K| < \beta$ & $\delta >$ DIFF-THRESHOLD$(|K|, i, \theta, \beta, N)$ **then** $\triangleright$ **- in budget**
22:             $K \leftarrow K \cup k$
23:           **else if** $\delta >= \delta_{min}$ **then** $\triangleright$ **over budget**
24:             Remove from K one of the keyframes in the closest pair.
25:             $K \leftarrow K \cup k$
26:         $E \leftarrow f_i$ $\triangleright$ **new event**

   FUNCTIONS

27: **Function** $f =$ SELECT-KEYFRAME$(data)$
28:    $f \leftarrow \underset{x \in data}{\arg \min}\, d(x, \text{mean}(data))$

29: **Function** $\delta =$ KEYFRAME-DIFF(f_1, f_2)
30:    $h_i \leftarrow$ hist16(hue(f_i)) $\triangleright$ Normalised 16-bin Hue histogram
31:    $\delta = \frac{1}{16} \sum\limits_{j=1}^{16} |h_1(j) - h_2(j)|$

32: **Function** $\theta_{new} =$ DIFF-THRESHOLD$(n_k, t, \theta, \beta, T)$
33:    $n_t \leftarrow \beta \times t/T$ $\triangleright$ Expected number of keyframes, assuming linear distribution
34:    **if** $n_t == \beta$ **then**
35:      $\theta_{new} = 0$
36:    **else**
37:      $\theta_{new} \leftarrow \frac{\theta \times (\beta - n_k) + (n_k - n_t)}{\beta - n_t}$

---

keyframe. This approach is suitable for clearly distinguishable shots (events) [12]. For application to egocentric videos, in this paper we adapt the approach to allow for less well-defined shots. In addition, the budget constraint provides a means of defining an expected or desired number of events to be captured. Egocentric videos are not easily split into coherent events. To improve the event detection, we compare a selected keyframe with its immediate predecessor. If the keyframes of the adjacent events are deemed similar, the new event is ignored, without extracting a keyframe. The tolerance for accepting similarity between frames varies in relation to how close to the overall budget the existing set of keyframes is, and how many more events may be expected in the video. Note that this assumes prior knowledge of roughly how long the video will be. If the budget for keyframes is reached while frames are still being captured, keyframes from any additional events are only saved if the keyframe set is made more diverse by the substitution of the new keyframe for an existing keyframe.

Assume a video stream is presented as a sequence of frames, $F = \{f_1, \ldots, f_N\}$, $f_i \in \mathbb{R}^L$, where L indicates the dimensions of the frame descriptor. For any upcoming frame, the similarity of consecutive frames f_i and f_{i-1} is calculated using Euclidean distance $d(.,.)$ in $\mathbb{R}^L$. Denote $d_i = d(f_i, f_{i-1})$. In the process of monitoring quality control, the probability p of an object being defective is known from the product specifications or trading standards. This probability is the quantity being monitored. For the event boundary detection in videos, we need to monitor the distance d_i. The initial values can be calculated by taking average values of the first b distances: $\mu = \frac{1}{b-1} \sum_{i=2}^{b} d_i$, and computing the standard deviation value of the first b distances as: $\sigma = \sqrt{1/(b-1) \sum_{i=2}^{b}(d_i - \mu)^2}$. At time point $i+1$, the distance value d_{i+1} is calculated and compared with the μ and σ at time point i. A change is detected if $d_{i+1} > \mu + \alpha\sigma$. The value of α typically is set to 3, but other alternatives are also possible.

The measure of similarity between two selected adjacent keyframes follows the study of de Avila et al. [4]. Those keyframes are represented by 16-bins histograms of the hue value (H). Keyframes are similar if the Minkowski distance between their normalised histograms is less than a threshold θ, and are dissimilar otherwise.

The proposed algorithm requires four parameters: the initial buffer size (b), the minimum event length (m), the pre-defined threshold value for keyframe similarity (θ), and the maximum number of keyframes (β).

3.2   Choosing Parameter Values

An empirical value for the desired number of the keyframes, β, has been obtained following the study by Le et al. [9]. The authors collected a total of 80 image sets from 16 participants from 9am to 10pm using lifelogging devices. An average of 28 frames per image set were chosen by the participants to represent their day. Therefore, in our experiment we set this parameter to $\beta = 28$. We sample one frame per second for each video. The buffer size b was selected to be equal to one minute, $b = 60$. The minimum event length was set to thirteen seconds, $m = 13$. The threshold value for keyframe similarity was set to $\theta = 0.7$.

3.3 Selecting a Feature Representation

The proposed algorithm is not tailor-made for any particular descriptor, therefore any type of feature space may be applied. For an online application, two factors must be considered when choosing a descriptor: good representation ability and low computational cost. Following a preliminary study involving 7 descriptors, including two convolutional neural networks, we chose the RGB feature space as the best compromise between the two criteria. This work is presented at Computer Graphics and Visual Computing 2018, ("Selecting Feature Representation for Online Summarisation of Egocentric Videos"). The RGB colour moments (mean and standard deviation) are obtained by dividing an image uniformly into 3×3 blocks. The mean and the standard deviation for each block and colour channel are computed, giving a feature space of dimensionality $L = 9 \times 6 = 54$.

4 Experimental Results

4.1 Dataset

The algorithm performance was evaluated on the Activity of Daily Living (ADL) dataset[2] [17]. This dataset was recorded using a chest-mounted GoPro camera and consists of 20 videos (each lasting about 30 min to one hour) of subjects performing their daily activities in the house.

4.2 Evaluation

Evaluation of keyframe video summarisation for egocentric videos is still a challenging task [5,7]. Yeung et al. [24] suggested to evaluate summaries through text using the VideoSET method[3]. In their experiments, the author provided text annotations per frame for the video to be summarised. The VideoSet method converts the summary into text representation. Then the content similarity between this representation and a ground truth text summary was measured through Natural Language Processing (NLP).

Motivated by [24], we annotated the ADL dataset rather using numbers than text. The numbers are organised to describe sequences of events. We made a list of events in each video, using an action list from [17]. The frames are labelled with their relevant event, or as not informative if the event cannot be recognised from the frame (semantic information). Consequently, any informative frame from the event can be considered ground truth for that event. Given a video summary, the number of matches and then the F-measure can be subsequently calculated.

---

[2] https://www.csee.umbc.edu/~hpirsiav/papers/ADLdataset/.

[3] http://ai.stanford.edu/~syyeung/videoset.html.

4.3 Online Summarisation Methods

We compared the following methods:

(a) BCC. The proposed Budget-constrained Control Chart algorithm.
(b) SCX. Submodular convex optimisation [6].
(c) UE. Uniform Events (baseline method). To implement the UE algorithm, the video is uniformly divided into ϵ number of events (segments). The ϵ value follows the number of keyframes extracted by our online algorithm. The closest frame to the center of each segment (in $\mathbb{R}^L$) is taken to represent the event.

To have a fair comparison we tuned the SCX and the UE for each video to their best performance. Doing that, the value for ϵ was adjusted with the number of keyframes extracted by our online algorithm. The same adjustment applied for the SCX.

Table 1. F-values for the comparison of the proposed method (BCC), and the two rival methods (SCX and UE) on the 20 videos in ADL video database.

Video	Number of frames	F-measure			Parameters	
		BCC	SCX	UE	SCX (λ)	UE (ϵ)
P_{01}	1,794	**0.73**	0.45	0.60	0.33	13
P_{02}	2,860	0.63	0.35	**0.67**	0.07	27
P_{03}	2,370	0.50	0.37	**0.56**	0.15	19
P_{04}	1,578	**0.52**	0.31	0.44	0.25	18
P_{05}	1,475	**0.42**	0.30	**0.42**	1	5
P_{06}	1,550	**0.67**	0.53	0.47	0.2	20
P_{07}	2,643	**0.81**	0.43	0.54	0.17	18
P_{08}	1,592	0.56	0.40	**0.60**	0.08	27
P_{09}	1,288	**0.67**	0.61	0.56	0.15	25
P_{10}	956	**0.80**	0.40	**0.80**	0.7	8
P_{11}	493	**0.87**	0.52	0.78	0.6	10
P_{12}	844	**0.69**	0.43	**0.69**	0.3	14
P_{13}	1,768	**0.63**	0.28	0.51	0.11	24
P_{14}	1,531	**0.78**	0.54	0.63	0.09	23
P_{15}	1,585	**0.59**	0.37	**0.59**	0.25	13
P_{16}	840	**0.89**	0.64	0.59	0.19	13
P_{17}	885	**0.44**	**0.44**	0.22	0.28	9
P_{18}	1,150	**0.47**	**0.47**	0.40	0.095	21
P_{19}	3,797	**0.77**	0.33	0.57	0.08	28
P_{20}	1,609	**0.69**	0.31	0.50	0.17	16

4.4   Keyframe Selection Results

Table 1 shows the F-value for the match between the summaries generated through BCC, SCX and UE, and the semantic-category ground truth for the

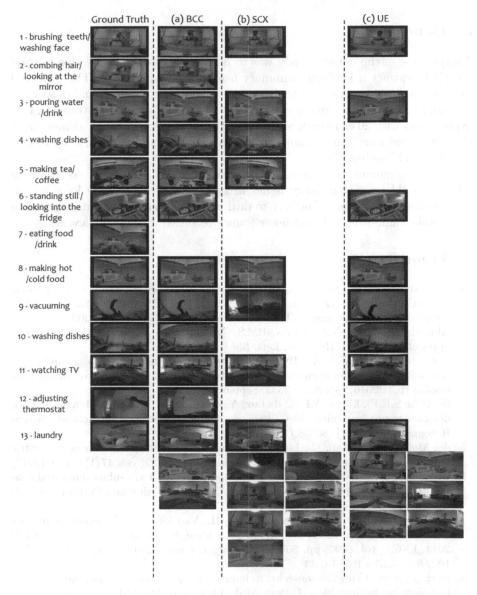

Fig. 2. Example of keyframe summaries obtained by the (a) BCC, (b) SCX and (c) UE methods and their matched frames with the ground truth, for ADL dataset video #16. The total number of events in ground truth for this video is 13, and the BCC just missed one event on eating food/drink.

20 videos. As seen from these results, the proposed online method performs consistently better than the two competitors.

Figure 2 displays the summaries obtained by the BCC, SCX and UE methods, highlighting matched frames with the ground truth. Our BCC method misses one event in the ground truth (Fig. 2a) resulting in the F-value of 0.89.

5   Conclusion

The purpose of the current study was to introduce a fast and effective method (BCC) to extract a keyframe summary from a streaming video. The proposed method applies control charts to detect event boundaries online, and observes a maximum limit on the number of selected keyframes (budged-constrained). Our experiments with 20 egocentric videos from the ADL video database demonstrate that BCC performs well in comparison with two existing methods, state-of-the-art SCX and baseline UE.

The requirement to store all frames for an event before the keyframe is selected could present memory issues in the event of excessively long, sedentary events, e.g. sleeping. One way to deal with this issue is the introduction of a dynamic frame-rate, with far fewer frames recorded during such events.

References

1. Abd-Almageed, W.: Online, simultaneous shot boundary detection and key frame extraction for sports videos using rank tracing. In: IEEE 15th International Conference on Image Processing (ICIP 2008), pp. 3200–3203, October 2008
2. Almeida, J., Leite, N.J., Torres, R.d.S.: Vison: video summarization for online applications. Pattern Recognit. Lett. **33**(4), 397–409 (2012)
3. Anirudh, R., Masroor, A., Turaga, P.: Diversity promoting online sampling for streaming video summarization. In: IEEE International Conference on Image Processing (ICIP2016), pp. 3329–3333, September 2016
4. de Avila, S.E.F., Lopes, A.P.B., da Luz, A., Araújo, A.d.A.: VSUMM: a mechanism designed to produce static video summaries and a novel evaluation method. Pattern Recognit. Lett. **32**(1), 56–68 (2011)
5. del Molino, A.G., Tan, C., Lim, J.-H., Tan, A.-H.: Summarization of egocentric videos: a comprehensive survey. IEEE Trans. Hum. Mach. Syst. **47**(1), 65–76 (2017)
6. Elhamifar, E., Kaluza, M.C.D.P.: Online summarization via submodular and convex optimization. In: IEEE Conference on Computer Vision and Pattern Recognition (CVPR2017), pp. 1818–1826, July 2017
7. Gygli, M., Grabner, H., Riemenschneider, H., Van Gool, L.: Creating summaries from user videos. In: Fleet, D., Pajdla, T., Schiele, B., Tuytelaars, T. (eds.) ECCV 2014. LNCS, vol. 8695, pp. 505–520. Springer, Cham (2014). https://doi.org/10.1007/978-3-319-10584-0_33
8. Kerr, J., et al.: Using the sensecam to improve classifications of sedentary behavior in free-living settings. Am. J. Prev. Med. **44**(3), 290–296 (2013)
9. Le, H.V., Clinch, S., Sas, C., Dingler, T., Henze, N., Davies, N.: Impact of video summary viewing on episodic memory recall: design guidelines for video summarizations. In: Proceedings of the 2016 CHI Conference on Human Factors in Computing System (CHI 2016), New York, USA, pp. 4793–4805. ACM, May 2016

10. Lee, M.L., Dey, A.K.: Lifelogging memory appliance for people with episodic memory impairment. In: Proceedings of the 10th International Conference on Ubiquitous Computing, UbiComp 2008, New York, USA, pp. 44–53. ACM (2008)
11. Matthews, C.E., Kuncheva, L.I., Yousefi, P.: Classification and comparison of online video summarisation methods. Machine Vision and Applications (2018, Submitted)
12. Matthews, C.E., Yousefi, P., Kuncheva, L.I.: Using control charts for on-line video summarisation. In: International Joint Conference on Computer Vision and Pattern Recognition (CCVPR 2018) (2018, Submitted)
13. Mei, S., Guan, G., Wang, Z., Wan, S., He, M., Feng, D.D.: Video summarization via minimum sparse reconstruction. Pattern Recognit. **48**(2), 522–533 (2015)
14. Monekosso, D.N., Remagnino, P.: Behavior analysis for assisted living. IEEE Trans. Autom. Sci. Eng. **7**(4), 879–886 (2010)
15. O'Loughlin, G., et al.: Using a wearable camera to increase the accuracy of dietary analysis. Am. J. Prev. Med. **44**(3), 297–301 (2013)
16. Ou, S.-H., Lee, C.-H., Somayazulu, V.S., Chen, Y.-K., Chien, S.-Y.: On-line multi-view video summarization for wireless video sensor network. IEEE J. Sel. Top. Signal Process. **9**(1), 165–179 (2015)
17. Pirsiavash, H., Ramanan, D.: Detecting activities of daily living in first-person camera views. In: IEEE Conference on Computer Vision and Pattern Recognition (CVPR 2012), pp. 2847–2854. IEEE , June 2012
18. Plummer, B.A., Brown, M., Lazebnik, S.: Enhancing video summarization via vision-language embedding. In: IEEE Conference on Computer Vision and Pattern Recognition (CVPR 2017), pp. 1052–1060, July 2017
19. Rasheed, Z., Shah, M.: Scene detection in Hollywood movies and TV shows. In: Proceedings of the IEEE Computer Society Conference on Computer Vision and Pattern Recognition (CVPR 2003), vol. 2, p. 343. IEEE, June 2003
20. Shewhart, W.A.: Economic Control of Quality of Manufactured Product. Van Nostrand Company, New York (1931)
21. Song, M., Wang, H.: Highly efficient incremental estimation of Gaussian mixture models for online data stream clustering. In: Intelligent Computing: Theory and Applications III, SPIE, vol. 5803, pp. 174–184 (2005)
22. Truong, B.T., Venkatesh, S.: Video abstraction: a systematic review and classification. ACM Trans. Multimed. Comput. Commun. Appl. (TOMM) **3**(1), 3 (2007)
23. Woodberry, E., Browne, G., Hodges, S., Watson, P., Kapur, N., Woodberry, K.: The use of a wearable camera improves autobiographical memory in patients with Alzheimer's disease. Memory **23**(3), 340–349 (2015)
24. Yeung, S., Fathi, A., Fei-Fei, L.: VideoSET: video summary evaluation through text. CoRR, arXiv preprint arXiv:1406.5824 (2014)

p-Laplacian Regularization of Signals on Directed Graphs

Zeina Abu Aisheh, Sébastien Bougleux, and Olivier Lézoray[✉]

Normandie Univ, UNICAEN, ENSICAEN, CNRS, GREYC, 14000 Caen, France
{zeina.abu-aisheh,sebastien.bougleux,olivier.lezoray}@unicaen.fr

Abstract. The graph Laplacian plays an important role in describing the structure of a graph signal from weights that measure the similarity between the vertices of the graph. In the literature, three definitions of the graph Laplacian have been considered for undirected graphs: the combinatorial, the normalized and the random-walk Laplacians. Moreover, a nonlinear extension of the Laplacian, called the *p*-Laplacian, has also been put forward for undirected graphs. In this paper, we propose several formulations for *p*-Laplacians on directed graphs directly inspired from the Laplacians on undirected graphs. Then, we consider the problem of *p*-Laplacian regularization of signals on directed graphs. Finally, we provide experimental results to illustrate the effect of the proposed *p*-laplacians on different types of graph signals.

Keywords: Directed graphs · *p*-laplacian · Graph signal Regularization

1 Introduction

With the development of new sensors, signals can now be generated from many different sources providing images, meshes, social or biological networks, to quote a few. These signals often have a structure much more irregular than a classical Euclidean grid but they can be represented by graphs [9]. When data vectors are associated with graph vertices, a so-called *graph signal* is obtained. The new research field of signal processing on graphs aims at extending the classical discrete signal processing tools to signals living on an underlying irregular graph (see [14] for a review) and one of its key ingredients is the graph Laplacian. Indeed, the graph Laplacian plays an important role in describing the structure of a graph signal from weights that measure the similarity between the vertices of the graph [3]. Several definitions of the graph Laplacian have been considered so far for undirected graphs [10]: the combinatorial Laplacian, the normalized Laplacian and the random-walk Laplacian. These Laplacians have become

This work received funding from the Agence Nationale de la Recherche (ANR-14-CE27-0001 GRAPHSIP), and from the European Union FEDER/FSE 2014/2020 (GRAPHSIP project).

© Springer Nature Switzerland AG 2018
G. Bebis et al. (Eds.): ISVC 2018, LNCS 11241, pp. 650–661, 2018.
https://doi.org/10.1007/978-3-030-03801-4_57

increasingly popular in graph signal processing [8,13,16] and machine learning [10,11]. Some extensions of the Laplacian have been also proposed for directed graphs [1,4,7]. A nonlinear extension of the Laplacian also exists that is called the p-Laplacian. This latter operator has been considered for undirected graphs and enables to recover analogues (when $p = 2$) of the combinatorial Laplacian [2,6] and of the normalized Laplacian [18]. Unfortunately there exists actually no formulation of the p-Laplacian for the general case of directed graphs and we propose in this paper three different formulations for the latter (i.e., combinatorial, normalized, and random-walk, similarly to the Laplacian on undirected graphs). Then, we consider the problem of p-Laplacian regularization of signals on directed graphs that minimizes a loss function plus a regularization term. To the best of our knowledge this is the first time that the use of the p-Laplacian on directed graphs is considered for graph signal regularization. Finally we show some results for the filtering of different graph signals.

2 Notations

We introduce in this section the notations that will be used in the paper. A graph represents a set of elements and a set of pairwise relationships between those elements [9]. The elements are called vertices and the relationships are called edges. Formally, a graph $\mathcal{G}$ [5] is defined by the sets $\mathcal{G} = (\mathcal{V}, \mathcal{E})$ in which $\mathcal{E} \subseteq \mathcal{V} \times \mathcal{V}$. We denote the ith vertex as $v_i \in \mathcal{V}$. Since each edge is a subset of two vertices, we write $e_{ij} = \{v_i, v_j\}$. A graph is called directed when each edge e_{ij} contains an ordering of the vertices. A directed edge from v_j to v_i will be denoted $v_j \to v_i$. The edges of a graph can be weighted with a function denoted by $w : \mathcal{E} \to \mathbb{R}^+$. The adjacency matrix representation of directed graph is a $|\mathcal{V}| \times |\mathcal{V}|$ matrix $\mathbf{W}$ where $\mathbf{W}_{ij} = w(v_i, v_j)$ if $v_i \to v_j \in \mathcal{E}$ and 0 otherwise. For undirected graphs the matrix $\mathbf{W}$ is symmetric and $\mathbf{W}^T = \mathbf{W}$. This will not be the case in this paper since we consider directed graphs and if $v_i \to v_j \in \mathcal{E}$ this will not necessarily imply that $v_j \to v_i \in \mathcal{E}$ or that $w(v_i, v_j) = w(v_j, v_i)$. The out-degree of a node v_i, $\mathrm{d}^+(v_i)$, is equal to $\mathrm{d}^+(v_i) = \sum_{v_i \to v_j \in \mathcal{E}} w_{ij}$. The in-degree of a node v_i, $\mathrm{d}^-(v_i)$, is equal to $\mathrm{d}^-(v_i) = \sum_{v_j \to v_i \in \mathcal{E}} w_{ji}$. Note that in an undirected graph, $\mathrm{d}^+(v_i) = \mathrm{d}^-(v_i)$, $\forall v_i \in \mathcal{V}$ and is denoted $\mathrm{d}(v_i)$. The out-degree matrix $\mathbf{D}_+$ is a diagonal matrix with $\mathbf{D}_{+ii} = \mathrm{d}^+(v_i)$, and similarly for $\mathbf{D}_-$. When the graph is undirected, one has $\mathbf{D}_+ = \mathbf{D}_- = \mathbf{D}$. For undirected graphs, several Laplacian formulation exist [10]. The combinatorial Laplacian is the matrix $\mathbf{L} = \mathbf{D} - \mathbf{W}$. The normalized Laplacian is $\tilde{\mathbf{L}} = \mathbf{D}^{-1/2}\mathbf{L}\mathbf{D}^{-1/2} = \mathbf{I} - \mathbf{D}^{-1/2}\mathbf{W}\mathbf{D}^{-1/2}$. The random walk Laplacian is $\mathbf{L}^{rw} = \mathbf{D}^{-1}\mathbf{L} = \mathbf{I} - \mathbf{D}^{-1}\mathbf{W}$. Now we define the space of functions on graphs (i.e., for graph signals). Let $\mathcal{H}(\mathcal{V})$ be the Hilbert space of real-valued functions defined on the vertices of a graph, a graph signal is a function $f : \mathcal{V} \to \mathbb{R}^n$ of $\mathcal{H}(\mathcal{V})$ that maps each vertex to a vector $\mathbf{f}(v_i)$. The space $\mathcal{H}(\mathcal{V})$ is endowed with the usual inner product $\langle f, h \rangle_{\mathcal{H}(\mathcal{V})} = \sum_{v_i \in \mathcal{V}} f(v_i)h(v_i)$, where $f, h : \mathcal{V} \to \mathbb{R}$. Similarly, let $\mathcal{H}(\mathcal{E})$ be the space of real-valued functions defined on the edges of $\mathcal{G}$. It is endowed with the inner product $\langle F, H \rangle_{\mathcal{H}(\mathcal{E})} = \sum_{e_{ij} \in \mathcal{E}} F(e_{ij}) H(e_{ij})$, where $F, H : \mathcal{E} \to \mathbb{R}$ are two functions of $\mathcal{H}(\mathcal{E})$.

3 p-Laplacian on Directed Graphs

3.1   Definitions

To define the p-Laplacian we need first to introduce several operators that operate on directed graphs. The formulation of these operators is similar to the one found in [18] but are expressed here on directed graphs. It is important to note that in contrast to undirected graphs, there has been few studies on Laplacian for directed graphs [4] and even less for the p-Laplacian [19]. The directed difference operator of a graph signal $f \in \mathcal{H}(\mathcal{V})$, called $d_w : \mathcal{H}(\mathcal{V}) \to \mathcal{H}(\mathcal{E})$, over a directed edge $v_i \to v_j$ is denoted by $(d_w f)(v_i, v_j)$. We do not explicitly provide now the definition of this difference operator and will show that with different definitions, different p-Laplacian on directed graphs can be formulated. The adjoint operator $d_w^* : \mathcal{H}(\mathcal{E}) \to \mathcal{H}(\mathcal{V})$, of a function $H \in \mathcal{H}(\mathcal{E})$, can then be expressed at a vertex $v_i \in \mathcal{V}$ by using the definition of the inner products since $\langle H, d_w f \rangle_{\mathcal{H}(\mathcal{E})} = \langle d_w^* H, f \rangle_{\mathcal{H}(\mathcal{V})}$. The gradient operator of a function $f \in \mathcal{H}(\mathcal{V})$, at vertex $v_i \in \mathcal{V}$, is the vector of all the weighted directed differences $(d_w f)(v_i, v_j)$, with respect to the set of outgoing edges $v_i \to v_j \in \mathcal{E}$:

$$(\boldsymbol{\nabla_w f})(v_i) = ((d_w f)(v_i, v_j))^T, \forall (v_i \to v_j) \in \mathcal{E} \ . \tag{1}$$

Its $\mathcal{L}_p$ norm is defined by

$$\|(\boldsymbol{\nabla_w f})(v_i)\|_p = \left[\sum_{v_i \to v_j \in \mathcal{E}} |(d_w f)(v_i, v_j)|^p \right]^{1/p} . \tag{2}$$

Then, the p-Laplacian $\Delta_w^p f : \mathcal{H}(\mathcal{V}) \to \mathcal{H}(\mathcal{V})$ can be formulated as the discrete analogue of the continuous one by [6]:

$$\Delta_w^p f(v_i) = \frac{1}{2} d_w^* \left(\|\boldsymbol{\nabla_w f}(v_i)\|_2^{p-2} (d_w f)(v_i, v_j) \right) = \frac{1}{2} d_w^* \left(\frac{(d_w f)(v_i, v_j)}{\|\boldsymbol{\nabla_w f}(v_i)\|_2^{2-p}} \right) \tag{3}$$

where $p \in (0, +\infty)$. If we choose specific formulations for the directed difference operator, we can end-up with new formulations of the p-Laplacian on directed graphs, that we propose in the sequel. Details are provided only for the first formulation due to paper length constraints.

3.2   Combinatorial p-Laplacian on Directed Graphs

First we consider

$$(d_w f)(v_i, v_j) = w(v_i, v_j)(f(v_j) - f(v_i)) \tag{4}$$

as a directed difference operator on the edge $v_i \rightarrow v_j$. This is similar to the one used for the combinatorial Laplacian on undirected graphs. Using the definitions of the inner products in $\mathcal{H}(\mathcal{E})$ and $\mathcal{H}(\mathcal{V})$, we can express the adjoint operator

$$(d_w^* H)(v_i) = \sum_{v_j \rightarrow v_i} H(v_j, v_i) w(v_j, v_i) - \sum_{v_i \rightarrow v_j} H(v_i, v_j) w(v_i, v_j) \ . \qquad (5)$$

Proof.

$$\langle H, d_w f \rangle_{\mathcal{H}(E)} = \sum_{(v_i, v_j) \in E} (d_w f)(v_i, v_j) H(v_i, v_j) = \sum_{(v_i, v_j) \in E} w(v_i, v_j)(f(v_j) - f(v_i)) H(v_i, v_j)$$

$$= \frac{1}{2} \sum_{v_i \in V} \left(\sum_{v_i \rightarrow v_j} H(v_i, v_j) w(v_i, v_j)(f(v_j) - f(v_i)) + \sum_{v_j \rightarrow v_i} H(v_j, v_i) w(v_j, v_i)(f(v_i) - f(v_j)) \right)$$

$$= \frac{1}{2} \sum_{v_i \in V} \left(2 \sum_{v_j \rightarrow v_i} H(v_j, v_i) w(v_j, v_i) f(v_i) - 2 \sum_{v_i \rightarrow v_j} H(v_i, v_j) w(v_i, v_j) f(v_i) \right)$$

$$= \sum_{v_i \in V} f(v_i) \left(\sum_{v_j \rightarrow v_i} H(v_j, v_i) w(v_j, v_i) - \sum_{v_i \rightarrow v_j} H(v_i, v_j) w(v_i, v_j) \right) = \langle d_w^* H, f \rangle_{\mathcal{H}(V)}$$

The adjoint operator measures the difference between the in- and outgoing flows at a vertex and can be associated to the divergence operator denoted by $-d_w^*$. Then, using Eq. (3) and the definitions of d_w, d_w^* and $\|\nabla_w\|$, a combinatorial *p*-Laplacian formulation on directed graphs can be expressed by:

$$\Delta_w^p f(v_i) = \frac{1}{2} \left(f(v_i) \left(\sum_{v_j \rightarrow v_i} \frac{w(v_j, v_i)^2}{\|\nabla_\mathbf{w} \mathbf{f}(v_j)\|_2^{2-p}} + \sum_{v_i \rightarrow v_j} \frac{w(v_i, v_j)^2}{\|\nabla_\mathbf{w} \mathbf{f}(v_i)\|_2^{2-p}} \right) \right.$$
$$\left. - \left(\sum_{v_j \rightarrow v_i} \frac{w(v_j, v_i)^2}{\|\nabla_\mathbf{w} \mathbf{f}(v_j)\|_2^{2-p}} f(v_j) + \sum_{v_i \rightarrow v_j} \frac{w(v_i, v_j)^2}{\|\nabla_\mathbf{w} \mathbf{f}(v_i)\|_2^{2-p}} f(v_j) \right) \right) \qquad (6)$$

On the opposite to the classical formulation on undirected graphs [2,6], the latter takes into account both ingoing and outgoing edges from vertices. However, with a specific (directed or undirected) graph and a given value of p, we can recover several state-of-the-art Laplacian formulations (up to a power of 2 on the weights). With undirected graphs, the formulation of [2] is recovered, with symmetric directed graphs the formulation of [7] is recovered. With $p = 2$, other formulations have been proposed on directed graphs but they only use in-degrees as $\Delta_w^2 f = (\mathbf{D}_- - \mathbf{W}) f$ [15] or out-degrees as $\Delta_w^2 f = (\mathbf{D}_+ - \mathbf{W}) f$ [12]. Our proposal encompasses these. In particular, for $p = 2$, Eq. (6) can be expressed as $\Delta_w^2 f = \frac{1}{2}(\mathbf{D}_- + \mathbf{D}_+ - \mathbf{W} - \mathbf{W}^T) f$ in matrix expression. With undirected graphs and the classical combinatorial Laplacian $\Delta_w^2 f = \mathbf{L} f$ is recovered [3].

3.3 Normalized *p*-Laplacian on Directed Graphs

Second we consider

$$(d_w f)(v_i, v_j) = w(v_i, v_j) \left(\frac{f(v_j)}{\sqrt{d^-(v_j)}} - \frac{f(v_i)}{\sqrt{d^+(v_i)}} \right) \qquad (7)$$

as a directed difference operator on the edge $v_i \to v_j$. This is close to the one used for the normalized Laplacian on undirected graphs, except that we normalize with both in- and out-going degrees since we consider directed graphs. Using the definitions of the inner products in $\mathcal{H}(\mathcal{E})$ and $\mathcal{H}(\mathcal{V})$, we can express the adjoint operator

$$(d_w^* H)(v_i) = \sum_{v_j \to v_i} \frac{H(v_j, v_i) w(v_j, v_i)}{\sqrt{\mathrm{d}^-(v_i)}} - \sum_{v_i \to v_j} \frac{H(v_i, v_j) w(v_i, v_j)}{\sqrt{\mathrm{d}^+(v_i)}} . \tag{8}$$

Then, using Eq. (3) and the definitions of d_w, d_w^* and $\|\nabla_\mathbf{w}\|$, a normalized p-Laplacian formulation on directed graphs can be expressed by:

$$\tilde{\Delta}_w^p f(v_i) = \frac{1}{2} \left(f(v_i) \left(\sum_{v_j \to v_i} \frac{w(v_j, v_i)^2}{\mathrm{d}^-(v_i) \|\nabla_\mathbf{w}f(v_j)\|_2^{2-p}} + \sum_{v_i \to v_j} \frac{w(v_i, v_j)^2}{\mathrm{d}^+(v_i) \|\nabla_\mathbf{w}f(v_i)\|_2^{2-p}} \right) \right.$$
$$\left. - \left(\sum_{v_j \to v_i} \frac{w(v_j, v_i)^2 \|\nabla_\mathbf{w}f(v_j)\|_2^{p-2}}{\sqrt{\mathrm{d}^-(v_i)\,\mathrm{d}^+(v_j)}} f(v_j) + \sum_{v_i \to v_j} \frac{w(v_i, v_j)^2 \|\nabla_\mathbf{w}f(v_i)\|_2^{p-2}}{\sqrt{\mathrm{d}^+(v_i)\,\mathrm{d}^-(v_j)}} f(v_j) \right) \right) \tag{9}$$

As previously we can recover several state-of-the-art formulations. With directed graphs, $p = 2$ and weights replaced by their square root, the formulation can be reduced to

$$\tilde{\Delta}_w^2 f(v_i) = f(v_i) - \frac{1}{2} \left(\sum_{v_j \to v_i} \frac{w(v_j, v_i) f(v_j)}{\sqrt{\mathrm{d}^-(v_i)\,\mathrm{d}^+(v_j)}} + \sum_{v_i \to v_j} \frac{w(v_i, v_j) f(v_j)}{\sqrt{\mathrm{d}^+(v_i)\,\mathrm{d}^-(v_j)}} \right) \tag{10}$$

or as $\left(\mathbf{I} - \frac{1}{2} \left(\mathbf{D}_-^{-1/2} \mathbf{W} \mathbf{D}_+^{-1/2} + \mathbf{D}_+^{-1/2} \mathbf{W}^T \mathbf{D}_-^{-1/2} \right) \right) f$ in matrix form. This formulation is closely related to the normalized Laplacian for symmetric directed graphs proposed in [7,17] and expressed as $\left(\mathbf{I} - \frac{1}{2} \left(\mathbf{D}^{-1/2} \mathbf{W} \mathbf{D}^{-1/2} + \mathbf{D}^{-1/2} \mathbf{W}^T \mathbf{D}^{-1/2} \right) \right) f$. As it can be seen they normalize only by $\mathbf{D}$ since the graph is symmetric, in contrast to our approach. A similar remark can be made for the formation of [4] for symmetric directed graphs that are strongly connected. With undirected graphs, our formulation reduces to $\tilde{\Delta}_w^2 f(v_i) = f(v_i) - \sum_{v_j \in V} \frac{w(v_j, v_i)}{\sqrt{d(v_i) d(v_j)}} f(v_j)$ which is exactly the normalized Laplacian $(\mathbf{I} - \mathbf{D}^{-1/2} \mathbf{W} \mathbf{D}^{-1/2}) f$ for undirected graphs [3].

3.4   Random-Walk p-Laplacian on Directed Graphs

Third we consider

$$(d_w f)(v_i, v_j) = \frac{w(v_i, v_j)}{\sqrt{\mathrm{d}^+(v_i)}} \left(f(v_j) - f(v_i) \right) \tag{11}$$

as a directed difference operator on the edge $v_i \rightarrow v_j$. This is similar to the one used for the random-walk Laplacian on undirected graphs. Using the definitions of the inner products in $\mathcal{H}(\mathcal{E})$ and $\mathcal{H}(\mathcal{V})$, we can express the adjoint operator

$$(d_w^* H)(v_i) = \sum_{v_j \rightarrow v_i} \frac{H(v_j, v_i)w(v_j, v_i)}{\sqrt{d^+(v_i)}} - \sum_{v_i \rightarrow v_j} \frac{H(v_i, v_j)w(v_i, v_j)}{\sqrt{d^+(v_i)}} . \tag{12}$$

Then, using Eq. (3) and the definitions of d_w, d_w^* and $\|\nabla_\mathbf{w}\|$, a random-walk p-Laplacian formulation on directed graphs can be expressed by:

$$\Delta_w^{p,rw} f(v_i) = \frac{1}{2} \left(f(v_i) \left(\sum_{v_j \rightarrow v_i} \frac{w(v_j, v_i)^2}{d^+(v_j) \|\nabla_\mathbf{w}f(v_j)\|_2^{2-p}} + \sum_{v_i \rightarrow v_j} \frac{w(v_i, v_j)^2}{d^+(v_i) \|\nabla_\mathbf{w}f(v_i)\|_2^{2-p}} \right) \right.$$
$$\left. - \left(\sum_{v_j \rightarrow v_i} \frac{w(v_j, v_i)^2}{d^+(v_j) \|\nabla_\mathbf{w}f(v_j)\|_2^{2-p}} f(v_j) + \sum_{v_i \rightarrow v_j} \frac{w(v_i, v_j)^2}{d^+(v_i) \|\nabla_\mathbf{w}f(v_i)\|_2^{2-p}} f(v_j) \right) \right) \tag{13}$$

Again, with a specific (directed or undirected) graph and a given value of p, we can recover several state-of-the-art Laplacian formulations (up to a power of 2 on the weights). In particular, for $p = 2$, Eq. (13) can be expressed as $\Delta_w^{2,rw} f = (\mathbf{I} - \frac{1}{2}\mathbf{D}_+^{-1}(\mathbf{W} + \mathbf{W}^T))f$ in matrix expression. With directed graphs and $p = 2$ the formulation in matrix expression of [7] is recovered, and with undirected graphs and $p = 2$ the classical random-walk Laplacian $\Delta_w^{2,rw} f = \mathbf{L}^{rw} f$ is recovered [10]. With $p = 2$, a similar formulation for directed graphs has been expressed as $(\mathbf{I} - \mathbf{D}_+^{-1}\mathbf{W})f$ in [1].

4 p-Laplacian Regularization on Directed Graphs

In the previous section, we have proposed general formulations for combinatorial, normalized and random-walk p-Laplacians on directed graphs. From these, we consider the problem of p-Laplacian regularization of signals on directed graphs that minimizes a loss function plus a regularization term. Let $f^0 : \mathcal{V} \rightarrow \mathbb{R}$ be a noisy graph signal of a clean graph signal $g : \mathcal{V} \rightarrow \mathbb{R}$ corrupted by a given noise n such that $f^0 = g + n$. To recover the uncorrupted function g, a commonly used method is to seek for a function $f : \mathcal{V} \rightarrow \mathbb{R}$ which is regular enough on $\mathcal{G}$, and also close enough to f^0. This inverse problem can be formalized by the minimization of an energy functional, that typically involves a regularization term plus an approximation term (also called loss). The proposed graph p-Laplacians can be used to define a regularization functional $R_w^p : \mathcal{H}(\mathcal{V}) \rightarrow \mathbb{R}^+$ on directed graphs by

$$R_w^{p,*}(f) = \langle \Delta_w^{p,*} f, f \rangle_{\mathcal{H}(\mathcal{V})} = \langle d_w f, d_w f \rangle_{\mathcal{H}(\mathcal{E})} = \sum_{v_i \in \mathcal{V}} \|(\nabla_\mathbf{w}f)(v_i)\|_2^p \tag{14}$$

where $\Delta_w^{p,*}$ is among Eqs. (6), (9) or (13). Since $R_w^{p,*} \geq 0$, $\Delta_w^{p,*}$ is positive semi-definite. From this we consider the following variational problem of p-Laplacian regularization on directed graphs

$$g \approx \min_{f:\mathcal{V}\to\mathbb{R}} \left\{ E_w^{p,*}(f, f^0, \lambda) = \tfrac{1}{p} R_w^{p,*}(f) + \tfrac{\lambda}{2}\|f - f^0\|_2^2 \right\}, \qquad (15)$$

where the regularization functional $R_w^{p,*}$ can be induced from one of the proposed p-Laplacians on directed graphs. When $p \geq 1$, the energy $E_w^{p,*}$ is a convex functional of functions of $\mathcal{H}(\mathcal{V})$. To get the solution of the minimizer (15), we consider the following system of equations

$$\frac{\partial E_w^{p,*}(f, f^0, \lambda)}{\partial f(v_i)} = 0, \forall v_i \in \mathcal{V} \qquad (16)$$

For all the p-Laplacians we have proposed, it can be proved that $\frac{1}{p}\frac{\partial R_w^{p,*}}{\partial f(v_i)} = 2\Delta_w^p f(v_i)$ (this is a direct consequence of Eq. (14)) and the system of equations is then re-written as follows:

$$2\Delta_w^{p,*} f(v_i) + \lambda(f(v_i) - f^0(v_i)) = 0 \qquad (17)$$

By substituting the expression of $\Delta_w^{p,*} f(v_i)$ by one of the proposed p-Laplacians (Δ_w^p, $\tilde{\Delta}_w^p$, $\Delta_w^{p,rw}$) into Eq. (17), the system of equations can be solved using a linearized Gauss-Jacobi iterative method. Let t be an iteration step, and $f^{(t)}$ be the solution at step t, then the following iterative algorithm is obtained for each of the proposed p-Laplacian on directed graphs.

$$f^{t+1}(v_i) = \frac{\lambda f^0(v_i) + \left(\displaystyle\sum_{v_j \to v_i} \frac{w(v_j, v_i)^2 f^t(v_j)}{\phi(v_j, v_i)\|\nabla_w f^t(v_j)\|_2^{2-p}} + \sum_{v_i \to v_j} \frac{w(v_i, v_j)^2) f^t(v_j)}{\phi(v_i, v_j)\|\nabla_w f^t(v_i)\|_2^{2-p}} \right)}{\lambda + \displaystyle\sum_{v_j \to v_i} \frac{w(v_j, v_i)^2}{\gamma_1(v_j, v_i)\|\nabla_w f^t(v_j)\|_2^{2-p}} + \sum_{v_i \to v_j} \frac{w(v_i, v_j)^2}{\gamma_2(v_i, v_j)\|\nabla_w f^t(v_i)\|_2^{2-p}}}$$

$$(18)$$

where ϕ, γ_1 and γ_2 are defined as follows, depending on the chosen directed p-Laplacian $\Delta_w^{p,*}$:

- Combinatorial p-Laplacian: $\phi(v_j, v_i) = \gamma_1(v_j, v_i) = \gamma_2(v_i, v_j) = 1$,
- Normalized p-Laplacian: $\phi(v_j, v_i) = \sqrt{d^-(v_i)\,d^+(v_j)}$, $\gamma_1(v_j, v_i) = d^-(v_i)$ and $\gamma_2(v_i, v_j) = d^+(v_i)$,
- Random-walk p-Laplacian: $\phi(v_i, v_j) = d^+(v_i)$ and $\gamma_1(v_j, v_i) = \gamma_2(v_i, v_j) = d^+(v_i)$.

5   Experiments and Results

In this section we provide sample results for the filtering of three different types of graphs signals for different directed graphs topologies and p-Laplacians. PSNR values will be used to compare the results. To weight the edges of the graphs, we use a parameterless function $w(v_i, v_j) = 1 - \dfrac{\|F_\tau^{f^0}(v_i) - F_\tau^{f^0}(v_j)\|_2}{\max\limits_{v_k \to v_l \in \mathcal{E}} \|F_\tau^{f^0}(v_k) - F_\tau^{f^0}(v_l)\|_2}$. The vector

$\mathbf{F}_\tau^{f^0}(v_i) = \left(f^0(v_j) : v_j \in \mathcal{N}_\tau(v_i) \cup \{v_i\} \right)^T$ corresponds to the set of values around v_i within a τ-hop $\mathcal{N}_\tau(v_i)$ (for images this is a patch of size $(2\tau + 1)^2$). We will consider two types of directed graphs: 8-adjacency directed grid graph (denoted $\mathcal{G}_0$, that connects each vertex to its 8 spatially closest neighbors), and k-nearest neighbor directed graphs (denoted $\mathcal{G}_k^{\alpha,\tau}$, that connects each vertex to its k nearest neighbors in terms of $\mathbf{F}_\tau^{f^0}$ L_2 norm within a α-hop). Figure 1 illustrates the influence of the graph construction: nearest neighbors with patch-based distances better capture the image geometry and this can be beneficial for latter processing.

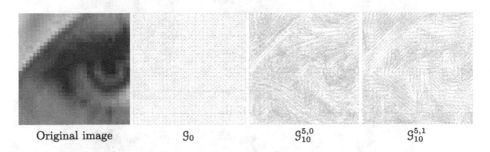

Original image $\mathcal{G}_0$ $\mathcal{G}_{10}^{5,0}$ $\mathcal{G}_{10}^{5,1}$

Fig. 1. Examples of directed graphs for an image. From left to right: original image, a symmetric 8-grid graph, 10-nearest neighbor graphs (inside a 11×11 window with color-based or 3×3 patch-based distances).

5.1   Images

The first type of graph signal we consider is 2D color images (see Fig. 2) and $f : \mathcal{V} \to \mathbb{R}^3$. An image has been corrupted by Gaussian noise and we filter the latter with p-Laplacian regularization with different configurations: a 8-adjacency directed grid graph (with $\lambda = 0.05$, $p = 1$), and a 8-adjacency directed grid graph augmented with a 10-nearest neighbor graph within a 5-hop ($\lambda = 0.09$ with patches of size 3×3). The nonlinear 1-Laplacian always provides better results than the linear 2-Laplacian. With $\mathcal{G}_0$ the graph is directed but symmetric and the filtering reduces to the undirected case [6], whereas with $\mathcal{G}_0 \cup \mathcal{G}_{10}^{5,1}$ the graph is not symmetric. As it can be seen, adding directed edges to the graph can enhance the results. We have observed that for the directed normalized p-Laplacian the results can degrade when low values of the in-degree occur. This is not the case for $\Delta_w^{p,rw}$ that always enables to obtain better results whatever the configurations we tested.

5.2   Database of Images

The second type of graph signal we consider is an image database (see Fig. 3) and $f : \mathcal{V} \to \mathbb{R}^{28 \times 28}$. We selected a subset of 90 images from the MNIST database for digits $0, 1, 3$ and corrupted the images with Gaussian noise of standard devision

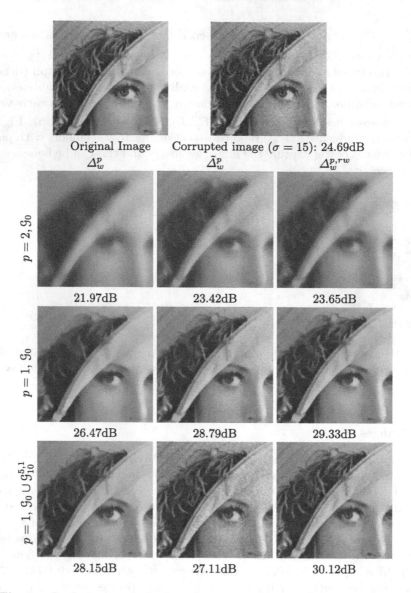

Fig. 2. p-Laplacian regularization of a corrupted image. See text for details.

σ. Then a directed 5-nearest neighbor graph is constructed on the whole dataset ($\alpha = \infty$). This graph is not symmetric. As it can be seen in Fig. 3, the filtering with the $\tilde{\Delta}_w^1$ enables to remove the noise while preserving the main structures. Table 1 presents additional results for different amounts of noise. Again, better results are obtained with $p = 1$ but the best results are obtained with different p-Laplacians, the normalized Laplacian having this time a much better behavior than for images.

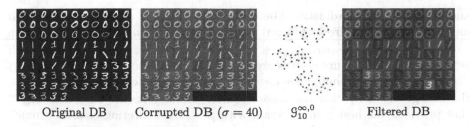

Original DB   Corrupted DB ($\sigma = 40$) $\mathcal{G}_{10}^{\infty,0}$ Filtered DB

Fig. 3. *p*-Laplacian regularization of a corrupted image database (with $\tilde{\Delta}_w^p$, $p = 1$, and $\lambda = 10^{-4}$). See text for details.

Table 1. Image database regularization on directed graphs ($\lambda = 10^{-4}$). Best results (in terms of PSNR) are bold faced.

σ	20			40		
$\Delta_w^{p,*}$	Δ_w^p	$\tilde{\Delta}_w^p$	$\Delta_w^{p,rw}$	Δ_w^p	$\tilde{\Delta}_w^p$	$\Delta_w^{p,rw}$
$p = 2$	14.54	**14.63**	14.56	12.91	**13.08**	12.88
$p = 1$	16.37	**16.83**	16.80	**14.01**	13.11	13.73

5.3 Meshes

Finally, we consider 3D colored meshes as a last graph signal and $f : \mathcal{V} \to \mathbb{R}^3$. The meshes are 3D scans from an ancient building and a person. The color is noisy due to the scanning process and the objective is to filter the vertices colors

Fig. 4. 3D colored mesh regularization on directed graphs (From left to right: original mesh, filtering with $\Delta_w^{p,rw}$, $\lambda = 0.05$, with $p = 2$ and $p = 1$).

and not their 3D coordinates. The considered graph is a symmetric directed mesh graph (provided from the scan) augmented with a 5-nearest neighbor graph within a 3-hop. To compare vertices we use $F_1^{f^0}$. However, since the mesh graph is not regular, the feature vectors are not of the same size. We cannot use a L_2 distance to compare them, so we use instead the Earth Mover Distance between the histograms of $F_1^{f^0}$. For space constraints, we show results only with $\Delta_w^{p,rw}$ that provided the best results. Again with $p = 1$ the filtering enables a much better preservation of the signal sharp edges while removing noise (Fig. 4).

6 Conclusion

In this paper we have proposed three formulations for p-Laplacians on directed graphs. They used specific difference operators on directed graphs that are inspired from the combinatorial, the normalized and the random-walk laplacians. These formulations of p-Laplacians on directed graphs had never been addressed before unless for specific graphs (symmetric and with $p = 2$ [7]). Our proposal goes beyond this. From these formulations, we have considered the problem of p-Laplacian regularization of graph signals and proposed a solution to the latter. Finally, some experimental results show the benefit of the approach for the filtering of three types of graph signals: images, images' databases, and 3D colored meshes. Given the results, none of the proposed p-Laplacians on directed graphs can be considered as always providing the best results which motivates the need for several formulations. Directed and non symmetric graphs have also shown their interest with respect to classical symmetric undirected graphs. In future works, we will consider other optimization schemes as well as the introduction of non symmetric weights for directed symmetric graphs with applications in image semi-supervised segmentation.

References

1. Bauer, F.: Normalized graph Laplacians for directed graphs. Linear Algebra Appl. **436**(11), 4193–4222 (2012)
2. Bougleux, S., Elmoataz, A., Melkemi, M.: Local and nonlocal discrete regularization on weighted graphs for image and mesh processing. Int. J. Comput. Vis. **84**(2), 220–236 (2009)
3. Chung, F.R.: Spectral Graph Theory. CBMS Regional Conference Series in Mathematics, vol. 92, pp. 1–212 (1997)
4. Chung, F.: Laplacians and the cheeger inequality for directed graphs. Ann. Comb. **9**(1), 1–19 (2005)
5. Diestel, R.: Graph Theory. Graduate Texts in Mathematics, 4th edn., vol. 173. Springer, Heidelberg (2012)
6. Elmoataz, A., Lezoray, O., Bougleux, S.: Nonlocal discrete regularization on weighted graphs: a framework for image and manifold processing. IEEE Trans. Image Process. **17**(7), 1047–1060 (2008)
7. Hein, M., Audibert, J., von Luxburg, U.: Graph Laplacians and their convergence on random neighborhood graphs. J. Mach. Learn. Res. **8**, 1325–1368 (2007)

8. Kheradmand, A., Milanfar, P.: A general framework for regularized, similarity-based image restoration. IEEE Trans. Image Process. **23**(12), 5136–5151 (2014)
9. Lézoray, O., Grady, L.: Image Processing and Analysis with Graphs: Theory and Practice. Digital Imaging and Computer Vision. CRC Press/Taylor and Francis, Boca Raton (2012)
10. von Luxburg, U.: A tutorial on spectral clustering. Stat. Comput. **17**(4), 395–416 (2007)
11. Ng, A.Y., Jordan, M.I., Weiss, Y.: On spectral clustering: analysis and an algorithm. In: Proceedings of the 14th International Conference on Neural Information Processing Systems: Natural and Synthetic, pp. 849–856 (2001)
12. Olfati-Saber, R., Murray, R.M.: Consensus problems in networks of agents with switching topology and time-delays. IEEE Trans. Automat. Contr. **49**(9), 1520–1533 (2004)
13. Pang, J., Cheung, G.: Graph laplacian regularization for image denoising: analysis in the continuous domain. IEEE Trans. Image Process. **26**(4), 1770–1785 (2017)
14. Shuman, D.I., Narang, S.K., Frossard, P., Ortega, A., Vandergheynst, P.: The emerging field of signal processing on graphs: extending high-dimensional data analysis to networks and other irregular domains. IEEE Signal Process. Mag. **30**(3), 83–98 (2013)
15. Singh, R., Chakraborty, A., Manoj, B.S.: Graph Fourier transform based on directed Laplacian. In: 2016 International Conference on Signal Processing and Communications (SPCOM), pp. 1–5 (2016)
16. Tremblay, N., Gonçalves, P., Borgnat, P.: Design of graph filters and filterbanks. ArXiv e-prints (2017)
17. Zhou, D., Huang, J., Schölkopf, B.: Learning from labeled and unlabeled data on a directed graph. In: Proceedings of the Twenty-Second International Conference on Machine Learning (ICML 2005), Bonn, Germany, 7–11 August 2005, pp. 1036–1043 (2005)
18. Zhou, D., Schölkopf, B.: Regularization on discrete spaces. In: Kropatsch, W.G., Sablatnig, R., Hanbury, A. (eds.) DAGM 2005. LNCS, vol. 3663, pp. 361–368. Springer, Heidelberg (2005). https://doi.org/10.1007/11550518_45
19. Zhou, D., Schölkopf, B., Hofmann, T.: Semi-supervised learning on directed graphs. In: Advances in Neural Information Processing Systems 17 (Neural Information Processing Systems, NIPS 2004, 13–18 December 2004, Vancouver, British Columbia, Canada, pp. 1633–1640 (2004)

A Dense-Depth Representation for VLAD Descriptors in Content-Based Image Retrieval

Federico Magliani[✉], Tomaso Fontanini, and Andrea Prati

IMP Lab, D.I.A., University of Parma, 43124 Parma, Italy
federico.magliani@studenti.unipr.it,
http://implab.ce.unipr.it

Abstract. The recent advances brought by deep learning allowed to improve the performance in image retrieval tasks. Through the many convolutional layers, available in a Convolutional Neural Network (CNN), it is possible to obtain a hierarchy of features from the evaluated image. At every step, the patches extracted are smaller than the previous levels and more representative. Following this idea, this paper introduces a new detector applied on the feature maps extracted from pre-trained CNN. Specifically, this approach lets to increase the number of features in order to increase the performance of the aggregation algorithms like the most famous and used VLAD embedding. The proposed approach is tested on different public datasets: Holidays, Oxford5k, Paris6k and UKB.

Keywords: Content-Based Image Retrieval · CNN codes VLAD descriptors

1 Introduction

The recent growth of available images and videos motivated researchers to work on Content-Based Image Retrieval (CBIR). There are many type of tasks in CBIR: the most studied is the instance-level image search, that consists in retrieving the most similar images starting from an image, used as a query. This task presents several challenges in terms of accuracy, search time and memory occupancy. Another relevant problem lies in the images themselves, which may present noisy features (*e.g.*, trees, person, cars, ...), different lightning conditions, viewpoints and resolution.

The image retrieval systems are based on a pipeline usually composed by: extraction of local features from the image, aggregation of the extracted features in a compact representation and retrieval of the most similar images. Initially, the focus was on the feature aggregation step and hence different types of embeddings were proposed in order to reduce the memory used and obtain a more representative global descriptor. Recently, due to the excellent results obtained in many tasks of computer vision, the deep learning approaches have become dominant also in image retrieval tasks. Particularly, Convolutional Neural Networks

© Springer Nature Switzerland AG 2018
G. Bebis et al. (Eds.): ISVC 2018, LNCS 11241, pp. 662–671, 2018.
https://doi.org/10.1007/978-3-030-03801-4_58

(CNNs) are adopted for the feature detection and description phase. They allow to densely extract features from images, that are better than the ones extracted with hand-crafted methods like SIFT [16] or SURF [4], because they can catch more details on the images through the high number of convolution layers.

Following the recent advances, this paper introduces a dense-depth detector applied on CNN codes extracted from InceptionV3 [30] network. This strategy augments the number of features in order to reach higher accuracy with a variant of VLAD [13] descriptors, called locVLAD [17]. It outperforms the previous VLAD implementation on several public benchmarks, thanks also to the use of Z-score normalization [32]. Furthermore a complete comparison and analysis among the other variants of VLAD is presented.

This paper is organized as follows. Section 2 introduces the general techniques used in the state of the art. Section 3.1 reviews the methods used for feature extraction. Next, while Sect. 3.2 exposes the Dense-Depth Representation, Sect. 3.3 describes VLAD algorithm. Section 4 reports the experimental results on four public datasets: Holidays, Oxford5k, Paris6k and UKB. Finally, concluding remarks are reported.

2   Related Work

In the last years, the problem of Content-Based Image Retrieval was addressed in many different ways. The first technique that has been developed, was the Bag of Words (BoW) [28]. It is a simple method that reaches good results, but consumes a large amount of memory. After the development of the BoW approach, researchers tried to overcome its weaknesses and implemented several embedding techniques: Hamming embedding [12], Fisher Vector [22] and VLAD [13]. VLAD [13] is the most used embedding techniques that tries to reduce the dimensionality of features, whilst preserving the recognition accuracy. A VLAD vector is a concatenation of the sum of the difference between the features and the relative closest centers, computed by using K-means clustering. There are many different variants of VLAD presented in the literature in order to solve the weakness of the VLAD descriptors: CVLAD [35], CEVLAD [36], HVLAD [6], FVLAD [14], gVLAD [32] and locVLAD [17]. CEVLAD [36] applies entropy for the aggregation of the features, FVLAD [14] modifies the aggregation steps using two codebooks: a descriptor one and a residual one, HVLAD [6] introduces a hierarchy of codebooks, that allows to create a more robust version of VLAD descriptors. Then, gVLAD [32] creates different VLAD using the orientation of the features, that are concatenated. This process increases the performance, but requires extra time.

Recently, with the development of new powerful GPUs, the deep learning approach has shown its superior performance in many tasks of image retrieval. Arandjelovic et al., in [1], applied a VLAD layer at the end of a CNN architecture, showing that the CNN-based pipeline reaches excellent results in the retrieval task. Another improvement of deep learning techniques is in the feature extraction phase. This process is known as "transfer learning" and consists in tuning the parameters trained in one feature space in order to work in another feature space [21]. Some methods that use transfer learning are: Spatial pooling [25], MOP-CNN [7], Neural codes [3], Ng *et al.* [34], CCS [33], OC [26], R-MAC [31], Gordo *et al.* [8] and Magliani *et al.* [18]. Also, fine-tuning global descriptors [9] on a similar image dataset, allows to highly improve accuracy results, but with an extra time effort due to the training phase on the new dataset.

3   System Architecture

In the following subsections, the proposed approach for features extraction and encoding using CNN features and locVLAD embedding is described.

3.1   CNN Codes

CNN codes are feature vectors extracted from pre-trained networks using the knowledge gained while solving one problem and applying it to a different, yet related, one through the process of transfer learning. There are several different pre-trained CNN architectures (like VGG16 [27], GoogLeNet [29], ResNet [10]) that allow to easily extract features from their layers. The choice of the layers depends on the type of problem and the selected network. Obviously, the deeper the network is, the better the results obtained by the extracted features are.

In this paper, the selected network is the recent Inception V3 [30], because it allows to obtain a more proper representation than VGG16 thanks to the concatenation of different convolutions. From it, the CNN codes in this paper are extracted from the 8th inception pooling layer (called mixed8 in the Keras implementation). Both the network and the layers have been chosen since they achieved the best results in our experiments. An ablation analysis of different networks has been conducted and it is reported in the Sect. 4.

3.2   Dense-Depth Representation

Since VLAD-based embedding works better with dense representations, we introduced a novel representation scheme.

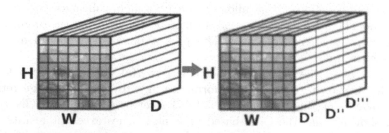

Fig. 1. Dense-depth detector

The features extracted from mixed8 are grouped into a larger set of features of lower dimensionality in order to augment the VLAD descriptive quality. Given a feature map of dimension $W \times H \times D$ (W = width, H = height and D = depth), we split it along the depth axis in order to obtain a high number of features of lower dimension, as it can be seen in Fig. 1. Splitting along D allows to maintain the geometrical information of the feature maps, because features that have different position on $H \times W$ are not aggregated. Following this method, the number of descriptors changes from $H \times W$ to $H \times W \times \frac{D}{splitfactor}$. The *splitfactor* indicates the dimension of every single descriptor obtained after the split along the depth axis. This value needs to be a trade-off between the number of features and their discriminative quality. As an example, a feature map of $8 \times 8 \times 1280$, with *splitfactor* = 128, will be transformed in a set of $8 \times 8 \times 10$ = 640 descriptors of 128D. Thereinafter, we will refer to this as *Dense-Depth Representation* (DDR).

After the extraction, the CNN codes are normalized using the root square normalization described in [2].

We will demonstrate in the experiments that the newly proposed DDR achieves higher performance.

3.3 VLAD and locVLAD

Starting from a codebook $C = \{\mathbf{u_1}, \ldots, \mathbf{u_K}\}$ of K d-dimensional visual features, generated from K-means clustering on the CNN codes, every local descriptor $X = \{\mathbf{x_1}, \ldots, \mathbf{x_m}\}$, extracted from the image, is assigned to the closest cluster center of the codebook:

$$q : \mathbb{R}^d \to C \tag{1}$$

$$q(\mathbf{x}) = \mu_i | i = \arg\min_{i=1,\ldots,K} ||\mathbf{x} - \mu_i|| \tag{2}$$

where $|| \cdot ||$ is a proper d-dimensional distance measure and d is the size of the descriptors ($d = 128$ in the aforementioned example).

The VLAD vector $\mathbf{v}$ is obtained by computing the sum of residuals, that is the difference between the feature descriptor and the corresponding cluster center:

$$\mathbf{v}^i = \sum_{\forall \mathbf{x} \in X : q(\mathbf{x}) = \mu_i} \mathbf{x} - \mu_i \tag{3}$$

The last step is the concatenation of the $\mathbf{v}^i$ features, resulting in the unnormalized VLAD vector $\mathbf{v}$. This vector often includes repeated (duplicated) features that make the recognition more difficult. To solve this problem, the vector $\mathbf{v}$ is normalized using the Z-score normalization [32], which consists in a residual normalization that is an independent residual L_2 norm of every visual word $\mathbf{v}^i$:

$$\tilde{\mathbf{v}}^i = \sum_{\forall \mathbf{x} \in X : q(\mathbf{x}) = \mu_i} \frac{\mathbf{x} - \mu_i}{||\mathbf{x} - \mu_i||} \tag{4}$$

Next, the resulting vector is further normalized as follows:

$$\hat{\mathbf{v}}^i = \frac{\tilde{\mathbf{v}}^i - m}{\sigma} \tag{5}$$

where m and σ represent the mean and the standard deviation of the vector, respectively. Finally, the vector is further L_2 normalized.

Recently, with the introduction of locVLAD [17], the accuracy in retrieval has been increased in an intuitive way. The VLAD vector is calculated through the mean of two different VLAD descriptors: one computed on the whole image and one computed only on the central portion of the image. The idea behind this method is that the most important and useful features in the images are often in the central region. LocVLAD is applied only to the query images, because the database images contain different views of the same landmark, as well as zoomed views.

At the end, VLAD descriptors are PCA-whitened [11] to 128D.

4   Experimental Results

The proposed approach has been extensively tested on public datasets in order to evaluate the accuracy against the state of the art.

4.1   Datasets and Evaluation Metrics

The performance is measured on four public image datasets:

- Holidays [12] is composed by 1491 images representing the holidays photos of different locations, subdivided in 500 classes. The database images are 991 and the query images are 500, one for every class.
- Oxford5k [23] is composed by 5062 images of Oxford landmarks. The classes are 11 and the queries are 55 (5 for each class).
- Paris6k [24] is composed by 6412 images of landmarks of Paris, France. The classes are 11 and the queries are 55 (5 for each class).
- UKB [19] is composed by 10200 images of diverse categories such as animals, plants, etc., subdivided in 2550 classes. Every class is composed by 4 images. All the images are used as database images and only one for category is used as a query image.

The vocabulary for the VLAD descriptors was created on Paris. Instead, when testing on Paris, the vocabulary was created on Oxford.

For the evaluation of the retrieval performance, mean Average Precision (mAP) was adopted. Instead, for the calculation of the distances between the query VLAD descriptor and the database VLAD descriptors, L_2 distance was employed.

In terms of actual implementation, the detector and descriptor used is CNN-based described in Sect. 3.1, that runs on a NVIDIA GeForce GTX 1070 GPU mounted on a computer with 8-core and 3.40 GHz CPU. All experiments have been run on 4 threads. To implement the feature extractor system, the Keras library was used.

4.2 Results on Holidays

Table 1 reports the results obtained extracting the features with CNN pre-trained on ImageNet [5]. Different CNN architectures have been tested: VGG19 [27] and InceptionV3 [30].

All the experiments were executed using a vocabulary of $K = 100$ visual words, created on Paris dataset through the application of K-Means [15] clustering technique, initialized following the K-Means++ [20] strategy. At the beginning, the initial configuration was to extract features from the block4_pool of VGG19 with an input image of the dimensions equal to 224×224, that is the predefined input image of VGG19. Changing, the dimension of the input image, the results were improved. Also, the choice of the layer in which extract the feature maps is important: from block4_pool to block5_pool of VGG19 there was an improvement equal to 2%. The breakthrough was the use of InceptionV3. Thanks to the depth of this CNN architecture, the feature maps extracted allowed to create a more representative VLAD descriptor. The first experiment executed on InceptionV3 reached a mAP equal to 81.55%, which is almost 4% more than VGG19. After we found the best configuration for the parameters: Network and Layer we focused on the other parameters. The application of locVLAD instead of VLAD for the feature aggregation phase allowed to improve the performance (improvement of 3%). Also, the root square normalization slightly improved the retrieval accuracy. Following the idea that features extracted on the image resized to square not respect the aspect ratio it is not a good idea, we modified the input image of InceptionV3 allowing to have an input of variable size, that was adaptable to the different dimensions of the images. Finally, the application of PCA-whitening reduced the dimension of the descriptors and removed the noisy values, also improving the performance.

Table 1. Results on Holidays. * indicates cases where the image aspect ratio is maintained.

Network	Layer	Input image	DDR	Root square norm.	Encoding	PCA-whit.	mAP
VGG19	block4_pool	224×244	✓	✗	VLAD	✗	74.33
VGG19	block4_pool	550×550	✓	✗	VLAD	✗	75.95
VGG19	block5_pool	550×550	✓	✗	VLAD	✗	77.80
InceptionV3	mixed_8	450×450	✓	✗	VLAD	✗	81.55
InceptionV3	mixed_8	450×450	✓	✗	locVLAD	✗	84.55
InceptionV3	mixed_8	562×562	✓	✗	locVLAD	✗	85.34
InceptionV3	mixed_8	562×562	✓	✓	locVLAD	✗	85.98
InceptionV3	mixed_8	562×662*	✓	✓	locVLAD	✗	86.70
InceptionV3	mixed_8	562×662*	✓	✓	locVLAD	128D	87.38
InceptionV3	mixed_8	562×662*	✗	✓	locVLAD	128D	85.63
InceptionV3	mixed_8	562×662*	✓	✓	locVLAD	256D	89.93
InceptionV3	mixed_8	562×662*	✓	✓	locVLAD	512D	90.46

It is worth to note that all the VLAD and locVLAD vectors are then finally normalized using Z-score normalization. Furthermore, the application of DDR allowed to higly improve the retrieval performance, as reported in the fourth last row of the Table 1.

Table 2. Comparison of state-of-the-art methods on different public CBIR datasets.

Method	Dimension	Oxford5k	Paris6k	Holidays	UKB
VLAD [13]	4096	37.80	38.60	55.60	3.18
CEVLAD [36]	128	53.00	–	68.10	3.093
FVLAD [14]	128	–	–	62.20	3.43
HVLAD [6]	128	–	–	64.00	3.40
gVLAD [32]	128	**60.00**	–	77.90	–
Ng *et al.* [34]	128	55.80	58.30	83.60	–
DDR locVLAD	128	57.52	**64.70**	**87.38**	**3.70**
NetVLAD [1]	512	59.00	70.20	82.90	–
DDR locVLAD	512	**61.46**	**71.88**	**90.46**	**3.76**

4.3 Comparison with the State of the Art on Holidays, Oxford5k, Paris6k and UKB

Table 2 reports the comparison with VLAD approaches on some public datasets.

All the descriptors of the VLAD-based methods are PCA-whitened, except the first one. Our method outperforms the others on all the presented datasets, reaching good results on the public benchmarks, in particular on the Holidays dataset. Unfortunately, on Oxford5k, gVLAD obtained an accuracy slightly better than our due to the concatenation of different VLAD, calculated following the orientation of local features. On the other hand, augmenting the dimension of the descriptor from 128D to 512D, our method performs better than the others even on Oxford5k. The high accuracy is the result of the focus on the central features of the images due to locVLAD and the dense representation of DDR.

5 Conclusions

The paper presents a new Dense-Depth Representation that allows, combined with locVLAD descriptors, to outperform the state of the art related to VLAD descriptors on several public benchmarks. The combination of the dense representation (DDR) and the focus on the most important part of the images of locVLAD allowed to obtain a better representation of each image and, therefore, to improve the retrieval accuracy without the need to augment the dimension of the descriptor that still remains 512D. The future work will be on a different embedding like R-MAC. Also, the application of fine-tuning could help to improve the final accuracy results.

Acknowledgment. This work is partially funded by Regione Emilia Romagna under the "Piano triennale alte competenze per la ricerca, il trasferimento tecnologico e l'imprenditorialità".

References

1. Arandjelovic, R., Gronat, P., Torii, A., Pajdla, T., Sivic, J.: NetVLAD: CNN architecture for weakly supervised place recognition. In: Proceedings of the IEEE Conference on Computer Vision and Pattern Recognition, pp. 5297–5307 (2016)
2. Arandjelović, R., Zisserman, A.: Three things everyone should know to improve object retrieval. In: 2012 IEEE Conference on Computer Vision and Pattern Recognition (CVPR), pp. 2911–2918. IEEE (2012)
3. Babenko, A., Slesarev, A., Chigorin, A., Lempitsky, V.: Neural codes for image retrieval. In: Fleet, D., Pajdla, T., Schiele, B., Tuytelaars, T. (eds.) ECCV 2014. LNCS, vol. 8689, pp. 584–599. Springer, Cham (2014). https://doi.org/10.1007/978-3-319-10590-1_38
4. Bay, H., Tuytelaars, T., Van Gool, L.: SURF: speeded up robust features. In: Leonardis, A., Bischof, H., Pinz, A. (eds.) ECCV 2006. LNCS, vol. 3951, pp. 404–417. Springer, Heidelberg (2006). https://doi.org/10.1007/11744023_32
5. Deng, J., Dong, W., Socher, R., Li, L.J., Li, K., Fei-Fei, L.: Imagenet: a large-scale hierarchical image database. In: IEEE Conference on Computer Vision and Pattern Recognition, CVPR 2009, pp. 248–255. IEEE (2009)
6. Eggert, C., Romberg, S., Lienhart, R.: Improving VLAD: hierarchical coding and a refined local coordinate system. In: ICIP, pp. 3018–3022 (2014)
7. Gong, Y., Wang, L., Guo, R., Lazebnik, S.: Multi-scale orderless pooling of deep convolutional activation features. In: Fleet, D., Pajdla, T., Schiele, B., Tuytelaars, T. (eds.) ECCV 2014. LNCS, vol. 8695, pp. 392–407. Springer, Cham (2014). https://doi.org/10.1007/978-3-319-10584-0_26
8. Gordo, A., Almazán, J., Revaud, J., Larlus, D.: Deep image retrieval: learning global representations for image search. In: Leibe, B., Matas, J., Sebe, N., Welling, M. (eds.) ECCV 2016. LNCS, vol. 9910, pp. 241–257. Springer, Cham (2016). https://doi.org/10.1007/978-3-319-46466-4_15
9. Gordo, A., Almazan, J., Revaud, J., Larlus, D.: End-to-end learning of deep visual representations for image retrieval. Int. J. Comput. Vis. **124**(2), 237–254 (2017)
10. He, K., Zhang, X., Ren, S., Sun, J.: Deep residual learning for image recognition. In: Proceedings of the IEEE Conference on Computer Vision and Pattern Recognition, pp. 770–778 (2016)
11. Jégou, H., Chum, O.: Negative evidences and co-occurences in image retrieval: the benefit of PCA and whitening. In: Fitzgibbon, A., Lazebnik, S., Perona, P., Sato, Y., Schmid, C. (eds.) ECCV 2012. LNCS, pp. 774–787. Springer, Heidelberg (2012). https://doi.org/10.1007/978-3-642-33709-3_55
12. Jégou, H., Douze, M., Schmid, C.: Hamming embedding and weak geometry consistency for large scale image search-extended version. In: Proceedings of the 10th European Conference on Computer Vision: Part I, pp. 304–317 (2008)
13. Jégou, H., Douze, M., Schmid, C., Pérez, P.: Aggregating local descriptors into a compact image representation. In: CVPR, pp. 3304–3311 (2010)

14. Liu, Z., Wang, S., Tian, Q.: Fine-residual VLAD for image retrieval. Neurocomputing **173**, 1183 (2016)
15. Lloyd, S.: Least squares quantization in PCM. IEEE Trans. Inf. Theory **28**(2), 129–137 (1982)
16. Lowe, D.G.: Object recognition from local scale-invariant features. In: The Proceedings of the Seventh IEEE International Conference on Computer Vision, vol. 2, pp. 1150–1157. IEEE (1999)
17. Magliani, F., Bidgoli, N.M., Prati, A.: A location-aware embedding technique for accurate landmark recognition. In: ICDSC, pp. 9–14 (2017)
18. Magliani, F., Prati, A.: An accurate retrieval through R-MAC+ descriptors for landmark recognition. In: Proceedings of the 12th International Conference on Distributed Smart Cameras. ACM. arXiv preprint arXiv:1806.08565 (2018)
19. Nister, D., Stewenius, H.: Scalable recognition with a vocabulary tree. In: 2006 IEEE Computer Society Conference on Computer Vision and Pattern Recognition, vol. 2, pp. 2161–2168. IEEE (2006)
20. Ostrovsky, R., Rabani, Y., Schulman, L.J., Swamy, C.: The effectiveness of LLOYD-type methods for the k-means problem. In: 47th Annual IEEE Symposium on Foundations of Computer Science, FOCS 2006, pp. 165–176. IEEE (2006)
21. Pan, S.J., Yang, Q.: A survey on transfer learning. IEEE Trans. Knowl. Data Eng. **22**(10), 1345–1359 (2010)
22. Perronnin, F., Liu, Y., Sánchez, J., Poirier, H.: Large-scale image retrieval with compressed fisher vectors. In: 2010 IEEE Conference on Computer Vision and Pattern Recognition (CVPR), pp. 3384–3391. IEEE (2010)
23. Philbin, J., Chum, O., Isard, M., Sivic, J., Zisserman, A.: Object retrieval with large vocabularies and fast spatial matching. In: Proceedings of the IEEE Conference on Computer Vision and Pattern Recognition (2007)
24. Philbin, J., Chum, O., Isard, M., Sivic, J., Zisserman, A.: Lost in quantization: improving particular object retrieval in large scale image databases. In: CVPR (2008)
25. Razavian, A.S., Sullivan, J., Carlsson, S., Maki, A.: Visual instance retrieval with deep convolutional networks. ITE Trans. Media Technol. Appl. **4**(3), 251–258 (2016)
26. Reddy Mopuri, K., Venkatesh Babu, R.: Object level deep feature pooling for compact image representation. In: Proceedings of the IEEE Conference on Computer Vision and Pattern Recognition Workshops, pp. 62–70 (2015)
27. Simonyan, K., Zisserman, A.: Very deep convolutional networks for large-scale image recognition. arXiv preprint arXiv:1409.1556 (2014)
28. Sivic, J., Zisserman, A.: Video Google: a text retrieval approach to object matching in videos. In: ICCV, vol. 2, pp. 1470–1477 (2003)
29. Szegedy, C., et al.: Going deeper with convolutions. In: CVPR, pp. 1–9 (2015)
30. Szegedy, C., Vanhoucke, V., Ioffe, S., Shlens, J., Wojna, Z.: Rethinking the inception architecture for computer vision. In: Proceedings of the IEEE Conference on Computer Vision and Pattern Recognition, pp. 2818–2826 (2016)
31. Tolias, G., Sicre, R., Jégou, H.: Particular object retrieval with integral max-pooling of CNN activations. arXiv preprint arXiv:1511.05879 (2015)
32. Wang, Z., Di, W., Bhardwaj, A., Jagadeesh, V., Piramuthu, R.: Geometric VLAD for large scale image search. arXiv preprint arXiv:1403.3829 (2014)
33. Yan, K., Wang, Y., Liang, D., Huang, T., Tian, Y.: CNN vs. SIFT for image retrieval: alternative or complementary? In: Proceedings of the 2016 ACM on Multimedia Conference, pp. 407–411. ACM (2016)

34. Yue-Hei Ng, J., Yang, F., Davis, L.S.: Exploiting local features from deep networks for image retrieval. In: Proceedings of the IEEE Conference on Computer Vision and Pattern Recognition Workshops, pp. 53–61 (2015)
35. Zhao, W.L., Jégou, H., Gravier, G.: Oriented pooling for dense and non-dense rotation-invariant features. In: BMVC (2013)
36. Zhou, Q., Wang, C., Liu, P., Li, Q., Wang, Y., Chen, S.: Distribution entropy boosted VLAD for image retrieval. Entropy 18(8), 311 (2016)

Virtual Reality II

Augmented Reality System for Training and Assistance in the Management of Industrial Equipment and Instruments

Edison A. Chicaiza$^{(\boxtimes)}$, Edgar I. De la Cruz$^{(\boxtimes)}$, and Víctor H. Andaluz

Universidad de las Fuerzas Armadas ESPE, Sangolquí, Ecuador
{eachicaiza1, eide, vhandaluz1}@espe.edu.ec

Abstract. This article proposes the development of a smartphone application on the Android platform as a recognition tool, focused on the digitization of real objects using image processing techniques. The application is oriented to the process of training and assistance in the handling of equipment and industrial instruments within the field of engineering such as electronics, mechanics, electromechanics, mechatronics, being a technological tool that allows users to interact in the reality environment Increased, it presents a friendly and intuitive environment, thus improving the process of handling industrial equipment and changing the paradigms of the use of physical manuals and giving use to new technologies such as smartphones with digital information.

Keywords: Augmented reality · Object recognition · Characteristic points

1 Introduction

The ever-increasing use of TIC has produced a new scenario that is affecting the most important elements in the development of the society being the industrial fundamental mainstay destined to develop the economy of a nation with intellectual capacity, moral and emotional people who contribute to the development of society [1, 2]. These technological developments have influenced the industry very strongly through the creation of new diffusion tools, and new structures of creation and advancement in prisoner of training and personnel within the industrial sector [3]. Within the system of management and assistance have been implemented new ideas, methods and lines of action that are related to the technology, instead of theoretical - practical that are aimed at improving the traditional production process [4]. The technological tools for training and assistance in the management of equipment and Instrument in comparison to the usual techniques present better result when applied, because the technology combined with the work or study increases the effectiveness of the knowledge acquisition processes [2, 5].

Augmented reality (AR) has been defined as a system that fulfills three characteristics [4, 6]: first, it combines the real and virtual world; second, it allows interaction in real time; third, align real objects or places and digital information in 3D. AR technology has existed for more than 50 years, but only the recent proliferation and consumption of

© Springer Nature Switzerland AG 2018
G. Bebis et al. (Eds.): ISVC 2018, LNCS 11241, pp. 675–686, 2018.
https://doi.org/10.1007/978-3-030-03801-4_59

smartphone technologies (for example, smartphone, tablets) have been available AR systems available to the general public. In parallel, another technology that has been highlighted by the advances are the smartphones [7, 8], these smartphones require features that allow the processing of information to develop the app with augmented reality, before it the basis to generate the AR environment is the recognizing of the site or object with which it will interact. Currently the AR is developed in 4 levels; the first level includes applications that hyperlink the physical world through the use of bar codes and 2D, these codes only serve as hyperlinks to other content, so there is no record in 3D or tracking of markers, at this level they have been developed "Mobile Augmented Reality of Tourism-Yilan Hot Spring", which uses QR fast response codes [9, 10]; in the second level consists applications that use markers, black and white images, quadrangular and with schematic drawings, usually for the recognition of 2D patterns, more advanced form of this level also allows the recognition of 3D objects, at this level they have developed works such as: "Authorship and Analytics of Multimodal Educational Mobile Applications", which handles recognition of 2D and 3D objects [9, 11]; the third level has applications that substitute the use of markers by the GPS and the compass of the smartphones to determine the location and orientation of the user and superimpose points of interest on the images of the real world, this level of the AR, this level of consists of works such as "Digitalization of Tourist Destinations: Tool for Government Planning and Management, "based on geposing, and" Augmented Reality and Pedestrian Navigation through its Implementation in M-Learning and E-Learning: Evaluation of an Educational Program in Chile "which is based on smartphone maping [9, 12]; The fourth level consists of devices such as Google Glass, high-tech contact lenses or others that, in the future, will be able to offer a fully contextualized, immersive and personal experience, such as: "An Augmented Lecture Feedback System to Support Learner and Teacher Communication ", which is based on Google Glass [8, 13].

Within the technology for learning is the fusion of the real environment and an environment with augmented reality, promoting the interaction of the operators with the contents for the training and assistance of the handling of industrial equipment, and thus improve the performance in the production process [2, 14]. For the use of the AR the success is the recognition of the objects or the environment with which one is going to interact there are several techniques as it was described in the levels of AR, according to the levels of AR, the development of our work is it is immersed in level 3, through the use of image processing for recognition, being the most efficient and effective process with smartphone due to its low data processing capacity [9, 10, 14].

This research proposes the development of an AR application aimed at supporting the process of training and assistance in the management of industrial equipment and instruments within engineering, taking advantage of the technology available to the smartphone and exploiting its benefits to the maximum by incorporating TIC in production processes [11, 15], and immersion with AR, using image processing techniques, aimed at recognizing objects and presenting multimedia content, creating a space in AR, with the aim of facilitating training and assistance, providing interactive, user-friendly training environments [16, 17].

This article is divided into 4 sections: the first section consists of the introduction, then the second section consists of the recognition and development technologies of the multimedia environment; in the third section the results are presented and their respective analysis of results, the fourth and last section consists of conclusions of the work developed.

2 Development of the Application

The development of the proposed application is shown in Fig. 1, which considers four main stages in which a specific task is defined, in addition, one or several processes that allow executing the workflow tasks of the application for smartphone: (i) *Layer 1* in this layer allows the creation of the 3D Object Target and the digitization of the industrial instrument, with the Vuforia Object Scanner application; Vuforia is the popular SDK for the creation of applications in a wide selection of smartphone, provides tracking, image recognition, recognition of objects encompassed patterns in which the categorization of input data into identified classes, by means of extraction of significant characteristics or attributes of the data extracted from a medium containing irrelevant details.

The extraction of characteristic points is a step frequently used to get to define the object itself within an image. The obtaining of the characteristic points of the object that allows to identify again the object from these points. The first step is to detect the position of each characteristic point. Subsequently its content is define by one or more characteristic regions. More specifically, two tasks are use, namely:

Detection: The detection consists of finding the place of the image where typical points exist; the detection is the process in which there are located the regions of the image that contain a few certain characteristics, due to his form or texture.

Description: The description is realized after the detection, once located the place, one proceeds to describe by means of one or more characteristics the region placed about typical detected point. These characteristics are stored frequently in a vector for his later use.

Vuforia Object Scanner is based on image processing determining points and regions characteristic of objects, image processing is based on the algorithm Speeded up Robust Features (SURF), and it is the accelerated algorithm of characteristic points providing better results in terms of repeatability, distinction and robustness.

SURF uses an algorithm based on the hessian matrix for detection, which looks for a balance between the approximation of methods and the conservation of good results, managing to create a rapid algorithm and with high repeatability. The utilization of Gaussian for the creation of the space of scales; concretely, in an approximation of the determinant of the hessiana matrix. By means of this approximation there is obtained a much more rapid calculation of the space of scales. To understand the approximation of SURF one must show before what aspect they have the partial derivatives that compose the hessiana matrix.

After locating the position and size of the characteristic points, the next step is to describe those points; this process is carried out by calculating the characteristic region surrounding each point, a concept known as local description. This process of obtaining characteristic points is achieved with the application Vuforia Object Scanner, as the

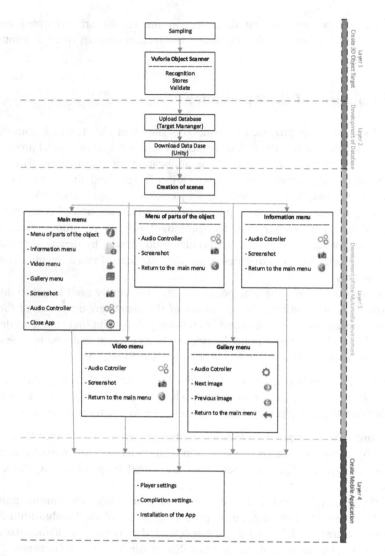

Fig. 1. Multilayer scheme of the application.

first instance it is essential to determine the objective of scanning objects, the objective of object exploration is used to establish the position of its object objective in relation with its local origin. This origin is represented by (0, 0, 0) in the lower left corner of the grid region of the object exploration target and corresponds to the local (0, 0, 0) of the bounding box of the prefabricated instance of Object objects, this is observed in the Fig. 2, the positioning of the instrument in the bounding box.

Object recognition encompasses patterns in the category of input data in identified classes, through the extraction of features or data extracted from a medium containing irrelevant details; The validation of the 3D Object is carried out by means of the

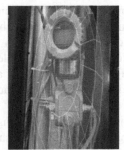

(a) Point of origin for the creation of the 3D Object

(b) Taking of characteristic points of the 3D Object

(c)   Object validated as 3D Object

Fig. 2. Positioning of the instrument in the delimiter and the process of obtaining characteristic points.

Vuforia Object scanner application and the camera of the smartphone for to verify the correct creation of our pattern, this can be seen in the Fig. 2(c).

(ii) *Layer 2* is responsible for generating the database in the Target Manager and provides 3D Object files with compatible features to use in the development of the application; the type 3D Object pattern is stored in the database, of the Vuforia platform to be used according to the user's needs. The Target Manager allows the download of stored patterns with an extension compatible with the Unity platform.

(iii) *Layer 3* consists of the development of the application where three scenarios were created which consist of: main menu, menu of parts of the object, and general information menu of the whole object that it recognizes, within which, in the main menu, as well as in the other menus, a label of text type is included that will indicate the name of the recognized object that is shown in the upper right part of the screen of the smartphone, the information button will appear that will direct to the corresponding scene, the options button for the audio control that is found by default, the information button of parts of the object that will direct to this scene, and the close button which closes the application.

In the information menu of parts of the object a script is developed for the handling of the Box Collider that will detect the AR Camera when it is located above the object's position, showing the name with the corresponding text color in the upper left, it also presents the return button that will direct you to the main menu scene.

In the Information menu, textual information is presented with 3D text showing characteristic content of each object, the Lean Touch script is also included to rotate and scale the information presented on the smartphone screen. For the presentation of the video, the Video Playback Controller script is used to manage the video shown on the screen through the AR Camera, allowing starting, pausing, and resuming the playback of the displayed video, also adding the Lean Touch script to rotate and scale the video.

Last, (iii) *Layer 4* is observed in Fig. 3, the Player Settings in Unity is configured prior to the compilation of the application, selecting the left orientation by default, placing parameters such as the name of the company and product developed, the version number of the application, and the minimum API (Application Programming Interface) level from which the application will work.

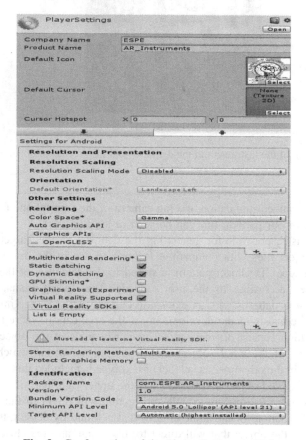

Fig. 3. Configuration of the Player Settings in Unity

After the configuration the Android application is compiled, generating an APK file (Android Application Package), the file is copied to the smartphone and the installation is carried out.

3 Experimental Results

This section presents the experimental performance of the application of augmented reality oriented to the process of training and assistance in the handling of industrial instruments, the application is used as a tool to improve the process of training and management of industrial equipment and changing the paradigms of the use of physical manuals and the use of new technologies such as smartphones with digital information.

In this section, it shows how the application of augmented reality facilitates the process of recognition and interaction with the recognized object by providing relevant information of industrial instruments. In this case the user can make use of the application to obtain specific information of the industrial instruments, to start with the application of recognition it is necessary that previously the APK is install on the smartphone.

When the application is running for the first time, a welcome splash of the application is show, as shown in Fig. 4(a); later the start screen appears where you can see the main menu of the application, such as it is show in Fig. 4(b). The application recognizes objects that are in the database, from the Industrial Instrumentation Laboratory, as shown in Fig. 5(a), the user uses the augmented reality application on his mobile device, as shown in Fig. 5(b), the Foxboro IAP 20 instrument is from the Pressure Station of the Industrial Instrumentation Laboratory, as shown in Fig. 5(c).

(a) Presentation of the splash with the theme of the application

(b) Presentation of the main menu screen

Fig. 4. Start and presentation of the application.

Once detected the desired object, allows the interaction with the object for it in the information icon *i*, allows showing information about the object, this information can be text or graphic, by means of which general information of the Foxboro Transmitter IAP 20 is provide, as shown in Fig. 6(a). The information presented can be rotted and scaled according to the needs of the user, as show in Fig. 6(b).

By means of the audio configuration buttons ⚙, we control the predefined audio of the application that allows us to stop - play the audio and upload - lower the volume, and with the button ◀, return to the main menu of the application. With the information menu provided by the application allows you to obtain the possibility of observing a multimedia video, related to the object that is detected according to the

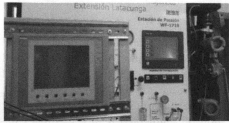

(a)   Pressure station of the industrial instrumentation laboratory

(b)   Use of the application on the smartphone
by the user

(a)   Foxboro IAP 20 Pressure transmitter information

Fig. 5. Use of the application in the pressure station in the Industrial Instrumentation Laboratory.

(a)   General information about the Foxboro
Transmitter IAP20

(b)   Information rotated and scaled by the
user

Fig. 6. General information about the Foxboro Transmitter IAP 20, with its characteristics and operation.

database, in this menu we can see the video with possibility to put play, raise - lower the audio volume, zoom and rotate the video with the next button 📹, allows you to configure the audio options and return via a button to the main menu ◀, this menu is shown in the following Fig. 4(b). Using the textual information button 📋, allows showing information in augmented reality of the detected objects as shown in Fig. 6.

The information is present in augmented reality on the mobile device as shown in the following Fig. 7(a), textual information of the Siemens S7-1500 PLC is present as show in Fig. 7(b), the audio information and video of the recognized device is show in Fig. 7(c).

(a) Presentation of information on the smartphone

(b) General information of the Siemens S7-1500 PLC

(c) Video in augmented reality of PLC S7-1500

Fig. 7. General information about the Siemens S7-1500 PLC, with its features and audio and video information.

Within the options of the application allows the recognition of specific parts of the objects detected, as show in Fig. 8, another of the benefits provided by the application is the ease of making screenshot using the button 📷, through this button you can save images in a local database of the same smartphone which is accessed through the button 🖼, this gallery of images is specifically for this application, when entering the gallery you can browse the images by means of the following buttons ➡ ⬅, this is show in Fig. 9, finally with the button ⏻ we abandoned the application.

The results presented below indicate the validity of the usability of augmented reality environments, to carry out an industrial instruments management, in our specific case: in the training process and operator, assistance in the handling of equipment and

(a) General recognition of Rosemount 3051s transmitter parts

(b) Detection of Rosemount 3051s transmitter parts

Fig. 8. Detection of detected object parts.

(a) Screen captured from the Foxboro
IAP20 Transmitter

(b) Screen captured from the S7-200 PLC

Fig. 9. Gallery of images of the screenshot.

instruments immersed in the industry. For this purpose, the SUS summary evaluation method is used [17]. Generally providing the style scale that generates a single number, represented by an average composed of the usability of the smartphone application, as shown in Table 1.

The total number, obtained from the sum of the operation in each question, results in 31. Based on this result, the SUS score is calculated and expressed by a multiplication of 2.5, which means that the application is feasible for training and assistance in the handling of industrial equipment and instruments, provides assistance to the operator, obtaining a percentage of 78.43%, representing a high usability of this type of technological tools.

Table 1. Results of the questionnaire.

Questions	Punctuation					Operation
I would like to use often the application				2	9	3.82
I found the App with increased reality it is unnecessarily and complex	9	2				3.82
It was easy to use the App with augmented reality				3	8	3.73
You need the support of a technician to be able to use this application	11					4
The different functions of the application are well integrated		1			10	4.1
There was too much flexibility in the application			1		10	0.18
I imagine that most people would learn very quickly to use the application				1	10	3.91
I found the application very difficult to use	9			1	1	0.27
I felt very confident in the navigation of the application				2	9	3.82
I need to learn many things before using the application	8	3				3.73
Total						31.37

For the precision in the detection of the objects, the same object was focused with the smartphone in 10 different angles, of which in 9 of them the detection is fast and instantaneous providing the information corresponding to the scene in which it is inside. The application, thus being 90% accurate in the detection of objects, this appreciation depends on the lighting in which the tests are performed and the focus of the smartphone camera, the environment must have a natural or artificial lighting higher than 100 lx.

4 Conclusions

The increased reality contributes to the training and assistance of the managing equipment and industrial instruments, providing benefits that they contribute to the suitable use of the equipment's in the industrial field, offering a training to the users and orientating to the correct managing and utilization of the equipment's, increasing the useful life of the equipment's, this way also omitting failures of functioning for erroneous maneuvers. The work shows the development of the application Assistance. AR that offers relevant, adaptable information of the equipment's and industrial instruments to the environment in which they are. In turn, the application allows the interaction of the user for the managing of the information presented in the recognition of the objects, from the screen of the mobile device. Finally, the application presents options of managing of the audio and video in the graphical interface developed of agreement to the needs of the user.

Acknowledgements. The authors would like to thanks to the Corporación Ecuatoriana para el Desarrollo de la Investigación y Academia – CEDIA for the financing given to research, development, and innovation, through the Grupos de Trabajo, GT, especially to the GTeTURISMO; also to Universidad de las Fuerzas Armadas ESPE, Universidad Técnica de Ambato, Escuela Superior Politécnica de Chimborazo, Universidad Nacional de Chimborazo, and Grupo de Investigación en Automatización, Robótica y Sistemas Inteligentes, GI-ARSI, for the support to develop this work.

References

1. Joo-Nagata, J., Abad, F.M., Giner, J.G.B.: Augmented reality and pedestrian navigation through its implementation in m-learning and e-learning: evaluation of an educational program in Chile. Elsevier Transl. J. Comput. Educ. **111**, 1–3 (2017)
2. Wu, H.-K., Lee, S.W.-Y., Chang, H.-Y., Liang, J.-C.: Current status, opportunities and challenges of augmented reality in education. Elsevier Transl. J. Comput. Educ. **62**, 41–49 (2013)
3. Zhanga, C.J.: The development and evaluation of an augmented reality-based armillary. Elsevier Transl. J. Comput. Educ. **73**, 178–188 (2014)
4. Blum, J.R., Greencorn, D.G., Cooperstock, J.R.: Smartphone sensor reliability for augmented reality applications. In: Zheng, K., Li, M., Jiang, H. (eds.) MobiQuitous 2012. LNICST, vol. 120, pp. 127–138. Springer, Heidelberg (2013). https://doi.org/10.1007/978-3-642-40238-8_11

5. Gallardo, C., et al.: Augmented Reality as a New Marketing Strategy. In: De Paolis, L.T., Bourdot, P. (eds.) AVR 2018. LNCS, vol. 10850, pp. 351–362. Springer, Cham (2018). https://doi.org/10.1007/978-3-319-95270-3_29

6. Huamaní, J.A.: Augmented reality: a digital resource between the real and the virtual world. Hamut'Ay **2**, 50–57 (2016)

7. Iván Ruiz, D.: Autoría y analítica de aplicaciones móviles educativas multimodales, vol. 1, pp. 1–6. Springer, España (2016)

8. Almenara, J.C.: Productions of learning objects production in Augmented Reality: the experience of SAV of the University of Seville. Int. J. Educ. Res. Innov. (IJERI) **6**, 110–123 (2016). España

9. Olivencia, L.: Tecnologías de Geolocalización y Realidad Aumentada en Contextos Educativos: experiencias y herramientas didácticas, RACO Transl. J. Didáctica, Innovacion y Multimedia, p. 31, Abril 2015

10. Espinosa, C.P.: Augmented Reality and Education: Analysis of Practical Experiencies, EBSCO, Enero, pp. 187–203 (2015)

11. Cabero Almenara, F.R.J.: Mobile devices and augmented reality in the learning process of university students. Int. J. Educ. Res. Innov. **20**, 110–123 (2016)

12. Sevilla, A.V.: Realidad Aumentada en Educación. Int. J. Educ. Res. Innov. **77**, 39 (2017)

13. Hui, L., Hung, F.Y., Chien, Y.L.: Mobile augmented reality of tourism-Yilan hot spring. In: 7th International Conference on Ubi-Media Computing and Workshops (UMEDIA), Mongolia, pp. 148–152 (2014)

14. Acioly, S.G.: Mobile augmented reality systems applied to food packaging—a heuristic evaluation. In: IEEE Transaction on Realidad Virtual y Aumentada (RVS), pp. 127–131 (2017)

15. Acosta, A.G., et al.: Digitalization of Tourist Destinations: Tool for Government Planning and Management. In: DePaolis, L.T., Bourdot, P. (eds.) AVR 2018. LNCS, vol. 10850, pp. 162–170. Springer, Cham (2018)

16. Torres, D.R.: Augmented reality and Cultural Heritage: new perspectives for the knowledge and dissemination of the cultural object. IEEE Trans. Realidad Virtual Aumentada **2**, 78–86 (2015)

17. Andaluz, V.H., et al.: Multi-user industrial training and education environment. In: De Paolis, L.T., Bourdot, P. (eds.) AVR 2018. LNCS, vol. 10851, pp. 533–546. Springer, Cham (2018). https://doi.org/10.1007/978-3-319-95282-6_38

Alternative Treatment of Psychological Disorders Such as Spider Phobia Through Virtual Reality Environments

Joseph Armas[✉] and Víctor H. Andaluz

Universidad de las Fuerzas Armadas ESPE, Sangolquí, Ecuador
{jearmas, vhandaluz1}@espe.edu.ec

Abstract. This article proposes a tool to support the psychotherapist in the process of treating spider phobia through a system that combines both software and hardware elements to present immersive virtual reality environments to the treated patient. To create the feeling of immersion, environments and models created in Unity are used in conjunction with the patient's movement tracked through the Kinect motion sensor. For the development of the system, the psychotherapeutic treatment method of systematic desensitization is used, so that the patient can overcome his fear and present non-phobic interactions with spiders. The process of developing the system and redacting this document was supported and supervised by a psychologist specialized in the treatment of phobias. Finally, tests were performed to obtain feedback from specialists and potential patients with a medium degree of phobia, in which the results were very positive and satisfactory.

Keywords: Spider phobia · Systematic desensitization · Virtual reality
Unity 3D · Kinect

1 Introduction

The knowledge of phobias themselves is very old, in the time of the Egyptians there were already scrolls that referred to the cirps hippocraticum with reference to excessive or irrational fears [1], nowadays phobias are known as the persistent fear which is unleashed in the presence of a specific object or situation [2]. In the 17th century it was Boissier who described the fear of heights, calling it hysterical vertigo now called acrophobia, and it was Morei who first classified phobias and other neuroses [1]. Phobic disorders are characterized by physiological, behavioral, and cognitive symptoms that are present and interact with each other in each of the anxious episodes presented by phobic subjects [3].

Studies with adults have found that the average age of onset of specific phobias is 9.7 years. However, at an early age there is a great deal of therapeutic neglect, because there is a tendency to confuse specific phobias with childhood fears that are transient and play an adaptive role [4, 5]. Phobia is without a doubt the most frequently found in psychopathology in relation to insects, this phobia called entomophobia is found within specific phobias, according to the American Psychiatric Association, in its classification

© Springer Nature Switzerland AG 2018
G. Bebis et al. (Eds.): ISVC 2018, LNCS 11241, pp. 687–697, 2018.
https://doi.org/10.1007/978-3-030-03801-4_60

of Mental Disorders DSM-IV. However, only 17% of patients with this phobia visit a psychiatrist [6].

Many people have a fear of spiders, although it is often controllable and will rarely actively avoid the possibility of encountering these animals. Several studies have been conducted on arachnophobia, one of which is Seligman's for example, who suggested that simple phobias are a response to stimuli that in the course of evolution have represented a real danger to mankind. This theory could explain entomophobia, or more specifically spider phobia [6]. A person becomes spider phobic due to a traumatic event or negative thoughts disclosed by close people, it is an anxiety disorder that gradually increases if not controlled [7].

The first appearance of virtual reality in Clinical Psychology focused on the treatment of acrophobia [8], in which the patient overcame his fear of heights after being exposed to virtual reality environments that put him in acrophobic situations. The use of this technology implies that one can have simulations of reality instead of the patient's imagination or procedures such as role-playing, giving the therapist full control over events [9], this gave way to further researches.

The advantages that virtual reality has over real exposure are important, many of the visual stimuli for the treatment of phobias can be expensive, virtual reality gives complete control of events to the therapist, which guarantees the safety of the patient; however, it also has its disadvantages, *e.g.* it does not completely replace reality because the patient will sooner or later be exposed to a real situation in order to complete his or her recovery, in addition to the fact that there are certain patients unable to fully fuse with virtual reality environments [10, 11].

Psychologists and researchers in the field of virtual reality have paid special attention to the treatment of phobias and other anxiety disorders, publishing several studies on the subject; the most relevant are [8, 12–14] in which various phobias are treated, *e.g.* acrophobia, dentist phobia, even using mobile devices for the treatment of dog phobia, however, there is other research that focuses especially on the treatment of spider phobia, which concludes that, despite some improvements to conventional treatments such as protocols and standardization, the difference between live exposure versus the use of virtual reality is not significant [15–19].

2 System Structure

The virtual reality system proposed for the treatment of spider phobia is designed to allow the user to interact easily with the system; the use of both input and output hardware devices allows the user to interact immersively with the system. The block diagram shown in Fig. 1 details the structure of the proposed system through a series of steps that it follows to achieve its objective.

The patient's interaction with the motion detection device provides real-time treatment for the patient, making rehabilitation more interactive and immersive, introducing the user to virtual reality environments created with the goal of overcoming the user's fear of spiders. On the other hand, as it is a virtual environment, the patient can leave when he feels that his fear is uncontrollable and he can no longer control himself, which increases the feeling of personal control at the moment of rehabilitation.

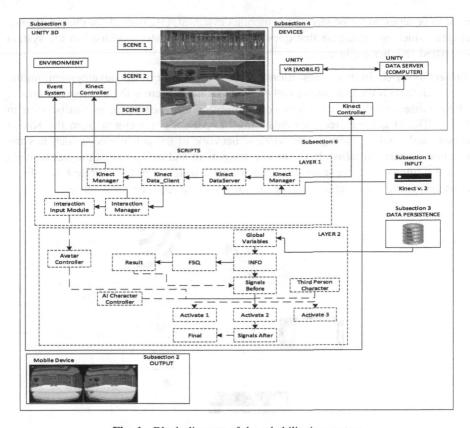

Fig. 1. Block diagram of the rehabilitation system

Likewise, by minimizing the effects and risks of live exposure and being something new for the patient, it significantly reduces therapeutic abandonment.

Figure 1 presents input, output, and data processing devices, as well as necessary scripts, logical objects, and a data persistence engine through which the proposed system becomes functional; the interaction of the variety of elements listed above recreates an immersive environment which is presented to the patient for the rehabilitation process. The patient's interaction with the entire system will give the sense of realism that is desired for successful rehabilitation. Application development can be subdivided into six subsections, (1) Input device, (2) Output device, (3) Persistence engine, (4) DataServer (Computer), (5) Processing interface (Mobile) and (6) Scripts.

Subsections 1–3. The proposed system has as its functional basis the detection of movements through the Kinect sensor as an input device [20, 21], for which through specific scripts, the data provided by the tool is interpreted in order to track the patient's movements to avatar animations within the treatment scene. As an output device we consider virtual reality glasses in order to give the patient a greater immersion in the rehabilitation process. Please note that the mobile device must be a smartphone and have Android 6.0 operating system or higher, while the virtual reality glasses will only need to be adjusted to the size of the mobile device. SQLite is used for the persistence engine, which is a database that does not represent a greater workload in the system compared to other engines.

Subsections 4–5. In these subsections there is the product of the development, on the one hand, there is the DataServer and on the other hand, there is the treatment interface. These subsections have a wireless communication between them, as can be seen in Fig. 2. The DataServer receives data from the patient's movement from the Kinect sensor, and sends it through the wireless network to the cell phone, which has the functional system installed. In the mobile the patient and the specialist interact actively with the software, at the same time, the software installed in the mobile has a direct connection with the database engine, which gives the required persistence.

Fig. 2. Communication between devices

Subsection 6. This subsection is the main part of the system as it contains all the logic applied for its development. This in turn is divided into two essential parts, (i) Layer 1, which aims at device connectivity and data interpretation, while (ii) Layer 2 will prioritize system functionality and data persistence.

(i) Layer 1. In this layer is found the Script that interconnects the devices wirelessly, taking as parameters the IP's of each equipment. The Kinect Data Server located on the server side (computer) determines the IP of the server and makes it visible to the server side so that there is a dynamic connection between the mobile phone and the computer. The Kinect Manager script located on both server and client, is the one that receives the patient's movements through the Kinect sensor, interprets them and makes them understandable for the Unity video game engine. Finally, there is the Avatar Controller, which allows the app to collect data from previous scripts, and based on this data, obtain and replicate the patient's movements and give motion to the avatar that's inside the environment.

(ii) This layer is responsible for the main functionality of the system, as it contains all the treatment logic, where the patient will have to go through virtual reality environments which depending on the patient have three different levels of intensity. These environments differ in: (a) *Comfort*. Which is the level of comfort provided by the environment in question, (b) *Realism*. It is the level of detail of the spider model, this feature enhances the therapeutic process through the modification of the 3D model, and in (c) *Animations*. Which are the type of movements the model has inside the virtual environment [22].

3 Virtual Interface

The system is developed in three different sections: (1) Interaction with the user, (2) Interaction with the specialist and, finally, (3) Virtual interaction with the patient.

3.1 User Interaction

This section focuses on the patient, a login process is presented so that the software stores each user and remembers all the results associated with it, both those obtained in the questionnaire and those provided to the system by the doctor during each session. Also, a questionnaire (FSQ) is presented which will inform both the specialist and the system about the level of phobia that the patient possesses, therefore, an interaction of the patient's hands with the buttons placed in the environment is needed, so that they can select the answer of their preference see Fig. 3.

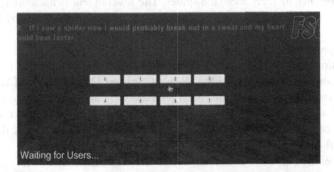

Fig. 3. Question number 18 from a bank of questions belonging to the FSQ, through which the patient's degree of phobia is obtained.

By completing the questionnaire, the system is able to present the scenario that best suits the patient depending on their degree of phobia. This avoids unnecessary interaction of the specialist with the system.

3.2 Specialist Interaction

This section is based on the interaction of the specialist with the system, it is about the input of certain variables that are needed in each session to follow the patient during his treatment, see Fig. 4.

Fig. 4. Data entry forms for the specialist, before and after the treatment session. On the left, input of the date of the current session and the patient's heart rate; on the right, input of the patient's fear level, presence level and heart rate prior to the session.

The variables to be measured are a selection of the variables presented in previous research [23, 24], which are listed below:

- Self-Reported Measures
  Here the state of the patient is used, the subjective units of disturbance scale (SUDs) will be used, where 0 is no disturbance or neutral and 10 is the maximum disturbance that the patient can imagine, with this range the patient must, after 10 to 40 s of exposure, rate the level of fear he feels of the spider, and after 20 to 50 s, rate the level of presence he feels about the spider. The level of fear is the anxiety the patient feels while the level of presence is if the patient feels the spider nearby after seeing it.
- Fear of Spiders Questionnaire
  The questionnaire will be taken from the patient before and after the treatment, the questionnaire was taken from FSQ (Fear of Spiders Questionnaire) [25].
  The FSQ consists of 18 questions each with answers on a scale of 0 to 7 where 0 is not at all and 7 is totally. The patient is asked to evaluate within this scale the similarity of his or her reaction to such situation with the reaction of the question.
- Behavioral Measures
  As for behavioral measurements, the heart rate measured with a sphygmo-manometer before and immediately after the treatment will be used, in this way, the values obtained can be compared and the impact of the treatment on the patient can be observed session by session [26].

3.3   Virtual Interaction

The proposed system has several virtual reality environments which are used as a treatment for patient phobia, through interaction with the most realistic 3D spider models possible, the patient should learn with the guidance of the specialist and the system to face the fear. For this purpose, it is taken into account that there are currently several methods for the treatment of phobias, one of which is systematic desensitization, which is based on the psychological principle that the body cannot be in a state of relaxation and anxiety at the same time, therefore, the patient should be taught how to relax in a situation of anxiety, and gradually become used to remain relaxed in front of the object responsible for the phobia.

Therefore, this research is based on what has been explained above and this concept is used to create virtual reality environments that allow this method to be applied. The system will have its functionality in treatments with constant and programmed sessions, in order for the rehabilitation to be a success.

4 Use Case

The results of the system developed as an alternative treatment for psychological disorders such as spider phobia are presented in this section. During the process, a group of patients with a high degree of spider phobia is treated, and a test subject is chosen to collect the results of this research. Next, the patient's treatment process is highlighted. First, the entire environment is prepared to proceed with the treatment. In order for the application to have its full functionality and be able to retrieve data from patient movement, an instance is required within a Data Server computer.

From the data retrieved from the Kinect sensor and sent through the local network where the server and client are connected by the Data Server, the application works at full capacity, at the beginning it displays a menu, which has the options of registering and logging in with a user. Once logged in the system displays some important information about the patient, see Fig. 5.

Fig. 5. Shows the information retrieved from the database for the user, in this interface the most relevant data of the patient is shown, such as user name, FSQ scores and the options to follow from that point onwards. On the left, information on the test subject, presented in the first instances of his or her treatment; on the right, the result of the patient's FSQ on the first day of treatment.

The patient's treatment is specified according to his degree of phobia, for this purpose the system has a spider fear questionnaire, which consists of 18 questions, with which a total is obtained and the patient is classified according to his level of fear, in this case, the patient presented a degree of phobia of 90, categorizing him as a highly phobic person [27]. There are 3 treatment levels within the system, see Fig. 6. In this case, the treatment starts with the most basic scene possible. Continuing with the treatment, the specialist enters the date of the session along with the patient's pre-treatment heart rate for future comparisons. The patient then interacts directly with the virtual environment guided by the therapist, thus the virtual part of the treatment begins.

(a) Basic intensity scene, where the pacient began   (b) Medium intesity scene

(c) High intensity scene

Fig. 6. Scenes divided by treatment levels.

The first scene is used as a basis for treatment because it does not constitute a major threat to the patient, in this scene the spider waits quietly for the patient, and at a certain distance begins to follow him. The following scene increases in difficulty for the phobic person as in this case the spider attacks the patient when he gets too close, see Fig. 7. Finally, the most difficult scene is the one where the patient has no idea where the threat comes from, so the alert status is higher, at the same time the number of spiders is higher.

Fig. 7. Sequence of images of the attack animation within scenario number 2

Once the session is over, the specialist re-enters the vital signs and other variables considered, and the system returns a history of the patient's data and all the results.

5 Analysis and Conclusions

The proposed tool is oriented towards the diagnosis of specific phobia CIE10 F40.2 (Spider Phobia), the therapeutic process consists of two phases, the preparatory phase, in which emotional control techniques such as relaxation, breathing, safe place, among others, are applied to the patient with the objective of making the patient feel as calm and comfortable as possible. Once this phase is over and the emotional state that the therapist requires has been achieved, the next phase proceeds to the use of the proposed system, focusing clearly on the rehabilitation of the patient.

The psychotherapeutic treatment is enhanced by the ease with which realism can be managed through the modification of the 3D model of the spider and the environment in general, in addition, the tool helps to reduce therapeutic abandonment through important factors within the treatment such as the increased sense of personal control, the novelty of the rehabilitation technique and the safety it provides by minimizing the effects of live exposure.

The proposed system was tested with a group of 10 patients with a medium degree of phobia and 3 specialists including the supervising research psychologist. In order to obtain feedback from the system, a bank of questions was prepared for both patients (Qp) and specialists (Qs) see Table 1, which are answered on a scale of 0 to 10 where 0 is disagreement and 10 is agreement (Fig. 8).

Table 1. Questions for patients and the specialist to obtain feedback on the proposed system

	Questions
Qp1	I am familiar with the handling of devices that facilitate the immersion in virtual environments.
Qp2	Handling virtual environments is relatively easy.
Qp3	The execution of the interface is simple and intuitive.
Qp4	The limitations given by external noise (light, depth) are imperceptible.
Qp5	The equipment used does not cause any discomfort.
Qs1	Patients are enthusiastic about these types of rehabilitation options.
Qs2	The system facilitates obtaining information on the progress of the patient's treatment.
Qs3	The increasing complexity of tasks accelerate the recovery of the patient.
Qs4	The system is robust enough to determine slight missteps in the sequences.
Qs5	The system can be easily implemented in institutions dealing with this phobia.

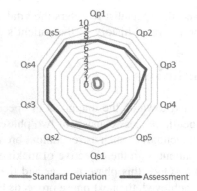

Fig. 8. Feedback results

Consequently, the proposed system is proven to be user-friendly and proves to provide a very useful tool for the therapist when treating arachnophobia. These positive and satisfactory results demonstrate the feasibility of implementing this tool in an institution or clinic that deals with this type of phobia.

Acknowledgements. This research was carried out thanks to the collaboration of Clinical Psychologist Jorge Rosero EMDR specialist endorsed by EMDR Iberoamerica, for his support with all the technical aspects of this article, also thanks to Rumen Filkov of the University of Applied Sciences Vorarlberg, Austria (https://rfilkov.com/about/), for his support to this research with the Unity assets necessary for the development of virtual environments integrating Kinect for Virtual Reality.

In addition, the authors would like to thanks to the Corporación Ecuatoriana para el Desarrollo de la Investigación y Academia–CEDIA for the financing given to research, development, and innovation, through the CEPRA projects, especially the project CEPRA-XI-2017-06; Control Coordinado Multi-operador aplicado a un robot Manipulador Aéreo; also to Universidad de las Fuerzas Armadas ESPE, Universidad Técnica de Ambato, Escuela Superior Politécnica de Chimborazo, Universidad Nacional de Chimborazo, and Grupo de Investigación en Automatización, Robótica y Sistemas Inteligentes, GI-ARSI, for the support to develop this paper.

References

1. Díez, S.: Evaluación de sesgos cognitivos (mnésicos y atencionales) en la vulnerabilidad a la aracnofobia (2005)
2. Caballo, V.: Manual para el tratamiento cognitivo-conductual de los trastornos psicológicos. Siglo Veintiuno Ed., Madrid (1998)
3. Díez, S., Cabaco, A., Lancho, M., Gil, S.: Evaluación de sesgos atencionales en sujetos con alta vulnerabilidad a la aracnofóbia mediante una Tarea Stroop emocional. Int. J. Dev. Educ. Psychol. **2**, 103–110 (2016)
4. LeBeau, R.T., et al.: Specific phobia: a review of DSM-IV specific phobia and preliminary recommendations for DSM-V. Depress. Anxiety **27**, 148–167 (2010)
5. Bados, A.: Fobias específicas. In: Pareja, M.A. (ed.) Manual de Terapia de Conducta. Dykinson, Madrid (1998)

6. Nasarre, A.: Artrópodos y psicopatologia: Aproximación a dos entidades clinicas. Los Artrópodos y el Hombre Bol. SEA **20**, 217–221 (1997)
7. Rufián Ortega, R.: Estudio de la araneofauna presente en la comarca metropolitana de Jaén (municipios de Martos y Torredelcampo) (2016)
8. Rothbaum, B., Hodges, L., Kooper, R., Opdyke, D.: Virtual reality graded exposure in the treatment of acrophobia: a case report. Behav. Ther. **26**, 547–554 (1995)
9. Arbona, C., García-Palacios, A.: Realidad virtual y tratamientos psicológicos. Cuad. Med. **82**, 17–31 (2007)
10. Bonet, J.: Tratamientos psicológicos eficaces para las fobias específicas. Psicothema **13**, 447–452 (2001)
11. Lear, A.: Virtual reality provides real therapy. IEEE Comput. Graph. Appl. **17**, 16–20 (1997)
12. Raghav, K., Van Wijk, A., Abdullah, F.: Efficacy of virtual reality exposure therapy for treatment of dental phobia: a randomized control trial. BMC Oral Health **16**, 25 (2016)
13. Bruce, M., Regenbrecht, H.: A virtual reality claustrophobia therapy system—implementation and test. In: 2009 IEEE Virtual Reality Conference, pp. 179–182 (2009)
14. Hnoohom, N., Nateeraitaiwa, S.: Virtual reality-based smartphone application for animal exposure. In: 2017 International Conference on Digital Arts, Media and Technology
15. Cavrag, M., Lariviere, G., Cretu, A.-M., Bouchard, S.: Interaction with virtual spiders for eliciting disgust in the treatment of phobias. In: 2014 IEEE International Symposium on Haptic, Audio and Visual Environments and Games
16. Miloff, A., Lindner, P., Hamilton, W.: Single-session gamified virtual reality exposure therapy for spider phobia vs. traditional exposure therapy: study protocol for a randomized controlled non-inferiority trial. Trials **17**, 60 (2016)
17. Haworth, M.B., Baljko, M., Faloutsos, P.: PhoVR. In: Proceedings of the 11th ACM SIGGRAPH International Conference on Virtual-Reality Continuum and its Applications in Industry—VRCAI 2012, p. 171 (2012)
18. Garcia-Palacios, A., Hoffman, H., Carlin, A., Furness, T., Botella, C.: Virtual reality in the treatment of spider phobia: a controlled study. Behav. Res. Ther. **40**, 983–993 (2002)
19. Hoffman, H.: Virtual reality: a new tool for interdisciplinary psychology research. CyberPsychol. Behav. **1**(2), 195–200 (1998)
20. Andaluz, V.H., et al.: Bilateral virtual control human–machine with kinect sensor. In: 2012 VI Andean Region International Conference, pp. 101–104 (2012)
21. Quevedo, W.X., et al.: Assistance system for rehabilitation and valuation of motor skills. In: De Paolis, L.T., Bourdot, P., Mongelli, A. (eds.) AVR 2017. LNCS, vol. 10325, pp. 166–174. Springer, Cham (2017). https://doi.org/10.1007/978-3-319-60928-7_14
22. Andaluz, V.H., et al.: Virtual reality integration with force feedback in upper limb rehabilitation. In: Bebis, G., et al. (eds.) ISVC 2016. LNCS, vol. 10073, pp. 259–268. Springer, Cham (2016). https://doi.org/10.1007/978-3-319-50832-0_25
23. Berdica, E., Gerdes, A.B.M.: A comprehensive look at phobic fear in inhibition of return: phobia-related spiders as cues and targets. J. Behav. Ther. Exp. Psychiatry **54**, 158–164 (2017)
24. Peperkorn, H., Diemer, J., Alpers, G.: Representation of patients' hand modulates fear reactions of patients with spider phobia in virtual reality. Front. Psychol. **7**, 268 (2016)
25. Szymanski, J., O'Donohue, W.: Fear of spiders questionnaire. J. Behav. Ther. Exp. **26**, 31–34 (1995)
26. Öst, L., Stridh, B., Wolf, M.: A clinical study of spider phobia: prediction of outcome after self-help and therapist-directed treatments. Behav. Res. Ther. **36**, 17–35 (1998)
27. Basanovic, J., Dean, L.: Direction of stimulus movement alters fear-linked individual differences in attentional vigilance to spider stimuli. Behav. Res. Ther. **99**, 117–123 (2017)

The Skyline as a Marker for Augmented Reality in Urban Context

Mehdi Ayadi[1,2]($\boxtimes$), Leo Valque[1], Mihaela Scuturici[1], Serge Miguet[1],
and Chokri Ben Amar[2]

[1] University of Lyon, CNRS, University Lyon 2, LIRIS,
UMR5205, 69676 Lyon, France
{Mehdi.Ayadi,Mihaela.Scuturici,Serge.Miguet}@univ-lyon2.fr,
leo.valque@ens-lyon.fr
[2] University of Sfax, ENIS, REGIM-Lab: REsearch Groups
in Intelligent Machines, BP 1173, 3038 Sfax, Tunisia
chokri.benamar@ieee.org

Abstract. In recent years, augmented reality (AR) technologies have emerged as powerful tools to help visualize the future impacts of new constructions on cities. Many approaches that use costly sensors and height-end platforms to run AR in real-time have been developed. Little efforts have been made to embed AR on mobile phones. In this paper, we present a novel approach that uses the *Skyline* as a marker in an AR system. This lightweight feature enables real-time matching of virtual and real skyline on smartphones.

We use device's embedded instruments to estimate the user's pose. This approximation is used to insert a synthetic object in the live video stream. This first approach gives a very unrealistic impression of the viewed scene: the inserted objects appear to *hover* and *float* with the user's movements. In order to address this problem, we use the live video camera feed as additional source of information which provides a redundancy to the instruments estimation. We extract the Skyline (a set of pixels that defines the boundary between the building and the sky) as main visual feature. Our proposal is to use these *automatically extracted* points and track them throughout the video sequence, to allow synthetic objects to anchor these visual features, making it possible to simulate a landscape from multiple viewpoints using a smartphone. We use images of the Lyon city (France) to illustrate our proposal.

Keywords: Mobile augmented reality
Image to geometry registration · Image comparison metric
3D models · Skyline matching · Urban landscape

1 Introduction

Nowadays, preserving a good visual landscape, in terms of aesthetics, health, safety and build ability is an important criteria to enhance the quality of life in

© Springer Nature Switzerland AG 2018
G. Bebis et al. (Eds.): ISVC 2018, LNCS 11241, pp. 698–711, 2018.
https://doi.org/10.1007/978-3-030-03801-4_61

urban environments. With the development of Smart Cities around the world, policy makers and architects want to involve citizens in the process of city construction on an early stage. To increase this environmental awareness and assist users, new tools and methods are required. In this context, augmented reality (AR) is used as a landscape simulation system where 3D models are included in a live video stream. Most of these mobile AR systems are marker-based which limit their scope to small-scale environments and indoor objects. Outdoor systems, in the other hand, rely exclusively on noisy sensor data to calibrate the virtual view with the real one. This kind of approaches are generally inaccurate with a limited user experience. They fail to provide a meaningful augmentation.

In this paper, we present a system for a real-time video stream augmentation on mobile platforms. The proposed system combines many features: large-scale (3D city model), visual (skyline) and contextual (instruments) information to augment the live video with 3D models in the correct location and perspective.

The proposed system allows a user to navigate in the urban environment and visualize the impact of a construction projects on the urban landscape using their smartphones (or tablet). The goal is to precisely insert in the image flow the new building model with the most realistic experience for the user. We propose an hybrid approach where the user's pose is first estimated using the smartphone's embedded instruments and then corrected with the skyline, as explained in Sect. 5. In other words, we cast the image/model matching problem into a curve matching problem which makes it a possible solution for real-time mobile application. Our AR system is running on a mobile platform (iPhone 6) with A8 processor.

The remainder of this paper is structured as follows:

In Sect. 2, we summarize the related previous works on video/GIS registration followed by literature on skyline matching methods. Next, Sect. 3 gives an overview of the proposed system. Section 4 describes the synthetic image generation process followed by Sect. 5 for our skyline matching methods and image comparison metrics. Results are presented in Sect. 6 followed by the conclusions and future work.

2 Related Work

One of the first mobile solutions for AR was *The Touring machine*. Other approaches, in [3] or [1], were introduced to overlay information on the camera image. These approaches are well suited to present illustrative informations but are not directly suited for visualization in urban environment or augmenting scenes with urban objects, as presented in this paper. In this context, Video/GIS registration technique is considered as a solution for large-scale augmented reality applications [2]. The problem consists in aligning pixels from the virtual world (3d city model, LiDAR scans, point clouds, ...) with the real image ones. We are in the case where the problem of image to point cloud registration is casted to an iterative process of image to image registration. To solve this problem, an implicit operation is done: the point cloud is turned into a synthetic picture. The real picture is then registered with the virtual one. In the following we present related works on video/GIS registration and skyline matching methods.

Existing approaches rely especially on 2D-features. The most explored methods in the literature use feature points such as SIFT or SURF points. The feature points are extracted from real and synthetic 2D images to be matched. This implies that the point clouds should have a texture, a color information or a reflectance value. In [4], a reflectance image is generated, from which SURF points are extracted. In [5], the image to image registration step relies on the RGB coloration of the point cloud using ASIFT descriptors. In this paper, we propose also to use a textured 3D city model, from which the rendering is a 3D textured object. However, the matching process is based only the on geometric features defined by the skyline.

For the real/virtual image registration step, [6] uses the Mutual Information between the two images. [7] proposes an improved approach, where a *Gradient Orientation Measure (GOM)* is used to compute the difference of the gradient orientation angle between the synthetic image and the real image. These methods are computationally expensive and memory consuming making them inappropriate for mobile real-time rendering. They also stay impractical for a large point clouds, as proposed in this paper.

[8] tries to improve camera orientations using multiple sensors, cameras and laser scans. This first approximation is then corrected with a skyline matching method based on an ICP algorithm. Other methods rely on specific 2D feature points, namely *the skyline*. This skyline matching step was also explored in the literature. In [9], a generic fisheye camera pointing upward and a 3D urban model were used to generate two an omni-directional real and virtual skylines. A matching step between the two images using a *chamfer* matching algorithm and a shortest path algorithm gives a precise GPS localization. We introduce a novel image comparison metric respecting the real-time constraint on mobile devices.

In [10], panoramic 3D scans are acquired from which the extracted skyline is encoded as a string. The step of skylines matching is then casted to a string matching problem. [11] uses the overall Skyline feature to estimate yaw angle (camera's viewing direction) from the image while having zero pitch and roll. The panoramic skyline is divided into four joint images from which a Cross-Similarity function is calculated to find the azimuth. An extension of this work in [12] overcomes this limitations with calculating the pitch and toll angle using a vertical vanishing points detection algorithm. More recent work in [13] uses a wide-angle synthetic image generated from 3D geometry model and the its associated image. The skyline matching metric is based on Normalized Mutual Information (NMI) and Histogram or Oriented Gradients (HOG).

As mentioned in [14], a city's skyline is defined as *the unique fingerprint of a city*, and therefore characterizes the uniqueness of urban environments or images. It also represents the overall geometric feature of the image in the real and virtual world. As explained in Sect. 5, we use it in our matching step. Our image/model matching problem is then transformed into a curve matching problem where the two skylines are matched with our similarity metric. This significantly reduce the computation complexity of our algorithm which makes it possible for testing on mobile platforms while respecting the real-time constraint.

3 Proposed System

Our method (Fig. 1) takes as input a live video stream from the smartphone's camera and a point cloud of the neighborhood urban scene. We propose a two-step registration method to refine the estimated camera's pose, knowing the camera's intrinsic parameters: first, a live video-stream is acquired with the smartphone's camera from which a *real skyline (1)* is extracted using a skyline extraction algorithm [15]. Then, a camera pose is estimated in world coordinate system with its 6 degrees of freedom due to the combination of smartphone's embedded sensors, as explained in Sect. 4.2: magnetic compass, gyroscope, accelerometer and barometer. This first camera pose allows us to place a virtual camera in the 3D city model and so generate a synthetic image of what the user should sees at this position. From this virtual image, a *virtual skyline (2)* is extracted. Our skyline matching method, detailed in Sect. 5, matches these *real* and *virtual* skylines and refines the camera's pose.

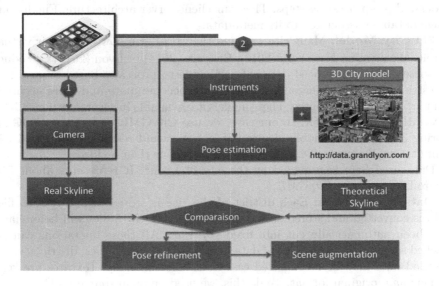

Fig. 1. System

4   Synthetic Image Generation

We first generate the synthetic image at an estimated user's pose. The camera pose estimation process is explained in Sect. 4.2. In the following, we detail our synthetic image generation process. We adopt a pinhole camera model, where the camera pose is expressed as a projection matrix P, giving the *2D pixel coordinate in image coordinate system* from the *3D vertex coordinates in the world coordinate system*. This projection matrix can be decomposed into three main components:

$$P = K * R * [I - t]$$

where K is the camera intrinsic parameter matrix; R is the rotations matrix and t the translations vector.

We do not detail the camera calibration step. We perform it with an *iOS-SDK* and *OpenCV* framework. This calibration step gives us the camera's intrinsic parameters as well as the distortion parameters (3 radial and 2 tangential).

4.1   Dataset

In this subsection, we present the data used in our experiments for the synthetic image generation step. First, we present the 3D city model used in here and associated pre-processing steps. Then our client-server architecture. Finally our image database associated to its meta-data.

3D City Model: Many cities around the world own nowadays their virtual double. We mention New York (2016), Brussels (2014) or Lyon (2012)[1]. Producing these 3D geo-referenced data is feasible due to processes based on aerial or terrestrial acquisition campaigns. These data become more and more accurate and particularly open source. These models are available in several formats: 3DS, CityGML, KMZ, DirectX. In our case, we use CityGML format from (OGC). Storing 3D model on mobile device is too heavy, and reading them (XML) is computationally expensive. A preprocessing stage is then bedded.

Data used here is provided by the city of Lyon[2]. It represents about 550 square kilometers in *CityGML*.

Data Preparation: Each district of the city is stored in a *CityGML* file. Data is converted and stored as text files. These *CityGML* files will beforehand have been automatically cut into fixed size tiles. All these operations can be batched server-side. In the case of data modification (other cities, districts, etc.), the tiled data may be recomputed easily and automatically. Textures are kept as their *png* original format. To do this, we used an open source tool[3].

We visualize in real-time the 3D city data of the user's neighborhood position. For this, we use a framework based on a mobile client/light server architecture, as described in Fig. 2. The server receives a request from the mobile device with its GPS position and sends back the corresponding tiled data in JSON format.

---

[1] https://www.citygml.org/3dcities, 2018.
[2] http://data.grandlyon.com, 2018.
[3] https://github.com/MEPP-team/3DUSE.

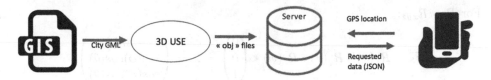

Fig. 2. Data exchange pipeline

4.2   Pose Estimation

We position our virtual camera in the 3D city model at the exact user's position, viewing direction and orientation.

The user's position (x, y, z) is estimated with a simple rough translation vector:

- (x, y) acquired directly by the smartphone's GPS (longitude, latitude);
- For the altitude (z), depending on smartphone, we retrieve data from:
  - Digital Elevation Model, giving an *absolute measure*;
  - Barometer, for most recent smartphones, giving a *relative altitude*;

Finally, the rotation matrix R is estimated by combining data from both smartphone's triaxial accelerometer and magnetic compass. The output of the accelerometer can be modeled as follows:

$$\vec{a_S} = \begin{pmatrix} a_{Sx} \\ a_{Sy} \\ a_{Sz} \end{pmatrix} = \vec{a_B} + R * \vec{g}$$

where:

$$\begin{cases} \vec{a_S} & \text{Accelerometer output} \\ a_{Sx} & \text{Acc. along x-axis} \\ \vec{a_B} & \text{Acc. experienced by the moving body} \\ \vec{g} & \text{Gravity} \\ R & \text{Rotation matrix} \end{cases}$$

All of these vectors are oriented according to the North-East-Down convention. The rotation matrix R allows to project the gravitational vector $\vec{g}$ from the *terrestrial inertial referential* to the *moving object referential*.

To solve this equation, we must first take a look at the rotation matrices expressions, along x, y and z axis. Since we want to perform the three rotations successively, we must multiply the matrices between them. Or, matrices multiplication is not commutative. We must choose an arbitrary order for these multiplications. Comparing all possible results, we can notice that only R_{xyz} and R_{yxz} are exploitable solutions, allowing us to resolve the equation (depend only on θ and ϕ).

For $R = R_{xyz}$:

$$\vec{a_S} = R_x(\phi) * R_y(\theta) * R_z(\psi) * \begin{pmatrix} 0 \\ 0 \\ 1 \end{pmatrix} = ... = \begin{pmatrix} -sin(\theta) \\ sin(\phi)cos(\theta) \\ cos(\phi)cos(\theta) \end{pmatrix}$$

We obtain the following expressions: $\begin{cases} \phi = tan^{-1}(\frac{a_{Sy}}{a_{Sz}}) \\ \theta = tan^{-1}(\frac{-a_{Sx}}{\sqrt{a_{Sy}^2 + a_{Sz}^2}}) \end{cases}$

At this step, we found out the user's orientation along two axis: pitch and yaw. The roll is directly obtained from the magnetic compass, as detailed in Fig. 3.

We are now able to build the projection model: we place our virtual camera at this previous estimated pose. We illustrate in Figs. 4 and 5 both real and its corresponding virtual image at same time and location.

5   Skyline Matching

Traditional methods use several textural features from the real and virtual images. These methods are quite computationally expensive and heavily depends on the quality of extracted features (SIFT, SURF, etc.), which is not suitable for our mobile AR context. We propose here to exploit scene's geometric features: the *skyline*. In fact, most images taken in urban environments contain a skyline which is defined as the border between sky and non-sky region. The proposed method assumes the existence of one significant sky regions inside the image. In [11], where images are horizontally rectified (zero tilt), we here authorize the six degrees of freedom.

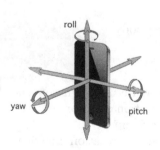

Fig. 3. Smartphone's axis

Fig. 4. Real image with Skyline

Fig. 5. Virtual image with skyline

Both skylines (Figs. 4 and 5) are assumed to be extracted from the same camera position. In order to, we rely on the similarity of their shapes. This allows us to find the correction that should be applied to the user's pose.

The objective is then to move the virtual skyline in the image plane on the x, y and θ coordinates to match it with the real one. As an approximation, we consider that small pitch and yaw rotations are estimated as translations in the image plane. The problem is to minimize a distance according to the x, y and θ parameters. The minimization algorithm used here is a Gradient descent (simplex) from *OpenCV* optimization modules, *Downhill Solver*. The rendering and the matching steps are real time. We also define an image comparison metric to determine the distance between the skylines. It's clear that, if the camera pose corresponds to the pose that yields the real image, this comparison metric should be minimum. In our case, this metric should be resilient to multiple factors: noise due to errors in skyline extraction process, incomplete data, jagged skyline, too much vegetation, missing data (..).

Our skyline matching pipeline contains three steps: skyline simplification, polygonal approximation and downhill solver.

Skylines systematically contain many straight lines due to noise-related pixels derived from the skyline extraction process or due to their presence in the real world but not in the virtual one (trees, chimney, clouds, ...). Added to that, the original skyline contains a little more than 300 pixels (image's width). Starting the matching step using this vector size would compromise the real-time constraint. A simplification step is then needed to eliminate noise pixels. This step is divided into two steps: outliers removal followed by a *polygonal approximation* step. This reduces the skylines to a few dozens of points that clearly define the shape of the scene.

Finally, to minimize our objective function, we launch a dynamic programming based on the Nelder-Mead method, namely: Downhill Solver. This allow us to find the global minimum while using a cost function based on one of our comparison metrics.

5.1   Skyline Simplification

Algorithm 1. Aberrant pixel removal

---

  for $i = 1$, $i++$, while $i < sizeof(input)$ **do**
    if $|input[i + 1].y + input[i - 1].y - 2 * input[i].y| < precision$ **then**
      $output \leftarrow input[i]$
    end if
  end for

Where "input" is the original skyline vector, "output" is the resulting vector and "precision" is a parameter reflecting the magnitude of vertical jump between two consecutive pixels.

We illustrate our results in our open source database for skyline extraction and simplification. The skyline is extracted from the real image. Then, outliers are removed based on Algorithm 1, obtaining, on average, a skyline vector of

25 pixels. The polygonal approximation step comes after skyline simplification, which approximate the skyline curve with a new one with less vertices such that the distance between them is less than the precision parameter[4]. These pre-treatments (outliers removal + polygonal approximation) allow us to obtain, on average, skylines vectors of around 25 pixels.

5.2   Comparison Metric

L_1 : We try to minimize a distance with the parameter x, y and θ. The first idea explored is to use distance L_1.

$$L_1(A, B) = \int_x \mid y_A(x) - y_B(x) \mid dx \qquad (1)$$

This distance is simply the area between the two curves. This solution is also used as a cross-similarity function in [12] and works well for skylines that are very similar. It already provides quite satisfactory results. But the two input skylines often contain important differences:

– lack of precision of the 3D model (building are sometimes reduced to their simplest shape);
– some recent buildings are not yet represented in the 3D model;
– absence of street lights, lamp posts, electrical panels, power lines and other artifacts in the 3D model.

When the real and theoretical (extracted from the 3D model) skylines present these differences, the matching step goes wrong. For this, we introduce a second comparison metric.

L_{-1} : The objective is to find a way to manage these differences while having the following features:

– close curves are strongly valued;
– distant curves are not too penalized: the curves must to be able to deviate in one point if it allows to be identical in others;
– distant lines and very distant ones have the same importance.

Among the tested metrics, one respects these criteria well. We define it as:

$$L_{-1}(A, B) = M - \int_x \frac{1}{\mid y_A(x) - y_B(x) \mid + c} dx \qquad (2)$$

We denote A and B the real and virtual skylines. The constant "c" avoids divergences and allows the behavior to be adjusted: the smaller it will be, the more it will apply strongly the criteria at the risk of creating a lot of local minimums affecting the convergence of the minimization algorithms. On the

---

[4] http://en.wikipedia.org/wiki/Ramer-DouglasPeuckerAlgorithm.

contrary, the bigger it will be, the closer we will get to the behavior of the first metric (1).

This metric follows well the criteria defined above and is much better robust to the cases where skylines present important differences.

However, it fails when matching vertical lines and is far from *good matches* for some entries, including fairly simple entries where our first metric find better solutions. This is not quite the expected result and it is therefore necessary to adjust this metric to be able to use it.

L_{final}: The two previous metrics are combined to get advantages of each one: the first one works well for simple cases but not for complicated ones. The second works better for complicated cases but not for all simple. For this, we have to combine these two metrics. The typical way to combine two functions in an objective one is to use a weighted linear combination of the two, while adding a parameter $alpha$, e.g $L_{final} = alpha * L_1 + (1 - alpha) * L_{-1}$. For this, we must make one of the following hypothesis:

- It exists more simple cases than complicated ones, and then, $alpha > 0.5$;
- In contrary, more complicated than simple cases, and then, $alpha < 0.5$.

Due to the variability of the scenes (simple or complicated cases), we chose to not add such weighted combination and abstract our final metric of any hypothesis. Our final metric is then:

$$L_{final}(A, B) = L_1(A, B) * L_{-1}(A, B) \qquad (3)$$

6 Results and Discussion

In order to test the accuracy and robustness of our method, we conducted several experiments. Tests have been made on real 3D data provided by the city of Lyon (France) covering more than $500 \, km^2$ of territory. Tests were made in different weather conditions and multiple types of areas. We take into account objects that can be found in real environment but not in 3D city model: along urban areas, mainly trees form the skyline of the foreground objects as can be found in our open source database images. Added to that, buildings and road furniture such as traffic lights, lamp posts, or street signs lead to wrong real skylines, that cannot be later matched with virtual one.

We conducted our experiments, and constructed a database of around 300 images. Global results are given in Table 1 and examples are illustrated in Fig. 6. All image database are available in [17]. For each image, we define multiple anchor points for residual error calculation, as the difference along the horizontal and vertical directions of those points. In Figs. 6a to d, we define these anchor points, that are essential in our evaluation protocol, and that have to be non-coplanar. For each image, the residual error is denoted $(\Delta x, \Delta y)$, in terms of the number of pixels, and is calculated as the average of all anchor points pixel error. Then, for each image with each of proposed comparison metrics, we

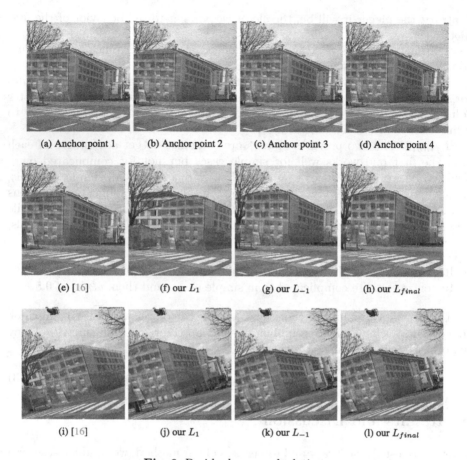

(a) Anchor point 1   (b) Anchor point 2   (c) Anchor point 3   (d) Anchor point 4

(e) [16]   (f) our L_1 (g) our L_{-1} (h) our L_{final}

(i) [16]   (j) our L_1 (k) our L_{-1} (l) our L_{final}

Fig. 6. Residual error calculation

choose, when possible, to use the same anchor points in the evaluation protocol, as illustrated in Figs. 6e to h. Then, as discussed previously, we authorize
the six-degree of freedom. Figures 6i and l illustrate the same scene with two
different perspectives (tilt angle). We notice in Figs. 6e to h, how this complicated case (presence of a tree on the left of the image) gives different results.
With [16], error is acceptable $((\Delta X, \Delta Y) = (28, 3))$. With our L_1 metric, we
obtain very bad results $((\Delta X, \Delta Y) = (99, 13))$. Then L_{-1} metric gives a little better result $((\Delta X, \Delta Y) = (24, 14))$ and finally L_{-1} metric the best one
$((\Delta X, \Delta Y) = (4, 13))$. We compare our method to [16] with our different metrics. We calculate, for each image, the residual error. These results verify the
high accuracy of our system for near and far objects.

Then, as a human-machine comparison step, we manually match the virtual
skyline with the real one, and then generate a manually generated alignments.
As the automatic pose estimation procedure, this step is also based only on
translation in the image plane. We add rotations in the virtual environment

and sees in real-time the virtual skyline moving in the image place. We denote this database: *manually alignment*. We compare our results to this manually alignments using the same residual error calculation method.

The developed system run on a smartphone with standard specifications (iPhone 6), including an Apple iOS 11.4 operating system and Open GL-ES 3.0. In Table 1, we show results of our system: we compare our result (virtual images) to the real ones, then to the manual generated alignments. We compare our results also to experiment 9 of [16]. We give in the table result for images shown in Fig. 6. The system runs in real-time on iPhone 6. Depending on the complexity of the rendered scene (number of buildings, complexity of the buildings, etc.), on average, the rendering process takes 12 ms and the matching step 11 ms.

Table 1. Residual error results

Image			Comparison to real images				Comparison to manual alignments		
			[16]	L_1	L_{-1}	L_{final}	L_1	L_{-1}	L_{final}
Frame 58: Figs. 6e to h	ΔX		28,5	−98	15	−20	−106	−29	−30
	ΔY			−3	−9	6	8	−10	9	8
Frame 62: Figs. 6i to l	ΔX		73	56	32	49	45	41	46
	ΔY			11	30	−12	−7	30	−8	−6
Database	ΔX	Absolute average	10	3	10	3	4	9	2
		Std Dev	70	82	66	66	92	61	59
	ΔY	Absolute average	15	20	14	14	24	17	18
		Std Dev	18	36	28	28	38	32	30

7 Conclusion and Future Work

We investigated the possibility of using skyline features as a marker for augmented reality. We proposed a system where the estimated pose with smartphone's instruments is corrected using the skyline. Our skyline matching method allows us to transform the image to model matching problem into a curve matching one. This reduced significantly the computation complexity (on an iPhone 6), allowing us to test our system in real-time video. The accuracy and robustness was tested on a set of 300 images, with synthetic and real images. Our different comparison metrics gives promising results for simple and complicated cases. However, results suffers from cases, where occlusions are present (tall trees, etc.). On the other hand, our matching process here is in the image plane. We will try to add a matching process with six degree of freedom on the world coordinate referential.

References

1. Schmalstieg, D., Langlotz, T., Billinghurst, M.: Augmented Reality 2.0. In: Brunnett, G., Coquillart, S., Welch, G. (eds.) Virtual Realities, pp. 13–37. Springer, Vienna (2011). https://doi.org/10.1007/978-3-211-99178-7_2
2. Langlotz, T., Mooslechner, S., Zollmann, S., Degendorfer, C., Reitmayr, G., Schmalstieg, D.: Sketching up the world: in situ authoring for mobile augmented reality. Pers. Ubiquitous Comput. **16**(6), 623–630 (2012)
3. Gotow, J.B., Zienkiewicz, K., White, J., Schmidt, D.C.: Addressing challenges with augmented reality applications on smartphones. In: Cai, Y., Magedanz, T., Li, M., Xia, J., Giannelli, C. (eds.) MOBILWARE 2010. LNICST, vol. 48, pp. 129–143. Springer, Heidelberg (2010). https://doi.org/10.1007/978-3-642-17758-3_10
4. Wiggenhagen, M.: Co-registration of terrestrial laser scans and close range digital images using scale invariant features. Plastverarbeiter.De, pp. 208–212 (2010)
5. Moussa, W., Abdel-Wahab, M., Fritsch, D.: An automatic procedure for combining digital images and laser scanner data. ISPRS Int. Arch. Photogramm. Remote. Sens. Spat. Inf. Sci. **XXXIX-B5**, 229–234 (2012)
6. Taylor, Z., Nieto, J.: Automatic calibration of lidar and camera images using normalized mutual information, p. 8 (2012)
7. Taylor, Z., Nieto, J., Johnson, D.: Automatic calibration of multi-modal sensor systems using a gradient orientation measure. In: 2013 IEEE/RSJ International Conference on Intelligent Robots and Systems, pp. 1293–1300, November 2013
8. Hofmann, S., Eggert, D., Brenner, C.: Skyline matching based camera orientation from images and mobile mapping point clouds. ISPRS Ann. Photogramm. Remote. Sens. Spat. Inf. Sci. **II-5**, 181–188 (2014)
9. Ramalingam, S., Bouaziz, S., Sturm, P., Brand, M.: Skyline2gps: localization in urban canyons using omni-skylines. In: 2010 IEEE/RSJ International Conference on Intelligent Robots and Systems, pp. 3816–3823, October 2010
10. Nüchter, A., Gutev, S., Borrmann, D., Elseberg, J.: Skyline-based registration of 3d laser scans. Geo Spat. Inf. Sci. **14**(2), 85 (2011)
11. Zhu, S., Pressigout, M., Servières, M., Morin, L., Moreau, G.: Skyline matching: a robust registration method between Video and GIS. In: Conference of the European COST Action TU0801 - Semantic Enrichment of 3D City Models for Sustainable Urban Development Location: Graduate School of Architecture, Nantes, France, pp. 1–6, October 2012
12. Zhu, S., Morin, L., Pressigout, M., Moreau, G., Servières, M.: Video/GIS registration system based on skyline matching method. In: 2013 IEEE International Conference on Image Processing, pp. 3632–3636, September 2013
13. Guislain, M., Digne, J., Chaine, R., Monnier, G.: Fine scale image registration in large-scale urban lidar point sets. Comput. Vis. Image Underst. **157**, 90–102 (2017). Large-Scale 3D Modeling of Urban Indoor or Outdoor Scenes from Images and Range Scans
14. Yusoff, N.A.H., Noor, A.M., Ghazali, R.: City skyline conservation: sustaining the premier image of Kuala Lumpur. Procedia Environ. Sci. **20**, 583–592 (2014)

15. Ayadi, M., Suta, L., Scuturici, M., Miguet, S., Ben Amar, C.: A parametric algorithm for skyline extraction. In: Blanc-Talon, J., Distante, C., Philips, W., Popescu, D., Scheunders, P. (eds.) ACIVS 2016. LNCS, vol. 10016, pp. 604–615. Springer, Cham (2016). https://doi.org/10.1007/978-3-319-48680-2_53

16. Fukuda, T., Zhang, T., Yabuki, N.: Improvement of registration accuracy of a handheld augmented reality system for urban landscape simulation. Front. Arch. Res. **3**, 386–397 (2014)

17. Skyline Database: $dionysos.univ-lyon2.fr/mayadi/ISVC'18/skylineDatabase$

Oil Processes VR Training

Víctor H. Andaluz[1]([⊠]), José L. Amaquiña[2],
Washington X. Quevedo[1]([⊠]), Jorge Mora-Aguilar[1,2]([⊠]),
Daniel Castillo-Carrión[1]([⊠]), Roberto J. Miranda[1]([⊠]),
and María G. Pérez[2]([⊠])

[1] Universidad de las Fuerzas Armadas ESPE, Sangolquí, Ecuador
{vhandaluz1, wjquevedo, jlmora2, dacastillo,
rjmiranda}@espe.edu.ec
[2] Escuela Politécnica Nacional, Quito, Ecuador
maria.perez@epn.edu.ec

Abstract. In this paper a virtual reality solution is developed to emulate the environment and the operations of the pitching and receiving traps of pipe scrapers (PIG), with the aim of reinforcing the training of operators in oil camps. To develop this, the information was collected on various pitching and receiving traps of the real pipeline operating companies in the country, thus defining the basic and specific parameters for the virtual recreation of a typical trap model. The 3d models obtains from P&ID's diagrams to interact with user. The environment, interaction and behavior of pipes was developed in a graphic engine, to make training tasks with real state procedures on the oil industry. The goal is save time, money, resources in the training and learning specific oil industry; and make available a base to simulate another complex process.

Keywords: Oil processes · Virtual training · Virtual reality
Immersive training

1 Introduction

Industrial processes since its inception have been forced to incur in advances in technology to be more competitive in the market [1–3], whose market strategy has focused on satisfying the demands of the new generations of the consumers that, among others, relates to the quality of a product, its features, the materials and also its relationship and impact with the environment [4, 5].

The specific features of an industrial environment are the big facilities (processing plants, maritime refining platforms) and several complex processes and subprocesses that operate at their maximum capacity continuously during the 365 days of the year, in extreme climatic conditions [6]. Therefore, this type of industry requires not only having staff who are constantly trained in the management and operation of equipment and systems, but also that they know and apply the industrial safety measures that are necessary [7], with the purpose of avoiding emergency situations that not only affect the integrity of the individual and their coworkers, in addition, to avoid damages in the plant and shutdown of production processes, which causes great economic losses and shortages of the final product in the market [8].

© Springer Nature Switzerland AG 2018
G. Bebis et al. (Eds.): ISVC 2018, LNCS 11241, pp. 712–724, 2018.
https://doi.org/10.1007/978-3-030-03801-4_62

In this context, virtual reality in the oil and gas sector can be used mainly in the following fields: exploration, operation and maintenance, training and training. In exploration, the different techniques of virtual reality have been used so that the actors within the world of oil and gas [9] such as engineers, geologists, scientists, operators, managers, etc., can explore different environments like oilfields; in which the use of 3D models through the different available resources (use of virtual tools and specific CAD-type programs) [10] allow us to create an environment that combines the information coming from different sources of seismic data revealing the structural characteristics, well registration, permeability and other properties involved in the analysis [11]. This procedure also allows manipulate a process in order to investigate specific cases of behavior using the data provided, being more comprehensive than the explanation of the exploration of a process in previous years through the use of a non-interactive graphical representation [9].

It should be mentioned that training in the industrial, oil and gas industries, the training programs are seen as short-term educational processes that are developed in a systemic and organized manner, due to the incorporation of new personnel or that is being carried out an update and improvement of technical skills to the oil-workers, which are covered in the area of hygiene and industrial safety, [12]; Thus, in this field, virtual reality has played an important role with reactive 3D models, simulations and visualizations with specific purposes [13].

2 Problem Formulation

Actually, industrial operations require compliance with new and more demanding challenges: efficiency, safety, and environmentally friendly environments, which has forced companies to improve training practices and standards operations for their oil-workers. This training requires precise planning to ensure minimum interruptions in production [14].

Oil transportation operations are continuous almost all year round, plant maintenance shutdowns must be scheduled and very well coordinated, this means that the time allocated for training with real equipment and facilities is reduced to a few weeks a year [15]. This type of training becomes complicated when training new personnel or subcontractors at any time of the year, in addition to using the facilities in situ to train staff increases the risk of accidents, equipment damage, not programmed shutdowns and possible environmental impact. According to the Statistical Report [16] the Transecuatoriano Pipeline System SOTE paralyzed its operations 32 h and 50 min in the year 2016, of which 19 h were as part of scheduled maintenance, and the others due to several unscheduled incidents. This period of time is insignificant to carry out an adequate training and with the own facilities to the operative personnel. To survive this new reality, companies must find new strategies, which allow them to be more competitive, reduce their costs and satisfy the demands of the new generations that demand greater care of the environment.

In terms of training, companies have generated virtual alternatives for their workers and subcontractors that allow them to access information, inductions, online courses and technical certifications using online platforms that interact directly with the previously registered user and show their content. through any technological interface (computer, iPad and smartphones). These practices although they have optimized the traditional way of transmitting theoretical knowledge, have not been able to develop the practical knowledge that the industry requires. The virtual training module proposed in this article, is intended to be a practical complement to the theoretical instruction that operators receive before manipulating the teams in the field, strengthening the two main dimensions of learning [17].

The features and advantages that training allows through the use of virtual reality is that employees can get involved and see what the platform, refinery, exploitation field, etc., is like and above all, know the work they will perform within it; Furthermore, within the virtual environment, employees can be simulated and prepared for eventual situations, creating a critical situation that in another training modality is not feasible to simulate (work accidents, fires, emergencies); That is why this training option not only turns out to be effective, fast, safe and efficient, but also saves economic resources for its development and logistics. Additionally, the training module becomes an educational complement to comply with the security policies of pipeline operators. For example, within the Strategic Business Plan of Petroecuador, the chapter on Business Policies mentions that "Good practices in the hydrocarbon industry for the prevention of pollution and occupational hazards" must be applied, in addition to "Ensuring that all employees and contractors they understand that safe work and the protection of the environment is a requisite to carry out their activities and that each of them is responsible for their own safety, those around them and the environment" [18].

3   Development

By having the P&ID diagrams available as a reference element of the representations to be represented, it is important to bear in mind that these are plans in two dimensions, so they must be converted into 3D models to be used in the graphic engine that will develop the environment virtual. For this reason, a series of processes are considered until the final model is obtained [19]. Figure 1 shows the block diagram of the transformation of the P&ID diagrams to 3D models.

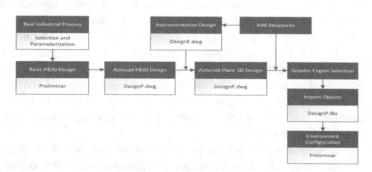

Fig. 1. Flow of conversion of a P&ID diagram of an industrial process to a 3D model

The 3D model of the P&ID diagram is obtained using AutoCAD Plant 3D, with scale and industrial connection standards, and allows to modify the physical layout of pipes and elements automatically or manually, see Fig. 2.

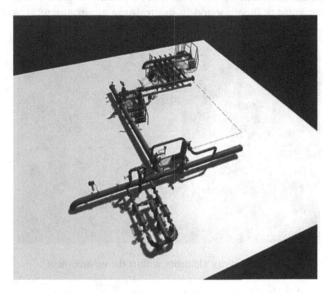

Fig. 2. 3D model of the oil plant from a P&ID diagram

3.1 Environment Development

The 3D model is imported into the environment created in Unity in *. fbx format to proceed with the texturing of the individual objects that make up the 3D model in order to resemble the actual plant used as a reference. Figure 3 presents one of the imported stations, applied textures and final position corrections within the preset training environment.

Fig. 3. 3D model of the plant in a virtual environment

It is considered as part of the industrial environment the security signage implemented whose location in a real station are regulated internationally and allow an adequate performance of the operators generating guarantees for personnel, environment and equipment that make up the system in its totality. Figure 4 shows the security elements and the signage incorporated in the training environment.

Fig. 4. Security elements within the environment

With the intention of increasing the degree of immersion of the user, its definite the procedure performed by an operator within an industrial plant is not the only task executed at that moment and that other operators perform other activities simultaneously. For this reason, the inclusion of avatars is established with artificial intelligence task coded, which have been imported into Unity obtaining as a result what is shown in Fig. 5(a) and for the locomotion of the user, the standard teleportation system has been implemented through the use of translation lines that identify the area to which the person will be redirected, as shown in Fig. 5(b).

(a) Industrial operator avatar   (b) Screenshot of locomotion system

Fig. 5. Use of avatars and locomotion system

3.2   User-Objects-Environment Interaction

The training system bases its operation on the preparation and manipulation of the pipe scraper for its launch and subsequent reception. This reason generates the need to represent the task of entering and extracting the scraper at the launching and receiving stations respectively. In addition to the direct interaction of the user with the primary elements such as: valves and gates. The main analysis will be carried out in the handling of the pipe scraper. This element does not have a standardized model within the industry. But its construction has a high level of importance according to the degree of interaction that is required. For the creation of the pipe scraper, own elements generated in Unity are used, grouped and hierarchized to form a uniform body, resulting in a structure like the one presented in Fig. 6.

Fig. 6. Build of pipe scraper

So that the development of the training is carried out intuitively, as part of the implemented programming, a color change has been established that indicates the interaction of the user with a component of the environment, in this case, the main valves of each station, as well as, the gates to the launch and reception chambers of the scraper. The script that controls the manipulation of objects allows that at the moment that a collision of the control with the object is made, the material disposed in the valves or the gates is changed; so, its original color that is red, will change to green while interacting with that element. Once the manipulation of the object is finished, the original color of the element is restored, as shown in Fig. 7.

An emergency situation is established as part of all the options available within the training environment. These situations are activated under certain parameters of malfunction by the user, which if not controlled can achieve an impact for the entire environment. The main emergencies are represented visually for a better understanding of the user and are made up of color changes in the pipes when there is elevated pressure concentrated in a point, or visual effects of spillage and in the extreme case explosions are shown, see Fig. 8.

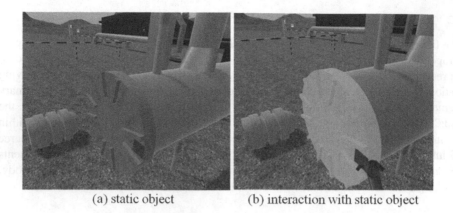

(a) static object   (b) interaction with static object

Fig. 7. Object behaviour

Fig. 8. Simulation of emergencies within the environment

3.3   Calculation of Operability

To measure the behavior of the pipes and other elements of the field station before the proposed training task, the following calculations are taken into account. These values are implemented in Matlab to interact with Unity through a shared memory software [20]. For valve B fully open (100% opening), closed valves A and C (0% opening) is known as initial condition and normal function for both stations, that is, it is fulfilled when it is not required to launch or it is not expected to receive the PIG (device used for cleaning pipes). In this case, the flow through the traps will have a single path corresponding to the main line and associated with the Bypass valve B, according to Fig. 9. For both the pitching and receiving trap, a flow equal to 255BBL/min

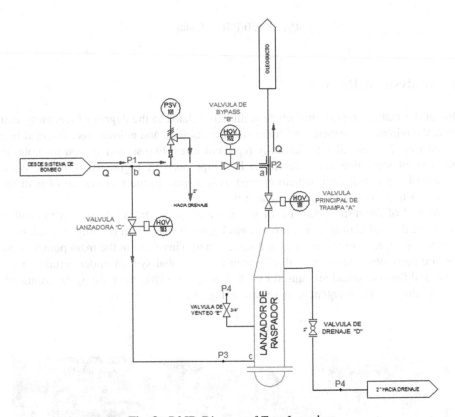

Fig. 9. P&ID Diagram of Trap Launcher

Data:

$$Q_1 = 255\frac{BBL}{min} * \frac{min}{60s} * \frac{m^3}{6.29BBL} = 0.6757\left[\frac{m^3}{s}\right]$$

$$\phi_B = D_1 = 25.66'' * \frac{m}{39.37''} = 0.65[m]$$

$$API = \frac{141}{GE} - 131.5; API = 24 \quad \text{therefore}$$

$$\rho = 910\frac{Kg}{m^3}$$

$$P_1 = 1800[PSI] \rightarrow 1800PSI * \frac{6894.757Pa}{PSI} = 12410562.6[Pa]$$

$$P_1 = 12410562.6[Pa] \quad \text{Launcher}$$

$$P_{11} = 150[\text{PSI}] \quad \text{Catcher}$$

4 Analysis of Results

One of the main results of this article is directly related to the degree of similarity that the real environment presents, with the facilities, objects and animations presented in a virtual way. It is intended to faithfully represent a real two-station system for training the tasks of launching and receiving a PIG pipe scraper. Figure 10 show the comparison of the virtual environment created with respect to the real system of both the launching trap (a) and the receiving trap (b).

As part of the results, the task of sending the scraper from one station to another following the instructions of the process has been considered. In training, the values of the variables (pressure transmitters and valves status) involved in the main points of the trap are presented, the changes that happen in the global system under certain conditions, and the risk situations caused by a bad practice within the training environment, even leading to an emergency, as shown in Fig. 11.

(a) Launch station virtual vs. real

(b) Catching station virtual vs real

Fig. 10. Comparison of virtual and real stations

Given the conditions where valves A, C and D are completely closed while valve B works with a 100% opening, it is said that it works in normal mode, the results obtained in the pressure measurement points are show in Fig. 12.

For emergency situations where the user has not followed the established training protocol, changes are observed in the color of the pipeline in which a pressure overload is being generated. If the error is corrected in time, this state can lead to a spill of oil or even an industrial fire as shown in Fig. 13.

Fig. 11. User within the training program

(a) Handling of Valve A at 0%

(b) Registration of values in pressure transmitters

Fig. 12. Training task execution

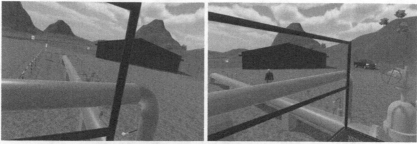

(a) Color change in pipeline

(b) Warning message on screen

Fig. 13. Consequences of procedural error in training

5   Conclusions

For the development and implementation of the virtual platform, the information collected from two-real stations of Petroecuador, such as the P&ID diagrams, was taken as a starting point and focused on the operations within the trapper and receiver trap. Although both stations show a similar behavior, at the time of implementing the platform, the physical, mathematical and operative factors that differentiate them were taken into account: geometrical heights, losses, sequence of operation, risk factors, etc.

The present simulator in virtual reality becomes the base on which is possible develop several industrial applications in a virtual way, not only with the objective of training staff, but also to be able to recreate the conditions of the plant process with the objective to know the responses of the process to a certain situation, for example: simulators of confined sites, refining plans, marine platforms, meteorological systems, etc.

Acknowledgements. The authors would like to thanks to the Corporación Ecuatoriana para el Desarrollo de la Investigación y Academia - CEDIA for the financing given to research, development, and innovation, through the Grupos de Trabajo, GT, especially to the GT-eTURISMO; also to Universidad de las Fuerzas Armadas ESPE, Universidad Técnica de Ambato, Escuela Superior Politécnica de Chimborazo, Universidad Nacional de Chimborazo, and Grupo de Investigación en Automatización, Robótica y Sistemas Inteligentes, GI-ARSI, for the support to develop this work.

References

1. Liu, D., Sun, D.W., Zeng, X.A.: Recent advances in wavelength selection techniques for hyperspectral image processing in the food industry. Food Bioprocess Technol. **7**(2), 307–323 (2014)
2. Schmidt, R., Möhring, M., Härting, R.-C., Reichstein, C., Neumaier, P., Jozinović, P.: Industry 4.0—potentials for creating smart products: empirical research results. In: Abramowicz, W. (ed.) BIS 2015. LNBIP, vol. 208, pp. 16–27. Springer, Cham (2015). https://doi.org/10.1007/978-3-319-19027-3_2
3. Meyr, H., Wagner, M., Rohde, J.: Structure of advanced planning systems. In: Stadtler, H., Kilger, C. (eds.) Supply Chain Management and Advanced Planning, pp. 99–106. Springer, Berlin (2015). https://doi.org/10.1007/978-3-662-04215-1_5
4. Cordeiro, J.J., Tewari, M.: Firm characteristics, industry context, and investor reactions to environmental CSR: a stakeholder theory approach. J. Bus. Ethics **130**(4), 833–849 (2015)
5. Pepe, M.: Concrete industry: waste generation and environmental concerns. In: Pepe, M. (ed.) A Conceptual Model for Designing Recycled Aggregate Concrete for Structural Applications. ST, pp. 7–16. Springer, Cham (2015). https://doi.org/10.1007/978-3-319-26473-8_2
6. Haghighi, M., Taghdisi, M.H., Nadrian, H., Moghaddam, H.R., Mahmoodi, H., Alimo-hammadi, I.: Safety Culture Promotion Intervention Program (SCPIP) in an oil refinery factory: an integrated application of Geller and Health Belief Models. Saf. Sci. **93**, 76–85 (2017)
7. Żywicki, K., Zawadzki, P., Górski, F.: Virtual reality production training system in the scope of intelligent factory. In: Burduk, A., Mazurkiewicz, D. (eds.) ISPEM 2017. AISC, vol. 637, pp. 450–458. Springer, Cham (2018). https://doi.org/10.1007/978-3-319-64465-3_43
8. Mons, M., et. al.: Petroleum applications of virtual reality technology: introducing a new paradigm. SEG Technical Expanded Abstracts, pp. 699–702 (1998)
9. Zhou, Z., et al.: Virtual reality based process integrated simulation platform in refinery: virtual refinery and its application. China Pet. Process. Petrochem. Technol. **13**, 74–84 (2011)
10. Quevedo, W.X., et al.: Virtual reality system for training in automotive mechanics. In: De Paolis, L.T., Bourdot, P., Mongelli, A. (eds.) AVR 2017. LNCS, vol. 10324, pp. 185–198. Springer, Cham (2017). https://doi.org/10.1007/978-3-319-60922-5_14
11. Pu, X., et al.: Geologic features of fine-grained facies sedimentation and tight oil exploration: a case from the second Member of Paleogene Kongdian Formation of Cangdong sag, Bohai Bay Basin. Pet. Explor. Dev. **43**(1), 26–35 (2016)
12. Cros, D., Tchounke, B., Nkague-Nkamba, L.: Training genomic selection models across several breeding cycles increases genetic gain in oil palm in silico study. Mol. Breed. **38**(7), 89 (2018)
13. Gavish, N., et al.: Evaluating virtual reality and augmented reality training for industrial maintenance and assembly tasks. Interact. Learn. Environ. **23**(6), 778–798 (2015)
14. Meza, G.: El internet y la Realidad virtual en la implementación de un prototipo de interfaz gráfica para la visualización de modelos de yacimientos. 3era Convención Técnica de la ACGGP (2004)
15. Daglas, H., Coleman, G.: Virtual reality 3D training for pipeline employees. Gas Pipeline J. **239**, 44–49 (2012)
16. EP Petroecuador: Informe Estadístico. Ecuador, Quito (2016)

17. Kolb, A.Y., Kolb, D.A.: Experiential learning theory. In: Seel, N.M. (ed.) Encyclopedia of the Sciences of Learning, pp. 1215–1219. Springer, Boston, MA (2012). https://doi.org/10.1007/978-1-4419-1428-6_227
18. EP Petroecuador: Plan estratégico Empresarial 2018-2021. Quito, Ecuador (2018)
19. Andaluz, V.H., et al.: Immersive industrial process environment from a P&ID diagram. In: Bebis, G., et al. (eds.) ISVC 2016. LNCS, vol. 10072, pp. 701–712. Springer, Cham (2016). https://doi.org/10.1007/978-3-319-50835-1_63
20. Andaluz, V.H., et al.: Unity3D-MatLab simulator in real time for robotics applications. In: De Paolis, L.T., Mongelli, A. (eds.) AVR 2016. LNCS, vol. 9768, pp. 246–263. Springer, Cham (2016). https://doi.org/10.1007/978-3-319-40621-3_19

ST: Intelligent Transportation Systems

Multiple Object Tracking in Urban Traffic Scenes with a Multiclass Object Detector

Hui-Lee Ooi[✉], Guillaume-Alexandre Bilodeau, Nicolas Saunier, and David-Alexandre Beaupré

Polytechnique Montréal, Montreal, Canada
{hui-lee.ooi,gabilodeau,nicolas.saunier,
david-alexandre.beaupre}@polymtl.ca

Abstract. Multiple object tracking (MOT) in urban traffic aims to produce the trajectories of the different road users that move across the field of view with different directions and speeds and that can have varying appearances and sizes. Occlusions and interactions among the different objects are expected and common due to the nature of urban road traffic. In this work, a tracking framework employing classification label information from a deep learning detection approach is used for associating the different objects, in addition to object position and appearances. We want to investigate the performance of a modern multiclass object detector for the MOT task in traffic scenes. Results show that the object labels improve tracking performance, but that the output of object detectors are not always reliable.

Keywords: Multiple object tracking · Road user detection
Urban traffic

1 Introduction

The objective of multiple object tracking (MOT) is extracting the trajectories of the different objects of interest in the scene (camera field of view). It is a common computer vision problem that is still open in complex applications. This paper deals with one of these complex applications, urban traffic, that involves different kinds of road users such as drivers of motorized and non-motorized vehicles, and pedestrians (see Fig. 1). The various road users exhibit different properties of moving speeds and directions in the urban environment. Their size vary because of perspective. Besides, road users are frequently interacting and occluding each other, which makes it even more challenging.

In this work, we want to investigate the performance of a modern multiclass object detector [2] for the MOT task in traffic scenes. We are interested in testing MOT in urban traffic settings with road users of varying sizes using an object detector while most previous works in such applications employ background subtraction or optical flow to extract the objects of interest regardless of their size. Our contributions in this work is an assessment of a typical model

G. Bebis et al. (Eds.): ISVC 2018, LNCS 11241, pp. 727–736, 2018.
https://doi.org/10.1007/978-3-030-03801-4_63

object detector for tracking in urban traffic scenes, and the introduction of label information for describing the objects in the scenes. Due to the variability of objects found in urban scenes, the label information should be a useful indicator to distinguish and associate the objects of interests across frames, thereby producing a more accurate trajectory. In this paper, the improvements obtained thanks to classification labels are evaluated with respect to a baseline tracker that uses a Kalman filter, bounding box positions and color information.

The results show that using classification labels from a detector improves significantly tracking performances on an urban traffic dataset. Therefore, multiple object trackers should capitalize on this information when it is available. However, they also show that the outputs of a multiclass object detector are not always reliable and not always easy to interpret.

Fig. 1. A frame from the urban traffic dataset that shows several road users in an intersection.

2   Related Works

MOT in urban traffic scenes was previously studied in [3], where the use of background subtraction is proposed for detecting the objects of interest followed by updating the object model with a state machine that uses feature points and spatial information. In fact, most previous work in MOT uses background subtraction or optical flow to detect the objects. The reason is that historically, methods based on pre-trained bounding box detectors are difficult to apply to road user tracking scenarios because it is difficult to design a detector that can detect and classify every possible type of road user from various viewpoints. However, recent progress in deep learning [2,21] make this avenue now possible and worth investigating.

When using background subtraction, the detection results give blobs that can correspond to parts of objects, one object, or many objects grouped together. The task is then to distinguish between merging, fragmentation, and splitting of objects. This is the main drawback of this method, since under congested traffic conditions, road users may partially occlude each other and therefore be merged into a single blob. Examples of trackers based on background subtraction include the work of Fuentes and Velastin [18], Torabi et al. [16], Jun et al. [13], Kim et al. [12], Mendes et al. [10], and Jodoin et al. [20]. For data association, they typically use the overlap of foreground blobs between two frames or a graph-based model for data association using appearance information, such as textures, color or keypoints. These approaches track objects in a merge-split manner as objects are tracked as groups during occlusion. The Hungarian algorithm is a classical graph-based choice for solving object assignment problems. To compensate for the missing detections, the Kalman filter is a popular option for estimating the location of the object of interest. A basic implementation of multiple object tracking is proposed in [4] using this approach.

With optical flow, objects are detected by studying the motion of tracked points in a video. Feature points that are moving together belongs to the same object. Several methods accomplish this process using the Kanade-Lucas-Tomasi (KLT) tracker [15]. The following researchers have proposed such trackers, often called feature-based: Beymer et al. [17], Coifman et al. [14], Saunier et al. [11] and Aslani and Mahdavi-Nasab [19]. For example, the algorithm proposed by Saunier et al. [11], named Traffic Intelligence, tracks road users at urban intersections by continuously detecting new features. The main issue is to select the right parameters to segment objects moving at similar speeds, while at the same time not oversegmenting smaller non-rigid objects such as pedestrians. Because objects are identified only by their motion, nearby road users moving at similar speed are often merged together. The exact bounding box occupied by the road user is unknown because it depends on the position of sparse feature points. Furthermore, when an object stops, its features flow becomes zero and feature trajectories are interrupted, which leads to fragmented object trajectories. Using a deep learning-based detector on road users is expected to provide objects that are less fragmented and that can be tracked whether they are moving or not.

3 Method

The proposed method consists of two main components: object detection and data association. It is illustrated in Algorithm 1. Object detection involves the extraction of objects of interest from the frames for further processing. Data association determines the tracking architecture to ensure the formation of the trajectories of each object in the scene. In order to match the objects correctly, an assignment cost based on a measure of similarity is computed for all the potential matches.

3.1 Object Detection

The road users from each frame are detected by using a deep-learning object detection model from the Region-based Fully Convolutional Network (RFCN) [2] framework due to its efficiency and accuracy. This detector was selected because it was the best performing approach on the MIO-TCD localization challenge [1]. The pre-trained model is further refined by using the MIO-TCD dataset [1] to provide the labels of the different road users found in traffic scenes, belonging to one of the eleven categories or labels: articulated truck, bicycle, bus, car, motorcycle, motorized vehicle, non-motorized vehicle, pedestrian, pickup truck, single unit truck and work van.

A non-maximal suppression (NMS) method [7,8] is applied to reduce the redundant detections of the same road users in each frame.

3.2 Data Association

The object assignment or data association is essentially performed on a set of detected objects from the current frame and a list of actively tracked objects that are accumulated from previous frames.

For the matched pairings, the latest position of the corresponding object in the track list is updated from the detected object. In the case of new detection, a new object will be initialized and added to the track list. In the case of objects in the track list without a matched candidate from the detection list, i.e. a missing detection, a Kalman filter [9] is applied to predict its subsequent location in the scene and the track information is updated using the prediction.

For the matching of objects across frames, if the total cost of assigning object pairs is higher than a set threshold T_{match}, the paired object would be reassigned to unmatched detection and unmatched track respectively due to the high probability of them not being a good match.

Actively tracked objects that are not assigned a corresponding object from the new detections after $N_{timeout}$ frames are removed from the list, under the assumption that the object has left the scene or the object was an anomaly from the detection module.

Object Assignment Cost. Once objects are detected, the subsequent step is to link the correct objects by using sufficient information about the objects to compute the cost of matching the objects. The Hungarian algorithm [5] is applied to match the list of active objects with the list of new detections in the current frame so that the matchings are exclusive and unique. The bipartite matching indicates that each active object can only be paired with one other candidate object (the detection) from the current frame. The algorithm can make use of different costs of assignment, with higher costs given to objects that are likely to be different road users.

Label Cost. In order to describe the properties of the detected objects, the labels and corresponding confidence score from the detections are taken into account. Setting the range of scores between 0 and 1, object pairs across frames that are more similar will be given a lower cost. Using the classification labels, object pairs with different labels are less likely to be the correct matchings, therefore they will be given cost of 1. Meanwhile, when the pairing labels are the same,

---

Algorithm 1 MOT algorithm

1: **procedure** MOT
2:     **for** i^{th} **frame do**
3:         Extract detections with multiclass object detector
4:         **if** $i == 1$ **then**
5:             Assign all detections as tracks
6:         **else**
7:             **for** each detection **do**
8:                 Compute cost of detection with respect to each track
9:             Run Hungarian algorithm for assigning pairing of detection and track
10:             **for** each matched detection **do**
11:                 **if** $Cost > T_{match}$ **then**
12:                     Reassign as unmatched detection and unmatched track
13:                 **else**
14:                     Update the track information from the detection
15:             **for** each unmatched detection **do**
16:                 Initialize as new track
17:             **for** each unmatched track **do**
18:                 **if** $N > N_{timeout}$ **then**
19:                     Remove track
20:                 **else**
21:                     Update track information using prediction from Kalman filter

---

the average of the confidence score of each detection are being taken as the label cost. The label cost is defined as

$$C_{label} = \begin{cases} 1 - 0.5 \times (\text{Conf}_i + \text{Conf}_j) & \text{if } L_i = L_j \\ 1 & \text{if } L_i \neq L_j \end{cases} \tag{1}$$

where L_n denotes the label of detection n and $Conf_n$ denotes the confidence of the corresponding label of the nth detection.

Jaccard Distance-based Position Cost. The bounding box coordinates of the detected objects are a useful indicator for matching the objects across frames as well. To judge the similarity of two bounding boxes in terms of proximity and size, the Jaccard distance is computed from the coordinates of the paired object, where the ratio of intersection over union of the bounding boxes is computed. This is calculated using

$$C_{position} = 1 - \frac{|Box_i \cap Box_j|}{|Box_i \cup Box_j|} \tag{2}$$

where Box_n denotes the set of pixels of the bounding box of the detected object n.

Color Cost. The visual appearance of the objects is characterized by their color histograms that are used to compute the color cost. In this work, the Bhattacharyya distance is applied to compute the distance of the color histogram of detections across frames with

$$C_{color} = \sqrt{1 - \frac{1}{\sqrt{\bar{H}_i \bar{H}_j N^2}} \sum \sqrt{H_i H_j}} \qquad (3)$$

where H_i denotes the color histogram of detection i, H_j denotes the color histogram of detection j and N is the total number of histogram bins.

4   Results and Discussion

To test the RFCN multiclass object detector in MOT and to assess the usefulness of the classification labels, we used the Urban Tracker dataset [3] since it contains a variety of road users in an urban environment. Figure 2 shows some sample frames from the Urban Tracker dataset with RFCN detections. The MOT performance is evaluated by using the CLEAR MOT metrics [6]:

- multiple object tracking accuracy (MOTA) that evaluates the quality of the tracking, if all road users are correctly detected in the frames they are visible and if there are no false alarms;
- and multiple object tracking precision (MOTP) that evaluates the quality of the localization of the matches.

To test the contribution of using labels in MOT, the proposed baseline method is applied with and without object classification labels in the cost computation for data association. The following parameters are used in the experiments: T_{match} is set at 1.5 and the value of $N_{timeout}$ is set at 5.

Table 1 summarizes the results obtained with the baseline tracker. First of all, we were not able to obtain interesting results on the René-Lévesque video. From the evaluation, it is observed that the size of the objects greatly influences the performance of the proposed method because of the shortcomings of RFCN. When the size of the road users is too small, there are not enough details for the detector to distinguish the different types of objects reliably. Mis-detections are common in such cases, as observed in video René-Lévesque, for example in Fig. 3. Since the frames are captured at a higher altitude than the other urban scenes, the object detector has difficulties in detecting and classifying the objects clearly due to the lack of details. On the other hand, larger objects such as buildings have the tendency of being detected as they share similarities with the features learned by the detector.

Secondly, it can be noticed from Table 1 that the MOTA results are negative and disappointing. This comes from the difficulty of interpreting the detections of RFCN. The same object is sometimes detected as several instances from the object detection module, as shown in Fig. 4. This often causes confusion and unnecessarily increases the number of detected objects and degrades the reported tracking performance. When there are no consecutive redundant detections, these redundant instances of the same object will usually be removed after a few frames since the object assignments are exclusive.

Fig. 2. Samples frames with detections from the Urban Tracker dataset.

Fig. 3. Typical detections obtained from the René-Lévesque video.

Table 1. Comparison of MOTA and MOTP scores for three videos of the Urban Tracker dataset with the inclusion and exclusion of label cost in the data association (the best results are in boldface).

	No. objects	MOTP		MOTA	
		With labels	Without labels	With labels	Without labels
Rouen	16	0.6870	**0.6893**	**−0.1877**	−0.4176
Sherbrooke	20	**0.7488**	0.7324	**0.0266**	−0.0023
St-Marc	28	**0.7234**	0.7136	−0.3657	**−0.2749**

Furthermore, contrarily to background subtraction or optical flow-based methods, RFCN gives detection outputs also for cars that are parked or for a car on a advertising billboard. Therefore, the data association process is distracted by many irrelevant objects. In such cases, standard NMS is not very useful in a traffic scene. Although NMS is used, it is insufficient to eliminate all the redundancies.

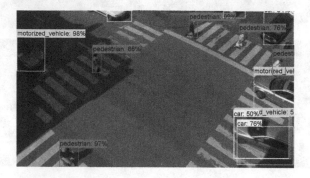

Fig. 4. An example of the redundant detection output for the same object.

Since the proposed method is intrinsically dependent on the results from the detection module, the mis-detections propagate and deteriorate the overall MOT performance. In this case, the existence of redundant tracks severely affects the MOTA score such that it falls into the negative range, as shown in Table 1. The MOTA takes into account the number of misses, false positives and mismatches from the produced trajectories.

However, it can be noted that MOT with inclusion of classification label generally gives higher MOTA. Among the different classes of labels from the detection module, the non-motorized vehicle label is currently excluded in the tracking framework since the occurrence of non-motorized vehicles is very rare in this experiment while parts of the background are sometimes mistakenly identified as objects from this class. MOTP is sometimes slightly better without labels as there are cases where tracking of an object fails in successive frames due to the switch of labels from the detection results. This is because with the labels, some matches are penalized and rejected because they are higher than the cost threshold. Therefore, the total number of matches is different, leading to slightly different values for MOTP. This occurrence is common among classes that share similarities such as pedestrians, bicycles and motorcycles, resulting in redundant tracks or fragmented tracks for the same object and thus lowering the overall tracking performance.

5 Conclusion

In this paper, the use of a modern multiclass object detector was investigated for the MOT task in traffic scenes. It was integrated in a baseline multiple object tracker. Results show that classification labels can be beneficial in MOT. However, the outputs of the multiclass object detector are hardly usable because they include a large number of false detections, or detections of objects that are not of interest in the current application (e.g. parked cars). Small objects are also difficult to detect. As a result, to use such a detector, its output needs to be combined with another detector that can focus more precisely on objects of interest such as background subtraction or optical flow.

Acknowledgement. This research is partly funded by Fonds de Recherche du Quebec -Nature et Technologies (FRQ-NT) with team grant No. 2016-PR-189250 and Polytechnique Montréal PhD Fellowship. We gratefully acknowledge the support of NVIDIA Corporation with the donation of the Titan X GPU used for this work.

References

1. Luo, Z., et al.: MIO-TCD: a new benchmark dataset for vehicle classification and localization. IEEE Trans. Image Process (2018)
2. Dai, J., Li, Y., He, K., Sun, J.: R-FCN: object detection via region-based fully convolutional networks. In: Advances in Neural Information Processing Systems, pp. 379–387 (2016)
3. Jodoin, J.-P., Bilodeau, G.-A., Saunier, N.: Tracking all road users at multimodal urban traffic intersections. IEEE Trans. Intell. Transp. Syst. **17**(11), 99–110 (2016)
4. Bewley, A., Ge, Z., Ott, L., Ramos, F., Upcroft, B.: Simple online and realtime tracking. In: 2016 IEEE International Conference on Image Processing (ICIP) on Proceedings, pp. 3464–3468 (2016)
5. Kuhn, H.W.: The Hungarian method for the assignment problem. Nav. Res. Logist. Q. **2**(5), 83–97 (1955)
6. Bernardin, K., Stiefelhagen, R.: Evaluating multiple object tracking performance: the CLEAR MOT metrics. J. Image Video Process. **2008**, 246309 (2008)
7. Malisiewicz, T., Gupta, A., Efros, A.A.: Ensemble of exemplar-SVMS for object detection and beyond. In: 2011 IEEE International Conference on Computer Vision (ICCV), pp. 89–96 (2011)
8. Felzenszwalb, P.F., Girshick, R.B., McAllester, D., Ramanan, D.: Object detection with discriminatively trained part-based models. IEEE Trans. Pattern Anal. Mach. Intell. **32**(9), 1627–1645 (2010)
9. Kalman, R.E.: A new approach to linear filtering and prediction problems. J. Basic Eng. **82**(1), 35–45 (1960)
10. Mendes, J.C., Bianchi, A.G.C., Júnior, A.R.P.: Vehicle tracking and origin-destination counting system for urban environment. In: Proceedings of the International Conference on Computer Vision Theory and Applications (2015)
11. Saunier, N., Sayed, T.: A feature-based tracking algorithm for vehicles in intersections. In: The 3rd Canadian Conference on Computer and Robot Vision, p. 59 (2006)
12. Kim, Z.W.: Real time object tracking based on dynamic feature grouping with background subtraction. In: IEEE Conference on Computer Vision and Pattern Recognition (CVPR), pp. 1–8 (2008)
13. Jun, G., Aggarwal, J.K., Gokmen, M.: Tracking and segmentation of highway vehicles in cluttered and crowded scenes. In: Proceedings of the 2008 IEEE Workshop on Applications of Computer Vision, pp. 1–6 (2008)

14. Coifman, B., Beymer, D., McLauchlan, P., Malik, J.: A real-time computer vision system for vehicle tracking and traffic surveillance. Transp. Res. Part C Emerg. Technol. **6**(4), 271–288 (1998)
15. Shi, J., Tomasi, C.: Good features to track. In: Computer Vision and Pattern Recognition, pp. 593–600 (1994)
16. Torabi, A., Bilodeau, G.-A.: A multiple hypothesis tracking method with fragmentation handling. In: Canadian Conference on Computer and Robot Vision, pp. 8–15 (2009)
17. Beymer, D., McLauchlan, P., Coifman, B., Malik, J.: A real-time computer vision system for measuring traffic parameters. In: IEEE Computer Society Conference on Computer Vision and Pattern Recognition, pp. 495–501 (1997)
18. Fuentes, L.M., Velastin, S.A.: People tracking in surveillance applications. In: Image and Vision Computing, pp. 1165–1171 (2006)
19. Aslani, S., Mahdavi-Nasab, H.: Optical flow based moving object detection and tracking for traffic surveillance. Int. J. Electr. Robot. Electron. Commun. Eng. **7**, 773–777 (2013)
20. Jodoin, J.P., Bilodeau, G.A., Saunier, N.: IEEE Winter Conference on Applications of Computer Vision, pp. 885–892 (2016)
21. Redmon, J., Divvala, S., Girshick, R., Farhadi, A.: You only look once: unified, real-time object detection. In: Proceedings of the IEEE Conference on Computer Vision and Pattern Recognition, pp. 779–788 (2016)

Autonomous Bus Boarding Robotic Wheelchair Using Bidirectional Sensing Systems

Shamim Al Mamun$^{(\boxtimes)}$, Hisato Fukuda, Antony Lam, Yoshinori Kobayashi, and Yoshinori Kuno

Saitama University, 255 Shimo-Okubo, Sakura-ku, Saitama City, Saitama 338-8570, Japan
{shamim,hisato,antony,yoshinori,kuno}@cv.ics.saitama-u.ac.jp

Abstract. Research interest in robotic wheelchairs is driven in part by their potential for improving the independence and quality-of-life of persons with disabilities and the elderly. Moreover, smart wheelchair systems aim to reduce the workload of the caregiver. In this paper, we propose a novel technique for 3D sensing using a conventional Laser Range Finder (LRF). We mounted two sensing systems onto our new six-wheeled robotic bus boarding wheelchair to locate the bus door and its determine its dimensions. Additionally, we have implemented a Single Shot Multibox Detector (SSD) to detect the bus doorsteps to allow for boarding. For precise movements, we successfully measure the height of the bus doorsteps and door width of the bus. Our step measurements and bus doorsteps detection technique for the wheelchair also enables the wheelchair to autonomously board a bus. Our experiments show the effectiveness and applicability of our system to real world robotic wheelchair freedom of movement.

Keywords: Robotic wheelchair · Bidirectional sensing
Lager range sensor

1 Introduction

In recent years, several smart wheelchairs possessing user-friendly interfaces and/or autonomous functions for enabling the elderly or disabled to travel have been proposed to meet the needs of aging societies [1,2]. Although ideally, wheelchair users may wish to go out alone, they are in practice, often accompanied by companions. Therefore, it is critical we determine how we can reduce the companion's workload and support their activities. Moreover, researchers have pointed out that when a wheelchair is moving in terrain, it needs to be able to avoid obstacles and classify road conditions [3,4]. In addition, smart wheelchairs intended to run autonomously in environments designed for humans must also be able to climb up steps in order to say, board a bus or train. Consequently, in

G. Bebis et al. (Eds.): ISVC 2018, LNCS 11241, pp. 737–747, 2018.
https://doi.org/10.1007/978-3-030-03801-4_64

this paper, we devised a new mechanism for a robotic wheelchair in collaboration with Toyota Motor Corporation and the University of Tokyo [5] that can detect steps and have the capability to move onto bus doorsteps.

For bus boarding, wheelchairs need 3D measurements to get precise measurements of the doorstep's height and door width. Vision based systems can be a good option for this kind of information [6]. A 3D depth camera can also be used for terrain mapping with depth information. But for outdoor applications, saturation issues may occur due to sunlight. Moreover, the computational cost can be too high for real time applications in bus boarding robotic wheelchairs and the measurements may be inaccurate.

Moreover, the wheelchair can acquire accurate measurements of the bus doorsteps and width of the bus door with updated laser sensing devices. Regarding this, researchers are working on building accurate models to overcome these difficulties with 3D laser sensors [7]. They rely on 3D laser range data for finding a given stair's planar surfaces from the observed point cloud to reconstruct models of staircases. Additionally, 3D mapping [8,9] can be a good tool for terrain mapping and obstacle detection for smooth navigation. But the price of such 3D sensors may prohibit deployment of current robots in real applications.

For precise movement of the smart wheelchair, it is very important to identify the observable area ahead of the wheelchair with faster detection tools. However, we note that most robotic wheelchairs use one or more 2D laser devices to avoid hazards like narrow passes, slopes, stairs, etc. [10]. In particular, much of the previous work concerns the use of 2D Laser Range Finder (LRF) sensors for obstacle detection. However, using multiple sensors or any moving mechanism for sensing results in a more complex system, thus increasing computational cost and the need for maintenance. Although, instead of using 3D sensors, in [11] the authors presented some 3D sensing systems using 2D LRFs. In those systems, multiple LRF sensors installed in different directions were mounted on a rotating unit to sense environmental hazards or for terrain classification. Fujita and Kondo [12] developed a sensing system using an arm-type sensor movable unit, which can sense in horizontal and vertical spaces to model stairs and gaps. The authors showed that their robot could measure the step size of stairs fairly well. Likewise, they had a 5.8% error in calculating the step height and width, where our previous approach [13] of height measurement with a single bidirectional measurement sensor, yielded a 1% error, which is more acceptable for wheelchairs to board onto buses.

In this paper, we propose a novel concept for sensing with a single 2D laser sensor that can obtain horizontal and vertical scan data simultaneously. To achieve bidirectional sensing, we have subdivided 2D sensors with 270° field of views into three equal segments. We attached three undistorted reflecting mirrors surrounding the sensor in each segment scanning path at an angle of 45°. In such an arrangement of mirrors, we virtually make the equivalent of three 2D sensors each with a 90° field of view. Moreover, we can install it in either way so that it can gives one vertical sensing lines and two horizontal sensing line or vice versa. In our previous works on step measurement techniques, we setup this system to get two vertical and one horizontal sensing lines as we used one system only to calculate precise step measurements of stairs.

For our Bus-boarding Mobility Robot (BMR) wheelchair, we used two Bidirectional Sensing Systems (BSS) to support the autonomous functionality of our robotic wheelchair, which can precisely measure the door's distance and height as well as board onto the bus. This system gives two vertical sensing lines by the wheels of our wheelchair to observe obstacles and from the horizontal lines, helps to find the height of the bus door. Moreover, the whole sensing system covers $1\,m^2$ of the area ahead of wheelchair to make observations for boarding. Through experiments, we found the vertical measurements along both sides of wheelchair provides an additional layer of safety to avoid collisions with the door while boarding. We also show that our setup is highly effective for finding steps on stairs, which allows for smooth climbing with our newly designed type of robotic wheelchair. Of course, a bus boarding wheelchair system needs to be able to detect the bus and bus door before boarding it. For that, we also installed a vision-assisted system to detect the bus and doorsteps of the bus with the help of a Single Shot Multibox Detector (SSD) [14] as its image recognition method.

2 System Overview

2.1 BMR Hardware

Figure 1 shows the overall system hardware setup of our bus-boarding wheelchair, the BMR and system flow diagram. We deploy our BSS on this six-wheeled smart wheelchair equipped with heavy suspensions for lifting itself. The wheelchair can move all its wheels according to the terrain and the BMR controller has functionalities to move forward, backward, and auto-board up onto doorsteps. Moreover, the wheelchair is equipped with a standard wide camera (iBuffalo) and two Laser Range Sensors (LRS) installed using a HOKUYO UTM-10LX unit at 75 cm above the ground plane and tilted downward. Besides, for visualization of laser data, we map sensor data on camera image and the calibrated wide camera is install in middle of the sensors axis so that we can map two BSS data on camera image which is explained in Sect. 4 in brief. Additionally, an Image Recognition System (IRS) is also deployed with the wheelchair to detect the bus, bus door, and doorstep. An intra-network system is built for the BMR, where the sensors, BMR controller, and Step Detection module are connected with a RJ-45 connector to a hub. The camera image is sent to the IRS for bus and bus door detection and sensor data is used for precise calculation of the bus door height and width. Although, the movement of the wheelchair partially depends on the IRS, once a bus and its door are detected, the wheelchair runs its step detection and position correction systems and autonomously instructs the BMR controller for boarding. A detailed description of the sensor system for precise measurement is in Sect. 4.

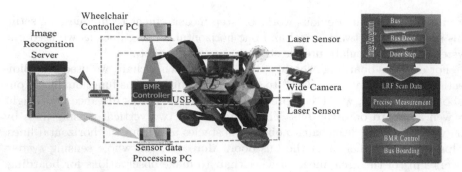

Fig. 1. Hardware of Smart Wheelchair System and system flow diagram

2.2   Detection Software

For devising a new bus boarding system, we need to be concerned with precise measurements of the door's location and height information. Before measurement, we have to locate the bus first for initial information gathering about the bus and bus door location. To do so, a camera vision system is used for detecting the bus and its sub-parts for proper information. We can recognize the bus, bus door, and doorstep successfully with our IRS module. Section 3 describes our overall implementation of the IRS in brief. Figure 1 illustrates the overall system flow of our bus boarding wheelchair's tasks where detection is the initial step via the vision system. For bus boarding, it is very important to measure the doorstep precisely otherwise the wheelchair could cause an accident while boarding. Therefore, after doorstep detection, we use the sensing mechanism to get accurate measurements of the door width and the doorstep height from the ground is calculated. Completing these steps, the measurement module of our software sends instruction to the wheelchair to get its distance from the bus door and boards. The BMR has its own automatic functionality to operate its wheels to overcome the calculated height.

3   Bus, Bus Door and Footstep Detection

Nowadays, deep learning networks are better at image classification than humans, which shows just how powerful this technique is. As a prerequisite, the wheelchair has to be able to acquire detection of the bus at the bus stop and locate the doorstep for boarding. Regarding this, we note that semantic segmentation [15] of the image is very helpful for our purposes. In particular, semantic segmentation approaches [16] yield good solutions for object detection using a variation of Convolutional Neural Networks in which a new def-pooling layer and learning strategies such as in Region-based Convolutional Neural Networks or Deep Belief Networks are employed. Great strides have been made in recent years but processing speed still presents challenges to applications in realtime systems. That is why some researchers have proposed regression models [17] for deep learning to speed up processing time such as with YOLO and SSD. The authors of those papers proposed that they discretize the output space of the bounding boxes into a set of default boxes over different aspect ratios and scales per feature map location. At prediction time, the network generates scores for the presence of each object category in each default box and produces adjustments to the box to better match the object shape. Moreover, they frame object detection as a regression problem to spatially separated bounding boxes and associated class probabilities. And they showed that their system runs at 59–67 FPS with mAP 76.85, which outperforms with other detection methods.

We used SSD for its high performance in precise bounding box location on the image and high 67 FPS speed. They use a multibox technique to locate the object in the image and draw the box near ground truth values. For real time applications, its not feasible to install it on the wheelchair so we use a pre-trained model for bus class identification and run it on a server. The wheelchair controller PC is connected to it remotely so that it can send a frame to the server and get the detected frame for further step calculation. In total, 400 images were used for training our bus, bus door, and bus doorstep detectors. For bus detection, we observed 100% accuracy in training, whereas we only attained 82% and 88% accuracy for our validation test set of different types of bus detections (Fig. 2). This was not problematic as we observed that buses would eventually be detected in some frames so that once the bus is detected, wheelchair stops sending frames to server and can perform its boarding. We ran a real scenario as video on our server and it successfully located our classes on video (Fig. 3). We could also detect the doorstep from our mock-up bus using the IRS.

Fig. 2. Different types of bus detections using SSD

4   Bidirectional Sensing System (BSS)

4.1   Sensor System

In this paper, we propose a new sensing mechanism using 2D laser sensors which can scan both in the horizontal and vertical directions. Conventionally, 2D laser sensor have a wide angle horizontal field of view. We use the HOKUYO 2D LRF with a horizontal field of view 270°, with a measuring interval angle of 0.25°. A single scan from the LRF captures 1,080 distance values in 25 ms but we do

(a) Bus Detection   (b) Bus Door Detection   (c) DoorStep Detection

Fig. 3. Image detection using SSD

not need to scan all 270° in the horizontal field of view for measuring height. However, we do need some vertical scan data to detect steps. Figure 6 shows the data acquisition apparatus, equipped with a HOKUYO UTM-10LX and three surrounding undistorted reflecting mirrors. The mirrors are placed at 45° angles around the 2D laser devices. The collected data from a single LRF is divided into three different segments where each mirror's associated data block consists of 360 values with angle coverage of 90°. From the LRF's scan, the first block of 360 values corresponds with the top side mirror within 0° to 90°, the middle block of 360 values are the angles between 90° to 180°, and the last block is from the bottom mirror corresponding to the 180° to 270° angles. As a result, the single laser sensor functions as three virtual laser sensors, each with a 90° field of view. In left part of the Fig. 4, the top and bottom part of the sensor shows two virtual horizontal scanners and one vertical. To avoid outliers, the data coming from the joint between two mirror segments is avoided. Therefore, we discard values from first and last 10° of each block. In this orientation of the laser, the top and bottom data from sensor in segment blocks 0 to 360 and 721 to 1080 are plotted in the $x - z$ plane and the vertical sensing data in the segment blocks 361 to 720 are plotted in the $y - z$ plane.

For bus boarding, we need two vertical scanning lines set apart at a distance the same as the wheelchair width so that it can avoid collisions with the bus door. Therefore, we use two BSS and equip them along the same axis on a 78 cm long bar edge tilted to the ground. This gives two vertical sensing lines from the far left and right of the sensors and four horizontal sensing lines across the vertical lines. Theoretically, we merge the horizontal data from the top and bottom so that we can receive a single distance value from both sensors. The vertical sensing positions of sensors start from 3 cm by the front wheels to check for obstacles.

Our sensing area also covers 1 m of distance ahead of wheelchair. The upper area of the top sensing line is important to find other obstacles like other passengers, bus seats, or luggage. When the wheelchair is instructed to board the bus, our system can sense this area as free to board, otherwise it sets itself back. This feature add an extra safety measure for our wheelchair. The right part of the Fig. 4 shows a 3D projection of the scanning data when the wheelchair is docked in front of the bus door. The pink lines show what comes from the left

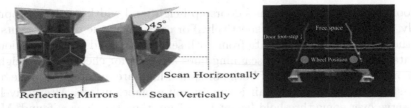

Fig. 4. Bidirectional Sensing System (BSS) and 3D projection of sensor data

sensor and yellow lines are from the right sensor. The free space for boarding inside the bus lies in between the two vertical lines above the top horizontal scanning lines. Mapping sensor data on the camera image plane is important for matching the bus doorstep detection on image for cross referencing with the scanning data values. Scanning data is used for step measurement and correcting the wheelchair position according to the door of the bus. In this paper, we also mapped our sensor data on real time image plane to visualize and analyze the 3D projection points for measuring doorsteps height and door width.

5   Experimental Setup

Our main goal of the experiment is to make our wheelchair autonomous and able to identify the bus and bus door while also being able to measure the bus door height precisely. For frequent experiments, it not always possible to test our system on a real bus. In our experiments, we set up a mock-up bus with printed image on a large sheet to simulate a real bus environment. Figure 5 shows the setup of our mock-up bus for our bus boarding case study and also we do several experiment on real bus scenario to measure its effectiveness.

Fig. 5. Real bus experiment setup and mock-up bus for indoor experiments

5.1   Step Detection and Position Correction

For bus boarding, it is essential to get precise measurements of the doorstep's height and door width. The doorstep's height is used for wheel movement in the upward direction and door width is necessary for avoiding collisions with the door's sides. Ideally, the bus's doorstep height and width would be approximately 15.0 cm and 110.0 cm respectively. For calculating the measurements, we took the horizontal scanning data from both sensor's top and bottom portions of the data. The top and bottom scanning lines are used for checking the height of the doorstep and door width. If both horizontal lines are in the same plane, then it is assumed that the wheelchair is running on a plane surface. Alternatively, if we observe over some threshold height i.e. 12 cm, then the door is found. Moreover, if the wheelchair is docked straight to the door then the average distance from both sensor's end segments of the data is approximately equal, otherwise the wheelchair is on the left side or right side of the door and accordingly our wheelchair can able to tune its position for boarding bus (Fig. 6).

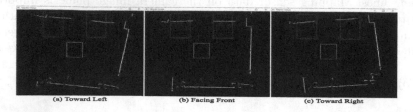

Fig. 6. Wheelchair position in respect to bus (a) Toward Left (b) Facing Front (c) Toward Right

Additionally, for measuring the door width, we applied a simple method where a dot product is used for calculating the width of the door. The horizontal data comes from top and bottom segment of the sensors and the total amount of data is 360 in each segment. We convert all the 2D data into 3D point cloud and take a patch of 5 data points. Then calculate the vector magnitude and dot product from 2nd point to 1st and 5th, which we called as feature for surface or door. If door appears on data it will gives 0 otherwise 1 or −1 as ideally, the angle between two vector in any patch would be 0° or 90° or 180°. From first sensor we take first feature of door as a start point of door and second sensor gives us end point of the door. Then compute the Euclidean distance between these two points to get the actual width of the door.

5.2   BMR Control

We have been collaborating with Toyota Motor Corporation to make a smart wheelchair that can board buses and escalators to grant freedom of movement to users. The BMR is equipped with six motor wheels. For normal movements, the wheelchair uses the front and rear wheels while the middle wheels support its balance while boarding. The dimensions of the smart wheelchair are

72.0 × 95.0 × 72.0 in cm. It can carry a typical weight of approximately 95 kg. The BMR can be controlled either via remote control or joystick. Although it can be manually maneuvered, we implemented autonomous control through programmed instructions with door detection from scan data and control its movements. It has also the capability to automatically board buses based on any found height. We implemented our algorithm on it to find the bus and bus door with proper measurement of height and the door with the help of bidirectional sensing using 2D lasers.

6   Experiment Results

We conducted our experiments for bus boarding with a newly trained image recognition server that can detect buses and bus doors as well as doorsteps. Figure 7 illustrates the outcomes of our system on camera images where we plot our sensor's data onto the image plane. The blue lines come from the left sensor and the cyan lines data come form the right sensor. The illustration shows the laser data in the 3D world space on the 2D images while the BMR approaches to the door. When the wheelchair observes a certain height (i.e. >12 cm) wheelchair plays a sound indicating, "The door has been detected." The sound playing is another feature for our wheelchair to make other passengers aware and cooperate with the wheelchair for safe boarding. In Fig. 7(b), we see that the horizontal line aligns with the height of the door. After that, the wheelchair moves forward a little bit to correct its position for boarding where the horizontal lines are aligned flat as shown in Fig. 7(d). Figure 8, depicts the actual moving of our wheelchair in six phases with boarding preparation in real bus scenarios. For boarding, the wheelchair lifts its front wheel to the height found using the laser sensor. The wheelchair then executes a series of movements to overcome that height and successfully board the bus. We have done this experiment by setting different heights of the doorstep and our wheelchair successfully detects the height and boards the bus.

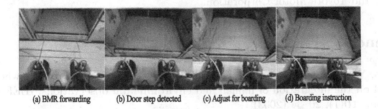

(a) BMR forwarding   (b) Door step detected   (c) Adjust for boarding   (d) Boarding instruction

Fig. 7. Visual camera images for boarding: (a) Running State (b) Detected bus doorstep (c) Adjusting its distance for safe boarding (d) Boarding

Fig. 8. Our wheelchair system autonomously boarding the bus in real scenarios

7   Conclusions

In this paper, we introduce a new mechanism of sensing for getting the heights of bus doorsteps for autonomous bus boarding. Our experiments were conducted in an indoor and outdoor environment and we demonstrated successfully operation of the proposed system using our method for measuring the height of the bus doorstep. Moreover, the wheelchair plays a warning sound for its movements while its boarding to help other passenger cooperate with the wheelchair. According to our results in step detection and measurement, our system is able to detect the bus door and measure the approximate height of the doorstep, which grants freedom of movement to the wheelchair user. Our wheelchair has successfully demonstrated autonomous bus boarding in real world scenarios. Though the real bus boarding experiment is conducted in controlled environment like height of the bus doorstep is assumed to be fixed but Of course, real world scenarios are a bit different so in the future, we will conduct more experiments in real environments at bus stops and also identify moving objects with sensor data such as escalator steps. Thereby making it so the BMR could ride on escalators and increase its mobility.

Acknowledgement. This work was supported by the Saitama Prefecture Leading-edge Industry Design Project and JSPS KAKENHI Grant Number JP26240038, and in collaboration with Dr. Tomoyuki Takahata and Prof. Iaso Shimoyama at the University of Tokyo, and Toyota Motor Corporation.

References

1. Kuno, Y., Shimada, N., Shirai, Y.: Look where you're going: a robotic wheelchair based on the integration of human and environmental observations. IEEE Robot. Autom. **10**(1), 26–34 (2003)
2. Leaman, J., La, H.M.: A comprehensive review of smart wheelchairs: past, present, and future. IEEE Trans. Hum. Mach. Syst. **47**(4), 486–489 (2017)
3. Kobayashi, Y., Kinpara, Y., Takano, E., Kuno, Y., Yamazaki, K., Yamazaki, A.: Robotic wheelchair moving with caregiver collaboratively. In: Huang, D.-S., Gan, Y., Gupta, P., Gromiha, M.M. (eds.) ICIC 2011. LNCS (LNAI), vol. 6839, pp. 523–532. Springer, Heidelberg (2012). https://doi.org/10.1007/978-3-642-25944-9_68

4. Mamun, S.A., Suzuki, R., Lam, A., Kobayashi, Y., Kuno, Y.: Terrain recognition for smart wheelchair. In: Huang, D.-S., Han, K., Hussain, A. (eds.) ICIC 2016. LNCS (LNAI), vol. 9773, pp. 461–470. Springer, Cham (2016). https://doi.org/10.1007/978-3-319-42297-8_43
5. Ishikawa, M., et al.: Travel Device, Patent Number: WO2016/006248 A1 (2016)
6. Schwarze, T., Zhong, Z.: Stair detection and tracking from egocentric stereo vision. In: IEEE International Conference on Image Processing (ICIP), pp. 2690–2694 (2015)
7. Hwang, Y., Lee, J.: Robust 3D map building for a mobile robot moving on the floor. In: IEEE International Conference on Advanced Intelligent Mechatronics (AIM) (2015)
8. Nemoto, Z., Takemura, H., Mizoguchi, H.: Development of small-sized omnidirectional laser range scanner and its application to 3D background difference. In: Proceedings of IEEE 33rd Annual Conference Industrial Electronics Society (IECON), pp. 2284–2289 (2007)
9. Poppinga, J., Birk, A., Pathak, K.: Hough based terrain classification for real time detection of drivable ground. J. Field Robot. 25(1–2), 67–88 (2008)
10. Lv, J., Kobayashi, Y., Hoshino, Y., Emaru, T.: Slope detection based on orthogonal assumption. In: IEEE/SICE International Symposium on system Integration (SII) (2012)
11. Sheh, R., Kadous, M., Sammut, C., Hengst, B.: Extracting terrain features from range images for autonomous random step field traversal. In: Proceedings of IEEE International Workshop on Safety, Security and Rescue Robotics (2007)
12. Fujita, T., Kondo, Y.: Robot Arms, 9 June 2011. Book edited by Satoru Goto. ISBN 978-953-307-160-2
13. Mamun, S.A., Lam, A., Kobayashi, Y., Kuno, Y.: Single laser bidirectional sensing for robotic wheelchair step detection and measurement. In: Huang, D.-S., Hussain, A., Han, K., Gromiha, M.M. (eds.) ICIC 2017. LNCS (LNAI), vol. 10363, pp. 37–47. Springer, Cham (2017). https://doi.org/10.1007/978-3-319-63315-2_4
14. Liu, W., et al.: SSD: single shot MultiBox detector. In: Leibe, B., Matas, J., Sebe, N., Welling, M. (eds.) ECCV 2016. LNCS, vol. 9905, pp. 21–37. Springer, Cham (2016). https://doi.org/10.1007/978-3-319-46448-0_2
15. Voulodimos, A., Doulamis, N., Doulamis, A., Protopapadakis, E.: Deep learning for computer vision: a brief review. Comput. Intell. Neurosci. 2018, Article ID 7068349, 13 pages (2018)
16. Dong, J., Chen, Q., Yan, S., Yuille, A.: Towards unified object detection and semantic segmentation. In: Fleet, D., Pajdla, T., Schiele, B., Tuytelaars, T. (eds.) ECCV 2014. LNCS, vol. 8693, pp. 299–314. Springer, Cham (2014). https://doi.org/10.1007/978-3-319-10602-1_20
17. Redmon, J., et al.: You only look once: unified real-time object detection. In: Proceedings of the IEEE Conference on Computer Vision and Pattern Recognition, pp. 779–788 (2016)

Road User Abnormal Trajectory Detection Using a Deep Autoencoder

Pankaj Raj Roy[✉] and Guillaume-Alexandre Bilodeau

LITIV Laboratory, Department of Computer and Software Engineering,
Polytechnique Montréal, Montreal, Canada
{pankaj-raj.roy,gabilodeau}@polymtl.ca

Abstract. In this paper, we focus on the development of a method that detects abnormal trajectories of road users at traffic intersections. The main difficulty with this is the fact that there are very few abnormal data and the normal ones are insufficient for the training of any kinds of machine learning model. To tackle these problems, we proposed the solution of using a deep autoencoder network trained solely through augmented data considered as normal. By generating artificial abnormal trajectories, our method is tested on four different outdoor urban users scenes and performs better compared to some classical outlier detection methods.

Keywords: Deep autoencoder · Unsupervised learning
Data augmentation · Abnormal trajectory detection

1 Introduction

Abnormal event detection has been an intriguing research subject for many years, namely because of the fact that the definition of an abnormal event can be very unclear. The classification of abnormal events can be a challenging task when the number of possible abnormalities can easily exceed our knowledge of abnormal behaviors. Also, it is usually a very tedious job to obtain abnormal data. There can be many different possibilities of abnormalities and some of them can even be subjective. In order to tackle this problem, many authors suggest the hypothesis that all the abnormalities are outliers of the normality distribution. By taking that into account, one can notice that abnormalities are context/scene dependent and that a uniform definition of abnormal events cannot be generalized for all kinds of scenarios other than the assumption of these being the opposite of normal events.

The goal of this paper is to detect abnormal trajectories at road intersections where the objects of interest can be identified as pedestrians, cyclists or vehicles. The problem with trajectory data at intersections is that it does not follow any particular probabilistic rules. Therefore, the best way for classifying them is to use statistical or machine learning approaches that can learn the normal trajectories in an unsupervised manner and be trained to detect outliers, which can be

© Springer Nature Switzerland AG 2018
G. Bebis et al. (Eds.): ISVC 2018, LNCS 11241, pp. 748–757, 2018.
https://doi.org/10.1007/978-3-030-03801-4_65

classified as abnormal trajectories. Various statistical approaches can solve the issue of trajectory anomaly detection. But, this problem becomes challenging when the dataset is not large enough for trajectory data classification. In this work, we want to devise a method that can use a small number of trajectory samples and that gives the best precision on the classification of normal and abnormal trajectories compared to other outliers detection methods.

To solve the abnormal event detection problem, our contribution is to propose a deep autoencoder model coupled with a data augmentation method. This allows us to encode information about normal trajectories while removing irrelevant information. Results show that our proposed method outperforms classical methods such as one-class support vector machine (SVM).

2 Related Work

In the work of Mousavi et al. [7], the detection of abnormal crowd behavior is based on Histograms of Oriented Tracklets (HOT), the Latent Dirichlet Allocation (LDA) and an SVM that is used for the classification of frames. A spatio-temporal model based on background subtraction in the form of a co-occurrence matrix is proposed in [1] for detecting objects following suspicious paths. This method cannot detect abnormal events overlapping normal paths. The Mixture of Dynamic Textures (MDT), in [6], is used for the anomaly detection in crowded scenes by modeling the appearance and the representation of dynamics of the scenes. This method is not designed to interpret trajectories. In [2], an interaction energy potentials method is proposed. An SVM is used in order to classify the abnormal activities based on the standard bag-of-word representation of each video clip. In [5], detection is implemented using a dictionary of normal patterns represented by the training features from a region in a video, which are the 3D gradient features of a spatial-temporal cubes of five frames. This method cannot be used to interpret trajectories. The covariance matrix for optical flow based feature is applied in [13]. In [12], the authors demonstrated how a Convolutional Neural Network (CNN), a Long Short Term Memory (LSTM) and an SVM can be learned from very few videos and used for detecting abnormal events. Even though this method achieves 95 % accuracy, the abnormal activity detection is only limited to binary classification and is not applicable to abnormal trajectory. The convolutional auto-encoder (CAE), proposed in [10], learns the signature of normal events with the training data. This method takes the frames, the appearance features extracted via Canny edge detector and the motion features from optical flow in the input of the CAE model and outputs the regularization of reconstruction errors (RRE) for each frame.

Abnormal event detection is fundamentally an outlier detection problem. Therefore, any classical outlier detection approach can be used. In [11], a One-Class SVM algorithm is proposed for unlabeled data, which can be used for the novelty detection. This latter form of detection is basically an outlier detector that does not require any abnormal data during the training process of the classification model [9]. In [4], the Isolation Forest method isolates anomalies instead of profiling normal points and also works well with large datasets.

3   Proposed Method

Before applying any statistical or machine learning methods for the detection of outliers, the input data is processed in order to extract its trajectories. Unlike the standard classification problem where each frame of a video represents a sample, in the case of trajectory, multiple frames are needed to define a trajectory sample. Even for thousands of frames, the number of trajectory samples extracted will be insufficient for training properly any statistical or machine learning methods, especially Neural Networks (NN) based methods. Therefore, it is necessary to apply data augmentation for increasing the number of trajectory samples. The general idea behind our abnormal trajectory detection is the following (see Fig. 1). First, tracking results are used to extract trajectories assumed to be normal. Then, data augmentation techniques are used in order to increase the number of normal trajectories. A deep autoencoder (DAE) is then trained to learn normal trajectories and classification can be applied on new data.

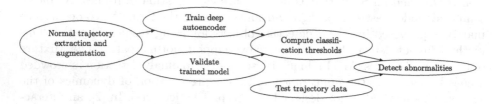

Fig. 1. The main steps of our abnormal trajectory detection method.

3.1   Background on Autoencoders and Deep Autoencoders

The simplest form of autoencoder (AE), called Vanilla Autoencoder (VAE), can be used for the abnormal trajectory detection. Regular AEs are made out of fully-connected NNs that are configured to reproduce the inputs to the outputs of the network. They follow an unsupervised learning method which does not require input data to be labeled. First, this type of NNs compresses the original input into a latent-space representation, which is the space that lies in the bottleneck (hidden) layer, also known as Compressed Feature Vector (CFV). This latter form of representation is produced by an encoding function representing the encoder. Then, the decoder side of this NN reconstructs the CFV input into the output resembling the original input of the encoder side. Figure 2 shows the simplest form of an AE, which is basically made out of three layers, one input, one hidden layer (CFV) and one reconstructed output.

   The advantage of utilizing this kind of NNs is that it can be used for learning the normality of the input data. By using only normal data for training of the AE network, the encoder and the decoder are adapted for the normal data and will produce a reconstructed data where the Mean Square Error (MSE) with the

Roy and Bilodeau

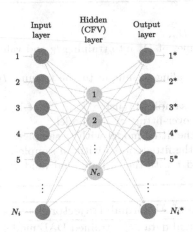

Fig. 2. Diagram showing a Vanilla Autoencoder.

original one varies within some specific defined range, which will be elaborated in the next subsection. When testing the trained AE with abnormal input data, it will produce a reconstruction error (RMSE) exceeding the threshold value calculated from the trained and validated RMSE values.

Deep Autoencoder (DAE). Even though the VAE can be used for the detection of anomalies, intuitively, it is not enough for learning the complex nature of normal trajectories in road intersections. By adding multiple hidden layers in the AE network, the model is able to learn a more complex feature representation, which can be useful for classifying more realistic abnormal trajectories.

3.2 Abnormal Event Detection with a Deep Autoencoder

Algorithms 1 and 2 summarize the main steps required for the training of the DAE model and for detecting abnormalities using the trained network. During the training process of the DAE model, there are two types of validation samples: one that is used internally through cross-validation during the fitting of the networks with the input training set, called va_{cv} samples, and the other called va_e is used externally to validate the scoring of the normality of normal input data. Note that the cross-validation data is necessary during the training process of the network in order to prevent over-fitting.

The scores S are based of the MSE between normalized original z and reconstructed output $\hat{z}$ for each sample, as shown in Eq. 1.

$$S = \mathrm{MSE}\,(z, \hat{z}) \tag{1}$$

The threshold value τ is learned from the data and is used for separating normal from abnormal data. It is determined through Eq. 2, where STD stands

---

Algorithm 1. Training of the Deep Autoencoder Model.

Input: normal data D_n

1. Shuffle the samples of D_n.
2. Split the shuffled samples of D_n into training tr and validation sets va.
3. Build the DAE model.
4. Apply normalization scaling technique to the training tr and validation sets va samples.
5. Fit the model with tr samples by using $P_{va_{cv}}$ % of it as the cross-validation set va_{cv} in order to avoid over-fitting of the model.
6. Get the scores S_{tr} of the fitted model with tr samples.
7. Get the scores S_{va} of the fitted model with va samples.
8. Compute the threshold τ with the training and validation scores (S_{tr} and S_{va}).

Algorithm 2. Detection of Abnormal Trajectories using Trained Autoencoder.

Input: Normal and abnormal data D_{an}, trained DAE model i
Output: classification decisions

1. Apply normalization scaling method to the test trajectory samples in D_{an} between 0 and 1 (z_{scaled}).
2. Open the saved trained model i and the corresponding computed threshold value τ.
3. Get the scores S_z of the trained model with sample z in D_{an}.
4. Detect the abnormalities using S_z and the previously computed threshold τ and output the results.

---

for standard deviation, and, S_{tr} and S_{va} are the scores for the training and the validation sets respectively.

$$\tau = \text{mean}(S_{tr}) + \text{mean}(S_{va}) + 3 \times (\text{STD}(S_{tr}) + \text{STD}(S_{va})) \qquad (2)$$

Then, the following rule applies for the classification C of a trajectory sample z:

$$C(z) = \begin{cases} \text{Normal,} & \text{if } S_z \leq \tau \\ \text{Abnormal, otherwise,} \end{cases} \qquad (3)$$

where S_z is the score obtained by applying the trained DAE model to the trajectory sample z.

4   Experiments

4.1   Deep Autoencoder Implementation Details

The Table 1 presents the values of hyper-parameters that resulted in the best convergence of the deep autoencoder network. The implementation of the DAE was done using Keras Python package.

Table 1. Hyper-parameters used for the training of the DAE.

Parameter	Value	Definition
H_i	125	Input trajectory sample size
H_{h_1}	128	Number of units in the first hidden layer
H_{h_2}	64	Number of units in the second hidden layer
H_{h_3}	32	Number of units in the third hidden layer
H_{h_4}	16	Number of units in the fourth hidden layer
H_c	8	Number of units in the CFV layer
N_{batch}	128	Batch size used each time
N_{epoch}	100	Number of epochs
Optimiser	RMSprop	RMSProp optimizer
σ	0.001	Default learning rate of RMSProp optimizer
Loss	MSE	Mean Squared Error

Notice that the first hidden layer in the encoder side of the DAE has a number of units which is slightly greater than the input size. This configuration helps to transform the input size into a number that is a power of two. In fact, by having large layer size in the first hidden layer, the network learns a more detail representation of the input data. Then, by having decreasing unit sizes of power of two in the subsequent layers, the CFV layer gets a more abstract representations of the normal trajectory samples, which can help to detect more complex level of outliers. Also, note that the hidden layers use ReLu activation and the output layer use Sigmoid.

Before feeding the input data into the network, it is scaled with a min and max scaler of 0 and 1. We apply a normalization scaling technique, because the input trajectory data does not follow any specific probabilistic distribution. Also, by scaling the input data before feeding it to the DAE network, we avoid the possibility of having the knock-on effect on the ability to learn the normality of the training data.

4.2 Experimental Protocol

We applied N iterations of Repeated random sub-sampling validation for validating our model, because the shuffling of the input normal data, combined with the splitting into training and validation sets, has an impact on the accuracy of the normality/abnormality detection. Therefore, by doing N iterations, we can determine the average of our method's performance to assess its power of generalization and get the best model giving the highest values of True Positive (TP) and True Negative (TN), and the lowest values of False Positive (FP) and False Negative (FN). We compared our method with OC-SVM and IF that are implemented in `sklearn` Python package [8].

4.3   Input Data, Data Augmentation and Processing

We used the Urban Tracker Dataset [3] that contains four different types of scenarios involving pedestrians, vehicles (including cars and large vehicles) and bikes. Figure 3 shows all the original trajectories of the four scenarios, all of which are considered as "normal" trajectories.

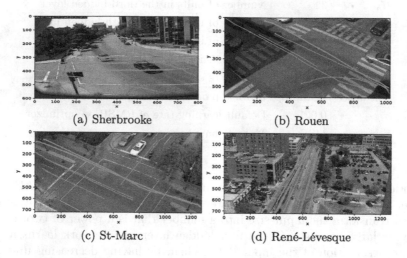

(a) Sherbrooke   (b) Rouen

(c) St-Marc   (d) René-Lévesque

Fig. 3. Original annotated trajectories of the Urban Tracker Dataset. Red, green and blue represent pedestrians, cars and bikes respectively. (Color figure online)

The Sherbrooke video contains the trajectories of 15 cars and 5 pedestrians. The Rouen video includes 4 vehicles, 1 bike and 11 pedestrians. For the St-Marc video, 1000 frames were chosen, with 7 vehicles, 2 bicycles and 19 pedestrians. Finally, the René-Lévesque video includes 29 vehicles and 2 bikes. We used the ground truth locations of the moving objects for every frames of the urban intersection videos. These locations are composed of bounding box positions. Algorithm 3 describes the fundamental steps for the extraction and augmentation of the trajectories.

Note that we choose to generate trajectory samples by applying a sliding-window approach in which the trajectory window, composed of 31 positions, slides the complete trajectory of an object with a stride of 10 frames. This is done to learn the continuity of the trajectory and therefore prevents the network to learn the wrong representation of trajectory coordinates.

4.4   Abnormal Trajectory Generation

For testing the trained model, abnormal trajectory data is needed. Abnormal events can be a different trajectory path for a car, or a car following the path of pedestrians. For demonstrating the validity of our method, we have generated

---

Algorithm 3. Trajectory Extraction and Augmentation.

Input: bounding boxes
Output: trajectory samples

1. Extract the positions x and y corresponding to the center of the bounding box positions and its related velocities v_x and v_y of the object n.
2. Generate 50 augmented trajectories by randomly generating positions x_a and y_a around the real ones x and y and its related velocities v_{x_a} and v_{y_a}.
3. Decompose the extracted and augmented trajectories into sub trajectory frames composed of 31 positions and velocities.
   - Stretch the complete trajectory of the object n in order for it to be decomposable according to the specific sliding stride value.
4. Add the appropriate label depending on the type of the object. The label "0" identifies a pedestrian, "1" is for a car and "2" specifies a bike.
5. Flatten all the sub trajectories in the following Packed format (125 elements): $[label, x_1, y_1, v_{x_1}, v_{y_1}, x_2, y_2, v_{x_2}, v_{y_2}, ..., x_{31}, y_{31}, v_{x_{31}}, v_{y_{31}}]$.

---

two types of abnormal data, one which consists of straight lines with constant velocities and the other, more realistic abnormal trajectories inspired by the real normal ones. The realistic ones are resulting from the transformation of the original trajectories, which keeps the same degree of fluctuation in the positions and the velocities. The Fig. 4 shows some of the generated abnormalities.

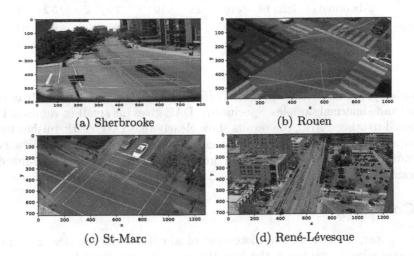

(a) Sherbrooke

(b) Rouen

(c) St-Marc

(d) René-Lévesque

Fig. 4. Generated realistic abnormal trajectories. Red, green and blue represent pedestrians, cars and bikes respectively. (Color figure online)

4.5   Experimental Results

Table 2 presents the results obtained by applying the trained models on the normal and abnormal trajectories of the dataset. The true positive rate (TPR) and the false positive rate (FPR) are defined as the detected normality/abnormality from normal/abnormal and abnormal/normal samples respectively. Here, we only considered the realistic version of the generated abnormal data. Also, note that the data augmentation technique is applied before training each of these models.

Table 2. Results obtained by applying the trained model on trajectory samples. Bold-face values indicate the best results. Status: label indicating normal/abnormal samples, Size: number of samples, OC-SVM: One-class SVM, IF: Isolation forest, VAE: Vanilla AE, DEA: Deep AE.

			Method (%)							
			OC-SVM		IF		VAE		DAE (Ours)	
Data	Status	Size	TPR	FPR	TPR	FPR	TPR	FPR	TPR	FPR
Sherb.	Normal	20606	90	83	89	82	99	**98**	99	**20**
	Abnormal	406	17	10	18	11	**2**	1	**80**	1
Rouen	Normal	11884	90	87	90	91	**100**	96	**100**	15
	Abnormal	234	13	10	9	10	4	**0**	**85**	0
St-Marc	Normal	40139	90	82	90	79	**99**	99	**99**	68
	Abnormal	789	18	10	21	10	1	1	**32**	1
Rene-L.	Normal	45341	90	80	89	80	**99**	99	**99**	61
	Abnormal	891	20	10	20	10	1	1	**39**	1

Globally, our method outperforms others in terms of TPR and FPR in both normal and abnormal samples. Specifically, DAE gives the smallest values of FPR compared to others. Also, the results show clearly that DAE distinguishes better the normal and abnormal data compared to VAE. Therefore, it is necessary to have multiple layers in AE network in order for it to avoid getting over-fitted by the training normal data.

5   Conclusion

In this paper, we studied the detection of abnormal trajectories in common traffic scenarios. Considering the hypothesis of abnormalities behaving as outliers, we have proposed a method with a DAE which uses only normal data in the training process. We also applied an automated data augmentation technique for increasing the number of training samples. By generating interactively abnormal realistic trajectories, our method, compared to others like OC-SVM, IF and VAE, yielded the best performance in terms of TPR and FPR of the normal/abnormal detection in most videos.

Acknowledgement. This research was supported by a grant from IVADO funding program for fundamental research projects.

References

1. Benezeth, Y., Jodoin, P.M., Saligrama, V., Rosenberger, C.: Abnormal events detection based on spatio-temporal co-occurences. In: 2009 IEEE Conference on Computer Vision and Pattern Recognition, pp. 2458–2465, June 2009. https://doi.org/10.1109/CVPR.2009.5206686
2. Cui, X., Liu, Q., Gao, M., Metaxas, D.N.: Abnormal detection using interaction energy potentials. In: CVPR 2011, pp. 3161–3167 (2011). https://doi.org/10.1109/CVPR.2011.5995558
3. Jodoin, J.P., Bilodeau, G.A., Saunier, N.: Urban tracker: multiple object tracking in urban mixed traffic. In: IEEE Winter Conference on Applications of Computer Vision, pp. 885–892, March 2014. https://doi.org/10.1109/WACV.2014.6836010
4. Liu, F.T., Ting, K.M., Zhou, Z.H.: Isolation forest. In: 2008 Eighth IEEE International Conference on Data Mining, pp. 413–422, December 2008. https://doi.org/10.1109/ICDM.2008.17
5. Lu, C., Shi, J., Jia, J.: Abnormal event detection at 150 fps in matlab. In: 2013 IEEE International Conference on Computer Vision, pp. 2720–2727, December 2013. https://doi.org/10.1109/ICCV.2013.338
6. Mahadevan, V., Li, W., Bhalodia, V., Vasconcelos, N.: Anomaly detection in crowded scenes. In: 2010 IEEE Computer Society Conference on Computer Vision and Pattern Recognition, pp. 1975–1981, June 2010. https://doi.org/10.1109/CVPR.2010.5539872
7. Mousavi, H., Mohammadi, S., Perina, A., Chellali, R., Murino, V.: Analyzing tracklets for the detection of abnormal crowd behavior. In: 2015 IEEE Winter Conference on Applications of Computer Vision, pp. 148–155, January 2015. https://doi.org/10.1109/WACV.2015.27
8. Pedregosa, F., et al.: Scikit-learn: machine learning in python. J. Mach. Learn. Res. **12**, 2825–2830 (2011)
9. Pimentel, M.A., Clifton, D.A., Clifton, L., Tarassenko, L.: A review of novelty detection. Signal Process. **99**, 215–249 (2014). https://doi.org/10.1016/j.sigpro.2013.12.026. http://www.sciencedirect.com/science/article/pii/S016516841300515X
10. Ribeiro, M., Lazzaretti, A.E., Lopes, H.S.: A study of deep convolutional auto-encoders for anomaly detection in videos. Pattern Recognit. Lett. **105**, 13–22 (2018). https://doi.org/10.1016/j.patrec.2017.07.016. http://www.sciencedirect.com/science/article/pii/S0167865517302489. Machine Learning and Applications in Artificial Intelligence
11. Schölkopf, B., Platt, J.C., Shawe-Taylor, J.C., Smola, A.J., Williamson, R.C.: Estimating the support of a high-dimensional distribution. Neural Comput. **13**(7), 1443–1471 (2001). https://doi.org/10.1162/089976601750264965
12. Vignesh, K., Yadav, G., Sethi, A.: Abnormal event detection on BMTT-PETS 2017 surveillance challenge. In: 2017 IEEE Conference on Computer Vision and Pattern Recognition Workshops (CVPRW), pp. 2161–2168, July 2017. https://doi.org/10.1109/CVPRW.2017.268
13. Wang, T., Qiao, M., Zhu, A., Niu, Y., Li, C., Snoussi, H.: Abnormal event detection via covariance matrix for optical flow based feature. Multimed. Tools Appl. **77**, 17375–17395 (2017). https://doi.org/10.1007/s11042-017-5309-2

Traffic Flow Classification Using Traffic Cameras

Mohammad Shokrolah Shirazi[1](✉) and Brendan Morris[2]

[1] Cleveland State University, Cleveland, OH, USA
m.shokrolahshirazi@csu.ohio.edu
[2] University of Nevada, Las Vegas, NV, USA
brendan.morris@unlv.edu

Abstract. Traffic flow classification is an integrated task of traffic management and network mobility. In this work, a feature collection system is developed to collect the moving and appearance-based features of traffic images, and their performance are evaluated by different machine learning techniques including Deep Neural Networks (DNN), and Convolutional Neural Networks (CNN). The experimental results for a challenging highway video with three traffic flow classes of light, medium and heavy indicates the highest performance of CNN with 90% accuracy.

1 Introduction

Due to recent advances in computer vision and machine learning techniques, traffic cameras are known as great resources for traffic analysis. The main advantages are their low cost, unintrusive characteristic and heterogeneous applications [1]. For instance, computer vision techniques can provide vehicle count, classes [2] and queue length estimate [3] simultaneously.

The traditional method of vehicle detection in traffic surveillance relies on utilizing vehicle motion cue for foreground segmentation. For instance, Zhang et al. [2] extracted a background image from a video sequence to detect presence of vehicles, and calculated vehicle lengths for classification. Nemade et al. [4] proposed a framework for vehicle count and license plate detection during day and night time. However, the performance of mentioned studies degrade for heavy traffic flow and cluttered scenes (See Sect. 2).

An alternative motion-based method is to use visual feature points to track and count vehicles [5] with optical flow. Although the method is robust against partial occlusion, the detection of good features to track is subjected to image resolution, and the real-time applicability of the system degrades for highly clustered scenes [1].

Deep learning methods have recently shown promising results in object detection and image classification, and they have attracted a great degree of attention for Intelligent Transportation Systems (ITS) applications such as traffic phase inference [6] and traffic flow estimation [7,8]. For instance, Ma et al. [8] proposed a method based on convolutional neural network (CNN) that learns traffic as

© Springer Nature Switzerland AG 2018
G. Bebis et al. (Eds.): ISVC 2018, LNCS 11241, pp. 758–767, 2018.
https://doi.org/10.1007/978-3-030-03801-4_66

images and predicts large-scale, network-wide traffic speed with a high accuracy. However, the data collection source is GPS and originated speeds form matrices and images. Fouladgar et al. [7] presented a deep learning-based method for congestion detection. Similarly, the average speed constructs the image matrices as input for deep traffic flow convolution network.

In this work, we investigate the performance of the handwritten and deep learning-based features for traffic flow classification task. Our work is different than presented works in [7,8], since we directly classify congestion through traffic camera images. The contributions of the paper are as follow:

1. The paper presents a simple way to determine a category of traffic flow regardless of developing a tracking system through learning moving and appearance-based features.
2. Variety of machine learning techniques including deep neural networks and convolutional neural networks are evaluated and their performance are compared against traditional methods with handwritten features.

2   Vehicle Tracking System

A vehicle tracking system is developed initially to provide the classification of traffic flow. The idea is to recognize traffic classes by the number of tracks available in the road [2,5]. The vehicle tracking is conducted by integration of two different modules named vehicle detection and tracking systems.

The main concept behind the detection system is to estimate an adaptive background using Gaussian mixture model (GMM) [9] and subtract it from each coming frame using background subtraction (BS) method. Moving vehicles are detected as pixel intensity values which do not fit in any of the N background Gaussian models.

The tracking system utilized a bipartite graph to find the closest neighbors between each two frames instead of overlapping ratio [10]. The matrix consists of two columns of detection and tracking that finally is updated if a detection appropriately fits both a dynamic model and an appearance constraint. More details about the tracking system can be found in [11].

Figure 1 shows snapshots of the tracking system for two videos of light and heavy traffic flows. The figure implies that the number of misdetected vehicles are accumulated when number of vehicles are increased in a highway. For example, Fig. 1a shows seven vehicle tracks while two of them are the nearby vehicles. However, the congested one (i.e., Fig. 1b) introduces more misdetected vehicles since only ten tracks are recognized by the tracking system.

The main reason for such an undesired scenario is due to degrade of the tracking system performance for the congested traffic. The tracking system is not able to keep track of the occluded and nearby vehicles since their blob characteristics no longer follow the vehicle appearance model learned in prior frames. As an outcome, the common tracking methods based on motion with background subtraction [2] are not sufficient to perform the traffic classification task.

(a) Light traffic flow   (b) Heavy traffic flow

Fig. 1. Tracking video snapshots

3   Feature Collection System

Since a road user's level of motion is influenced by the traffic congestion level, our work aims to recognize the traffic flow categories of light, medium and heavy through observing moving features and obtaining appropriate models using machine learning techniques. The moving features are extracted from a video using optical flow and background subtraction techniques and their specific characteristics are measured to construct feature vectors.

3.1   Blob Features

Background subtraction is a common way of road user detection in traffic surveillance due to its speed, simplicity and efficiency with normal traffic flow [12]. The background subtraction method has been developed along with the vehicle tracking system to improve tracking performance (See Sect. 2).

The measured blob characteristics are collected and prepared into feature vectors for training purposes. Figure 2a shows movement areas called blob after performing background subtraction for the frame 65. The feature vector is created by measuring fundamental characteristics of a foreground blob such as $f = \{x, y, w, h, area, eccen, orien\}$ where x, y are the centroid coordinates of a blob, w, h are the width and height of the fitted bounding box around the blob, $area$ is total number of white pixels, $eccen$ is the eccentricity of the fitted ellipse within the blob, and $orien$ is the angle of the fitted ellipse.

3.2   Optical Flow Features

In order to find pixel matches in sequence of frames, optical flow (OF) is utilized to find a displacement vector (i.e., pixel translation) under two assumptions of brightness constancy and pixel movement of more than one pixel [13].

The sparse optical flow is utilized by identifying key feature points on moving objects and find matches through an optimization process. This helps to keep processing time low while increasing the accuracy of detecting features on vehicles. The feature detection is performed using the popular Harris corner method [13] and the patches around the features are considered to find the match through the OF. The famous optical flow tracker such as the Kanade-Lucas-Tomasi tracker [14] is used to find the matches.

Figure 2b presents detected corner features between two frames for a typical highway video. The feature vector is created by $f = \{x_1, y_1, x_2, y_2, m, \theta\}$ where x_1, y_1 and x_2, y_2 are feature point coordinates for current and next frames, $m = \sqrt{(x_2 - x_1)^2 + (y_2 - y_1)^2}$, and $\theta = tan^{-1}(\frac{y_2 - y_1}{x_2 - x_1})$. There are some noisy feature points on the background that can be further filtered out through the patch comparison around the feature points for each two frames.

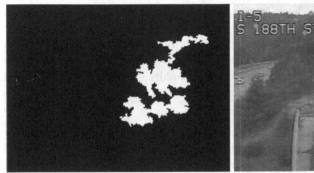 

(a) Blob areas by background subtraction   (b) Harris corners by optical flow

Fig. 2. Moving feature collection (frame: 65)

3.3 Convolutional Neural Network Features

Convolutional neural network (CNN) features are utilized as category of appearance-based techniques to distinguish traffic flow classes. In contrast to handwritten features (e.g., blob features), CNN features are learned concurrently with a training process by variety of convolution operations on input images through different layers of the CNN.

The convolutional layers convolve the input image with bank of filters (i.e., kernels) which have relatively small receptive field through the forward pass. Since image labels are provided, the hierarchy of filters with different complexity are learned that best fit the classification task through the training process.

4 Training Methods

The collected features are labeled according to their traffic flow class (e.g., light = 1, medium = 2, heavy = 3) for the training purpose. Different machine learning algorithms are deployed based on their popularity in solving the classification problem for ITS applications.

4.1 Traditional Machine Learning Methods

K Nearest Neighborhood (KNN): It is widely used in ITS applications for classification and regression problems due to its simplicity, and prediction power [6]. KNN is a non-parametric method that assigns a class to an object based on majority vote of its neighbors. However, its speed becomes limited for a large training dataset since it needs to measure distance and sort all the training data at each prediction step.

Naive Bayes (NB): Bayesian networks are extensively used in variety of ITS applications (e.g., vehicle turning recognition [1]) since they facilitate use of prior knowledge and allow us to learn about causal relationships. For classification problem, we conclude that $P(c|x) = P(x_1|c)P(x_2|c)...P(x_n|c)P(c)$ where $P(c|x)$ is a posterior probability and $P(c)$ is a prior probability. Other probabilities like a $P(x_n|c)$ indicates the likelihood that a feature (i.e., x_n) belongs to the class c. Performing full Bayesian learning is computationally expensive and they tend to perform deficiently on high dimensional data.

Neural Network (NN): Neural Networks are common frameworks utilized by various forecasting and recognition problems in ITS applications such as vehicle and pedestrian classification [15]. A neural network is a nonlinear model that is easy to use and understand compared to statistical methods. The utilized shallow neural network has one hidden layer with ten nodes and Tan-Sigmoid activation functions. However, the last layer consists of three nodes with linear transfer function for three label flow classes. Although NN is able to learn and model non-linear and complex relationships, its black box learning cannot interpret relationships between input and outputs.

4.2 Deep Learning Methods

A deep learning framework has achieved great accuracy for classification problems in ITS [16] due to its excellent feature learning process through high volume data samples. Deep neural networks and convolutional neural networks are evaluated in this work for the traffic flow classification problem.

Deep Neural Network (DNN): Since handwritten features such as blob and optical flow features are collected which have relatively large size, deep neural networks are utilized to improve the classification performance [6]. As an outcome, the addition of more hidden layers and rectifiers (e.g., *ReLUs*) helps to learn more complex patterns with better accuracy.

Table 1. DNN architectures for blob and optical flow features

(a) Blob

Layer	Node #	Parameters #
Dense(1)	140	166460
Dense(2)	280	39480
Dense(3)	60	16860
Dense(4)	80	4880
Dense(5)	20	1620
Dense(6)	8	168
Dense(7)	3	27

(b) Optical flow

Layer	Node #	Parameters #
Dense(1)	2000	2378000
Dense(2)	1000	2001000
Dense(3)	2000	2002000
Dense(4)	500	1000500
Dense(5)	800	400800
Dense(6)	200	160200
Dense(7)	100	20100
Dense(8)	20	2020
Dense(9)	3	63

Table 1 shows DNN architectures for two introduced handwritten features. The input feature size for optical flow and blob methods are 280 and 1188 after up-sampling features and equalizing their length to the maximum feature one. The total number of trainable parameters are 229,495 and 7,964,683 for the blob and optical flow related architectures respectively.

Convolutional Neural Network (CNN): Convolutional Neural Networks receive raw input images with labels directly which allows them to encode certain properties into their architecture. A typical CNN has convolutional, pooling, and fully connected layers. For traffic flow classification task, the softmax layer is embedded as a last layer after flatting whole features into one vector through fully network connections.

Table 2 shows the CNN architecture details utilized in this work for training traffic images. The architecture learns 1,212,643 parameters from three different image sets extracted from traffic videos corresponding to three classes of light, medium and heavy traffic. Furthermore, the extracted handwritten features (e.g., blob features) at each frame arrange into a matrix to form the images for CNN training. Each side of the image matrix is calculated as $w = \sqrt{l}$ where l is the feature vector length. As an outcome, the final images will have small sizes of 17×17 and 35×34 for the blob and optical flow features respectively.

5   Experimental Results

The vision-based tracking system and feature collection system were implemented in C++ using OpenCV 2.3 and they were run on a quad core Intel

Table 2. CNN architecture

Layer	Output Shape	Param #
Convolution(1)	[148, 148, 32]	896
Activation(1)	[148, 148, 32]	0
Max_pooling(1)	[74, 74, 32]	0
Convolution(2)	[72, 72, 32]	9248
Activation(2)	[72, 72, 32]	0
Max_pooling(2)	[36, 36, 32]	0
Convolution(3)	[34, 34, 64]	18496
Activation(3)	[34, 34, 64]	0
Max_pooling(3)	[17, 17, 64]	0
Flatten(1)	[18496]	0
Dense(1)	[64]	1183808
Activation(4)	[64]	0
Dropout(1)	[64]	0
Dense(2)	[3]	195
Activation(5)	[3]	0

i7 processor with 6 GB RAM. The system evaluated videos of a highway with three different traffic flows of light, medium and heavy [17].

The Keras wrappers with Python scripts was run on top of Theano to train deep learning frameworks. Training and testing experiments were performed on a dedicated, high-end PC with a quad core intel i7-7700 3.6 GHz processor, 16 GB RAM and an Nvidia Geforce GTX 1070 GPU. For traditional machine learning techniques (i.e., KNN, NB, and NN), the collected handwritten feature were trained using MATLAB R2016a.

5.1 Feature Preparation and Training

Video frames were directly extracted and labeled for CNN training and each feature vector also created an image as explained in Sect. 4.2. The final dataset produces two separated train and test datasets according to 70%–30% split of each traffic flow category [15].

5.2 Accuracy Evaluation

The collected features and images are trained with the mentioned training methods explained in Sect. 4. After a training step and obtaining a model, the predictions are performed on train and test datasets. The accuracy (Acc) results are calculated as summation of correct predictions according to the traffic flow labels over the total number of samples.

For KNN method, the K is selected as half of the feature vector size due to a better trade off between accuracy and speed of the method to distinguish three different classes. For NN, a feed-forward network is trained using Levenberg-Marquardt method due to its speed and performance [6].

Table 3. The accuracy results of traditional machine learning techniques

		KNN	NB	NN
Blob features	Training Acc	48%	65%	85%
	Test Acc	37%	51%	49%
Optical flow features	Training Acc	58%	57%	73%
	Test Acc	43%	52%	46%

Table 3 shows the accuracy results for traditional machine learning method. Due to the challenging nature of the traffic flow classification, the collected features of three different classes are not easy to separate using traditional methods. The highest accuracy on training data set is achieved by neural networks. However, the bigger input size of optical flow features reduces the accuracy on both train and test dataset for neural network. The highest accuracy is achieved by optical flow using NB classifier.

Table 4. The accuracy results for deep learning techniques

	DNN+OF	DNN+Blob	CNN+OF	CNN+Blob	CNN+Org
Training Acc	100%	90%	89%	80%	96%
Test Acc	52%	52%	60%	61%	90%

For DNN, the main optimizer is Stochastic Gradient Descent (SGD) with learning rate of $1e - 6$, and two activation functions are rectifier and softmax. The batch size of 4 and 300 epochs are considered for the training process. The model with best accuracy on test dataset is recorded during training phase.

Similar to DNN, SGD with lower learning rate of $1e - 4$ is used with CNN for training convergence to a local minimum cost. Moreover, the same batch size of 4 and 300 epochs are considered for the training task. Since CNN is more efficient with large amount of data, image samples are augmented via a number of random transformations. As an outcome, model would never see twice a same image. The data augmentation process during training incorporates rotation change, translate pictures vertically and horizontally (i.e., width shift), re-scale, shear range, zoom range, and horizontal flip.

Table 4 shows the accuracy results for deep learning methods including DNN and CNN. DNN trained with handwritten features called DNN+OF and DNN+Blob. However, CNN trained with images extracted from videos named CNN+Org. The images constructed from optical flow features and blob features

Table 5. Confusion matrices for CNN methods on test data

(a) CNN+OF

	L	M	H
L: 687	381	108	198
M: 689	50	445	194
H: 689	62	210	417

(b) CNN+Blob

	L	M	H
L: 684	458	87	139
M: 689	56	455	178
H: 690	45	309	336

(c) CNN+Org

	L	M	H
L: 688	684	4	0
M: 690	12	566	112
H: 692	1	87	604

called CNN+OF and CNN+Blob respectively. The deep learning experiments shows the great accuracy of 90% on test data, when the raw images are directly utilized by CNN. This implies that CNN features learned from raw images works better than images constructed from the manually handwritten features which are more prone to over-fitting problem. The problem is shown through the large gap of accuracy between training and test datasets of DNN+OF and DNN+Blob. Moreover, CNN shows better performance than DNN since it has better accuracy for test datasets.

Table 5 shows the confusion matrices for prediction of low (L), medium (M) and high (H) traffic classes of test image datasets. Each row shows the total number of test image samples for each category and predictions to L, M and H traffic classes. The confusion matrices implies the difficulty of the prediction task to distinguish medium and high traffic classes.

6   Conclusion

This work presents the classification of traffic flows by variety of machine learning techniques including deep neural networks and convolutional neural networks. The experimental results shows promising results when the CNN features are directly learned from the traffic images. The future work will focus on congestion detection for different road types including unsignalized intersections to highlight the waiting time information for road users (e.g., pedestrians) and design traffic signals for transportation engineers.

References

1. Shirazi, M.S., Morris, B.T.: Looking at intersections: a survey of intersection monitoring, behavior and safety analysis of recent studies. IEEE Trans. Intell. Transp. Syst. **18**, 4–24 (2017)
2. Zhang, G., Avery, R., Wang, Y.: Video-based vehicle detection and classification system for real-time traffic data collection using uncalibrated video cameras. Transp. Res. Rec. J. Transp. Res. Board **2007**, 138–147 (1993)
3. Shirazi, M.S., Morris, B.: Vision-based vehicle queue analysis at junctions. In: 2015 12th IEEE International Conference on Advanced Video and Signal Based Surveillance (AVSS), pp. 1–6 (2015)

4. Nemade, B.: Automatic traffic surveillance using video tracking. Procedia Comput. Sci. **79**, 402–109 (2016). Proceedings of International Conference on Communication, Computing and Virtualization (ICCCV) 2016

5. Saunier, N., Sayed, T.: A feature-based tracking algorithm for vehicles in intersections. In: Proceeding 3rd Canadian Conference on Computer and Robot Vision, p. 59, Canada, Quebec (2006)

6. Shirazi, M.S., Morris, B.: Traffic phase inference using traffic cameras. In: 2017 IEEE Intelligent Vehicles Symposium (IV), pp. 1565–1570 (2017)

7. Fouladgar, M., Parchami, M., Elmasri, R., Ghaderi, A.: Scalable deep traffic flow neural networks for urban traffic congestion prediction. CoRR abs/1703.01006 (2017)

8. Ma, X., Dai, Z., He, Z., Wang, Y.: Learning traffic as images: a deep convolution neural network for large-scale transportation network speed prediction. CoRR abs/1701.04245 (2017)

9. Stauffer, C., Grimson, W.E.L.: Adaptive background mixture models for real-time tracking, pp. 246–252 (1999)

10. Fang, W., Zhao, Y., Yuan, Y., Liu, K.: Real-time multiple vehicles tracking with occlusion handling. In: Proceedings of the International Conference on Image and Graphics, San Juan, Puerto Rico, pp. 667–672 (2011)

11. Shirazi, M.S., Morris, B.T.: Vision-based turning movement monitoring:count, speed & waiting time estimation. IEEE Intell. Transp. Syst. Mag. **8**, 23–34 (2016)

12. Shirazi, M.S., Morris, B.: Vision-based turning movement counting at intersections by cooperating zone and trajectory comparison modules. In: Proceeding 17th International IEEE Conference on Intelligent Transportation Systems, Qingdao, China, pp. 3100–3105 (2014)

13. Harris, C., Stephens, M.: A combined corner and edge detector. In: Proceedings of Fourth Alvey Vision Conference, pp. 147–151 (1988)

14. Tomasi, C., Kanade, T.: Detection and tracking of point features. Technical report, International Journal of Computer Vision (1991)

15. Shirazi, M.S., Morris, B.: Contextual combination of appearance and motion for intersection videos with vehicles and pedestrians. In: Bebis, G., et al. (eds.) ISVC 2014. LNCS, vol. 8887, pp. 708–717. Springer, Cham (2014). https://doi.org/10.1007/978-3-319-14249-4_68

16. Krizhevsky, A., Sutskever, I., Hinton, G.E.: Imagenet classification with deep convolutional neural networks. In: Pereira, F., Burges, C.J.C., Bottou, L., Weinberger, K.Q. (eds.) Advances in Neural Information Processing Systems, vol. 25, pp. 1097–1105. Curran Associates, Inc. (2012)

17. Chan, A.B., Vasconcelos, N.: Probabilistic kernels for the classification of autoregressive visual processes. In: 2005 IEEE Computer Society Conference on Computer Vision and Pattern Recognition (CVPR 2005), vol. 1, pp. 846–851 (2005)

Author Index

Abdelpakey, Mohamed H.   463
Abu Aisheh, Zeina   650
Al Mamun, Shamim   737
Alexis, Kostas   529, 565
Álvarez, Andrés M.   371
Álvarez, Mauricio A.   371
Álvarez-Meza, Andrés   116
Amaquiña, José L.   712
Andaluz, Víctor H.   193, 395, 675, 687, 712
Andersen, Ole Kæseler   552
Angulu, Raphael   157
Arguissain, Federico G.   552
Armas, Joseph   687
Ayadi, Mehdi   698

Badger, Jonathan C.   500
Bappanadu, Aravind   511
Bashir, Raja Muhammad Saad   286
Bashiri, Fereshteh S.   500
Bayana, Mayibongwe H.   157
Beaupré, David-Alexandre   727
Ben Amar, Chokri   698
Ben Chattah, Thoraya   587
Bilodeau, Guillaume-Alexandre   309, 727, 748
Bouachir, Wassim   309
Bougleux, Sébastien   587, 650
Brunner, Iris   552
Buele, Jorge   215
Bushra, Naila   226

Carruth, Daniel   226
Castillo-Carrión, Daniel   712
Chang, Gregory   576
Chen, Cheng   576
Chen, Honglin   68
Chen, Kaiyuan   15
Chen, Yang   106, 619
Cheng, Xiang-zheng   382
Chicaiza, Edison A.   675
Chicaiza, Fernando A.   395
Chiluisa, Max G.   193
Clark, Kevin   237

Craig, George   359
Cuellar-Fierro, Jhon F.   371

D'Souza, Roshan M.   500
Damen, Dima   274
De la Cruz, Edgar I.   675
Deb, Shuchisnigdha   226
Dias, Paulo   57
Ding, Lu   487
Du, Shengzhi   147, 445
Duarte, José   57

Easton, James   93, 629
Espinoza, Jhon   215

Fagertun, Jens   264
Fernández-Ramírez, Jorge   116
Fischer, Gregory S.   167
Fontanini, Tomaso   541, 662
Fraz, Muhammad Moazam   286, 423
Fu, Shan   487
Fukuda, Hisato   737
Fusek, Radovan   433

Galarza, Eddie D.   215
Galarza, Eddie E.   215
Gdawiec, Krzysztof   47
Gościniak, Ireneusz   47
Guha, Indranil   598
Guo, Ye   79

Hamouda, Atef   587
Hanser, Karsten   359
Haque, Mohammad A.   552
Hebborn, Anna Katharina   299
Höhner, Nils   299
Hotta, Kazuhiro   607

Jafri, Fareed ud din Mehmood   344
Jørgensen, Anders   264, 552

Kakadiaris, Ioannis A.   126
Karmaker, Debajyoti   332

Kenyon, Garrett T. 455
Khan, Waqar 251
Khattak, Shehryar 529, 565
Khosla, Deepak 106, 619
Khurram, Imran 423
Kjeldsen, Simon S. 552
Klein, Ole 359
Klette, Reinhard 251
Kobayashi, Yoshinori 737
Kuncheva, Ludmila I. 640
Kuno, Yoshinori 737
Kurkure, Uday 511

Laganière, Robert 320, 487
Lagunes-Fortiz, Miguel 274
Lam, Antony 737
Laroche, Daniel 320
LaRose, Eric 500
Lee, Dah-Jye 382
Lee, Seugnkyu 139
Leitte, Heike 359
Lewis, Brittany 167
Lézoray, Olivier 587, 650
Li, Chunming 34
Li, Zhenxi 309
Liu, Ke 79
Loffredo, Donald 93, 237, 629
López, Victoria M. 215
Lukácová-Medvidová, Mária 359
Luo, Xinbin 487

Magliani, Federico 541, 662
Mastora, Ermioni 126
Matsuzuki, Daisuke 607
Matthews, Clare E. 640
Mayol-Cuevas, Walterio 274
Medeiros, Henry 474
Miao, Xi-kui 382
Miguet, Serge 698
Miranda, Roberto J. 712
Moeslund, Thomas B. 264, 552
Mohamed, Mostafa M. 463
Mora-Aguilar, Jorge 712
Moreira, José 57
Morita, Satoru 205
Morris, Brendan 758
Mozhdehi, Reza Jalil 474
Mueller, Martin Fritz 344

Müller, Stefan 299
Mullo, Rubén D. 193

Nakada, Masaki 68
Nasrollahi, Kamal 552
Nielsen, Jørgen F. 552
Nikou, Christophoros 126
Nycz, Christopher J. 167

Ooi, Hui-Lee 727
Orozco, Álvaro A. 371
Orozco-Gutiérrez, Álvaro 116
Ors, Ali Osman 320

Papachristos, Christos 529, 565
Peissig, Peggy 500
Pérez, María G. 712
Piatkowski, Marian 359
Pilatasig, Marco 215
Pokharel, Shiraj 407
Porr, William 93, 629
Prati, Andrea 541, 662

Quevedo, Washington X. 712

Reuter, Patrick 395
Reznichenko, Yevgeniy 474
Rieck, Bastian 359
Roy, Pankaj Raj 748

Sadlo, Filip 359
Sagristà, Antoni 359
Saha, Punam K. 576, 598
Salih, Omran 25
Santana, Jaime 395
Saunier, Nicolas 727
Scalzo, Fabien 3, 15
Schiffner, Ingo 332
Scuturici, Mihaela 698
Selz, Tobias 359
Shahzad, Muhammad 286, 423
Shehata, Mohamed S. 463
Shen, Jingyue 15
Shi, Xue 34
Shirazi, Mohammad Shokrolah 758
Siddique, Abubakar 474
Simmons, Sean 93, 237, 629

Sivaraman, Hari   511
Srinivasan, Mandyam V.   332

Tang, Alice   3
Tang, Lijun   34
Tavakkoli, Alireza   93, 237, 629
Terzopoulos, Demetri   68
Tu, Chunling   147, 445

Uhlenbrock, Ryan   106

Valque, Leo   698
Vargas-Cardona, Hernán Darío   371
Venkatasubramanian, Krishna K.   167
Viriri, Serestina   25, 157
Vrigkas, Michalis   126
Vu, Lan   511

Wang, Yong   320, 487
Watkins, Yijing   455

Wiebe, Bettina   359
Wilson, Michael   332

Xiong, Huaixin   180
Xu, Xiaoyin   320

Yang, Xiao-yu   382
Yezzi, Anthony Joseph   344
Yousefi, Paria   640
Yu, Seunghwa   139
Yu, Zeyun   79, 500

Zambrano, Pablo A.   215
Zhang, Shaoxiang   34
Zhang, Xiaoliu   576
Zhang, Xinhua   455
Zhang, Zhiyuan   3
Zheng, Boyan   359
Zhu, Changyun   320
Zhu, Ying   407

Printed in the United States
by Bookmasters

Printed in the United States
By Bookmasters